OXFORD WORLD'S CLASSICS

THE OXFORD SHAKESPEARE

General Editor · Stanley Wells

The Oxford Shakespeare offers new and authoritative editions of Shakespeare's plays in which the early printings have been scrupulously re-examined and interpreted. It includes all Shakespeare's non-dramatic output in the present volume. In the play editions, an introductory essay provides all relevant background information together with an appraisal of critical views and of the play's effects in performance. The detailed commentaries pay particular attention to language and staging. Reprints of sources, music for songs, genealogical tables, maps, etc. are included where necessary; many of the volumes are illustrated, and all contain an index.

COLIN BURROW, the editor of *The Complete Sonnets and Poems* in the Oxford Shakespeare, is Senior Research Fellow at All Souls College, University of Oxford. He is the author of *Shakespeare and Classical Antiquity* (OUP, 2013), among other works.

THE OXFORD SHAKESPEARE

OXFORD WORLD'S CLASSICS

WILLIAM SHAKESPEARE

The Complete Sonnets and Poems

Edited by
COLIN BURROW

OXFORD
UNIVERSITY PRESS

OXFORD

UNIVERSITY PRESS

Great Clarendon Street, Oxford OX2 6DP

Oxford University Press is a department of the University of Oxford.
It furthers the University's objective of excellence in research, scholarship,
and education by publishing worldwide in

Oxford New York

Auckland Bangkok Buenos Aires Cape Town Chennai
Dar es Salaam Delhi Hong Kong Istanbul Karachi Kolkata
Kuala Lumpur Madrid Melbourne Mexico City Mumbai Nairobi
São Paulo Shanghai Singapore Taipei Tokyo Toronto

with an associated company in Berlin

Oxford is a registered trade mark of Oxford University Press
in the UK and in certain other countries

Published in the United States
by Oxford University Press Inc., New York

First published 2002
Reissued 2008

British Library Cataloguing in Publication Data

Data available

Library of Congress Cataloging in Publication Data

Shakespeare, William, 1564–1616.
[Selections, 2002]
Shakespeare: the complete sonnets and poems / edited by Colin Burrow.
p. cm.—(The Oxford Shakespeare)
Includes index.
1. Sonnets, English.   I. Title: Complete sonnets and poems.   II. Burrow, Colin.   III. Title.
PR2841.B8 2002 821'.3—dc21 2001036734

ISBN 978-0-19-953579-8

17

Typeset in Photina MT
by Best-set Typesetter Ltd., Hong Kong
Printed in Great Britain by
Clays Ltd, Elcograf S.p.A.

PREFACE

THIS has been a big labour, which would have been impossible had I not been able to share ideas with (and to borrow from) many colleagues and past editors. Several recent editors of the poems have been exceptionally kind in offering advice and additional assistance. John Kerrigan has been particularly helpful and encouraging, especially since his edition of the Sonnets is such an impossibly fine example to follow. His careful reading of the typescript saved me from many errors. Katherine Duncan-Jones has offered many wise words, in print and in person, without which this edition would be much poorer than it is. A helpful conversation with Helen Vendler on punctuation has also left its mark on many lines of the Sonnets, and John Roe has offered many helpful comments over several years. Hyder Rollins's monumental Variorum editions have been daily and invaluable companions.

Many other colleagues and friends have helped me in many ways. Ian Donaldson lent me his extensive and meticulously arranged notes on *Lucrece*. Gavin Alexander assisted with transcriptions of some manuscript material. Anne Barton nobly read the complete typescript, and her shrewd comments have spared me many a blush. Quentin Skinner provided extremely helpful comments and references on the political context of *Lucrece*. Stuart Gillespie gave many useful pointers for reading. I have benefited from conversations with Patrick Cheney, who allowed me to see much of his forthcoming work on Shakespeare's poetic career. MacDonald P. Jackson gave me very early access to some of his most important work on the ordering and date of the Sonnets. Brian Vickers gave me an early view of his sceptical work on *A Funeral Elegy*, and sent copies of some of his extremely valuable essays on the rhetoric of the Sonnets. Heather Dubrow offered some valuable advice as well as showing me copies of recent work. I am especially grateful to Martin Dzelzainis and Roy Booth, the convenors of a stimulating (and for me most timely) conference on Shakespeare's Narrative Poems in the summer of 2000. All the contributors to that conference, especially (but not only) Catherine Belsey, Anthony Mortimer, Mark Rasmussen, Sasha Roberts, and

James Schiffer, provided great stimulus in the final stages of the project, and I fear that the acknowledgements of their ideas in the introduction do not adequately indicate how much I owe to them. Several colleagues at Caius, including John Mollon, Brian Outhwaite, and Vic Gattrell, have given me helpful pointers and references. I am particularly grateful to the series editor, Stanley Wells, and to Frances Whistler at OUP.

I am grateful to librarians at the Cambridge University Library, Trinity College, Cambridge, St John's College, Cambridge, the Bodleian, the British Library, the Folger Shakespeare Library, to Mr Robert Yorke, archivist at the College of Arms, and to the archdeacon of Salop, for their help with queries about manuscript material. I am grateful too to the Master and Fellows of Gonville and Caius College, to the English Faculty at Cambridge, and (above all) to my family for granting me some periods of quiet in which it has been completed.

Some of the arguments in the introduction have been aired at greater length in 'Life and Work in Shakespeare's Poems', The British Academy Chatterton Lecture 1997, *Proceedings of the British Academy* 97 (1997), 15–50—reprinted in Stephen Orgel and Sean Keilen, eds., *Shakespeare: The Critical Complex: Shakespeare's Poems* (New York and London, 1999)—and in 'Editing Shakespeare's Sonnets' (a review article on Helen Vendler, *The Art of Shakespeare's Sonnets* and Katherine Duncan-Jones, ed., *Shakespeare's Sonnets*), *The Cambridge Quarterly* 29 (1999), 1–14. I am grateful to Henry Woudhuysen and Eric Rasmussen for drawing to my attention a number of errors, which are corrected in this impression.

COLIN BURROW

CONTENTS

Contents

LIST OF ILLUSTRATIONS

INTRODUCTION

Shakespeare the Poet

Many editions of Shakespeare's poems, and of the Sonnets in particular, present themselves as having solved some or all of the many unanswered questions which surround these works. The questions have varied with each age, as have the answers. Commentators since the late eighteenth century have argued over the identity of 'Mr W.H.' to whom the Sonnets volume is dedicated, and have worked themselves into a fine froth over the nature of Shakespeare's sexuality. Of late *Venus and Adonis* and *Lucrece* have generated suggestive but equally inconclusive debates over a string of slightly different questions: critics have argued about whether *Lucrece* is a republican poem, over the sexual politics of *Venus and Adonis*, and over the ways in which Shakespeare represents sexual desire. The main aim of this edition is not to offer definitive answers to any of these questions, but to provide its readers with enough information to take up an informed position on most of them, and to feed that information back into the way they read the poems. Since its focus is on helping readers to read, this edition makes some use of the rather patchy evidence of how Shakespeare's early readers responded to his poems. It also includes a group of poems which he is unlikely to have written but which were believed to be by him by his early readers. Some of these appeared in *The Passionate Pilgrim* of 1599, and some were ascribed to him in manuscripts which date from after his death. The latter group are included in an appendix in order to help modern readers understand what kind of poet Shakespeare was thought to be by the creators of manuscript miscellanies. None of them can safely be ascribed to Shakespeare, but they are an index of the beliefs which early readers had about the kind of poet Shakespeare was.

And the chief aim of this edition is to pose the question, 'What sort of poet was Shakespeare?' Should we think of him as having produced something which resembles a non-dramatic oeuvre? By uniting the narrative poems with the sonnets, and by printing them along with a number of poems attributed to Shakespeare in the seventeenth century, this volume stands as a physical encouragement to readers to think about these poems together, and to explore what they might have in common. This has been done surprisingly rarely (Heather Dubrow's *Captive Victors* is a notable exception to this rule). Shakespeare in the past century was perceived primarily as a dramatic poet, and his poems tended to be split into two groups, the Sonnets and the rest, each of which stimulated a different kind of critical attention. From the early nineteenth to the twentieth century the Sonnets were seized upon as objects of biographical speculation. By the late 1930s they also became a central testing-ground for the literary methods of the New Criticism. *Venus and Adonis* and *Lucrece*, long on rhetoric, void of biography, did not suit either of these literary critical fashions. With the exception of some brilliant appreciation by Coleridge the poems languished in a pool of faint praise mingled with outright condemnation from the 1790s until the 1970s, when readers began to recognize the power of Shakespeare's early responses to Ovid, and to relish their implied view of personal identity as the improvised product of rhetoric and play.[1]

An earlier string of institutional accidents effectively divided the poems (often unthinkingly stigmatized by the dire privative prefix of 'the *non*-dramatic works') from the plays. The poems were not included in the First Folio of Shakespeare's *Comedies, Histories and Tragedies* of 1623. This was partly because many of those responsible for putting the volume together were men of the theatre. But it was also partly because *Venus and Adonis* and *Lucrece* were extremely popular, and remained marketable commodities in their own right throughout the seventeenth century. Their printers would have been very unlikely to wish to surrender their rights to print them, even if they had been asked to do so by the compilers of the Folio. In the eighteenth-century collected editions of Shakespeare (which in many respects constructed the playwright whom we still read today), the poems and sonnets were usually either left out altogether, or shuffled off into final volumes or appendices to the dramatic works. Supplementary volumes, several of which sought to masquerade as the final volumes of prestigious collected editions of the plays, gave eighteenth-century readers the impression the

---

[1] The best recent survey of critical opinion is Philip C. Kolin, ed., *Venus and Adonis: Critical Essays* (New York and London, 1997).

poems were an optional extra: so Gildon produced a supplement containing the poems to augment Rowe's edition of 1709, and George Sewell did the same for Pope's Shakespeare in 1725. Even Edmond Malone's great edition of the poems in 1780 was a supplementary volume added to George Steevens's edition. Fashion played its part in consigning the poems to the realm of the supplement. In an age in which Steevens could say of the Sonnets that 'the strongest act of Parliament that could be framed, would fail to compel readers into their service', the poems were never likely to help sales of a collected edition of Shakespeare.

These historical accidents have cast a greying residue over the poems, which has proved hard to shift, despite some splendid reappraisals over the last fifty years. Most collected editions of Shakespeare's complete works continue to relegate the poems to the edges of the canon: the poems are dispersed in the chronological sequence of the Oxford and Norton Shakespeares. In the Riverside edition they moulder at the back. The collected Arden alone reverses the trend, but oddly prints the Sonnets (published in 1609) first in its sequence, apparently for no other reason than that more readers will have heard of them than of *Venus and Adonis* (printed in 1593). If collected editions wished to reflect how Shakespeare wished to be thought of in the 1590s, or how he was generally regarded before the folio of 1623, then *Venus and Adonis* should be at the front of those editions: this was the first work to which he attached his name, and it was the work which made his name. Now, though, even the standard catalogue of early modern printed books, the *Short-Title Catalogue of Books Printed in England . . . 1475–1640*, gives bibliographical details of Shakespeare's plays first, then it lists the Shakespearian apocrypha, then it lists the poems. And so *A Yorkshire Tragedy* is made to seem more central to Shakespeare's output—despite the fact that he did not write it—than *Venus and Adonis*, of which there were sixteen editions before 1640 (there were five of *Hamlet* in the same period). Economic pressures and simple limitations of space have usually meant that modern annotated editions of the Sonnets (usually now with *A Lover's Complaint* in its rightful place as the conclusion to the sequence) have appeared in separate volumes from the other narrative poems

---

¹ Quoted in Rollins 2, ii. 337–8, from The Advertisement to the Plays of William Shakespeare (1793).

and *The Passionate Pilgrim*. All of these material forces have conspired to make it seem unnatural to ask the question, 'What sort of poet was Shakespeare?'—unless one wants the answer, 'Well, there are some good lines in *Hamlet*.'

The picture of Shakespeare the poet which emerges from this volume is not one of a writer who wanted to be a poet *rather than* a dramatist, nor is it a picture of someone who sought programmatically to follow any of the number of career patterns available to early modern poets. Being a poet in the period from 1590 to 1610 was not easy, and gave room only for circumscribed autonomy. Poets worked with and within traditions which were made for them (although many poets besides Shakespeare decisively transformed the genres they received). They also learnt, often with frenzied speed and some rapacity, from other poets. Fashions changed rapidly and markedly, and poets who wished to attract the benison of patrons had to adapt themselves to these changes or die. Poets also had to work within the complicated and often haphazard processes by means of which early modern printing presses produced books. The treatment of copy in this period—which was owned not by its author but by the first printer to obtain a manuscript and pay 6*d*. to have it 'entered' in the Stationers' Register, and which might be set by compositors of varying levels of experience and skill—meant that authorial control over texts, their layout, and even the timing of their publication, was always less than complete. Even if Shakespeare had laid out for himself a literary career, running through Ovidian narrative poetry in *Venus and Adonis*, to the 'graver' offering of *Lucrece*, through Sonnets, to a concluding Complaint, it would have been something which he would have had neither the time nor the power to shape entirely for himself. His non-dramatic works were in many respects the products of occasion: it is likely that periods of plague, during which the theatres were closed, in 1592–4 led to a burst of work on *Venus and Adonis* and *Lucrece*; and it is possible that later periods of plague enabled periods of revision and augmentation of the Sonnets. In the middle of Shakespeare's career as a poet sits the extraordinary, other-worldly lyric 'Let the bird of loudest lay' (the received title 'The Phoenix and the Turtle' is dropped in this edition, since it has no Shakespearian authority, and is first found in 1807), a poem which it is impossible to fit into any sort of planned career.

Shakespeare's career as a poet is likely to have jolted along in fits and starts during periods of enforced idleness (the dominant sense of 'career' in this period was still what a horse does when it bolts under you); but the periods of idleness enabled the emergence of something which looks like an oeuvre, with a distinctive set of pre-occupations. Every reader will find a slightly different configuration of concerns here; but the poems in this volume repeatedly meditate on the perverse effects and consequences of sexual desire, on sacrifice and self-sacrifice, on the ways in which a relationship of sexual passion might objectify or enslave both the desirer and the desired, and they repeatedly complicate simple binary distinctions between male and female. The poems are also all marked by a continual and brilliantly various experimentation in juxtaposing speech and narrative circumstance, and, from *Venus and Adonis* to the early Sonnets, recurrently explore how even the most elaborate rhetoric can fail to persuade its addressee. Even the shady volume of mostly non-Shakespearian pieces, *The Passionate Pilgrim* (1599), in part builds on, and in part makes up a 'Shakespearian' poetic identity, as its printer, William Jaggard, sought to create a volume of poems which could just about persuade its readers that it represented the hitherto hidden works of Shakespeare the poet.

Each of the poems included in this volume adopts different angles and perspectives in a manner which is distinctively that of a dramatist—of a dramatist who could think about sexual desire in *Measure for Measure* from the viewpoint of a votaress, a Duke's deputy, and the laddish Lucio—and with a combination of cool spectatorship and impassioned participation. The poems, like the plays, meditate on relations between rhetoric, persuasion, self-persuasion, gender, politics, action, and passion. And they do so with a directness and a clarity which marks them not as offshoots of the dramatic works, but as the works in which Shakespeare undertook much of the foundational thought which underpins his dramatic work. In the Sonnets and the narrative poems Shakespeare thinks through what it is to love someone whom you know to be the wrong person to love, and in them too he attempts to construct subject-positions and rhetorical methods to accommodate these multiple perspectives. The poems and Sonnets should not be split apart, and they should not be consigned to the ghetto of 'the non-dramatic verse': they should be regarded as central to an understanding of Shakespeare.

Venus and Adonis

Publication and Date of Composition. *Venus and Adonis* was entered in the Stationers' Register on 18 April 1593 by Richard Field,[1] a printer who was born, like Shakespeare, in Stratford. Field had printed some of the most notable literary works of the 1590s. His list included works which encouraged vernacular authors to use the art of rhetoric in verse, such as George Puttenham's *Art of English Poesy* (1589), and the second edition of Henry Peacham's *Garden of Eloquence* (1593). He had also printed the most elaborately produced work of vernacular literature of the 1590s, Sir John Harington's translation of Ariosto (1591), a work which also included a 'Brief Apology of Poetry'. Field's shop produced books which looked good and which made claims to high literary status, as well as works which sought to define what high literary status was—and it may be notable in this respect that there is a striking lack of theatrical texts among the works he printed. His typesetting was also 'as good as any to be found in London at the time'.[2] These were good reasons for Shakespeare to use him as the printer of *Venus and Adonis*, the highly crafted and pointedly rhetorical work in which he sought to make his mark on the world of print. Field was also an appropriate printer for an Ovidian poem. He had inherited his business and his presses from Thomas Vautrollier, whose widow he had married. Vautrollier had enjoyed a monopoly in the printing of Ovid in Latin.[3] Field had reprinted Vautrollier's edition of the *Metamorphoses* in 1589 and was to reprint Vautrollier's text of the *Heroides* in 1594.[4]

Field had copies of the elegantly presented Quarto edition of *Venus and Adonis* ready for sale by mid-June 1593. The dedicatory epistle to Henry Wriothesley, Earl of Southampton, was signed 'William Shakespeare'. This was the first time that Shakespeare's name had been attached to a printed work. (It was quite usual in this period for authors' names to be attached to dedicatory epistles rather than appearing on the title-page.) On 12 June 1593 Richard Stonley recorded in his diary that he bought a copy of the poem for sixpence, which makes him the first known purchaser of a printed

[1] Arber, ii.630.
[2] W. W. Greg, 'An Elizabethan Printer and his Copy', *The Library* 4 (1923–4), 117.
[3] Arber, ii.746.   [4] Arber, i.144.

work attributed to Shakespeare.[1] The standard of printing in the first Quarto is extremely high, with so few evident errors that it is likely Field worked from a carefully prepared fair copy. Field's compositors doubtless standardized the spelling and punctuation of the manuscript from which they worked, as they are known to have done in the case of Harington's translation of Ariosto (in this case the manuscript from which Field worked survives).[2] In all respects Q1 is as good a text as any editor could wish for.

There are known to have been at least sixteen editions of the poem by 1640. Few copies of most of these editions survive, which suggests that many eager readers read their copies to pieces. It is likely that there were other editions which were completely destroyed by their eager consumers. Editions after the first of 1593 have no independent authority: they all ultimately derive from the first Quarto (in general each new printing was set from the most recent available edition). Each subsequent edition introduces some compositorial emendations, as well as some errors. The collation to this edition lists readings from late Quartos only when they appear to offer intelligent responses to apparent error.

The very success of the poem is likely to be a major reason why it came to be regarded as peripheral to the canon of Shakespeare's works. Venus and Adonis remained a marketable work through the seventeenth century: the right to print the copy was transferred from publisher to publisher, presumably for a fee, and the transactions were recorded in the Stationers' Register.[3] As we have seen, this may be one reason why Venus and Adonis, like Lucrece, did not appear in the first Folio of 1623: since the poems remained popular

[1] Schoenbaum, 175–6.

[2] BL MS Add. 18920. On Field's setting of Harington see Greg, 'An Elizabethan Printer', 102–18; Philip Gaskell, From Writer to Reader: Studies in Editorial Method (Oxford, 1978), 11–28. On Field's career see A. E. M. Kirwood, 'Richard Field, Printer, 1589–1624', The Library 12 (1931–2), 1–39.

[3] Full details are given in Rollins I, 369–79. See also Henry Farr, 'Shakespeare's Printers and Publishers, with Special Reference to the Poems and Hamlet', The Library 4th ser. 3 (1923), 225–50. Field assigned the copyright to John Harrison, Sr., on 25 June 1594 (Arber, ii.655); Harrison assigned it to William Leake on 25 June 1596 (Arber, iii.65); Leake assigned it to William Barrett on 16 February 1617 (Arber, iii.603); Barrett assigned it to John Parker on 8 March 1620 (Arber, iii.666); Parker assigned it to John Haviland and John Wright on 7 May 1626, who re-entered the title on 4 September 1638 (Arber, iv.160, 431); Wright passed it on to his brother Edward on 27 June 1646, Edward Wright assigned it to William Gilbert-son on 4 April 1655 (Eyre, i.236, 470).

it would have been difficult and expensive to obtain the right to print them. And by the early eighteenth century both *Venus and Adonis* and *Lucrece* had become thoroughly marginal to Shakespeare's works. They were persistently printed in supplementary volumes to the collected editions of the plays. Several of those volumes, such as that by Gildon (added to Rowe's edition in 1709), or George Sewell (added to Pope's in 1725), appear to have been unauthorized attempts to supplement and cash in on collected editions.[1] This pattern did not change at the end of the eighteenth century. Edmond Malone's first great edition of the non-dramatic verse, which appeared first in 1780 and played a major part in the rehabilitation of the Sonnets, was introduced on its title-page as a 'supplement' to George Steevens's edition of the plays. The labour of editing these works, which were still believed to be unimportant and of low quality, was taken on by a younger, and in 1780, lesser-known man.

Venus and Adonis was probably composed in the months immediately before its publication. Some earlier critics felt that the poem was written by a Shakespeare who still had the loam of Warwickshire on his boots,[2] presumably on the odd assumption that he was unlikely to have been able to write vividly about hares, horses, and snails unless he could see them through his window. The poem is so smartly attuned to London literary fashions of the early 1590s that it must have been written if not in London, then in its literary atmosphere. On 23 June 1592 plays had been suspended as a result of disagreements between the civic authorities and the players.[3] By August the plague had broken out in London, and on 7 September city plague orders extended the prohibition on playing. The public theatres remained closed until June 1594, with the exception of brief periods in the winters of 1593 and 1594. On 28 January 1593 the Privy Council wrote to the aldermen of London stating that 'we think it fit that all manner of concourse and public meetings of the

---

[1] For a detailed discussion of this, and the possible connection between the spate of editions of the non-dramatic works and the copyright act of 1710, see Colin Burrow, 'Life and Work in Shakespeare's Poems', *Proceedings of the British Academy* 97 (1997), 15–50; repr. in Stephen Orgel and Sean Keilen, eds., *Shakespeare's Poems*, Shakespeare: The Critical Complex 4 (New York and London, 1999), 1–36.

[2] Notably Charles Armitage Brown, *Shakespeare's Autobiographical Poems* (1838). On his heirs see Rollins I, 412–15.

[3] J. R. Dasent, ed., *Acts of the Privy Council of England (1542–1604)*, 35 vols. (1890–1907), xxii.549.

people at plays, bear-baitings, bowlings, and other like assemblies for sports be forbidden'[1] for fear of spreading the plague which was to kill around 10,000 people in London that year. The theatres reopened again briefly for the winter of 1593–4, but on 3 February 1594 the Privy Council issued a further proclamation against the performance of plays during the plague.[2] The public theatres were therefore effectively closed for almost two years, with no regular playing in London until 3 June 1594. The final permission to resume playing came on 8 October 1594. The most reasonable supposition is that Shakespeare composed both *Venus and Adonis* and *Lucrece* during this extended period in which he could not be sure of any kind of financial return for a composition for the public theatres. The year 1594 did coincide with a sudden upsurge in the number of plays entered in the Stationers' Register, which rose from around four per year to twenty-three. This indicates that theatrical companies were attempting to use print to realize their assets when they could not put on plays in the city.[3] The authors of those plays would probably have received nothing for their publication, since the texts were usually the property of the companies which performed them; but from *Venus and Adonis* and *Lucrece* Shakespeare might expect at least a reward from his patron or a fee from a bookseller.

The likelihood that Shakespeare wrote the narrative poems during the plague of 1592–4 is sometimes used to argue that nondramatic verse was peripheral to his interests. There is no reason to suppose this to be the case. The narrative poems could have been composed out of necessity, as Shakespeare sought a source of income from the patronage of the Earl of Southampton. But it could equally well be that the poems reflect a long-standing intention to make a mark as a poet, or, as Patrick Cheney has argued, as a poet-playwright after the model of Ovid (who composed a lost

---

[1] Dasent, ed., *Acts*, xxiv.32. The Privy Council register is missing for the period August 1593–October 1595.

[2] E. K. Chambers, *The Elizabethan Stage*, 4 vols. (Oxford, 1923), iv.345–51; ii.122–4; W. P. Barrett, ed., *Present Remedies against the Plague* (1933), p. xii reproduces the general civic plague order 'That restraint be made of interludes and plays, assemblies of fencers, or other profane spectacles . . .'. For a general account of the plague, see Leeds Barroll, *Politics, Plague, and Shakespeare's Theatre* (Ithaca and London, 1991), 70–116.

[3] Barrett, *Present Remedies*, p. xvii.

tragedy about Medea).[1] Certainly the promise in the dedication to
Venus and Adonis of 'some graver labour' suggests that the poems
formed part of a continuing project. The dedication is keen to pre-
sent *Venus and Adonis* as 'the first heir of my invention', in effect the
beginning of Shakespeare. And for his earliest readers, Shake-
speare was a poet.

Dedication. Both *Venus and Adonis* and *Lucrece* were dedicated to
Henry Wriothesley (pronounced 'Risely'), third Earl of Southamp-
ton. Southampton was born on 6 October 1573. He was not quite
20 and still a minor when *Venus and Adonis* appeared some time
before mid-June 1593. On his father's death in 1581 Southampton
had become a royal ward until he reached the age of 21. He was ini-
tially a ward of Lord Howard of Effingham, but was then trans-
ferred to the guardianship of William Cecil, Lord Burghley, who
was master of the court of wards. Wardship was in theory a recog-
nition that noblemen held their land from the king, and that there-
fore the crown had some rights over the land when it passed to a
minor. In practice it often meant that the wardship was sold to a
guardian, who might lease out the minor's lands for his own profit,
and who might also arrange a lucrative marriage between the
ward and a member of the guardian's family.[2] Burghley tended to
be an enlightened guardian, but none the less in 1589 he attempt-
ed to arrange a marriage between Southampton and his grand-
daughter Lady Elizabeth Vere. Southampton resisted this match.
This reluctance to marry may have been for reasons of family alle-
giance: in 1598 he eventually married Elizabeth Vernon (whom he
had made pregnant).[3] She was the cousin of the Earl of Essex,
Southampton's close ally.

Burghley's attempt to marry Southampton to his granddaugh-
ter in 1589 may have played a small part in the genesis of Shake-
speare's poem about a man who resists the charms of the very

[1] Patrick Cheney, unpublished paper delivered at the University of London con-
ference on the Narrative Poems, 27–29 July 2000: 'Mirrors for the Millennium:
Francis Meres and the Historic Hall of Shakespeare'.

[2] See Joel Hurstfield, 'Lord Burghley as Master of the Court of Wards, 1561–98',
Transactions of the Royal Historical Society 4th ser. 31 (1949), 95–114. Akrigg, 23–40.

[3] For the view that the taint of illegitimacy surrounding Elizabeth Vere played its
part, see Patrick M. Murphy, 'Wriothesley's Resistance: Wardship Practice and
Ovidian Narratives in Shakespeare's *Venus and Adonis*', in Philip C. Kolin, ed., *Venus
and Adonis: Critical Essays* (New York and London, 1997), 323–40, esp. 334–5.

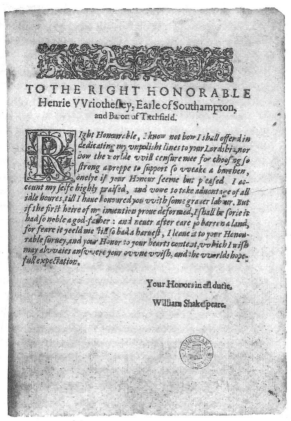

2. Dedication to *Venus and Adonis* (1593).

goddess of love herself. In 1591 John Clapham, one of Lord Burghley's secretaries, composed a highly Ovidian Latin poem called *Narcissus*, which he dedicated to Southampton.[1] The poem may have been designed as a rebuke to the wilful ward from a prominent member of Burghley's entourage, since it describes the selfish failure of Narcissus to respond to the love of Echo. Clapham's *Narcissus* was the first work of any kind dedicated to

---

[1] See Colin Burrow and Charles Martindale, 'Clapham's *Narcissus*: A Pre-Text for Shakespeare's *Venus and Adonis*', *English Literary Renaissance* 22 (1992), 147–76.

Southampton.[1] The second was *Venus and Adonis*. It has been claimed that Shakespeare's poem was an answer to Clapham's, and that the resistance of Adonis to Venus is an oblique defence of the Earl for his resistance to the charms of Elizabeth Vere.[2] This is unlikely: the fate of Adonis—gored by a boar, turned into a flower, and then plucked—is scarcely powerful propaganda for remaining a bachelor. Richard Field had some connections with Burghley and his interests, and had dedicated Puttenham's *Art of English Poesy* to Burghley in 1589.[3] It is highly unlikely that he would have risked a relationship with one of the most powerful men in England by printing a work which could be seen as encouraging one of Burghley's wards to rebel against him. It is more likely that Shakespeare found in the creaky apparatus of Clapham's poem a form of moralized, neo-Latin Ovidianism which he could outstrip in the vernacular. At several points his poem seems to be consciously attempting to outdo Clapham's monochrome classicism in technicolour English. So Clapham's Echo sings a lengthy echo song of lament, each line of which ends with an artful Latin pun (ll. 178–208); Shakespeare's Venus also sings an echo song, but it is pointedly not reproduced in the poem, as though it is simply too passé ('Her heavy anthem still concludes in woe, | And still the choir of echoes answer so. | Her song was tedious, and out-wore the night', ll. 839–41). Clapham's Narcissus eventually gallops off on a ponderously allegorical horse called 'caeca Libido' ('Blind Desire', l. 151). It is likely that here too Shakespeare was determined to complicate and enrich Clapham's skeletal allegory by creating the vernacular horse of fire described in lines 259–318, which tramples, whinnies, and bolts with an energy which comprehensively outruns Clapham's jaded allegory.

It was a shrewd move on Shakespeare's part to dedicate a poem to a nobleman who was just about to attain seniority (and so would shortly have control over the income from his estates), who cut a fine figure at court, and who had a taste for Ovidian poems.

[1] Franklin B. Williams, *Index of Citations and Commendatory Verses in English Books before 1641* (1962), 204 (no entries for Southampton are in the emendations to the index in *The Library* 5th ser. 30 (1975), Supplement).

[2] Akrigg, 196: 'Knowing how Southampton had begged old Burghley for more time before taking a bride, Shakespeare . . . could envisage his patron giving an approving nod.'

[3] Field's first publication was Burghley's *The Copy of a Letter sent out of England to Don Bernadin Mendoza* (1588).

By 1594 Thomas Nashe, dedicating *The Unfortunate Traveller* to Southampton, described him as 'a dear lover and cherisher as well of the lovers of poets as of the poets themselves'.[1] A little later John Florio recorded that he had lived 'in his pay and patronage for some years'.[2] Southampton evidently offered more than promises to those who dedicated works to him. And the fact that Shakespeare went on to dedicate *Lucrece* to the Earl in 1594, and did so in notably warm terms, suggests that Southampton gave him something. Whether it was friendship, love, hospitality during the plague, or money, or any or all of these things will probably never be known. The earliest evidence concerning what Southampton may have offered Shakespeare is extremely unreliable. Rowe recorded in 1709, on the authority of Davenant, that Southampton gave Shakespeare £1,000.[3] This is wildly improbable, since the total income from Southampton's estate on his majority was only around £3,000 per annum,[4] and there are plausible reports that Burghley imposed a crippling debt of £5,000 on his rebellious ward in 1594 for his refusal to marry Elizabeth Vere.[5] Southampton also would certainly have had to pay a fee to the crown for the resumption of his lands when he achieved his majority. It is probably no coincidence that after Southampton turned 21 there is no clear indication that Shakespeare wrote for him again, nor that any other writer (apart from A. Darcie, the translator of Du Moulin in the 1620s) dedicated more than one work to him. Southampton did not inherit wealth in 1594: he was broke. And writers seem to have jumped smartly off the bandwagon. Nashe's *Unfortunate Traveller* was reprinted in 1594 without the dedication to Southampton. This may indicate that Southampton disapproved of the dedication, which has all of Nashe's perky just-this-side-of-insolent style to discommend it to his patron.[6] But it may also imply that by late 1594 Southampton had little money to spare to lavish on writers. There is a spate of dedications to him in the later 1590s, including

---

[1] Nashe, ii.201. Nashe graduated BA in 1585–6 from St John's College, where Southampton matriculated in 1585.

[2] John Florio, *A World of Words* (1598), sig. a3ᵛ.

[3] *Works*, ed. Nicholas Rowe (1709), i, p. x; Schoenbaum, 178–9.

[4] Akrigg, 38.

[5] C. C. Stopes, *The Life of Henry, Third Earl of Southampton, Shakespeare's Patron* (Cambridge, 1922), 86. Burghley was fully entitled to do this; Akrigg, 39.

[6] McKerrow speculates that Nashe may have had 'a patron who was not on good terms with Southampton' by late 1594, Nashe, iv.255.

a translation of the Greek prose romance *Clitophon and Leucippe*, Florio's *World of Words*, and the biblical paraphrases of Henry Lok. In the seventeenth century several poets, including Samuel Daniel, Joshua Sylvester, and George Chapman, may have hoped that Southampton would revive the patronage formerly offered by his executed friend the Earl of Essex. But there is little sign that in his later life Southampton offered significant support to poets, and there is no sign of any contact with Shakespeare after the publication of *Lucrece* in 1594.

Southampton has, however, frequently been linked with Shakespeare's Sonnets, and has often been identified with the 'Mr W. H.' to whom the volume is dedicated. There are reasons to be sceptical about this identification, as there are about all the attempts to find a single biographical key to the Sonnets (see below, pp. 100–3), but some aspects of his later career may cast light on Shakespeare's poems. Southampton joined with the Earl of Essex in 1596 for the Cadiz expedition, and followed him again to the Azores in 1597, and to Ireland in 1599. It was in this period of his life that William Reynolds claimed Southampton gave physical expression to male friendships:

I do marvel also what became of Pierce Edmonds, the Earl of Essex's man . . . he was Corporal general of the horse in Ireland under the earl of Southampton. He ate and drank at his table and lay in his tent . . . the earl Southampton would coll [embrace] and hug him in his arms and play wantonly with him.[1]

Reynolds was a madman by the standards of any age (he repeatedly wrote long and marvellously deranged letters to Queen Elizabeth). His accusation is typical of many attempts by hostile witnesses to characterize intense and tactile male friendships, and particularly relationships between masters and servants, as symptoms of the capital offence of sodomy.[2] But this description of the Earl does set up resonances with the resistant Adonis, and perhaps too with the beloved young man who will not breed who is addressed by the early Sonnets. In 1601 Southampton joined the

[1] Cecil Papers 83, fo. 62^r; BL microfilm M/485/41, transcribed in Katherine Duncan-Jones, 'Much Ado With Red And White: The Earliest Readers Of William Shakespeare's "Venus and Adonis" (1593)', *RES* 44 (1993), 485.

[2] Allan Bray, 'Homosexuality and the Signs of Male Friendship in Elizabethan England', in Jonathan Goldberg, ed., *Queering the Renaissance* (Durham, NC and London, 1994), 40–61, esp. 48.

Earl of Essex in his rebellion, and was condemned to death. His former guardian Lord Burghley ensured that his sentence was commuted to life imprisonment. Southampton was freed from the tower on 10 April 1603, after the accession of James I (an event which some have linked with 'My love looks fresh' in Sonnet 107; see 107.10 n.). It is, however, likely that any association with Shakespeare ended in 1594.

Literary Milieu. *Venus and Adonis* was a hit. But what kind of poem was it? It is hard to know how the many early readers who rushed to buy it would have described what they had bought. The terms usually used today—'narrative poem', 'minor epic', 'epyllion'—were not current in the 1590s. Its early readers would probably not have used a generic term of the poem at all. They would have either described it as a 'pamphlet',[1] or they would have characterized it by a descriptive epithet derived from the sensuousness of its verse. 'Honey-tongued' became the favoured epithet to apply to Shakespeare after the publication of the poem. The use of a compound adjective to describe Shakespeare is no accident, since such adjectives are part of the stylistic fingerprint of *Venus and Adonis* from its very first stanza.[2] The first reader to leave a record of his responses to the poem noted not its genre but its persistent play of colour. William Reynolds, who read the poem in 1593, thought that Venus was a thinly veiled allegory of Elizabeth I, whilst noting (in a rare moment of lucidity) that the poem made 'much ado with red and white'.[3] Its hyper-rich language and its continual minglings of crimson and pale (Adonis suspended ' 'Twixt crimson shame, and anger ashy pale' (l. 76), the battle in Venus between the red and white of passion (ll. 346–7), the milky tusks of the boar mingled with the gore of his victim, the chequered red and white of the Adonis-flower) were what first hit its readers' eyes. Red and white were burned into the imaginations of Londoners in 1593: those infected with the plague in the city carried red wands to warn passers-by; in the country they carried white.[4]

---

[1] *Allusion Book*, i.174 and 189.

[2] See e.g. Meres (*Allusion Book*, i.46) and Weever (*Allusion Book*, i.24).

[3] Duncan-Jones, 'Much Ado', 488.

[4] Barrett, *Present Remedies*, p. xiv. Compare *Oenone and Paris by T.H.*, ed. Joseph Quincy Adams (Washington, DC, 1943), l. 156, when Paris blushes: 'The white and red were in his face at strife.'

But most early readers would have known that *Venus and Adonis* was an intervention in a recognizable project. Over the previous decade a number of writers had created erotic narrative poems by extracting and elaborating single tales from Ovid's *Metamorphoses*. Early readers would have seen the poem as contributing to this genre, even if they did not know what to call it.[1] Richard Carew in 1595 linked Marlowe's *Hero and Leander* with *Venus and Adonis* as the modern equivalents of Catullus.[2] He is presumably thinking of Catullus's 64th poem, an artful brief epic on the abandonment of Ariadne by Theseus, which is seen by modern critics as the first Latin epyllion. (These were short mini-epics rooted in the aesthetics of the Greek poet Callimachus, who insisted that poets should eschew the extended narrative of epic in favour of a short fable encrusted with learned mythological allusions and digressions.[3]) Other learned readers might also have recognized that the work was one of the vast number of European poems from the mid-sixteenth century onwards which had taken single tales from Ovid's *Metamorphoses* and turned them into free-standing narrative poems. There were a number of versions of the story of Venus and Adonis in this tradition, several of which, like Shakespeare's version, divide the poem between Venus's courtship of Adonis and her eventual lament for his death, in the manner of Bion's 'Lament for Adonis'.[4]

Shakespeare's poem was primarily a contribution to an English genre, however, and one which had two distinct features: it was a form adopted by young men (and often by young men associated with the theatre, such as Marlowe, Lodge, and Beaumont); and it was a form which those young male poets used to display their tal-

[1] Valuable book-length studies of what are variously called 'erotic narrative poems' and 'minor epic' include Clarke Hulse, *Metamorphic Verse: The Elizabethan Minor Epic* (Princeton, 1981) and William Keach, *Elizabethan Erotic Narratives* (New Brunswick, 1977). Useful anthologies include Sandra Clark, ed., *Amorous Rites: Elizabethan Erotic Narrative Verse* (1994), and Nigel Alexander, ed., *Elizabethan Narrative Verse*, Stratford-upon-Avon Library 3 (1967).

[2] *Allusion Book*, i.27.

[3] But see Walter Allen, Jr., 'The Non-existent Classical Epyllion', *SP* 55 (1958), 515–18.

[4] See Anthony Mortimer, *Variable Passions: A Reading of Shakespeare's Venus and Adonis* (New York, 2000), 171–96. For French contributions, see Anne Moss, *Poetry and Fable: Studies in Mythological Narrative in Sixteenth-century France* (Cambridge, 1984).

ents to a wide audience in print. The epigraph to the volume, which translates as 'Let the common herd be amazed by worthless things; but for me let golden Apollo provide cups full of the water of the Muses' (Ovid, *Amores* 1.15.35–6), claims that what follows stands out from the herd. Each writer who composed an Ovidian narrative poem aimed to make his mark by adapting and exceeding what earlier exponents of the form had achieved. It is not known whether Shakespeare's poem antedates or imitates Marlowe's *Hero and Leander* (printed in 1598, but composed before Marlowe's death in June 1593, and entered in the Stationers' Register on 28 September 1593, just after the publication of *Venus and Adonis*).[1] But in Marlowe's poem there is a tiny description of the love of Venus and Adonis lurking on the hem of Hero's gown:

> Her wide sleeves green, and bordered with a grove,
> Where Venus in her naked glory strove
> To please the careless and disdainful eyes
> Of proud Adonis, that before her lies.[2]

Shakespeare may have plucked this detail from (almost literally) the margin of Marlowe's poem, or Marlowe may have decided to enfold the subject-matter of his rival's poem into a tiny embroidered patch at the very start of his work. Either way, the detail reveals a primary feature of the aesthetic of Elizabethan Ovidian poems: in them marginal details are amplified until they become central, and what seems central is often miniaturized until it becomes marginal. Contributors to the genre loved to miniaturize the poems they were imitating, or to make whole poems from tiny details in earlier contributions to the genre. T[homas] H[eywood] played this trick on Shakespeare when at the start of *Oenone and Paris* (registered on 17 May 1594, less than a year after *Venus and Adonis* had appeared) he truncated the subject of Shakespeare's poem into a simile: 'As once the goddess Cytherea came | To find Adonis following of his game'[3] Shakespeare's poem may also blow up into a full story a tiny passage from the margins of Spenser's *Faerie Queene*, in which Venus is described as a sly ensnarer of Adonis in a description of a tapestry on the walls of Malecasta's castle:

---

[1] Arber, ii.636.   [2] *Hero and Leander*, ll. 11–14. Quotations modernized from Gill.
[3] *Oenone and Paris*, ll. 53–4.

A worke of rare deuice, and wondrous wit.
First did it shew the bitter balefull stowre,
Which her assayd with many a feruent fit,
When first her tender hart was with his beautie smit.

Then with what sleights and sweet allurements she
  Entyst the Boy, as well that art she knew,
  And wooed him her Paramoure to be;
  Now making girlonds of each flowre that grew,
  To crowne his golden lockes with honour dew;
  Now leading him into a secret shade
  From his Beauperes, and from bright heauens vew,
  Where him to sleepe she gently would perswade,
Or bathe him in a fountaine by some couert glade.

(*FQ* 3.1.34–5)

Shakespeare may also have responded, in a similarly sceptical and resistant way, to Spenser's use of the myth in the Garden of Adonis (3.6), where the relationship between Venus and Adonis becomes a sage and serious allegory of the origins of life and the need for it to continue. One of the principal aims of Ovidian poetry in the 1590s was to take a detail and weave ornaments around it, and in the process to rewrite the priorities of an earlier writer: Spenser's sleep-inducing, procreative goddess is answered by Shakespeare's ceaselessly eloquent and active Venus. His goddess runs, and sweats, and faints, and talks, and talks. The poem owed its birth to the highly competitive market-place for printed books among the young men of late Elizabethan London. Shakespeare wanted the poem to impress its patron, but he also wished it to make his mark among the book buyers who wandered around the precincts of St Paul's Cathedral (the main area for printing and selling books) as someone who could outdo his predecessors in the arts of miniaturization and ornamentation.

The Fable of Ovid Treating of Narcissus, which appeared anonymously in 1560, and Thomas Peend's *Pleasant Fable of Salmacis and Hermaphroditus* (1565) were the earliest English poems to expand stories from Ovid's *Metamorphoses* into free-standing publications (although Ovidian tales leave a rich imprint on the work of Chaucer and Gower). But effectively the first English Ovidian narrative poem to operate within and in part create the ambience of *Venus and Adonis* was Thomas Lodge's *Scylla's Metamorphosis* (1589), which dwells on the ways in which men can yearn for women and women can yearn for men. It also insists that these states of yearning are sequential rather than simultaneous. This aspect of Lodge's poem responds to one of the main interests of Ovid. The *Metamorphoses* repeatedly explore the ways in which sexual desire simply will not do what it should, and the ways in which desire fails to find fulfilment even where it should. Metamorphosis often enters Ovid's tales as a means of exploring the ways in which desire warps and transforms those who experience it. Ovid's tale of Echo and Narcissus (which weaves in and out of most of the English examples of the Ovidian narrative poem) dwells on how desire never manages to be mutual: as Echo pines into nothingness through her longing for Narcissus, Narcissus gazes at his own image and fades into a shadow. That story is only one of Ovid's many explorations of the ways in which mutual love, a recognition of oneself in the other which also acknowledges the difference of the other, is so elusive a thing as to be all but unattainable. But it is absolutely at the heart of the Ovid which Shakespeare read. This episode, the chief source of Clapham's *Narcissus*, repeatedly surfaces in Shakespeare's poem. Venus threatens Adonis with the fate of Narcissus, who 'died to kiss his shadow in the brook' (l. 162); she also promises a form of sexual fulfilment which famishes the appetite it feeds, in an echo of Narcissus's cry of 'inopem me copia fecit' (abundance makes me want) at *Metamorphoses* 3.466: 'And yet not cloy thy lips with loathed satiety, | But rather famish them amid their plenty' (ll. 19–20). She is fond of echoing figures such as epizeuxis, the emphatic repetition of a word or phrase ('Say shall we, shall we?', l. 586) or of delicately remodelled echoes ('"Give me my hand", saith he . . . | "Give me my heart", saith she', ll. 373–4). When she is left alone at night she sings songs to echo, as she is driven by the resistance of the self-loving Adonis nearly to metamorphose, like Echo, into a disembodied voice (ll. 829–46).[1]

  Shakespeare found the story of Venus and Adonis in the tenth book of Ovid's *Metamorphoses*. He probably read the story in Latin,

---

[1] On the narcissism of Adonis, see Coppélia Kahn, 'Self and Eros in *Venus and Adonis*', *Centennial Review* 20 (1976), 351–71. This aspect of the poem has generated some fine readings founded on Lacanian conceptions of desire: see Catherine Belsey, 'Love as Trompe-l'oeil: Taxonomies of Desire in *Venus and Adonis*', *Shakespeare Quarterly* 46 (1995), 257–76, and James Schiffer, 'Shakespeare's *Venus and Adonis*: A Lacanian Tragi-Comedy of Desire', in Kolin, ed., *Venus and Adonis*, 359–76; reprinted as 'Shakespeare's *Venus and Adonis*: Flower of Desire', *Q/W/E/R/T/Y* 8 (1998), 117–26.

and probably also in the translation by Arthur Golding (1567). It is likely, however, that he did not just pluck the story out of its context. Ovid embeds the story of Venus and Adonis in a long sequence of tales about loves which go wrong in a variety of ways. The whole of Book 10 is related by the singer Orpheus, who, in Ovid's version, turns to the love of boys after the death of his wife Eurydice. The tale of Adonis concludes the stories told by Orpheus, but the majority of the book relates the stories of his parents and grandparents. Adonis's genealogy as told by Ovid begins with Pygmalion, who made and fell in love with an ivory statue. Pygmalion courts and touches his creation, and, thanks to the intervention of the goddess Venus, it eventually comes to life. His union with his own artefact produces Paphus (as sixteenth-century texts called him), whose child, in turn, is Cinyras. Cinyras has a daughter, Myrrha, who conceives an incestuous passion for her father, which she eventually consummates by deceiving him as to her identity. She flees in terror when he discovers who she is, and eventually begs to be metamorphosed into a tree. From that incestuous union between the grandchild and the great-grandchild of a statue Adonis is born, and he enters the world by ripping through the bark of the tree into which his mother has been transformed. Venus, the goddess of love whose metamorphosis of Pygmalion's statue began the whole dynasty, then falls in love with Adonis, and, in Ovid's version, wins him.

Ovid's story, however, is not by any means a simple genealogy. Book 10 plays artful games with narratorial perspectives, to which Shakespeare actively responded. Much of the story of Venus and Adonis is taken up with a long tale related by Venus herself. When Adonis tells her that he plans to hunt the boar, the goddess tries to delay him by telling the tale of Atalanta and Hippomenes. This story, told by the loquacious Venus, occupies one hundred and forty-seven of the two hundred and nineteen lines which Ovid devotes to the story of Venus and Adonis. The tale told by Venus does not directly figure in Shakespeare's version of the Venus and Adonis story, but it fuels many of the concerns of his poem: Venus tells it in order to delay her lover from hunting, and it is a tale about delay (Hippomenes runs a race against the maiden Atalanta, whom he defeats by throwing down golden balls in her path; she delays to pick them up). It is also a tale about disastrous sexual passion, since Atalanta has received a prophecy that when she marries she is doomed, and she and Hippomenes are duly turned to lions for their ingratitude to Venus. As Jonathan Bate has noted, the tale also draws attention to the way in which tales about love are shaped by the motives of the teller: for Orpheus, the narrator of the whole book, the story stands as a warning to avoid love (or the love of women at any rate); for Venus, its immediate narrator, it is a warning to Adonis that he should obey her.[1] The presence of two narrators in the inset tale of Atalanta also enables Ovid to bend and confuse his readers' preconceptions about gender. Atalanta is a boyish girl. And when Ovid describes Orpheus, the lover of boys, describing Venus (in love with a girlish boy) describing the girl Atalanta as she runs from Hippomenes any assured sexual bearings dive for cover:

> Her count'nance and her grace
> Was such as in a boy might well be called a wench's face,
> And in a wench be called a boy's.
>
> (Golding 10.429–36)

A little later the confusion spreads, as Hippomenes sees Atalanta:

> He saw her face and body bare, (for why the Lady then
> Did strip her to her naked skin) the which was like to mine,
> Or rather (if that thou wert made a woman) like to thine:
> He was amazed.
>
> (Golding 10.673–6)

This deliberately queers the vision. Is she desirable because she is like a boy, or because she is a girl, or both? Is Adonis lovely as a girl? And to what extent is Orpheus, who has loved women and now loves boys, a presence here?

Renaissance readers of Ovid responded vigorously to this aspect of his art, which is not anything so reassuringly stable as 'homosexual': it makes any reader who is committed to reading with his or her sexual desires alive experience sexuality as a dislocating force. Once you choose to gaze erotically, eros could pull your desires in any direction, towards men, towards women, or towards hermaphroditic adolescents. This was a live element in the Ovidian poetry of the 1590s, and remained a live element in Shakespeare's Sonnets. Francis Beaumont's erotic narrative poem *Salmacis and Hermaphroditus* (which tells the Ovidian tale of how the nymph

[1] Bate, 57.

Salmacis falls in love with the boy Hermaphroditus, and eventually absorbs his body into hers) begins with an epigraph to the reader: 'I hope my poem is so lively writ | That you shall turn half maid for reading it'. The poem tries to make its male readers turn womanish in their desires, and repeatedly Elizabethan Ovidian poems seek to make men desirable by men, and to blur the divide between genders. The glorious moment in *Hero and Leander* when the God Neptune laps and winds around the body of Leander as he swims the Hellespont knowingly makes its readers imagine the licking of water over a smooth body:

> He watched his arms and, as they opened wide
> At every stroke, betwixt them would he slide
> And steal a kiss, and then run out and dance,
> And, as he turned, cast many a lustful glance,
> And threw him gaudy toys to please his eye,
> And dive into the water, and there pry
> Upon his breast, his thighs, and every limb,
> And up again, and close beside him swim,
> And talk of love. Leander made reply,
> 'You are deceived; I am no woman, I.'
> (*Hero and Leander*, ll. 667–76)

The poetry of the 1590s is frequently homosocial, and frequently is written, as *Venus and Adonis* was, by poorer male poets to richer and more powerful male patrons in order to persuade them to provide material support. That relationship often takes on a homoerotic charge. To engage a male reader's desire for a male author's male creation is one way of transforming the material exchange of poem for money into an act of quasi-sexual intimacy.[1]

It is often said that Shakespeare took the idea of a resistant Adonis from Ovid's tale of the nymph Salmacis and the reluctant ephebe Hermaphroditus.[2] The poem is also haunted, as we have seen, by the figure of Narcissus. But more than that, Shakespeare's poem reads the Ovidian tale of Venus and her reluctant lover with a dramatist's ear for the significance of silences and hesitations. Ovid's Adonis says little, and sits patiently while his would-be mistress tells him the tale of the reluctant Atalanta's efforts to escape

---

[1] See Jeffrey Masten, *Textual Intercourse* (Cambridge, 1997), 44–5.
[2] For the poem's sources in Ovid, see Bullough, 161–76; Bush, 137–48; Bate, 48–65.

her lovers. Before she begins the story she tells him peremptorily to sit down on the ground, like a wayward dog ('humo', *Met.* 10.552). His silence and his subordination to Venus become in Shakespeare's retelling of the tale fraught with significance, and from the momentary curtness of the Ovidian goddess Shakespeare developed his provocative reading of the relationship of power between the two characters. Shakespeare knew well the dramatic effect of having a character onstage who fails to speak (his Adonis utters only eighty-eight lines in the entire poem), and he read that dramatic effect into the silence of Ovid's Adonis. And the moment he breaks his silence prompts Venus to her archest teasing:

> 'What, canst thou talk?' quoth she, 'Hast thou a tongue?'
>
> (l. 427)

Part of the comedy and the pathos of the poem is that Venus both wants Adonis to speak and desperately does not want him to speak in order to reject her, and part of what the poem asks of its readers is to imagine how her eloquence is being deflected or rejected by Adonis as she speaks.

The poem is in other respects the product of a theatrical intelligence enjoying leave from the material restrictions of the stage. It often gives cues to its readers to imagine its setting, the passage of time, or the gestural relations between the two speakers. At several key points the physical positions of the two lovers are evoked, sometimes with a wry glimpse at the physical power of Venus (as when she tucks Adonis under her arm, or reminds us he is wriggling: 'Lie quietly, and hear a little more; | Nay, do not struggle, for thou shalt not rise', ll. 709–10, or when she says 'What seest thou in the ground?', l. 118). And throughout there are direct appeals to a reader to 'look', which extend into the poem's normal way of introducing a simile, which is by 'Look how'. This formula struck the eye of Shakespeare's most responsive imitator, Richard Barnfield: 'Look how a brightsome planet in the sky, | (Spangling the Welkin with a golden spot) | Shoots suddenly from the beholder's eye.'[1] And well it might: in Shakespeare's dramatic works the phrase 'look how' is not used to introduce similes, but to convey a verbal stage-direction or an instruction to an audience to imagine

---

[1] Richard Barnfield, *The Complete Poems*, ed. George Klawitter (Selinsgrove, Pa. and London, 1990), 'Cassandra', ll. 145–7; *A lusion Book*, i.19.

a gesture or a scene before them (as in *Merchant* 5.1.58–9: 'Look how the floor of heaven | Is thick inlaid with patens of bright gold'). The poem uses this trick of stage-setting to create a pictorial mode of writing, in which similes become part of the visually imagined scene. Voices do not simply echo off the page in this poem in a glorified version of the *suasoriae* (or formal speeches of persuasion) which Shakespeare is likely to have practised at Stratford Grammar School. They take on bodies.

Shakespeare probably had an extensive training in the art of rhetoric at school, where he is very likely to have been required to imagine speeches which would fit particular characters, and to argue on either side of a complex question, such as whether or not it is a good thing to marry.[1] A commonplace of the art was that rhetoric was a form of irresistible power (a frequent emblem for rhetoric in this period was that of an orator dragging his audience around by golden chains tied to their ears). Another was that rhetoric was aligned to virtue: Cato Uticensis's doctrine that the orator was a good man skilled in speaking ('vir bonus, dicendi peritus') was cited with approval by Quintilian (12.1.1), and re-echoed in innumerable textbooks in the period. These sober principles are subjected to merciless teasing in this poem: Venus is not a man, and her rhetoric is certainly not motivated by anything so straightforward as virtue. Moreover, it manages to have no effect on the recalcitrant body of Adonis, even when she is physically on top of him.[2] One of Adonis's methods of attacking Venus's arguments is to claim that they are no more than a 'theme', or a formal topos for schoolroom debate (ll. 422, 770). The poem owes almost as much to the art of rhetoric as it does to Ovid (himself a staple of the early-modern classroom); but it is ostentatiously a poem for people who have outgrown the pieties they learnt at school, and a poem which asks questions about the relationship, or misrelationship, between rhetoric, virtue, and the practical effects of the art of persuasion. Its voices are not those of Ciceronian virtuous orators

[1] For an exhaustive discussion of the likely curriculum of Stratford Grammar School, see T. W. Baldwin, *William Shakspere's Small Latine and Lesse Greeke*, 2 vols. (Urbana, Ill., 1944). On arguments on either side of the question see Joel B. Altman, *The Tudor Play of Mind: Rhetorical Inquiry and the Development of Elizabethan Drama* (Berkeley and London, 1978).

[2] See further Richard Lanham, *The Motives of Eloquence: Literary Rhetoric in the Renaissance* (New Haven, 1976), 82–110.

who successfully persuade their fellow-citizens to follow a virtuous course; rather they emanate from bodies positioned within a landscape in precise relation to each other, who can neither persuade nor be persuaded. Words and bodies refuse simply to marry in the poem: however hard Venus persuades, she still fails to make Adonis desire her.

A great part of the pleasure of reading the poem, however, comes from repeatedly almost forgetting the scene and the bodily presences from which its words spring. Venus's courtship of Adonis is gloriously and scandalously inappropriate. She is given the full repertoire of the clichéd language which men in the Petrarchan tradition use to seduce women: breed, reproduce yourself, pluck the flower of youth, avoid the fate of Narcissus. The main trick of the poem is to ask a simple question: how do these clichés sound when they are put in the mouth of a woman? Some of the hostility and unease which readers have felt towards Venus (which is considered below) derive from this simple transposition of a recognizably gendered mode of rhetoric to someone of what is, conventionally speaking, the 'wrong' sex. Her speeches, however, often continue for so long that they usurp their narrative frame, and make it possible almost to forget who is speaking. This effect is more apparent in an unmodernized text, in which speech-marks were not used. Playwrights, of course, can only write for distinct bodies; but in a printed poem distinct voices can blend and dip into one another before an aside or an allusion to the physical setting reminds a reader that they are distinct. As Venus speaks, her readers are alternately absorbed by the masculine persuasive force of her voice and then reminded of her physical presence. She becomes an eloquent manly woman, and then often herself drops a cue to remember that it is a woman speaking and not an orthodox male Petrarchist: 'Within my bosom, whereon thou dost lie, | My boding heart pants, beats, and takes no rest' (ll. 646–7).

The poem's willingness to confuse its readers about gender and setting was clearly recognized by its early readers. In Thomas Heywood's play *The Fair Maid of the Exchange* (printed in 1607) Bowdler (who is a man) uses Venus's words to court a woman:

> *Bowdler*: I never read anything but *Venus and Adonis*.
> *Cripple*: Why that's the very quintessence of love.
> If you remember but a verse or two,

> I'll pawn my head, goods, lands and all 'twill do.
>   *Bowdler*: Why then, have at her.
> Fondling I say, since I have hemmed thee here,
> Within the circle of this ivory pale,
> I'll be a park.
>   *Mall Berry*: Hands off, fond Sir!
>   *Bowdler*: —And thou shalt be my deer;
> Feed thou on me, and I will feed on thee,
> And love shall feed us both.
>   *Mall Berry*: Feed you on woodcocks. I can fast a while.
>   *Bowdler*: Vouchsafe, thou wonder, to alight thy steed.
>   *Cripple*: Take heed, she's not on horseback.
>   *Bowdler*: Why then she is alighted.[1]

Bowdler, the exuberant opposite of his prudish namesake, is sure that he (a man) can borrow the eloquence of Venus, and the most erotic section of it at that, to win his mistress. The passage hints too that readers appreciated the muscle which lurks behind Venus's entrapment of Adonis: 'She locks her lily fingers one in one' just before she creates the conceit of herself as the park and Adonis as a deer (and this highly erotic passage was also copied down in commonplace books by early readers of the poem).[2] Bowdler does not just quote from the poem: he tries to re-enact it by embracing the unfortunate Mall Berry as he quotes its words. The scene is a playwright's reading of a playwright's poem, which is aware of the ways in which speech can imply actions. But it also has a joke at the expense of Bowdler for his failure to remember the physical setting implied by the poem: when he quotes Venus's first words to Adonis, 'Vouchsafe, thou wonder, to alight thy steed', he forgets that Adonis is on horseback, and his mistress is not. The learned spoof on witty university men, *The Return from Parnassus* (printed in 1606), similarly represents a *man* using Venus's words as part of an unsuccessful seduction, and again makes a character snatch Venus's words out of their context, while the playwright slyly remembers where they come from:

[1] *Allusion Book*, i.177.

[2] Hilton Kelliher, 'Unrecorded Extracts from Shakespeare, Sidney, and Dyer', *English Manuscript Studies* 2 (1991), 163–87, notes that the East-Anglian gentleman Henry Colling transcribed this section of the poem into his commonplace book (CUL, MS Mm.3.29, fo. 63ᵛ) probably *c*.1596. Heywood's *Oenone and Paris* (1594) tries its hand at a revision of Venus's ivory pale, ll. 463–6: Oenone offers 'Be thou Pigmalion, I his ivory work | (Though woman-like, a cold and senseless stone), | Suffer me in thy naked bed to lurk, | Clip, kiss, coll, love me like Pigmalion.'

Gullio: Pardon, fair lady, though sick-thoughted Gullio makes amain unto thee, and like a bold-faced suitor gins to woo thee.

Ingenioso: (We shall have nothing but pure Shakespeare and shreds of poetry that he hath gathered at the theatres!).

Gullio goes on:

> Thrise fairer than myself (—thus I began—)
> The gods fair riches, sweet above compare,
> Stain to all nymphs, more lovely than a man . . .[1]

The final quotation from Venus's first address to Adonis lets the original setting of these words drift incongruously back into view. 'More lovely than a man' means one thing when it is addressed by a goddess to a man ('as a youth you are lovelier than a man; as a human you are almost a god'); when it is addressed by a man to a woman it carries the presumably unwanted suggestion that Gullio may usually find men more lovely than women. These dramatizations of extracts from *Venus and Adonis* suggest that early readers appreciated its sophisticated tangling of conventional perceptions of gender, and that they also relished the way its rhetoric can be read at one time within its dramatic setting, and at another independently of it.

As place and persons dissolve and then re-form continually in *Venus and Adonis*, so too time comes and goes. The poem creates a continual interplay between the time it takes to read a particular speech or episode and the literal passage of time. It is punctuated by moments which classical rhetoricians would call 'chronographies', or descriptions of particular times of day. These too caught the eye of several of the poem's early readers and imitators: Thomas Heywood's *Oenone and Paris* begins with a flush of dawn, and the unscrupulous Paris tries to end his conversation with the woman he has abandoned at nightfall.[2] *Venus and Adonis* begins with the purple glow of dawn. The heat of noon strikes at lines 177–8. We are suddenly reminded that night has fallen in line 821, and dawn breaks gorgeously again in lines 853–8: 'Lo here the gentle lark, weary of rest, | From his moist cabinet mounts up on high.' These temporal indicators are so pronounced, and make it so clear that the action of the poem lasts for a period of two days, that they have led Alastair Fowler and Christopher Butler to argue for exact

---

[1] *Allusion Book*, i.67.   [2] *Oenone and Paris*, ll. 1–12 and 703–8.

numerological significance within the poem: each 43 lines, they argue, represents one hour of action, and the whole poem (which consists of twenty times sixty lines minus six) evokes the short summer's day of the twenty years of the Earl of Southampton.

The poem's time-scheme, however, is likely to be more psychological than numerological. Venus promises that

> 'A summer's day will seem an hour but short,
> Being wasted in such time-beguiling sport.'
> (ll. 23–4)

And there are indeed moments in the poem when time seems to slow down almost to a standstill, as Venus holds her human addressee still and silent for extraordinarily long speeches. There are other moments when time gallops, as the narrator refuses to adapt the time of the poem to the passage of time as it is felt by the characters within the poem. Venus's night of lament, for instance, seems to her tediously long, but is dispatched by the narrator with a briskness which is close kin to brusqueness:

> Her song was tedious, and out-wore the night,
> For lovers' hours are long, though seeming short;
> If pleased themselves, others they think delight
> In suchlike circumstance, with suchlike sport.
> (ll. 841–3)

The shortness of the night may indicate that the events related in the poem do indeed occupy 'a summer's day', which, in England, consists of long hours of daylight and brief hours of darkness. This would suit the time of publication of the poem, which was probably close to mid-summer, but would conflict with seasonal indicators buried in the text: its flowers are all flowers of the spring, such as primroses, violets, and (finally) the anemone into which Adonis is transformed. The poem is about an encounter between a fully mature woman and a beardless boy. Its seasonal setting consequently straddles the springtime under-ripeness of Adonis *and* the full summer bloom of Venus. It also repeatedly psychologizes time, overlaying its literal passage with a string of emotional dawns: so, when Adonis threatens to rebuke Venus his red mouth is 'Like a red morn that ever yet betokened | Wrack to the seaman, tempest to the field' (ll. 453–4); when Venus comes round from her faint 'The night of sorrow now is turned to day', and her eye becomes both the sun which 'cheers the morn' and a moon which reflects the light of Adonis's face. Night and day blend for her as she wakes and wonders 'What hour is this? Or morn or weary even?' (l. 495). The contraction and expansion of the passage of time in the poem is one of its most powerful techniques for moving in and out of its characters' experiences. Sometimes the narrator allows the characters' emotions to drag the poem to a standstill, or to intercalate a whole imaginary day into the action, and at other times he pointedly refuses to stretch time out in order to match the way in which his characters experience it.

The time taken to narrate, and read, the poem, is greatly influenced by its digressions—chief among which are the lengthy description of Adonis's horse (ll. 259–324), and Venus's tale of the hunting of Wat the hare (ll. 673–714). Digressions were a primary component in Elizabethan erotic poems, which continually invite their readers to wonder about the relationship between plot and ornament, centre and periphery. Shakespeare's first and most striking digression, the description of Adonis's horse as it bolts after a jennet, occupies sixty-five lines, and was dismissed by Dowden as 'a paragraph from an advertisement of a horse sale'.[1] In fact the episode artfully contributes to the poem's careful indecision about whether passion is an unbridled force which can carry you away, or a natural instinct to which Adonis is perversely resistant: the horse might be allegorized as unbridled desire (as it was in Clapham's poem) or naturalized (as Venus wishes it to be) as an embodiment of what men should do. The digression also serves a more mundane function: to stop the poem ending, as it has just almost done:

> 'Pity', she cries, 'Some favour, some remorse.'
> Away he springs, and hasteth to his horse.
>
> (ll. 257–8)

But the horse, mercifully for Venus and Shakespeare's readers, is not there, so Adonis cannot go home. Adonis's actions repeatedly try to bustle the poem into ending, and the poem refuses to do his bidding. Shakespeare's digressions make him stay, and serve to continue the endless courtship of Venus. Venus herself is in principle committed to dilating tales into as full a form as possible (and

---

[1] Edward Dowden, *Shakspere: A Critical Study of his Mind and Art* (1875), 51.

in this respect she is like the Venus who tells the story of Atalanta to her lover in Ovid). She and Shakespeare are also both particularly artful in combining intensity of feeling with duration of telling.

The second major digression, on the hunting of Wat the hare, lasts nearly forty lines. It is related by Venus rather than the narrator, and is part of her plot to thwart the passage of time. It is designed seductively to appeal to Adonis's love of hunting and to redirect it towards gentler adversaries, as well as serving to delight many of those early readers who might also have bought Turbervile's works on hunting and Blundeville's works on horsemanship (from which Shakespeare extensively draws). The Wat episode, however, does not offer quite what a Renaissance theorist of rhetoric would have wanted from a digression within a speech or poem. As Henry Peacham observed, 'the digression ought always to pertain and agree to those matters that we handle, and not to be strange or far distant from the purpose.'[1] The tale of Wat's fearful running from the hunt does appear initially to be far from Venus's purpose: its sympathy for the hare cuts against her wish to use it to persuade Adonis to hunt hares rather than boars. But in other ways it serves her purposes completely. At this point of the poem she has Adonis on top of her. To tell a long tale (and one which involves a lot of wriggling and weaving) has a practical point. It is designed by Venus to enable her to spend as long as she can underneath her lover. And if he wriggles in sympathy with the hare, then so much the better. The hare-hunt is placed at this climactic moment of sexual non-fulfilment in order to give readers from the 1590s the combined pleasure of hearing at length about a hunt, and of imagining, also at length, a woman attempting to rape a man. But it also becomes its own world, as a reader follows the hunt, and ducks into brakes, weaving and indenting with poor Wat. The poem's digressions function in a multiplicity of ways: they draw out the delight of the reader, and they prolong Venus's frustrated attempt at sexual delight. They also work to defuse the eroticism of the poem for a censorious reader. Who could possibly object to a description of a hare-hunt? Or of a sexually aroused stallion? The poem is very keen to deny, or at least to make deniable, its own eroticism. It does that partly by enabling its readers to become so absorbed in an apparent digression that the fact

---

[1] Peacham, sig. U4^r.

that the digression is designed to draw out a sexual encounter gets forgotten.

Venus's rhetoric, however, is by no means always in control of the passage of narrative time in the poem. Time slips away from her despite her attempts to seize the day, or draw it out slowly by stories. There are times too when her own lengthy rhetoric can thwart her control over the plot. At the end of Ovid's version of the story of Venus and Adonis the goddess herself decides to make Adonis into a flower. This is both a display of her power and an expression of her desire to make a memorial of her grief:

> From year to year shall grow
> A thing that of my heaviness and of thy death shall show
> The lively likeness. In a flower thy blood I will bestow.
> Hadst thou the power, Persephone, rank-scented mints to make
> Of women's limbs? and may not I like power upon me take
> Without disdain and spite, to turn Adonis to a flower?
>
> (Golding 10.849–54)

At the end of Shakespeare's poem the goddess laments, and while she curses love so that future lovers will share her sorrow, Adonis just melts away. The transformation of Adonis seems to happen behind her back, as she lets slip her grip on time:

> By this the boy that by her side lay killed
> Was melted like a vapour from her sight.
>
> (ll. 1165–6)

'By this' (a favourite phrase in the poem for jerking time on despite the wishes of its characters) means 'by this time' rather than 'as a result of this prayer'. How long has her lament taken? Long enough for Venus to have lost the power over her story which her Ovidian predecessor enjoys.

Time and how you spend it also is an important element in the moral argument of the poem, and is vital to the distinctions it makes between different ways of living. The two characters in the poem (and monologue and duologue are the staples of both *Venus and Adonis* and *Lucrece*) have a very different attitude to time as an economic commodity. Adonis is not simply a man of action forced into slow-motion by the 'time-beguiling' rhetoric of the goddess of love. He is someone who thinks time should be spent in laborious activity, and who instinctively thinks that even the sun, in making its rounds, is working hard:

> 'Look the world's comforter, with weary gait,
> His day's hot task hath ended in the west;
> The owl (night's herald) shrieks; 'tis very late.'
>
> (ll. 529–31)

Adonis notices that dusk is falling about three hundred lines before night actually falls. The lines that intervene between his sensing the dusk and darkness falling are filled by the eloquence of Venus, who manages to make the short hour between dusk and darkness expand to fill almost a third of the poem. This period of time is extended because it is the most critical period of day for a wooer: it is the point at which loquacious delay could keep the seducee out dangerously late.

There is both playfulness and purpose in this concertinaing of time at dusk. It enables Venus to produce an inverted version of an aubade, in which her eloquence delays the coming of night and the departure of Adonis. But it also reflects a subliminal unease which runs throughout the poem about its own delightful abuses of the noble art of rhetoric. Is reading an erotic poem a proper way to spend time? Is writing one a proper way to advance a poetic career? The pressure to be serious, to use time well, runs through the poem: the dedication promises Southampton that its author will 'take advantage of all *idle* hours, till I have honoured you with some graver labour'. Idle hours are what the poem presents, with the voice of Adonis and of labour being recurrently stilled within it. It beguiles its readers into delaying over it by promising a sexual fulfilment which it does not deliver and a 'graver labour' which lies in the future rather than in the present. Venus barters and haggles over the cost of a kiss, and claims to seek 'increase' (both children and wealth, ll. 169–70) in payment for her rhetoric. She tries too to make her rhetorical play of courtship appear to be an economic exchange, sealed with a 'seal manual' (l. 516) of a kiss, whilst continually taking more kisses than she has claimed to want. But at the end of the poem she wants him still, and never earns the consummation for which she has laboured so long.

For writers in the 1590s, trained in an eloquence with which they were intended to serve the state as lawyers or secretaries to the nobility, the use and abuse of rhetoric was an issue of great concern. As Richard Helgerson has shown, the myth of the prodigal son provided a recurrent reminder that the work which professional writers were engaged in might be only frivolous expenditure of time—or, to use the main Elizabethan term for fun, a pastime.[1] *Venus and Adonis* has half an eye on these arguments about how poets were using their learning and their time. It engages the reader with the rhetoric of the prodigal Venus ('Be prodigal. The lamp that burns by night | Dries up his oil to lend the world his light', ll. 755–6), which eats up their idle hours despite Adonis's curt and abrupt eagerness to get away. As well as delighting and teasing and pleasing its readers the poem reminds them that its rhetorical display is not quite work, and that its sumptuous rhetoric is not deployed for the serious purposes of advising monarchs or earning material 'increase'.

The under-presence of unease about time and its abuse is one aspect of the very delicate and carefully controlled way in which the poem creates beneath its sportive surface a pressure to read it morally. Some of its early readers would have been aware of allegorizations of the tale of Venus and Adonis. These were frequently printed in Latin mythological handbooks and in commentaries on Ovid (such as the widely influential one by Sabinus, which had been reprinted in Cambridge in 1584). Allegorical commentaries on Ovidian myths were also available in the vernacular (Arthur Golding's translation of Ovid is prefixed by an epistle which gives brief moral interpretations of many of Ovid's tales). The allegorical readings of the story of Venus and Adonis presented in these learned works were usually cosmological or seasonal. A representative example appeared in Abraham Fraunce's *Countess of Pembroke's Ivychurch* in 1592:

By Adonis is meant the sun, by Venus, the upper hemisphere of the earth . . . by the boar, winter: by the death of Adonis, the absence of the sun for the six wintery months; all which time, the earth lamenteth. Adonis is wounded in those parts which are the instruments of propagation: for, in winter the sun seemeth impotent, and the earth barren.[2]

---

[1] See Richard Helgerson, *The Elizabethan Prodigals* (Berkeley, Los Angeles, and London, 1976), *passim*, and R. W. Maslen, 'Myths Exploited: The Metamorphoses of Ovid in Early Elizabethan England', in A. B. Taylor, ed., *Shakespeare's Ovid: The 'Metamorphoses' in the Plays and Poems* (Cambridge, 2000), 15–30.

[2] Abraham Fraunce, *The Countess of Pembroke's Ivychurch* (1592), fo. 45ᵛ. A similar allegory is presented by Georgius Sabinus, whose commentary on Ovid was reprinted in Cambridge in 1584: Adonis is the sun, the boar is Capricorn. When the sun enters Capricorn in winter it loses its rays, and Venus, the earth, mourns. *Metamorphosis seu Fabulae Poeticae, Frankfurt, 1589, The Renaissance and the Gods* (New York and London, 1976), 364–5.

A number of critics (particularly those who wish to present the joyous play of reading poems as a form of moral labour) have felt that the poem is a moral allegory. It has been suggested, for instance, that beyond the apparent petulance of Adonis lies a moral commitment to love rather than lust (as he himself claims in lines 799–804), or to the independence of beauty from desire.[1] Early readers too sometimes picked out from the dedicatory promise of 'some graver labour' the wish that Shakespeare had used his skill to write on a 'graver subject' than love.[2] The poem does not preclude these impulses towards gravity—though the priestly tones adopted by some of their proponents are hard to reconcile with the poem's sexiness and humour—nor does it finally side with them. It asks its readers to think about ease and labour, and to wonder how they are spending (and the financial metaphor is active in the poem) their time even as they are being beguiled by sport.

Venus has had a particularly bad press from the moralists. C. S. Lewis memorably wrote of her:

Shakespeare's Venus is a very ill-conceived temptress. She is made so much larger than her victim that she can throw his horse's reins over one arm and tuck him in under the other, and knows her own art so badly that she threatens, almost in her first words, to 'smother' him with kisses. Certain horrible interviews with voluminous female relatives in one's early childhood inevitably recur to mind.[3]

Allen called her 'a forty-year-old countess with a taste for Chapel Royal altos'.[4] The anti-Venusians have some meat to chew on. Love is often presented in the poem as a form of predatory chase. The kisses (the word and its variants occur twenty-eight times in the poem) which Venus seeks from Adonis can become consuming. And her kind of love does seem often to transform mother love into smother love. Her first hungry kisses prompt an animal simile:

[1] See e.g. Baldwin, 83–4; Don Cameron Allen, 'On *Venus and Adonis*', *Elizabethan and Jacobean Studies Presented to Frank Percy Wilson* (Oxford, 1959), 100–11, reads Adonis's horse as an embodiment of desire and Venus as a temptation to the 'soft hunt' of love. A. C. Hamilton, '*Venus and Adonis*', *SEL* 1 (1961), 1–15, reads Adonis as beauty beset by love in all its variety.

[2] *Allusion Book*, i.69. Judicio says in *The Return from Parnassus*: 'His sweeter verse contains heart-throbbing line, | Could but a graver subject him content, | Without love's foolish lazy languishment.'

[3] C. S. Lewis, *English Literature in the Sixteenth Century Excluding Drama* (Oxford, 1954), 498.

[4] Allen, 'On *Venus*', 101.

'Even as an empty eagle sharp by fast | Tires with her beak on feathers, flesh, and bone' (ll. 55–6). The association of sexual desire and the hunt culminates in the final image of Adonis, nuzzled lovingly in the flank by the boar. Ovid often associates sexual violence with the hunt and woodland pursuits (Shakespeare had brought this association to life onstage in *Titus Andronicus*, a play written at roughly the same time as *Venus and Adonis*) both in the *Metamorphoses* and in the *Ars Amatoria*.[1] The way love-as-hunt comparisons hound Venus does appear to push her into the nets of those who wish, like Lewis, to attribute the tragedy of the poem to an over-muscled, over-sexed, and overbearing goddess.

Moral readings of the poem and of Venus, however, do not reckon with the volatility of both the poem and the goddess who is its chief character. One of the poem's deepest debts to Ovid is its fleetingness and fascination with changefulness. Ovid's Venus changes: at one moment she benignly answers Pygmalion's timid request for a wife who is like his ivory maid, at another she dresses like Diana to hunt with Adonis, and at another she savagely punishes Atalanta and Hippomenes. Shakespeare's poem draws on this flux: his Venus is powerfully seductive, engagingly absurd, desperately persuasive, a little over-large, as light as the air, wincingly wounded, and near-vindictive in grief. There is a delicacy in this mutability, which does not allow Venus to be identified with an undesirable and predatory form of 'lust' as Adonis would wish (and even he is not always quite sure he dislikes her). When Venus faints there is a sudden shift in how both she and Adonis are presented. At this point her passion is not described as being in any way predatory, and Adonis comes close to succumbing to her, as well as almost himself becoming a potential predator. It is not Venus's but Adonis's words which are compared to a wolf which 'doth grin before he barketh' 'Or like the deadly bullet of a gun' (ll. 459–61). And it is Adonis who kisses her as she faints, and who seems half-bashful, half-won when he says, apologetically, when she has come round, 'Measure my strangeness with my unripe years' (l. 524). Immediately after the faint, too, the lovers touch in a way that promises for the first and only time in the poem to be both mutual and fusing, as

[1] Hugh Parry, 'Ovid's *Metamorphoses*: Violence in a Pastoral Landscape', *Transactions and Proceedings of the American Philological Association* 95 (1964), 268–82; M. L. Stapleton, 'Venus as *Praeceptor*: The *Ars Amatoria* in *Venus and Adonis*', in Kolin, ed. *Venus and Adonis*, 309–21.

the poem almost shifts away from its volatile confusions of male and female passions to allow the two to enjoy a hermaphroditic union of desire with desire: 'Incorp'rate then they seem; face grows to face' (l. 540).

The poem, though, does not rest with that vision of union, despite the fact that it comes at the end of a stanza: in the very next line the ever-busy Adonis breathlessly 'disjoined' from Venus. It is at this point that the image of the hunt returns with a vengeance. Once partially satisfied, Venus's appetite to feed becomes destructively hungry once more: 'having felt the sweetness of the spoil, | With blindfold fury she begins to forage. | Her face doth reek and smoke, her blood doth boil, | And careless lust stirs up a desperate courage' (ll. 553–6). Shakespeare's Venus is a mobile creation, and so is his Adonis. His presentation of her draws (distantly) on a wide range of mythographical traditions: as the mythographer Natales Comes put it, 'since there are various Venuses, the modes of worshipping her vary too':[1] she is the Venus of Ovid who attempts to imitate her sister Diana and become a huntress; she is Venus Victrix, the conqueror of Mars ('leading him prisoner in a red-rose chain', l. 110); she is a Venus vulgaris (goddess of sensual love), and a Venus mechanitis (Venus practised in love's verbal artifices); and she is finally (though by no means solely) Venus Genetrix, the mother, as she finally nurses the flower which is Adonis in her arms. These representations of Venus are never allowed to rest unqualified, nor are they ever allowed to rest. Venus has moments of stillness and beauty, and moments of frantic and predatory energy. There are moments of maternal anguish ('She wildly breaketh from their strict embrace, | Like a milch-doe, whose swelling dugs do ache, | Hasting to feed her fawn, hid in some brake', ll. 874–6), and there are moments when her 'lust' seems entirely innocent of the negative associations which the word was to take on shortly after the composition of Shakespeare's poem.[2]

Venus was often represented in Renaissance mythographical handbooks by figures which simultaneously represent a multipli-

---

[1] Natales Comes, *Mythologiae (Venice 1567)*, The Renaissance and the Gods (New York and London, 1976), 121. See further A. D. Cousins, *Shakespeare's Sonnets and Narrative Poems* (Harlow, 2000), 14–28.

[2] See Belsey, 'Love as Trompe-l'oeil'.

city of aspects;[1] but to press the analogy between the poem and pictorial arts runs the risk of underestimating the temporal flux on which this time-obsessed and changeable work depends for its effects. Venus's attributes are not graphically and simultaneously presented in one image as they are in Renaissance emblem books. They are sequentially related. Venus will not be still. Even at the end she flies off to Paphos, leaving the poem in motion. And before her flight, in what is indeed an almost pictorial tableau of her and her Adonis flower, Shakespeare's representation of her is far from static:

> 'Here was thy father's bed, here in my breast.
> Thou art the next of blood and 'tis thy right.
> Lo, in this hollow cradle take thy rest:
> My throbbing heart shall rock thee day and night.
>   There shall not be one minute in an hour
>   Wherein I will not kiss my sweet love's flower.'
>   (ll. 1183–8)

For Coppélia Kahn Venus becomes at this moment the all-encompassing mother, who unites sex with death, and who finally succeeds in dominating the narcissistic Adonis.[2] The scene might also throw up dark suggestions of an incestuous union between Venus the mother, and Adonis the father and son, and remind readers of the incestuous union between Cinyras and Myrrha from which Adonis was born.[1] It might too suggest pictures of the *mater dolorosa*, in which Mary cradles her dead son in her arms. Venus is blithely (perhaps divinely) unaware of what Adonis has suffered, and this comes through in her final little echo of Echo here: 'here in my breast' echoes the previous line's 'To wither in my breast', and may preserve a little of its threat of destruction. But it is also a picture of a woman grieving, putting a flower between her breasts and kissing it in her grief. A reader might give priority to the metaphors which make this a description of motherhood, inheritance, and sexual union, but another reader might equally

[1] S. Clarke Hulse, 'Shakespeare's Myth of *Venus and Adonis*', PMLA 93 (1978), 95–105.

[2] Kahn, 'Self and Eros'.

[1] Bate, 55: 'The Myrrha story, then, provides an ironic, darkening pre-text for the tale of Venus and Adonis, which points to the perverse origins of desire'; Mortimer disagrees, *Variable Passions*, 139.

legitimately see a scene which is of a flower, a woman, and grief. Any reader might also want to rock to and fro over the phrase 'my sweet love's flower'. The possessive forms here are unresolvable: does Venus mean (egoistically) 'the flower which embodies my passion', or does she mean 'the flower which belongs to my love Adonis', or 'the fruition of my love'? Love, the poem suggests, is like that: it does not allow those who feel it to distinguish between possessive fantasies and the delicate cherishing of another person, and it does not allow those who witness it to make such distinctions either. Venus cannot finally separate her subjective experience of love from the physical being of her lover, and readers who try to do so for her, and to read her as *either* predatory *or* maternally loving, are wilfully detaching themselves from the multiplicity of perspectives on which the poem insists.

The poem was designed to be printed, and was designed to appeal to many different kinds of reader. Readers close to the Earl of Southampton might conceivably have read it as a coterie work, larded with privy allusions to the Earl's reluctance to marry; but the poem's success depended on its being open to the great variety of readers. And this is why it is so profoundly and finally interested in creating a multiplicity of perspectives, and why the existence of multiple ways of reading and responding to the world is what it celebrates. After the wounding of Adonis Venus sees his body, and her tears split and refract his body and its wounds into multiple forms:

> Upon his hurt she looks so steadfastly
> That her sight, dazzling, makes the wound seem three.
> And then she reprehends her mangling eye,
> That makes more gashes where no breach should be.
>> His face seems twain, each several limb is doubled;
>> For oft the eye mistakes, the brain being troubled.
>>> (ll. 1063–8)

From the start *Venus and Adonis* is much concerned with looking: as early as line 67 its readers are invited to become unimpassioned spectators of love ('Look how a bird lies tangled in a net, | So fastened in her arms Adonis lies'). By its end it comes to concentrate on the ways in which the passions of the observer can change what they see. There is a kind of destructive egoism here in grief (and there *is* a kind of destructive egoism in grief) which makes

Venus see more wounds for every tear. Her love does not make
her see things as single. It makes them multiple. Being susceptible
of feeling and seeing means continually experiencing many reali-
ties at once in a way that makes Venus shrink from what she sees
'as the snail, whose tender horns being hit, | Shrinks backward in
his shelly cave with pain, | And, there all smothered up, in shade
doth sit, | Long after fearing to creep forth again' (ll. 1033–6).
Venus experiences a pain which is secret and wincing and
which makes her grief separate her from the experience of those
around her.

In Shakespeare's mature dramas, and especially in the tragedies
of love, the ability to see things several ways at once is a major
source of pain, and also makes painful distinctions between what
characters onstage see and what an audience sees: when Troilus
sees Cressida kissing Diomed he sees too many realities at once to be
able to know which one he inhabits, and yet all those realities are
available at once to an audience. *Venus and Adonis* is working at the
same seam and opening it out for the first time: the poem is found-
ed on the recognition that you can know what is true and still feel
what you feel; that rhetoric can make an overwhelming case for a
given belief, and yet you will still not be persuaded to feel in a differ-
ent way about the world. In a way that is perhaps more powerful
than the plays, because it is so intimately tied in with the reading
experience of the poem, *Venus and Adonis* also makes its readers
go through a variety of perspectives and attitudes, to feel them in
sequence and also at once. The passage quoted above evokes per-
sonal hurt by recording a discrepancy between what the grieving
lover feels and what is presented as being true. In this respect, as we
shall see, it builds a vital part of the groundwork of ideas on which
the Sonnets are based. Multiple perspectives and self-deception are
as early as 1593 central to Shakespeare's poems, and the poems are
foundational to his oeuvre.

The end of *Venus and Adonis* also enters the psychological realm
(and the regal metaphor matters here) which was to come to dom-
inate Shakespeare's next major poem, *Lucrece* (1594). Venus's sight
of the dead Adonis prompts the most sustained and complex piece
of syntax in the whole poem, as her mind becomes a state in tur-
moil. The full effect of the passage depends on its extended refusal
to end tidily with each stanza, and so it needs to be quoted in its
entirety:

> So at his bloody view her eyes are fled
> Into the deep-dark cabins of her head,
>
> Where they resign their office, and their light
> To the disposing of her troubled brain,
> Who bids them still consort with ugly night,
> And never wound the heart with looks again,
> > Who, like a king perplexèd in his throne,
> > By their suggestion gives a deadly groan,
>
> Whereat each tributary subject quakes,
> As when the wind imprisoned in the ground,
> Struggling for passage, earth's foundation shakes,
> Which with cold terror doth men's minds confound.
> > This mutiny each part doth so surprise
> > That from their dark beds once more leap her eyes,
>
> And, being opened, threw unwilling light
> Upon the wide wound that the boar had trenched
> In his soft flank . . .

$$\text{(ll. 1037–53)}$$

Critics have said remarkably little about this passage, but it is the part of the poem from which Shakespeare learnt most in his later works. It will not stop, despite the fact that Field's compositors solemnly end-stopped each stanza. As it surges uncontrollably on, it evokes a radically disturbing picture of the mind. Who is in control of it? The eyes retreat into solitude, like the tender horns of cockled snails; the brain, a wise councillor of the royal heart, banishes them; and yet they still make the heart, the king of Venus's body, groan; the groan creates a volcanic mutiny, and the eyes are forced once more to work. The eyes' own retreat from vision is the ultimate cause of their return. The king of this body in rebellion has no control over events, as the 'variable passions' (l. 967) of Venus take over the poem, and, in a simile at least, shake the whole foundations of the world. This picture of the mind in tumultuous rebellion feeds a central preoccupation of Shakespeare's next poem, *Lucrece*.

Lucrece

Publication and Date of Composition. 'A book entitled *The Ravishment of Lucrece*' was entered to John Harrison in the Stationers'

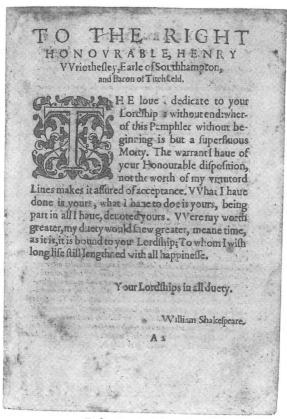

TO THE RIGHT
HONOVRABLE, HENRY
VVriothesley, Earle of Southhampton,
and Baron of Titchfeld.

HE loue I dedicate to your
Lordship is without end:wher-
of this Pamphlet without be-
ginning is but a superfluous
Moity. The warrant I haue of
your Honourable disposition,
not the worth of my vntutord
Lines makes it assured of acceptance. VVhat I haue
done is yours, what I haue to doe is yours, being
part in all I haue, deuoted yours. VVere my worth
greater, my duety would shew greater, meane time,
as it is, it is bound to your Lordship; To whom I wish
long life still lengthned with all happinesse.

Your Lordships in all duety.

William Shakespeare.

A 2

2. Dedication to *Lucrece* (1594).

Register on 9 May 1594.[1] The title-page of the first Quarto reads
'LVCRECE | [Anchora Spei device; McKerrow 222] | LONDON. |
Printed by Richard Field, for John Harrison, and are | to be sold at
the signe of the white Grehound | in Paules Church-yard. 1594.'
Field assigned the copyright of *Venus and Adonis* to Harrison in June
of that year. It is likely that *Lucrece* appeared in the summer of 1594
at roughly the same time as the second Quarto of *Venus and Adonis*.

[1] Arber, ii.648.

The two volumes, with almost identical ornaments on their title-pages,[1] would have made an attractive pair of books to buy at Harrison's shop at the sign of the White Greyhound in the Churchyard of St Paul's. *Lucrece* is presumably the work which Shakespeare had in mind when he promised 'some graver labour' to the Earl of Southampton in the dedication to *Venus and Adonis*. That gravity is typographically marked: twenty-three lines are marked as memorable *sententiae*, which the 'wiser sort', as Gabriel Harvey termed those who admired this poem,[2] could note down in their commonplace books. Shakespeare almost certainly worked on the poem during the latter part of the period in which the theatres were closed for the plague from 1592 to October 1594. The dedication to the Earl of Southampton (whose connection with Shakespeare is discussed in the introduction to *Venus and Adonis*) is notably warmer than that to *Venus and Adonis*, and shows that Shakespeare was already in the early 1590s experimenting with fusing the language of devoted love with that of patronage in a manner which was to become a central element in the Sonnets.

The text of the 1594 *Lucrece* is carefully printed, although the experimental compression of the poem's language forces a couple of nasty cruces from Field's compositors (discussed in the notes to lines 639, 1544). There are two different states of several gatherings of Q1, one unrevised (Qa) and the other which contains a number of 'press variants' (Qb), as stop-press corrections to the text are called.[3] The press variants are the kinds of correction which one would expect from a careful printer such as Field. His punctilious compositors probably replaced Shakespeare's technically incorrect form 'Collatium' with 'Collatia' (l. 50). Other variants appear to be over-systematizations, but some yield clear sense, and may have been based on reference back to the manuscript copy. As with *Venus and Adonis* the copyright of *Lucrece* remained

---

[1] Q1 of *Lucrece* has McKerrow 222 in the centre of its title-page, *Venus* has the slightly smaller version of Field's 'Anchora Spei' device (McKerrow 192) in order to accommodate the epigraph. Both volumes fill the area above the title with the same ornament.

[2] *Allusion Book*, i.56. See further John Roe, 'Pleasing the Wiser Sort: Problems of Ethics and Genre in *Lucrece* and *Hamlet*', *Cambridge Quarterly* 23 (1994), 99–119.

[3] Press variants occur in ll. 24, 31, 50, 125, 126, 1182, 1335, 1350. The copy of Qa in the Bodleian Library (Malone 34, of which there is a Scolar Press facsimile) and the copy in Yale retain earlier readings in sigs. B, I, and K; other copies contain early readings in sigs. I and/or K.

valuable property, and was carefully transferred from printer to printer well into the seventeenth century.[1] *Lucrece* appears to have been less popular than *Venus*; copies survive from eight editions before 1640, as against the sixteen editions of *Venus* which survive from the same period. In the eighteenth century it is usually printed with *Venus and Adonis*, and shares the general fate of Shakespeare's poems in that period, of being relegated to supplementary volumes tacked on to the end of prestigious editions of the plays.

The seventeenth-century Quartos show clear signs of compositorial errors and editorial tinkerings with metre and phrasing, some of which are intelligent attempts to emend the sense of Q1, others of which bear witness to changes in taste or idiom, but none of which derive from Shakespeare.[2] Some modifications in the late Quartos do, however, significantly change the reading-experience of the poem. Q has the sparse title *Lucrece* on the title-page (which is followed in this edition). This is likely to be a damping down of the title as originally registered: the half-title which precedes the text of the poem as well as the running-titles calls it 'The Rape of Lucrece'. The spicier title first appeared on the title-page of Q6 (1616), the first edition to be produced after Harrison had sold his rights to the poem.[3] That edition tries to add a gloss of novelty to the poem by claiming to be 'Newly revised', by containing a number of new readings (which are not Shakespearian), and by dividing the poem into sections. In its table of contents Q6 describes the newly named section 7 in lurid terms: 'Tarquin all impatient interrupteth her, and ravisheth her by force.' Readers who shared Tarquin's impatience, and who turned to what was clearly flagged as the hottest bit of the poem, worked up in this newly revised edition, perhaps, to be as sexy as *Venus and Adonis*, are given a more reflective marginal note, which shows that the printer Roger Jackson or his annotator had responded to the poem's intricate debates about the nature of consent, as well as to its frequent association of Lucrece with rooms and cities under siege: 'Tarquin all impatient

---

[1] John Harrison passed the copyright to Roger Jackson on 1 March 1614 (Arber, iii.542); Harrison's widow sold the copyright to John Stafford and William Gilbertson on 15 March 1655 (Eyre, i.468).

[2] A full collation can be found in Rollins 1, and full details of the editions are found on 406–13.

[3] Editions after Q1 are in fact octavos rather than quartos. For the sake of clarity I follow the normal practice of referring to subsequent editions as Q2 etc., rather than O1 etc.

interrupts her and denied of consent breaketh the enclosure of her chastity by force.' By Q9 (1655) the marginal notes have become chapter headings, and Shakespeare's poem is printed together with Quarles's *Tarquin Banished, or the Reward of Lust*, which dwells on the remorse of Tarquin ('Lucretia, ah, Lucretia! Thou didst find | A rapèd body, I a rapèd mind' (p. 10)). Quarles's Tarquin laments with Philomel, like Lucrece, and is eventually sung to death by vengeful nightingales, who peck out his eyes for good measure. Q9 shifts the focus of the poem firmly towards crime and punishment, and mutes the suggestions in the work as it was first printed that the story of Lucrece changes the constitution of Rome. The tendency among earlier twentieth-century critics to focus on 'the rape of Tarquin',[1] rather than on the political consequences of his banishment, may owe something to Quarles's view of the poem as a work concerned with individual crime and punishment rather than with politics.

A few manuscript transcriptions of passages from the poem survive, which similarly testify to the varied ways in which the poem was read. The majority of these transcriptions, like those of *Venus and Adonis*, are likely to derive from printed versions. Sir John Suckling's *Fragmenta Aurea* (1646) contains 'A Supplement of an imperfect copy of verses of Mr Wil. Shakespeare's', which develops the passage in which Tarquin gazes on Lucrece as she sleeps. Suckling's poem is in the six-line stanzas of *Venus and Adonis*, rather than in the rhyme royal of *Lucrece*, which has been taken to indicate that he possessed a manuscript which recorded a section from an earlier draft of the poem.[2] It is more likely, however, that Suckling found an inaccurate scribal version of the passage and worked it up, or that for him 'Shakespearian' verse meant verse in the *Venus and Adonis* stanza, and that he rewrote the section from *Lucrece* accordingly. The gazing Tarquin did stoke up excitement among copyists: in one manuscript version a scrambling of pronouns makes it appear that Lucrece is lying with her hand under his cheek, rather than her own. This transforms the scene into a vision of post-coital fulfilment rather than imminent rape:

---

[1] See Sam Hynes, 'The Rape of Tarquin', *Shakespeare Quarterly* 10 (1959), 451–3.

[2] See Roland Mushat Frye, 'Shakespeare's Composition of *Lucrece*: New Evidence', *Shakespeare Quarterly* 16 (1965), 289–96. The other examples of six-line versions of *Lucrece* which Frye cites do not tip the balance in favour of his claim: all show signs of scribal reshaping.

Her lilly hand his rosy cheekes lyes under
Cooseninge ye pillow of a lawfull kisse[1]

The poem may, as Gabriel Harvey said, have 'pleased the wiser
sort', but it also appealed to those readers who had enjoyed
Venus and Adonis, who sought in this poem the consummation so
artfully denied to the goddess of love in its predecessor and
companion-piece.

The Argument, Sources, and Politics. The story of Lucretia, the
chaste wife whose rape precipitated the ejection of the kings from
Rome, has been subjected to varieties of interpretation from the
earliest period of Roman historiography.[2] Shakespeare could have
read versions by Ovid, Livy (or by Livy in Painter's translation), by
Dionysius Halicarnassus, Gower, and Chaucer, and any number of
popularized versions of these.[3] Each version differs slightly in
detail, as well as in its ethical and political attitudes to the central
character. Lucretia stood at the centre of a variety of intersecting
ethical and political debates. She was often briefly cited in both
poetry and prose as an example of feminine virtue, whose suicide
reflected the purity of her mind. But most post-classical inter-
preters of her story were also aware of St Augustine's critical treat-
ment of it. Augustine argues at length that chastity is a virtue of
the mind, and so 'what man of wit will think he loseth his chastity,
though his captived body be forced to prostitute unto another's
bestiality?'[4] He consequently presented the suicide of Lucretia as a
case which raised a mass of awkward questions about responsibil-
ity and punishment: either she did not consent to the rape, in which
case only Tarquin was guilty of a crime and she unjustly con-
demned herself to death; or else 'she herself did give a lustful con-
sent' and so rightly punished herself. He concludes, 'this case is in
such a strait, that if the murder be extenuated, the adultery is con-
firmed, and if this be cleared the other is aggravated'.[5] By 1610 the

---

[1] BL MS Add. 27406, fo. 74.   [2] Donaldson is the authority here.
[3] On the sources, see Bullough, 179–99. Extensive discussion is in Wilhelm Ewig,
'Shakespeare's *Lucrece*: Eine litterarhistorische Untersuchung', *Anglia* 22 (1899),
1–32. Earlier views are surveyed in Rollins I, 416–39. For the view that Gower is the
main influence on how Shakespeare dramatized the tale, see R. Hillman, 'Gower's
Lucrece: A New Old Source for *The Rape of Lucrece*', *Chaucer Review* 24 (1990),
263–7.
[4] St Augustine, *Of the City of God*, trans. John Healey (1610), 28.
[5] Augustine, *City of God*, 31.

full text of Augustine's *City of God* was available in English (by an odd quirk of fortune it was printed at almost exactly the same time, and in the same print-shop, as Shakespeare's Sonnets). In its post-classical forms the story of Lucretia prompts uneasy arguments about relations between body and will, consent and pollution.

In most of the versions which precede Augustine Lucretia's story is politically charged. Her rape lies at the start of the Roman Republic, and writers who like republics regard it in a very different way from those who do not. According to Livy, her violation led to the banishment of the kings from Rome and the institution of government by consuls, and thus enabled the emergence of later forms of Roman republican government. This was a profoundly influential view of her significance, but was by no means the only way of glossing the political consequences of her rape. For a tradition deriving from Tacitus, the consular government to which her rape gave rise was as much a form of slavery as the monarchy from which it was notionally an escape. William Fulbecke in his *An Historical Collection of the Continual Factions, Tumults, and Massacres of the Romans and Italians* (printed by Richard Field in 1601) wrote of the transfer of power from kings to consuls which followed the expulsion of the Tarquins, 'what could be more unjust, or more contrary to the free estate of a city, than to subject the whole common weal to the rule of many potentates, and to exclude the people from all right and interest in public affairs?' (p. 1).[1] By 1574 Justus Lipsius was praising Tacitus for having concentrated on examining life inside the courts of princes, and the flattery and treachery which occur under a tyrant, rather than dwelling on the 'speciosam Lucretiae necem', the misleadingly beautiful death of Lucrece.[2] These arguments about the political significance of Lucretia's story have not stopped: some twentieth-century readers have felt that the republican panegyrists who leapt to praise the republic which resulted from Lucretia's fate are too readily founding their form of liberty on a woman's violation, and that republican ideals and the justification of rape are not just bedfellows in this story, but are sinisterly and consistently intertangled.[3]

[1] Quentin Skinner notes (privately) that Fulbecke is here echoing Livy 3.9.3–5.

[2] Justus Lipsius, ed., *C. Cornelii Taciti Opera quae Exstant* (Antwerp, 1589), sig. *2ᵛ. The dedication to Maximilian (in which this remark occurs) appeared in editions from 1574.

[3] See Stephanie H. Jed, *Chaste Thinking: The Rape of Lucretia and the Birth of Humanism* (Bloomington and Indianapolis, 1989).

So the question 'Which sources did Shakespeare follow?' does not just mean comparing in painful detail versions of the story in which Lucrece sends out two messengers to tell her family about her rape, and those in which she sends only one. It means deciding which sides (and the plural is necessary) Shakespeare took in these many arguments about Lucrece: is her story about rape, or about liberty? Does telling her story distract attention from an analysis of what tyranny is and how it works? The question as to which sources Shakespeare drew on also reverberates with two other questions: what are the politics implicit in the poem? And what is the relationship between the poem and the prose Argument which is prefixed to it? These three questions are intervolved because the Argument shows clear signs of a debt to Livy, and shows an implicit allegiance with a republican form of government (or, to be more precise, an elective consulship). It concludes: 'Wherewith the people were so moved that, with one consent and a general acclamation, the Tarquins were all exiled, and the state government changed from kings to consuls.' The vital word here is 'consent', and the key concept which it appears to support is the belief that the government of the state should reflect a popular voice.[1] The poem, however, differs from the Argument in several respects, some relatively insignificant, and some central to its moral emphasis and meaning.[2] In the poem Lucrece sends one messenger to her father and husband, whereas in the Argument she sends 'messengers'; in the poem Tarquin does not seem to have visited Lucrece's house before the rape, whereas the Argument says he and Collatine had surprised the other Roman matrons at play the night before, and had discovered the chaste Lucrece busily sewing. The most significant difference of emphasis, however, emerges in the very last lines of the poem:

> The Romans plausibly did give consent
> To Tarquin's everlasting banishment.
>
> (ll. 1854–5)

---

[1] Annabel Patterson, *Reading Between the Lines* (1993), 306. 'Shakespeare has written a brief epic which, unlike Virgil's long epic, is Republican in sentiment and focus', Michael Platt, *Rome and Romans According to Shakespeare*, rev. edn. (New York and London, 1983), 35.

[2] The most sustained denial that the Argument is by Shakespeare remains J. R. Tolbert, 'The Argument of Shakespeare's *Lucrece*', *Texas Studies in English* 29 (1950), 77–90.

Here the Romans only 'give consent' to the punishment of Tarquin, and there is no reference to a change in the mode of government. The word 'consent' is echoed from the Argument, but seems muffled by the echo: here it is as though the Romans are simply applauding the performance of Tarquin's punishment in order to give it a retrospective seal of approval, rather than actively participating in a transformation of their state.

What is going on here? Was a more Livian and more political Argument tacked on to an only peripherally political poem? Richard Field printed a number of political works, including William Fulbecke's *Historical Collection*, and, in 1594, Justus Lipsius's highly Tacitean *Six Books of Politics*. His print-shop certainly had connections with people who were capable of writing a preface to Shakespeare's poem which was informed by detailed knowledge of Roman historians. The pagination of the Quarto left him with a blank page after the dedication (A2^v), which the Argument fills up neatly.[1] Perhaps it was put there just before publication, to flesh out the narrative and historical context to what the Dedication describes as a pamphlet 'without beginning'. Alternatively, Shakespeare may have read or reread Livy (perhaps in Painter's translation) before he wrote the Argument.[2] Or, like Spenser, whose 'Letter to Ralegh' gets almost all of his own *Faerie Queene* wrong, he might have forgotten details of the poem when he came to describe it in prose.

The simplest and most radical hypothesis, however, is that Shakespeare read the version of the story of Lucretia in Ovid's *Fasti* side by side with the more explicitly political prose versions by Livy and the Greek historian Dionysius Halicarnassus, and that by adding the prose Argument to his poem he invited his readers to read the Lucretia story in the same way, as two generically distinct things. A single book would have given Shakespeare a grasp of all these variant versions of the story. This was Paulus Marsus's edition of Ovid's *Fasti*, which was frequently reprinted in the sixteenth century.[3] There are strong grounds for believing Shakespeare

[1] It is, however, unlikely that Field wished to save paper and reduce costs: the volume collates 4°: A2, B–M⁴, N¹. Had the Argument been omitted and the poem begun on A2^v he would have been spared the need to end the volume with a singleton.

[2] Baldwin, 115.

[3] Baldwin, 108. The commentaries of Antonius Constantius (Antonio Costanzi of Fano) and of Paulus Marsus (Paolo Marsi) were originally written in 1480 and 1482

knew this version. Before the rape of Lucretia, Ovid's Tarquin pretends to the Gabii that he has been cast out by his family. He then betrays the tribe who have taken him in. At this point both Marsus and his fellow commentator Constantius compare Tarquin to Sinon.[1] This detail is almost certainly what prompted Shakespeare, who was attempting a 'graver', quasi-epic, labour in *Lucrece*, to insert the description of the sack of Troy into his poem, at the climax of which Tarquin is compared to Sinon, the Greek who wins the pity of the Trojans and then persuades them to take in the Trojan horse.

But whether or not Shakespeare owned or read Marsus's Ovid, the edition gives an exemplary instance of how early-modern readers read the tale of Lucretia, and casts a bright light on the relationship between the poem and its Argument. To read Ovid's *Fasti* in Marsus's edition is to experience the story of Lucretia in multiple versions at the same time. Massive quotations from Livy physically surround the elegiac couplets of Ovid, and sometimes all but push them off the page. Marsus prints so much of Livy because he believed that Ovid imitated the Roman historian, and he urges his readers to make comparisons between the versions in prose and verse.[2] He also ends his commentary on the story with an encomium of the liberty which the Romans obtained after the banishment of the kings, which he compares to the liberty which he himself had obtained several years before, and which he celebrates each year.[3] The most influential recent accounts of the way Livy was read in the late sixteenth century suggest that he was taken as a practical guide to political life;[4] the example of Marsus's Ovid indicates that readers in this period also read comparatively, with an

---

respectively. The helpful account in Ann Moss, *Ovid in Renaissance France: A Survey of the Latin Editions of Ovid and Commentaries Printed in France before 1660*, Warburg Institute Surveys 8 (1982), 17–18 emphasizes the pedagogical intention of Marsus's commentary.

[1] Marsus, 142.　　[2] Marsus, 140.

[3] Marsus, 151: 'The poet himself has delayed greatly, and perhaps we too have delayed excessively in glossing him down to the banishment of the kings and the birth of liberty for the city of Rome. But that very delay, and the placing together of these histories, was more pleasing to me in as much as liberty herself is pleasing. After I myself had achieved liberty nine years ago, I have celebrated each year the feast of liberty at the end of September, and will continue to do so for the rest of my life.'

[4] Anthony Grafton and Lisa Jardine, '"Studied for Action": How Gabriel Harvey Read his Livy', *Past and Present* 129 (1990), 30–78.

eye to variant versions rather than to the practical applications of what they read. Marsus encourages his readers to think about the elegiac Lucretia of Ovid and the republican Lucretia of the Roman historians side by side, and clearly applied the political argument of the latter to his own circumstances. This set of reading practices is very likely to explain the presence of two discrepant versions of the story in the volume which Field printed, and may well indicate that for Shakespeare, as for Marsus, the story was two things at once: a poem which was partly about how to give suffering a voice, and a republican prose history. The 'wiser sort' of Shakespeare's readers would have not been surprised to be invited to think about the story in two distinct ways by the physical form of a book.

Does the presence of the Argument and the likelihood that it is by Shakespeare mean, though, that *Lucrece* is a republican poem? Ovid's poem and the historians' prose versions have distinct and complementary emphases. Ovid emphasizes moments at which Lucretia is unable to speak, when her voice sticks in her throat, and Marsus's annotations frequently draw attention to Lucretia's hesitations and stammerings (and Shakespeare's Lucrece repeatedly breaks off or rethinks sentences as passions draw her mind another way).[1] But Marsus is also keen to quote from the historians extensive passages of exhortative rhetoric by men: whereas Brutus's speech persuading the Romans to banish Tarquin is passed over in indirect speech in Ovid, Marsus's commentary quotes an extensive digest of Dionysius Halicarnassus, in which Brutus's rhetoric stirs the populace to action.[2] The relationship between text and commentary presses for both a generic distinction between different versions of the story, and for a gendered differentiation between modes of speech: passion chokes a woman's voice in Ovid's poem; men, meanwhile, speak out to transform the state into a republic.

This aspect of the commentary alerts us to the fact that Shakespeare's response to the versions of Lucretia's story which came down to him is in one respect extraordinarily radical. Shake-

---

[1] 'ter conata loqui' ('Three times she tried to speak', *Fasti* 2.823) prompts a long note, Marsus, 148, as does 'quid faciat?' ('what should I do?' *Fasti* 2.801), which prompts Marsus (147) to say: 'Nullae vires erant Lucretiae ad loquendum, ob pavorem, nec erat sibi mens ulla' ('Lucretia had no strength to speak, because of her fear, nor did she have any power of thought').

[2] Marsus, 150–1.

speare's Lucrece is astonishingly, unstoppably, all-but endlessly eloquent. She has her moments of elegiac choking of the voice, of the pathetic silence of the Ovidian heroine (e.g. ll. 1604–8); but she has also taken over the eloquence of the men who speak so loudly and so long from the margins of the Renaissance Ovid. And one moment when Shakespeare allows his heroine to speak, and speak like a man, has a massive bearing on the question of the poem's politics. Unlike any other Lucretia before her, Shakespeare's Lucrece urges Tarquin not to rape her, and she does so using a vocabulary which is distinctively male, and for readers in 1594 distinctively political:

> 'This deed will make thee only loved for fear,
> But happy monarchs still are feared for love.
> With foul offenders thou perforce must bear,
> When they in thee the like offences prove.
> If but for fear of this, thy will remove.
>   For princes are the glass, the school, the book,
>   Where subjects' eyes do learn, do read, do look.
>
> 'And wilt thou be the school where lust shall learn?
> Must he in thee read lectures of such shame?
> Wilt thou be glass wherein it shall discern
> Authority for sin, warrant for blame
> To privilege dishonour in thy name?
>   Thou back'st reproach against long-living laud,
>   And mak'st fair reputation but a bawd.

                                                (ll. 610–23)

This builds on, but goes far beyond, the transposition of a male voice of seduction to a female voice in *Venus and Adonis*. Lucrece speaks here with the voice of a Renaissance royal counsellor, and echoes Cicero's injunction that it is better to be loved than feared.[1] The last couplet of the first stanza here quoted was excerpted in W.B.'s *The Philosopher's Banquet* of 1633 under the heading 'Of

---

[1] *De Officiis* 2.7.23. See Barry Nass, 'The Law and Politics of Treason in Shakespeare's *Lucrece*', *Shakespeare Yearbook* 7 (1996), 301: 'Articulated moments before her rape, Lucrece's devout recapitulation of official Tudor precepts does not so much validate them as reveal how inadequate such discourse is to the violence and lawlessness of her princely adversary.' Lucrece's rebuke may owe something to the apostrophe to Tarquin delivered by the narrator in *LGW* 1819–22: 'Tarquinius, that art a kynges eyr, | And sholdest, as by lynage and by ryght, | Don as a lord and a verray knyght, | Whi hastow don this lady vilanye'. Gower reflects on Tarquin's tyranny at *Confessio Amantis* 7.4839 and 4998.

Princes',[1] and the lines are themselves a culling of commonplaces. Antonio Guevara in his *Dial of Princes*, for example, insists that Princes should govern themselves before they can govern their state. He claims too 'that if the miserable Tarquin [whom Guevara conflates with his father the king] had been beloved in Rome, he had never been deprived of the realm, for committing adultery with Lucretia'.[2] The advice which Lucrece gives to Tarquin here is a textbook example of political oratory in this period: the civic aspect of rhetoric in Elizabethan England was not displayed by speaking to the Senate, but by giving counsel. Early readers of the poem would have heard behind the voice of Lucrece at this point that of Erasmus ('The tyrant strives to be feared, the king to be loved'),[3] or any one of a dozen contributors to the genre of humanist prince-books. Her words would have won an easy nod of assent from early readers, who would instinctively feel that princes *should* seek to be feared through love, and *should* provide exemplary government. They should 'govern all', or regulate their appetites. These comfortable, and, by the 1590s decidedly old-fashioned,[4] Erasmian orthodoxies then abruptly end:

> 'Have done,' quoth he. 'My uncontrollèd tide
> Turns not, but swells the higher by this let.'
> (ll. 645–6)

Tarquin will not be counselled. Shakespeare takes a paradigm instance of what should be politically effective rhetoric within the tradition of humanist political thought, and he puts it into the place where readers familiar with Ovid would expect either silence from Lucrece or a pathetically ineffective lament. The result of this hybridization of elegy and the discourse of humanist prince-books is an explosive piece of rhetorical cross-dressing: the forms of counsel which should prevent monarchy sliding into tyranny simply do not work in this poem. They become the words of a woman

---

[1] *The Philosopher's Banquet* (usually attributed to Sir Michael Scott, STC 22061.5), 103.

[2] Antonio de Guevara, *The Diall of Princes*, trans. Thomas North (1557), sig. M6ᵛ.

[3] Desiderius Erasmus, *The Education of a Christian Prince*, trans. Neil M. Cheshire and Michael J. Heath, ed. Lisa Jardine (Cambridge, 1997), 28.

[4] Martin Dzelzainis has suggested (privately) that the failure of Lucrece's rhetoric may show that the old-fashioned pieties of early humanist political rhetoric fail to influence the new-style Tacitist prince Tarquin.

who is about to be raped. And she is raped by a man who cannot govern his own passions.

Jonathan Bate has suggested that 'Shakespeare's poem . . . is more interested in desire than in politics'. Ian Donaldson has suggested that 'Shakespeare cannot have wished to be thought to be questioning, even in a very indirect way, the system of monarchical government under which he lived and to which he owed allegiance'.[1] Michael Platt and Annabel Patterson have, conversely, seen *Lucrece* as either overtly republican or as a work which is rooted in the discourse of republicanism.[2] The variety of these judgements testifies to the complexity of the poem, and all may have their truths. But the widespread analogy between the supremacy of the reason over the passions and of the just monarch over a nation made the passions of a prince and their regulation an inescapably political matter in this period. 'Government'—Lucrece urges Tarquin to 'govern all'—meant both the regulation of passions and of the nation. The poem is not 'royalist' if that is taken to mean that it is founded on a belief in the absolute supremacy of the will of the prince. It is also not likely to be a 'republican poem', in the sense of one which advocated the abolition of monarchy, since such a thing was not a publishable, perhaps not even a fully thinkable, thing in the England of the 1590s. So what is it?

For many of the most influential political thinkers of the late Elizabethan period England was a form of mixed monarchy, in which the Queen in parliament interacted with the Queen in Council in ways which could attribute considerable power to any one of these three elements. The moment of the rape in *Lucrece* dramatizes a collapse in the complex interrelationship between monarch and counsel. In the context of what Patrick Collinson has described as 'the Elizabethan monarchical republic' this is a terrifying event. The ideal tempering of a monarch's passions by reason and counsel is shown only in a state of radical dysfunction. Theoretical formulations of mixed monarchy in the Elizabethan period are thin on the ground; but even Lord Burghley, who was by no means a radical thinker, could envisage formal measures for ensuring that the

---

[1] Bate, 73; Donaldson, 116.

[2] See Platt, *Rome and Romans*, 13–51, which is a revised version of his 'The Rape of Lucrece and the Republic for which it Stands', *Centennial Review* 19 (1975), 59–79; and Patterson, *Reading Between the Lines*, 297–317.

Privy Council would continue to govern during the interregnum which might follow the death of Elizabeth; others, such as Thomas Digges, could imagine Parliament remaining in session after the Queen's death in order to determine the succession.[1] By the end of Elizabeth's reign the Queen's femininity was shifting traditional views of what counsel should be, and the voices of female members of the privy chamber might often have almost as much influence on her actions as male members of her Privy Council.

Lucrece does not directly comment on these aspects of the political scene, nor does it provide a viable republican alternative to conciliar monarchy. It transposes the rhetorical trick which Shakespeare had learned in writing *Venus and Adonis* into a political key: it puts the discourse appropriate to one kind of speaker—a male counsellor—into the mouth of another kind of speaker—a victim of rape—and in doing so raises unanswered and urgent questions about both gender roles and politics. A woman who speaks like a counsellor, and then is raped—this subject-matter darkly intimates that a polity founded on the notional ability of counsellors to curb the will of the prince encounters a black and insoluble problem if the prince cannot control himself. And Shakespeare's *method* of raising this insoluble problem makes any political radicalism in the poem immediately deniable, even when its critical position is most apparent to its readers. If Lucrece's words to Tarquin were quoted out of their context (and Shakespeare, as we have seen, had learned to allow printed words to drift free of their context in *Venus and Adonis*) they would become a commonplace of impeccable orthodoxy—as they duly became when quoted by W.B. in *The Philosopher's Banquet*. In their original context, in a poem in which even a prince is unable to persuade himself not to follow the 'worser course', and in which a woman is destroyed as a result of her failure to persuade him, and in which a prose argument intimates that there are alternatives to monarchy, Lucrece's words ask awkward and unanswerable questions about unregulated monarchy. Rhetoric once again, as in *Venus*, fails to persuade. But here it cannot persuade to good, nor can it save a state from decline towards tyranny.

---

[1] See Patrick Collinson, 'The Monarchical Republic of Elizabeth I', in John Guy, ed., *The Tudor Monarchy* (1997), 110–34.

Reading (in) Lucrece. Shakespeare learnt from and ingeniously transformed what he read. One of the things he read and from which he learnt most was Shakespeare. *Lucrece* is part complement, part sequel to *Venus and Adonis*. Where the action of *Venus and Adonis* had spread itself in a leisurely way across two days, *Lucrece* spins almost twice as many lines from a single night and morning. *Venus* had shrunk and expanded time with a delicious wantonness: in *Lucrece* the only thing that happens quickly is travel to and from Collatium. Tarquin arrives at the poem's start in a flash of dark fire; Collatine and the other Roman lords enter abruptly at its end with 'But now' (l. 1583). Lucrece's body is 'published' on the streets of Rome with such 'speedy diligence' (l. 1853) that it takes only a single line to accomplish. Once characters are within the domestic space into which Lucrece is herself oppressively locked, however, time is forced into slow motion. Tarquin's long slow passage to Lucrece's chamber makes every tiny object become an obstacle: the wind blows him back, a needle tries heroically to become a sword. It is as though the poem's slow expansiveness is the chief guarantee that it is indeed the 'graver labour' promised in the dedication to *Venus and Adonis*: just as its rhyme royal stanza extends and slows the brisk six-line form of *Venus and Adonis*, so its treatment of time delays action and forces its characters to reflect on what they are doing, and on what has been done to them. This poem cannot flit lightly through the woods, as *Venus and Adonis* could, nor does it fleetingly compress the complaints of a woman at night as *Venus and Adonis* had done (ll. 829–52): Lucrece spends lines 747–1078 filling the hours of darkness with complaints, and repeatedly seeks new means of making moan. Even the sound of morning birdsong coming in from the outside world is transformed inward into lament (ll. 1107 ff.), as Lucrece weaves the notes of her sad song into the melancholy tale of the raped Philomel. The fleeting moment of sexual consummation which was missing from *Venus and Adonis* becomes, in the slow-motion domestic spaces of *Lucrece*, a source of pained reflection and regret, and all but endless eloquence.

Although *Lucrece* radically decelerates *Venus and Adonis*, its imaginative starting-point is the final section of the earlier poem, when Venus complains against death, curses love, and time seems to stand still as the body of Adonis melts beside her. The final phase of *Venus and Adonis* also moves towards a physically inward setting, as Venus's eyes shrink back into her head like the tender horns of cockled snails, and the goddess finally flits off, meaning to (though perhaps not actually performing her intention) 'immure herself and not be seen'. Lucrece spends her poem immured within her house, until her body is finally displayed in Rome. And throughout the poem Tarquin's assault on her is represented as a raid on the inner regions of a domestic space. As he hovers over the sleeping Lucrece, her body becomes a castle under siege:

> Whose ranks of blue veins as his hand did scale
> Left their round turrets destitute and pale.
>
> They, must'ring to the quiet cabinet
> Where their dear governess and lady lies,
> Do tell her she is dreadfully beset,
> And fright her with confusion of their cries.
> She, much amazed, breaks ope her locked up eyes,
>   Who, peeping forth this tumult to behold,
>   Are by his flaming torch dimmed and controlled.
>
> Imagine her as one in dead of night,
> From forth dull sleep by dreadful fancy waking,
> That thinks she hath beheld some ghastly sprite,
> Whose grim aspect sets every joint a-shaking.
> What terror 'tis! But she in worser taking,
>   From sleep disturbèd, heedfully doth view
>   The sight which makes supposèd terror true.
>
>   (ll. 440–55)

At the centre of *Venus and Adonis* a goddess discovers that 'all is imaginary', and at the end of the earlier poem Venus's mind and perceptions are thrown into rebellious tumult by the sight of Adonis dead. Those passages lie behind the extract from *Lucrece* quoted above, but are rewritten in a darker key that suits the claustrophobic interiority of *Lucrece*. Her veins become desperate servants scrambling to wake their governess as she sleeps in her 'quiet cabinet'. It places Lucrece in a tiny, intimate room within a castle, surrounded by walls within walls. Then the real and the imaginary blend, as a reader is first asked to imagine her imaginings, and then to realize that she awakes and finds her imagination truth. A dreaming queen within a simile of siege who *is* really a woman under attack: the effect is of claustrophobia within claustrophobia, of truth within a dream within a siege. *Lucrece* never lets its readers forget that it is a chamber work in a literal sense of being set in a chamber: the word 'chamber' is rung on in lines 302, 337, 365, 1626.[1] Here she occupies a 'cabinet', an intimate inner room designed for private occupation, to which only personal servants and family would have access. This image of a little room hems in the heroine: at the end of the poem Lucrece herself recalls and attempts to purify her violated inner regions by insisting that her mind 'Doth in her poisoned closet yet endure' (l. 1659), as a clean inhabitant within a polluted, private room.[2] The rape is figured as a violation of domestic spaces, and in this respect feeds off widespread late sixteenth-century anxieties about burglary and theft.[3]

But the attempt at violation of the domestic sphere rebounds on the rapist. In a passage which is designed to make its readers do a double-take, it is Tarquin's soul, rather than that of Lucrece, which is exposed to a siege and ravished:

> Besides, his soul's fair temple is defacèd,
>   To whose weak ruins muster troops of cares,
>   To ask the spotted princess how she fares.
>
> She says her subjects with foul insurrection
> Have battered down her consecrated wall,
> And by their mortal fault brought in subjection
> Her immortality, and made her thrall
> To living death and pain perpetual,
>   Which in her prescience she controllèd still,
>   But her foresight could not forestall their will.
>
> (ll. 719–28)

'She': the pronoun matters acutely. Tarquin becomes a rebel against himself, who destroys his own soul's private and consecrated places, and his invasive male pride forces on him a feminine sense of violation.[4] This detail illustrates how in this poem

---

[1] For the association between chambers and female chastity, see G. Zeigler, 'My Lady's Chamber: Female Space, Female Chastity in Shakespeare', *Textual Practice* 4 (1990), 73–100.

[2] 'The closet in every house, as it is a reposement of Secrets, so is it only . . . at the owner's, and no other's commandment', Angel Day, *The English Secretorie* (1625), 103. For the intimacy of the closet, see Alan Stewart, 'The Early Modern Closet Discovered', *Representations* 50 (1995), 76–100.

[3] See Heather Dubrow, *Shakespeare and Domestic Loss* (Cambridge, 1999), 45–61.

[4] Hynes 'The Rape of Tarquin'.

Shakespeare was not just building on, but going far beyond the ending of *Venus and Adonis*. *Lucrece* generates a slow-moving interior realm where all action seems violent and abrupt, and in which men of action have to readjust themselves to the reflective pace and expansive volume of female rhetoric, and find themselves becoming victims of interiority. Tarquin and Collatine are men at war who are suddenly plunged into a setting and a pace of life with which they are occupationally unable to cope. Lamenting, thinking on consequences, debating the pros and cons of actions—these things are forced on the men in the poem, and make their rhetoric seem inadequate to the domestic realm. The way *Lucrece* deliberately brings warriors and images of warfare into a domestic sphere marks it as one of the seminal moments in Shakespeare's career. The long slow pause after, or in anticipation of, or in the midst of a battle is a setting to which he recurs again and again. The awkwardness of men, especially martial men, misplaced in domestic environments for which neither their language nor their conduct quite suits them becomes the substance of many of the tragedies: *Macbeth* begins after a battle, forcing its hero to reflect about action rather than act; the oppressive domestic closeness of *Othello* is forced on its hero by the sudden and unexpected end of the battle against the Turks. Slowness, reflection, domestic space, and a preoccupation with how deeds and desires and persuasion interconnect: these themes and moods Shakespeare came to first in *Lucrece*. And they are absolutely central to Shakespeare.

Even readers who recognize the significance of *Lucrece* within Shakespeare's career, however, have felt that it is overstocked with words. Few who have read Lucrece's complaints against Night, Opportunity, and Time would wish that she had found further personifications to berate (although Shakespeare's treatment of the complaint tradition is carefully used to characterize his heroine).[1] The poem interweaves a wide range of imagery from seemingly divergent areas: there is a little of the hunting imagery that runs through *Venus and Adonis*, there are recurrent allusions to merchant venturers in search of profit, there is a mass of heraldry, some smoke, and a more or less equal amount of fire. There are

---

[1] Heather Dubrow, 'A Mirror for Complaints: Shakespeare's *Lucrece* and Generic Tradition', in B. Lewalski, ed., *Renaissance Genres: Essays on Theory, History and Interpretation* (Cambridge, Mass., 1986), 400–17.

many seas, which extend from the boundless tide of Tarquin's will as he rapes Lucrece into the eddying tidal waters of Collatine's grief at the end of the poem. Both of these floods seem to flow together in the dark waters of blood which finally ebb from and surround the 'island' of Lucrece's body. Commentators have often felt these riches of imagery do not work comfortably together, and that their diversity compounds inconsistencies and uncertainties in the ethical design of the poem. It has been said that the poem is caught uncomfortably between two incompatible ethical models: Lucrece has a soul, and a profound sense of inward guilt; she also has a keen sense of family honour and is overwhelmed by the shame that goes with the violation of that public honour by Tarquin.[1] Is the poem concerned with interior guilt or public shame, with insides or with outsides? Is it primarily interested in the material question of who owns Lucrece, or in the immaterial question of who is dishonoured by the rape?

The poem does raise these questions, and does not offer conclusive answers to them. But the fact that it does so is not indicative of a flawed design. Like its sister poem *Venus and Adonis*, it relishes multiplicity, and is fascinated by perspectival experimentation: it invites its readers to feel with Tarquin the dazzling brightness of Lucrece's face as he pulls back the curtain from her bed (and this moment of wonder prompts one of the very few reprises of the 'Look' formula (l. 372) that regularly introduces similes in *Venus and Adonis*); it also wants its readers then suddenly to shift perspective and to be inside Lucrece's eyelids as she opens them to see the carnal ghost who has violated her chamber. The poem builds on the tearful diffractions of sight which Venus experiences at the end of *Venus and Adonis*, and refuses to see things singly. But it does much more than this. The poem is partly *about* the different ways in which readers read, and the distinct ways in which different people and different sexes respond to material realities. It is also the result of deep thinking about the ways in which human actions may be described in a number of ways which are not compatible with each other. Its Argument, as we have seen, draws attention to the fact that there are various ways of reading the story of Lucrece. And reading—how one does it, how experience changes how one does it—is one of the central preoccupations of the poem. Both books

[1] Donaldson, 45–6.

and people are physical things and more than physical things, and this poem presses repeatedly on this similarity between people and texts. It begins to do so when Lucrece fails to read Tarquin's intentions from his eyes:

> But she that never coped with stranger eyes
> Could pick no meaning from their parling looks,
> Nor read the subtle shining secrecies,
> Writ in the glassy margins of such books.
>
> (ll. 99–102)

The poem was written to be printed. Here, though, it suggests that at the centre of people's minds are secret thoughts which readers of their faces can miss. The verb 'writ' suggests that Tarquin's privy intentions might be either printed notes which explain an arcane allusion, or handwritten marginalia jotted down according to principles known only to the annotator and illegible to Lucrece.[1] Tarquin's face has both the impersonality of print and the idiosyncrasy and near illegibility of a manuscript annotation.

Do readers read aright? The heroine of the poem is throughout conscious that she may be read, and read awry, that people will see her face and infer from it an inner crime which she did not commit. One of her primary concerns is to ensure that she will not become an exemplum of ill for those who debate in future over her life. She is also, at the start of the poem, a simple reader who believes that books and their margins should tell the same story, and that inner feelings should be physically printed on the material form of the face. She wants to be a legible, physical emblem of grief, where her inner sorrow is simply published in her face:

> 'And grave, like water that doth eat in steel,
> Upon my cheeks what helpless shame I feel.'
>
> (ll. 755–6)

At the same time she fears such publication of her sorrow if it meant that the source of her shame would become legible to all. She fears that the sour-faced groom, and even those who cannot read, will be able to perceive her private experiences published in her expression:

---

[1] 'Marginalia—traces left in a book—are wayward in their very nature . . . The marginal gloss, however, responds to another frame of mind: the need to spell everything out'. Laurence Lipking, 'The Marginal Gloss', *Critical Inquiry* 3 (1977), 612.

> Yea, the illiterate that know not how
> To cipher what is writ in learnèd books
> Will quote my loathsome trespass in my looks.
>
> (ll. 810–12)

At this stage of her story her face does not in fact carry the story behind her grief graven upon it, although she thinks it does. But by the end of the poem her tears have fretted visible characters in her countenance, and her grief is written clearly for all to see:

> with a joyless smile, she turns away
> The face, that map which deep impression bears
> Of hard misfortune, carved in it with tears.
>
> (ll. 1711–13)

Grief gradually etches emotion onto the face, making it a map of woe legible by all. This is in a way the end of a process of metamorphosis, which turns Lucrece into a physical form which is immediately and unambiguously legible, and which parallels the movement of the poem from the heroine's chamber to the public world of Rome. Private experiences are finally published in the face. This moment also prepares the way for Lucrece's reception into a literary tradition as an exemplary violated heroine, whose chastity is legibly printed in her countenance.

The odd thing about the poem is that while Lucrece is becoming an increasingly legible figure of grief, her own view of what reading is undergoes a radical change. And it changes in a direction which is diametrically opposed to the direction in which her own person is tending. She comes to read in a way that *is* aware of the subtle shining secrecies written in the margins of people's faces. The crucial transitional moment in this process is her response to the picture of the siege of Troy. That picture is initially introduced from what it is tempting to call an impersonal perspective. It is not quite right to call it 'impersonal' however, since this phase of the description repeatedly addresses the reader of the poem as 'you' ('There might *you* see'), or as an impersonal 'one' which instinctively carries a male pronoun ('That *one* would swear *he* saw them quake and tremble'). As the narrator describes the picture he emphasizes the way that it inscribes the characters of the Greek heroes in their painted faces:

> In Ajax and Ulysses, O what art
> Of physiognomy might one behold!

> The face of either ciphered either's heart;
> Their face their manners most expressly told.
>
> (ll. 1394–7)

'One' (male) immediately reads the heroes' manners ciphered in faces. The battle for the city is still raging when the picture is observed by the narrator's detached gaze: Achilles is still alive, and Troy's walls still stand. But when Lucrece comes to the painting it undergoes a sudden change. She sees things in the public, material form of the artwork which had been invisible to the narrator and his audience of male connoisseurs. When Lucrece begins to look at it, the picture becomes unmistakably an image of the very last days of Troy: Hecuba laments; Sinon, like Tarquin, betrays the town. The painting is presumably a multi-panelled historical narrative series, which graphically presents all of Troy's history at once. Lucrece, though, is a motivated reader who zooms in to the moment in the sequence onto which she might best project her own sense of violation. And the figure of Sinon makes her rewrite her responses to the picture:

> 'It cannot be', quoth she, 'that so much guile—'
> She would have said 'can lurk in such a look',
> But Tarquin's shape came in her mind the while,
> And from her tongue 'can lurk' from 'cannot' took.
> 'It cannot be' she in that sense forsook,
>   And turned it thus: 'It cannot be, I find,
>   But such a face should bear a wicked mind.'
>
> (ll. 1534–40)

As we have seen, Shakespeare the sophisticated reader of classical texts probably formed the idea of adding the description of the sack of Troy when he came across a comparison between Sinon and Tarquin in the marginal notes to Marsus's edition of Ovid's *Fasti*. At this point in the narrative Lucrece becomes a reader almost as sophisticated as her author. As well as reading her own experiences into the picture of Sinon, Lucrece brings to it a knowledge of the story which surrounds it. She sees the apparently innocent face of Sinon; and she adds to that innocence her knowledge of the part he will play in the fall of Troy. She no longer looks directly at the face before her for outward visible signs of its moral nature, but interprets its expression in the light of what has happened to her, and in the light of what will happen to Priam. Reading a narrative picture means now for her not just taking physiognomy as a physical sign of intent; it means taking account of circumstance, of prior and future events, and of stories which cling around the story before her. It means almost reading the scene like an annotator, who is aware of circumambient history in the way that Marsus's marginal notes to Ovid's story of Livy encourage his readers to be aware of the larger historical setting.

So reading matters in *Lucrece*. And the main characters in the poem do it very differently. Lucrece seems not to be aware at all of the medium in which Troy is depicted, and even the narrator fails to note what it is painted on or of, or what its colours, materials, and pigments are. She is interested entirely in the private significance it carries for her; he in its technique. When Tarquin looks at Lucrece as she sleeps, however, he reads her in a different way again. The description of the sleeping Lucrece is, as Nancy Vickers has shown, a blazon dominated by the male gaze.[1] Tarquin is not a bookish character, but even he reads objects in a way that carries the impress of his nature. He reads Lucrece as though she is simply a material thing:

> Her breasts, like ivory globes circled with blue,
> A pair of maiden worlds unconquerèd:
> Save of their lord no bearing yoke they knew,
> And him by oath they truly honourèd.
> These worlds in Tarquin new ambition bred,
>   Who like a foul usurper went about
>   From this fair throne to heave the owner out.
>
> What could he see, but mightily he noted?
> What did he note, but strongly he desirèd?
> What he beheld, on that he firmly doted,
> And in his will his wilful eye he tirèd.
> With more than admiration he admirèd
>   Her azure veins, her alabaster skin,
>   Her coral lips, her snow-white dimpled chin.
>   (ll. 407–20)

This was, as we have seen, one of the most popular passages among manuscript miscellanists. A section from it appears in the

---

[1] Nancy Vickers, '"The Blazon of Sweet Beauty's Best": Shakespeare's *Lucrece*', in Patricia Parker, Geoffrey Hartman, and David Quint, eds., *Shakespeare and the Question of Theory* (New York and London, 1985), 95–115.

popular anthology *England's Parnassus* (1601), and another part of it was imitated and elaborated by Suckling. The desire to record, and at times to rewrite, this passage, may have been prompted by the obvious complicity which it establishes between a male reader and a male viewer. But readers may have been prompted to write it down partly because of its writerly language: 'mightily he *noted*? | What did he *note*'. This voyeur has his commonplace book to hand, and is ready to make Lucrece's appearance into his property by writing it down (as Jachimo does in the closely analogous scene in which he spies on the sleeping Innogen in *Cymbeline* 2.2). But Tarquin is above all preoccupied with what Lucrece is made of. In Renaissance art the value of constituent materials composed a vital part of the meaning of art objects. Azure was an especially expensive pigment; coral a precious and rare commodity believed to bring good luck. Ivory too was an expensive raw material. Much of this vocabulary of costly materials is of course common in erotic blazons from the period, but the combination of so many materials of value here evokes a very particular kind of looking. Tarquin is a rich patron drooling over a costly work of art, working out how much the artist has spent on materials and dwelling long-ingly on the bits that cost the most. The 'pair of ivory globes' of Lucrece's breasts belong, for Tarquin, in a cabinet of curiosities. Globes were not in fact made of ivory in this period, but of papier mâché onto which 'gores' or triangular sections of a map (usually paper) were glued by a skilled workman. This made them a rare thing: an early modern artefact which was valuable purely because of the skill of the workman in transforming paste and paper into an accurate instrument. But Tarquin metamorphoses globes into images of conquest and precious materials. Unlike Lucrece he does not read a work of art in the light of what it might mean for him, or for the emotional senses which might emerge from its material form. He reads in order to own a thing of costly worth, which he sees as simply something to possess.

The poem's fascination with reading, and how to read the mind's construction in the face, reflects light on several points in it which critics have found puzzling. People are like texts: they can have secret meanings and they can have public, printed meanings. These two are unlikely ever to coincide, since no two readers read in exactly the same way. This fascination with the varieties of reading also helps to clarify the peculiarities of the poem's beginning and ending. Critics have been disturbed and intrigued by the fact that the rape of Lucrece in the poem originates with Collatine's boast to Tarquin and his fellow warriors about his wife's chaste beauty. This conflicts with the account of the matter in the Argument, in which Tarquin goes with Collatine to see Lucrece as the Roman lords test their wives' chastity. In the poem, however, it is Collatine's rash 'publication' of his wife's beauty that prompts Tarquin's desire. And the poem invites its readers to ask why Collatine published his wife's beauty so promiscuously:

> Or why is Collatine the publisher
> Of that rich jewel he should keep unknown
> From thievish ears, because it is his own?
>   (ll. 33–5)

Collatine's exposure of his wife's beauty has been variously interpreted by modern readers as a failure to protect her reputation,[1] or as a moment which suggests that rape is the price paid by a woman for being described.[2] To emphasize Collatine's culpability here, however, may be to attach too little significance to the role played by readers in the poem, and the wider question about how different people respond to published works. That the poem is thinking about such matters is indicated by the return to the word 'publish' at its end: the body of Lucrece is used to 'publish Tarquin's foul offence' (l. 1852). This preoccupation is not surprising: Lucrece was only the second printed work to which Shakespeare's name was attached. The poem is aware that it will be read by unknown readers who will have unpredictable responses to what they read (and by 1594 it is likely that Shakespeare had some idea of how strongly readers of Venus and Adonis had responded to the erotic charge of that poem). That anxiety over publication and interpretation feeds into the central action of the poem, since it was not unusual in this period to associate publication with sexual exposure, or with the leaking of secrets from a private chamber into a public sphere. Thomas Nashe's preface to the pirated edition of Sidney's Astrophil and Stella represents the printing of Sidney's private works as the result of a thieving violation of a private chamber. Although, Nashe claims, poetry 'be oftentimes imprisoned in ladies' casks,

---

[1] Dubrow, Domestic Loss, 51–5.
[2] Rape is the price Lucrece pays for being described', Vickers, ' "The Blazon" ', 102.

and the precedent books of such as cannot see without another man's spectacles, yet at length it breaks forth in spite of his keepers, and useth some private pen (instead of a picklock) to procure his violent enlargement'.[1] *Lucrece* explicitly links together intimacy violated—the chamber of Lucrece is broken into—and publication. But throughout the poem asks whether what people experience or feel coincides with the way in which they are read.[2] Collatine 'publishes' Lucrece; but how does he know how Tarquin might respond to his publication? How far is Brutus using the 'published' body of Lucrece to serve his own ends at the conclusion of the poem? These questions the poem cannot lay to rest.

Rape and Consent. *Lucrece* is about a rape, and about how women and men respond to rape. It also responds acutely and in detail to early modern thinking about the crime of rape and its nature. The common-law offence of rape in the late sixteenth century encompassed not one, but two distinct kinds of crime. The first form of rape was defined as intercourse with a woman over the age of 10 against her will. This was a felony against the woman, which, under the Elizabethan statute 18. Eliz. cap. 7, was punishable by death without benefit of clergy, and for which a woman could bring an appeal of felony. The second kind of crime referred to in this period as 'rape' was the abduction of a woman along with her husband's property, or in an attempt to acquire the heritable possessions of her father by a forced marriage.[3] This form of rape was seen as a violation of the proprietary rights of the husband of a married woman or of the father of an unmarried woman. In cases of rape-as-abduction the woman's family might suffer material loss, and so were regarded in law as deserving compensation. The two forms of rape are often blended in the writing of the period, so that rape was widely represented and thought of as both a crime against property and a crime against a person. The Elizabethan law

---

[1] *Sir P.S. His Astrophel and Stella* (1591), sig. A3^r.

[2] Wendy Wall, *The Imprint of Gender: Authorship and Publication in the English Renaissance* (Ithaca and London, 1993), 218. Wall builds on Vickers, '"The Blazon"'.

[3] *The Law's Resolution of Women's Rights* (1632) distinguishes between 'a hideous hateful kind of whoredom in him which committeth it, when a woman is enforced violently to sustain the fury of brutish concupiscence, but she is left where she is found, as in her own house or bed, as Lucrece was, and not hurried away, as Helen by Paris', and abduction.

of rape-as-sexual-violation was further confused by an extremely odd and unfair treatment of consent. A refusal to consent at the moment of rape was, as now, a central element in definitions of rape-as-sexual-violation. Subsequent events could, however, retrospectively affect whether or not a woman was deemed to have consented, and so could determine the severity of the crime.[1] If the victim consented to marriage to the rapist after the event this could remove grounds for the victim to make an appeal of felony, or might mitigate the punishment given to the offender. Legal textbooks from the period also frequently stated that if a woman conceived she cannot have been raped, since conception was taken to imply consent: 'rape is the carnal abusing of a woman against her will. But if the woman conceive upon any carnal abusing of her, that is no rape, for she cannot conceive unless she consent.'[2]

These multiple currents within the common-law offence of rape have a shaping influence on the imagery and argument of *Lucrece*. The crime of rape raised questions about property and ownership, but it also created an overlap between these material concerns and immaterial questions about volition, and about what it is to 'consent' to an act. Rape was both a material violation of family and property, and an immaterial violation of a woman's will. This is the determining reason why the imagery of the poem refers frequently to jewels and treasure, and why Tarquin is presented as a thief or merchant venturer, gambling what he has in order to gain something he cannot own, and why these material concerns are habitually translated into, or yoked with, metaphors for desire.[3] Rape straddles these realms, since it was both a crime against wealth and a crime against will. Tarquin does not abduct Lucrece, of course, and that becomes part of the point of the poem: he desires to possess her, but his form of possession consists in forcing her to have sex with him against her will rather than in obtaining the use of her or her husband's property. He slips from desiring rape as a form of material enrichment to achieving it as a violation and contamination of another's will. That desire issues only in the destruction of desire at the moment when its object is achieved is an idea to which

[1] See the lucid account in Sokol, 319–24, and Barbara J. Baines, 'Effacing Rape in Early Modern Representation', *ELH* 65 (1998), 69–98.

[2] Henry Finch, *Law, or a Discourse thereof in Four Books* (1627), 204.

[3] Although it also reflects contemporary anxieties about burglary and 'the violation and contamination of a dwelling place *per se*', Dubrow, *Domestic Loss*, 48.

Shakespeare recurred in the sonnets (notably in *129*), and which is
a ground-tone of thought in *Macbeth* and *Antony cnd Cleopatra*. For
Tarquin a crude desire to possess an object ends in his possessing
nothing which has any material value at all:

> Those that much covet are with gain so fond
> That what they have not—that which they possess—
> They scatter and unloose it from their bond,
> And so by hoping more they have but less,
> Or gaining more, the profit of excess
>   Is but to surfeit, and such griefs sustain,
>   That they prove bankrupt in this poor-rich gain.
>
> (ll. 134–40)

And as Tarquin skulks from the poem Shakespeare presents us with
the paradox of a man who has sought a material thing, a 'jewel', a
possession, and who is tricked by the double nature of rape into
achieving only a spiritual and physical violation which contami-
nates his own soul, while leaving him with nothing.

It is not only Tarquin whom the poem leaves in this position. At
the end of *Lucrece* the male members of Lucrece's family haggle
over who 'possesses' the victim, and who should most mourn her
death. This scene again has its foundation in the Elizabethan law
of rape: if a rape victim died, either the father of an unmarried
woman or the husband of a married woman could seek redress.
But although both men are feeling that they have lost a material
possession, the poem mocks them with the emptiness of their claim
to possess Lucrece:

> The one doth call her his, the other his,
> Yet neither may possess the claim they lay.
> The father says 'She's mine.' 'O mine she is',
> Replies her husband . . .
>
> (ll. 1793–6)

and:

> 'My daughter' and 'My wife' with clamours filled
> The dispersed air, who, holding Lucrece' life,
> Answered their cries, 'My daughter and my wife.'
>
> (ll. 1804–6)

Words often vainly oppose words in this poem without resolving
themselves into an outcome. Here words which claim possession

over Lucrece vanish into air (and in the first Quarto, which does not contain speech marks, it is not even clear who says 'O mine she is' in line 1792). Is rape primarily about possession of goods or of a woman? The poem mocks those who want to see it purely in this light: they set out like Tarquin to possess Lucrece, then find that the air has as good a claim on her as they do.

The Elizabethan law of rape raised questions about ownership and family honour, and connected those questions with imponderable and intangible concerns with volition and agency. The most slippery and intangible aspect of rape in this period was the question of what 'consent' might be. Absence of consent to sex could take the form of explicit refusal, or it could be an interior matter; but, as we have seen, it also might be qualified by later events which were completely beyond the will of the woman, such as conception. These darker reaches of the Elizabethan law of rape are registered in Lucrece's actions. Her determination to kill this 'bastard graff' (L 1062) along with herself is not simply an expression of her horror that she might bear Tarquin's child and so defile Collatine's lineage. It also reflects a fear that if she conceived she might be thought to have consented to the rape. Pronouns throughout the latter part of the poem suggest that, as many rape victims do, she feels the crime is partly hers: 'O hear me then, injurious shifting Time, | Be guilty of my death, since of my crime' (ll. 930–1). She means 'the crime against me', but her language suggests she cannot regard herself as free of complicity. The extraordinary inside-out inversion with which the men of Rome seek to console her also tries hard not to mean what it says: they say, 'Her body's stain her mind untainted clears' (l 1710). This means that her untainted mind makes her body free of pollution, but the inverted syntax makes it seem to say the reverse. These areas of uncertainty within the poem interact in complex ways with the multiplicity of versions of the Lucretia story which Shakespeare inherited, not all of which are clear about the choices Lucretia does or does not make. In most versions of the story Lucretia is given the classic Hobson's choice by Tarquin: she can choose either to be raped and killed and shamed for ever by being placed in bed next to a dead slave, or she can agree to be violated by Tarquin. Her response to this non-choice was treated in a variety of ways in different versions of the story. The version of the story in Dio's Roman history states that Lucretia chose to yield to Tarquin rather than lose her reputation:

when he threatens to kill a slave and 'spread the report that he had found them sleeping together and killed them, she could no longer endure it, but, fearing it might really be believed that this had so happened, chose to yield to him and die after giving an account of the affair rather than lose her good name in perishing at once'.[1] Is this a choice? And does making such a choice amount to consent? And does the decision that Lucretia makes in this version to control the stories which are subsequently told about her give her anything which amounts to self-determination?

Most modern readers would think the only possible answer to these questions would be 'no'. Shakespeare and his heroine, however, are extremely uncertain and uneasy about the extent to which her will might be contaminated by Tarquin's crime. This is compounded by the fact that the poem does not represent the actual moment of violation (to have done so might well have risked the suppression of the volume). The result is that the moment of rape becomes a blur, which extends both to a reader's visual and ethical perception:

> 'No more,' quoth he: 'By heaven I will not hear thee.
> Yield to my love; if not, enforcèd hate
> Instead of love's coy touch shall rudely tear thee.
> That done, despitefully I mean to bear thee
>> Unto the base bed of some rascal groom
>> To be thy partner in this shameful doom.'
>
> This said, he sets his foot upon the light,
> For light and lust are deadly enemies.
> Shame folded up in blind concealing night,
> When most unseen, then most doth tyrannize.
>
> (ll. 667–76)

Darkness falls, and Lucrece says nothing in response to Tarquin's offer of a simulacrum of choice. The moment of the rape is a critical one in differing versions of the Lucretia story: Chaucer's heroine faints at this point; Ovid's is overcome by the fear of infamy; and in Livy 'her resolute modesty was overcome by his victorious lust'—a moment which is itself blurred by textual corruption: modern texts, but not the early modern versions available to Shakespeare, emend the odd grammar of Livy here to read 'as if by

---

[1] *Dio's Roman History*, ed. with an English translation by Ernest Cary, Loeb Classical Library, 9 vols. (Cambridge, Mass. and London, 1914–27), ii.17.

force'.[1] Shakespeare's narrator loads sententious observation on
sententious observation in order to fill in the time taken by the
physical act of rape. What happens while he moralizes? All we
witness suggests that Tarquin presents the non-choice—either she
must 'yield', or else she will be raped and killed and defamed—and
is then so overwhelmed by desire that he does not stay for an
answer (and this is how the marginal notes to Q6 present it: 'Tar-
quin all impatient interrupts her and denied of consent breaketh
the enclosure of her chastity by force'). Lucrece's chastity—that is,
her freedom from any taint of having given any form of consent to
sex with a man who is not her husband—is preserved by Tarquin's
haste and by the poem's reluctance to represent the moment of
rape, since she does not say or do anything in response to the
options he offers. And yet Tarquin has staged the rape as being her
choice, despite the fact that it is manifestly an act of coercion.

This is one of the cruelest aspects of his crime. But it is a vital
one, since it goes some way towards explaining why both Lucrece
and the poem are so undecided about the extent to which she is in
control of her fate, and about whether her inner mind as well as
her family honour is tainted by the crime. Has she 'consented' to
the rape? And does the concept of consent have any purchase on a
moment where the choice is between rape or death with perpetual
infamy? For many readers her cry that 'I am the mistress of my
fate' (l. 1069) rings true: she manages to ensure by her actions that
she will go down in history as an exemplum of a chaste wife. Her
complaints, and her efforts to establish a bond of sympathy with
Philomela and Hecuba, have also been seen as creating a feminine
language of woe, and as therefore bringing about a form of ex-
pressive victory from a physical defeat.[2] She is indeed manifestly
concerned to shape her own story, and not become a theme for
disputation or an example of lust, and this concern for her own
future exemplary status is presented as one of the chief motives for
her actions. Her suicide is a decisive act of choice, and it is care-
fully staged in order to win the consent of her family to revenge
before her death. Yet the poem interweaves each of these threads of
autonomy with darker matter. Her lament with Philomel joins the

[1] *LGW* ll. 1812–18; *Fasti* 2 810; Livy 1.58.5.
[2] For a strong statement of the view that Lucrece seeks to use, and simultane-
ously suspects, a masculine persuasive language, see Philippa Berry, 'Woman, Lan-
guage, and History in *The Rape of Lucrece*', *Shakespeare Survey* 44 (1992), 33–9.

two violated women in a single song, but their voices are not in perfect consonance as they sing of different stories: 'For burden-wise I'll hum on Tarquin still, | While thou on Tereus descants better skill' (ll. 1133–4). When she laments with Hecuba she '*shapes* her sorrow to the beldam's woes' (l. 1458), and the phrasing here suggests that seeking to identify across a huge gulf of time with the sorrow of another woman leads her to *reshape* her own suffering rather than simply to give it voice. Finding a source and a parallel for her suffering involves also warping it. She and Hecuba are both victims of male aggression, but Hecuba has not been raped, and the gulf of ages which separates the two women is replicated by a gulf between their experiences. Lucrece's grief seeks to find vehicles, but the vehicles it finds are other people's stories rather than her own, approximations to grief rather than expressions of 'her grief's true quality' (l. 1313).

And, like many rape victims, she feels guilt and a sense of inner taint. At least part of this guilt has to do with the shadow of a choice with which Tarquin has presented her (and I should emphasize that my argument here is not intended to blame the victim of rape, but to explain the circumstances in which the victim comes to blame herself). Lucrece urges her hand to 'Kill both thyself and her for yielding so' (l. 1036). The word 'yield' is rung on through the poem: Lucrece's doors 'yield' to Tarquin's battery, and immediately before the rape he urges her to 'yield' to him. The word belongs exactly to the ambience of this poem: immaterial things (and people) can 'yield' in the sense of physically giving way; people can also in some sense voluntarily yield themselves subject to a superior when they are defeated. 'Yielding' occupies a hazy world between volition and compulsion in which the balance between the two is painfully unclear. The poem traps Lucrece and her readers within this dark terrain. The concept of 'yielding' slips from the compulsory to the semi-voluntary, and Lucrece is agonizingly uncertain about where to locate herself on that scale. That slippage is not one which modern readers wish to experience, and for good reason. It leads to painful questions about the autonomy of victims in circumstances in which a man is clearly and devilishly to blame.

Nevertheless, the intersection between the multiple versions of the story and the multiple strands within the Elizabethan law of rape creates an area of conceptual darkness at the heart of this poem. Lucrece is left feeling both that her family honour is violated and that her will is contaminated by 'yielding'. And some early readers took an even darker view of her than that: one seventeenth-century reader left a note of his scepticism about the conduct of Lucrece when she entertained Tarquin in a British Library copy of Q1: 'whoever made a feast for a single guest?'[1] The suggestion that Lucrece may have 'yielded' in part voluntarily goes a long way towards explaining why the poem shuffles between Christian conceptions of guilt and pagan conceptions of shame: Lucrece's private guilt comes from the shadow of a choice which she has been given; her public shame is a necessary response to the fact that rape was in this period viewed as a crime against the family, its status, and its heritable possessions. The poem's journey through these dark realms, where choices seem not really to be choices at all, also helps to explain why that crucial word 'consent' seems to mutate from the strong claim in the Argument that the Roman people 'with one consent' agreed to change the state into one that is governed by consuls to its less muscular usage at the end. At the end of the poem 'The Romans plausibly did give consent | To Tarquin's everlasting banishment' (ll. 1854–5), and in applauding the banishment they implicitly assent to a transformation in their state which, according to Fulbecke's Tacitean vision of Roman history at least, substitutes one form of tyranny for another. 'Consent' of the kind that is exercised by a post-Kantian individual who freely chooses to determine the direction of her actions, irrespective of material pressures, just does not exist in this poem. *Lucrece* works off a variety of discourses, of ownership, of self-determination, of material enclosure, of liberty and tyranny. And it darkly pinions its heroine and readers within the indeterminate areas of overlap between those different discourses. The poem is not confused in doing this: it is asking dark but profound questions of the way in which the individual will intersects with circumstances, about how our bodies are both public objects and receptacles of hidden inner emotions. If it does not resolve these questions it is because they are irresolvable. What the poem does achieve, however, is to make those questions matter.

[1] Shelfmark G 11178, sig. E1^{v}.

The Passionate Pilgrim

By the later 1590s *Venus and Adonis* and *Lucrece* were established as two of the most popular and widely imitated poems in English. And by 1598–9—crucial years in the development of Shakespeare's reputation—his name had become a valuable commodity. In 1598 the name 'William Shakespeare' appeared for the first time on the title-page of a play (*Richard II*). In 1598 too Francis Meres wrote that 'the sweet witty soul of Ovid lives in mellifluous and honey-tongued Shakespeare' and sought to excite the reading public of early-modern London by referring to Shakespeare's 'sugared Sonnets among his private friends'.[1] If Shakespeare was not to produce a volume of poems in that year, then the atmosphere was so thick with his influence that it was almost inevitable that one should have been invented.

The title-page of the first edition of *The Passionate Pilgrim*, a small octavo volume containing twenty poems (STC 22341.5), does not survive.[2] It was printed by T. Judson for William Jaggard (probably in 1599, though conceivably as early as September 1598 when Judson is first known to have set up his press). The volume was poorly produced on a miscellaneous stock of paper by a printer whose career was short and unsuccessful. It was clearly designed to exploit the excitement which surrounded the name of Shakespeare in that year. Jaggard placed two sonnets by Shakespeare (versions of what became Sonnets *138* and *144*) at the start of the volume, and augmented the collection with several poems which he must have known were by other hands (the Court of Assistants had ordered in 1598 that no books in pica letters without pictures should be sold for more than two sheets for a penny; there were therefore material rewards for bulk).[3] His printer also took the relatively unusual step of beginning each new poem on a new recto.

<hr />

[1] Smith, ii. 317.

[2] Earlier scholars, including the all-but-infallible Rollins, believed that the copies in Trinity College and the Huntington Library were the first edition. Joseph Quincy Adams decisively proved that these in fact represented the second edition in his introduction to his facsimile edition of the Folger copy of *The Passionate Pilgrim* (New York and London, 1939). Only sigs. A3–A7, C2–7 survive from this edition. Hence O1 is control text in this edition only for Poems 1, 2, 3, 4, 5, 16, 17, 18. O2 is adopted as control text for the remainder.

[3] Edwin E. Willoughby, *A Printer of Shakespeare* (1934), 32.

The second edition (*The passionate pilgrime. Or certaine amorous sonnets*, STC 22342) appeared in 1599. Its title-page is revealing about Jaggard's ambitions for the volume:

THE | PASSIONATE | PILGRIME. | *By* W. *Shakespeare.* | [Ornament] | *AT LONDON* . Printed for W. Iaggard, and are | to be sold by W. Leake, at the Grey- | hound in Paules Churchyard. | 1599. |

Leake had owned the copyright of *Venus and Adonis* since 25 June 1596.[1] Jaggard was in all probability trying to ensure that book-collectors picked up copies of *The Passionate Pilgrim by W. Shakespeare* as a companion volume to the narrative poem.[2]

Few copies survive, and O1 survives only in fragments. This may indicate that the volumes pleased their target audiences so much that they were read to pieces. O2 was set from O1, but by a different compositor. He seems not to have realized that only new poems were afforded the luxury of a new recto, and started off setting the poems exclusively on rectos. As a result the original three-and-a-half sheets of O1 (which collated A–C^8, D^4) had to be expanded to four full sheets (A–D^8). There are signs that the printer may have initially thought this new arrangement would not fill the thirty-two pages of the volume. This may explain the addition of a separate title-page on sig. C3^r:

SONNETS | To sundry notes of Musicke. | [Ornament] | *AT LONDON* | Printed for W. Iaggard, and *are* | to be sold by W. Leake, at the Grey- | hound in Paules Churchyard. | 1599.

The two parts of the volume could not have been sold separately, since the new title-page occurs in the middle of a gathering. Adams's speculation that the second title-page was added as a result of complaints by Shakespeare at the attribution of the poems to him is not convincing:[3] the sole evidence for this is the testimony of Thomas Heywood in 1612 that Shakespeare was 'much offended with M. Jaggard'. This is a reference to the publication of O3 in 1612 (which is discussed below) and is not reliable evidence that Shakespeare took a proprietorial interest in his name or his writings as early as 1599. Furthermore, Poem 16, the second poem after the new title-page, is indisputably of Shakespeare's authorship, since it is found in *Love's Labour's Lost* (which had appeared,

---

[1] Arber, iii.65.   [2] Adams, ed., p. xv.   [3] Adams, ed., p. xxxvi.

'newly corrected and augmented by W. Shakespeare', in 1598). The title-page is therefore likely to be a misjudged attempt to pad the volume out. This plan was misjudged indeed: the printer had to abandon his earlier lavishness with paper in the last few pages of the volume: the last three stanzas of Poem 18 had to be crammed onto a single page, and the last two poems (19 and 20) had to be compressed onto the recto and verso of the remaining four leaves in order to avoid the expense of an additional sheet. It is possible too that the final few stanzas of the reply to 'Live with me and be my love' had to be omitted in order to keep the volume within four sheets. It is bad work.

Of the twenty poems in the volume, five are known to be by Shakespeare (1, 2, 3, 5, and 16), four can confidently be attributed to other authors (8 and 20 are by Barnfield, 11 is by Bartholomew Griffin, 19 is attributed to Marlowe in *England's Helicon* (1600)), and eleven (4, 6, 7, 9, 10, 12, 13, 14, 15, 17, and 18) are of unknown authorship. The volume is most notable for its inclusion of versions of Sonnets *138* and *144*. The variants between these versions and those which were printed in 1609 are significant. In the case of *138* they are too extensive to be simply the product of scribal or compositorial tinkering. The *Passionate Pilgrim* version of *138* may well represent an early state of the sonnet. Jaggard had clearly obtained a hot property in the form of two genuine sonnets by Shakespeare.

The origins of these and the other texts included in the volume are, however, a mystery. There is insufficient evidence to reach a certain conclusion about how these poems came into Jaggard's hands, or about the kind of copy from which the printer of the volume was working. In the absence of clear external or internal evidence about authorship it is impossible to be certain how closely the poems are related to Shakespeare. There is a wide spectrum of possibilities:

1. A manuscript which had belonged to Shakespeare came into Jaggard's hands. It included poems by Shakespeare as well as transcriptions of and variations upon poems by other authors. He printed it with minimal changes.
2. A manuscript which had circulated among a group of poets, including Shakespeare, Barnfield, Marlowe, and Griffin, came into Jaggard's hands which he then printed.

3. A manuscript miscellany consisting of copies at some remove from their earliest versions came into Jaggard's hands. He recognized a number of poems as Shakespeare's and jumped to the conclusion that the whole collection was by him.

4. Jaggard obtained copies of two sonnets by Shakespeare. He recognized that they were valuable copy, but too slight to warrant publication in book form. He sought out a number of poems, including some lyrics from recently printed plays by Shakespeare, some sonnets on the theme of Venus and Adonis, and a number of miscellany pieces of unknown authorship which he set about compiling into a volume of verse.

Most editors incline more to option 4 than to option 1. This is largely because in 1612 Jaggard produced a third augmented edition of *The Passionate Pilgrim*, floridly entitled

THE PASSIONATE | PILGRIME. | OR | *Certaine Amorous Sonnets,* | *betweene* Venus *and* Adonis, | *newly corrected and aug-* | mented. | *By W. Shakespere.* | The third Edition. | VVhere-unto is newly ad- | ded two Loue-Epistles, the first | from *Paris* to *Hellen,* and | *Helens* answere backe | againe to *Paris.* | Printed by W. Iaggard. | 1612.

This contained two of Thomas Heywood's translations from Ovid's *Heroides* ('The Amorous Epistle of Paris to Helen' and 'Helen to Paris') and nine poems culled from Thomas Heywood's *Troia Britannica* of 1609. Jaggard's use of this material prompted an angry outburst from Heywood in his *Apology for Actors,* in which he implies that Shakespeare too was offended by the misattribution of the poems to him:

Here likewise, I must necessarily insert a manifest injury done me in that work [*Troia Britannica,* which Jaggard had printed in 1609], by taking the two epistles of *Paris to Helen,* and *Helen to Paris,* and printing them in a less volume [*The Passionate Pilgrim* of 1612], under the name of another [Shakespeare], which may put the world in opinion I might steal them from him; and he to do himself right, hath since published them in his own name: but as I must acknowledge my lines not worthy his [Shakespeare's] patronage, under whom he [Jaggard] hath published them, so the author [Shakespeare] I know much offended with M. Jaggard (that altogether unknown to him) presumed to make so bold with his name.[1]

---

[1] Thomas Heywood, *Apology for Actors* (1612), sigs. G4[a–b].

The augmented edition of 1612 seems to mark *The Passionate Pilgrim* as a purely opportunistic publication, since the material it includes builds so evidently on the claim of Meres that 'the sweet witty soul of Ovid' lived on in Shakespeare.[1] Jaggard probably hoped to persuade readers that Shakespeare metempsychosed not just the Ovid of the *Metamorphoses*, but also the Ovid of the *Heroides*. It is enough to make many critics dismiss *The Passionate Pilgrim* as the product of an unscrupulous piratical printer, who somehow got hold of two sonnets by Shakespeare and who made something of them by adding poems which his contemporaries would have some reason to attribute to his name. This position cannot be readily dismissed: the texts of the two poems by Barnfield (8 and 20) are so close to the versions printed a year before by Jaggard's brother that it is highly probable they were set from the printed texts, and that their publisher was therefore aware that he was passing off as Shakespeare's poems which were clearly by someone else.

Before we damn Jaggard as an unscrupulous opportunist, however, we should perhaps pause over the list of alternative possibilities (1–4) above. The first and the fourth of them assume too tidy a division between authorial agency and a printer's mercantile unscrupulousness. We should also pause over the contents of the third edition of *The Passionate Pilgrim* in 1612. Jaggard was not simply passing Heywood's poems off as Shakespeare's: the 'two Love epistles' added to the volume are referred to after the mention of Shakespeare on the title-page. Nor, technically, was he pirating the poems (Swinburne referred to him as an 'infamous pirate, liar, and thief' who produced in *The Passionate Pilgrim* a 'worthless little volume of stolen and mutilated poetry, patched up and padded out with dirty and dreary doggrel').[2] Jaggard had entered *Troia Britannica* in the Stationers' Register on 5 December 1608.[3] This meant that he owned the right to print the poem, and was legally entitled to reprint it. Heywood's testimony that Shakespeare was offended

[1] Smith, ii.317.

[2] Algernon Charles Swinburne, *Studies in Prose and Poetry* (1894), 90.

[3] The entry includes the slightly unusual proviso: 'Provided that if any question or trouble grow hereof, then he shall answer and discharge it at his own loss and cost' (Arber, iii.397). This was presumably because of fears that the work might engage in potentially controversial historical parallels rather than in anticipation of a dispute between printer and author.

by the publication is also not free from bias. Heywood had had an extended dispute with Jaggard over the printing of *Troia Britannica*. According to Heywood's account (included in the *Apology for Actors*) Jaggard had refused to print a list of errata along with *Troia Britannica*, but would 'rather let his own fault lie upon the neck of the author'. The reprinting of Heywood's poems along with Shakespeare's appears to have been the final straw as far as Heywood was concerned. What we are seeing here is not necessarily evidence that Shakespeare was by 1612 sufficiently concerned about his literary property to have his Sonnets printed 'in his own name' (Heywood's chronology in any case is wrong here: *Shakespeares Sonnets* appeared in 1609, three years before the third edition of *The Passionate Pilgrim*). It may well be evidence that Heywood, in common with a number of writers in the first decades of the seventeenth century, was becoming increasingly irritated by the lack of control which he could assert over his texts once a printer had won the copyright of them. Jaggard may have had to reissue the volume with a new title-page, which omits all reference to Shakespeare.[1]

The poems which have the most tantalizing relation to the demonstrably Shakespearian corpus of verse are the 'Venus and Adonis Sonnets' (4, 6, 9, and 11), to which Jaggard so proudly gave prime billing on the title-page of O3.[2] Jaggard was by 1612 evidently aware that the publication of Shakespeare's Sonnets in 1609 had stolen whatever thunder was left in his meagre crop of two indisputably Shakespearian sonnets. The title-page of O3 capitalizes on what he had: sonnets on an indisputably Shakespearian theme which were at least of disputable, and possibly of Shakespearian authorship. And the most significant question to ask of

---

[1] The Bodleian copy, formerly Malone's, includes two title-pages, one of which (the first, bound into the volume so as to face the second) omits the name of Shakespeare. According to STC this was 'probably intended as a cancel'. Jaggard's printers may have missed out the all-important name of Shakespeare on their first attempt, and may have been instructed to reset the page. This is borne out by the Bodleian copy, in which the two title-pages face each other. The title-page without the name of Shakespeare (which is bound in first) is noticeably less worn than that which includes Shakespeare's name. This suggests that the volume was originally circulated with Shakespeare's name on the outermost leaf of the volume, and that Malone had the pages bound in their present order, having found the cancelled title-page originally inside the volume.

[2] The most extensive discussion remains C. H. Hobday, 'Shakespeare's Venus and Adonis Sonnets', *Shakespeare Survey* 26 (1973), 103–9.

the poems printed in 1599 is whether or not the 'Venus and Adonis' sonnets (Poems 4, 6, 9, 11) were written by Shakespeare.

Almost certainly not. They read like reflections at one remove on the Venus and Adonis story as told by Shakespeare, and in at least one case seem almost to be attempts at Shakespearian pastiche. The opening of 6, 'Scarce had the sun dried up the dewy morn', bows to the opening lines of *Venus and Adonis* in a way that is typical of Richard Barnfield, whose works frequently sought to mingle themselves with Shakespeare's (and one of whose poems concludes Jaggard's volume). Shakespeare was as bawdy as the next poet, but his bawdy is always mingled with pleasures for the ear. Poem 6 in particular tries to please the eye but neglects the finer senses: 6.10, 'And stood stark naked on the brook's green brim', congregates, coagulates, sounds which Shakespeare always used sparingly: 'st' is hard on the mouth; 'stood stark naked' is harder on the mouth than anything in Shakespeare, and is trying to shock, both acoustically and graphically. Venus's proud display of the gash in her thigh in 9.13 is also likely to be the product of a crude reimagining of the delightfully hidden brakes and fountains of the Shakespearian Venus rather than a glimpse of an earlier, more salacious treatment of the Venus and Adonis theme which was then toned down for print. That another Venus and Adonis sonnet, number 11, first appeared in Bartholomew Griffin's *Fidessa* may indicate the rest are also by Griffin. Whoever wrote them (and it is possible that more than one poet was involved), these poems are likely to indicate the kinds of things *Venus and Adonis* did to the imaginations of poets of respectable ability who wished to write in an unrespectable way, rather than giving us Shakespeare's early thoughts on what Venus and Adonis may have done with each other.

Of the rest of the poems in *The Passionate Pilgrim* the best that one can say is that most of them give their readers just enough to enable them to believe they are by Shakespeare if they really want to. The Shakespearian poems are artfully disposed so as to make the most of apparent continuities with the non-Shakespearian pieces. Jaggard, or whoever ordered the poems, knew that readers want to make sequences out of series. The phrase 'Thou being a goddess' in Poem 3 is a simple piece of hyperbole in its original setting in *Love's Labour's Lost*. But placed as it is in *The Passionate Pilgrim* it resonates with the angels and devils of the version of Sonnet 144 that precedes it, and makes a bridge between that poem and the following one, which is about the literal goddess Venus. Moments such as this serve as a valuable reminder that sonnets can work with the poems which surround them in a variety of ways, even if their author has had nothing to do with the ordering, and that printers in this period might have good readerly ears. Poem 16, 'On a day', also from *Love's Labour's Lost*, is grouped with the 'Sonnets to Sundry Notes of Music'. In its new setting, with its wording carefully tweaked to remove clues about its original setting, the poem's triple repetition of 'Air' seems to allude to the musical form of that name, and to blend its lines into the non-Shakespearian pieces which surround it, in which music and musical language do sound loudly. 'On a day' manages to draw the short lines of 20 (which is by Barnfield) into a Shakespearian ambience, interacting with Barnfield's vaguely *Lucrece*-like plangency to make the poem sound like a slightly new Shakespearian mode. Poem 16 works its magic too on Poem 13, a meditation on beauty which is unascribable and in its way perfect: its reflective form builds on the glistening beauty which it describes ('A shining gloss that vadeth suddenly'). Its delicacy and evanescence link it with the blossom 'playing in the air' in the Shakespearian 16. Perhaps as a result of this connection 13 was enthusiastically claimed as Shakespeare's, and manuscripts of it were duly invented to prove the ascription, in the eighteenth century.[1] It is lovely, but it gives no indications at all of who wrote it. Indeed, part of its loveliness is the sense it gives of having been generated more from rhetorical patterning than from deliberate thought of a kind which might bear the imprint of its owner.

The watching Poem 14, too, full of longing for dawn, has a music to it. Whether that music is quite that of Shakespeare in lyric mode ('I post unto my pretty') is doubtful. And the doubt grows with the other pieces in the volume. The solitary pastoral speaker of 17 ('My flocks feed not, my ewes breed not') reads as though his monologue was generated by a desire to produce completely unidentifiable poems for a pastoral (one is tempted to say pasteurized) anthology such as *England's Helicon*. That poem takes its readers into a world in which anonymity seems not only to be deserved, but actively sought.

[1] Rollins I, 292.

Although the poems it contains are of uneven quality and of uncertain origin, *The Passionate Pilgrim* is none the less an artefact of considerable historical significance. It shows that by 1599 the name of Shakespeare was a valuable addition to a title-page. It is unlikely to contain any works by Shakespeare apart from those which are attributed to him elsewhere, but it does give some indication of the kinds of works which could be sold as his at the height of his fame as a poet. Reading it does also sharpen one's unease about how ascriptions are made in the case of short lyric pieces. Careful choice of material and careful ordering can create a wishful projection of an author's identity even in a sequence of works put together by a less than completely scrupulous printer. Jaggard did not just invent a volume of poems by Shakespeare: he gave his readers just enough of Shakespeare to make them collaborate with his invention. In that respect he was not the thief and scoundrel Swinburne took him for, but a sharp publisher and a shrewd reader.

'Let the bird of loudest lay'

This poem is usually called 'The Phoenix and the Turtle'. That title was first used in 1807,[1] and has no connection with Shakespeare. It has therefore not been used in this edition. The poem first appeared without a title and with Shakespeare's name attached to it in 1601. It was the fifth in a group of fourteen poems otherwise by Marston, Chapman, Ben Jonson, and an unknown poet, which were appended to a long, digressive narrative poem called *Love's Martyr* by an obscure poet called Robert Chester. Chester's poem has the portentous title 'LOVES MARTYR: | OR, | ROSALINS COMPLAINT. | *Allegorically shadowing the truth of Loue,* | In the constant Fate of the Phoenix | *and Turtle.*' It was printed by Richard Field, the printer of *Venus and Adonis* and *Lucrece.* The group of poems containing Shakespeare's piece was set off from the rest of the work by a separate title-page:

HEREAFTER | FOLLOW DIVERSE | Poeticall Essaies on the former Sub- | iect; viz: the *Turtle* and *Phoenix.* | *Done by the best and chiefest of our* | moderne writers, with their names sub- | scribed to their particular workes: | *neuer before extant.* | And (now first) consecrated by them all

[1] Rollins 1, 560–1.

generally, | *to the love and merite of the true-noble Kright,* | Sir Iohn Salis-
burie. | *Dignum laude virum Musa vetat mori.* | [Device: Anchora Spei] |
MDCI.'

This section of the volume is signed and paginated in sequence
with Chester's poem. Despite its endorsement by 'the best and
chiefest of our modern writers', the poem was not a success: sheets
from the first edition were reissued by a new printer (Matthew
Lownes) with a new title-page in 1611. The new title was 'The
Anuals [*sic*] of Great Brittaine. Or a Most Excellent Monument',
and thus renamed it sought to exploit the early seventeenth-centu-
ry fashion for antiquarian works on British monuments. The story
it relates is simple, but it takes Chester nearly two hundred pages of
the *Venus and Adonis* stanza to mar it in the telling. The Goddess
Nature finds the Phoenix mourning over the attacks of Envy. She
banishes this wicked spirit and takes the Phoenix to Paphos, the
island of Venus. They go on a circuitous route over Europe and
England. This provides a pretext for chorographical excursuses,
which include a lengthy history of King Arthur. Eventually they
arrive at the isle of Paphos, and a long account is given of its
plants, trees, fishes, gems, minerals, animals, and (finally) its birds.
This catalogue ends with the Turtle Dove, which is grieving for the
loss of its mate. The Phoenix is moved by sympathy for his unhap-
piness (Chester's is, unusually for poetic turtle doves, a male), and
the pair immolate themselves. As she enters the flames the Phoenix
declares: 'I hope of these another Creature springs, | That shall
possess both our authority'. The poem is rounded off by a moral
commentary spoken by a Pelican, and by a prophecy that children
will arise from the couple.

Chester's poem has received a great deal of hostile commentary
(when Matchett refers to it as 'an agglomeration of diverse ma-
terials' he is being more polite than most),[1] and has been interpret-
ed in many ways. Several significant features of it have none the
less gone unremarked. It is clearly a contribution to, and probably
an attempt to develop, the main currents in Ovidian narrative

---

[1] William H. Matchett, *The Phoenix and the Turtle: Shakespeare's Poem and
Chester's 'Loues Martyr'*, Studies in English Literature Vol. 1 (London, The Hague,
and Paris, 1965), 60. The helpful summary of past criticism of the poem, Richard
Allan Underwood, *Shakespeare's 'The Phoenix and Turtle': A Survey of Scholarship*,
Salzburg Studies in English Literature: Elizabethan Studies (Salzburg, 1974), 32,
offers this: 'It is sufficient to say of Chester's work . . . that it is awful.'

poems in the 1590s: it combines encyclopaedic, chorographical, historical, and erotic elements together with complaint in a manner which is clearly indebted to Spenser and Samuel Daniel. It could not have been written before 1590. The presence in the poem of some possible allusions to *Venus and Adonis* and to *Lucrece* may suggest that it was attempting to attract the smart urban readers who bought Shakespeare's narrative poems in the early 1590s, and may also indicate that Chester was keen to have Shakespeare write one of the poems appended to it.[1] Chester was a rare thing for the 1590s, a genuinely provincial poet in a dominantly urban literary scene. It is probable that he was a member of the household of John Salusbury of Llewenni in Denbighshire (*c.*1566–1612), to whom this and several surviving manuscript poems are dedicated.[2] Chester appears to have printed the volume to celebrate his patron's knighthood in June 1601, and was evidently attempting to impress Salusbury with a contribution to several of the most fashionable literary forms at once. He missed the mark, however, by at least five years, since by the time his poem reached print its particular fusion of generic elements would have seemed passé, and his attempts to integrate history, amatory verse, and encyclopaedism would have appeared distinctly creaky.

Interpretations of Chester's poem have consequences for the interpretation of Shakespeare's 'Let the bird of loudest lay'. Many commentators on *Love's Martyr* take their cue from Chester's inclusion of the phrase '*Allegorically shadowing the truth of Loue*' in his title, and have assumed that the word 'allegorically' indicates that the poem makes reference to specific events and people. For Alexander Grosart the Phoenix was Elizabeth and the Turtle was the Earl of Essex, and the whole poem urged Elizabeth to marry Essex—this despite the fact that Essex was married, and that Sir John Salusbury, the dedicatee of the volume, was actively involved

[1] The dedicatory poem alludes to the semi-epic status of *Lucrece*: 'Of bloody wars, nor of the sack of Troy, | . . . Of Lucrece' rape, being ravished by a King, | Of none of these, of sweet conceit I sing', *Robert Chester, Love's Martyr, or Rosalins Complaint (1601) with its supplement, 'Diverse Poeticall Essaies' on the Turtle and Phoenix by Shakspere, Ben Jonson, George Chapman, John Marston, etc.*, ed. Alexander B. Grosart, New Shakspere Society Series 8, no. 2 (1878), 6. There is also a reference to Ovidian tales of Lucretia on p. 46; and a reference which may be to Shakespeare's first poem, 'under this | Faire *Venus* from *Adonis* stole a kisse', occurs on p. 18.
[2] The case is made in *Poems by Sir John Salusbury and Robert Chester*, ed. Carleton Brown, EETS ES 113 (1914), pp. xlvii–liv.

in disputes with supporters of the Earl of Essex in his native Denbighshire. The theory has had its supporters since.[2] Carleton Brown treated the poem as a belated tribute to the marriage of John Salusbury (the turtle) in 1586 to Ursula Stanley (the phoenix), the illegitimate but acknowledged daughter of the Earl of Derby—this despite the fact that a significant proportion of Salusbury's poems appear to declare affection for his sister-in-law Dorothy Halsall (which might make the subject of married love a rather awkward one for Salusbury), and despite the poem's evident affinities with poems composed after 1590.[3] The grief of the Turtle is related to the sorrow of Salusbury at the execution of his brother for involvement in the Babington plot. A more plausible school of thought sees Chester's poem (and Shakespeare's) as an allegory of succession. The Phoenix, sad and ageing, is Elizabeth I; the Turtle is the devotion of her subjects (and of the poem's dedicatee, John Salusbury, who had been an esquire of the Queen's body since 1594 and was knighted for his service shortly before the poem's publication). It is only when love is exchanged between monarch and subject that the succession can be smoothly achieved; given such love the death of one monarch is swallowed up in the victorious succession of another, and subject and ruler become indistinguishable. It has also been suggested that the poem makes specific allusion to the sadness of the Queen and the discontent among many English people after the execution of the Earl of Essex. The Phoenix's banishment of envy becomes on this reading an allegorical representation of attempts to defuse the widespread discontent which surrounded the Earl of Essex's ill-judged rebellion in 1601.[4]

Sustained though they are by considerable learning, it is hard to believe that any of these interpretations would have been proposed

[1] See Grosart's introduction. Salusbury's attitudes to Essex wavered, however; it is likely that he did not commit himself to opposition to the Earl until after the Essex rebellion. See Mark Bland, '"As far from all reuolt": Sir John Salusbury, Christ Church MS 184 and Ben Jonson's First Ode', *English Manuscript Studies* 8 (2000), 43–78.

[2] Notably Matchett, *The Phoenix and the Turtle*. The relationship of the poem to Essex is also assumed in Richard McCoy, 'Love's Martyrs: Shakespeare's "Phoenix and Turtle" and the Sacrificial Sonnets', in Claire McEachern and Debora Shuger, eds., *Religion and Culture in Renaissance England* (Cambridge, 1997), 188–208.

[3] *Poems by Sir John Salusbury*, pp. liv–lxxiv.

[4] See Marie Axton, *The Queen's Two Bodies* (1977), 116–30, and the refinement of the position in Anthea Hume, 'Love's Martyr, "The Phoenix and the Turtle", and the Aftermath of the Essex Rebellion', *RES* 40 (1989), 48–71.

had Chester not hinted in his title that his poem was allegorical. All such interpretations of Chester's poem encounter serious problems: if the Phoenix is designed to be identifiable as Elizabeth I, then Chester's emphasis on the bird's sorrow and age becomes extraordinarily tactless in 1601. By 1601 the Queen was extremely sensitive to representations of herself as old. It is quite impossible that Chester could have suggested, even beneath the thickest veil of allegory, that she should marry Essex and have children at the age of 68. The view that the poem represents love of monarch and subject has more to recommend it, but still leaves major elements of Shakespeare's poem unaccounted for. Why end with the bleak flatness of these 'dead birds' if the people so represented are supposed to be the Queen of England and her subjects?[1] Was it quite so miserable to worship a sovereign in 1601? And why, above all, does Shakespeare apparently not grant the pair any offspring, despite the fact that Chester's poem ends with the reproduction of the Phoenix? This would make the poem a dark meditation indeed.

Some of these questions can be laid to rest if one reads Chester's title-page beyond the problematic adverb 'allegorically'. The poem is described as '*Allegorically shadowing the truth of Love*'. A poem which works 'allegorically' does not need to shadow forth the fate of individuals: it might meditate on an abstract idea, and relish the possibility which that offered of making multiple applications to several individuals. Indeed, Shakespeare's poem is remarkable for its interest in *lack* of individuality (in its modern sense of 'separate persons'): its central mystery is that of there being 'two distincts, division none' in the union of Phoenix and Turtle. Its logical conceit, and much of its tone, depend on the horror (is it?) or delight (is it?) of imagining two entities becoming identical with each other. This is a source both of mourning, since each entity is lost, and joy, since they are combined in a super-entity which transcends the language of logic, and presses it towards theological wonder.[2]

Since the poem is about these amalgamations of identities, it

[1] Matchett is unable to explain why 'his calling not only Essex but the Queen a "dead bird" presents no insuperable challenge to the historical probability of the thesis I have been developing', *The Phoenix and the Turtle*, 159.

[2] On the theological resonances of the poem's language, see J. V. Cunningham, ' "Essence" and the Phoenix and the Turtle', *ELH* 19 (1952), 265–76.

does itself create uncertainties about who is who. These begin with its first sentence. The 'bird of loudest lay' is unidentifiable. The Phoenix was believed to have a loud voice, and was thought to inhabit the Arabian tree. This creates an acute uncertainty right at the start of the poem: is the Phoenix—the 'bird of loudest lay'— miraculously able to be present at its own obsequies? Or has its death left a void which can only be filled by some other, unknown bird? These uncertainties over voices and how to separate them run on through the poem. At line 21 there appears to be a shift of voice into a priestly register with 'Here the anthem doth commence'. But where does the anthem, or song by the priest or congregation, stop? Does it continue to include the voice of Reason, who begins to voice his perplexity at the miraculous union of the Phoenix and the Turtle in line 45? And if so, who is to be imagined singing the 'Threnos'? Is it Reason (as 'Whereupon it made this threne', l. 49, would suggest)? And is the voice of Reason singing the Threnos still imagined as being part of the anthem, and hence is it absorbed into the voice of the priest or congregation at the obsequies?

There are no answers to these questions, but posing them is one way of understanding how the poem comes to be, as I. A. Richards put it, 'the most mysterious poem in English', or as Barbara Everett has it in her fine essay on the poem, 'the reader halts, never quite sure what it is, to *read* this poem. We seem, even while finding it exquisite, to lack some expertise, some password.'[1] The poem slips between theological and logical registers, and blends voice on voice in a polyphony that has the resonance of ritual worship. This is partly an effect of its dominantly seven-syllable trochaic lines, which end with a single stressed syllable. This metrical form begins and ends with a weighty syllable, allowing the poem to lift off the ground in the centre of the line: so 'Two distincts, division none' (l. 27) welds abstractions within the solid buttresses of 'Two' and 'none'. The poem's mingling of gravity and airy lightness enables the physical and the spiritual to interblend. Those who mourn and praise the dead pair seem themselves to be losing their unity and 'distinction' (or logical separateness) in a growing thunder

[1] I. A. Richards, 'The Sense of Poetry: Shakespeare's "The Phoenix and the Turtle"', *Daedalus* 87 (Summer 1958), 86; Barbara Everett, 'Set Upon a Golden Bough to Sing: Shakespeare's Debt to Sidney in "The Phoenix and Turtle"', *TLS* 5,107 (16 Feb. 2001), 13–15.

of metaphysical speculation. The poem also, perhaps inevitably, works the minor miracle of being two poems in one: the 'Threnos' begins on a new leaf in *Love's Martyr* and has its own title, whilst also being implicitly presented as a continuous part of the voice of Reason and so an inseparable part of the whole. 'Let the bird of loudest lay' is not only about the dissolution of separate identities into a single whole: it enacts it.

That is to describe the poem, rather than to explain it. But explanations will always fall short of this poem. It is hard to see why Shakespeare should have written it for this volume: he is notable for having written no commendatory poems apart from 'Let the bird of loudest lay', and even this is scarcely a poem of fulsome praise of a living author. Ben Jonson had some connection with the Salusbury family, since an autograph copy of his Ode on James, Earl of Desmond, figures in a manuscript miscellany which was in the possession of the family.[1] Given that Jonson was to collaborate with Chapman and Marston in 1605 over *Eastward Ho!* it is possible that he orchestrated the efforts of the other poets who contributed to the volume. Shakespeare had no known connection with the family (unless he is identified, as Honigmann would wish, with one 'William Shakeshafte' who was associated with the household of the Derbyshire Stanleys in the 1580s, and who moved on to be one of the Earl of Derby's men).[2] But the chief motivation of Chapman and Jonson, at least, in contributing to this volume was clearly a desire for patronage and its rewards. The political events of 1601 had had one major consequence for many poets, including George Chapman: the Earl of Essex was a powerful and, it seems, also a relatively generous literary patron (and his return from Ireland is one of the very few historical events to which Shakespeare makes an explicit and immediately recognizable allusion in the prologue to Act 5 of *Henry V*). The first instalment of Chapman's Homer had been dedicated to the Earl in 1598, and it has recently been argued that Ben Jonson was manoeuvring for the patronage of Essex in the

[1] Christ Church, Oxford, MS 184; early drafts of Jonson's 'Proludium' and 'Epos' are in Salusbury MS 5390 D in the National Library of Wales. This MS also contains an anonymous poem 'To my good freandes m^r John Hemings & Henry Condall' on the publication of Shakespeare's first Folio, which may indicate some continuing links between Shakespeare and the Salusbury family.

[2] Honigmann, 90–113. Honigmann's argument, like that of Brown, depends on an improbably early date for both Chester's and Shakespeare's poem. Roe, 47–9, is judiciously sceptical.

months before his fall from favour.[1] After the execution of Essex, however, many English poets lost their most obvious source of support. The group of poets who contributed to *Love's Martyr* may have hoped that Salusbury might have helped to fill that vacuum, or that he would offer them some form of introduction to further patronage. They produced works which ostentatiously go beyond the habitual poetic forms of the 1590s: the word 'Threnos' is found in Peacham's handbook of rhetoric (as noted in the commentary); but the second part of Shakespeare's poem appears to be the first in English to have adopted that title; Jonson's poem in the volume is the first in English to be called an Epode. While it is not quite true to say, with Empson, that 'Let the bird of loudest lay' is Shakespeare's 'only consistent use of the Metaphysical style'[2] (it is far too disengaged from the outcome of its argumentation to resemble Donne any more than distantly), Shakespeare's poem is clearly pushing in the direction of an innovative and abstract poetic vocabulary (probably, as Everett has argued, with the precedent of the eighth Song in *Astrophil and Stella* to aid it).[3]

The conscious innovation of the poems appended to Chester's volume, and arguably also their high level of abstraction, grow in part from the social and financial needs of a poet in this period, to write verses of praise which are both new and sufficiently abstract to be applied to a number of circumstances, and which could therefore appeal to a number of potential patrons. Jonson's 'Ode Enthusiastic' from *Love's Martyr* was subsequently dedicated to Lucy, Countess of Bedford: its abstract reflections on love and appetite are grounded in no particular realities, and so could be adapted to suit any patron willing to find his own virtue in the poem.[4] The sad, solemn ritual of Shakespeare's poem seems to be motivated by something higher than the wish to praise a potential patron about whom in all probability he knew little, and by this stage of his career it is unlikely that he needed or actively sought courtly patronage. His poem feels as though it is coming from another world, and as though it grows from thinking, and thinking gravely,

[1] See Bland, ' "As far from all reuolt" '.

[2] William Empson, ' "The Phoenix and the Turtle" ', *Essays in Criticism* 15 (1966), 147.

[3] See Everett, 'Shakespeare's Debt to Sidney'.

[4] Bernard Newdigate argued, on the basis of scanty evidence, that Lucy, Countess of Bedford was Jonson's as well as Shakespeare's phoenix, 'The Phoenix and Turtle: Was Lady Bedford the Phoenix?', *TLS*, 24 Oct. 1936, 862.

about sacrifice in love, and about where Elizabethan poetry might move next. But the difficulty of attaching his poem to particular circumstances may partly derive from the work which it is attempting to achieve: to keep the name of Shakespeare alive and to keep it associated with new forms, and to create a poem which could adapt itself to many circumstances by virtue of its refusal to individualize.

If 'Let the bird of loudest lay' is considered in the context of Shakespeare's career as a poet, rather than as a covert commentary on political or personal events, its elusiveness does not diminish. And the ritual wonder which it creates by its refusal to pin its words to particular speakers should not be reductively presented as the product of material need. But to think of the poem as a work which *needs* to be abstract in order to mean the most to the greatest number of readers at least enables us to understand why it is so elusive, so like music pitched just beyond the reach of hearing. The poem contains many verbal innovations which are recorded in the commentary; but *Love's Martyr*, the poem to which it is attached, looked back to the chorographical and historical poems of the previous decade. The fact that Shakespeare contributed a poem to a volume printed early in the seventeenth century which harked back to the previous decade and forward to the next is in itself significant. It helps to cast light on what Shakespeare thought he was doing as a poet in the early years of the seventeenth century. In 1609 there was printed in his name a collection of Sonnets, which look back to and revise one of the major literary forms of the later 1580s and 1590s, and *A Lover's Complaint*, which, in an extraordinary blend of archaizing and innovatory language, reappraises the tradition of female complaint which had flourished in the 1590s. That the collection in which 'Let the bird' appeared was also one in which references to living individuals seem to be absorbed in an abstract interest in love and the delights and pains of identifying completely with another being is also significant. The Sonnets, as we shall see, have a similar set of concerns with the sacrifice of identity necessary to love, and with the teasing inapplicability of poems about love to identifiable individuals.[1]

<hr>

[1] This is by no means to agree with Wilson Knight, *The Mutual Flame: Shakespeare's Sonnets and 'The Phoenix and the Turtle'* (1955), 194: 'Shakespeare may have had more than one ardent love, and *The Phoenix and the Turtle* need be referred to no particular person or event. Even so, we shall, I think, be right in allowing

Shakespeare's Sonnets

Publication and Circulation. The title *Shakespeare's Sonnets* sounds conclusive,[1] as though in 1609, a decade after the main vogue for the Elizabethan sonnet sequence,[2] Shakespeare had decided to leave his imprint on the form for posterity. However, there remain so many unanswered questions about the publication of the Sonnets in 1609 that it is impossible to be entirely sure that Shakespeare wished them to appear in exactly the form in which they were printed and at exactly that time, and whether he saw them as the culmination of his career as a poet. The passionate rationality of the poems can only have been the product of considered work, and, as we shall see, it is very likely that Shakespeare at least provisionally put the sonnets into the order in which they appear in the 1609 Quarto. But we do not know certainly when they were written, whether or to what extent they might spring from actual relationships which Shakespeare may have had, or whether Shakespeare wished them to be printed and dedicated to the mysterious Mr W.H. Many critics have tried to resolve these uncertainties; others have said that they are simply irrelevant to the poems. Neither of these positions will quite do. The question 'when, and to whom was this written?' is one which the poems repeatedly invite their readers to pose, and which they quite deliberately fail to answer. We have seen that *Venus and Adonis* and *Lucrece* frequently create an unsteadying counterpoint between who is speaking and what is said. The Sonnets are best viewed not as Shakespeare's final triumphant assertion of poetic mastery, but as poems which develop the methods of the earlier narrative poems to their utmost point—a point at which one is not quite sure who is male and who is female, who is addressed or why, or what their respective social roles are. If the Sonnets are viewed in this light, then the many empirical uncertainties as to when and to whom they were written seem less like

it to include, to gather up and transmute, the experience of the Sonnets', by which Knight means that the poem is an allegorical representation of Shakespeare's bisexuality.

[1] Katherine Duncan-Jones, 'What are Shakespeare's Sonnets Called?', *Essays in Criticism* 47 (1997), 1–12.

[2] Duncan-Jones shows that in the first decade of the seventeenth century several poets, particularly Scots, printed sonnet sequences. A glance at the list of major sonnet sequences on pp. 168–9 below shows, however, that the vast majority of sequences appeared in 1592–6.

damaging gaps in our knowledge, and more like an enabling condition of the delighted mystification which all readers of these poems have felt, and which they repeatedly invite.

Still, there are some facts. Shakespeare's Sonnets were published in 1609 by Thomas Thorpe. The title-page reads:

Shake-Speares | Sonnets. | Neuer before Imprinted. | At London | By G. Eld for T. T. and are | to be solde by *John Wright*, dwelling | at Christ Church gate. | 1609.

There is a variant issue which was 'to be solde by William Apsley'. It is likely that the two booksellers and the publisher shared the costs and risks of publication between them. Thorpe had established his ownership of the copy on 20 May 1609 by the following entry in the Stationers' Register: 'Entred for his copie under the handes of master Wilson and master Lownes Warden a Booke called SHAKESPEARES *sonnettes* vjd.'[1] The volume contains 154 sonnets, which are followed by *A Lover's Complaint*. The latter poem begins on the verso of a leaf (K1) and so can never have been sold separately from the sonnet sequence which it concludes. The volume was set by two compositors, who varied in their spelling-preferences and in their level of accuracy.[2] No manuscripts of the Sonnets or *A Lover's Complaint* survive in Shakespeare's hand, but some features of the printed text suggest that the copy from which Eld's compositors worked may have been hard to read or that it may not have been finally revised: Q contains the odd line that does not rhyme (25.9, 69.3, 113.6), a couplet that is repeated in two poems (36 and 96), a fifteen line-sonnet (99), a sonnet with a second line which repeats, unmetrically, a phrase from its first line (146), and a repeated error in which 'their' is printed for 'thy', an error which mysteriously stops at Sonnet 128, at a point in the sequence when some unusual spellings also begin to appear.[3] The

---

[1] Arber, iii.410. An earlier entry of 3 January 1599/1600 of 'a booke called *Amours* by J.D. with *certen other sonnetes* by W.S.' (Arber, iii.153) has been seen as a sign that Shakespeare wished to prepare an edition of his Sonnets in response to *The Passionate Pilgrim* (Duncan-Jones, 3–6). 'Sonnets' on a title-page could, however, cover a multitude of ills, and W.S. was not a rare set of initials.

[2] MacDonald P. Jackson, 'Punctuation and the Compositors of Shakespeare's *Sonnets*, 1609', *The Library* 5th ser. 30 (1975), 1–23. The notes record moments at which one or other compositor appears to have made an error.

[3] Q confuses 'their' and 'thy' at 26.12, 27.10, 35.8, 37.7, 43.11, 45.12, 46.3,

copy from which Eld's compositors worked was probably the product of one or more scribes, who may have had difficulty deciphering a revised authorial draft, which in places may have contained excisions and revisions. It is impossible entirely to exclude the possibility that the sequence was set from different manuscripts, or from a single manuscript containing different hands, and that the more disparate group of poems after *126* was conceived by its author as a separate series. The printed title, *Shake-speares Sonnets*, is consistently maintained from the entry in the Stationers' Register through to the title and running-heads of the printed volume.[1]

A second edition of the Sonnets appeared in *1640*. John Benson, the publisher of the volume, abandoned the order in which the poems appeared in the Quarto, and combined several poems under generic titles.[2] He changed three masculine pronouns to feminine pronouns in the text of the poems, and clearly assumed, or wished his readers to assume, that most of the sonnets were addressed to a mistress: *122* is entitled 'Upon the receipt of a Table Book from his

---

46.8, *46.13*, *46.14*, *69.5*, *70.6*, *128.11*, *128.14*, and possibly also at *85.3*. As Jackson's analysis of compositorial preferences in the Sonnets ('Punctuation and the Compositors'), shows, the error is usually made by compositor B, although *35.8* and *37.7* were set by compositor A. The most probable explanation (offered by Malone) is that the copy contained two letter abbreviations for the personal pronoun in which 'they' and 'thy' looked alike, but the absence of errors after *128* is striking. The mistress is consistently addressed as 'thou', which may conceivably have helped the compositor to unscramble illegible copy; but this would of course also make instances of the possessive pronoun very high (around 2.1 instances per poem as against 1.5 instances per poem for the earlier part of the sequence, or 1.6 if one includes the occurrences erroneously set as 'their') and so multiply the opportunity for error. This suggests that the copy for the poems after *128* may have significantly differed in orthography from the early part of the sequence. This is also suggested by some unique or unusual spellings: 'Broake' is found only in *143.2* and *152.3*; 'bouldnes' is unique; 'ynough', *133.3* occurs also in Q1 of *Troilus* (also printed in 1609 by Eld, so this could be a compositorial quirk); *142.14* 'mai'st' appears to be unique; 'wofull' occurs thirty-two times elsewhere in the canon and is usually pre-1600. This hypothesis sits suggestively beside the recent claim on stylometric grounds that Sonnets *126–54* are among the earliest poems in the sequence. See A. Kent Hieatt, Charles W. Hieatt, and Anne Lake Prescott, 'When did Shakespeare Write *Sonnets* 1609?', *SP* 88 (1991), 69–109.

[1] Duncan-Jones, 'What are Shakespeare's Sonnets Called?'

[2] R. M. Alden, 'The 1640 Text of *Shakespeare's Sonnets*', *Modern Philology* 14 (1916), 17–30; Joan W Bennett, 'Benson's Alleged Piracy of *Shake-Speare's Sonnets* and Some of Jonson's Works', *Studies in Bibliography* 21 (1968), 235–48.

Mistress' and *125* 'An entreaty for her acceptance'.[1] (Sonnet *2* is also treated by manuscript miscellanists as a poem to a woman: so in several versions it is entitled 'to one that would die a maid', and in other manuscripts it is grouped with poems which urge women to use their beauty by having children.)[2] Benson also reprinted the poems from the 1612 edition of *The Passionate Pilgrim*. He aimed to refashion Shakespeare's sonnets for a market attuned to Cavalier lyric, as well as to produce a tiny accompaniment to the 1632 Folio, which was also printed by Thomas Cotes.[3] His text was reprinted in the majority of eighteenth-century editions of the poems, in which the Sonnets generally appeared in supplementary volumes along with *Venus and Adonis* and *Lucrece*. Many of these collections sought to exploit the vogue in the early eighteenth century for 'Miscellany Poems' which addressed a range of occasions.[4] It was not until 1711 that Lintot reprinted the Quarto in the order of 1609. He probably did this in order to secure the rights to reprint the volume, and in the belief that the 1609 Sonnets were a distinct piece of property from the text presented by Benson.[5] The Sonnets were then reprinted by Edmond Malone in 1780 in the order in which they are found in Q. Since 1780 the Sonnets have generally been reprinted (as they are here) in the order of the 1609 Quarto, although there have been persistent (and unconvincing) attempts to reorder them.[6]

Earlier editors in general believed the Sonnets were surreptitiously obtained from Shakespeare by the unscrupulous Thomas Thorpe, who was thought to have printed them poorly and in an

[1] *Pace* Margreta de Grazia, 'The Scandal of Shakespeare's Sonnets', *Shakespeare Survey* 46 (1996), 35–49, who argues that Benson did not attempt to eradicate the male addressee from the poems, and that those who blame him for doing so are displacing onto him the modern dilemma of 'what to do with the inadmissible secret of Shakespeare's deviant sexuality'.

[2] e.g. BL Add. MS 21433, fo. 114^v.

[3] Margreta de Grazia, *Shakespeare Verbatim: The Reproduction of Authenticity and the 1790 Apparatus* (Oxford, 1991), 166–7.

[4] Sewell's edition of 1725 refers to 'Mr Shakespeare's miscellany poems'. Both Gildon and Sewell had been involved in producing miscellany poems: Gildon's 'Miscellany Poems upon various occasions' appeared in 1692; Sewell wrote the preface for Addison's 'Miscellanies in Verse and Prose' in 1725.

[5] For detailed argument to this effect, see Colin Burrow, 'Life and Work in Shakespeare's Poems', *Proceedings of the British Academy* 97 (1998), 1–7.

[6] Among the more critically valuable attempts to reorder the sequence is Brents Stirling, *The Shakespeare Sonnet Order: Poems and Groups* (Berkeley, 1968). See also Bray.

order which their author had not intended. This position has been overturned in the past twenty years or so, and has effectively been replaced by a new orthodoxy. According to this, *Shake-speare's Sonnets* were printed with the author's consent and in an order which reflects their author's wishes.[1] Katherine Duncan-Jones has argued that the career of Thomas Thorpe was not as black as it was painted by earlier scholars, and that his links with theatrical circles would have put him in a good position legitimately to obtain the manuscript of the poems from Shakespeare himself. As a result, she argues, Q should be taken as a reliable guide to what Shakespeare wished to print. While there are good grounds to believe that the order of poems in Q is authorial (discussed below), there are grounds for being less certain than Duncan-Jones that Q represents that ideally convenient thing for an editor, an 'authorized' final version which accurately reflects its author's intentions. 'Authorized' can mean many things. At its most minimal it would mean that Shakespeare assented to publication of the volume. At its maximal it would mean that Shakespeare assented to publication of the volume and that he gave Thorpe a manuscript which accurately reflected his final intentions, and that those final intentions were completely realized in the book which resulted. If one accepts the minimal thesis of authorization it does not imply any aspect of the maximal. If one accepted the maximal it would still be the case that the volume which resulted would be subject to the thousand material uncertainties which preyed on early modern printed texts: foul case (type which had got into the wrong box), foul papers (rough working manuscript copy), shortages of type, and tired compositors. Many bibliographers now argue that printed copy always and necessarily reflects not just what its author may have intended, but also the material business of printing it.[2] The missed

---

[1] Katherine Duncan-Jones 'Was the 1609 SHAKE-SPEARES SONNETS Really Unauthorized?', *RES* NS 34 (1983), 151–71 For the view that 'The 1609 edition represents not that dream of a traditional textual editor, the author's final intention, but rather a set of poems in various stages of composition', see Heather Dubrow, ' "Incertainties now crown themselves assur'd": The Politics of Plotting in Shakespeare's Sonnets', *Shakespeare Quarterly* 47 (1996), 299. Arthur F. Marotti, 'Shakespeare's Sonnets as Literary Property', in Elizabeth D. Harvey and Katharine Eisaman Maus, eds., *Soliciting Interpretation: Literary Theory and Seventeenth-Century English Poetry* (Chicago and London, 1990), 50–4, is also sceptical about Duncan-Jones's thesis, and voices a similar opinion about the miscellaneity of the sequence.

[2] See e.g. D. F. McKenzie, *Bibliography and the Sociology of Texts* (Cambridge, 1999).

rhymes and manifest errors of Thorpe's Quarto indicate that, whatever the origins of the text he printed, the book which he produced falls some way short of that which would fit a 'maximal' thesis of authorization.

What of the minimal thesis that Shakespeare assented to publication? This question would only have been at the fringes of the interests of early modern readers, for whom authorial ownership of intellectual property was an emergent concept (if that). Copy in this period belonged to the printer who entered it as his or hers in the Stationers' Register. Authors might protest about what printers printed or the errors which they introduced, but they enjoyed no ownership of the products of their labour. Thorpe's earlier career does not give certain guidance as to how he may have obtained the manuscript of Shakespeare's Sonnets. He had printed Ben Jonson's *Sejanus* in 1605, *Volpone* in 1607, and a variety of other theatrical texts, and had presented those texts with care. It is possible that Shakespeare might indeed have consigned a manuscript of poems to him. But Thorpe was also capable of underhand manoeuvres: his first entry in the Stationers' Register had to be cancelled because the work had already been entered to another printer.[1] He was also quite capable of making jokes in prefaces about how he had obtained his copy, and of creating doubts in the minds of his readers as to the level to which the author had been involved in publication. On at least one occasion he printed a text which was clearly not his to print.[2]

The question 'did Shakespeare want these poems to be printed' cannot definitely be answered. It is also the wrong sort of question to be asking. The text of the Quarto is often examined as though it provides a set of clues from which can be inferred the nature and provenance of the manuscript from which it was set. If the Quarto is considered in a different light, as an object which called for par-

---

[1] Thorpe attempted with William Apsley to register a piece of copy, 'a panegyric or congratulation for the concord of the kingdomes of great Britaine in the unitie of religion under king JAMES' on 23 June 1603. This entry was cancelled because the work was already registered to 'Master Seaton', Arber, iii.37.

[2] As in the prefatory matter to Marlowe's translation to Lucan. See W. W. Greg, 'The Copyright of *Hero and Leander*', *The Library* 4th ser. 24 (1944), 165–74. In the prefatory matter to Gorges's translation of Lucan, Gorges's son Carew (then only 10 years old) claims that he stumbled on the poem 'in my father's study, amongst many other of his Manuscripts' (sig. A3^v). Thorpe indisputably printed copy which he did not own in the case of Thomas Coryate's *Odcombian Banquet* (STC 5810).

ticular forms of attention from its early readers, then there is some chance of moving beyond the uncertainties which surround its origins. Early modern books, as much as their twenty-first-century descendants, gave off a set of semi-formalized signals which might indicate to their potential purchasers what kind of book it was that they were about to buy. And a close examination of the physical appearance and layout of Thorpe's Quarto suggests that it would have sent off a set of conflicting signals to its early readers. Its lay-out is unusual among sonnet sequences. It has the author's name on its running-titles ('Shake-speares Sonnets'), and the sonnets it contains are often split at awkward points by page divisions. It also has a dedication (discussed in more detail below) which is not by its author. Most sonnet sequences from the 1590s have no running-titles; a few use the title of the fictional addressee at the top of each page. They also in general have an authorial dedication, rather than one signed by the printer, and most of them carefully dispose one or two complete poems per page with an ornamental border at the top and sometimes also at the bottom of each page.[1] This conventional way of laying out sonnets was beginning to lose its hold in the seventeenth century: William Alexander's *Aurora* (1604) was printed with numbered sonnets broken across pages. But the only other printed sonnet sequence to share all the features displayed by Thorpe's Quarto was the 1591 edition of *Sir P.S. His Astrophel and Stella*. This edition was suppressed, probably at the instigation of the Sidney family. Thomas Nashe's preface proudly boasted that it was the printed offshoot of a manuscript which had walked away from its rightful owner.[2] This unauthorized volume

---

[1] Exceptions are rare: Barnabe Barnes's *Parthenophil and Parthenophe* (1593), sig. A2ᵛ, contains an epistle from the Printers: 'The Author though at the first unknown, yet enforced to accord to certain of his friends' importunity herein, to publish them by their means, and for their sakes ...'. The poems that follow are disposed chaotically across openings. The general pattern, especially marked in sequences such as Bartholomew Griffin's *Fidessa* (1596) and Richard Barnfield's *Cynthia* which were printed for Humphrey and Matthew Lownes, is to present one sonnet per page with ornamental borders at the top and bottom of each page.

[2] The case for attending to physical similarities between these two volumes has been persuasively made by Marotti, 'Literary Property', 154–5. For the converse and equally defensible view, that the resemblances to the 1591 edition of *Astrophil and Stella* should be interpreted as signs that Shakespeare's sequence is the summation of its genre, at once recalling and overgoing its origin, see Duncan-Jones, 'What are Shakespeare's Sonnets Called?'

also blazoned the unmistakable initials of Sir Philip Sidney over every page in the running-titles.

How might these features of the printed volume have influenced its early readers? The resemblances to the pirated *Astrophil and Stella* can be interpreted in two quite contradictory ways: they could tell readers that this was another publisher's coup, in which a work by a notable author was smuggled into print by an unscrupulous printer; or they could support the view that Shakespeare's sequence consummates the Sidneian tradition by recognizing its great predecessor in its physical form. Thorpe's Quarto is a radically ambiguous thing. Viewed under one aspect it manages to look like a monumental revival of Sidney's achievement; viewed under another aspect it appears to be a heavily revised manuscript copy hyped into print by an eager printer, who may or may not have liberated it from the author's private closet. And these features of the volume are not simply bibliographical curiosities. They resonate with the poems contained in the sequence, which frequently switch between constructing a public monument to the friend and preserving him as a secret treasure: he is compared to a jewel hidden away 'Within the gentle closure of my breast' (48.11), or as 'time's best jewel', or as a store and treasure-house of nature's sweets; he is also immortally transformed to public property when other poems proclaim that he will be remembered forever as a result of the black lines of the poems, that 'Your name from hence immortal life shall have' (81.5)—though the name of course is (teasingly) never given. The volume both publishes the youth's beauty, and jealously reserves his identity in a way that perpetuates the undercurrent of unease about publication which, as we have seen, runs beneath *Lucrece*. Sonnets in this period were often represented as private works which began life as private exchanges between a poet and his circle, and which found their way into print by accident or as a result of a printer's unscrupulousness. The appearance of Thorpe's volume powerfully reinforces this view of the sonnet as a form which was located at the intersection between private papers and printed record. Whether or not Shakespeare intended his volume to be presented in this way will never be known.

Dedication. This aspect of the volume is reinforced by its enigmatic dedication, which has since the nineteenth century become a dank pit in which speculation wallows and founders. Thorpe's

TO.THE.ONLIE.BEGETTER.OF.
THESE.INSVING.SONNETS.
M^r.W.H. ALL.HAPPINESSE.
AND.THAT.ETERNITIE.
PROMISED.

BY.

OVR.EVER-LIVING.POET.

WISHETH.

THE.WELL-WISHING.
ADVENTVRER.IN.
SETTING.
FORTH.

T. T.

3. Dedication to *Shake-speares Sonnets* (1609).

Quarto is prefixed by a dedication to 'Mr W. H.' which is signed
'T. T.'. Thomas Thorpe otherwise only signed prefatory matter if
the author of the work was dead or out of the country. This makes
it very probable that Shakespeare was not in London while the
sequence was being set, and indicates that he was not immediately
involved in the final stages of printing.[1] Thorpe's words, laid out

[1] Thorpe also provided dedications for Marlowe's translation of Lucan and the
1616 edition of John Healey's translation of Epictetus, both of which were printed
posthumously. See Burrow, 'Life and Work', 34–6.

like a Roman inscription, have given rise to endless speculation. Who is Mr W. H.? And is he to be identified with the youth addressed in the first sonnets in the volume? Nathan Drake first proposed in 1817 that these initials should be identified as those of Henry Wriothesley, Earl of Southampton (H.W.; W.H.; what's in a sequence?), the dedicatee of *Venus and Adonis* and *Lucrece*.[1] There is no evidence that Shakespeare had any contact with Southampton after 1594. This would not preclude the possibility that versions of, say, Sonnets 1–17 might at one point have been addressed to Southampton (conceivably around the time of his proposed marriage to Elizabeth Vere in 1589) and then revised: similarities between these sonnets and Venus's arguments to Adonis are often noted, and could conceivably imply identity between their historical addressees.

For those who want to identify W.H. with the young man, the other major candidate is William Herbert, third Earl of Pembroke (1580–1630), to whom the first Folio of Shakespeare's dramatic works was dedicated.[2] Pembroke would have been about the right age to serve as a plausible addressee for many of the poems, and it has been suggested that Sonnets 1–17, the 'marriage sequence', were composed on or around his seventeenth birthday in 1598.[3] Pembroke was a serial bachelor, having resisted marriage to Elizabeth Carey in 1595, to Bridget Vere in 1597, to Lady Hatton in 1598, and to a niece of Charles Howard in 1599. It is, however, extremely unlikely that an Earl should be addressed by a printer as 'Mr'. For a printed poem by a commoner to address an Earl as the 'master mistress of my passion' would be audacious beyond belief. Thomas Thorpe addresses Pembroke as 'your Lordship' six times in a single paragraph of his dedication to the second edition of John Healey's translation of *Epictetus his Manual,* humbly begging him to 'pardon my presumption, great Lord, from so mean a man, to so great a person' (sig. A4ʳ). Thorpe's dedication to Pembroke of Healey's translation of *The City of God,* which was going through Eld's press at the same time as the Sonnets, presents the work as Healey's 'legacy

---

[1] Rollins 2, ii.186–95; recent advocates of Southampton include Jonathan Bate, *The Genius of Shakespeare* (1997), 46, and Akrigg.

[2] First suggested by Boaden in 1832; Rollins 2, ii.195–213. Duncan-Jones presents the most convincing recent arguments for identifying W.H. with Pembroke, 55–69.

[3] Dover Wilson, p. c.

laid at your Honour's feet', which 'is rather here delivered to your Honour's humbly thrice-kissed hands by his poor delegate' (sig. A3ʳ). Unless Thorpe had forgotten how to grovel by the time Shakespeare's Sonnets were printed it seems very unlikely that he would have stripped Pembroke of his title, even if his purpose in doing so was to save him the direct embarrassment of association with poems by a man which seem mostly to be to a man. But Pembroke is a more probable suggestion than the other myriad beings proposed as the object of Shakespeare's love: from Oscar Wilde's engaging fantasy of an actor called Willy Hughes in *The Portrait of Mr W.H.* (1889), through William Hathaway or William Hall (who have been thought to be 'begetters' of the sequence in the sense of 'the person who obtained the manuscript'), to Donald Foster's party-pooping claim that 'W. H.' is a misprint for 'W. S.' or 'W. SH.' and that Thorpe was dedicating Shakespeare's poems to Shakespeare,[1] noone has ever successfully answered Shakespeare's own question, 'What is your substance, whereof are you made?'

The dedication is sometimes dismissed as merely a printer's preface (which it clearly is)[2] or a red herring (which it may be), but it cannot simply be wished away. It is a para-text: as much as the poems' *mise-en-page*, the dedication is part of how the book invites its readers to respond to it. And it embeds the sequence in some well-established beliefs about the kinds of relations which poetry might court with 'life' in this period. Targeted anonymity was a deep-seated convention in Elizabethan erotic verse, as well as in 'autobiographical' narratives in the period. The autobiography of the Elizabethan music master Thomas Whythorne records how its author (a comical Malvolio-figure) used love poems as part of his many attempted seductions of his socially superior mistresses. At one point he records that he found an amorous poem in the strings of a gittern, which 'I could not well judge whether it were written by a man or a woman'.[3] He pens a reply, hoping to discover that the author of the poem is his mistress, and finds to his great disappointment that it is only her maid. Poems do not target their addressees with exact precision in this period. They were addressed to the person who found themselves addressed by them, and they

[1] Donald Foster, 'Mr W.H., RIP', *PMLA* 102 (1987), 42–54.

[2] Kerrigan, 10–11.

[3] Thomas Whythorne, *The Autobiography*, ed. James M. Osborn (1962), 21.

often evoked emotions which could derive from a variety of possible circumstances. George Gascoigne's *Adventures of Master F.J.* deals in fictional versions of Whythorne's experiences. The work is laced with teasing initials: from the 'F.J.' of the title they run riot in an introductory epistle, which is supposedly from someone called H.W., but is almost certainly by Gascoigne himself. The epistle relates how the manuscript passed to H.W. from someone called G.T. to his printer A.B.[1] F.J.'s courtship, like that of Thomas Whythorne, is conducted by means of love lyrics dropped in the path of the married lady Eleanor, his proposed addressee, who has to infer that they are addressed to her. The editor of the prose narrative frequently interjects critical comments on the poems F.J. uses in his courtship, which claim that the poems were not written by F.J. to Eleanor, but by other poets to other addressees. Initials create an atmosphere of furtive but deniable biographical allusion, and readers from the 1580s onwards were well used to the uncertain pleasures to which these tricks could give rise. *Willobie his Avisa* (1594), a verse narrative purportedly about an affair, has frequently been invoked in biographical studies of Shakespeare's Sonnets, especially by Southamptonites. This is because its hero, Henry Willoughby (H.W.; Here We-go-again) is urged on by an old player called 'W.S.' to court the ever-chaste Avisa. The poem contains the first printed reference to Shakespeare's *Lucrece*, so the temptation to assume the old player W.S. is William Shakespeare has proved irresistible for many of its readers. *Willobie his Avisa* offers further teasing details which invite its readers to relate the poem to real places and people: Avisa is described as living below 'the badge | Of England's saint'; so, the ever ingenious Southamptonite Arthur Acheson found a tavern under the sign of St George in Oxford and suggested that Shakespeare stopped off there to seduce the (dark, naturally) landlady.[2]

Thorpe's dedication should not be read with this painful literalism. It should be taken within a context of suggestive semi-anonymity, in which the use of initials creates possible, but deniable, connections with the lives of particular people. Thorpe made money from selling books; one way in this period of selling books was to suggest seductively that there might be private allu-

---

[1] *A Hundreth Sundrie Flowres bound up in one Small Poesie* (1573), fo. 201.
[2] *Shakespeare's Sonnet Story* (1922), 120–56.

sions to unknown individuals hidden within them. W.H. (Who He?) may be someone; but he may be part of an invitation to readers of a printed edition of what is presented as a coterie work to believe themselves on the outer fringes of a hidden inner circle of drama. While nineteenth-century readers of the poem were convinced, as Wordsworth put it in 1827 in 'Scorn not the Sonnet' (ll. 2–3), that 'with this key, | Shakespeare unlocked his heart', the collection's earliest readers may have seen it as a work which locked them out whilst waving a key before their eyes. They might have muttered with Browning, 'If so, the less Shakespeare he!'[1] Printed poems could be presented in such a way as to make their readers feel that they were both inside and outside a charmed circle of knowledge.[2] Thorpe's publication of Shakespeare's Sonnets is designed to play to those expectations. Given that Shakespeare was unlikely to have been in London during its production (it was a time of plague) the safest assumption is that this is Thorpe's design rather than Shakespeare's.

Date and Sequence. When were the poems written? This is not an easy question to answer. The external evidence is scanty: at least some sonnets by Shakespeare were circulating by 1598, when Francis Meres in *Palladis Tamia* referred to Shakespeare's 'Sonnets to his private friends'.[3] In 1599 versions of Sonnets *128* and *144* appeared in *The Passionate Pilgrim*. That is all the external evidence we have about the composition of the poems before they appeared in print a decade later.

Recent stylometric work, however, has strongly suggested that the sequence had an extended genesis. Different groups of poems display markedly different frequencies of 'late rare words' (that is, words which occur between three and nine times in works of Shakespeare known to have been composed after 1600) and 'early rare words' (words which fulfil these criteria and which occur in works written before 1600).[4] These indicators have proved a

[1] Robert Browning, 'House', l. 40.
[2] See Wendy Wall, *The Imprint of Gender: Authorship and Publication in the English Renaissance* (Ithaca and London, 1993), 23–109, and the suggestive account of the sonnet form in Patricia Fumerton, *Cultural Aesthetics: Renaissance Literature and the Practice of Social Ornament* (Chicago and London, 1991), 67–110.
[3] Francis Meres, *Palladis Tamia* (1598), sigs. 2O1^v–2O2^r.
[4] See Hieatt *et al.*, 'When did Shakespeare Write *Sonnets* 1609?'

reliable means of confirming other methods of dating the dramatic works. The detailed arguments derived from stylometry suggest that the sequence may well not have been composed in the order in which it appeared in the Quarto. The first study based on this method found that *1–60* were likely to have been composed early (*c.*1591–5) and then revised up to 1609 (which would tally with arguments that later seventeenth-century manuscripts preserve early versions of Sonnet 2);[1] that *61–103* were early (*c.*1591–5) and unrevised; that *104–26* were later (1597–1603); and that *127–54* were indisputably early (1591–5). More recent work, founded on a division of Shakespeare's career into four, rather than two, phases has pushed the dates of the earliest phase of composition a little later, into the mid-to-late 1590s,[2] and proposes that the presence of both early and late rare words in *1–60* is a sign of composition in the late 1590s, rather than of early work which was then revised. This makes sense of the strong presence (noted in the commentary) of parallels in this group to plays from the later 1590s, although the revision hypothesis cannot be ruled out. Sonnets *104–26* do persistently appear to bear the fingerprints of Shakespeare's style in the early seventeenth century. Poems in this group are very likely to be the products of the latest phase of composition, as well as, it appears, marking the end of the affair with the friend. It is also beyond reasonable doubt that the much more disparate group *127–54* contains the earliest sonnets to have been composed. The evidence at present suggests that the poems were written roughly in the following periods: [3]

[1] Gary Taylor, 'Some Manuscripts of Shakespeare's Sonnets', *Bulletin of the John Rylands Library* 68 (1985), 210–46.

[2] MacDonald P. Jackson, 'Vocabulary and Chronology: The Case of Shakespeare's Sonnets', *RES*, forthcoming, and 'Rhymes in Shakespeare's Sonnets: Evidence of Date of Composition', *NQ* 244 (1999), 213–19, has refined their conclusions. The datings offered in this introduction are chiefly based on his work, and I am grateful to Professor Jackson for giving me early access to his conclusions. Less systematic precedents include J. M. Nosworthy, 'All too Short a Date: Internal Evidence in Shakespeare's Sonnets', *Essays in Criticism* 2 (1952), 311–24, and Eliot Slater, 'Shakespeare: Word Links between Poems and Plays', *NQ* 220 (1975), 157–63, as well as A. Kent Hieatt, T. G. Bishop, and E. A. Nicholson, 'Shakespeare's Rare Words: "Lover's Complaint", *Cymbeline*, and Sonnets', *NQ* 232 (1987), 219–24.

[3] This tabulation is based on the findings of Hieatt, Hieatt, and Prescott as modified by MacDonald P. Jackson. Jackson argues that Hieatt and his collaborators probably give too early a date for the earliest phase of composition.

1–60	composed *c.*1595–6 (possibly revised thereafter)
61–103	composed *c.*1594–5
104–26	composed *c.*1598–1604
127–54	composed *c.*1591–5[1]

There are many grey areas in these approximate findings, and the greyest areas are the most critical: there is no certainty when Shakespeare began to write sonnets, and there is no certainty that his revisions and rewritings continued beyond about 1604–5.[2] Many individual sonnets contain neither early nor late rare words. This means that there are some sections of the sequence, and many individual poems, which cannot be firmly allocated to a particular period for any other reason than their contiguity with poems which do contain stylistic indicators of their date. The groups are therefore best thought of as sections which may contain greater or lesser concentrations of early and late periods of work on the sequence, rather than as definitive means of dating individual poems. There are some groups within groups, such as *77–87* (which includes the 'rival poet' sonnets), which contain significant concentrations of rare words found in the middle period of Shakespeare's career.[3] Many poems within each group interconnect with each other in theme or language, or are linked by rhyme-words. This could indicate that they were composed at a similar period, but they might equally well go to show that poems with similar vocabularies and moods were placed together. Shakespeare often experimented with new words and rhymes in non-dramatic verse before letting them loose on the stage. This means that any of the conjectural dates might plausibly be pushed back by a year or so (and my suggested date for the earliest poems in *127–54* is earlier than some authorities would have it).

The breaking down of the Sonnets into groups with different periods of composition may leave some unresolved questions, but it does ignite critical sparks from other evidence about the poems'

[1] This initial date is earlier than Jackson would like. The presence of *145* (which appears very early), the incidence of word-links with *Comedy of Errors*, and Shakespeare's tendency, noted by Jackson, to experiment with rhymes and rare words in non-dramatic verse before they are registered in the dramatic verse all incline me to favour an earlier date for at least some poems in this group.

[2] Although there is some evidence from word-links that *A Lover's Complaint* may date from *c.*1608: see Hieatt *et al.*, 'Shakespeare's Rare Words'.

[3] Jackson, 'Vocabulary and Chronology'.

composition. The suggestion that *127–54* are early (they contain no late rare words) tallies with the appearance of *138* and *144* in *The Passionate Pilgrim* of 1599, and reinforces the traditional and reasonable belief that a new mini-sequence begins at that point (that it appears likely to be an 'old' sequence raises, as we shall see, some intriguing critical possibilities). The octosyllabic *145*, which plays with the name of Shakespeare's wife Anne Hathaway, is also found in this group, and may well be the earliest sonnet in the sequence.¹ Even these early poems, however, may have been revised in the course of the 1590s. The variants between the versions of *138* and *144* in *The Passionate Pilgrim* and in the 1609 Quarto probably indicate that Shakespeare retouched at least some sonnets in this group during the later 1590s. Most sonneteers did revise and reorder their poems, and several radically reconceived their sequences in the process of an extended genesis: Samuel Daniel added some more impersonal sonnets on fame and immortality to his *Delia* for its authorized edition in 1592; Shakespeare's fellow Warwickshireman Michael Drayton extended and revised his *Ideas' Mirror* into *Idea* over a twenty-five-year period (1594–1619). Shakespeare worked with a similar sense that sonnet sequences erode, slip, and reshape with time, and he may well have altered images or phrases in particular poems in order to tie them in with their neighbours.

Twenty-five manuscript versions of individual sonnets are known, all of which date from after Shakespeare's death, some from as late as the 1660s. Some clearly derive from the Quarto,² others are evidently scribal adaptations of the poems to suit musical settings.³ Other cases are less clear: Sonnet 2 has an unusually extensive manuscript tradition, and a modernized text of the manuscript versions is reproduced here at the end of the sequence

¹ See Andrew Gurr, 'Shakespeare's First Poem: Sonnet 145', *Essays in Criticism* 21 (1971), 221–6.
² e.g. St John's College MS S.23, fo. 38ʳ⁻ᵛ. Folger MS V.a.162, fo. 26 is also likely to derive from Q's text of Sonnet 32. For a full list see Beal, 452–4.
³ The version adapted by Henry Lawes of *116* in the New York Public Library Music Division MS Drexel 4257, no. 33 is clearly for setting; so, probably, is the version of *8* divided into stanzas and entitled 'In laudem Musice et opprobrium Contemptoris eiusdem', British Library Add. MS 15226, fo. 4ᵛ. ('Contemptoris' is usually transcribed as the ungrammatical 'Contemptorii': there is a dot in the MS over the terminal 's'.) The version of *128* in Bodleian MS Rawl. Poet. 152, fo. 34ᵛ seems also to have been transcribed because of its musical allusions.

in Q.[1] It is just possible that these witnesses distantly record what may have been an earlier authorial version of this sonnet. It is equally possible that these manuscripts may derive from a version by a transcriber who missed a number of puns: Q's 'Thy youth's proud livery so gazed on now | Will be a tattered weed of small worth held' corresponds to the manuscript tradition's 'Thy youth's fair liv'ry so accounted now | Shall be like rotten weeds of no worth held'. 'Rotten weeds' shades less delicately than 'tattered weed' from the imagery of clothes to that of plants, and is the kind of phrase that a copyist is likely to have misremembered. Q's 'treasure of thy lusty days' could have been memorially reconstructed as 'lustre of thy youthful days' in the manuscript tradition, where 'lustre' registers both 'treasure' and 'lusty'. Many of the highly literate men and women who kept manuscript miscellanies in the early seventeenth century were happy to adapt and alter the poems they received. This may have happened with Sonnet 2. It seems almost certain to have happened in the case of other manuscript versions. So when the first line of Sonnet 106 ('When in the chronicle of wasted time') appears in one manuscript as 'When in the Annals of all wastinge Time',[2] a miscellanist has done some flattening and some updating: the 1570s and 1580s were the peak years for the big baggy histories called 'Chronicles'; by the early seventeenth century Tacitus's *Annals* was the model to which many trend-setting historians aspired. Shakespeare's poem exploited that conscious oldness of the word 'Chronicles' in 1609; by the 1620s it felt musty, and the copyist altered it, also flattening 'wasted' ('thin', and also 'used up to no avail') into the monophony of 'wasting'.

Despite what appears to have been a very extended genesis, and whether or not the poems in it were revised, the sequence as it is printed in Q does have some fixed points which indicate that the order in which the poems appear had been carefully considered, at least in the part of the sequence up to 126. Stylometric evidence suggests that Sonnet 60 (which is packed with words favoured by the later Shakespeare) marks the end of a chronologically linked

---

[1] Taylor, 'Some Manuscripts'. Duncan-Jones puts a strong and sceptical case that the manuscript versions do not preserve authorial variants, but illustrate the reception history of the poems, 453–66.

[2] Pierpont Morgan Library, MA 1057, 95. Facsimile in *Autograph Letters and Manuscripts: Major Acquisitions of the Pierpont Morgan Library 1924–74* (New York, 1974), plate 12.

group.[1] That this sixtieth poem dwells on minutes and hours can hardly be an accident, and Shakespeare may well have worked up this poem in order that it should sustain a particular weight in the sequence.[2] Other sonnets seem positioned in a way that strongly suggests a deliberate counterpoint between their subject and their numbering within the sequence. Sonnet 63—the age at which bodies were thought to undergo a 'grand climacteric' after nine weeks of years—relates a crisis. Sonnet 49—the age at which people were believed to undergo a 'minor climacteric' after seven weeks of years—interrupts a mini-sequence about travel and separation in order to muse on death. These poems begin with a chiming attempt to fortify the friend against time: 'Against that time' begins 49: 'Against my love shall be as I am now' echoes 63. Sonnet 126, twice 63, slices off the friend's life with the irresistible payment of his account to Nature.

Ingenious eyes can see a lot in numbers, and ears can make sequences of sounds where none is meant. But a random sequence could not have produced the waves of consonant moods, of sounds and rhythms of thought, which link almost every sonnet with a neighbour or near-neighbour, and which parallel the tireless interconnections within individual sonnets of sound with sound and quatrain with couplet.[3] Readers of the poems in their sequence in Q are not invited to weld them into an immutable numerologically determined structure, but to make sequences, of time, of sound, of sense, of narrative, and of argument. The satisfaction offered by each of these differing systems is left so artfully partial that some poems seem to call to others from which they are separated by long intervals, and to invite rearrangement.[4] Sonnet 42, for instance,

---

[1] Hieatt *et al.*, 'When did Shakespeare Write *Sonnets* 1609', 94.

[2] See the judiciously pragmatic essay by René Graziani, 'The Numbering of Shakespeare's Sonnets: 12, 60, and 126', *Shakespeare Quarterly* 35 (1984), 79–82.

[3] See MacDonald P. Jackson, 'Aspects of Organisation in *Shakespeare's Sonnets*', *Parergon* NS 17 (1999), 109–34. On the internal organization of the poems, see Stephen Booth, *An Essay on Shakespeare's Sonnets* (New Haven, 1969). Vendler is a fine study of the poems' aural magic, and on their rhetorical patterning and its emotional effects see Brian Vickers, 'Rhetoric and Feeling in Shakespeare's *Sonnets*', in Keir Elam, ed., *Shakespeare Today: Directions and Methods of Research* (Florence, 1984), 53–98.

[4] Richard Lanham, *The Motives of Eloquence: Literary Rhetoric in the Renaissance* (New Haven, 1976), 116, puts it sharply: 'Obviously all the rearrangers cannot be right. Yes they can. The sonnets present orderless order, *invite* rearrangement. *All* the rearrangers are right.'

which bewails the loss of the young man to a woman, seems too close to the biographical context of the unfaithful mistress in 127–52 not to be related in some way to those poems. But in its direct use of a second-person pronoun to a male addressee it clearly cannot be moved from where it is: the 'thou' of poems after 127 is usually either implicitly a woman or Cupid, but is never categorically male. There are jolts and sudden shifts of tack between groups, but links between rhymes and themes and moods among successive poems create shifting alliances even between groups and sub-groups which seem distinct. Some poems sit restlessly beside each other, teasing darker senses from words on which earlier poems had relied, or forcing lighter senses to emerge. Sonnet 32 begins 'If thou survive my well-contented day' and muses on death. The juxtaposition with the glorious dawn of 33, 'Full many a glorious morning have I seen', seems more of a breach than a link, until 34 reminds us that 'day' can mean both the day of death *and* a promise of a lovely dawn and good weather: 'Why didst thou promise such a beauteous day'. Sonnet 32 and 34 rhyme on the word 'day', forcing the kinds of intimacy between divergent senses which repetition and echo create best.

Sonnet 104, which introduces what is likely to be the last group to have been composed, also contains a significant allusion to the passage of time, which had caught commentators' eyes long before stylometry was dreamed of:

> Three winters cold
> Have from the forests shook three summers' pride,
> Three beauteous springs to yellow autumn turned
> In process of the seasons have I seen,
> Three April perfumes in three hot Junes burned,
> Since first I saw you fresh, which yet are green.

The poem looks back on time past, and may also mark the resumption of work on the sequence after the literal passage of time, maybe even three years, or perhaps after two years, the twice fifty-two weeks which would total the poem's number. Even here, though, the apparent divisions between datable units of sonnets are enmeshed with other forms of sequential artifice: 104 does not begin the sequence anew or break decisively from the poems which precede it. It works together with the surrounding poems, all of which meditate on past, present, and future. Sonnet 100 rebukes the muse for forgetting to praise for so long, and prepares readers of the sequence to find a hiatus in composition. Sonnet *105* seeks a permanent present of praise in the hymn-like insistence that ' "Fair, kind and true" is all my argument', as though attempting to arrest the passage of time by ritual repetition. This is in turn followed by the poetic retrospect of *106*, in which the poet looks back to the 'descriptions of the fairest wights' in 'the chronicle of wasted time'. The word 'wights', combined with the chronicle of past beauties which it is used to describe, suggests that this poem is thinking back to the 1590s, to that great epic of time's passage, Spenser's *Faerie Queene*,[1] and is consciously recording a break in literary history, as well as perhaps in personal history. Sonnet *104* sits amid poems about time, time misspent, time present and time future, and is artfully placed to work with and against poems which may have been written before or after it. The literal passage of the time it took to compose the poems is one force in the sequence; but it needs to be constantly weighed against other forms of structure and other principles of ordering. The sequence—and that word, with its suggestion of linearity and its promise of unity was not used of sonnet books in the period[2]—weaves together a multiplicity of forms of order, none of which predominates. As a result it demands readerly activity of a peculiar kind. The sequence at times seems to build up a body of recurrent structures and preoccupations, and at some moments seems to shape itself around particular moods or events. And then it seems not to. A story converges from the lyrics, and then it vanishes. Surprise at this is right: the sequence calls for a form of disappointed wonder, as readers make and remake different methods of unifying the sequence. The Sonnets ask their readers to think about how their responses are mak-

---

[1] See Patrick Cheney, ' "In praise of ladies dead and lovely knights": Shakespeare's Sonnet 106, Spenser's National Epic, Counter-Petrarchism', *ELR* 31 (2001), forthcoming.

[2] On the miscellaneity of sonnet sequences, see Germaine Warkentin, ' "Love's sweetest part, variety": Petrarch and the Curious Frame of the Renaissance Sonnet Sequence', *Renaissance and Reformation* 11 (1975), 14–23. Carol Thomas Neely, 'The Structure of English Renaissance Sonnet Sequences', *ELH* 45 (1978), 359, notes that 'The Italian model—fragmentary composition followed by careful selection and arrangement into a sequence—both justifies the expectation of structure in the seq. ence and predicts its loose elastic nature'. On the origins of the term 'sonnet seql.ence', see William T. Going, 'Gascoigne and the Term "Sonnet Sequence" ', *NQ* 199 (1954), 189–91, and 'The Term "Sonnet Sequence" ', *Modern Language Notes* 62 (1947), 400–2.

ing a sequence out of a series, and about why they have pulled one possible pattern from material which seems so heavily patterned that almost any form could be seen in it.

Sources. The sequence does not have any simple source, and only a few poems (such as the relatively weak and formally aberrant 99) have clear analogies in the English sonnet tradition. Petrarch is some sort of influence, but the Petrarch who may have influenced Shakespeare is not the frequently imitated and more frequently parodied Petrarch of freezing fires and icy mistresses; it is the Petrarch who is preoccupied with fame and with thoughtful solitude.[1] Precedents for poems addressed to a male beloved can be found in Michelangelo; poems which share Shakespeare's recurrent concern with the inner secrecies of the mind can be found in Sidney's *Astrophil and Stella*, the first great English sonnet sequence; and close parallels for the exhortations to marry which run through the early sonnets can be found in a speech by Erasmus.[2] Shakespeare is also humorously conscious of the clichés of the sonnet tradition, that mistresses have cherry lips and hairs of golden wire, and artfully seeks to differentiate his mistress from the tired blondes of Petrarchan convention.

But the most clearly identifiable models for Shakespeare's sonnets are structural rather than verbal. Shakespeare drew from Daniel's *Delia* the conception of a series of sonnets which resonated with its final complaint, and shares with Daniel a recurrent, tolling concern with time and its thievish passage to eternity. But

---

[1] See Gordon Braden, 'Love and Fame: The Petrarchan Career', in Joseph H. Smith and William Kerrigan, eds., *Pragmatism's Freud: The Moral Disposition of Psychoanalysis*, Psychiatry and the Humanities 9 (Baltimore, 1986), 126–58, the same author's 'Shakespeare's Petrarchism', in James Schiffer, ed., *Shakespeare's Sonnets: Critical Essays* (New York and London, 1999), 163–83, and his 'Ovid, Petrarch, and Shakespeare's Sonnets', in A. B. Taylor, ed., *Shakespeare's Ovid: The 'Metamorphoses' in the Plays and Poems* (Cambridge, 2000), 96–112. For a valuable study of English Petrarchism, see Heather Dubrow, *Echoes of Desire: English Petrarchism and its Counterdiscourses* (Ithaca and London, 1995).

[2] On connections with Michelangelo, see John Kerrigan, 'Between Michelangelo and Petrarch: Shakespeare's Sonnets of Art', in Yasunuri Takada, ed., *Surprised by Scenes: Essays in Honour of Professor Yasunuri Takahashi* (Tokyo, 1994), 142–63, reprinted in his *On Shakespeare and Early Modern Literature: Essays* (Oxford, 2001); for connections with Sidney, see Anne Ferry, *The 'Inward' Language: Sonnets of Wyatt, Sidney, Shakespeare, Donne* (Chicago and London, 1983). Debts to Erasmus are explored in Katharine M. Wilson's *Shakespeare's Sugared Sonnets* (1974), 146–65.

Daniel is not exactly a source, and 'source' is itself the wrong sort
of metaphor for describing how and where Shakespeare's sonnets
originated. They do not flow downstream from a pure classical ori-
gin: they take topoi, often from classical, but sometimes also from
Petrarchan works, and muse on them.[1] The poems relish the elas-
ticity of sonnet conventions, and their author shows his strength
by toying with, and sometimes parodying, those conventions. In
the process the topoi are mutated from their originals, and, on their
later recurrence in the sequence, changed even from their Shake-
spearian starting-points. The best poem to take as an example of
this process, and of how it interacts with the sequence and shaping
of the series of poems, is Sonnet 60.

> Like as the waves make towards the pebbled shore,
> So do our minutes hasten to their end,
> Each changing place with that which goes before,
> In sequent toil all forwards do contend.
> Nativity, once in the main of light,
> Crawls to maturity, wherewith being crowned
> Crookèd eclipses 'gainst his glory fight,
> And Time that gave doth now his gift confound.
> Time doth transfix the flourish set on youth,
> And delves the parallels in beauty's brow,
> Feeds on the rarities of nature's truth,
> And nothing stands but for his scythe to mow.
>> And yet to times in hope my verse shall stand,
>> Praising thy worth, despite his cruel hand.

This poem in some sense comes from the meditation on change
which is spoken by the philosopher Pythagoras in the final book of
Ovid's *Metamorphoses*:

> 'In all the world there is not that that standeth at a stay.
> Things ebb and flow: and every shape is made to pass away.
> The time itself continually is fleeting like a brook.
> For neither brook nor lightsome time can tarry still. But look
> As every wave drives other forth, and that that comes behind
> Both thrusteth and is thrust itself: even so the times by kind

---

[1] Still valuable on this, despite its inconclusiveness over precise influences, is J. B.
Leishman, *Themes and Variations in Shakespeare's Sonnets* (1961). On the metaphor of
the source, potent in many Renaissance poems, see David Quint's suggestive study
Origin and Originality in Renaissance Literature: Versions of the Source (New Haven and
London, 1983).

Do fly and follow both at once, and evermore renew.
For that that was before is left, and straight there doth ensue
Another that was never erst. Each twinkling of an eye
Doth change.'

(Golding 15.197–206)

Despite the evident affinities between Sonnet 60 and this passage it is misleading to say that Ovid is a 'source' for Shakespeare. Shakespeare's poem is implicitly an anti-source poem.[1] Influence (and that word too has hidden within it the fluvial metaphors which so often shape our inherited language for describing poetic origins) is here replaced by the erosive movement and counter-movement of the sea. 'Sequent toil' might suggest an effort on the part of a successor to overgo or surpass its original, but that word 'sequent' ducks back into the sea of sense, as it recalls the phrasing of Ovid's poem ('dum sequuntur') and imports it into English. *OED* presents Shakespeare's usage of the word here as the first in the sense (3b) 'Characterized by continuous succession; forming an unbroken series or course; consecutive', but it has a touch of 'that which succeeds' (*OED* 1b) and its conjunction with 'toil' gives an overtone of 'striving to overgo'. The structure of the poem itself presents a working energy which attempts to build up a sustained momentum. The first four lines present an energetic process of endless, surging replacement as the sea works on and yet stays still. This creates an expectation, if not of forward progress, then at least of endless change, which is fulfilled in the birth of a child who crawls to maturity. The 'crooked eclipses' then force a return to a reappraisal of the image of the sea: it was the forceful return of wave on wave, their mutually thwarting energy, which was the point of the comparison. 'Crowned' rhymes not with 'renowned', but with 'confound', and the energy of the sonnet becomes all Time's, as he reaps and gouges lines and wounds in the face of beauty. 'And . . . and . . . and'—the poem builds up destructive forces relentlessly, then it turns 'And' round into a adversative form with 'And yet'. The couplet sits there as awkwardly assuring itself of poetic permanence in a world of change as does Ovid's famous coda to the *Metamorphoses*, from which it principally derives:

[1] See further Jonathan Bate, 'Ovid and the Sonnets; or, Did Shakespeare Feel the Anxiety of Influence', *Shakespeare Survey* 42 (1989), 65–76.

> Now have I brought a work to end which neither Jove's fierce wrath,
> Nor sword, nor fire, nor fretting age with all the force it hath
> Are able to abolish quite. Let come that fatal hour
> Which (saving of this brittle flesh) hath over me no power,
> And at his pleasure make an end of mine uncertain time.
> Yet shall the better part of me assurèd be to climb
> Aloft above the starry sky. And all the world shall never
> Be able for to quench my name. For look how far so ever
> The Roman empire by the right of conquest shall extend,
> So far shall all folk read this work. And time without all end
> (If poets as by prophecy about the truth may aim)
> My life shall everlastingly be lengthened still by fame.
>
> (Golding 15.984–95)

However, one notable difference between Shakespeare's declaration of the immortality of his verse and that of Ovid is the way that for Shakespeare the original guarantor of the value of his verse is the friend, rather than his own immortal art ('thou art all my art', 78.13). And this is a recurrent feature of the sequence: its authority, permanence, and fame are frequently said to be founded not on the power of the poet, but on the beauty of its subject.[1] It is the young man who is the archetype of Adonis and Helen of Troy in Sonnet 53, and it is the 'living record of his memory' which is imagined to 'pace forth' in order to defeat time in Sonnet 55. He is imagined not only as the sustaining source of the value of Shakespeare's poem, but as the archetype of value towards which earlier poets aspired:

> When in the chronicle of wasted time
> I see descriptions of the fairest wights,
> And beauty making beautiful old rhyme
> In praise of ladies dead, and lovely knights;
> Then in the blazon of sweet beauty's best,
> Of hand, of foot, of lip, of eye, of brow,
> I see their antique pen would have expressed
> Even such a beauty as you master now.
>
> (106.1–8)

As we have already seen, this sonnet is consciously establishing a chronological gap between itself and earlier Elizabethan litera-

---

[1] On the use of the beloved as a source of the endlessly frustrated desire of the sonneteer, see Jacqueline T. Miller, *Poetic License: Authority and Authorship in Medieval and Renaissance Contexts* (Oxford, 1986), 121–75.

ture, and echoes Spenser and Daniel to make that point more force-
fully. The present, the 'now' of beauty, accelerates literary history,
and makes all past poems seem to be trying to be poems about the
friend. It is a clear paradox that the friend is unnamed, and that
the survival of his beauty is dependent on the poet's description of
him. And the sonnets which present the friend as a source of value
all more or less inconspicuously register that for him to function as
a source of value he needs to be alive, or to have a poet to praise
him, or a lover to worship him: 'Even such a beauty as you master
now' lightly points the evanescence of his beauty; the '*living* record
of your memory' too notes that the young man has to be experi-
enced by people who are alive, and in whom the faculty of memory
persists, in order to remain valuable. In this respect the first seven-
teen poems, which urge the friend to marry, are a crucial part of
the design of the whole sequence: they propose a means by which
the source of value in the sequence might literally be sustained for
ever by biological reproduction. But it is also a crucial aspect of the
sequence that these persuasions to marry fail of their rhetorical
effect, just as Venus's persuasions of Adonis had failed to make him
succumb to her. Much of the rest of the sequence urgently asks
whether poetry can provide a form of permanent beauty which
would function as a substitute for biological reproduction (and it is
in this context a suggestive detail that a commonplace of Renais-
sance imitation theory, after Seneca's 84th Epistle, was that an
imitator should seek to imitate his predecessor as a child resembles
his father). The question as to whether words in themselves can
create an archetype and permanent source of beauty is in one
respect the subject of the whole sequence up to 126: the young
man will not breed, and so will change and decay; the source of the
poems' value will erode; the poet's love, which is the precondition
of his desire to praise and see the young man as a source of beauty,
may fade if the friend is fickle (and suggestions that he is suscepti-
ble to stains grow from Sonnet 33 onwards). When the friend is
finally reminded that nature must 'render thee' (126.12) as a debt,
the sequence breaks off, still asking whether poetic power can pro-
vide an alternative to the biological decay of the principal source of
its vitality.

Shakespeare's Sonnets do not provide either a strongly positive
or a firmly negative answer to this question. By Sonnet 126 it seems
far too simple to believe that there might be a single source of value

or beauty. Its readers have been introduced to the multiple aspects of the friend—his androgyny, his mutability, his cruelty. Readers have also experienced recurring different versions of familiar ideas—that poetry can conquer time, that perhaps it cannot, that love unites lover and beloved, or perhaps it does not. Many sonnet sequences give the impression that the author is writing and rewriting the same poem over and over again. In the worst of them this can become a mark of imaginative poverty. But Shakespeare's Sonnets use the methods of repetition and reapproximation which are central to the sonnet sequence to powerful effect. The changeful process of rereading and reimagining the perfection of the young man, of thinking and rethinking the relationship between time and beauty, gives the effect that the sequence is building not on an external source of value, nor, finally, on the external beauty of the friend. The sequence seems rather to be sourced in itself, and to be made up of readings and rereadings of its own poems. Sonnet 126, the final poem addressed to the friend, re-echoes a number of words and images which had been used earlier in the sequence (audits, sickles, debts, the plucking of plants). This poem seems to draw most of its vitality from the preceding sequence, and to invite a reappraisal of the poems which have come before. And Sonnet 60 again in this respect enacts in little the processes of reading required by the whole group of poems. Its structure seems to insist that each image and each thought could go in two or more directions: waves could be endlessly recurrent, or they could erode the shore to nothing. It also makes each quatrain work off against its predecessor like thought and after-thought. And it weights the couplet with a grandeur of resolution which it seems almost consciously to be unable to sustain. The poem seems fragile and labile; and yet set against these points of fragility is a cool framework of order and steadying artifice. Poem 60; sixty minutes. The hands of a clock go round in a circle as well as moving destructively onwards. While the poem relates directly to the argument of change presented in Sonnet 59, its positioning makes it seem to do so from a distance created by artifice, an artifice which reinforces the couplet's fragile claim to permanence. Perhaps this work of art, it seems to suggest, can incorporate within itself the passage of time and the changes which it wreaks, and achieve some mastery of Time's destructive actions. Sonnet 60 changes Ovid's great poem of change, and it glories in that fact even as it deplores the fragility of living. Time figures often in the sequence as a destructive force, as an auditor of accounts, or a force which can write its presence into the most beautiful of faces. But the sonnets are always themselves using the passage of time to urge their readers to read them anew.

And this process of reading anew continues right to the end of the sequence, although the brilliance with which this technique is used becomes dulled after *126*. The very last poems in the collection present little allegories about Cupid. These are often seen as a detached coda to the sequence of poems to the mistress, since the fires and hot baths which they describe darkly allude to venereal diseases and their cures in the sweating tubs. Sonnets *153* and *154* are also often seen as poems which modulate the generic mood of the work towards *A Lover's Complaint*, as Spenser's *Amoretti* (1595) uses a set of light anacreontic rhymes to bridge the transition to the *Epithalamion* or as Daniel shifts from *Delia* to the *Complaint of Rosamond* via an intermediary Ode. These two poems, though, are also alternative versions of each other and of a poem (which Shakespeare might have encountered in any one of a multitude of disguises) by Marianus Scholasticus in the Greek Anthology: 'Beneath these plane trees, detained by gentle slumber, Love slept, having put his torch in the care of the Nymphs; but the Nymphs said to one another "Why wait? Would that together with this we could quench the fire in the hearts of men." But the torch set fire even to the water, and with hot water thenceforth the Love-Nymphs fill the bath.'[1] The fact that these poems both relate quite closely to this source is often invoked as grounds for separating them from the sequence proper—and if the 'sequence' were in fact a printer's interpretation of a manuscript commonplace book with several groups of entries in it these poems could have been just a couple of trial runs at a familiar theme from European love poems which happened to have been sketched in at its end. But these two poems could equally well be seen as a final exploration of the quizzical relationship of sonnet-writing to sources: the process of reading seems at the end of the whole collection to have become a process of watching the poet rewrite and refashion the poems which have gone before.

---

[1] See James Hutton, 'Analogues of Shakespeare's Sonnets 153–4', *Modern Philology* 38 (1941), 385–403.

Reading the Sonnets. There is strong evidence that at least the poems up to *126* were arranged carefully in order, and there is strong evidence that the poems in the collection were composed over an extended period. As a result there is no reason to assume that the Sonnets are 'about' one relationship, that they are systematically organized on a single numerological or biographical principle,[1] or that *1–126* are addressed to one man—although the layers upon layers of tones of voice and feeling which they dramatize have the thickness, and at times the twistedness, of poems which seem to have their roots in experience rather than in literary experimentation. They are a structured miscellany of recurrent themes, passions, and thoughts, rather than a story or a mathematically ordered sequence. The fables which have grown up around the sequence—Shakespeare loved a noble young man; the young man was unfaithful to the poet with a Dark Lady and a Rival Poet; the poet himself became unfaithful to the youth, and then, after a period of some years of froideur, came weeping back to him—are ingenious but misguided responses to the milieu of targeted anonymity in which Thorpe's dedication embeds the volume. They derive from a wish to find a story in a set of poems which shadows many possible stories.[2] The Sonnets, which may or may not have originally been addressed to a variety of people, in their (new?) place in the Quarto become the culmination of the methods which Shakespeare had explored in the earlier narrative poems. *Venus and Adonis* and *Lucrece* play off voice against circumstance, whilst keeping circumstances and setting always at least half in mind. The earlier poems do always come back to a literal narrative setting against which the word of the speaker can be calibrated. In the dramatic works, too, different characters may have a different understanding of what a given speech means because of the different kinds of knowledge which they have, but an audience always has a framework against which they can judge what the character means by his words. So, in *Measure for Measure*, the returned Duke speaks in praise, it appears, to Angelo. The Duke knows that Angelo has monstrously abused his trust, but Angelo thinks the Duke does not know this:

---

[1] For rigorous numerological readings see Thomas P. Roche, *Petrarch and the English Sonnet Sequences* (New York, 1989), and Alastair Fowler, *Triumphal Forms* (Cambridge, 1970), 183–97.

[2] 'The author did not arrange these sonnets in a way that tells a clear story', Dubrow, 'Incertainties', 293.

> O, your desert speaks loud, and I should wrong it
> To lock it in the wards of covert bosom
> When it deserves with characters of brass
> A forted residence 'gainst the tooth of time
> And razure of oblivion.
>
> (5.1.9–13)

The vocabulary of this passage has richer associations with the Sonnets than any other passage of similar length from the dramatic works. The 'wards' one meets as the poet safely locks away his goods (but not the young man) in 48.4; the razure of oblivion grates through the sequence up to 126, 'characters' and 'brass' both leave a heavy imprint on the sequence. But this speech is addressed precisely to its circumstances, and it speaks doubly to two distinct audiences. The Duke is adopting the language of panegyric to praise Angelo, but there is a cutting edge to his praise; so Angelo is imagined not to be able to hear that 'desert' can mean both good or bad desert, and that memorialization of someone's 'desert' can mean recording it as an example of ill as well as making a monument of praise. A dramatic audience is party to a multiplicity of circumstances and so can hear at once the speech as it sounds to Angelo and the speech as it reflects on what the Duke knows that Angelo has done.

Many of the poems of praise to the young man work in the way that this extract from *Measure* works, except that in the case of the Sonnets it is impossible to segregate the varieties of possible meanings into meanings *to* particular characters, or to fix their meanings in relation to a known set of events. This leaves readers attempting to construct anterior circumstances which would allow each apparent current of sense within the Sonnets to be active, and at the same time enable critical decisions to be made about which of those currents is the primary one. This desire to embed the Sonnets in a story has been endemic in their reception history. It is not simply wrong-headed, since the poems implicitly claim to be embedded in exterior and anterior events. It only becomes wrong-headed when a critic fails to realize that judgements of tone endlessly feed back into beliefs about what has happened between the poet and his addressee, and vice versa, as in Sonnet 94:

> They that have power to hurt and will do none,
> That do not do the thing they most do show,

> Who, moving others, are themselves as stone,
> Unmovèd, cold, and to temptation slow:
> They rightly do inherit heaven's graces,
> And husband nature's riches from expense.
> They are the lords and owners of their faces,
> Others but stewards of their excellence.
> The summer's flower is to the summer sweet,
> Though to itself it only live and die,
> But if that flower with base infection meet,
> The basest weed outbraves his dignity:
> > For sweetest things turn sourest by their deeds;
> > Lilies that fester smell far worse than weeds.
>
> (94)

Is this praise? Is it right that those who move others whilst being themselves as stone should inherit heaven's graces, or does a wave of hurt rise up through 'rightly'? Proverbs take on meaning by being related to circumstances, and from the part they are made to play in conversational acts. But the proverbs here are used in a form which is devolved from the circumstances from which they are presumed to derive. The result is strategic uncertainty, in which it is impossible to separate praise of laudable restraint from dispraise of criminal insensibility. This creates a bewildering cycle of uncertainty: imagined circumstances feed back into how one judges tone and register; how one judges tone and register feeds back into what one thinks may have prompted a poet implicitly to compare his beloved to a festering lily.

The poems to the friend relish these uncertainties. They frequently offer fragmentary allusions to material relationships (here the opposition of 'lords and owners' to 'stewards' implicitly aligns the addressee with those who own large estates rather than with those who simply maintain them for others). Different poems grant the friend 'charters' of his worth, or allusively hint that he should be a good husbandsman and preserve the material wealth of his estate from decay by begetting an heir.[1] But these hints never simply settle into a clear description of the friend or of his material relationship with the poet:

[1] See Thomas M. Greene, 'Pitiful Thrivers: Failed Husbandry in the Sonnets', in Patricia Parker and Geoffrey Hartman, eds., *Shakespeare and the Question of Theory* (New York, 1985), 230–44, and John Barrell, 'Editing Out: The Discourse of Patronage in Shakespeare's Twenty-Ninth Sonnet', in his *Poetry, Language and Politics* (Manchester, 1988), 18–43.

Being your slave, what should I do but tend
Upon the hours and times of your desire?
I have no precious time at all to spend,
Nor services to do, till you require.
Nor dare I chide the world-without-end hour
Whilst I (my sovereign) watch the clock for you,
Nor think the bitterness of absence sour
When you have bid your servant once adieu.
Nor dare I question with my jealous thought
Where you may be, or your affairs suppose,
But like a sad slave stay and think of naught.
Save where you are how happy you make those.
   So true a fool is love, that in your will
   Though you do anything, he thinks no ill.

(57)

The tone of voice in which this poem is read depends on how far its
reader is prepared to accept that the speaker *is* the friend's 'slave'. If
he is a servant or a household retainer, then the poem could be
read as a piece of abject praise from one whose social standing does
not permit him to love or to question his love's conduct. But the
poem resists this simple reading: the opening rhetorical question
does not allow a reader to rest entirely comfortably with the idea
that the poet should simply wait, and the couplet, darkly playing
with the sexual possibilities of the word 'will', reinvents the poet as
one who is only a metaphorical slave, fooled by love into servile
acquiescence in infidelity.

Repeatedly sonnets of abject praise to the young man generate
undertows of irony and criticism which resist the implied social
division between poet and patron-beloved. Often too the poet
makes his largest claims through a voice of professed abjection, as
in Sonnet 71:

No longer mourn for me when I am dead
Than you shall hear the surly sullen bell
Give warning to the world that I am fled
From this vile world with vilest worms to dwell:
Nay, if you read this line, remember not
The hand that writ it, for I love you so
That I in your sweet thoughts would be forgot,
If thinking on me then should make you woe.
O, if (I say) you look upon this verse
When I (perhaps) compounded am with clay,

> Do not so much as my poor name rehearse;
> But let your love even with my life decay,
>   Lest the wise world should look into your moan
>   And mock you with me after I am gone.

One way of reading this is to imagine that the poem was written from oblivion in the face of neglect, and that that is why it tries to turn the act of forgetting into a positive act: so it could be crudely paraphrased as 'you have forgotten me now; so go on, forget me completely when I am dead', with all the claims to attention that such extremes of abjection invariably make. This poem also, like many in the sequence, plays with different audiences. It sets off an intimacy of address to a single person, who implicitly knows the anterior circumstances of the poem, against the distance created by addressing a readership in print. 'If you read this line' to the intimate audience of one means 'these poems are ephemeral and although they are testaments of love, well, I know that you won't even bother to read them' (and it is tempting to add to that paraphrase a parenthetical '(sniff)'). To a print readership it starts out from the page: 'this intimate record has somehow come to you, and you do not fully know who the "you" to whom it was addressed might be; and you, responding to this poem not as a manuscript epistle but as a printed monument, are right on my side because you know that these poems are valuable and not ephemeral at all.' So the very delicate balance of the poem between an abjection which is potentially manipulative and a dignified pride in the worth of verse comes from the implicit presence of two (at least) groups of readers. There is also a magical effacing of that pride even as it is asserted: do not rehearse my name even as you read it, says a poem which sits, a touch proudly perhaps, under the running title 'SHAKE-SPEARES SONNETS'. It manages to be an ephemeral epistle asking for oblivion, and a claim for emotional attention, and a claim to be remembered and something approaching a monument. This sonnet, in common with many, addresses a multitude of both anterior and posterior circumstances, and seems as a result to be designed for an amphibian life between readers who know about its circumstantial origins and those who can only speculate about them. It resonates with the bibliographic puzzle prompted by Thorpe's setting forth of the Sonnets: are we hearing a private poem which has been stolen into print, or a public monument to selfless love?

Many of the poems in the group 1–126 which since Malone have been treated as poems to a 'young man' carefully skirt around even giving a fixed gender to their addressee. These poems enable their readers to feel the lure of homoerotic attraction, the pull of ethical admiration, the power of love, and the underpresences of fear, hurt, and disappointment which are the darker side of worship. The poems partly ask their readers to imagine persons or a set of circumstances which would give rise to the poems; but they also ask their readers to hear them as a voice seeking its own bearings in relation to what it desires. 'The young man' of biographical critics, in his doublet with his roses and his golden curls and his country estate, is never actually called the 'young man' in this group of poems, several of which are about how hard it is to define their addressee. There is a 'youth', 'sweet boy' and 'friend', a 'thou' and a 'you' and a 'he'. Each of these terms has its own register, and most of them are notably double: a 'friend' can be a lover as well as a moral equal and confidant; 'thou' can be respectfully poetic, contemptuous, or intimate, and can embrace both a fictional addressee and a reader in bonds of intimacy; 'sweet boy' (108.5) carries a strong claim to closeness (the phrase is used by Falstaff just before Hal rejects him: part of what happens in that scene is that the older friend oversteps the mark by using such an intimate address in public (*2 Henry IV* 5.3.43–5)). The addressee is a different thing depending on how he or she is addressed, and on how the epithet by which he or she is addressed is inflected in its context. To impose a single scenario on the poems is to deny this vital poetic fact. The commentary to this edition uses 'the friend' as a shorthand way of referring to the addressee of poems before 127; this is not part of an attempt to reduce the manifest erotic energy of these poems into a laddish companionship, or to fix the ungendering delights of the poems: 'friend' can mean mistress or male companion in this period, and is a double-gendered word in the way in which many of the poems are double-gendered. The 'friend' drifts in and out of material being. Part of the poet's frustration and delight with his object of desire is that it will not be one thing:

> What is your substance, whereof are you made
> That millions of strange shadows on you tend?
>
> (53.1–2)

Here, as so often in the Sonnets, the super-charging of metaphor and the packing in of sense on sense make multiple realities converge and dissolve into each other: 'substance' can mean 'material being'; it can also mean 'wealth'. 'Shadows' can mean 'representations'; it can also mean 'ghosts', or 'servile followers'. The friend is rich and thronged with toadies; he is a beauty so dazzling that he can only be represented as being better than his representations; he is also a ghostly fantasy. The boyish Adonis, and the loveliest woman, Helen of Troy, are his shadows. He is many things, material and immaterial, including, quite often, a sort of she.

What sort of she? This leads to one of the most contentious areas in the interpretation of the Sonnets. Does the sequence describe a homoerotic attachment which is physically consummated? Does it indicate that Shakespeare was a homosexual?[1] What has been said so far should make it clear these are the wrong questions to ask: the poems flirt with but refuse to be fixed in settings, and they wonder about the boundaries between sexual desire, love, and admiration. They are also the wrong sort of question to put to poems of this period.[2] The 'thou's and 'you's of the poem's address resist these fixities: they skate across time, addressing now an intimate audience of one, now the reader directly, and at other points they speak out to future ages.[3] 'Shakespeare's homosexuality' is a readerly fiction generated by a desire to read narrative coherence into a loosely associated group of poems: the poems present a multiplicity of structural patterns and overlapping groups and semi-sequences. To fix their sexuality is to seek to lock them in, where most, perhaps, they seek to be free.

Still, a poet who refers to his addressee as 'sweet boy' and 'my lovely boy' does raise questions which go beyond simple curiosity about the decorum of different modes of address. What kind of thing was love between men in the late Elizabethan period? Twentieth-century language for describing sexual behaviour (and

[1] Joseph Pequigney, *Such Is My Love: A Study of Shakespeare's Sonnets* (Chicago and London, 1985), puts the case strongly; more subtly inflected is Bruce R. Smith, *Homosexual Desire in Shakespeare's England* (Chicago and London, 1991), 228–65.

[2] See Peter Stallybrass, 'Editing as Cultural Formation: The Sexing of Shakespeare's Sonnets', *Modern Language Quarterly* 54 (1993), 91–103.

[3] On pronouns see Andrew Gurr, 'You and Thou in Shakespeare's Sonnets', *Essays in Criticism* 32 (1982), 9–25, and Bruce R. Smith, 'I, You, He, She, and We: On the Sexual Politics of Shakespeare's Sonnets', in Schiffer, ed., *Shakespeare's Sonnets*, 411–29.

even our tendency to prioritize sex as a leading human drive) does not fit the behaviour, or (which is all we have) the representations of behaviour of late sixteenth-century males. No one in the early modern period would have defined themself as a homosexual, since the word only entered English in medical contexts in the 1890s; indeed, no one in the period would have sought to define their identity by their sexual activity.[1] The language for describing same-sex sexual activity in the late sixteenth century is full of what seem to us to be gaps. That language is richest in epithets for passive, and usually by implication junior, partners: the coyly mythological 'Ganymede' and the slangy 'ingle' are both used of the recipients of sexual favours from more senior and more powerful men. The act of intercourse between men was often described by the violently pejorative 'sodomy' and 'buggery', which were crimes punishable by death, and accusations of which were frequently linked with accusations of bestiality and treason.[2] Enemies of the state and Catholic enemies of the state religion were likely also to be called 'sodomites'. Christopher Marlowe was accused by the government informer Richard Baines of having said that 'all who love not tobacco and boys were fools' and that 'St John the Evangelist was bedfellow to Christ and leaned always in his bosom, that he used him as the sinners of Sodoma'.[3] This does not tell us what Marlowe may have said, but what a government informer thought an enemy of the people should have said: such a person would combine heresy with sodomy, and might well have the mark of the devil on his body too. Playhouses were also widely represented, by their enemies at any rate, as sites of sodomy: so in Ben Jonson's *Poetaster* the father of Ovid learns that his son is to become a player and cries, 'What! Shall I have my son a stager now? An engle for players?'[4] The puritan Philip Stubbes thundered that once plays were over 'every mate sorts to his mate, everyone brings another homeward of their way very friendly, and in their secret conclaves

---

[1] See Alan Bray, *Homosexuality in Renaissance England*, 2nd edn. (New York, 1995), 16, and Smith, *Homosexual Desire*, 10–11.

[2] 25 Henry VIII c. 6 made sodomy a capital offence and linked it with Catholicism; the law against sodomy was made perpetual in 32 Henry VIII c. 3 (1540) and revived in 5 Eliz. c. 17.

[3] F. C. Danchin, 'Études critiques sur Christopher Marlowe', *Revue Germanique* 9 (1913), 570–2.

[4] *Poetaster*, ed. Tom Cain (Manchester, 1995), 1.2.15–16.

covertly they play the sodomites or worse'.[1] Stubbes, though, who hated plays and players, is no neutral witness, and does not specify the gender of those who 'play the sodomites': the term can encompass almost any sexual malpractice in the period (and it has been suggested that the real 'sodomy', in the early modern sense of transgressive sexual abuse, that goes on in Shakespeare's Sonnets is the adulterous liaison between the poet and the mistress).[2] The relishing engagement of the desires of a predominantly male audience for the boys who took women's parts in the plays of the period, however, does suggest that one of the pleasures of theatre-going was to test and query cultural expectations about whom one should desire.[3] The theatre is, indeed, the only institution in the period which can have any claim to have fostered anything which remotely resembled a same-sex subculture.

But in early modern England male friends shared books, beds, and occasionally also women (and in the Universities it was common practice for students to share sleeping quarters with their Tutors). Men embraced and kissed each other with far greater freedom than most Anglo-Saxon males do now. Such relationships could be presented by hostile outsiders as the outward indices of sodomy. As we have seen, Reynolds had claimed that Shakespeare's patron the Earl of Southampton was a close friend of one Piers Edmonds in 1601 while he was Commander of the Horse under Essex in Ireland, and clearly wished to insinuate that the two were sexual partners.[4] It is impossible at this historical distance to separate whatever physical intimacy Southampton and Edmonds may have shared from the malice of their reporter. Since sodomy was a capital offence, capital could be made out of alleging that an enemy engaged in it. Certainly, though, in learned circles there was a live acquaintance with Hellenic tolerance of pederasty.[5] Philemon Holland's translation of Plutarch's discourse 'On Love' from the *Moralia* begins by warning that 'This dialogue is more

[1] *The Anatomie of Abuses* (1583), sig. L8[v].

[2] Jonathan Goldberg, ed., *Queering the English Renaissance* (Durham NC and London, 1994), 6; de Grazia, 'The Scandal'.

[3] See Stephen Orgel, *Impersonations: The Performance of Gender in Shakespeare's England* (Cambridge, 1996), esp. 53–82.

[4] See above, p. 14.

[5] On the Hellenic roots of this tradition, see K. J. Dover, *Greek Homosexuality* (New York, 1980). For early Christian attitudes to homosexuality, see John Boswell, *Christianity, Social Tolerance and Homosexuality* (Chicago, 1980).

dangerous to be read by young men than any other treatise by
Plutarch, for that there be certain glances here and there against
honest marriage, to uphold indirectly and underhand, the cursed
and detestable filthiness covertly couched under the name of the
love of young boys'.[1] Plutarch's father in the dialogue eventually
puts forward orthodox Platonic arguments that love directs the
lover through the earthly to the divine; but on the way to ortho-
doxy we hear a variety of enthusiastic speakers praise the love of
boys as a higher form of love, as in the anonymous fragment which
one speaker quotes:

> So often as these eyes of mine behold
> That beardless youth, that smooth and lovely boy,
> I faint, I fall: then wish I him to held
> Within mine arms, and so to die with joy.[2]

Richard Barnfield, whose *Affectionate Shepherd* appeared in 1594,
wrote in similarly explicit terms of a love for a young boy called
Ganymede. In the Greek Romance *Clitophon and Leucippe*, trans-
lated in 1597 and dedicated to Shakespeare's patron the Earl of
Southampton, there is also a frank argument in favour of the
delights of boys rather than women. Literary traditions also gave
rich prominence to uncertainty over gender. Shakespeare drew the
tale of *Venus and Adonis* from Book 10 of the *Metamorphoses*, which
is related by the singer Orpheus, who, after the loss of his wife
Eurydice, has turned his attentions to boys. The *Metamorphoses* is
much preoccupied by likenesses and similitudes, and in Book 10
homoerotic affection is presented as a desire to be the other: when
Jove sees Ganymede Ovid says, 'et inventum est aliquid, quod
Iuppiter esse, | quam quod erat, mallet' (literally, 'something was
found which Jupiter would rather be than himself').[3] That yearn-
ing to be outside of oneself and to become a mirror image of the
object of desire plays a large part in the poetics of the Sonnets, from
the early allusions to the story of Narcissus to the later efforts to
resemble the beloved.

Same-sex relations in early modern England could be read
within a number of different and incompatible traditions, from the
political (according to which they were monstrous) to the Hellenic

---

[1] Plutarch, trans. Philemon Holland, *The Philosophy, Commonly Called the Morals*
(1603), 1130.

[2] Plutarch, *The Philosophy*, 1155.   [3] *Met* 10.156–7.

(which could present them as the highest form of love). This leads to a key aspect of the Sonnets. The sequence is extraordinarily responsive to areas of language and human conduct which are trespassed on by many different discourses and points of view. It delights in hybridizing many different areas of language, from the language of patronage to the language of love, from the language of householding to the language of the law. The form of sexuality presented in the Sonnets feeds off all the various ways of writing about love between men in this period, and delights in their incompatibility. It consequently upsets several dominant paradigms. One widespread model of same-sex affection in the period is of a social superior and older man who supports a younger social inferior, whom he might adopt as his favourite, whose career he might advance, and to whom he might give a place in his bed. The Greek model of pederastic love would have it that such relationships were stable until the younger partner began to grow a beard and to mature into a man.[1] The Sonnets begin with an experimental reversal of this form of relationship, in which the poet is older than and socially inferior to his addressee, and yet adopts the tone of a father or adviser to the young man. Sonnets *1–17*, which urge a youth to marry, repeatedly echo the sage authority of Erasmus, as though seeking to turn his cultural authority into social standing. And the socially inferior poet's authority over the 'lovely boy' grows as the sequence moves forward, as his immortalizing art comes to offer a physical permanence which the addressee himself, insistent on not breeding, cannot hope to achieve.

The Sonnets work on what many people in the period would have believed about same-sex love, and they work at every level by seductively fusing together a number of voices which will not comfortably be fused. To bear this in mind helps in reading the flirtatious suggestiveness of Sonnet *20*, which is quite as much a readerly poem as it is a poem about sexuality:

> A woman's face with nature's own hand painted,
> Hast thou, the master mistress of my passion;
> A woman's gentle heart, but not acquainted
> With shifting change as is false women's fashion;
> An eye more bright than theirs, less false in rolling,
> Gilding the object whereupon it gazeth;

---

[1] Plutarch, *The Philosophy*, 1157.

> A man in hue, all hues in his controlling,
> Which steals men's eyes and women's souls amazeth.
> And for a woman wert thou first created,
> Till Nature as she wrought thee fell a-doting,
> And by addition me of thee defeated,
> By adding one thing to my purpose nothing.
>> But since she pricked thee out for women's pleasure,
>> Mine be thy love, and thy love's use their treasure.

The games being played by this sonnet, which is the poetical equivalent of a broad wink, are multiple. One game is in its feminine rhymes (rhymes on two syllables in which the last is unstressed and hypermetrical). This form of rhyme was by 1600 gendered feminine, and often clusters at moments of transgressive passion. So Sir John Harington's translation of Ariosto's tale about a judge who agrees to be buggered by a Negro reaches its climax in a feminine rhyme:

> In fine, he made to him the like request
> As Sodomites did make for guests of Lot;
> The Judge his motion doth and him detest,
> Who though five times repulsed, yet ceaseth not,
> But him with so large offers still he pressed,
> That in conclusion, like a beastly sot,
> So as it might be done, in hugger mugger,
> The Judge agreed, the Negro him should (——).[1]

Buggery, for good politic reasons, is replaced by a dashing substitute for a feminine rhyme. Shakespeare's Sonnet *20* is also playing games with register and structure, and offers punning substitutes for Harington's dash: it comes very shortly after the poems which urge marriage and reproduction. It also comes on the heels of the first poem in the sequence to address a 'you', a form of address which probably makes claim for intimacy and equality.[2] The sober Erasmian counsellor of *1–17* metamorphoses into a sexual punster: the addressee is 'pricked out' in the sense of being given a prick, and in the sense of being chosen, and has 'one thing', a penis, which is 'to my purpose nothing'. 'Nothing' can mean a vagina; it can also mean 'something of no importance at all'. The

[1] Sir John Harington, trans., *Orlando Furioso*, ed. R. McNulty (Oxford, 1972), 43.133.
[2] Gurr, 'You and Thou'.

puns are fed by the uncertainty about the kind of person who is being addressed. Is it to a woman, a 'master mistress' in the sense of a mistress who completely controls the poet? The jolt in pronoun to 'A man in hue all hues in *his* controlling' shifts the gender malewards, but also away from direct address. And 'for a woman' makes gender hang on a preposition: 'for' means 'to be with a woman', but also 'to be a woman'. The final lines, which appear to disavow sexual interest in the person (who has by the end of the poem clearly become a male), will not let the game rest: the Quarto spelling allows for the possibility that the poet enjoys the sexual favours of the friend:

> But since she prickt thee out for womens pleasure,
> Mine be thy loue and thy loues vse their treasure.

As Stephen Orgel puts it, 'In this reading, "But" signals a reversal of the argument, and means "on the other hand": the "womens pleasure" the friend is "pricked out for" (i.e. selected for: see *OED* 5. prick III 15) is not the pleasure he gives women but his ability to take pleasure as women do; "loves" in the last line is then not a possessive but a plural, and "use" is a verb—the line without its modern apostrophe need not be a renunciation at all: "let my love be yours, and let your loves make use of their treasure."'[1] Strained? Maybe. But Shakespeare is in the Sonnets still the poet of *Venus and Adonis*, urging his readers to make it lewd, to stray towards the 'bottom grass'. Local mobilities of sense shift the reality from which the poems seem to spring. The only way to grasp the circumambient reality is to grasp hold of the totality of the poem's possible senses. And the range of possible senses is so broad that to grasp at it makes any single circumambient reality dissolve.

So should readers of the Sonnets give up on the real pleasure and the real and liberating disturbance which comes from thinking that Shakespeare was homosexual? Yes and no. The poems are printed poems 'to his private friends'. As we have seen, they call on their readers to take on the receptive stance of two audiences: a coterie audience who might know exactly what was going on (but who also might only be an ideal and imaginary audience created by the rhetoric of the volume's setting forth), and a print audience for whom 'William Shakespeare' is only an alluring name on a title-

---

[1] Orgel, *Impersonations*, 57.

page. They actively encourage their readers to imagine circumstances which would fit the poems, but they multiply the figures of multiple sense, paronomasia and antanaclasis, the more frenziedly the closer they get to sexual activity: in 136 the puns on 'will' climax as the poet teasingly makes his own name mean the sexual organs of both sexes and sexual desire ('Will will fulfil the treasure of thy love, | Ay, fill it full with wills, and my will one'). The closer the poems come to a carnal revelation, the more involved their resistance to final exposure becomes, and the more insistently their words resist the imposition of a single sense upon them.

And this is true of the poems' treatment of male–female sexual relations as well as their treatment of male–male relationships. The 'Dark Lady', like 'the Young Man', is never in the Sonnets called by the name she has been given by critical tradition. And that name is a noxious piece of pseudo-gentility: the mistress is called the 'dark lady' by the prurient in order to make her sound both sexy and upper-crust, and (within careful racially determined limits)[1] exotic. She is, rather, a complicated poetic creation, and like the 'friend' is a different sort of thing in different poems. Sometimes she is the negatively imagined loveable thing which escapes poetic conventions ('My mistress' eyes are nothing like the sun'); she may be the player on the virginals (no gender is specified for that poem) in 128 who is seen, but touched only by the imagination; she lies (in every sense); she may have venereal disease. She is usually addressed as 'thou' in the poems, and the pronoun can carry some contempt when it is used of her. She is referred to as 'the mistress' in the commentary, and that word, like 'friend', carries a range of senses: it can mean 'the woman who commands my affection' as well as 'the woman who illicitly takes the place of a wife'. Her role is slightly different in each poem, and there is no particular reason to think of her as one person. Her (or their) role in the sequence is to triangulate desire, in every sense of 'triangulate': the presence of a female outside the close and mostly male bonds of the earlier poems makes the love triangular; it also negatively defines and shapes the contours of the male–male love.[2] Rivalry is one of the forces at the heart of the sequence: Shakespeare attempts a longer and more

[1] See Marvin Hunt, 'Be Dark But Not Too Dark: Shakespeare's Dark Lady as a Sign of Colour', in Schiffer, ed., *Shakespeare's Sonnets*, 369–89.

[2] See Eve Kosofsky Sedgwick, *Between Men: English Literature and Male Homosocial Desire* (New York, 1985), 28–48.

complicated sequence than many earlier English sonneteers, and he makes rivalry between lovers and between poets a central element in the actions described in the sequence.[1] Losing someone to a rival is the point at which you love them most, and the point too at which it is most in your interests to think that they are not worth the effort of mourning; and it is this experience of loss as a provocation to desire which lies at the centre of the final poems in the sequence.

The poems after *126* are much less carefully ordered than the preceding group. They do not show obvious signs of having been positioned for numerological effect, although word-links and rhyme ties among this group are stronger than they would be if the sequence were randomly ordered.[2] Several poems in this very disparate group, though, dwell explicitly on the ways in which love can make the world seem different from how it is, even though the lover knows that the world is not in fact how love makes it appear. In this respect the poems to the mistress seem to sharpen and clarify some of the problems explored earlier in the sequence: the misrelation between the poet's desire to praise the young man and the ill deeds which he performs becomes in the later poems a stark triad of oppositions between the perceived 'fairness' of the mistress, her physical darkness, and her dark deeds. The 'dark' mistress who is 'fair' to the poet is more likely to be a product of Shakespeare's interest in how love changes the way the world is perceived than to be a fictional version of an actual woman with whom he had an affair. In the world of a sonnet a word of praise can transform a world of experience, turning dark to fair and vice versa, and the last poems in the sequence are bitterly self-conscious about this fact. Sonnet *152* is the dark outer reach of the poems to the mistress, and seems to mark the emergence in the sequence of a form of subjectivity founded on perpetual alienation between the poet and the object of love:

> For I have sworn deep oaths of thy deep kindness,
> Oaths of thy love, thy truth, thy constancy,
> And to enlighten thee gave eyes to blindness,

---

[1] See the perceptive discussion of what she terms 'diacritical desire', or the effort to make distinctions between male and female, self and other, in Dubrow, *Echoes of Desire*.

[2] Jackson, 'Aspects of Organisation'.

> Or made them swear against the thing they see.
> For I have sworn thee fair: more perjured eye,
> To swear against the truth so foul a lie.

The eye of love and the eye of knowledge are at war here, and praise becomes a self-deceit which the poet can simply condemn as perjury. This poem sharpens and hardens the division, which grows in Sonnets *104–26*, between the way the poet values the young man and the way the world responds to him (and we have seen how Shakespeare explores the disjunction between the world as it is and the world as the lover wants it to appear as early as the end of *Venus and Adonis*). Sonnet *152* seems to imply that the sequence has finally decided that it is centrally about a division between eye and heart, between what a lover wants to believe and what he knows is true.

Several influential interpretations of the sequence have seen in the sub-sequence *127–52* the core of the whole work. Joel Fineman's extremely influential *Shakespeare's Perjured Eye* presents the whole sequence as leading to this final disjunction between eye and truth, between praise and its object. He argues that the poems of praise to the young man press for a narcissistic identification between poet and subject, and for an identity between language and its object. This issues in the tautology of praise ('Therefore my verse, to constancy confined, | One thing expressing, leaves out difference. | "Fair, kind, and true" is all my argument, | "Fair, kind, and true" varying to other words', *105.7–10*). This simple relationship, Fineman argues, breaks down in the sequence to the mistress, which explores a split between praise and its object, and between the poet and his subject. For Fineman this shift of emphasis marks the transition from the Lacanian imaginary (which is founded on a narcissistic desire for the same) to the Lacanian symbolic (which grows from a recognition that the world is not as the subject desires it to be, and which plunges the subject into endless desire for the other). He also sees this phase of the sequence, in a radical (and radically unconvincing) extension of his argument, as marking the emergence of modern poetic consciousness.[1] Margreta de Grazia has argued for the significance and value of the poems to the mistress on the rather different grounds that they contain the real

[1] Joel Fineman, *Shakespeare's Perjured Eye: The Invention of Poetic Subjectivity in the Sonnets* (Berkeley, Los Angeles, and London, 1986).

'scandal' of Shakespeare's Sonnets: they dramatize an adulterous desire for a black woman which unstitches social and gender relations in a way in which the earlier deferential affection for the young man does not. Primogeniture, racial order, and social order, are all, in de Grazia's view, finally questioned by the poems to the mistress: 'The scandal in the Sonnets has been misidentified. It is not Shakespeare's desire for a boy; for in upholding social distinctions, that desire proves quite conservative and safe. It is Shakespeare's gynerastic longings for a black mistress that are perverse and menacing, precisely because they threaten to raze the very distinctions his poems to the fair boy strain to preserve.'[1]

These arguments are thought-provoking responses to the sequence of poems as it appears in the Quarto, which invites its readers to take 127–52 as conclusions to the sequence in argument as they are to its arrangement. But if it is true (and it is in my view so probable as to amount to a moral certainty) that the sub-sequence 127–52 includes the earliest poems to have been written, then both of these influential arguments should be slightly retuned. The stylometric and external evidence suggests that Shakespeare *began* work in the 1590s on poems addressed to a consciously unorthodox sort of mistress. The poems in this group focus sharply on distinctions between what the poet sees and what is, and as a result they seem far simpler than many of the poems before 126. They read more like a starting-point than a conclusion. Sonnet 138, one of the two sonnets to appear in *The Passionate Pilgrim* of 1599, ends on a note of throwaway world-weary acceptance that lovers lie with each other and to each other. It does so in a third-person reflective mode which is unusual in sonnets positioned earlier in the sequence:

> O, love's best habit is in seeming trust,
> And age in love loves not to have years told.
> Therefore I lie with her, and she with me,
> And in our faults by lies we flattered be.

This is sharp and bright, and is trying so hard to be worldly that it succeeds only in belonging to the world of those who are trying to be 'worldly'. It suggests a phase of composition which was concentrating on a set of problems about the relationships between praise

---

[1] De Grazia, 'The Scandal', 48.

and poetry, and between what we want to believe and what we know to be the case. These questions are treated as a third-person set of problems to be explored in the form of paradoxes (which were a voguish form for fashionable writers in the mid-to-late 1590s). Had Shakespeare stopped work on the sequence at this point in its composition it would have been brightly paradoxical. But it would not have been remembered except as a literary experiment which resembled the games played with the conventions of the love sonnet in *Love's Labour's Lost*.

What makes the sequence permanently valuable is that this early interest in divisions between belief and knowledge carries over into the chronologically later poems, many of which present themselves as being addressed (once more) to what readers would recognize as the 'wrong' sort of person: a young, nobly born man. In this later body of work the things which the poet wishes to say in praise of his addressee and what he recognizes to be true about him are intertangled to the point of anguished inseparability. Critics who value the poems to the mistress above those to the young man tend to regard the earlier poems in the sequence as simply poems of praise, or tokens of a desire for males to bond with males to the exclusion of the feminine.[1] They are wrong to do so. The poems which praise the young man painfully do not, as Fineman would have them, identify the lover with his object and deny difference, except in the exceptional hymn to tautology which is *105*. Rather they bring about a dramatic interaction between what is said in praise of the young man and the events which seem to surround what is said. They try to praise while gesturing towards circumstances which make praise untrue. If anywhere in the sequence Shakespeare 'invented modern consciousness' (and my suspicion is that coal, steel, and Descartes played a stronger part in the emergence of whatever this strange thing might be than any poet did) he did so in the poems to the young man. These poems fuse voices of desperate praise together with an anguished desire to condemn in a way that seems semi-consciously to be repressing the desire to condemn the beloved.

And this fusion of voices occurs above all in the final and finest group of poems to the young man (and they are latest both in their

[1] So Sedgwick, *Between Men*, 41, overstates the case considerably when she says: 'The Sonnets' poetic goes to almost any length to treat the youth as a moral monolith; while the very definition of the lady seems to be doubleness and deceit.'

sequence in Q and probably too in order of composition), 104–26. These poems make two truths or three truths coexist in the same work, and suggest that they are all blocked from recognition of each other. Several of these poems are also far more radical in their implicit social and political stance than any of the poems to the mistress, since they give the poet an unexpected power over the person he praises, inverting the expected relation of poet and patron and of lover and unmovable beloved. Your abject servant knows just what the nobleman is up to, and by the end of the sequence he has done whatever it is too; and, moreover, he has done it back to his insouciant lover:

> That you were once unkind befriends me now,
> And for that sorrow, which I then did feel,
> Needs must I under my transgression bow,
> Unless my nerves were brass or hammered steel.
> For if you were by my unkindness shaken,
> As I by yours, y' have passed a hell of time,
> And I, a tyrant, have no leisure taken
> To weigh how once I suffered in your crime.
> O that our night of woe might have rememb'red
> My deepest sense how hard true sorrow hits,
> And soon to you, as you to me then, tend'red
> The humble salve, which wounded bosom fits!
>   But that your trespass now becomes a fee;
>   Mine ransoms yours, and yours must ransom me.
>   (120)

Sonnet 120 does not allow the poet simply to identify with the friend, nor does it allow its speaker or its reader a firm grip on a single state of mind which he shares with the object of his devotion. The smooth integration of reconciliation and memory of past separations which the poem proffers makes it appear to be a simple poem of apology. But there is a sort of glory in the thought that it is time to be paid back for the friend's former 'unkindness', and in the thought that the poet through his very insouciance might have become a tyrant over his love: 'you owe me, you hurt me; now it is time to be paid back', is one strand in the poem's voice. But that potential vengefulness is qualified by the conjectural and hypothetical belief that the friend only *might* have suffered in the same way as the speaker has done: 'For *if* you were by my unkindness shaken, | As I by yours. . . .' The sonnet comes at a crucially important phase in the sequence, six poems before Sonnet 126 reminds the friend that his debt to nature will be paid by his death, and after a period in which the sequence has dwelt on the past. It is a poem which radically (and the word has a social inflection here) shifts the earlier relationship between the speaker and the young man: it both grants the poet 'power to hurt' and demands reciprocal suffering. And it may win a reciprocal hurt from its implied noble addressee—unless the friend is insensible, which he may be. This is the central point of differentiation between the poems to the mistress and those to the young man: in the poems to the mistress the poet *knows* she is untrue and that he is deceiving himself, and says as much; in the poems to the young man, on the other hand, knowledge is blurred and diffracted by self-persuasion that things might be otherwise than they appear, and by the actual opacity of the friend's emotion. The friend is never a narcissistic mirror of the poet's desire: even when the poet seems to be victorious over him, the victory is shadowed by the dark, uncertain question 'Does he feel like me? Has he felt anything like the pain I have felt?'

This is not a simple form of panegyric from which the poems to the mistress develop. It is the reverse. It is a complex exploration of how love can only be accommodated by blending voices of praise and dispraise around a love-object whose conduct and nature and sensibility are unknowable. And it is too a form of social scandal greater than the poet's love of a dark woman: a lowly poet, who begins sounding like a schoolmaster paid by a noble family to advise their son to marry, seems in the course of the sequence to have metamorphosed himself into a wounder and a victor, and to have turned himself almost into a version of a Petrarchan mistress who causes pain by insouciant misconduct. He is possessed of a wealth of suffering which can 'ransom' his wealthy beloved. By the time Shakespeare came to write the later sonnets to the friend he was writing in a mode where mere doubleness of perception seemed too little and too easy. What he came to recognize was that by positioning a poem of apparent praise in a setting which creates implicit doubt about the addressee's desert he could evoke not two realities, but a range of possible worlds which changed with a shift in emphasis on a single word. In learning that art he built on *Venus and Adonis*, *Lucrece*, and 'Let the bird of loudest lay', in which speaker and setting are made dynamically to shift in their relationship to each other; he also learnt from the sonnets to the mistress.

But he made from them something greater than any of these earlier works: poems in which praise and dispraise restlessly mingle and fuse, and in which love and praise and obeisance will not be separated cleanly from hurt, and a desire to hurt back.

The Sonnets have had a hard press. 'And as to their ultimate drift, as for myself, I can make neither head nor tail of it.'[1] So William Hazlitt on the Sonnets in 1821. The collection has had more scorn poured on it than any other work by Shakespeare with the possible exception of *Titus Andronicus*: for Wordsworth in around 1803 the Sonnets 'are abominably harsh, obscure, and worthless'[2] (though he was later to say that 'in no part of the writings of this Poet is found, in an equal compass, a greater number of exquisite feelings felicitously expressed');[3] Landor found 'much condensation, little delicacy' in them, 'like raspberry jam without cream, without crust';[4] for George Steevens, justifying his omission of the poems from his edition of 1793, 'the strongest act of Parliament that could be framed, would fail to compel readers into their service'.[5] The abuse was revived by John Crowe Ransom in 1938: 'generally they are ill-constructed'.[6] They are not easy poems. They thwart readers' desires to know, and they do so artfully and with a systematic elusiveness which can be frustrating. They are not confessional, and they do not give any insights into the heart of Shakespeare or what he did in the bedroom. But in their continual counterpointing of language against implied circumstance they are the culmination of Shakespeare's career as a poet.

A Lover's Complaint

Date and Attribution. The last eleven pages of *SHAKE-SPEARES SONNETS* are devoted to *A Lovers Complaint BY WILLIAM SHAKE-SPEARE* (sigs. K1ᵛ–L2ᵛ). The poem is in the same rhyme royal

[1] 'On Milton's Sonnets', in *Table Talk* (1821); quoted in the still valuable collection *Shakespeare: The Sonnets*, ed. Peter Jones (1977), 48.

[2] Marginalia to Robert Anderson's *Poets of Great Britain*, quoted in Jones, ed., *Shakespeare: The Sonnets*, 41.

[3] *Essay Supplementary to the Preface to 'Lyrical Ballads'*, quoted in Jones, ed., *Shakespeare: The Sonnets*, 43.

[4] *Imaginary Conversations*, Third Series (1828) from 'Southey and Landor', quoted in Jones, ed., *Shakespeare: The Sonnets*, 49.

[5] Quoted in Rollins 2, ii.337–8, from The Advertisement to the Plays of William Shakespeare (1793).

[6] 'Shakespeare at Sonnets', in *The World's Body* (New York, 1938), 273.

stanza as *Lucrece*, but contains no fewer than forty-nine words or forms not otherwise found in Shakespeare's works, including a number of archaisms. Malone had no doubts that the poem was by Shakespeare: 'In this beautiful poem, in every part of which the hand of Shakespeare is visible, he perhaps meant to break a lance with Spenser. It appears to me to have more of the simplicity and pathetic tenderness of the elder poet, in his smaller pieces, than any other poem of that time.'[1] Later critics were reluctant to accept Thorpe's attribution, chiefly because the poem was felt to be stiff and awkward in style and construction: its language is often compressed, and its initial frame, in which a narrator sees a young woman complaining on a hill, is never closed at the end.[2]

A body of convincing work in the sixties by Kenneth Muir and MacDonald P. Jackson, however, definitively ended discussion about the poem's attribution:[3] after the work of Hart it became widely recognized that canonical works by Shakespeare are distinguished by their willingness to absorb new vocabulary, to make new verbs from nouns, and to coin compound adjectives.[4] All of those features are present in *A Lover's Complaint*, which also showed strong links in vocabulary and theme with other works by Shakespeare. Since the majority of these connections are with works composed after 1600—critics have found parallels with Bertram and Helena in *All's Well that Ends Well*, between the 'reverend man' who hears the young woman's confession and the Duke in *Measure for Measure*, as well as significant word-links with

[1] Malone 1790, x.371.

[2] J. W. Mackail, 'A Lover's Complaint', *Essays and Studies* 3 (1912), 51–70.

[3] Kenneth Muir, '"A Lover's Complaint": A Reconsideration', in Edward A. Bloom, ed., *Shakespeare 1564–1964* (Providence, RI, 1964), 154–66; reprinted in *Shakespeare the Professional and Related Studies* (London, 1973), 204–19; MacDonald P. Jackson, *Shakespeare's 'A Lover's Complaint': Its Date and Authenticity*, University of Auckland Bulletin 72, English Series 13 (Auckland, 1965). The attribution has been question on stylometric grounds in W. E. Y. Elliot and R. J. Valenza, 'Glass Slippers and Seven-League Boots: Computer-aided Tests, Donald Foster, Claremont-Shakespeare-Clinic: C-prompted Doubts about Ascribing A "Funeral Elegy" and A "Lover's Complaint" to Shakespeare', *Shakespeare Quarterly* 48 (1997), 177–207.

[4] Alfred Hart, 'Vocabularies of Shakespeare's Plays' and 'The Growth of Shakespeare's Vocabulary', *RES* 19 (1943), 128–40 and 242–54. Studies of *A Lover's Complaint* deriving from Hart include Eliot Slater, 'Shakespeare: Word Links between Poems and Plays', *NQ* 220 (1975), 157–63; A. K. Hieatt, T. G. Bishop, and E. A. Nicholson, 'Shakespeare's Rare Words: "Lover's Complaint", *Cymbeline*, and *Sonnets*', *NQ* 232 (1987), 219–24.

Cymbeline[1]—the former orthodoxy that the poem was early and unformed work died the death it deserved. Brilliant critical and literary historical work by John Kerrigan, who was the first editor to see that the poem is integrally connected to the sonnet sequence it follows, has brought the poem to life as *echt* Shakespeare.[2] The date of the poem is still debated: stylometric evidence suggests that it had at least touches of Shakespeare's hand quite shortly before its publication in 1609, but that it may well have been begun as much as a decade before. If this is so (and the evidence is hard to interpret given that the language of the poem is in general so untypical of Shakespeare, and so rich in archaic forms), then the poem may have had the same kind of extended genesis as the Sonnets.

The Poem and its Context. There is no doubt that *A Lover's Complaint* belongs where it is found in the Quarto, as a coda to the Sonnets. Sonnet sequences are frequently followed by poems which modulate their obsessively close attention on the anguish of a male lover into other literary kinds: Samuel Daniel's *Delia* (1592) is followed by *The Complaint of Rosamond*, Lodge's *Phillis* (1593) is followed by *The Tragical Complaint of Elstred*, Spenser's *Epithalamion* follows his *Amoretti* (1595). These poems give their readers a final extra meditation on sexual desire and its consequences, which sits questioningly beside the sonnet form. The sonnet sequence in the late sixteenth century invited a consideration of love from a variety of perspectives and in a variety of generic forms. The triangle which *A Lover's Complaint* presents—an old man, a young woman, a seductive and rhetorically skilled young man (as well as an anonymous narrator)—recalls in shadowy form the triangular relationship between older poet, mistress, and dangerously seductive young man in the Sonnets. Even the poem's failure to close its

---

[1] Roger Warren, '"A Lover's Complaint", "All's Well", and The Sonnets', *NQ* 215 (1970), 130–2; Roger Warren, 'Why Does it End Well? Helena, Bertram and the Sonnets', *Shakespeare Survey* 22 (1969), 79–92; Richard Allan Underwood, *Shakespeare on Love: The Poems and the Plays. Prolegomena to a Variorum Edition of 'A Lover's Complaint'*, Salzburg Studies in English Literature, Elizabethan and Renaissance Studies 91 (Salzburg, 1985); Hieatt *et al.*, 'Shakespeare's Rare Words'; MacDonald P. Jackson, 'Echoes of Spenser's *Prothalamion* as Evidence Against an Early Date for Shakespeare's *A Lover's Complaint*', *NQ* 235 (1990), 180–2; Kerrigan 2, 39–40.

[2] Kerrigan 2, 39–51.

initial frame, in which a narrator watches an old man listen to the confession of a young woman, links it with the Sonnets' reluctance to root themselves in a single narrative setting. Readers of the Sonnets are invited to wonder who speaks, and how the emotional valuations presented by the speaker relate to what he may have seen or known to be the case. *A Lover's Complaint* works away at that refusal to offer fixed circumstances against which to calibrate the words of its main speakers, and it does so to such an extent that it finally allows its physical setting to vanish into a continuing voice.

The poem also intensifies the impression of eavesdropping on a private affair which the Sonnets had cultivated. Its opening presents an echoing hill, and a series of enigmatic images. A woman raises a handkerchief to her eye, and reads its 'conceited characters' (l. 17); she then destroys letters, 'schedules', and posied rings (ll. 43–9). Neither the poet, who is observing this scene, nor the readers who read his description of it, can see what is written on these objects, although they clearly have significance for the woman: they are wrapped up from prying eyes, and even the description of their concealment is wrapped in scarcely penetrable language: 'With sleided silk feat and affectedly | Enswathed and sealed to curious secrecy' (ll. 48–9). Later in the poem the young man who has seduced the woman describes material objects which have a similarly rich private history, and he too does so in language so full of innovation that it is difficult even to penetrate its literal sense, let alone to grasp what the objects which are being described mean to the participants in the story. So the young man offers the maid 'talents' (presumably tokens) of hair from his former lovers, 'With the annexions of fair gems enriched, | And deep-brained sonnets that did amplify | Each stone's dear nature, worth, and quality' (ll. 208–10). Early readers would have stumbled over 'annexions' (additions), and would have felt that the 'deep-brained sonnets' were being teasingly flashed before their eyes by an artist who had no intention of telling what exactly was in them. The poem plunges its readers into a world where interpretation is all: objects have a high emotional charge to the characters in it; but since the meaning of those objects depends on prior stories to which readers of the poem are not fully party those objects remain to them darkly laden with hidden significance. This effect of excluded intimacy with a love affair goes several steps further than the Sonnets: it is here as though a love affair is being seen, finally, from the outside, with all the excluding impersonality of the third person, 'sealed to curious secrecy'.

The poem actively seeks enigmas, both in its style and in its themes, and actively wants the ground to move under its readers. It repeatedly raises 'questions', *quaestiones* or topics for debate which give rise to open-ended and irresolvable discussion. Even the young man's horsemanship prompts a 'question' as to whether he or his horse is the primary mover in his equestrian displays (l. 110). He is a rhetorician whose words can serve any occasion: 'All kind of arguments and *question* deep, | All replication prompt and reasons strong, | For his advantage still did wake and sleep' (ll. 121–3). And this questioning of rhetoric means that the moral ground of the poem is as prone to vanish as the material setting in which the poem begins. This is because the bulk of *A Lover's Complaint* is speech, a monologue by a woman who has been seduced and abandoned. This 'fickle maid' introduced in line 5 has been identified with the unreliable dark mistress of the Sonnets; but the poem is less simply condemnatory in its attitudes to her than this comparison would suggest. She combines a number of elements from the preceding sonnet sequence: her ability to see that she has been deceived whilst still being deceived invites comparison with the voice of the poet in the Sonnets.[1]

The poem also creates a controlled uncertainty about who is speaking and what their gender is in ways that weld it to Shakespeare's earlier poems: the maid devotes lines 183–280 of her complaint to relating the words of the young man who seduced her. The absence of speech-marks in Q makes the male voice (which triumphantly recalls how he has been desired by others whom he has abandoned) blend into that of the female complainant. The maid's narrative is partly a confession to the father figure who sits down beside her at the opening of the poem; but it also intimates that the act of making a confession might seduce the person making the confession all over again: as she relates the young man's persuasive words, with the full knowledge of his

[1] Ilona Bell, ' "That which thou hast done": Shakespeare's Sonnets and *A Lover's Complaint*', in James Schiffer, ed., *Shakespeare's Sonnets: Critical Essays* (New York and London, 1999), 455–74.

untruth, she both confesses her earlier fault, and re-enacts his slippery persuasions.[1]

The maid's recollection of the young man's seductive plea to her also fuses two distinct forms of complaint, which were often aligned in this period with different genders. The first and overarching form of complaint in the poem is in the tradition of 'female complaint'. In this tradition an abandoned woman might appeal for redress, or simply lament her violation or abandonment (often in an empty landscape; often with an eavesdropper nearby). The second form of complaint, which Shakespeare does not allow to be fully distinguishable from the first, is that of a male lover who appeals to a woman that she have pity on his desire for her. This form of complaint is a recurrent element in Petrarchan sonnet sequences, in which male lovers repeatedly plead for pity from their mistresses. It may well be, as Mark Rasmussen has argued, that the presence of the male voice of longing in *A Lover's Complaint* is a means of belatedly incorporating Petrarchanism into a sequence which up to this point has notably lacked the voice of a male who pines for a female.[2] The effect of fusing together these two forms of complaint makes gender divisions blur, and it also makes time loop round on itself. The female form of complaint usually follows seduction; the male form of complaint might more often precede it (or might issue in unconsummated endless longing); but in this poem we hear a voice of male complaint *after* a seduction. This combination of different types of complaint works away at its readers' perceptions of how time passes: before seduction, a complaint; after seduction, a complaint.

This temporal looping is of a piece with the language of the poem, which invites its readers to think back over a decade of rapidly moving literary history to the idiom of Spenser, as well as inviting them to compare the poem with the newest literary productions of the early seventeenth century, in which neo-Spenserianism enjoyed a major vogue. Old and new, the voice of complaint takes its readers into a landscape in which words initially re-echo unsteadily from a landscape, and then seem to make

---

[1] I am indebted here to an unpublished paper by James Schiffer, delivered at the conference on Shakespeare's Narrative Poems at the University of London, 27–29 July 2000.

[2] Mark Rasmussen, unpublished paper given to the University of London conference on Shakespeare's Narrative Poems, 27–29 July 2000.

that landscape finally disappear altogether. The poem begins with an echo, 'From off a hill whose concave womb reworded | A plaintful story from a sist'ring vale, | My spirits t' attend this double voice accorded' (ll. 1–3), and it ends with a re-echoing 'O'. The maid concludes by saying that were she to hear the young man again the whole process of the poem would begin once more:

> 'O that infected moisture of his eye;
> O that false fire which in his cheek so glowed;
> O that forced thunder from his heart did fly;
> O that sad breath his spongy lungs bestowed;
> O all that borrowed motion, seeming owed,
> Would yet again betray the fore-betrayed,
> And new pervert a reconcilèd maid.'
>
> (ll. 323–9)

This is not shamelessness, nor is it an indication that the maid's testimony should be regarded as a less than accurate representation of what has happened. It reminds readers of the poem that memory can contribute to repentance, but that if this is so then repentance must always seem to be something almost indistinguishable from re-enactment. Even though the language here is charged with knowledge that the young man is false ('false fire', 'borrowed motion') the poem ends in a cycle of seduction: 'yet again' implies almost that the maid has already been seduced more than once, and the 'fore-betrayed' suggests that people are always already betrayed even before they are betrayed. Its 'O' of complaint takes on a disturbing affinity with the 'O' of panegyric wonder, as pain and desire and moral consciousness blend together in a confession that, yes, this might all begin again. And the letter 'O' is, of course, a circle on the page.

A Lover's Complaint also repeatedly reworks some of the readerly preoccupations which ran through Shakespeare's earlier verse. In *Lucrece*, as we have seen, *sententiae* and words of received wisdom do not always do the moral work for which they seem to be designed: the uncontrollable desires of Tarquin turn his own moral knowledge, and Lucrece's impassioned rhetoric, into an ineffective smoke of words. In the Sonnets, too, the lover knows that his eye is untrue whilst knowing at the same time that he cannot act according to that knowledge. *A Lover's Complaint* pulls together all these sceptical examinations of the power of rhetoric and exemplary wisdom. Not only does the maid not seem to repent as she remembers. She also states that moral aphorisms are bound not to have an effect on conduct. She knows she is wrong, and knows she knew at the time of her error that she was wrong. But desire just does not follow moral persuasions of received wisdom:

> 'For further I could say this man's untrue,
> And knew the patterns of his foul beguiling,
> Heard where his plants in others' orchards grew,
> Saw how deceits were gilded in his smiling.
> Knew vows were ever brokers to defiling,
> Thought characters and words merely but art,
> And bastards of his foul adulterate heart.

> 'And long upon these terms I held my city,
> Till thus he gan besiege me . . .'

(ll. 169–77)

The first line here means both 'I could say a great deal more about this man's lack of fidelity' and 'I was able at the time unambiguously to declare "This man's untrue."' This combination of senses is peculiar to the mood of *A Lover's Complaint*, in which desire and moral aversion are not opposites but intimate interdependants. A catalogue of the man's crimes could go on and on, and perhaps the maid even wants to continue that catalogue of wrongdoing; but she knows he is false. And yet she falls for him, and in memory falls for him again. Her sententious list of the man's crimes recalls the rhetorical mood of Shakespeare's earlier poem of complaint, *Lucrece* (and the comparison of the resistant woman to a city recalls *Lucrece*, ll. 463–9). For Lucrece, however, suicide offered a means to break out of the potentially endless process of complaining by transforming her into an exemplary wife, and by providing a stimulus for her family to revenge her violation. The maid in *A Lover's Complaint* has no such escape: she finds that exemplary instances of falsity generate not an aversion to falsity, but more desire.

The poem offers its readers no simple way out of the cycle of desiring and complaining in which the maid is trapped. A maiden-aunt might purse his or her lips (maiden aunts in literary criticism are more often male than female) and disapprove, but the maiden-aunt would have missed the painful insistence of the poem that the fickle maid knows exactly what a maiden-aunt would say, and would indeed say it and assent to it too. And yet she would be seduced again, because she was originally seduced in the first place by hearing the young man relate tales of his earlier seductions and abandonments. As when Tarquin stops Lucrece's sage words of counsel with the torrent of his rage, so here prudent advice can inflame rather than calm: 'Counsel may stop awhile what will not stay; | For when we rage advice is often seen | By blunting us to make our wits more keen' (ll. 159–61). Confessing, remembering seduction, accumulating instances of wrong, and condemning it all feed back into the cycle of seduction and complaint. There is no escaping from a loop in which someone is desired for having treated others so badly that they longed for him, and no escape from the consciousness that when you have been abandoned by him too that might make him even more desirable. That is why the poem just dissolves into the confession that the young man's rhetoric would only 'new pervert' the maid, rather than emerging back into the firm landscape of grief which is evoked at its beginning. And that is too why the poem works so well as a conclusion to the Sonnets, which move towards a position in which the poet is caught knowing that his mistress is false, whilst still desiring her. *A Lover's Complaint* reverberates with the central concerns of the canon of Shakespeare's verse: it explores misrelations between rhetoric and desire, between moral knowledge and passion. Even if, as the failure to close the initial frame makes it tempting to believe, the work is not quite finished, and even if its experimentations in archaism produce passages which are crabbed rather than simply beautiful, the poem is a rich offshoot of a larger poetic project.

Poems Attributed to Shakespeare in the Seventeenth Century

The majority of late sixteenth-century poets composed some occasional verse, and by the early seventeenth century the vogue for epigrams, funeral elegies, and epitaphs was so entrenched that it was hard for any writer to resist it. Shakespeare would have been unusual had he done so. The signs are, however, that he was indeed unusual in this as in so many other respects: the one occasional piece which can firmly be attributed to him, 'Let the bird of loudest lay', rises beyond its immediate occasion as a poem appended to *Love's Martyr* and fuses theology, logic, and mythology in a blend that seems not to come from this earth. What we know of

Shakespeare the poet suggests that he did not move towards writing epigrams to named individuals or funerary pieces at the start of the seventeenth century.

However, a number of miscellaneous pieces and epigrams were attributed to him in seventeenth-century manuscripts, a group of which is reprinted in an appendix to this volume. None of these poems can be securely attributed to Shakespeare; they are reproduced here purely to show the kinds of poem which Shakespeare was thought to have written by his contemporaries and near-contemporaries. Poems attributed to 'W.S.' are excluded: with William Strode, and William Strachey, and William Skipwith, and umpteen others to choose from, there are too many W.S.'s around in the seventeenth century to make it at all probable that a poem ascribed to those initials was composed by Shakespeare.[1] Even the attributions to 'William Shakespeare' seem mostly unsafe. But where printers might sell more copies by ascribing their copy to known writers, as Jaggard had sought to do in *The Passionate Pilgrim*, scribes and copyists of manuscript miscellanies did not have a financial stake in misascription. It is at least possible that Shakespeare wrote some of the funerary pieces which are ascribed to him.[2] Circumstantial evidence suggests he may have written the brief epitaph on Elias James, a brewer with premises close to Shakespeare's residence in Puddle Dock Hill.[3] It is not impossible that he composed his own epitaph, and it is just about conceivable that he wrote the verses on the Stanley tomb at Tong, since he had some links with the family (although there are some vexatious questions about chronology here which are discussed in full in the headnote to these poems). Even unsafe attributions by scribes and copyists can reveal something about what kinds of poem a particular author was thought by near-contemporaries to be likely to have written.

[1] Attributions of poems by 'W.S.' and its variants to Shakespeare tend to be unfortunate: see Peter Levi, *A Private Commission: New Verses by Shakespeare* (1988), and the convincing argument by James Knowles *TLS* 4,439 (29 Apr. 1988), 472, 485 that the poem concerned is by William Skipwith.

[2] The best positive account of the matter is J. Q. Adams, 'Shakespeare as a Writer of Epitaphs', in *The Manly Anniversary Studies in Language and Literature* (Chicago, 1923), 85–6. See also Honigmann, 77–83. A more sceptical view is in Chambers, i.550–5 and S. Schoenbaum, *Shakespeare's Lives*, 2nd edn. (Oxford, 1991), 41–6.

[3] See Leslie Hotson, *Shakespeare's Sonnets Dated* (1949), 111–24; see also Hilton Kelliher, letter to the *London Review of Books*, vol. 8, no. 9 (22 May 1986).

Scribes and miscellanists can, however, make mistakes. They might be struck by a parallel between an anonymous work and a known work by a named author; they might mistakenly expand initials into a name, assume that authorship of one poem in a miscellany implies authorship also of the next, or assume that because a poem is about someone from Stratford-upon-Avon it is by Shakespeare. The epigram on John Combe the usurer, for instance, seems to have been sucked into the ambit of Shakespeare's authorship as a result of seventeenth-century curiosity about the poet's life, fuelled by loquacious churchwardens, eager, no doubt, to please their visitors and secure a remuneration. In the case of most of the poems included in the appendix it is likely some such process resulted in misascriptions. Detailed discussions of manuscript sources and of the likelihood of Shakespeare's authorship are given in the headnotes to each poem. These are finicky and distinct for each work. In the majority of cases it is possible to construct a plausible account of how the ascription arose; and the more plausible such accounts become, the less likely it must be that Shakespeare wrote the poem. The epigram on the title-page of James I's works, for example, was probably assumed to be by Shakespeare because he was known as the leading playwright of the King's Men.

Seventeenth-century scribes gained nothing from ascribing a poem to Shakespeare; twentieth-century scholars could gain a reputation from doing so. The majority of the poems attributed to Shakespeare in the seventeenth century are slight in both scale and significance, and have given rise to little critical debate. Two poems ascribed to Shakespeare in the twentieth century have, however, given rise to a mass of discussion: 'Shall I die?' and *A Funeral Elegy*. These are given more detailed consideration below. (For those who prefer their Gordian knots sliced rather than nibbled through, I should briefly state that in my view neither of them is by Shakespeare; my conviction in the case of the latter is so strong that the poem does not form part of this edition.)

'Shall I die?' The poem is found in two manuscript miscellanies dating from the 1630s (Yale Beinecke MS Osborn b.197 and Bodleian MS Rawl. Poet. 160), both of which were compiled by scribes with a taste for Caroline lyric. The Yale MS reflects the tastes of its compiler, the Norfolk teenager Tobias Alston, and the tastes

of his relatives at Cambridge in the 1630s. The poem is unattributed in the Yale MS. The anonymous scribe of the Bodleian MS attributes it to 'William Shakespeare'. No other ascription has been so far discovered. Gary Taylor's announcement that the poem would appear in the Oxford Edition of the complete works of Shakespeare led to extensive discussion in the press, with the curious result that the case for attributing 'Shall I die?' to Shakespeare has had far fuller discussion than that for ascribing to him the poems printed under his name in *The Passionate Pilgrim*.[2] The Bodleian MS shows all the signs of being a miscellany composed by a professional scribe. A number of the poems are attributed, and those from the period 1613–30 are attributed with a reasonable degree of accuracy, although not without errors.[3] The manuscript contains relatively little verse from the late Elizabethan or early Jacobean periods, and the ascriptions of these poems are usually those established by tradition, whether or not tradition errs. That the bulk of the collection consists of lyrics written after Shakespeare's death gives grounds for treating the attribution of 'Shall I die?' with some scepticism (both Malone and Chambers inspected the manuscript but did not comment at all on the poem). That the poem is only found in two manuscripts, both of which can be dated with some confidence to c.1630, and both of which chiefly contain material written shortly before their compilation, is an indication that the poem may well date from after Shakespeare's death.

Taylor argued that the poem shows significant overlap of vocabulary with Shakespeare's works, and that it contains a sufficiently high proportion of early rare words to suggest that it could have been written by the Shakespeare of the 1590s. He also made use of Hart's work on Shakespeare's habits as a verbal innovator to show that the poem contained roughly the proportion of 'new' words (that is, words not previously found in the canon) which one would

---

[1] Peter Beal, correspondence on 'Shall I die?', *TLS* 4,321 (24 Jan. 1986), 88.

[2] Gary Taylor, 'A New Shakespeare Poem? The Evidence', *TLS* 4,316 (20 Dec. 1985), 1447–8, and Robin Robbins's reply 'And the Counterarguments', *TLS* 4,316 (20 Dec. 1985), 1449–50. The correspondence about the poem continues in the *TLS* until the following March. Taylor replied to his critics in ' "Shall I die" Immortalized?', *TLS* 4,322 (31 Jan. 1986), 123–4.

[3] See Peter Beal's correspondence on 'Shall I die?', *TLS* 4,318 (3 Jan. 1986), 13. This letter is the most judicious contribution to the debate, and my debt to it is great.

expect from a poem by an endlessly inventive verbal experimenter such as Shakespeare. Taylor's adversaries quickly pointed out an obvious weakness in this argument: that a large number of works *not* by Shakespeare also contain a significant proportion of words which are not used by Shakespeare. It is very unlikely that statistical analysis of a poem which contains only around four hundred and fifty words could provide enough evidence for a safe attribution. When confronted with such a poem, embedded in a manuscript milieu in which ascriptions often depend on tradition, post-romantic conceptions of authorship—a visible imprint of a creating mind—lose their purchase, and can proffer only unhelpful judgements about poetic quality. (It is a poem which it is very hard to read aloud, in my experience, without snorting at least once at its many inanities and points of metrical slackness; but judgements of quality are doubtless unhelpful.)

Perhaps, then, rather than asking directly 'Is it by Shakespeare?' we should first ask, 'What kind of poem is "Shall I die?" and how might such a poem have come to be attributed to Shakespeare?' The poem appears from its stanzaic pattern and from its frequent use of internal rhymes to have been a lyric, although at ninety lines it is unusually long for a poem which was designed to be sung. Its short internally rhyming lines have something in common with Puck's song (or magical chant) in *A Midsummer Night's Dream* 3.3.36–46 ('On the ground sleep sound. | I'll apply to your eye, | Gentle lover, remedy. | When thou wak'st thou tak'st | True delight in the sight | Of thy former lady's eye ...'), and could seem to some readers to have a ring of 'My flocks feed not', ascribed to Shakespeare in *The Passionate Pilgrim*. These similarities may explain the attribution. The poem is one of a group of lyrics composed in the early years of the seventeenth century which evoke the paralysis of a melancholy lover by means of reiterated questions, several of which begin 'Shall I ...'[1]. This formula was used by the lutenist John Dowland in his 'Shall I sue? Shall I seek for grace?' in his *Second Book of Songs or Airs* (1600). The section of the poem from stanza 4 onwards appears to extend the stasis of such melancholy meditations into an openly erotic blazon more typical of

---

[1] See Jeremy Maule and Erica Sheen, correspondence on 'Shall I die?', *TLS* 4,320 (17 Jan. 1986), 61. The suggestion that the poem might have been used as incidental music in a play was first made by Peter Beal, loc. cit.

Caroline than late Elizabethan lyric,[1] as though the author or authors of the piece had decided to make a melancholy lover snap out of it and decide not to die as a result of seeing the beauty of the mistress. It may be noteworthy that the latter section of the poem contains more scribal errors than its opening stanzas, as well as offering the majority of its more unusual turns of phrase ('As amazed, I gazed | On more than a mortal complexion. | You that love can prove | Such force in beauty's inflection'). None of these features gives more than inklings as to the poem's likely genesis, but they might indicate that 'Shall I die?' is an answer to a lyric similar to Dowland's, and that, rather than having an individual author, it may have a complex and hybrid growth. Answer poems were a frequent by-product of coterie manuscript circulation: they were one means by which a scribe-cum-poet could absorb and respond to poems which he had acquired, as 'Come live with me' is answered by 'If that the world and love were young' in *The Passionate Pilgrim*. Such a lyric (or a shorter version of it) might be used in a play, perhaps as a means of intimating that what initially appears to be a static love affair could emerge into active life at a later stage in the drama. It may be that the poem was used in a performance of one of Shakespeare's plays in the 1630s, and it has been suggested that its progression from melancholy paralysis to active courtship would be particularly appropriate to Orsino's initial melancholy feeding on music in *Twelfth Night* (although it is hard to reconcile the open eroticism of its end with the play as we know it). If the poem had been used in performance (and lyrics were frequently exchanged between plays, or adapted for new theatrical settings by a new author), this would give a reason for the scribe's erroneous attribution. John Benson's edition of the Sonnets in 1640 had assimilated Shakespeare to the vogue for amorous lyric in the Caroline period, and made him, effectively, a Caroline miscellany poet. *The Passionate Pilgrim* also shows that early readers could accept the attribution of erotic material to Shakespeare's name—he was, after all, principally known as the author of *Venus and Adonis* in the early years of the seventeenth century. It is clear that the scribe of Bodleian MS Rawl. Poet. 160 (or his source) had a sense that 'Shakespeare' was the kind of author who might have written an

---

[1] Muriel Bradbrook, correspondence on 'Shall I die?', *TLS* 4,322 (31 Jan. 1986), 115.

initially melancholy meditation which rises to eroticism. The ascription of the poem to Shakespeare in this manuscript is extremely unlikely to be a reliable indicator of his authorship, but it does show kinds of qualities which readers in the 1630s were prone to impute to him. Like the unascribable poems in *The Passionate Pilgrim*, 'Shall I die?' illustrates the kind of poet which Shakespeare was thought to be in the seventeenth century, and so justifies its place here, though only in an appendix.

A Funeral Elegy. This volume does not include *A Funeral Elegy*, a poem attributed to 'W.S.' on its title-page, which was entered in the Stationers' Register by Thomas Thorpe on 13 February 1612 and printed by George Eld in 1612.[1] The poem was written very shortly after the murder of William Peter by Edward Drew on 25 January 1612. It aims to restore Peter's reputation after he was stabbed in the back of the head at the end of a day of hard drinking with the Drew brothers. In 1989 Donald Foster published a study of the poem which gave extensive stylometric evidence for attributing it to Shakespeare, but which held off from a final definitive attribution. Foster argued that 'five words (*and, but, not, so, that*) may serve as a kind of stylistic Geiger counter',[2] and that the distribution of these words in the *Elegy* was in the expected range of the larger Shakespearian corpus; that the *Elegy* shared Shakespeare's distinctive taste for hendiadys; that its use of grammatically idiosyncratic forms, such as 'more better', fell within the expected range of Shakespeare's later works; that it showed the frequency of 'late rare words' which one would expect from a later work by Shakespeare; that it appealed to John Ford, one of Shakespeare's chief seventeenth-century admirers and imitators; and that it alluded frequently to Shakespeare's works. He then concluded, 'Whether either of these men [William Strachey and William Shakespeare] wrote the *Elegy* is more than I can say with certainty.'[3]

On the basis of further findings (particularly the fact that the instances of Shakespearian 'rare words' used in the poem are drawn more frequently from parts which may have been played by

[1] Arber, iii.477.

[2] *Elegy by W.S.: A Study in Attribution* (Newark, London, and Toronto, 1989), 141–2.

[3] Foster, *Elegy*, 79.

Shakespeare and from plays which were revived by the King's Men around the time of the poem's composition) Foster and Abrams argued in stronger terms for the attribution in 1995-6, with the result that the poem has since been included in several one-volume editions of Shakespeare's works, more, one suspects, in order to avoid the odium of having left something out than because of a full conviction that the case for the ascription to Shakespeare is sound. Abrams has gone so far as to argue that the apparent hostility to the stage in the poem corresponds to a movement away from the theatrical in later Shakespeare, a view which depends on a rather simple reading of some complex treatments of stagecraft and illusion in the late plays.[1] There has been extensive argument over the attribution, but since in such cases there are no agreed criteria of proof or disproof the matter has, shall we say, Petered out rather than being finally resolved. Recent and muscular work by Brian Vickers, however, has given strong support to the view that the poem is by Peter's fellow Devonian John Ford. Ford wrote several funeral elegies and was a habitual imitator of Shakespeare.[2]

Since the appendix to this volume contains only verse attributed to Shakespeare in the seventeenth century the poem does not

---

[1] R. Abrams, 'W[illiam] S[hakespeare]'s "Funeral Elegy" and the Turn from the Theatrical', *Studies in English Literature 1500-1900* 36 (1996), 435-60. A revised version of this article is '"Exercise in this kind": Shakespeare and the "Funeral Elegy" for William Peter', *Shakespeare Studies* 25 (1997), 141-70.

[2] The major contributions include: Donald Foster, 'A "Funeral Elegy": W[illiam] S[hakespeare]'s "best-speaking-witnesses"', *PMLA* 111 (1996), 1080 ff., reprinted in *Shakespeare Studies* 25 (1997), 115-40; W. E. Y. Elliot and R. J. Valenza, 'Glass Slippers and Seven-League Boots: Computer-aided Tests, Donald Foster, Claremont-Shakespeare-Clinic- C-prompted Doubts about Ascribing A "Funeral Elegy" and A "Lover's Complaint" to Shakespeare', *Shakespeare Quarterly* 48 (1997), 177-207; Stanley Wells, 'In Memory of Master William Peter: The Difficulties of Attributing A "Funeral Elegy" to Shakespeare', *TLS* 4,843 (1996), 28; R. Abrams, 'In Defense of WS: Reasons for Attributing A "Funeral Elegy" to Shakespeare', *TLS* 4,845 (1996), 25-6; Brian Vickers, 'Whose Thumbprints: A More Plausible Author for a "Funeral Elegy"', *TLS* 4,829 (1996), 16-18; Ian Lancashire, 'Empirically Determining Shakespeare's Idiolect', *Shakespeare Studies* 25 (1997), 171-85; Stanley Wells, '"A Funeral Elegy": Obstacles to Belief', *Shakespeare Studies* 25 (1997), 186-91; Katherine Duncan-Jones. 'Who Wrote A *Funerall Elegie*?' *Shakespeare Studies* 25 (1997), 192-210; Leah S. Marcus, 'Who was Will Peter? Or, a Plea for Literary History', *Shakespeare Studies* 25 (1997), 211-28; Stephen Booth, 'A Long, Dull Poem by William Shakespeare', *Shakespeare Studies* 25 (1997), 229-37. Correspondence in *TLS* from Katherine Duncan-Jones, Donald Foster, R. Abrams, I. A. Shapiro, Stanley Wells, and Brian Vickers (issues 4,851-63) adds heat and some light to the controversy. Brian Vickers's *Counterfeiting Shakespeare* (forthcoming from Cambridge University Press) drives additional nails deep into Peter's coffin.

appear here: an attribution to 'W.S.' is not an attribution to 'William Shakespeare'. But the criteria for including poems in this edition have been determined in this way partly because I find the attribution of *A Funeral Elegy* to Shakespeare improbable. Thorpe and Eld did not attribute the poem to Shakespeare in 1612, and this is enough in itself to make one doubt that it is by him: Jaggard in 1599 had eagerly recognized the commercial value of Shakespeare's name, and *Shake-speares Sonnets*, printed by Eld for Thorpe in 1609, had boasted of the author's name on every opening of the volume. Indeed, the story told in this introduction is substantially that of the growing significance of Shakespeare's name as a poet. It may be that the printer and publisher were obeying the wishes of the author in using only initials to attribute what appears to have been a privately printed memorial volume, but it seems highly likely that they would have made more of the authorship of the poem had they known it was by Shakespeare. No printer wilfully decides to sell fewer copies than he could.

The poem also displays distinctive and not evidently Shakespearian stylistic features. Its author has a penchant for a partitive genitive form ('best of time', l. 64; 'spring of days', l. 74; 'nine of years', l. 511), and rarely indulges in the contractions 'o'the' and 'i'th', which are frequent in Shakespeare's late works.[1] The frequency of 'in', 'in the', 'with', 'to', and 'by' is well outside the expected range of Shakespearian usage at this point in his career.[2] The frequency of 'of' in the poem is also remarkably high, and contributes a great deal to its monotony: 'of' occurs about twice as frequently in the *Elegy* (about 3.2% of its words are 'of') as it does in Shakespeare's known non-dramatic verse. 'Of' has a frequency of about 1.7% in *Two Noble Kinsmen* and *All is True*, the plays with which Foster believes the poem to have the greatest stylistic affinity. The formulae '[noun] of [noun]' and '[noun] | Of [adjective] [noun]' and 'noun | Of [pronoun] [noun], are frequent in the poem. 'Of' often falls as the unstressed first syllable of the line ('work | Of singleness', l. 44; 'crop | Of education', ll. 54–5; 'float | Of fond conceit', ll. 98–9; 'wane | Of plenty', ll. 141–2; 'eyes | Of men', ll. 257–8; 'vein | Of boast', ll. 326–7; 'traps | Of hell', ll. 369–70; 'scourge |

---

[1] Stanley Wells, letter in *TLS* 4,846 (1996), 17.
[2] MacDonald P. Jackson, Review of Foster in *Shakespeare Survey* 43 (1991), 258–61.

Of torture', ll. 395–6).[1] This stylistic tic is not found in the works usually attributed to Shakespeare. It is one reason why many readers find the poem metrically clumsy: we usually and reasonably think that poems are bad if they seem to have a very limited repertoire of tricks for making their lines scan. Further computer-aided tests, which employ different criteria from those employed by Foster, have cast doubt on the attribution on stylometric grounds (the same tests have also cast doubt on the attribution of *A Lover's Complaint* to Shakespeare, which may be an indication of the difficulty of adjusting such tests to take account of inflexions to a dominant style which can result from genre and conscious pastiche).[2] Stylistic fingerprinting can be used with some confidence in cases where the range of potential authors is limited, and where there is a large sample of material of similar kind by each potential candidate for authorship with which to compare the unattributed work. But it is a fallible tool to use on an early modern text for which the theoretical pool of authors is not limited, and where the full extent of that pool is not knowable.

There are also some awkward biographical questions surrounding the authorship of the poem. It was written with extreme speed after the murder of William Peter, a Devonian gentleman educated at Exeter College, Oxford. Shakespeare's brother Gilbert was buried in the middle of the three-week period of the poem's composition (3 February 1612). Foster's earlier study scrupulously notes that 'It is difficult to see how a friendship could have existed between an Oxford student and a largely untutored playwright, nearly twenty years his senior, who lived much of the time in London, fifty-five miles away'.[3] He also recognizes that unless the references on the part of the poet to himself as a 'youth' are metaphorical, then the attribution to Shakespeare, 47 at the time of the poem's composition, appears difficult to sustain (although references to the poet's age in the Sonnets often defy literal interpretation). Readers of the *Elegy* have frequently remarked on its piety, which has no parallel elsewhere in Shakespeare's oeuvre. The poem uses 'predestinated'

---

[1] About 3% of the *Elegy*'s lines start with 'Of' (ll. 138, 142, 172, 204, 258, 264, 270, 295, 327, 370, 384, 396, 430, 484, 492, 521, 544, 566); only about 0.5% of lines of *Venus and Adonis*, about 1% of ll. in *Lucrece*, and a similar proportion of the Sonnets. These figures are based on a rough count, but are striking even if one allows for a high margin of error.

[2] Elliot and Valenza, 'Glass Slippers', 177–207.   [3] Foster, *Elegy*, 201.

twice (ll. 1 and 497), with an apparent theological seriousness which is not otherwise found in Shakespeare. Its frequent nose-dives into awkwardly phrased moralism do not have clear Shakespearian precedent ('O, whither tends the lamentable spite | Of this world's teenful apprehension', ll. 269–70; 'Ruling the little ordered commonwealth | Of his own self', ll. 294–5; 'Blood, pomp, state, honour, glory and command | Without fit ornaments of disposition | Are in themselves but heathenish and profane', ll. 439–41). Its tendency to splice cliché awkwardly to cliché similarly suggests that its poet had a dull ear ('caught within the snares of making truth a pawn', l. 352). There are moments when the poem's penchant for overworking the obvious is worthy of Holofernes, the pedant in *Love's Labour's Lost* ('Though in the complemental phrase of words | He never was addicted to the vein | Of boast', ll. 325–8). Its piety cannot simply be attributed to the poem's genre, since many elegies in the period praise their subject in dominantly secular terms. Several scholars have proposed rival candidates for its authorship (including, most convincingly, John Ford; other candidates have included the clergyman William Sclater and the schoolmaster Simon Wastell).[1]

The poem does offer some clues to its authorship:

> Though I, rewarded with some sadder taste,
> Of knowing shame, by feeling it have proved
> My country's thankless misconstruction cast
> Upon my name and credit, both unloved
> By some, whose fortunes sunk into the wane
> Of Plenty and Desert, have strove to win
> Justice by wrong, and sifted to embane
> My reputation, with a witless sin;
> Yet Time, the Father of unblushing Truth,
> May one day lay ope malice which hath crossed it,
> And right the hopes of my endangered youth,
> Purchasing credit in the place I lost it.
> Even in which place, the subject of the verse
> (Unhappy matter of a mourning style
> Which now that subject's merits doth rehearse),
> Had education, and new being . . .
>
> (ll. 137–52)

---

[1] Duncan-Jones, 'Who Wrote *A Funerall Elegie*?', suggested Sclater; Vickers, 'Whose Thumbprints', suggested Simon Wastell.

This passage and the 'witless [possibly a nonce-usage for 'unwitting', but the word is unfortunate in the context of such a very bad piece of writing] sin' to which it alludes have both proved contentious. They have been connected by Abrams and Foster with the references to unspecified shame in Sonnets 33–8, 71–2, 111, 121, and by Leah Marcus to slanders which Shakespeare may have suffered after his purchase of an interest in tithes from Humphrey Colles.[1] The Stratford Council book for 1610 noted that Thomas Greene, Shakespeare's fellow purchaser, 'standeth secretly scandalised and unjustly slandered by unknown authors'. The passage illustrates the interminable cycles of feedback in which arguments over attribution tend to spin: critics who find the case for Shakespeare weak tend to say either that there is no specific evidence that he was shamed in Oxford, or that the 'place' referred to is more likely to be Devon, at which Peter received his 'education and new being' in the sense of 'being born and brought up', and that Shakespeare is not known to have spent any significant period in Devon.[2] If this passage were considered independently of the stylometric evidence, though, most readers would probably suppose that the poem was written by a man of roughly Peter's age who suffered some shame in a town with which the subject of the elegy was associated. This does not fit what we know about Shakespeare. It may fit John Ford.

The argument over the attribution of *A Funeral Elegy* finally rests on a balance of probabilities, and on the kinds of evidence to which one is disposed to attach greater weight. In my view it is highly improbable that Shakespeare, during the days surrounding his brother's death, rapidly wrote his one extended non-narrative poem to commemorate the life and virtue of an otherwise unknown Devonian with whom he cannot be proven to have had any contact. The poem is now widely available, and Foster's arguments raise interesting questions about canonicity and attribution. The poem does not find a place in this volume because no reader of Shakespeare before the twentieth century thought that the poem was his (with the possible exception of John Ford—unless he himself wrote it), and because there is sufficient evidence for a moral certainty that it is not by Shakespeare. Were the case that the poem

[1] Marcus, 'Who was Will Peter?', 224.
[2] Duncan-Jones, 'Who Wrote *A Funerall Elegie*?', 198.

is by John Ford to be finally proven, several small cans of worms would be reopened: did Thorpe then seek to mislead his readers into thinking the poem was Shakespeare's by attributing it to 'W.S.'? And if so, what dark light does this cast on the arguments about Thorpe's dealings with Shakespeare over the Sonnets? For the present, however, such questions must be lost in the cloud of obscurity with which the poem is still surrounded, and the worms must stay wriggling in the can.

EDITORIAL PROCEDURES

Spelling and punctuation have been modernized in accordance with the principles devised by Stanley Wells and outlined in *Modernizing Shakespeare's Spelling* (Oxford, 1979), although not all of my decisions have followed those of the one-volume Oxford Shakespeare. Quotations from early printed sources have been modernized even where the source of the quotation is unmodernized, except in the cases of quotations from Spenser, quotations from works composed before about 1450, and quotations where there is a particular point at issue which depends upon the old-spelling text. Variant readings in the collations have been modernized unless there is a particular difficulty or ambiguity arising from an old spelling. Manuscript variants are not modernized. The collation includes only selected substantive variants from early printed or manuscript sources. Later emendations are collated only if they have a good claim to be adopted, or if they illustrate a particular problem in interpretation. Since there are an unusual number of problems of interpretation in the Sonnets, the collation to that part of the edition reproduces a larger number of conjectural emendations from editions after Shakespeare's death than is usual for this series.

In order to make it easy to examine Shakespeare's sources, line references to and quotations from classical texts are wherever possible keyed to the appropriate volumes of the Loeb Classical Library, although on several occasions I have substituted my own translations for those in the Loeb. Classical texts and quotations have been checked against early modern editions for variants, which are noted if they are significant. Early modern translations of source materials have been quoted where they convey the sense, even if it is not certain that Shakespeare made use of them: so a reference to 'Golding' does not necessarily imply that Shakespeare is indebted to the wording of Golding's translation at that point, but may mean there is a general debt to Ovid. References to proverbs are to R. W. Dent, *Shakespeare's Proverbial Language*, which has been checked against Tilley's earlier collection. Commonplaces ('red as a rose') which Dent marks as proverbial are not always noted. I have sometimes retained references to proverbs found by Tilley but dismissed by the more austere Dent.

Words are glossed on their first occurrence in each work, rather than, as usually in the series, once only. The index gives cross-references to words glossed.

Abbreviations and References

Abbreviations in the collation and notes such as Q, Q2, etc. refer to the first and subsequent quartos of the text under discussion. Where the first edition is a quarto, all subsequent editions are referred to by the abbreviation Q2 etc. even if they are not in fact quartos. The second and subsequent editions of *Lucrece* are in fact octavos, as are the third and subsequent editions of *Venus and Adonis*, but to have begun a new sequence 'O1' etc. could only have caused confusion. The date of publication for each edition of each work is listed below. In some cases (notably the '1602' editions of *Venus and Adonis*) there is uncertainty surrounding the actual date of publication. I have followed the dates given in STC. The place of publication is London unless otherwise stated.

EARLY EDITIONS OF SHAKESPEARE

O1	First octavo, *The Passionate Pilgrim* (?1599; part only)
O2	Second octavo, *The Passionate Pilgrim* (1599)
O3	Third octavo, *The Passionate Pilgrim* (1612)
Q	First quarto: *Venus and Adonis* (1593), *Lucrece* (1594), *Shake-speares Sonnets* (1609)
Qa	Unrevised state of *Lucrece* (1594); Unrevised state of *Shake-speares Sonnets. Never before Imprinted* (1609)
Qb	Revised state of *Lucrece* (1594); Revised state of *Shake-speares Sonnets. Never before Imprinted* (1609)
Q2	Second quarto: *Venus and Adonis* (1594), *Lucrece* (1598; this and subsequent editions are octavo)
Q3	Third quarto: *Venus and Adonis* (?1595; this and subsequent editions are octavo), *Lucrece* (1600)
Q4	Fourth quarto: *Venus and Adonis* (1596), *Lucrece* (1600)
Q5	Fifth quarto: *Venus and Adonis* (1599), *Lucrece* (1607)
Q6	Sixth quarto: *Venus and Adonis* (1599), *Lucrece* (1616)

Q7	Seventh quarto: *Venus and Adonis* (?1602), *Lucrece* (1624)
Q8	Eighth quarto: *Venus and Adonis* ('1602'; probably 1607/8), *Lucrece* (1632)
Q9	Ninth quarto: *Venus and Adonis* ('1602'; probably 1608/9), *Lucrece* (1655)
Q10	Tenth quarto: *Venus and Adonis* ('1602'; probably 1610; title-page only)
Q11	Eleventh quarto: *Venus and Adonis* (1617)
Q12	Twelfth quarto: *Venus and Adonis* (1620)
Q13	Thirteenth quarto: *Venus and Adonis* (Edinburgh, 1627)
Q14	Fourteenth quarto: *Venus and Adonis* (1630)
Q15	Fifteenth quarto: *Venus and Adonis* (1630–6?)
Q16	Sixteenth quarto: *Venus and Adonis* (1636)

MANUSCRIPTS

BL1	British Library Add. MS 10309, fo. 143 (Sonnet 2)
BL2	British Library Add. MS 15226, fo. 4^v (Sonnet 8)
BL3	British Library Add. MS 21433, fo. 114^v (Sonnet 2)
BL4	British Library Add. MS 25303, fo. 119^v (Sonnet 2)
BL5	British Library Add. MS 30982, fo. 18 (Sonnet 2)
BL6	British Library Sloane MS 1792, fo. 45 (Sonnet 2)
Bod1	Bodleian MS Ashmole 38, p. 180 ('An Extempore Epitaph'), p. 181 ('On Ben Jonson')
Bod2	Bodleian MS Aubrey 6, fo. 10^r ('An Extempore Epitaph')
Bod3	Bodleian MS Rawlinson Poet. 117, fo. 269^v (Verses on the Stanley Tomb)
Bod4	Bodleian MS Rawlinson Poet. 152, fo. 34 (Sonnet 128)
Bod5	Bodleian MS Rawlinson Poet. 160, fos. 108–9 ('Shall I die?') and 41^r ('An Epitaph')
Bodley-Caldecott	Bodleian Library copy of Q1 of *Sonnets*, shelf-mark Arch. G.e.32
Fane	Shakespeare Birthplace Trust Records Office MS ER.93, p. 177 ('Upon a Pair of Gloves', 'An Extempore Epitaph', 'Epitaph on himself')
Fol1	Folger MS V.a.89, fo. 25^{r-v} (PP18)
Fol2	Folger MS V.a.103, Pt. 1, fo. 8 (Verses on the Stanley Tomb)
Fol3	Folger MS V.a.147, fo. 72 ('An Extempore Epitaph')

Fol4	Folger MS V.a.148, Pt. I, fo. 22 (Sonnet 2 and various sonnets)
Fol5	Folger MS V.a.162, fo. 12^v (Sonnet 71), fo. 26^r (Sonnet 32)
Fol6	Folger MS V.a.170, pp. 163–4 (Sonnet 2)
Fol7	Folger MS V.a.180, fo. 79^v ('An Extempore Epitaph'), fo. 79^v ('Epitaph on himself')
Fol8	Folger MS V.a.275, fo. 177 ('On Ben Jonson')
Fol9	Folger MS V.a.339, fo. 197 (PP4, PP6), fo. 197^v (Sonnet 138 [PP1], PP7, PP11), fo. 185^v (PP18)
Fol10	Folger MS V.a.345, p. 145 (Sonnet 2), p. 232 ('An Extempore Epitaph')
Fol11	Folger MS V.b.43, fo. 22 (PP4), fo. 21^v (PP1)
Harl.	Harleian MS 6910, fo. 156 (PP17)
John's	St John's College, Cambridge, MS S.23 (Sonnet 2)
M	Pierpont Morgan MA 1057, p. 96 (Sonnet 106)
Nott.	University of Nottingham Portland MS Pw V 37, p. 69 (Sonnet 2)
Plume 1	Archbishop Thomas Plume's MS 25, fo. 77 ('On Ben Jonson')
Plume 2	Archbishop Thomas Plume's MS 25, fo. 51 ('On Ben Jonson')
RO 1	Rosenbach Museum and Library MS 1083/16, p. 256 (Sonnet 106)
RO 2	Rosenbach Museum and Library MS 1083/17, fos. 132^v–133^r (Sonnet 2)
Tomb	The slab covering Shakespeare's grave, Holy Trinity Church, Stratford-upon-Avon
Tong	The monument to the Stanley Family in St Bartholomew's Church, Tong, Shropshire
W	Westminster Abbey MS 41, fo. 49 (Sonnet 2)
Yale1	Beinecke Library Osborn b.197, pp. 135–6 (Song)
Yale2	Beinecke Library Osborn b.205, fo. 54^v (Sonnet 2)

LATER EDITIONS

Beeching	H. C. Beeching, ed., *Sonnets*, Athenaeum Press Series (Boston, Mass. and London, 1904)
Bell	Robert Bell, ed., *Poems*, English Poets Annotated Edition (1855)

Benson	*Poems: Written by Wil. Sh.* (1640)
Booth	Stephen Booth, ed., *Shakespeare's Sonnets* (New Haven and London, 1977)
Boswell	James Boswell, ed., *Plays and Poems*, vol. 20 (1821)
Brathwait	Richard Brathwait, *Remains After Death* (1618), sig. L2^v, as reissued in P. Hannay's *A Happy Husband* (1619; STC 12747)
Bray	Denys Bray, *The Original Order of Shakespeare's Sonnets* (1925)
Brooke	Tucker Brooke, ed., *Shakespeare's Sonnets* (New Haven, 1936)
Bullen	A. H. Bullen, ed., *Works*, vol. 10 (Stratford-upon-Avon, 1907)
Butler	Samuel Butler, ed., *Shakespeare's Sonnets* (New York and Bombay, 1899)
Cambridge	W. G. Clark, John Glover, and W. A. Wright, eds., *Works*, vol. 9 (Cambridge, 1866)
Cambridge 1893	W. A. Wright, ed., *Works*, vol. 9 (Cambridge, 1893)
Capell	MS annotations by Edward Capell in a copy of Lintot's 1709–11 reprint of the Quarto now in the library of Trinity College, Cambridge
Collier	J. P. Collier, ed., *Works*, vol. 8 (1843)
Collier 1858	J. P. Collier, ed., *Shakespeare's Comedies, Histories and Tragedies*, vol. 6, 2nd edn. (1858)
Collier 1878	J. P. Collier, ed., *Plays and Poems of William Shakespeare*, vol. 8 (1878)
Delius	Nicolaus Delius, ed., *Werke*, vol. 7 (Elberfeld, 1860)
Deloney	Thomas Deloney, *The Garland of Good Will* (1631)
Dover Wilson	John Dover Wilson, ed., *The Sonnets* (Cambridge, 1966)
Dowden	Edward Dowden, ed., *Sonnets* (1881)
Duncan-Jones	Katherine Duncan-Jones, ed., *Shakespeare's Sonnets* (1997)
Dyce	Alexander Dyce, ed., *Poems*, Aldine Poets (1832)
Dyce 1857	Alexander Dyce, ed., *Works*, vol. 6 (1857)
Dyce 1866	Alexander Dyce, ed., *Works*, vol. 8 (1866)
EH	*England's Helicon*, ed. Hyder H. Rollins, 2 vols. (Cambridge, Mass., 1935)
Evans	*Poems*, Printed for Thomas Evans (1775)
Fidessa	Bartholomew Griffin, *Fidessa, more chaste than kind* (1596)

G. B. Evans	G. Blakemore Evans, ed., *The Sonnets* (Cambridge, 1996)
Gentleman	Francis Gentleman, ed., *Poems* (1774)
Gildon	Charles Gildon, ed., *Works*, vol. 7 (1710) (appended to Rowe)
Gildon 1714	Charles Gildon, ed., *Works*, vol. 9 (1714)
Globe	W. G. Clark and W. A. Wright, eds., *Works*, Globe Edition (Cambridge and London, 1864)
Hazlitt	William Hazlitt, ed., *Supplementary Works* (1852)
Hudson	H. N. Hudson, ed., *Works*, vol. 11 (Boston, Mass., 1856)
Hudson 1881	H. N. Hudson, ed., *Complete Works*, vol. 19 (Boston, Mass., 1881)
Ingram and Redpath	W. G. Ingram and Theodore Redpath, eds., *Shakespeare's Sonnets* (1964; 2nd edn. 1978)
Kerrigan	John Kerrigan, ed., *The Sonnets and A Lover's Complaint* (Harmondsworth, 1986)
Kerrigan 2	John Kerrigan, ed., *The Motives of Woe: Shakespeare and 'Female Complaint'. A Critical Anthology* (Oxford, 1991)
Knight	Charles Knight, ed., *Works: (Volume 2 Tragedies)* Pictorial Edition (1842)
Lever	J. W. Lever, ed., *The Rape of Lucrece* (Harmondsworth, 1971)
Lintot	Bernard Lintot, ed., *A Collection of Poems*, 2 vols. (1709, 1711)
Malone	Edmond Malone, ed., *Supplement to the Edition of Shakespeare's Plays Published in 1778* (1780)
Malone 1790	Edmond Malone, ed., *Plays and Poems*, vol. 10 (1790)
Maxwell	J. C. Maxwell, ed., *The Poems* (Cambridge, 1969)
Oulton	W. C. Oulton, ed., *Poems* (1804)
Oxford	Stanley Wells and Gary Taylor, eds., *William Shakespeare: The Complete Works* (Oxford, 1986)
Palgrave	F. T. Palgrave, ed., *Songs and Sonnets by William Shakespeare* (1878)
Pooler	C. K. Pooler, ed., *Sonnets*, The Arden Shakespeare, 2nd edn. (1931)
Prince	F. T. Prince, ed., *The Poems* (1960)
Ridley	M. R. Ridley, ed., *Sonnets* (1934)
Roe	John Roe, ed., *The Poems* (Cambridge, 1992)
Rollins 1	Hyder Edward Rollins, ed., *The Poems*, A New Variorum Edition (Philadelphia and London, 1938)

Rollins 2	Hyder Edward Rollins, ed., *The Sonnets*, A New Variorum Edition, 2 vols. (Philadelphia and London, 1944)
Rowe	N. Rowe, ed., *The Works of William Shakespeare* (1709), vol. I, p. xxxi ('An Extempore Epitaph')
Sewell	G. Sewell, ed., *Works*, vol. 7 (1725) (appended to Pope's edition)
Sewell 1728	G. Sewell, ed., *Works*, vol. 10 (1728)
Seymour-Smith	Martin Seymour-Smith, ed., *Shakespeare's Sonnets* (1963)
Staunton	Howard Staunton, ed., *Plays*, vol. 3 (1860)
Stow	John Stow, *Survey of London* (1633), p. 825 ('Epitaph on Elias James')
Tucker	T. G. Tucker ed., *The Sonnets* (Cambridge, 1924)
Tyler	Thomas Tyler, ed., *Sonnets* (1890)
Vendler	Helen Vendler, ed., *The Art of Shakespeare's Sonnets* (Cambridge, Mass., 1997)
Verity	A. W. Verity, ed., *Sonnets and Poems* in *Works*, vol. 8, Henry Irving Shakespeare (1890)
Weelkes	Thomas Weelkes, *Madrigals to 3, 4, 5, and 6 voices* (1597)
White	R. G. White, ed., *The Works of Shakespeare* (Boston, Mass., 1865)
Wyndham	George Wyndham, ed., *Poems* (1898)

OTHER WORKS AND ABBREVIATIONS

Abbott	E. A. Abbott, *A Shakespearean Grammar*, rev. edn. (1870)
Aen.	Virgil, *The Aeneid*, in *Virgil*, ed. with a translation by H. Rushton Fairclough, 2 vols., rev. edn. (Cambridge, Mass. and London, 1934)
Akrigg	G. P. V. Akrigg, *Shakespeare and the Earl of Southampton* (1968)
Allusion Book	*The Shakespeare Allusion-Book: A Collection of Allusions to Shakespeare from 1591–1700*, 2 vols., ed. John Munro, reissued with a preface by Sir Edmund Chambers (1932)
Arber	*A Transcript of the Registers of the Company of Stationers of London*, ed. E. Arber, 5 vols. (1875–94)
Baldwin	T. W. Baldwin, *On the Literary Genetics of Shakspere's Poems and Sonnets* (Urbana, Ill., 1950)
Bate	Jonathan Bate, *Shakespeare and Ovid* (Oxford, 1993)

Beal	Peter Beal, *Index of English Literary Manuscripts vol. 1* (London and New York, 1980)
Beaumont and Fletcher	Fredson Bowers, ed., *The Dramatic Works in the Beaumont and Fletcher Canon*, 10 vols. (Cambridge, 1966–96)
Bullough	Geoffrey Bullough, ed., *Narrative and Dramatic Sources of Shakespeare Volume 1: Early Comedies, Poems, Romeo and Juliet* (London, Henley, and New York, 1957)
Bush	Douglas Bush, *Mythology and the Renaissance Tradition in English Poetry* (Minneapolis, 1932)
Chambers	E. K. Chambers, *William Shakespeare: A Study of Facts and Problems*, 2 vols. (Oxford, 1930)
Dent	R. W. Dent, *Shakespeare's Proverbial Language* (Berkeley, Los Angeles, and London, 1981)
Donaldson	Ian Donaldson, *The Rapes of Lucretia: A Myth and its Transformations* (Oxford, 1982)
Dubrow	Heather Dubrow, *Captive Victors: Shakespeare's Narrative Poems and Sonnets* (Ithaca and London, 1987)
ELR	*English Literary Renaissance*
Eyre	George Edward Briscoe Eyre, *A Transcript of the Registers of the Worshipful Company of Stationers from 1640–1708 AD*, 3 vols. (1913–14)
Fasti	*Ovid*, edited with a translation by James George Frazer, vol. 5 (Cambridge, Mass. and London, 1976)
FQ	Edmund Spenser, *The Faerie Queene*, ed. A. C. Hamilton (1977)
Geneva	*The Bible and Holy Scriptures contained in the Old and New Testament* (Geneva, 1560)
Gill	Roma Gill, ed., *The Complete Works of Christopher Marlowe: Volume 1* (Oxford, 1987)
Golding	*Shakespeare's Ovid, being Arthur Golding's Translation of the Metamorphoses*, ed. W. H. D. Rouse (1961)
Harrison	William Harrison, *The Description of England*, ed. Georges Edelen (Washington, DC and New York, 1994)
Honigmann	E. A. J. Honigmann, *Shakespeare: The 'Lost Years'*, 2nd edn. (Manchester, 1998)
Hotson	Leslie Hotson, *Shakespeare's Sonnets Dated and Other Essays* (1949)
Kökeritz	Helge Kökeritz, *Shakespeare's Pronunciation* (New Haven and London, 1953)

Lettsom	See Walker (some conjectures privately conveyed to Dyce 1857)
LGW	*The Legend of Good Women* in *The Riverside Chaucer*, 3rd edn., ed. Larry D. Benson (Boston, 1987)
Livy	Titus Livius, *History of Rome Books I–II*, ed. with an English translation by B. O. Foster (Cambridge, Mass. and London, 1919)
Marsus	P. Ovidii Nasonis, *Fastorum Libri VI. Tristium V. De Ponto IIII. In Ibin. Cum Commentariis Doctiss. Virorum, Ant. Constantii Fanensis, Pauli Marsi, Barth. Merulae, Domitii Calderini, Zaroti: multo quam hactenus usquam, & elegantius & emendatius excusis* (Basle, 1550)
McKerrow	Ronald B. McKerrow, *Printers' and Publishers' Devices in England and Scotland. 1485–1540* (1913)
Met.	Ovid, *Metamorphoses*, ed. with an English translation by Frank Justus Miller, 2 vols. (Cambridge, Mass. and London, 1916)
Morley	Thomas Morley, *A Plain and Easy Introduction to Practical Music*, ed. R. Alec Harman (1952)
Nashe	*The Works of Thomas Nashe*, ed. Ronald B. McKerrow, rev. F. P. Wilson, 5 vols. (1958)
NQ	*Notes and Queries*
OED	*The Oxford English Dictionary*, 2nd edn. on CD ROM
OLD	*The Oxford Latin Dictionary*, ed. P. G. W. Glare (Oxford, 1982)
Partridge	Eric Partridge, *Shakespeare's Bawdy*, 3rd edn. (1968)
Partridge, *Grammar*	A. C. Partridge, *A Substantive Grammar of Shakespeare's Nondramatic Texts* (Charlottesville, Va., 1976)
Peacham	Henry Peacham, *The Garden of Eloquence* (1577)
Peacham (1593)	Henry Peacham, *The Garden of Eloquence* (1593)
Phaer	*The Thirteen Bookes of Aeneidos*, trans. Thomas Phaer and Thomas Twyne (1596)
Pliny	*The History of the World: Commonly called the Natural History*, trans. Philemon Holland, 2 vols. (1601)
Puttenham	George Puttenham, *The Arte of English Poesie*, ed. Gladys Doidge Willcock and Alice Walker (Cambridge, 1936)
Quintilian	*The Institutio Oratoria of Quintilian*, ed. with an English translation by H. E. Butler, 4 vols. (Cambridge Mass. and London, 1921–2)
RES	*Review of English Studies*

Schmidt	Alexander Schmidt, *Shakespeare Lexicon and Quotation Dictionary*, 3rd edn., rev. Gregor Sarrazin, 2 vols. (Berlin, 1902; repr. New York, 1971)
Schoenbaum	S. Schoenbaum, *William Shakespeare: A Compact Documentary Life* (Oxford, 1977)
SEL	*Studies in English Literature*
Sisson	C. J. Sisson, *New Readings in Shakespeare*, 2 vols. (Cambridge, 1956)
Smith	G. Gregory Smith, ed., *Elizabethan Critical Essays*, 2 vols. (Oxford, 1904)
Sokol	B. J. Sokol and Mary Sokol, *Shakespeare's Legal Language: A Dictionary* (London and New Brunswick, NJ, 2000)
SP	*Studies in Philology*
STC	*A Short-Title Catalogue of Books Printed in England, Scotland and Ireland, and of English Books Printed Abroad 1475–1640*, ed. A. W. Pollard and G. R. Redgrave, rev. W. A. Jackson, F. S. Ferguson, and Katharine F. Pantzer, 3 vols. (1976–91)
Tilley	M. P. Tilley, *A Dictionary of the Proverbs in England in the Sixteenth and Seventeenth Centuries* (Ann Arbor, 1950)
TLS	*The Times Literary Supplement*
Topsell	Edward Topsell, *The Historie of Four-Footed Beasts* (1607)
Turbervile	George Turbervile, *The Noble Arte of Venery or Hunting* (1576)
Walker	W. S. Walker, *A Critical Examination of the Text of Shakespeare*, ed. W. N. Lettsom, 3 vols. (1860)
Wilson	*Wilson's Arte of Rhetorique 1560*, ed. G. H. Mair (Oxford, 1909)

SONNET SEQUENCES AND APPROXIMATE DATES

Anon., *Zepheria* (1594)

William Alexander, *Aurora* (printed 1604; possibly composed *c.* 1592)

Barnabe Barnes, *Parthenophil and Parthenophe* (1593)

Richard Barnfield, *Cynthia* (1595)

E.C., *Emaricdulfe* (1595)

Henry Constable, *Spiritual Sonnets* (composed 1590s; first printed 1815)

Henry Constable, *Diana* (printed 1592)

Alexander Craig, *Amorous Songs, Sonnets, and Elegies* (1606)

Samuel Daniel, *Delia* (50 sonnets in 1592, 54 later in 1592, revised in 1594, 55 sonnets in 1595, 57 sonnets in 1601)

Sir John Davies, *Gulling Sonnets* (composed *c*.1594; first printed 1873)

Michael Drayton, *Idea's Mirror* 51 sonnets in 1594; revised and augmented as *Idea* in 1599, which was subsequently revised in 1600, when eight sonnets were added, in 1602, when one was added, in 1605, when seven were added, and in 1619, when ten more were added)

Giles Fletcher, *Licia* (1593)

Fulke Greville, Lord Brooke, *Caelica* (composed *c*.1590–1610; printed 1633)

Bartholomew Griffin, *Fidessa* (1596)

Thomas Lodge, *Phyllis* (1593)

Henry Lok, *Sundry Christian Passions* (1593)

R[ichard] L[ynche], *Diella* (1596)

David Murray, *Caelia* (appended to his *Sophonisba* of 1611)

William Percy, *Sonnets to the Fairest Coelia* (1594)

Sir Philip Sidney, *Astrophil and Stella* (first printed 1591)

William Smith, *Chloris* (1596)

Edmund Spenser, *Amoretti* (1595)

Thomas Watson, *Hecatompathia* (1582)

T[homas] W[atson], *The Tears of Fancy* (1593)

Venus and Adonis

Vilia miretur vulgus: mihi flavus Apollo
Pocula Castalia plena ministret aqua.

TO THE RIGHT HONOURABLE
Henry Wriothesley, Earl of Southampton,
and Baron of Titchfield.   5

Right honourable, I know not how I shall offend in dedi-
cating my unpolished lines to your Lordship, nor how the
world will censure me for choosing so strong a prop to
support so weak a burden; only if your Honour seem but
pleased I account myself highly praised, and vow to take   10
advantage of all idle hours, till I have honoured you with
some graver labour. But if the first heir of my invention

DEDICATION

1–2 *Vilia . . . aqua* 'Let the common herd be
amazed by worthless things; but for me
let golden Apollo provide cups full of
the water of the Muses', Ovid, *Amores*
1.15.35–6. The epigraph presents the
poem as a work which is inspired, set
apart from the common run of writing,
and which invites an elite readership.

4 **Henry   Wriothesley**   The   Earl   of
Southampton (aged 19 at the time of pub-
lication) is also the dedicatee of *Lucrece*.
Venus was only the second literary work
dedicated to him. For details of his life
and Shakespeare's reasons for dedicating
the poem to him, see Introduction, pp.
10–15.

7 **unpolished** It was conventional to empha-
size the lack of finish of a poem dedicated
to a noble patron, as in the envoy to
Thomas Watson's *Tears of Fancy* (regis-
tered in August 1593): 'Go, idle lines,
unpolished, rude and base'. Compare 'my
untutored lines', *Lucrece* dedication, l. 4
and Sonnet *16*.10.

11 **idle hours** The modesty topos continues,
but with a twist. The poet humbly sug-
gests that his hours of work are mere
nothings; at the same time he implies
that he is no common labourer, but a
person who has the leisure in which to
write.

12 **some graver labour** is generally thought
to allude to *Lucrece*, which was dedicated

to Southampton in the following year. For
readers in 1593 the *graver labour* might
have suggested epic (Patrick Cheney, pri-
vately). Although it was conventional for
love poets to promise to go on to address
'graver writs', *OED* cites this as the first use
of the comparative of *graver* in sense 2,
'weighty, important', as used of a work of
literature. 'Gravior' is regularly used by
classical poets who were mapping out
their future careers. This underlies
Shakespeare's usage here: the proem to
the pseudo-Virgilian *Culex* (translated by
Spenser as *Virgil's Gnat* in 1591) promises,
ll. 8–10: 'posterius *grauiore* sono tibi musa
loquetur | nostra, dabunt cum securos
mihi tempora fructus, | ut tibi digna tuo
poliantur carmina sensu', which Spenser
translated as 'Hereafter, when as season
more secure | Shall bring forth fruit, this
Muse shall speak to thee | In bigger notes,
that may thy sense allure'. The word is
also used by Golding in this sense when he
describes the 'epic' battle between the
Lapiths and Centaurs: 'I erst in graver
verse | The giants slain in Phlægra fields
with thunder, did rehearse' (10.155–6).
This corresponds to Ovid's 'plectro grav-
iore', and comes from the same book as
the tale of Venus and Adonis.

12 **first heir of my invention** The poem was
the first printed work to which Shake-
speare's name was attached.

173

prove deformed I shall be sorry it had so noble a godfa-
ther, and never after ear so barren a land, for fear it yield
me still so bad a harvest. I leave it to your honourable   15
survey, and your Honour to your heart's content, which
I wish may always answer your own wish, and the
world's hopeful expectation.

Your Honour's in all duty,

William Shakespeare.   20

14 **ear** plough
16 **survey** (a) 'literary examination' (*OED* 4);
(b) 'assessment of the scale and value of
the land', picking out the preceding agri-
cultural metaphors

Venus and Adonis

Even as the sun with purple-coloured face
Had ta'en his last leave of the weeping morn,
Rose-cheeked Adonis hied him to the chase.
Hunting he loved, but love he laughed to scorn.
    Sick-thoughted Venus makes amain unto him,   5
    And like a bold-faced suitor 'gins to woo him.

'Thrice fairer than my self', thus she began.
'The field's chief flower, sweet above compare,
Stain to all nymphs, more lovely than a man,
More white and red than doves or roses are: 10

8 field's] Q (fields); fields' OXFORD

VENUS AND ADONIS

1–6 The poem begins with a *chronographia*, 'when we do plainly describe any time for delectation's sake, as the morning, the evening, midnight . . . Examples. The morning: When the bright beams of the East hath driven away the dark shadow of the Night; when the lark doth first amount on high, and welcome the morning shine with her cheerful song', Peacham, sig. O4ᵛ.

1 **Even as** just when; but *even as* is more usually used by Shakespeare to mark a simile, which here connects Adonis with the heartless sun. *Even* is, as usually, monosyllabic. This opening was widely imitated almost immediately on publication, and became a generic indicator of the erotic epyllion: so Richard Barnfield's *Affectionate Shepherd* (1594), ll. 1–2: 'Scarce had the morning star hid from the light | Heaven's crimson canopy with stars bespangled'.
purple-coloured establishes the work as one in which compound adjectives (of which there are four in the first stanza) strive to make English compete in richness with Latin. *Purpureus* means 'red' and connotes 'imperial'; it is used in Ovid's *Amores* 1.3.14 to describe blushing modesty, and in *Amores* 1.13.10 to describe the flush of dawn.

3 **Rose-cheeked** A healthy flush contrasts Adonis's cheek with the sexually sated purple of the sun. Compare Christopher Marlowe's *Hero and Leander* ll. 91–3: 'The men of wealthy Sestos, every year, | (For his sake whom their goddess held so dear, | Rose-cheeked Adonis) kept a solemn feast'. (Quotations modernized from Gill.)
hied him hurried

4 **laughed to scorn** is a set phrase for contemptuous mockery. Its hubristic overtones are apparent from the promise of the witches in *Macbeth* 4.1.95–6 ('Laugh to scorn | The power of man'), which echoes ironically through 5.5.3 and 5.7 15.

5 **Sick-thoughted** love-sick
makes amain goes swiftly, with full force. *Make* as a verb of motion can carry a suggestion of aggressive or hostile intent in Shakespeare, and *amain* generally means 'with full strength': Venus is already presented as potentially a predator.

9 **Stain** source of shame (because he is more beautiful than they)

10 **white and red** Traditionally it is women whose faces are described as red and white (as in the description of the cheeks of the nymph Scylla in Thomas Lodge's *Scylla's Metamorphosis* (1589), l. 294: 'ruddy rose bespread on whitest milk'.

Nature that made thee with herself at strife,
Saith that the world hath ending with thy life.

'Vouchsafe, thou wonder, to alight thy steed,
And rein his proud head to the saddle-bow.
If thou wilt deign this favour, for thy meed   15
A thousand honey secrets shalt thou know.
    Here come and sit, where never serpent hisses,
    And being set, I'll smother thee with kisses,

'And yet not cloy thy lips with loathed satiety,
But rather famish them amid their plenty,   20
Making them red, and pale, with fresh variety:
Ten kisses short as one, one long as twenty.
    A summer's day will seem an hour but short,
    Being wasted in such time-beguiling sport.'

With this she seizeth on his sweating palm,   25
The precedent of pith and livelihood,
And trembling in her passion, calls it balm,
Earth's sovereign salve, to do a goddess good.

---

11 **at strife** Nature aspires to overgo herself in making Adonis who will not breed as she wishes. Compare ll. 953–4.

12 **world hath . . . life** Since Adonis is nature's best work the world will die with him. The argument anticipates Sonnet 11, and also *Romeo* 1.1.213: 'when she dies, with beauty dies her store.'

13 **Vouchsafe** graciously condescend (usually used of benefits granted by a superior, or by a lover)
alight alight from (Shakespeare's only transitive use)

14 **And rein . . . saddle-bow** Horses were restrained either by tying the reins to an object, or, as here, by looping the reins back onto the *saddle-bow* (the raised arch at the front of the saddle).

15 **deign** graciously grant
meed reward

18 **set** seated
smother The literal sense, 'suffocate', is strong here.

19–20 **not cloy . . . plenty** That desire creates an appetite which it cannot satisfy is a commonplace. Ovid's Narcissus cries 'inopem me copia fecit' (abundance makes me want) at *Met.* 3.466 and

Shakespeare's Cleopatra 'makes hungry | Where most she satisfies', *Antony* 2.2.243–4.

23 **an hour but short** no more than a brief hour

24 **wasted** spent. The word has strong associations with destruction and idleness, which Venus seeks carelessly to pass over.
time-beguiling 'Beguile' can mean simply to pass time pleasantly (*OED* 5), but *OED* 1, 'to delude, deceive, cheat', is in the background here.

25 **seizeth** She grabs him. 'Seize' in legal contexts means 'to take possession', so the verb implies a predatory aim.

26 **precedent . . . livelihood** A sweaty palm was taken in the period as a sign of radical moisture, and hence an indicator (*precedent*) of sexual vitality (*pith and livelihood*), as in Othello's suspicious 'This hand is moist, my lady' to Desdemona, *Othello* 3.4.36. Cf. Tilley (H86): 'A moist hand argues an amorous nature'.

28 **sovereign salve** is a Spenserianism, meaning 'a remedy for all ills'. It often has heavenly associations (as when the River of Life is described by Spenser in *FQ* 1.11.48 as 'A trickling streame of Balme,

Being so enraged, desire doth lend her force
Courageously to pluck him from his horse.   30

Over one arm the lusty courser's rein,
Under her other was the tender boy,
Who blushed and pouted in a dull disdain,
With leaden appetite, unapt to toy;
 She red, and hot, as coals of glowing fire,   35
 He red for shame, but frosty in desire.

The studded bridle on a ragged bough,
Nimbly she fastens (O how quick is love!);
The steed is stallèd up, and even now,
To tie the rider she begins to prove.   40
 Backward she pushed him, as she would be thrust,
 And governed him in strength though not in lust.

So soon was she along, as he was down,
Each leaning on their elbows and their hips.
Now doth she stroke his cheek, now doth he frown,   45
And 'gins to chide, out soon she stops his lips,

most soueraine', or when the medicine used to cure the wounded Marinell in 3.4.40 is described as 'soueraine balme and Nectar good | Good for both earthly med'cine, and heauenly food'). These associations are consciously inverted here: Adonis's earthly sweat becomes a cure-all for a goddess.

29 **enraged** Venus becomes both a warrior who tries *courageously* (l. 30) to unhorse her adversary with martial rage, and a lover overwhelmed with passion.

30 **pluck** The word grows to matter in the poem, where it is persistently associated with premature reaping, until Venus finally, surprisingly, *crops* rather than 'plucks' the flower Adonis at l. 1175. Cf. also ll. 416, 528, 574, 946, 1150.

31 **lusty** full of life and spirits (with a slight sexual suggestion)

33 **disdain** is often used of sexually unyielding mistresses (as also at l. 112 below).

34 **leaden . . . toy** Lead was associated with melancholy and hence with insusceptibility to sexual desire. So Adonis is

constitutionally unsuited to amorous play (*unapt to toy*).

37 **studded bridle** To have ornamented harness was a sign of supreme lavishness, as in the Lord's temptation of Christopher Sly, *Shrew*, Induction 2.40–1: 'Or wilt thou ride, thy horses shall be trapped, | Their harness studded all with gold and pearl.'
ragged rough

39 **stallèd up** tied up, prevented from moving. Compare *P. Pilgrim* 18.2.
even is here (unusually) two syllables.

40 **prove** attempt

41 **Backward . . . him** Ovid's Venus also abruptly gets Adonis to sit: 'libet hac requiescere tecum, | Et requievit; pressitque et gramen et ipsum', *Met.* 10.556–7 (' "It is pleasing to sit here with you." And she sat, and weighed down both the grass and him').

42 **And . . . lust** 'She was able to overcome him, but not to compel him to desire her.'

43 **along** reclining at her length beside him

46 **stops** The physical sense 'plug up' (*OED* 1) is active here.

And kissing speaks, with lustful language broken:
'If thou wilt chide, thy lips shall never open.'

He burns with bashful shame, she with her tears
Doth quench the maiden burning of his cheeks;   50
Then with her windy sighs, and golden hairs,
To fan, and blow them dry again she seeks.
  He saith she is immodest, blames her miss;
  What follows more, she murders with a kiss.

Even as an empty eagle sharp by fast   55
Tires with her beak on feathers, flesh, and bone,
Shaking her wings, devouring all in haste,
Till either gorge be stuffed, or prey be gone:
  Even so she kissed his brow, his cheek, his chin,
  And where she ends, she doth anew begin.   60

Forced to content, but never to obey,
Panting he lies, and breatheth in her face;
She feedeth on the steam, as on a prey,
And calls it heavenly moisture, air of grace,
  Wishing her cheeks were gardens full of flowers,   65
  So they were dewed with such distilling showers.

---

54 murders] Q (murthers); smothers Q7 56 feathers] Q; feather Q2 63 prey] Q (pray)

47 **broken** interrupted. The whole line leaves it masterfully unclear whether speech interrupts the real language of lovers, which is kissing, or vice versa. The effect is to mimic the tangled word-order of Ovid's description of Venus in *Met.* 10.559: 'sic ait, ac mediis interserit oscula verbis' ('thus she speaks and intersows kisses in the midst of words'—in which 'oscula', kisses, is artfully planted in the middle of the line).

50 **maiden burning** virginal glow. Up to *c.*1500 *maiden* could be used of a male virgin. Here it re-emphasizes Adonis's androgynous youth.

53 **miss** misbehaviour. Shakespeare's only usage in this archaic sense (although compare Sonnet 35.7).

55 **sharp by fast** eager through fasting. *Sharp* conveys predatory eagerness, and perhaps also thinness (as in 'My falcon now is sharp and passing empty', *Shrew* 4.1.176).

56 **Tires** tugs at (*OED* s.v. 'tire' *v.* 2, 2: 'Of a hawk: To pull or tear with the beak at a tough morsel given to it that it may exercise itself in this way'). Compare *3 Henry VI (True Tragedy)* 1.1.269–70: 'like an empty eagle | Tire on the flesh of me and of my son.'

61 **content** forced to give satisfaction (to her). *Content* (accented on the second syllable) functions chiefly as a verb with Venus as its implied indirect object (compare l. 213), but the verb can also mean 'to be content with what one has (even if it is unpleasant)'. The word may also function as a noun meaning 'a state of imposed acquiescence', as in *Othello* 3.4.118: 'So I shall clothe me in a forced content'.

63 **prey** is spelled 'pray' in Q, which was a rare but recognized form of 'prayer' in 1593. This anticipates the *heavenly moisture* and *air of grace* in the next line.

66 **So** provided that
distilling which condense from minute drops

178

Look how a bird lies tangled in a net,
So fastened in her arms Adonis lies.
Pure shame and awed resistance made him fret,
Which bred more beauty in his angry eyes: 70
   Rain, added to a river that is rank,
   Perforce will force it overflow the bank.

Still she entreats, and prettily entreats,
For to a pretty ear she tunes her tale.
Still is he sullen, still he lours and frets,   75
'Twixt crimson shame, and anger ashy pale,
   Being red she loves him best, and being white,
   Her best is bettered with a more delight.

Look how he can, she cannot choose but love;
And by her fair immortal hand she swears,   80
From his soft bosom never to remove,
Till he take truce with her contending tears,
   Which long have rained, making her cheeks all wet,
   And one sweet kiss shall pay this countless debt.

Upon this promise did he raise his chin,   85
Like a dive-dapper peering through a wave,

---

75 still he] Q; still she Q4

67 **Look how** The formula is the equivalent of 'just as', and is found in Marlowe ('Look how their hands, so were their hearts united', *Hero and Leander* l. 511), and occasionally in narrative poems which imitated *Venus and Adonis*. It is usually used in the dramatic works to urge an onstage audience to watch a particular character. This poem's repeated use of imperative forms of 'look' urges a reader to see the poem as a piece of pictorialism. Compare ll. 79, 289, 295, 529, 815, 925.

69 **awed resistance** intimidated efforts to resist

71 **rank** swollen. The word can also mean 'lustful' (*OED* 13).

76 **'Twixt . . . pale** He blushes with shame and turns white with rage. Ashes are proverbially pale (Dent A339).

78 **more** greater. Compare *Lucrece* l. 332.

80 **by her . . . swears** Oaths or troth-plightings are frequently made 'by this hand' (as in Benedict's vow to Beatrice 'By this hand, I love thee', *Much Ado* 4.1.525). Sometimes oaths made 'by this hand' can both act as a statement of good faith and present a threat of physical force, as in Stefano's catchphrase 'by this hand, I will supplant some of your teeth' (*Tempest* 3.3.50). Venus's oath here suggests a formal troth-plighting, but the threat of violence which underlies her oath emerges in her intention *never to remove* (like a siege) and in *truce*.

82 **take truce** make peace
   contending tears tears which are doing battle with him.

84 **countless** inestimable. Q's 'comptless' suggests 'for which an account cannot be given'. This use of the '-less' suffix makes the word a typical Shakespearian coinage. *OED* cites the near-contemporary *Titus* 5.3.158 as the first usage of the word.

86 **dive-dapper** a dabchick or little grebe, which appears to duck nervously away

Who being looked on, ducks as quickly in:
So offers he to give what she did crave,
    But when her lips were ready for his pay,
    He winks, and turns his lips another way.   90

Never did passenger in summer's heat,
More thirst for drink, than she for this good turn.
Her help she sees, but help she cannot get;
She bathes in water, yet her fire must burn:
    'O pity', gan she cry, 'flint-hearted boy,   95
    'Tis but a kiss I beg; why art thou coy?

'I have been wooed as I entreat thee now,
Even by the stern and direful god of war,
Whose sinewy neck in battle ne'er did bow,
Who conquers where he comes in every jar,   100
    Yet hath he been my captive, and my slave,
    And begged for that which thou unasked shalt have.

'Over my altars hath he hung his lance,
His battered shield, his uncontrollèd crest,
And for my sake hath learned to sport, and dance,   105

94 her fire] Q; in fire Q7

from observers. This behaviour (comical here) is not simply the result of shyness: grebes engage in elaborate courtship displays, including ritualized preening, head shaking, and diving.

87 **Who** is often used as neuter pronoun. See Abbott §264.

88 **offers** Adonis makes an action which gives a show of an intention to yield (*OED* 5b), rather than directly making a proposal (*OED* 4). But the momentary uncertainty as to how definite his acceptance is tricks both Venus and the reader.

89 **pay** payment

90 **winks** is a variant form of 'wince' (*OED* s.v. 'wink' *v.* 2), but Venus's comment at l. 121 suggests that Adonis closes his eyes as he flinches away.

91 **passenger** traveller on foot

92 **for this good turn** (a) in order to win the benefit of a kiss; (b) as a result of Adonis's virtuous swerving away from her. *Good turn* has erotic associations, as in *Antony*

2.5.58–9: '*Messenger*: He's bound unto Octavia. *Cleopatra*: For what good turn? *Messenger*: For the best turn i' th' bed.'

94 **She . . . burn** The familiar Petrarchan paradox that lovers freeze in fire and burn in ice is given a literal twist: Venus is still awash with tears, so *bathes in water*.

95 **'O pity . . . flint-hearted'** continues the inverted Petrarchanism: female mistresses are proverbially flint-hearted in this period (Dent H311).

98 **god of war** Venus was married to Vulcan, but became the lover of Mars. The story of his submission to her is related in Lucretius, *De rerum natura* 1.29–40. She omits one crucial detail: that both she and Mars were eventually trapped in her husband Vulcan's net.

99 **bow** To bow the neck is a formal recognition of defeat.

100 **jar** fight, encounter

104 **uncontrollèd** unvanquished
   crest feathers on the top of a helmet

105 **sport** play (with an erotic overtone)

To toy, to wanton, dally, smile, and jest,
   Scorning his churlish drum and ensign red,
   Making my arms his field, his tent my bed.

'Thus he that over-ruled, I over-swayed,
Leading him prisoner in a red-rose chain.   110
Strong-tempered steel his stronger strength obeyed;
Yet was he servile to my coy disdain.
   O be not proud, nor brag not of thy might,
   For mastering her that foiled the God of fight.

'Touch but my lips with those fair lips of thine   115
(Though mine be not so fair, yet are they red),
The kiss shall be thine own as well as mine.
What seest thou in the ground? Hold up thy head,
   Look in mine eye-balls, there thy beauty lies:
   Then why not lips on lips, since eyes in eyes?   120

'Art thou ashamed to kiss? Then wink again,
And I will wink, so shall the day seem night.
Love keeps his revels where there are but twain;
Be bold to play; our sport is not in sight:
   These blue-veined violets whereon we lean   125
   Never can blab, nor know not what we mean.

119 there] Q; where Q5   123 are] Q; be Q2   126 know not] Q; know they Q7

107 **churlish** rough, violent (but also 'common' or 'vulgar')
108 **arms his field** Venus's amorous arms become Mars's battlefield. There is also a play on *arms* meaning 'heraldic insignia' (*OED* 14a) and *field* meaning the coloured background on which insignia are set (*OED* 13a).
111 **obeyed** is spelt 'obayed' in Q to preserve the eye-rhyme.
113 **nor brag not** The double negative in Shakespeare is often emphatic.
115 **Touch but simply touch**
118 **What see'st ... ground** 'What is there in what you are looking at (the ground) that is worth your attention?' (Kittredge). The poem often presents these conversational stage-directions, which establish the gestures and spatial relationships of the speakers.
119 **there thy ... lies** Adonis is asked to see

himself reflected in Venus's eyes. Lovers 'look babies' in each other's eyes, as they see small images of themselves.
123 **keeps his revels** stages his entertainments
124 **in sight** in public view. The images here suggest a private, coterie performance of love's erotic drama.
125 **blue-veined violets** A much-imitated phrase (e.g. by Richard Barnfield in *The Affectionate Shepherd* st. 30). Violets are traditionally associated with evanescence (*Hamlet* 1.3.7–8: 'A violet in the youth of primy nature, | Forward not permanent, sweet not lasting').
126 **blab** blurt out our secrets
nor know not The double negative is emphatic. It may have been ambiguous or awkward to early readers, hence the compositorial emendation in Q7 (maintained in later Quartos) to 'know they'.

'The tender spring upon thy tempting lip
Shows thee unripe; yet mayst thou well be tasted.
Make use of time, let not advantage slip:
Beauty within itself should not be wasted,   130
    Fair flowers that are not gathered in their prime
    Rot, and consume themselves in little time.

'Were I hard-favoured, foul, or wrinkled old,
Ill-nurtured, crookèd, churlish, harsh in voice,
O'er-worn, despisèd, rheumatic, and cold,   135
Thick-sighted, barren, lean, and lacking juice;
    Then mightst thou pause, for then I were not for thee,
    But having no defects, why dost abhor me?

'Thou canst not see one wrinkle in my brow,
Mine eyes are grey, and bright, and quick in turning.   140
My beauty as the spring doth yearly grow,
My flesh is soft, and plump, my marrow burning.
    My smooth moist hand, were it with thy hand felt,
    Would in thy palm dissolve, or seem to melt.

'Bid me discourse, I will enchant thine ear,   145
Or like a fairy trip upon the green,
Or like a nymph, with long dishevelled hair,

127 **tender spring** light down that will become a beard
129–32 **Make . . . time** These lines anticipate some of the arguments of Sonnets *1–17*. Compare esp. l. 130 with Sonnet 9.11. They draw on a long tradition of poems which urge lovers to seize the flower of youth ('carpe florem'), such as Ovid, *Ars Amatoria* 3.59–80.
129 **advantage** favourable opportunity
133 **hard-favoured** harsh-featured. At l. 931 the word also implies tyrannical rigour; in *Lucrece* l. 1632 it suggests coarseness of feature.
133 **foul** ugly
134 **crookèd** deformed
135 **O'er-worn** worn out with age. Compare Sonnet 63.2.
    rheumatic The stress is on the first syllable. The word means 'dripping with rheum or catarrh'. To be *cold* and rheumy, as Venus imagines herself here, was thought to be characteristic of the old.

136 **Thick-sighted** poor-sighted. The skin on the eye was believed to wrinkle and thicken with age. See Sonnet 3.12 n.
    juice vigour. See l. 26 n.
138 **defects** is stressed on the second syllable.
140 **grey** probably corresponds to what we would now call 'blue', and is traditionally a sign of beauty.
142 **marrow burning** Marrow is often associated with sexual vitality (as in *All's Well* 2.3.278, 'Spending his manly marrow in her arms'). To have *marrow burning* was a near proverbial sign of sexual desire in the sixteenth century (*OED* s.v. 'marrow' 1b).
143 **moist hand** See l. 26 n.
146 **trip** 'To move lightly and nimbly on the feet' (*OED* 1)
147 **nymph** a semi-divine inhabitant of woods or waters, with a slightly more human appeal via the secondary sense of 'a young woman'

Dance on the sands, and yet no footing seen.
  Love is a spirit all compact of fire,
  Not gross to sink, but light, and will aspire.   150

'Witness this primrose bank whereon I lie:
These forceless flowers like sturdy trees support me;
Two strengthless doves will draw me through the sky,
From morn till night, even where I list to sport me.
  Is love so light, sweet boy, and may it be   155
  That thou should think it heavy unto thee?

'Is thine own heart to thine own face affected?
Can thy right hand seize love upon thy left?
Then woo thyself, be of thyself rejected.
Steal thine own freedom, and complain on theft.   160
  Narcissus so himself himself forsook,
  And died to kiss his shadow in the brook.

155 should] Q; shouldst Q2   160 on] Q; of Q4

148 **footing** footprint. Compare the elves
invoked in *Tempest* 5.1.34–5 'that on the
sands with printless foot | Do chase the
ebbing Neptune'.

149 **all compact** wholly compounded. *Compact* is often used in the period to describe
the combination of various humours
which makes up an individual temperament. In Shakespeare it is generally used
when one quality is dangerously pronounced, as in Theseus's 'The lunatic, the
lover, and the poet | Are of imagination
all compact', *Dream* 5.1.7–8. Compare
Lucrece l. 530.

150 **gross** heavy, earthy
  will aspire desires to ascend. Fire was
believed to have a desire to ascend to the
sphere above the earth in which it properly resided.

151 **primrose** As with the violets in l. 125, the
flora suggests a setting in March to April,
rather than the midsummer day which is
elsewhere implied. The Athenian festival
of Adonia, a fertility ritual which celebrated the death of Adonis, was held
annually in midsummer.

152 **forceless** powerless, weak

154 **list** please

155 **light** is meant by Venus to mean 'weightless' and hence 'insignificant'. The further sense 'wanton, unchaste' (*OED* 14b)
hangs rather heavily over her.

155 **sweet boy** For the erotic associations of
this phrase, see Sonnet 108.5 n.

156 **heavy** (a) wearisome; (b) having serious
consequences

157–62 The allusion marks a connection
with John Clapham's *Narcissus* (on which
see Introduction, pp. 11–12), as well as
anticipating the argument of Sonnet 1.

157 **affected** in love with

158 **seize love** The image is of a man so in love
with himself that he grasps his own hand
as a lover would. It is reinforced by a
strong association between the verb *seize*
and the moment of betrothal, as in
Lear (Folio) 1.1.252, when France accepts
Cordelia as his wife with 'Thee and
thy virtues here I seize upon.' Compare
l. 25 n.

160 **complain on** complain against. This is a
standard poetic formula (*OED* s.v. 'complain' 6b), which was dying out by the
seventeenth century, hence Q4's emendation in 1596 to 'complain of'. See l. 544.

162 **And died . . . brook** In Ovid's story of
Narcissus the hero turns into a flower
(*Met*. 3.508–10), but in a variant version,
common in the sixteenth century, he
drowned after falling into the stream. In
Marlowe's *Hero and Leander* ll. 74–5 he
'leapt into the water for a kiss | Of his own
shadow', and Clapham's *Narcissus* ends
in this way, ll. 240–2. The tradition is

'Torches are made to light, jewels to wear,
Dainties to taste, fresh beauty for the use,
Herbs for their smell, and sappy plants to bear.   165
Things growing to themselves are growth's abuse;
    Seeds spring from seeds, and beauty breedeth beauty:
    Thou wast begot: to get it is thy duty.

'Upon the earth's increase why shouldst thou feed,
Unless the earth with thy increase be fed?   170
By law of nature thou art bound to breed,
That thine may live, when thou thyself art dead:
    And so in spite of death thou dost survive,
    In that thy likeness still is left alive.'

By this the love-sick Queen began to sweat,   175
For where they lay the shadow had forsook them,
And Titan, tirèd in the midday heat,
With burning eye did hotly overlook them,
    Wishing Adonis had his team to guide,
    So he were like him, and by Venus' side.   180

And now Adonis, with a lazy sprite,
And with a heavy, dark, disliking eye,
His louring brows o'erwhelming his fair sight,

summarized in Baldwin, 18–21. Compare *Lucrece* ll. 265–6, and Francis Beaumont's *Salmacis and Hermaphroditus* (1602), ll. 397–400.

162 **shadow** reflection

163–74 These conventional arguments for procreation have close parallels in the first seventeen Sonnets, and in *Hero and Leander* ll. 223–54 and *Romeo* 1.5.46–8.

164 That 'Beauty is made for use' is proverbial (Dent B170.1).

165 **sappy plants to bear** It is the purpose of young wood to bear fruit.

166 **to themselves** A similar enclosed reflexive form is used also to condemn the self-love of the friend in Sonnet 94.10.

168 **get** beget

169–70 **increase . . . increase** (a) fruits, abundant growth; (b) offspring. The word is stressed on the second syllable. The use here anticipates Sonnet 1.1.

172 **thine** 'Those who are thine; thy people, family, or kindred' (*OED* 5b). Compare Sonnet 10.14.

177 **Titan** the sun
tirèd in (a) attired in; (b) tired by. The poem presents a goddess of love in love, and the sun god suffering from his own heat.

178 **hotly overlook** burn down on them. There is a suggestion of sexually inflamed voyeurism here, since *hotly* can mean 'passionately', as at *Lucrece* l. 715.

179 **his team** The chariot of the sun is pulled by a *team* of four horses.

180 **So** if only

181 **lazy sprite** sluggish mind. The suggestion is that Adonis is constitutionally slow, or phlegmatic, and so unresponsive to the fiery energy of Venus's propositions.

182 **heavy** gloomy, unanimated. Compare the quickness of Venus's eyes at l. 140.
louring glowering. Q's spelling 'lowring' may play on 'lowering': the brow physically sinks over his eye, *o'erwhelming* (hanging threateningly over) it.

183 **his fair sight** eyes (compare *Lucrece* l. 104); although the phrase could also

Like misty vapours when they blot the sky,
   Souring his cheeks, cries, 'Fie, no more of love: 185
   The sun doth burn my face, I must remove.'

'Ay me', quoth Venus, 'Young, and so unkind,
What bare excuses mak'st thou to be gone?
I'll sigh celestial breath, whose gentle wind,
Shall cool the heat of this descending sun: 190
   I'll make a shadow for thee of my hairs;
   If they burn too, I'll quench them with my tears.

'The sun that shines from heaven, shines but warm,
And, lo, I lie between that sun and thee:
The heat I have from thence doth little harm.   195
Thine eye darts forth the fire that burneth me,
   And were I not immortal, life were done,
   Between this heavenly and earthly sun.

'Art thou obdurate, flinty, hard as steel?
Nay more than flint, for stone at rain relenteth: 200

---

185 Souring] Q (So wring) *There is a small space between the 'o' and the 'w'*   193 shines but] Q; *altered to* shineth but *by hand in the unique copy*   198 earthly] Q *altered to* this earthly *by hand in the unique copy*; this earthly Q8

function as either a subjective or objective genitive: 'the fair sight of him', or 'his own (beautiful) ability to see'

184 **vapours** noxious mists drawn up from the earth by the sun

185 **Souring his cheeks** pursing his cheeks as though he had tasted something sour. The *OED* cites only this and a passage spoken by that other great Shakespearian narcissist *Richard II* (2.1.170), 'made me sour my patient cheek', to support sense 4c: 'To invest with a sour expression'. The unusual word may explain why a thin space crept into Q between 'so' and 'wring'.

187 **Young . . . unkind** That youth should be tender-hearted is a truism to which Lear resorts when Cordelia refuses to respond to his request for love: 'So young and so untender?' (*Lear* (Folio) 1.1.106).

188 **bare** shamelessly inadequate; undisguised

190 **descending sun** Since it is now just past

noon (see l. 177) this has literal force: the sun is at its hottest as it starts to descend (although Roe argues that *descending* is transferred from the rays, which do descend, to the sun, which does not).

192 **queach** extinguish

194 **lo** a favourite word, used also in ll. 259, 280, 320, 853, 1128, 1135, 1185.

196 **Thine eye . . . me** That the lover's eye produces a scorching flame is a standard Petrarchism. *Darts* is the first cited usage in *OED* for sense 3: 'to send forth, or emit, suddenly and sharply'. Earlier usages had referred to the hurling of missiles, so the usage here conveys a greater physical force than it would now.

199 **obdurate** is stressed on the second syllable.

200 **relenteth** is worn away. Petrarchan lovers frequently blamed their mistresses for being harder than stone, since they would not yield to their lovers' torrential tears. It was proverbial that 'constant dropping will wear the stone' (Dent D618).

Art thou a woman's son and canst not feel
What 'tis to love, how want of love tormenteth?
    O had thy mother borne so hard a mind,
    She had not brought forth thee, but died unkind.

'What am I that thou shouldst contemn me this?   205
Or what great danger dwells upon my suit?
What were thy lips the worse for one poor kiss?
Speak, fair, but speak fair words, or else be mute.
    Give me one kiss, I'll give it thee again,
    And one for int'rest, if thou wilt have twain.   · 210

'Fie, lifeless picture, cold, and senseless stone,
Well-painted idol, image dull, and dead,
Statue contenting but the eye alone,
Thing like a man, but of no woman bred:
    Thou art no man, though of a man's complexion,   215
    For men will kiss even by their own direction.'

This said, impatience chokes her pleading tongue,
And swelling passion doth provoke a pause.
Red cheeks, and fiery eyes blaze forth her wrong:

203 hard] Q; bad Q2   208 Speak,] Q7; ~ ˄ Q

201 **woman's son** compare Sonnet 41.7–8, and Lyly's *Campaspe* 5.4.68: 'In mine opinion thou wert never born of a woman, that thou thinkest so hardly of women'.

202 **want** lack

203 **thy mother** In Ovid's *Metamorphoses* Adonis is the son of Myrrha, who incestuously loves her father. His love of himself consequently has more in common with the perverse desire experienced by his mother than Venus realizes. The irony is more explicit in 'The Shepherd's song of Venus and Adonis', attributed to 'H.C'. in *England's Helicon* (1600), fo. Z1ᵇ: 'Myrrha thy fair mother, | Most of any other, | Did my lovely hests respect'. Venus draws on the near-proverbial saying (Tilley M1196) 'If thy mother had been of that mind [not to marry] when she was a maiden, thou hadst not now been born to be of this mind to be a virgin', Lyly, *Euphues: The Anatomy of Wit* (1578), 230.

204 **unkind** unnatural. It is also the normal epithet used to describe a woman who resists a wooer's advances.

205 **contemn** despise and spurn

205 **this** thus. This is the last example quoted by the *OED* of this archaic adverbial use of *this*. Alternatively it is just possible that the whole phrase means 'that you should contemptuously deny me this [thing]'.

210 **twain** two

213 **Statue** Adonis was descended from Pygmalion's statue (which begot Paphus, who begot Cinyras, who begot Myrrha, who begot Adonis through incestuous union with her father).

215 **complexion** appearance. Originally it meant the individual blend of humours which constituted a particular type of person; so also 'constitution, disposition'.

216 **by their . . . direction** of their own accord, by their own instruction. The instinctiveness of sexual desire is a recurrent element in erotic narrative poems in the 1590s.

217 **pleading** anticipates the legal imagery of l. 220 (*judge, cause*).

219 **blaze** like fire; also with a secondary sense (*OED v.* 2) from heraldry, 'to blazon forth', or 'publish'.

Being judge in love, she cannot right her cause.   220
    And now she weeps, and now she fain would speak,
    And now her sobs do her intendments break.

Sometime she shakes her head, and then his hand;
Now gazeth she on him, now on the ground;
Sometime her arms enfold him like a band: 225
She would, he will not in her arms be bound.
    And when from thence he struggles to be gone,
    She locks her lily fingers one in one.

'Fondling', she saith, 'Since I have hemmed thee here
Within the circuit of this ivory pale,   230
I'll be a park, and thou shalt be my deer:
Feed where thou wilt, on mountain, or in dale;
    Graze on my lips, and if those hills be dry,
    Stray lower, where the pleasant fountains lie.

'Within this limit is relief enough,   235
Sweet bottom grass, and high delightful plain,

---

223 Sometime] Q; Sometimes Q4   231 deer] Q (deare)   235 Within] Q (Witin)

---

220 Being . . . cause 'Although she is the supreme arbiter in cases of love, she cannot do justice to her own case.' It was proverbial that 'No man ought to be judge in his own cause' (Dent M341).

222 intendments intentions

228 one in one she intertwines each of her fingers between his (or her own)

229 Fondling foolish boy. This is Shakespeare's only use of the term.

229 hemmed restricted. The usage without an adverbial extension such as 'in' or 'about' was not unusual in the period.

230 ivory pale ivory fence. *Pale* also plays on the pallor of Venus's arms, which encircle Adonis. As William Harrison put it in 1577: 'Our parks are generally enclosed with strong pale made of oak', Harrison, 254. Harrison goes on to deplore those noblemen who, like Venus, enclose parks for their exclusive pleasure. The term *pale* has a jurisdictional as well as territorial force (*OED* s.v. 'pale' *n*. 1, 4a): Venus is enclosing Adonis as a piece of her territory.

231 park has now lost its regal associations, but in this period it was used of 'an

enclosed tract of land held by royal grant or prescription for keeping beasts of the chase' (*OED* 1a). The conceit is not just whimsy: it places both physical and legal constraint on Adonis, while implying that he is a piece of royal property.

231 deer puns on 'dear'. Harrison, 255 notes, 'venison in England is neither bought nor sold as in other countries but maintained only for the pleasure of the owner and his friends'.

234 pleasant fountains Venus's geography becomes anatomical.

235 relief feeding. This is a term of art from hunting (*OED* 8a: 'Of the hare or hart: The act of seeking food; feeding or pasturing'), and its associations are potentially threatening: Turbervile, 171 implies that hunted animals are especially vulnerable when they seek *relief*: 'Hounds will have better scent of an hare when she goeth towards the relief, than when she goeth towards her form'.

236 bottom grass grass growing in a valley (and so especially succulent). *Bottom* was not yet a word for the backside, but the passage invites a reader to extend wordplay into bawdy.

Round rising hillocks, brakes obscure and rough,
To shelter thee from tempest, and from rain:
    Then be my deer, since I am such a park.
    No dog shall rouse thee, though a thousand bark.'   240

At this Adonis smiles, as in disdain,
That in each cheek appears a pretty dimple;
Love made those hollows, if himself were slain,
He might be buried in a tomb so simple,
    Foreknowing well, if there he came to lie,   245
    Why there love lived, and there he could not die.

These lovely caves, these round enchanting pits,
Opened their mouths to swallow Venus' liking:
Being mad before, how doth she now for wits?
Struck dead at first, what needs a second striking?   250
    Poor Queen of Love, in thine own law forlorn,
    To love a cheek that smiles at thee in scorn.

Now which way shall she turn? What shall she say?
Her words are done, her woes the more increasing;
The time is spent, her object will away,   255
And from her twining arms doth urge releasing.
    'Pity', she cries, 'Some favour, some remorse.'
    Away he springs, and hasteth to his horse.

237 **brakes obscure** hidden thickets (pubic hair)
240 **rouse** is again a term of art from hunting: 'To cause (game) to rise or issue from cover or lair' (*OED* 2), as in Turbervile, 106: 'The huntsman . . . shall then go before them and rouse the deer'.
241 **as in disdain** Given that parks were kept for the express purpose of hunting, and that Adonis, as a huntsman, would know this all too well, his *disdain* is not surprising. Hunting in parks, as opposed to forests, was held in disdain in this period.
242 **That** so that
243 **if he himself** so that if he were
246 **Why . . . die** i.e. Cupid cannot be dead in the grave which is made from Adonis's dimple, because love (Venus) lived there.
247 **pits** dimples. The word could continue

the hunting allusions, although *OED* 1f, 'An excavation, covered or otherwise hidden to serve as a trap for wild beasts', is not cited before 1611. The association between pits and predatory sexuality is, though, very strong in the roughly contemporary *Titus* 2.3.
248 **liking** affection
250 **Struck dead . . . striking** Venus was so smitten by love at its first assault that the additional blow struck by Adonis's dimples is unnecessary.
251 **in thine . . . forlorn** abandoned without aid in a matter that falls within your own jurisdiction
254 **her woes . . . increasing** Silence is often presented as exacerbating misery: see l. 331 and n.
255 **object** (a) Adonis, the object of her love; (b) her goal
257 **remorse** compassion

But lo, from forth a copse that neighbours by
A breeding jennet, lusty, young, and proud   260
Adonis' trampling courser doth espy,
And forth she rushes, snorts, and neighs aloud.
   The strong-necked steed being tied unto a tree
   Breaketh his rein, and to her straight goes he.

Imperiously he leaps, he neighs, he bounds,   265
And now his woven girths he breaks asunder.
The bearing earth with his hard hoof he wounds,
Whose hollow womb resounds like heaven's thunder.
   The iron bit he crusheth 'tween his teeth,
   Controlling what he was controllèd with.   270

His ears up pricked, his braided hanging mane
Upon his compassed crest now stand on end.

260 **jennet** a small Spanish horse. The word is generally used when the horse is sprightly and well turned out. The description may owe something to Ovid's *Ars Amatoria* 1.280. According to Thomas Blundeville, *The Four Chief Offices Belonging to Horsemanship* (1593), 13ʳ: 'Aristotle saith, that the mare for her part is more desirous to be covered about the mid-day'.
   proud can suggest sexual arousal. See Sonnet 151.10 and n.

261 **trampling courser** a stallion which shows its vigour by pawing the ground

263–70 The description of the horse is a virtuoso over-going of a simile from Marlowe's *Hero and Leander* ll. 625–9 ('For as a hot proud horse highly disdains | To have his head controlled, but breaks the reins, | Spits forth the ringled bit, and with his hooves | Checks the submissive ground: so he that loves, | The more he is restrained, the worse he fares'). Clapham's Narcissus mounts and rides a horse called 'caeca Libido' (blind passion: *Narcissus*, ll. 131–9), which Shakespeare's horse may seek to overgo. He may also have had in mind the description of a stallion in Virgil's *Georgics* 3.75–94, translated by Barnabe Googe in *Four Books of Husbandry* (1586), 115ᵛ–116ʳ: 'High crested is his neck, and like his head is framèd small. | His belly gaunt, his back is broad, and breasted big withal | ... | He scraping stands and making a deep hole, he paws the ground. | Whiles as aloud

his hornèd hoof all hollowed seems to sound'. The association between unbridled horses and sexual desire is as old as Plato's *Phaedrus* 253d, and was a commonplace of Renaissance iconography.

266 **woven girths** The straps which hold on the saddle are woven, rather than being made of leather.

267 **bearing** which supports his weight. But there is a suggestion of violence against a generative mother, too, which is activated by *womb* in the next line.

269 **bit** Champing on the bit is a traditional sign of a stallion's vigour, as when Aeneas's horse, shortly before his master consummates his relationship with Dido, 'stat sonipes ac frena ferox spumantia mandit', *Aeneid* 4.135 (Phaer (1562) translates, 4.145–6: 'The palfrey stands in gold, attirèd rich, and fierce he stamps | For pride, and on the foamy bit of gold with teeth he champs'). Crushing a bit is a potent symbol of uncontrolled passion, since metaphors of 'reining in', or 'bridling', passion were frequent in the period.

271 **braided** plaited

272 **compassed crest** is usually glossed as 'arched or curved forelock', above which the mane appears. This may be supported by *bending crest* in l. 395. It is possible, however, that the forelock is *compassed* in the sense of 'having been bound round' (*OED* s.v. 'compass' *v.* 8) with ornamental thongs. This would make the parallel with *braided mane* more exact.

His nostrils drink the air, and forth again,
As from a furnace, vapours doth he send.
   His eye which scornfully glisters like fire   275
   Shows his hot courage and his high desire.

Sometime he trots, as if he told the steps,
With gentle majesty, and modest pride;
Anon he rears upright, curvets, and leaps,
As who should say 'Lo, thus my strength is tried.   280
   And this I do to captivate the eye
   Of the fair breeder that is standing by.'

What recketh he his rider's angry stir,
His flatt'ring 'Holla', or his 'Stand, I say!'
What cares he now for curb or pricking spur,   285
For rich caparisons or trappings gay?
   He sees his love, and nothing else he sees,
   For nothing else with his proud sight agrees.

---

272 **stand** The plural form with the singular subject *mane* is not unprecedented in Shakespeare, but could here result from an impression that *ears* (which also are standing on end) comprise part of the grammatical subject.

275 **scornfully glisters** glitters contemptuously. 'Glisters scornfully' would be less metrically awkward, and was a popular emendation among eighteenth-century annotators.

276 **courage** (a) 'spirit, disposition, nature' (*OED* 1); (b) desire. Adonis's horse has the fiery disposition which his master lacks. Horses in this period were believed, like human beings, to have temperaments which resulted from the mixture of elements in their constitutions. See Sonnet 44.11 n. They were also believed to imitate the mood of their master; as Holofernes says, '*imitari* is nothing. So doth the hound his master, the ape his keeper, the tired horse his rider' (*L.L.L.* 4.2.126–7).

277 **told** counted

279 **curvets** 'A leap of a horse in which the fore-legs are raised together and equally advanced, and the hind-legs raised with a spring before the fore-legs reach the

ground' (*OED*). Adonis's horse, like that of the young man in *A Lover's Complaint* ll. 107–9, is trained in manège, or the formal art of equestrianism. He is also behaving as stallions should in the presence of a mare: 'so soon as he seeth and smelleth the mare, he will immediately fetch three or four salts [leaps], and bound aloft with all four feet for joy', Blundeville, *Horsemanship*, 13ʳ.

280 **As who** like one who
   tried proven. Q spells 'tride' to preserve the eye-rhyme.

283 **What recketh he** what notice does he take of

284 **'Holla'** is a cry used to stop a horse in the manège. So *As You Like It* 3.2.239–40: 'Cry "holla" to thy tongue, I prithee: it curvets unseasonably'. Shakespeare is precise in reproducing the appropriate cries for specific activities: see l. 973 n.

286 **caparisons** 'A cloth or covering spread over the saddle or harness of a horse, often gaily ornamented' (*OED*). Since the first citation in *OED* is from 1602 (although the term is also found in Peele's *Polyhymnia* (1590)) it may be doubled here with its near synonym *trappings* in order to clarify the sense.

Look when a painter would surpass the life
In limning out a well-proportioned steed,   290
His art with nature's workmanship at strife,
As if the dead the living should exceed:
    So did this horse excel a common one
    In shape, in courage, colour, pace, and bone.

Round-hoofed, short-jointed, fetlocks shag and long,   295
Broad breast, full eye, small head, and nostril wide,
High crest, short ears, straight legs and passing strong,
Thin mane, thick tail, broad buttock, tender hide.
    Look what a horse should have he did not lack,
    Save a proud rider on so proud a back.   300

Sometime he scuds far off, and then he stares;
Anon he starts at stirring of a feather;
To bid the wind a base he now prepares,

301 and] Q (aud)

289 **Look when** just as when. Appeals to the visual imagination punctuate the poem (see l. 67 and n.) but this one has a precise point, as Shakespeare embarks on a *paragone*, or formal comparison between the vividness of the sister arts of poetry and painting.

290 **limning out** painting (the verb was modish in the 1590s)

291 **at strife** Several writers from the period explore how art strives to better nature. Spenser's Bowre of Blisse is the *locus classicus*: 'One would haue thought, (so cunningly, the rude | And scorned parts were mingled with the fine,) | That nature had for wantonesse ensude | Art, and that Art at nature did repine; | So striuing each th'other to vndermine, | Each did the others worke more beautifie' (*FQ* 2.12.59).

293 **one** was pronounced as a full rhyme with *bone*.

294 **courage** See l. 276 n.
bone frame

295–300 This description marks Adonis's horse as not just an eager breeder, but as the perfect stallion from which to breed. Blundeville, *Horsemanship*, 8ᵛ–9ʳ, describes the ideal stallion in very similar terms (he is translating Federico Grisone, who was widely taken as an authority): 'let him haue short and slender head, a wide mouth, and wide nostrils, slender jaws, great eyes and black . . . short ears and sharp pointed like a mouse, a neck rather long than short, great towards his breast, slender towards his head, the crest whereof would be rising in the midst . . . a broad breast, and full of apparent muscles . . . great round buttocks . . . strong legs and great joints . . . short pasterns, with long fetlocks, also round, smooth, black, hard, hollow, and sounding hooves'. Shakespeare's description was closely imitated by R.S. in *Phillis and Flora* (1598).

295 **fetlocks shag** The fetlock is the point at which hair grows out from behind the pasterns (a horse's ankle joint, effectively); shagginess here is a good sign: as Blundeville says, 'long fewter locks . . . are a sign of strength'.

299 **Look . . . lack** Blundeville was more forthright: a stallion should have 'a yard [penis] and stones [testicles] of mean [middle] size', *Horsemanship*, 9ʳ.

300 **proud** noble; also sexually active. See Sonnet 151.10 n.

301 **scuds** darts

302 **starts** jumps. Proverbial (Dent W5.1). Compare *All's Well* 5.3.236: 'Every feather starts you.'

303 **a base** *Base* is 'A popular game among boys; it is played by two sides, who occupy contiguous 'bases' or 'homes'; any player running out from his 'base' is chased by

And where he run, or fly, they know not whether:
> For through his mane and tail the high wind sings,   305
> Fanning the hairs, who wave like feathered wings.

He looks upon his love, and neighs unto her.
She answers him as if she knew his mind.
Being proud, as females are, to see him woo her,
She puts on outward strangeness, seems unkind,   310
> Spurns at his love, and scorns the heat he feels,
> Beating his kind embracements with her heels.

Then, like a melancholy malcontent,
He vails his tail, that like a falling plume
Cool shadow to his melting buttock lent.   315
He stamps, and bites the poor flies in his fume.
> His love perceiving how he was enraged,
> Grew kinder, and his fury was assuaged.

His testy master goeth about to take him
When, lo, the unbacked breeder, full of fear,   320

304 where] Q (where); whe'er MALONE   317 was] Q; is Q4

one of the opposite side, and, if caught, made a prisoner' (*OED* s.v. 'base' *n.* 2). To 'bid base' is to challenge someone to this game.

304 **where** may be a contracted form of 'whether'. The effect is markedly bewildering and would have been to a contemporary reader: 'And whether or wherever he ran or he flew, they had no idea where it was'.

306 **who** This uncoordinated relative ('which' would be the norm for the period here) is a Shakespearian trademark. Compare ll. 630, 891, 956.
feathered wings There is just a ghost of Pegasus here, the winged horse from whose hoof-print the river of Helicon sprang. Since Helicon is the home of the Muses, and since the description of the horse is a poetic *tour de force*, the faint allusion should be registered: this is a horse of almost mythical poetic power.

308 **mind** intention

311 **Spurns at** plays on 'to reject with contempt or disdain' (*OED* 6) and the literal sense (*OED* 3), 'To kick against or at something disliked or despised'. The latter is

developed at the end of the stanza, which describes how fillies and mares often kick at stallions who are attempting to mount them.

313 **melancholy malcontent** A spurned lover in the 1590s, especially if he had an eye for fashion, would put on an appearance of satirical discontent which could even extend to a display of madness. Ophelia's description of Hamlet (2.1.78–101) is the most notable Shakespearian example.

314 **vails** lowers. The verb is often used of military submission (reinforced by *plume*), in which a sword or an ensign is lowered.

316 **fume** rage (*OED* 7a)

317 **was** is commonly emended to 'is' (after Q4). The easy transfer between historic present and past tense in this stanza is not, however, un-Shakespearian. See l. 873 and n.

319 **testy** irritable

320 **unbacked breeder** unbroken mare. Compare l. 419 and *Tempest* 4.1.175–6: 'Then I beat my tabor, | At which like unbacked colts they pricked their ears'. There may be a vestigial sense of 'that had not previously been mated' in *unbacked*, since the verb 'back' can by

Jealous of catching, swiftly doth forsake him;
With her the horse, and left Adonis there.
   As they were mad unto the wood they hie them,
   Outstripping crows, that strive to overfly them.

All swoll'n with chafing, down Adonis sits,   325
Banning his boist'rous and unruly beast.
And now the happy season once more fits
That love-sick Love by pleading may be blest:
   For lovers say the heart hath treble wrong
   When it is barred the aidance of the tongue.   330

An oven that is stopped, or river stayed,
Burneth more hotly, swelleth with more rage:
So of concealèd sorrow may be said.
Free vent of words love's fire doth assuage;
   But when the heart's attorney once is mute   335
   The client breaks, as desp'rate in his suit.

He sees her coming, and begins to glow
Even as a dying coal revives with wind,

---

325 chafing] Q; chasing Q5

1658 mean 'to cover (used of animals in copulation)' (*OED* 11), and *OED* is often tardy in picking up sexual vocabulary.

321 **Jealous of catching** reluctant to be caught
forsake has a much weaker force in this period; more 'leave', than 'abandon a lover'.

323 **As they . . . them** (a) as though they were mad they rush to the woods (b) (with a pun on 'wood' meaning mad) since they were mad they went to the wood

324 **overfly** fly faster than (*OED* 2). First cited usage in this sense.

325 **swoll'n with chafing** bursting with rage

326 **Banning** cursing (slightly archaic)

327 **now . . . fits** and now the time is propitious again

328 **love-sick Love** Venus is sick of love

330 **aidance** assistance. Used by Shakespeare only here and in *2 Henry VI (Contention)* 3.2.165. It had been obsolete for more than a century.

331 **oven that is stopped** If the door of an oven is closed it draws more strongly, and

so burns more fiercely. The thought was proverbial (Dent O89.1). So *Titus* 2.4.36–7: 'Sorrow concealèd, like an oven stopped, | Doth burn the heart to cinders where it is'. That 'grief pent up will break the heart' was proverbial (Dent G449), as was the belief that 'griefs disclosed . . . are soon relieved' (Thomas Lodge, *Scylla's Metamorphosis* l. 222), and that 'the stream stopped swells the higher' (Dent S929).

334 **vent** utterance. The word is rare in this sense, and is used here to continue the image of a fire or river which has no outlet: compare John Davies of Hereford, *Microcosmos* (Oxford, 1605), 197 (l. 4997): 'For griefs do break the heart if vent they miss'.

335 **heart's attorney** The tongue is the heart's advocate. This sense of *attorney* (*OED* 4) is not recorded after Shakespeare.

336 **The client breaks** (a) the heart bursts (continuing the images of pressure pent up from the previous stanza); (b) the client goes bankrupt (*OED* s.v. 'break' 11b, as in *Romeo* 3.2.57: 'O break, my heart, poor bankrupt, break at once!').

And with his bonnet hides his angry brow,
Looks on the dull earth with disturbèd mind,   340
   Taking no notice that she is so nigh,
   For all askance he holds her in his eye.

O what a sight it was wistly to view
How she came stealing to the wayward boy,
To note the fighting conflict of her hue,   345
How white and red each other did destroy:
   But now her cheek was pale, and by and by
   It flashed forth fire, as lightning from the sky.

Now was she just before him as he sat,
And like a lowly lover down she kneels.   350
With one fair hand she heaveth up his hat;
Her other tender hand his fair cheek feels.
   His tend'rer cheek receives her soft hand's print,
   As apt as new-fall'n snow takes any dint.

O what a war of looks was then between them: 355
Her eyes petitioners to his eyes suing;

---

339 **bonnet** 'A head-dress of men and boys; usually soft, and distinguished from the *hat* by want of a brim. In England, superseded in common use (app. before 1700) by *cap*' *OED*). There is no suggestion of effeminacy here.

340 **dull earth** is a set phrase used to imply that the earth, as a heavy element, is conducive to melancholy and insensible to suffering. Compare *Romeo* 2.1.1–2: 'Can I go forward when my heart is here? | Turn back, dull earth, and find thy centre out'. **disturbèd** troubled

342 **all askance** out of the corner of his eye (with suspicion or disdain). The phrase is of deliberately uncertain meaning, and might hint that Adonis is keener to look at Venus than his posture would suggest.

343 **wistly** intently. See *Lucrece* l. 1355. The adverb floats between the reader/spectator ('wistly to view') and Venus ('wistly stealing').

344 **wayward** wilful, perverse. The word can be used in a strongly pejorative sense in this period, and was a favourite term to describe human perversity among Puritan divines.

346–8 Compare *Lucrece* ll. 52–73.

347 **But now** just now

350 **lowly . . . kneels** The humble Venus assumes the traditional position of someone who is beseeching a favour.

351 **heaveth** The verb need not imply great effort (see *Lucrece* ll. 111 and 638), and can correspond roughly to our 'lift'. The majority of usages in Shakespeare do imply effort, however. This, like the rest of the stanza, teasingly suggests that the encounter between Venus and Adonis involves barely concealed physical pressure.

353 **receives** 'To admit (an impression, etc.) by yielding or by adaptation of surface' (*OED* 4b). Adonis's face does not simply accept contact with Venus's tender hand, but takes a physical imprint from it.

354 **apt** 'easily impressed, impressionable' (Schmidt, 2). Shakespeare can use the word of docile women, as in *Othello* 2.3.312–13: 'so free, so kind, so apt, so blessed a disposition'. It functions adverbially here.
   dint impression

356 **suing** pressing of a case (agreeing with *Her eyes*, but there is a wishful flicker of confusion between the two lovers).

His eyes saw her eyes as they had not seen them;
Her eyes wooed still; his eyes disdained the wooing:
　And all this dumb-play had his acts made plain
　With tears which chorus-like her eyes did rain.　　　　360

Full gently now she takes him by the hand,
A lily prisoned in a gaol of snow,
Or ivory in an alabaster band,
So white a friend engirts so white a foe:
　This beauteous combat wilful and unwilling,　　　　365
　Showed like two silver doves that sit a-billing.

Once more the engine of her thoughts began:
'O fairest mover on this mortal round,
Would thou wert as I am, and I a man,
My heart all whole as thine, thy heart my wound,　　　　370
　For one sweet look thy help I would assure thee,
　Though nothing but my body's bane would cure thee.'

362 gael] Q (gaile)

359–60 **dumb-play . . . rain** 'The significance of this dumb-show was shown by her tears, which commented on the action.' *His* is neuter (as often in Shakespeare, Abbott §228), and agrees with *dumb-play*. Earlier Elizabethan plays were regularly preceded by a dumb-show which might silently enact the drama to come, or draw out its didactic and emotional significance. By the time of Thomas Kyd's *Spanish Tragedy* (1592) a choric figure might comment on the meaning of the preceding dumb-show, which is the role taken here by Venus's tears. Some early dumb-shows contained allegorical personages, and Venus herself was a favourite character in shows of this type. See Dieter Mehl, *The Elizabethan Dumb Show* (1965), 19, 35–6, 63–71. For a Shakespearian example, see *Hamlet* 3.2.129–30.

361 **Full** very (used often in Shakespeare as an intensifier)

362 **lily . . . snow . . . ivory . . . alabaster** are all types of whiteness (Dent L296, S591, I109, A95.2). The layering of white on white here invites a reader to make infinitesimal discriminations between varieties of perfect whiteness.
gaol Q spells 'gaile', possibly marking a pun on 'gale'.

364 **engirts** circles, surrounds. The word

enjoyed a vogue in the poetry of the 1590s. *Lucrece* l. 221 shows that Shakespeare, unusually, associated the word with military contexts (*friend . . . foe*).

365 **wilful willing** (not used in this sense by Shakespeare after 1600); more usually 'obstinately self-willed'. It takes an effort to exclude a potentially pejorative sense of the term used of Venus.

366 **Showed . . . a-billing** Doves are symbols of devoted affection: the scene looks like a perfect courtship. Q reads 'showed', with a non-syllabic final '-ed'. This sometimes occurs after 'w' or 'u'; compare *Lucrece* ll. 50, 111.

367 **engine . . . thoughts** her tongue, as in *Titus* 3.1.82. *Engine* is often used of weapons and machinery of war: Venus keeps up her assault.

368 **mover . . . round** creature with motion on this world; with a hyperbolic secondary comparison of Adonis with the *primum mobile*, or sphere which moves the other spheres

369 **wert** subjunctive form; cf. l. 445

370 **my wound** my heart (which is one big wound)

371–2 Venus means that if Adonis's heart did become, like her own, one big wound she would assure him of a cure, even if it would cause her *body's bane*, her death.

'Give me my hand,' saith he; 'Why dost thou feel it?'
'Give me my heart,' saith she, 'and thou shalt have it.
O give it me lest thy hard heart do steel it,   375
And being steeled, soft sighs can never grave it.
    Then love's deep groans I never shall regard,
    Because Adonis' heart hath made mine hard.'

'For shame,' he cries, 'let go, and let me go.
My day's delight is past; my horse is gone,   380
And 'tis your fault I am bereft him so.
I pray you hence, and leave me here alone,
    For all my mind, my thought, my busy care,
    Is how to get my palfrey from the mare.'

Thus she replies: 'Thy palfrey, as he should,   385
Welcomes the warm approach of sweet desire.
Affection is a coal that must be cooled,
Else, suffered, it will set the heart on fire.
    The sea hath bounds, but deep desire hath none;
    Therefore no marvel though thy horse be gone.   390

'How like a jade he stood tied to the tree,
Servilely mastered with a leathern rein;
But when he saw his love, his youth's fair fee,
He held such petty bondage in disdain;
    Throwing the base thong from his bending crest,   395
    Enfranchising his mouth, his back, his breast.

393 But] Q (Bnt)

Help is used in the sense 'Relief, cure, remedy' (*OED* 5a), hence she offers Adonis his cure, rather than her assistance.

375 **steel** (a) harden it; (b) steal it
376 **grave** engrave, make an impression in
381 **bereft him** deprived of him
382 **hence** go hence
384 **palfrey** a saddle horse (rather than a war-horse). In *FQ* (1590) palfreys are exclusively ridden by women, which would suggest that Adonis's choice of word has a trace of effeminacy. In Thomas Phaer's translation of the *Aeneid* (1562), however, the word is occasionally used of strong war-horses (e.g. 9.282–3: 'Thou sawest what palfrey steed, what armour brave king Turnus bare').

387 **Affection** (a) loving attachment; (b) 'Feeling as opposed to reason; passion, lust' (*OED* 3)
388 **suffered** allowed to burn
389 **hath bounds** plays on the near-proverbial boundlessness of the sea (Dent S169.1).
390 **though** if
391 **jade** 'a horse of inferior breed, e.g. a cart- or draught-horse as opposed to a riding horse' (*OED* 1)
393 **fee** due reward
395 **bending crest** arched neck (see l. 272 n.)
396 **Enfranchising** setting free (the usual sense in Shakespeare)
mouth . . . breast Throwing off the reins would liberate the mouth; Venus presses her argument to the point where the

'Who sees his true-love in her naked bed,
Teaching the sheets a whiter hue than white,
But when his glutton eye so full hath fed,
His other agents aim at like delight? 400
   Who is so faint that dares not be so bold
   To touch the fire, the weather being cold?

'Let me excuse thy courser, gentle boy,
And learn of him, I heartily beseech thee,
To take advantage on presented joy. 405
Though I were dumb, yet his proceedings teach thee.
   O learn to love: the lesson is but plain,
   And once made perfect, never lost again.'

'I know not love,' quoth he, 'Nor will not know it,
Unless it be a boar, and then I chase it. 410
'Tis much to borrow, and I will not owe it.
My love to love, is love but to disgrace it,
   For I have heard it is a life in death,
   That laughs and weeps, and all but with a breath.

397 sees] Q; seeks Q2

horse is imagined as having also thrown off its saddle-girths (*his back*) and achieved freedom for its desires (*his breast*).

397–400 'Who can see his lover naked in bed and whiter than white, and not want his other senses to indulge in a similar delight once he has feasted his sight?' The sentence changes subject midstream from *Who* to *his other agents*, as though the sensuous passions usurp the agent's own wishes.

397 **naked bed** The transferred epithet was common in this period: it is unlikely to be a direct echo of Kyd's Hieronymo, 'What outcries pluck me from my naked bed?' (*The Spanish Tragedy* 2.5.1) as earlier editors thought. There are many parallels (for example, in John Harington's translation of Ariosto's *Orlando Furioso* (1591), 17.75).

398 **Teaching . . . white** Compare l. 362 above, and Jachimo's description of Innogen when he steals into her bedchamber:

'Fresh lily, | And whiter than the sheets', *Cymbeline* 2.2.15–16.

401 **faint** spiritless

403 **courser** Venus metamorphoses the horse from a *palfrey* (l. 385) to a *jade* (l. 391) to a full martial charger in the course of her argument.

405 **advantage on** advantage of. Compare Sonnet 64.6.

406 **proceedings** actions

407 **but plain** quite evident

408 **perfect** learnt by rote (as an actor learns a script). See Sonnet 23.1 n.

409–12 Adonis's point is bluntly made and remade in the repeated feminine rhymes (on which see Sonnet 20.1 n.): his womanly resistance is founded on a male preference for hunting.

409 **Nor . . . not** The double negative is emphatic.

411 **owe it** acknowledge such a debt

412 **My love . . . it** 'The sole desire I feel towards love is a desire to scorn it.'

414 **all . . . breath** and all in the same breath. 'He can laugh and cry both with a breath' was proverbial by 1616 (Dent B640).

197

'Who wears a garment shapeless and unfinished?   415
Who plucks the bud before one leaf put forth?
If springing things be any jot diminished
They wither in their prime, prove nothing worth.
  The colt that's backed and burdened being young
  Loseth his pride, and never waxeth strong.   420

'You hurt my hand with wringing. Let us part,
And leave this idle theme, this bootless chat.
Remove your siege from my unyielding heart:
To love's alarms it will not ope the gate.
  Dismiss your vows, your feignèd tears, your flatt'ry,   425
  For where a heart is hard they make no batt'ry.'

'What, canst thou talk?' quoth she, 'Hast thou a tongue?
O would thou hadst not, or I had no hearing.
Thy mermaid's voice hath done me double wrong:
I had my load before, now pressed with bearing: 430
  Melodious discord, heavenly tune harsh sounding,
  Ears' deep sweet music, and heart's deep sore wounding.

432 Ears'] Q (Eares)

417 **springing** in their first growth
419 **backed** broken in, saddled. Compare l.
   320 n.
420 **pride** vigour, energy
   waxeth grows
421 **wringing** squeezing. The verb could be
   used of a simple handshake, but could
   also convey hard pressure (*OED* 2a: 'to
   force (a limb, etc.) *round* or *about* so as to
   cause a sprain or pain').
422 **theme** has a schoolroom ring to it: sub-
   ject for debate, even 'a school essay' (*OED*
   3), which would throw Venus's didacti-
   cism at ll. 407–8 back at her.
   bootless chat profitless talk
423 **unyielding** obdurate. This is the first
   cited usage in *OED* by about sixty years:
   early readers may have taken it in a nar-
   rowly literal sense, 'refusing to yield (to
   your siege)'.
424 **alarms** attacks; in stage directions
   from the period the word used of sounds
   of trumpets which indicated a new
   wave of battle. It was believed in the
   seventeenth century to derive from a cry
   of 'all arm', a cry sent up in cities under

siege, so it continues the imagery of
siege.
   ope is a metaplasmic (i.e. contracted) form
   of 'open' frequent in poetry of the period.
426 **batt'ry** originally means an attempt to
   enter a military position; here it is extend-
   ed to mean a successful military assault,
   as in *Pericles* Scene 21.35–7: 'She ques-
   tionless, with her sweet harmony | . . .
   would alarum | And make a batt'ry
   through his deafened ports'.
429 **mermaid** a Siren, a creature with a
   mythically tuneful voice capable of luring
   sailors to their deaths. See *Lucrece* l. 1411.
   The word could be slang for a prostitute in
   the period.
430 **pressed** overwhelmed almost to death.
   The verb could refer to a form of judicial
   killing in which a prisoner who would not
   plead was crushed to death by weights
   (Sokol, 310), which may be in play here
   since Venus has been (unusually) mute in
   the previous stanzas.
432 **sore** functions as both a noun (recalling
   Venus's *wound* in l. 370) and as an adjec-
   tive (painful, grievous).

'Had I no eyes but ears, my ears would love
That inward beauty and invisible,
Or were I deaf, thy outward parts would move   435
Each part in me that were but sensible.
    Though neither eyes, nor ears, to hear nor see,
    Yet should I be in love, by touching thee.

'Say that the sense of feeling were bereft me,
And that I could not see, nor hear, nor touch,   440
And nothing but the very smell were left me,
Yet would my love to thee be still as much;
    For from the stillatory of thy face excelling
    Comes breath perfumed, that breedeth love by smelling.

'But O, what banquet wert thou to the taste,   445
Being nurse and feeder of the other four
Would they not wish the feast might ever last,
And bid suspicion double-lock the door,
    Lest jealousy, that sour unwelcome guest,
    Should by his stealing in disturb the feast?'   450

Once more the ruby-coloured portal opened
Which to his speech did honey-passage yield,
Like a red morn that ever yet betokened
Wrack to the seaman, tempest to the field,

433–50 This passage is founded on the tradition of the 'banquet of sense' in which a lover feasts each of the senses in turn, moving from the immaterial (hearing, smell) to the increasingly carnal (sight, taste, and finally touch). George Chapman's *The Banquet of Sense* (1595) is the most extended treatment of the topos in the period. Venus promotes touch to an early point in the feast, and her version of the banquet repeatedly advances and then retreats from the more carnal senses, rather than proceeding in orderly sequence.

435 **outward parts** external beauties

436 **Each . . . sensible** every part of me that could feel. There is a moment here of super-sensitivity, as Venus goes beyond the traditional exploration of the five senses, and imagines that the whole body could respond to the beauty of Adonis. It is not until the end of the stanza that tactile sensation is located in the sense of touch, offering a moment when it seems as though the whole body could intuit his beauty. Touch is traditionally the final, most carnal stage in the banquet of sense.

437 **Though** neither although having neither

443 **stillatory** a still (which produces distilled scents). Compare Sonnet 5.13–14.
excelling exceedingly beautiful (with perhaps a vestigial play on 'exhaling')

446 **Being . . . four** Adonis nourishes the other four senses, but gives a banquet to the sense of taste. *Being* is a hanging participle which for a moment identifies Adonis with the sense of taste.

448 **double-lock** lock the door by two turns of the key First cited usage in *OED*.

451 **ruby-coloured portal** his red lips. *Portal* is an elaborately decorated door.

453–4 That 'A red morning foretells a stormy day' was (and is) proverbial (Dent M1175). See Matthew 16: 2–3.

Sorrow to shepherds, woe unto the birds, 455
Gusts and foul flaws to herdmen and to herds.

This ill presage advisedly she marketh,
Even as the wind is hushed before it raineth,
Or as the wolf doth grin before he barketh,
Or as the berry breaks before it staineth, 460
  Or like the deadly bullet of a gun,
  His meaning struck her ere his words begun.

And at his look she flatly falleth down,
For looks kill love, and love by looks reviveth.
A smile recures the wounding of a frown. 465
But blessèd bankrupt that by loss so thriveth!
  The silly boy, believing she is dead,
  Claps her pale cheek, till clapping makes it red.

And all amazed, brake off his late intent,
For sharply he did think to reprehend her, 470
Which cunning Love did wittily prevent.
Fair fall the wit that can so well defend her:

---

466 loss] HUDSON 1881 (*conj.* Walker); loue Q   469 all amazed] Q; all in a maze Q5; in a maze Q6

456 **flaws** squalls of wind (*OED n.* 2)
457 **presage** omen. Compare Sonnet 107.6.
  advisedly warily, intently. See *Lucrece* ll. 180 and 1527.
458 That 'little rain allays great winds' was proverbial (Dent R16), and so it was commonly remarked that the winds stop just before it rains: compare 3 *Henry VI (True Tragedy,* 1.4.146–7: 'For raging wind blows up incessant showers, | And when the rage allays the rain begins', and *Lucrece* ll. 1788–90.
459 **grin** bare his teeth
461 **Or . . . gun** i.e. someone can be wounded before they hear the report of the gun; hence there is a silence before a catastrophe, as in the earlier elements of the comparison.
462 **struck** plays on three main senses: (a) 'To hit with a missile, a shot, etc'. (*OED* 34); (b) 'To prostrate mentally' (*OED* 47); (c) 'Of a thought, an idea: To come into the mind of, occur to (a person)' (*OED* 64: Shakespeare is attributed with the earliest usages in this sense).

462 **begun** The usual form 'began' (l. 7 etc.) is modified for the rhyme.
463 **flatly** (a) on her back; (b) without more ado
465 **recures** heals
466 **loss** Q reads 'love'. Walker's emendation to 'loss' is attractive: the tails of the long double 's' in 'losse' might have been mistaken for the ascenders of a 'u' in 'loue'. The meaning is that as Venus faints her loss of consciousness brings her the attention of Adonis.
466 **thriveth** prospers
467 **silly** Senses in the period range from 'deserving of compassion' through 'unsophisticated' to 'helpless' and 'simple'.
468 **Claps** gives it a medicinal smack
470 **he did think** he had intended
471 **wittily** ingeniously
472 **Fair fall** good luck to (with a pun: she has fallen to the ground beautifully).
  her functions as a reflexive pronoun: 'herself'.

For on the grass she lies as she were slain,
Till his breath breatheth life in her again.

He wrings her nose, he strikes her on the cheeks,   475
He bends her fingers, holds her pulses hard.
He chafes her lips; a thousand ways he seeks
To mend the hurt that his unkindness marred.
   He kisses her, and she by her good will
   Will never rise, so he will kiss her still.   480

The night of sorrow now is turned to day.
Her two blue windows faintly she upheaveth,
Like the fair sun when in his fresh array
He cheers the morn, and all the earth relieveth.
   And, as the bright sun glorifies the sky,   485
   So is her face illumined with her eye,

Whose beams upon his hairless face are fixed,
As if from thence they borrowed all their shine.
Were never four such lamps together mixed,
Had not his clouded with his brows' repine: 490
   But hers, which through the crystal tears gave light,
   Shone like the moon in water seen by night.

484 earth] Q; world Q2

473 **as she** as though she
475 **wrings** probably implies a vigorous squeeze. Compare l. 421 and n.
478 'he tries to undo the harm caused by his unkindness'. The conjunction of *mend* and *mar* is common in proverbs, but none seem to be alluded to here (cf. Dent M875.1).
479 **by her good will** cheerfully
480 **so** expresses both a wish and a result. 'She will never rise, so that he will continue to kiss her' and 'Since she will not rise he continues to kiss her'.
482 **windows** probably 'eyelids', since Venus's eyes are *grey* at l. 140, and the comparison with the rising sun suggests that the eye (frequently compared to the sun) is peeping from under the lids. For 'windows' in this sense, see *Cymbeline* 2.2.20–3: 'and would underpeep her lids, | To see th' enclosèd lights, now canopied | Under these windows, white and azure-laced | With blue of heaven's own tinct', or *Antony* 5.2.310: 'Downy windows, close'.
487 **beams** continues the conceit of the sun. In this period the belief that vision depended on extramission from the eye of light, fire (as Plato has it in *Timaeus* 45b–d), or particles coexisted with intromissive theories, according to which rays of light were received by the optic nerve. Pliny (i.334–5) appears to hold an extramissive theory: 'It cannot be denied, that with the soul we imagine, with the mind we see, and the eyes as vessels and instruments receiving from it that visual power and faculty, send it soon after'.
490 **repine** discontent. The first cited usage of the noun in *OED*.

'O where am I?' quoth she, 'In earth or heaven,
Or in the ocean drenched, or in the fire?
What hour is this? Or morn or weary even?   495
Do I delight to die or life desire?
     But now I lived, and life was death's annoy,
     But now I died, and death was lively joy.

'O thou didst kill me; kill me once again.
Thy eyes' shrewd tutor, that hard heart of thine,   500
Hath taught them scornful tricks, and such disdain,
That they have murdered this poor heart of mine,
     And these mine eyes, true leaders to their queen,
     But for thy piteous lips no more had seen.

'Long may they kiss each other for this cure.   505
O never let their crimson liveries wear,
And as they last, their verdour still endure,
To drive infection from the dangerous year,
     That the star-gazers, having writ on death,
     May say the plague is banished by thy breath.   510

'Pure lips, sweet seals in my soft lips imprinted,
What bargains may I make still to be sealing?
To sell myself I can be well contented,
So thou wilt buy, and pay, and use good dealing.

500 shrewd] Q (shrowd)

494 **drenched** immersed; the sense 'drowned' is also still available in this period.

500 **shrewd** sharp, bad-tempered

503 **leaders** commanders, captains (who are loyal to their mistress). Cf. *Lucrece* l. 296.

505 **kiss each other** A lover's lips are also imagined to kiss each other in *Astrophil and Stella* 43.11: 'With either lip he doth the other kiss'.

506 **crimson . . . wear** The lips are imagined to be loyal retainers whose bright livery should never be allowed to wear out.

507 **verdour** fresh vitality. Shakespeare is especially prone to take shades of green as metaphors for freshness. See Sonnets 63.14 n. and 112.4 n. There is, though, as Malone (1821) suggested, a hint that the lips are compared to herbs which preserve

their power to drive off infection throughout the year.

509–10 **That . . . breath** In 1593 the plague killed approximately 10,000 Londoners. Cf. 'Methought she purged the air of pestilence', *Twelfth Night* 1.1.19.

509 **star-gazers** astrologers, or composers of almanacs. For other thwarted augurs, see Sonnet 107.6.

511 **seals** Venus imagines the imprint of Adonis's lips remains in her flesh as a seal in wax. Kisses are also presented as a seal of a bond of love in *Two Gentlemen* 2.2.7: 'and seal the bargain with a holy kiss'.

513 **sell myself** Venus's images of a sealed agreement degenerate rapidly into a mercantile exchange which is one step from prostitution.

514 **So** provided that

Which purchase if thou make, for fear of slips,   515
Set thy seal manual on my wax-red lips.

'A thousand kisses buys my heart from me,
And pay them at thy leisure, one by one.
What is ten hundred touches unto thee?
Are they not quickly told, and quickly gone?   520
    Say for non-payment that the debt should double,
    Is twenty hundred kisses such a trouble?'

'Fair Queen,' quoth he, 'If any love you owe me,
Measure my strangeness with my unripe years.
Before I know myself seek not to know me.   525
No fisher but the ungrown fry forbears;
    The mellow plum doth fall, the green sticks fast,
    Or being early plucked is sour to taste.

'Look the world's comforter, with weary gait,
His day's hot task hath ended in the west;   530
The owl (night's herald) shrieks; 'tis very late.

515 **slips** counterfeit coin (*OED* n. 4), voguish slang in the 1590s, sometimes used in contexts of duplicitous *amours*, as in Nashe's *Unfortunate Traveller*, Nashe, ii.258. 'Ay me, she was but a counterfeit slip, for she not only gave me the slip, but had well nigh made me a slipstring'.

516 **seal manual** signature; possibly 'personal seal (on a ring)', which would suit *wax-red*: Venus's lips are the sealing wax, his the seal.

517 **buys** Numbers (here 'a thousand') are also given a singular verb at ll. 519, and 522.

519 **touches** kisses (though 'sexual contact', *OED* 1b, is also present and 'blemish, stain', *OED* 17, may be faintly registered). A secondary sense is 'An official mark or stamp upon gold or silver indicating that it has been tested, and is of standard fineness' (*OED* 5b); hence genuine currency rather than *slips*.

520 **told** (a) related; (b) counted

521 **Say** just suppose

521–2 The bond to which Venus persuades Adonis to set his *seal manual* is a penal bond, which carries a forfeit for non-payment. See Sonnet 87.4 n. The apparent light-heartedness (*Say*) with which she transforms what appears to be a

single bond, to which no forfeit is attached, into a penal bond is reminiscent of Shylock in *Merchant* 1.3.143–9: 'Go with me to a notary, seal me there | Your single bond, and, in a merry sport, | If you repay me not on such a day, | ... let the forfeit | Be nominated for an equal pound Of your fair flesh'.

523 **Queen** This is the first time Adonis refers to Venus in this way. Since it comes after her offer to sell herself to him it may have a contemptuous overtone of the slang sense 'prostitute'.

523 **owe** bear

524 **Measure . . . years** attribute my coldness to my immaturity

525 **know** can have the sense 'to have sexual experience of'.

526 **No fisher . . . forbears** all fishermen spare the young fish. This sounds proverbial, but no analogues have been found.

527 **mellow** 'Soft, sweet, and juicy with ripeness' (*OED* 1a). 'Soon ripe soon rotten' is a proverb which may underlie Adonis's claim here (Dent R133), as it does in *Richard II* 2.1.154, 'The ripest fruit first falls'.

529 **world's comforter** the sun

531 The shriek of the owl was proverbially ill-omened (Dent R33).

The sheep are gone to fold, birds to their nest,
    And coal-black clouds, that shadow heaven's light,
    Do summon us to part and bid good-night.

'Now let me say good night, and so say you.   535
If you will say so, you shall have a kiss.'
'Good night,' quoth she, and ere he says adieu
The honey fee of parting tendered is.
    Her arms do lend his neck a sweet embrace:
    Incorp'rate then they seem; face grows to face,   540

Till breathless he disjoined, and backward drew
The heavenly moisture, that sweet coral mouth,
Whose precious taste her thirsty lips well knew,
Whereon they surfeit, yet complain on drouth.
    He with her plenty pressed, she faint with dearth,   545
    Their lips together glued, fall to the earth.

Now quick desire hath caught the yielding prey,
And glutton-like she feeds, yet never filleth.
Her lips are conquerors; his lips obey,
Paying what ransom the insulter willeth: 550
    Whose vulture thought doth pitch the price so high
    That she will draw his lips' rich treasure dry.

---

538 **tendered** is the technical term for presenting payment of a debt (with a pun on 'tender' as an adjective meaning 'soft').

540 **Incorp'rate** united in one body. The legal sense 'united into one corporation' (*OED* 2) may continue the imagery of bonds and contracts exchanged between the two lovers. The description recalls the metamorphic union of Salmacis and Hermaphroditus in *Met.* 4.371–9 (Golding 4.46c–470), in which a resistant youth is eventually won over by a voracious woman. Salmacis cries: '"Ye Gods of Heaven agree | That this same wilful boy and I may never parted be." | The Gods were pliant to her boon. The bodies of them twain | Were mixed and joinèd both in one. To both them did remain | One count'nance: like as if a man should in one bark behold | Two twigs both growing into one and still together hold. | Even so when through her hugging and her grasping of the t'other | The members of them mingled were and fastened both together, | They were not any longer two: but (as it were) a toy | Of double shape. Ye could not say it was a perfect boy, | Nor perfect wench: it seemèd both and none of both to been'.

540 **grows to** grows into (as grafted stock grows into its host). See Sonnet *18.12*.

541 **disjoined** separated.

542 **coral** A conventional epithet for a mistress's lips in sonnet sequences. See Sonnet *130.2* and n.

544 **complain on** See l. 160 n.
    drouth drought

545 **plenty pressed** oppressed by the abundance of her love, with also a hint that Venus's body is overwhelming.

550 **insulter** attacker. The word derives from Latin *insultare*, to leap at, attack. The verb 'insult' can mean 'attack' (*OED* 3) by the 1630s, and Shakespeare anticipates this usage. First citation in *OED*.

551 **vulture thought** predatory imagination. The only other adjectival use of *vulture* in Shakespeare occurs in *Lucrece* l. 556.

And, having felt the sweetness of the spoil,
With blindfold fury she begins to forage.
Her face doth reek and smoke, her blood doth boil,   555
And careless lust stirs up a desperate courage,
    Planting oblivion, beating reason back,
    Forgetting shame's pure blush and honour's wrack.

Hot, faint, and weary with her hard embracing,
Like a wild bird being tamed with too much handling,   560
Or as the fleet-foot roe that's tired with chasing,
Or like the froward infant stilled with dandling,
    He now obeys, and now no more resisteth,
    While she takes all she can, not all she listeth.

What wax so frozen but dissolves with temp'ring,   565
And yields at last to every light impression?
Things out of hope are compassed oft with vent'ring,
Chiefly in love, whose leave exceeds commission:
    Affection faints not like a pale-faced coward,
    But then woos best, when most his choice is froward.   570

---

551 **pitch** settle (*OED* 13b). The *vulture* of the same line suggests a pun on 'pitch' as a noun meaning 'The height to which a falcon or other bird of prey soars before swooping down on its prey' (*OED s.v.* 'pitch' *n.* 2, 18a).

552 **treasure** treasury (a sense already slightly archaic by 1593)

553 **spoil** both 'prey' and 'plunder' (uniting a hunt and a military conquest)

554 **forage** (a) search for provender like an army; (b) 'To glut oneself, as a wild beast; to raven' (*OED* 4, citing this passage as the first instance, and the close parallel in *Henry V* 1.2.108–10: 'Whiles his most mighty father on a hill | Stood smiling to behold his lion's whelp | Forage in blood of French nobility.')

555 **reek** drips with blood. Compare *Caesar* 3.1.159: 'Now, whilst your purpled hands do reek and smoke'. Cf. Sonnet 130.8 n. and *Lucrece* l. 799 n.

556 **careless** reckless

557 **Planting oblivion** causing forgetfulness of everything he ought to remember

558 **wrack** wreck

560 **Like . . . handling** Compare *Hero and Leander* ll. 771–5: 'Love is not full of pity (as men say) | But deaf and cruel where

he means to prey. | Even as a bird, which in our hands we wring, | Forth plungeth and oft flutters with her wing, | She trembling strove'.

562 **froward** fretful, wilful

564 **not . . . listeth** although not everything she desires. That 'Men must do as they can, not as they would' was proverbial (Dent M554).

565 **dissolves with temp'ring** becomes pliant after squeezing between the fingers. Compare *2 Henry IV* 4.2.125–7: 'I have him already tempering between my finger and my thumb, and shortly will I seal with him'.

567 **out of hope** beyond hope **compassed** achieved. It was proverbial that 'Nothing is impossible to a willing heart' (Tilley N299) and 'Nothing venture nothing have' (Dent N319).

568 **leave exceeds commission** who has permission to exceed the strict limits of his orders. *Commission* is a formal mandate which delegates specific powers (as in *Measure* 1.1.13–14: 'There is our commission, | From which we would not have you warp'); *leave* is a discretionary agreement to allow someone to do what they are not normally allowed to do.

569 **Affection** passion. See l. 387 n. It was

When he did frown, O, had she then gave over
Such nectar from his lips she had not sucked;
Foul words and frowns must not repel a lover.
What though the rose have prickles? Yet 'tis plucked;
    Were beauty under twenty locks kept fast,   575
    Yet love breaks through, and picks them all at last.

For pity now she can no more detain him:
The poor fool prays her that he may depart.
She is resolved no longer to restrain him,
Bids him farewell, and look well to her heart,   580
    The which by Cupid's bow, she doth protest,
    He carries thence encagèd in his breast.

'Sweet boy,' she says, 'this night I'll waste in sorrow,
For my sick heart commands mine eyes to watch.
Tell me, love's master, shall we meet tomorrow,   585
Say, shall we? Shall we? Wilt thou make the match?'
    He tells her no, tomorrow he intends
    To hunt the boar with certain of his friends.

'The boar?' quoth she, whereat a sudden pale,
Like lawn being spread upon the blushing rose,   590
Usurps her cheek. She trembles at his tale,

---

proverbial that 'Faint heart ne'er won fair lady' (Tilley H302).

571 **gave over** given up. For an analogous construction, see l. 176.

573 **Foul** harsh, unpleasant

574 Compare the proverb 'The sweetest rose hath his prickle' (Dent R182).

575 **twenty locks** That 'Love laughs at the locksmith' became proverbial (Dent L517.1). Compare Sonnet *48*.

580 **look well to** take good care of (a valediction usually used between those who are reluctant to part, as in *Antony* 3.2.45). That 'The lover is not where he lives but where he loves' was proverbial (Dent L565).

581 **The which** The use of the article with the relative *which* was archaic by 1593 (Partridge, *Grammar*, 27). Compare l. 683.

583 **Sweet boy** See l. 155 n.
    waste (a) spend; (b) waste away

584 **watch** stay awake. Cf. Sonnet *57* for a

comparison between a lover and servant condemned to wake.

588 **the boar** was traditionally regarded as 'the beast of this world that is strongest armed, and can sooner slay a man than any other', Edward, Duke of York, *The Master of Game*, ed. W. A. and F. Baillie-Grohman (1909), 46. The word 'boar' is properly used by huntsmen of an animal aged 4 years (John Manwood, *A Treatise of the Forrest Laws* (1598), fo. 25ᵛ).

589 **pale** pallor. Compare *The Shepherd's Song of Venus and Adonis*, attributed to H.C. in *England's Helicon* (1600), ll. 105–12: 'At the name of boar | Venus seemed dying: | Deadly-coloured pale | Roses overcast. | Speak, said she, no more | Of following the boar, | Thou unfit for such a chase; | Course the fearful hare . . .'. It is impossible to determine the direction of the influence here.

590 **lawn** fine white linen. For the contrast of roses and *lawn* see *Lucrece* ll. 258–9.

And on his neck her yoking arms she throws.
  She sinketh down, still hanging by his neck;
  He on her belly falls, she on her back.

Now is she in the very lists of love,   595
Her champion mounted for the hot encounter.
All is imaginary she doth prove;
He will not manage her, although he mount her,
  That worse than Tantalus is her annoy,
  To clip Elysium, and to lack her joy.   600

Even so poor birds deceived with painted grapes
Do surfeit by the eye, and pine the maw:
Even so she languisheth in her mishaps,
As those poor birds that helpless berries saw.
  The warm effects which she in him finds missing   605
  She seeks to kindle with continual kissing,

But all in vain. Good queen, it will not be.
She hath assayed as much as may be proved;
Her pleading hath deserved a greater fee.

601 so] Q; as Q10   605 effects| ●; affects Q12

594 **belly** is quite as corporeal in 1590 as
  now, but can be used in erotic contexts.
595 **lists** the pallisades which enclose a tilt-
  yard, with perhaps a pun on 'pleasure'
  (*OED* n. 4)
596 **mounted** *OED* 10 tentatively cites this
  passage to support the definition 'To get
  upon, for the purpose of copulation'. The
  tentativeness seems unnecessary. Com-
  pare *Winter's Tale* 2.5.17.
597 **All . . . prove** 'All that she experiences is
  mere imagination' (Kittredge); also 'she
  realises that everything is imaginary'.
  This is the central line of the poem, a
  point at which poets from the period fre-
  quently place royal or divine triumphs. It
  may well be by design that the failure of a
  goddess and the triumph of the merely
  imaginary figures at this point.
598 **manage** put her through her paces; run
  through the steps of formal horseman-
  ship or 'manège'
599 **That** so that
  Tantalus a son of Zeus who revealed the
  secrets of the gods, and was condemned
  to stand in Tartarus up to his chin in
  water which constantly receded as he

stooped to drink. Branches of fruit hung
  over him and fled from his fingers as he
  grasped at them.
600 **clip** embrace
  Elysium the abode of the blessed in Greek
  and Roman mythology. The word only
  entered English poetry in the 1590s, and
  this usage pre-dates the first citation in
  OED by six years. The word also appears
  in the Preface to Greene's *Menaphon*
  (1589).
601–2 This alludes to the story, widely cited
  in the period, of the painter Zeuxis, who
  'for proof of his cunning, brought upon
  the scaffold a table, wherein were clusters
  of grapes so lively painted that the very
  birds of the air flew flocking thither for to
  be pecking at the grapes', Pliny, ii.535.
602 **pine the maw** starve the stomach
602 **helpless** which gave no help. Compare
  Lucrece ll. 756 and 1027.
605 **effects** actions. Q12 emends to 'effects',
  passions; but see *Lucrece* l. 251 n.
608 **She . . . proved** she has tried out
  everything
609 **fee** reward (like a barrister, she expects a
  rich reward)

She's love, she loves, and yet she is not loved. 610
   'Fie, fie,' he says, 'you crush me. Let me go;
   You have no reason to withhold me so.'

'Thou hadst been gone,' quoth she, 'sweet boy, ere this,
But that thou told'st me thou wouldst hunt the boar.
O be advised, thou know'st not what it is 615
With javelin's point a churlish swine to gore,
   Whose tushes never sheathed he whetteth still,
   Like to a mortal butcher bent to kill.

'On his bow-back, he hath a battle set
Of bristly pikes that ever threat his foes; 620
His eyes like glow-worms shine when he doth fret,
His snout digs sepulchres where'er he goes;
   Being moved, he strikes whate'er is in his way,
   And whom he strikes his crooked tushes slay.

'His brawny sides with hairy bristles armed 625
Are better proof than thy spear's point can enter;
His short thick neck cannot be easily harmed;
Being ireful, on the lion he will venture;
   The thorny brambles and embracing bushes
   As fearful of him part, through whom he rushes. 630

628 venture] Q (venter)

612 **withhold** restrain, imprison (*OED* 3)
617 **tushes** tusks
   whetteth According to Turbervile, 150, the boar has four tusks 'whereof the two highest do not hurt when he striketh, but serve only to whet the other two lowest' (a belief also found in Edward, Duke of York, *The Master of Game*, 50).
618 **mortal butcher** deadly slaughterman. *Butchers* in this period killed the meat they sold.
   bent functions with both the *butcher*, who is 'determined' to kill (*OED* 3), and with *tushes*, which are 'curved' (*OED* 1).
619 **bow-back** arched or crooked back
   battle 'a body or line of troops in battle array' (*OED* 8a, citing this passage). The description recalls the Calydonian boar in Golding 8.376–80: 'Right dreadful was to see | His brawnèd neck, right dreadful was his hair which grew as thick | With pricking points as one of them could well by other stick. | And like a front of armèd pikes set close in battle ray | The sturdy bristles on his back stood staring up alway'.
620 **pikes** (a) 'A weapon consisting of a long wooden shaft with a pointed head of iron or steel' (*OED* s.v. 'pike' *n.* 5); also perhaps (b) 'a hedgehog's prickle or spine' (*OED* s.v. 'pike' *n. 1*, 2 a)
621 **fret** rage
623 **Being moved** when roused to anger, as in *Romeo* 1.1.5: 'I strike quickly, being moved.'
626 **better proof** stronger armour. Armour is *proof* has been tested for its efficacy.
630 **whom** which. On the uncoordinated relative, see l. 306 n.

'Alas, he naught esteems that face of thine,
To which love's eyes pays tributary gazes,
Nor thy soft hands, sweet lips, and crystal eyne,
Whose full perfection all the world amazes,
 But having thee at vantage (wondrous dread!) 635
 Would root these beauties, as he roots the mead.

'O let him keep his loathsome cabin still:
Beauty hath naught to do with such foul fiends.
Come not within his danger by thy will.
They that thrive well take counsel of their friends: 640
 When thou didst name the boar, not to dissemble,
 I feared thy fortune, and my joints did tremble.

'Didst thou not mark my face? Was it not white?
Saw'st thou not signs of fear lurk in mine eye?
Grew I not faint, and fell I not downright? 645
Within my bosom, whereon thou dost lie,
 My boding heart pants, beats, and takes no rest,
 But like an earthquake shakes thee on my breast.

'For where love reigns, disturbing jealousy
Doth call himself affection's sentinel; 650
Gives false alarms, suggesteth mutiny,

645 downright] Q (downe right)

631–3 These lines echo *Met.* 10.547–9 (Golding 10.634–6): 'Thy tender youth, thy beauty bright, thy count'nance fair and brave | Although they had the force to win the heart of Venus, have | No power against the lions, nor against the bristled swine'.

632 eyes pays Here *love* is thought of as the subject, hence the singular verb.

633 eyne archaic plural of eyes

635 having ... vantage being in a position of superiority over you

636 root 'Of swine: To turn up the soil by grubbing with the snout' (*OED* s.v. 'root' *v.* 2), an intransitive verb which Shakespeare is the first recorded writer to use transitively
mead meadow

637 cabin lair of a wild beast (rare in this sense; it is more usually used of lowly dwellings, and so is of a piece with

Venus's effort to present the boar as *churlish* or a *butcher*, the sorts of person the finical Adonis would not wish to meet)

638 foul fiends In popular usage this phrase was usually used to describe minor devils, as in *Lear* (Folio) 3.6.8: 'Pray, innocent, and beware the foul fiend'.

639 danger power to do harm

640 Proverbial in tone, but no parallel has been adduced.

641 not to dissemble to tell the truth

642 feared feared for

645 downright immediately; Q reads 'down right' which suggests also 'right down'

647 boding foreboding. *OED* cites this as the earliest use of the participle in this sense.

650 sentinel sentry (only introduced into English in the late 1570s)

651 suggesteth incites. The verb is often used of promptings from Satan to evil actions. Compare l. 1044 and *Lucrece* l. 37.

And in a peaceful hour doth cry "Kill, kill,"
Distemp'ring gentle love in his desire,
As air and water do abate the fire.

'This sour informer, this bate-breeding spy,   655
This canker that eats up love's tender spring,
This carry-tale, dissentious jealousy,
That sometime true news, sometime false, doth bring,
    Knocks at my heart, and whispers in mine ear,
    That if I love thee, I thy death should fear.   660

'And more than so, presenteth to mine eye
The picture of an angry chafing boar,
Under whose sharp fangs, on his back doth lie
An image like thyself, all stained with gore,
    Whose blood upon the fresh flowers being shed   665
    Doth make them droop with grief, and hang the head.

'What should I do, seeing thee so indeed
That tremble at th' imagination?
The thought of it doth make my faint heart bleed,
And fear doth teach it divination: 670
    I prophesy thy death, my living sorrow,
    If thou encounter with the boar tomorrow.

654 air] Q; earth *conj.* Oxford

652 'Kill, kill' was a command given for a
general assault on the enemy by English
troops, which was then adopted as a
battle cry. Compare *Lear* (Folio) 4.5.183.
653 **Distemp'ring** disturbing; more precisely,
putting love out of its natural balance
of humours, or 'temper', in the way that
exposure to adverse elements (*air and
water*) puts out *fire*.
655 **bate-breeding** causing strife or discord.
Bate (discord) was slightly archaic by
1593.
656 **canker** a worm which kills buds. See
Sonnet 35.4 n.
    spring tender new growth
657 **dissentious** quarrelsome
658 This line recalls Virgil's description of
Fama (rumour) as 'tam ficti pravique
tenax quam nuntia veri' ('as keen to
bear false and wicked news as truth'),
Aen. 4.188, a passage which underlies
Rumour's prologue to *2 Henry IV*.
662 **chafing** raging

663 **fangs** tusks. A boar's tusks were re-
garded as teeth by Turbervile, 150.
    his back i.e. Adonis's.
665–6 There is a distant recollection of the
death of the youth Euryalus in Virgil's
Aeneid (Phaer 9.451–5: 'Down falls
Euryalus in death, his limbs, his fair fine
flesh | All runs on blood, his neck down
fainting nods on shoulders nesh [tender]
| Well like the purple flower that cut
with plough letfalling lops | In languish
with'ring dies, or like weak necks of
poppy's crops | Down peising [weighing]
heavy heads, when rain doth lading
grieve their tops'). The image of the
drooping, bloodstained flowers antici-
pates Adonis's death (ll. 1055–6) and his
metamorphosis (ll. 1165–70).
667 **seeing thee so indeed** if I really were to
see you like this
668 **imagination** unreal mental image (four
syllables)
672 **encounter with** do battle against

'But if thou needs wilt hunt, be ruled by me;
Uncouple at the timorous flying hare,
Or at the fox which lives by subtlety,   675
Or at the roe, which no encounter dare:
    Pursue these fearful creatures o'er the downs,
    And on thy well-breathed horse keep with thy hounds.

'And when thou hast on foot the purblind hare,
Mark the poor wretch to overshoot his troubles,   680
How he outruns the wind, and with what care
He cranks and crosses with a thousand doubles.
    The many musets through the which he goes
    Are like a labyrinth to amaze his foes.

680 overshoot] Q (ouer-shut)

674 **Uncouple** 'To release (dogs) from being
fastened together in couples; to set free for
the chase' (*OED*)
   timorous . . . hare The hare is traditionally
regarded as timid: its Latin name is *lepidus
timidus*. Topsell, 296, records that 'If they
hear the dogs they raise themselves on
their legs and run from them; but if fear-
ful imagination oppress them, as they
oftentimes are very sad and melancholy,
supposing to hear the noise of the dogs
when there are none such stirring, then
do they run to and fro, fearing and trem-
bling, as if they were fallen mad'. Venus
is not here being merely pusillanimous,
however, since the hare was regarded as
'king . . . of all venery' (Juliana Barnes,
attrib., *The Boke of St Albans* (1530),
sig. A3ʳ), and as 'not the least in estima-
tion because the hunting of that seely
[defenceless] beast is mother to all the
terms, blasts, and artificial devices that
hunters do use' (Harrison, 327). Harrison
does go on to say that 'all which . . . are
pastimes more meet for ladies and gentle-
women to exercise . . . than for men of
courage to follow'. It is also an appropri-
ate beast for Venus since it is capable
of superfoetation: 'herein Nature hath
showed her bounty and goodness . . . The
hare is the only creature . . . which after it
be once with young, conceiveth again
upon it', Pliny, i.232.
676 **dare** the subjunctive form of 'dares',
which is also found in the early histories
(Abbott §361)
677 **o'er the downs** Downland is free of
undergrowth and is usually grazed; it

represents a domesticated alternative to
the wood, which, in Ovid (and through
Ovid in *Titus Andronicus*), is a place devot-
ed to hunting and to violence.
678 **well-breathed** sound of wind; fit
679 **on foot** in motion
   purblind Hares were traditionally believed
to have 'bad sight' (Edward, Duke of York,
The Master of Game, 17), and the hare is
called *purblind* in the Middle English poem
'The Names of the Hare' (*OED* s.v. 'pur-
blind' 2e). Topsell, 265: 'The eye-lids com-
ing from the brows are too short to cover
their eyes, and therefore is this sense very
weak in them'. Given the tragic out-
come of the poem, it is also significant
that hares were regarded as ill-omened
creatures.
680 **poor wretch** Sympathy for hunted hares
is not unusual in this period: Turbervile,
176–8 contains a poem called 'The Hare
to the Hunter' which begins 'Are minds of
men become so void of sense, | That they
can joy to hurt a harmless thing'.
   overshoot his troubles lose his pursuers.
Q's 'ouer-shut' is a variant spelling of
overshoot, a term from hunting usually
applied to dogs when they eagerly 'over-
shoot a chase through too much heat'
(Turbervile, 173).
682 **cranks** twists and turns about. First
cited usage in *OED*.
   doubles 'A sharp turn in running' (*OED*
6: first cited usage, although Turbervile,
161, writes of a hare's 'doublings and
crossings').
683 **musets** a hare's form or lair; also related
to 'meuse', a hole in a hedge through

'Sometime he runs among a flock of sheep   685
To make the cunning hounds mistake their smell;
And sometime where earth-delving conies keep,
To stop the loud pursuers in their yell;
   And sometime sorteth with a herd of deer:
   Danger deviseth shifts; wit waits on fear.   690

'For there his smell, with others being mingled,
The hot scent-snuffing hounds are driven to doubt,
Ceasing their clamorous cry, till they have singled,
With much ado, the cold fault cleanly out.
   Then do they spend their mouths; echo replies,   695
   As if another chase were in the skies.

'By this poor Wat, far off upon a hill,
Stands on his hinder legs with list'ning ear,
To hearken if his foes pursue him still.

which game weaves to avoid its pursuers. First cited usage in *OED*. Adopted by Shakespeare's imitator Richard Barnfield in *The Affectionate Shepherd* 2.11.13: 'Or with Hare-pipes (set in a muset hole) | Wilt thou deceive the deep-earth-delving coney?' Compare *earth-delving conies* at l. 687 below.

683 **the which** The use of the definite article before the relative *which* was archaic by 1593. See l. 581 n.

684 **amaze** bewilder. Since the phrase to 'be in a maze' was an alternative form of 'to be amazed' (as is apparent from the later Quarto variants for l. 469) the pun on *labyrinth/maze* would be apparent to early readers.

685 **sheep** Shakespeare here draws on Turbervile's account (165) of the hare's wiles: 'I have seen some hares oftentimes run into a flock of sheep in the field when they were hunted, and would never leave the flock'.

687 **earth-delving conies** rabbits which dig the earth. 'I have seen that [hare which] would take the ground like the coney', Turbervile, 165.
keep dwell

688 **yell** can be used of animals' cries, so refers to the barking of the dogs rather than to the cries of the huntsmen.

689 **sorteth with** keeps company with. Turbervile, 165, notes that dogs will always prefer to chase a hart rather than a hare 'because the venison of the hart is much more delicate and dainty than the hare's is'.

690 **shifts** stratagems
waits on accompanies, attends. Compare *Lucrece* l. 275.

693 **Ceasing . . . cry** Good hounds were trained to be silent unless they were on the scent.
singled separated. Often used in hunting for the action of separating the scent of a pursued animal from a group: so *Titus* 2.1.118–19: 'Single you thither then this dainty doe, | And strike her home by force, if not by words'.

694 **fault** 'Hunting. A break in the line of scent; loss of scent; a check caused by failure of scent' (*OED* 8a: first cited usage).

695 **spend their mouths** bay prodigiously (as a sign to the huntsman: see l. 693 n.). The metaphor is a common one in descriptions of hunting dogs (*OED* 9b).

697 **Wat** is a familiar name for a hare between 1500 and 1600, usually found in Norfolk and Cornwall. No reason is known for the name. For other names of the hare, see G. E. Evans and David Thomson, *The Leaping Hare* (1972), 200–12.

Anon their loud alarums he doth hear,   700
   And now his grief may be comparèd well
   To one sore sick, that hears the passing bell.

'Then shalt thou see the dew-bedabbled wretch
Turn, and return, indenting with the way.
Each envious briar his weary legs do scratch.   705
Each shadow makes him stop, each murmur stay,
   For misery is trodden on by many,
   And being low, never relieved by any.

'Lie quietly, and hear a little more;
Nay, do not struggle, for thou shalt not rise.   710
To make thee hate the hunting of the boar.
Unlike myself thou hear'st me moralize,
   Applying this to that, and so to so,
   For love can comment upon every woe.

'Where did I leave?' 'No matter where,' quoth he;   715
'Leave me, and then the story aptly ends·

705 do] Q; doth Q5

700 **alarums** war-cries. See l. 424 n.

702 **passing bell** the bell which was tolled for the soul of the dead. Roe notes that during the plague of 1592–4 in which the poem was almost certainly composed the *passing bell* would have tolled as a ceaseless reminder of mortality to the sick.

704 **indenting** zig-zagging. To 'indent' is 'To sever the two halves of a document, drawn up in duplicate, by a toothed, zigzag, or wavy line, so that the two parts exactly tally with each other ... This was done in the case of a deed, covenant, agreement, etc. in which two or more parties had an interest, so that one copy was retained by each party; the genuineness of these could be subsequently proved by the coincidence of their indented margins' (*OED* 2). Compare Golding 7.1013–16, in which a monster hunted by hounds 'Doth quickly give the grewnd [greyhound] the slip, and from his biting shrink: | And like a wily fox he runs not forth directly out, | Nor makes a windlass over all the champion fields about, | But doubling and *indenting* still avoids his en'my's lips'.

705 **envious** spiteful

  do Q5 and later editions emend to 'doth';

but the 'error of proximity', in which a plural noun *legs* is taken as the subject of the verb (rather than the singular *each briar*) is common (Abbott §412 and Partridge, *Grammar*, 27). Compare l. 840 n. and l. 1128 n.

707 Compare the proverb 'If a man once fall all will tread on him' (Dent M194).

708 **relieved** is used in *OED* sense 2a: 'To assist (the poor or needy) by gifts of money or necessary articles; to help in poverty or necessity'. It was proverbial that 'The poor have few friends' (Tilley P468).

712 **moralize** teach through exemplary tales

714 **comment** supply a (moral) commentary on

715 **leave** break off the subject (*OED* 11b; a slightly archaic sense by 1593). Epyllia frequently contain inset stories, and characters within them sometimes resist the charms of these narratives as Adonis does here so Leander objects to Neptune's story-telling in *Hero and Leander* ll. 685–8: 'Ere half this tale was done, | "Ay me," Leander cried, "th'enamoured sun | That now should shine on Thetis' glassy bower, | Descends upon my radiant Hero's tower."'

The night is spent.' 'Why, what of that?' quoth she.
'I am,' quoth he, 'expected of my friends,
    And now 'tis dark, and going I shall fall.'
    'In night,' quoth she, 'desire sees best of all.   720

'But if thou fall, O, then imagine this:
The earth, in love with thee, thy footing trips,
And all is but to rob thee of a kiss.
Rich preys make true men thieves: so do thy lips
    Make modest Dian cloudy and forlorn,   725
    Lest she should steal a kiss and die forsworn.

'Now of this dark night I perceive the reason:
Cynthia for shame obscures her silver shine,
Till forging Nature be condemned of treason,
For stealing moulds from heaven, that were divine,   730
    Wherein she framed thee, in high heaven's despite,
    To shame the sun by day, and her by night.

'And therefore hath she bribed the destinies
To cross the curious workmanship of nature,
To mingle beauty with infirmities,   735
And pure perfection with impure defeature,
    Making it subject to the tyranny
    Of mad mischances, and much misery.

'As burning fevers, agues pale and faint,
Life-poisoning pestilence, and frenzies wood,   740

718 **expected of** expected by (Abbott §170)
720 Compare Marlowe's *Hero and Leander* l. 191: 'dark night is Cupid's day', which became proverbial (Dent N167).
722 **footing** step
724 **Rich . . . thieves** It was proverbial that 'The prey entices the thief' (Dent P570). See Sonnet *48*. 14 n.
724 **true** honest
725 **modest Dian** Diana is the goddess of chastity and of the moon; also, ironically, of hunting.
726 **forsworn** having broken her vow of virginity
728 **Cynthia** the moon (another name for Diana, goddess of chastity and the moon)
729 **forging . . . treason** Nature is presented as having stolen divinely owned *moulds* and as having usurped a divine preroga-

tive to coin money in order to forge Adonis.
731 **framed** created
in . . . despite against the will of
732 **her** i.e. the moon
733 **destinies** the Fates, personified in Greek and Latin literature as Clotho, Lachesis, and Atropos
734 **cross** thwart
curious artful
736 **defeature** disfigurement. *OED* cites *Errors* 5.1.299–300 as the first usage: 'Careful hours with time's deformèd hand | Have written strange defeatures in my face'.
739 **agues** illnesses in which periods of high fever alternate with fits of shivering
740 **pestilence** could mean 'plague', which raged in London in 1592–4. See l. 509 n.
wood mad

The marrow-eating sickness, whose attaint
Disorder breeds by heating of the blood,
 Surfeits, impostumes, grief, and damned despair
 Swear Nature's death, for framing thee so fair.

'And not the least of all these maladies   745
But in one minute's fight brings beauty under,
Both favour, savour, hue and qualities,
Whereat th' impartial gazer late did wonder,
 Are on the sudden wasted, thawed, and done,
 As mountain snow melts with the midday sun. 750

'Therefore, despite of fruitless chastity,
Love-lacking vestals, and self-loving nuns
That on the earth would breed a scarcity,
And barren dearth of daughters and of sons,
 Be prodigal. The lamp that burns by night   755
 Dries up his oil to lend the world his light.

'What is thy body but a swallowing grave,
Seeming to bury that posterity
Which by the rights of time thou needs must have,
If thou destroy them not in dark obscurity?   760
 If so the world will hold thee in disdain,
 Sith in thy pride so fair a hope is slain.

748 **th' impartial]** Q2; the th' impartiall Q 754 **sons]** Q2; suns Q

741 **marrow-eating sickness** possibly vene-
real disease, the name of which of course
derives from that of Venus
 attaint infection (a sense peculiar to
Shakespeare, transferred from *OED*
'attaint' *ppl. a.* 2)
743 **Surfeits** illnesses brought on by excess
 impostumes abscesses; also moral
corruptions
745–6 **not . . . under** 'even the smallest of
these diseases can bring beauty into sub-
jection after only the briefest of battles'.
For this sense of *bring . . . under* see *OED*
s.v. 'bring' 26.
747 **favour** beauty
 hue beauty, complexion. See Sonnet
20.7 n.
748 **impartial** indifferent not swayed by
desire
749 **thawed** dissolved. Sometimes used of
emotions or moral qualities, as in *Lucrece*
l. 884.

751 **despite of** in defiance of
752 **vestals** virgins. Originally one of the
four priestesses, sworn to virginity, who
guarded the sacred fire of the Temple of
Vesta in Rome.
755 **Be prodigal** spend what you have
756 **Dries . . . oil** metaphorically: expends his
sexual energy. Cf. 'A candle (torch) lights
others and consumes itself' (Dent C39).
His, as often, means 'its'.
757–62 Compare Sonnets 3–6, and esp.
3.7–8.
759 **by . . . time** to which time has due
title
760 This is the only twelve-syllable line in the
poem.
762 **Sith** since
 in thy pride (a) through your haughti-
ness; (b) in your prime. For the sexual
associations of *pride* see Sonnet 151.10
n.

'So in thyself, thyself art made away,
A mischief worse than civil home-bred strife,
Or theirs whose desperate hands themselves do slay,   765
Or butcher-sire, that reaves his son of life.
   Foul cank'ring rust the hidden treasure frets,
   But gold that's put to use more gold begets.'

'Nay then,' quoth Adon, 'you will fall again
Into your idle over-handled theme.   770
The kiss I gave you is bestowed in vain,
And all in vain you strive against the stream:
   For by this black-faced night, desire's foul nurse,
   Your treatise makes me like you worse and worse.

'If love have lent you twenty thousand tongues,   775
And every tongue more moving than your own,
Bewitching like the wanton mermaid's songs,
Yet from mine ear the tempting tune is blown,
   For know my heart stands armèd in mine ear,
   And will not let a false sound enter there,   780

'Lest the deceiving harmony should run
Into the quiet closure of my breast,
And then my little heart were quite undone,
In his bed-chamber to be barred of rest.

781 run] Q (ronne)

763 **made away** killed. A common euphemism for murder in the sixteenth century.
766 **reaves** deprives
767 **frets** wears away
768 The analogy between breeding and usury is common: *Hero and Leander* ll. 232–4: 'What difference betwixt the richest mine | And basest mould but use? For both, not used, | Are of like worth'. The slight echo of the parable of the talents in Matthew 25: 14–30 adds to the sermonical tone. It was proverbial that 'Money begets money' (Dent M1053).
769 **you will fall** you are determined to return to
770 **over-handled theme** tired old subject for debate (and Venus's hands have been busy). On *theme*, see l. 422 n.
771 **The kiss I gave you** at l. 479
772 Compare the proverb 'It is in vain to strive against the stream' (Dent S927).
773 **nurse** nourisher. It was proverbial that 'Night (or opportunity) is whoredom's bawd' (Dent O70). In the classical tradition nurses very often inspire their mistresses to sexual licentiousness: in *Met.* 10.382–445 Myrrha's nurse assists the incestuous union from which Adonis is conceived.
774 **treatise** talk. Short, pious works from the period are often called 'A treatise of . . .'.
777 **mermaid** See l. 429 n.
778 **blown** blown away (as a song would be if the wind were in the wrong direction)
781 **run** Q spells 'ronne' in order to preserve the eye-rhyme.
782 **quiet closure** enclosure. Compare Sonnet 48.11 n.
784 **barred of** deprived of

No, lady, no; my heart longs not to groan,   785
But soundly sleeps, while now it sleeps alone.

'What have you urged that I cannot reprove?
The path is smooth that leadeth on to danger.
I hate not love, but your device in love,
That lends embracements unto every stranger.   790
    You do it for increase? O strange excuse,
    When reason is the bawd to lust's abuse.

'Call it not love, for love to heaven is fled,
Since sweating lust on earth usurped his name,
Under whose simple semblance he hath fed   795
Upon fresh beauty, blotting it with blame,
    Which the hot tyrant stains, and soon bereaves,
    As caterpillars do the tender leaves.

'Love comforteth like sunshine after rain;
But Lust's effect is tempest after sun;   800
Love's gentle spring doth always fresh remain;
Lust's winter comes ere summer half be done;
    Love surfeits not; Lust like a glutton dies:
    Love is all truth; Lust full of forgèd lies.

'More I could tell, but more I dare not say: 805
The text is old, the orator too green.

787 **reprove** (a) disprove (*OED* 5); (b) rebuke (*OED* 3)
788 Compare the proverb 'The path is smooth that leads to danger' (Dent P101.1).
789 **device** (a) manner of thinking (Schmidt, 4); (b) tricky artfulness
791 **increase** (a) procreation ^compare Sonnet *1.*1 and n.); (b) financial advantage (*OED* 4), hence *bawd* in the next line. Stressed on the second syllable.
792 **bawd** pimp, who takes a cut from a prostitute's takings. Venus could be associated with prostitution in the period: Stephen Gosson in *The School of Abuse* (1587), fo. E7ᵛ, describes how prostitutes 'live a mile from the city like Venus' nuns'.
    abuse wicked practice (with perhaps a sexual taint; compare *Lucrece* l. 1259 n.).
795 **Under . . . semblance** in whose harmless appearance
796 **blotting** can imply a moral stain. See Sonnet 36.3.

797 **Which . . . bereaves** which (i.e. beauty) lust contaminates and soon snatches away
799–804 This section of Adonis's answer to Venus takes the form of a *distinctio*, in which he tries to replace the terms which her argument has deployed by closely equivalent but morally pejorative language. This was a ploy widely advocated in classical rhetorical manuals for occasions when an orator wished to diminish the value of an action which his adversary was attempting to present as good. See Quintilian 9.3.65.
799 It was proverbial that 'After rain comes fair weather' (Dent R8).
802–3 Compare *Lucrece* ll. 48–9.
806 **text** subject, theme for disputation, received maxim; perhaps also 'The theme or subject on which anyone speaks; the starting-point of a discussion' (*OED* 4c). Adonis is a textbook orator, who sees the

Therefore in sadness now I will away.
My face is full of shame, my heart of teen;
    Mine ears, that to your wanton talk attended,
    Do burn themselves for having so offended.'   810

With this he breaketh from the sweet embrace
Of those fair arms which bound him to her breast,
And homeward through the dark laund runs apace,
Leaves love upon her back, deeply distressed.
    Look how a bright star shooteth from the sky;   815
    So glides he in the night from Venus' eye,

Which after him she darts, as one on shore
Gazing upon a late embarkèd friend,
Till the wild waves will have him seen no more,
Whose ridges with the meeting clouds contend: 820
    So did the merciless and pitchy night
    Fold in the object that did feed her sight.

Whereat amazed, as one that unaware
Hath dropped a precious jewel in the flood,
Or 'stonished, as night wand'rers often are,   825
Their light blown out in some mistrustful wood;

---

discussion as a schoolroom debate.

806 **green** inexperienced

807 **in sadness** (a) in earnest (compare *Romeo* 1.1.196: 'Tell me in sadness, who is that you love?'); (b) in low spirits

808 **teen** vexation, sorrow

810 **burn themselves** Their hot red flush becomes self-punitive.
so offended performed such a crime

813 **laund** glade, clearing in a wood

816 **glides** can be used of the graceful movement of a person (*OED* 1d), or of a heavenly body through the air (*OED* 1c); both senses co-operate here. Cf. Golding 14.978: 'There gliding from the sky a star straight down to ground was sent'.

815, 816 **from** This magical simile plays on *from*: it suggests that Venus is the point of Adonis's origin as the sky is the origin of the shooting star, and so presents the scene *from* her point of view; it also suggests with a simple objectivity that Adonis glides away *from* Venus's sight.

817–20 may recall the anxiety of Alcyone at the departure of Ceyx, her husband: Golding 11.539–45: 'And after that the land | Was far removèd from the ship, and that the sight began | To be unable to discern the face of any man, | As long as ere she could she looked upon the rowing keel. | And when she could no longer time for distance ken it well, | She lookèd still upon the sails that flaskèd with the wind | Upon the mast'. In the storm that follows waves and clouds join (573–4): 'The surges mounting up aloft did seem to mate the sky, | And with their sprinkling for to wet the clouds that hang on high'. The echo would be appropriate: both men meet violent ends. Compare *Cymbeline* 1.3.8–22.

817 **darts** shoots. The literal sense of 'hurls a weapon' is still active. See l. 196 n.

820 **ridges** crests (not an unusual word for the tops of waves in this period)

825 **'stonished** bewildered

826 **mistrustful** causing fear (the only example cited for this sense in *OED*)

Even so confounded in the dark she lay,
Having lost the fair discovery of her way.

And now she beats her heart, whereat it groans,
That all the neighbour caves, as seeming troubled,   830
Make verbal repetition of her moans:
Passion on passion deeply is redoubled.
　'Ay me,' she cries, and twenty times 'woe, woe',
　And twenty echoes, twenty times cry so.

She, marking them, begins a wailing note,   835
And sings extemporally a woeful ditty,
How love makes young men thrall and old men dote,
How love is wise in folly, foolish witty.
　Her heavy anthem still concludes in woe,
　And still the choir of echoes answer so.   840

Her song was tedious, and out-wore the night,
For lovers' hours are long, though seeming short;
If pleased themselves, others they think delight
In suchlike circumstance, with suchlike sport:

---

832 deeply] Q; doubly WHITE (*conj* Walker)

827 **confounded** confused
828 **fair discovery** the light cast by Adonis, which reveals her path
829–41 has its roots in Ovid's story of Echo and Narcissus (Golding 3.625–8): 'These are the words that last | Out of his lips beholding still his wonted image passed: | "Alas, sweet boy, beloved in vain, farewell." And by and by | With sighing sound the self-same words the Echo did reply'. The story has already been invoked in ll. 19–20 and 161–2, and is a prominent subtext both for its representation or misdirected and unfulfillable desire, and because it was the subject of the first poem dedicated to the Earl of Southampton, Clapham's *Narcissus*. See Introduction, pp. 11–12.
829 **heart** breast (*OED* 3a)
830 **neighbour** neighbouring. This transformation of a word's grammatical form was a rhetorical figure known as *permutatio* or *enallage*, and is the product of conscious artistry. See Quintilian 9.3.7.
831 **verbal** usually carries the sense 'merely to do with words rather than things' in this period. This usage may anticipate the sense 'word for word, verbatim' (*OED* 5a: first cited 1612).
832 **Passion** lamentation. See Sonnet 20.2 n. **deeply** (a) solemnly; (b) with deep emotion; (c) loudly (Schmidt, 5)
836 **ditty** is not necessarily a contemptuous term for a trivial song; see Sidney's Psalm 13.5: 'Still, therefore, of thy graces shall be my song's ditty'.
839 **heavy anthem** melancholy song. An *anthem* is a song of praise, and can connote solemnity, as in *Two Gentlemen* 3.1.238–9: 'breathe it in mine ear, | As ending anthem of my endless dolour.'
840 **answer** The singular *choir* is given a plural form of verb because of the proximity of *echoes*. Compare l. 705 n. and l. 1128 n.
841 **out-wore** outlasted
843–4 **If . . . circumstance** 'If lovers are themselves happy they assume that others are also delighted by similar joyful experiences.'

Their copious stories, oftentimes begun,   845
End without audience, and are never done.

For who hath she to spend the night withal,
But idle sounds resembling parasites?
Like shrill-tongued tapsters answering every call,
Soothing the humour of fantastic wits.   850
   She says ' 'Tis so'; they answer all ' 'Tis so',
   And would say after her, if she said 'no'.

Lo here the gentle lark, weary of rest,
From his moist cabinet mounts up on high,
And wakes the morning, from whose silver breast   855
The sun ariseth in his majesty,
   Who doth the world so gloriously behold
   That cedar tops and hills seem burnished gold.

Venus salutes him with this fair good morrow:
'O thou clear god and patron of all light,   860
From whom each lamp and shining star doth borrow
The beauteous influence that makes him bright,
   There lives a son that sucked an earthly mother
   May lend thee light, as thou dost lend to other.'

845 **copious** elaborated with verbal orna-
ment, in the manner advocated in
Erasmus's *De Copia*
847 **withal** with (the preferred emphatic
form at the end of a sentence; Abbott
§196 and 274)
848 **parasites** toadies, scroungers who
servilely repeat her words
849 **shrill-tongued** loud, and perhaps too
with unbroken voices
   tapsters people who draw beer for cus-
tomers in a tavern. They were famously
servile, as Francis is in *1 Henry IV* 2.4, and
were occasionally pimps, like Pompey in
Measure.
850 **fantastic wits** Smart young men about
town with foppish tastes and a high opin-
ion of their own verbal sharpness were
called 'fantastics'.
854 **moist cabinet** dewy lodging. A *cabinet*
can be a rustic dwelling or a private
apartment.
856–8 Compare Sonnet 33.1–4.

858 **cedar** is here in such *majestic* company
because it is traditionally regarded as the
king of trees.
860 **clear** (a) brightly shining (as in Song of
Solomon 6: 10: 'Fair as the moon, clear
as the sun'); (b) famous (from the Latin
claris)
861 **lamp** heavenly body
862 **influence** Powers and virtues were
believed to flow (Latin *influere*) from the
planets.
863 **earthly mother** Adonis was in fact
born from Myrrha after she was trans-
formed into a tree as a result of her
incestuous union with her father. Her
links with the earth were therefore
stronger than Venus appears to know:
'The *ground* did overgrow her feet, and
ankles as she spake. | And from her
bursten toes went roots, which writhing
here and there | Did fasten so the trunk
within the *ground* she could not stir'
(Golding 10.562–4).

This said, she hasteth to a myrtle grove,   865
Musing the morning is so much o'erworn
And yet she hears no tidings of her love:
She hearkens for his hounds and for his horn;
   Anon she hears them chant it lustily,
   And all in haste she coasteth to the cry.   870

And as she runs the bushes in the way
Some catch her by the neck, some kiss her face,
Some twined about her thigh to make her stay.
She wildly breaketh from their strict embrace,
   Like a milch-doe, whose swelling dugs do ache,   875
   Hasting to feed her fawn, hid in some brake.

By this she hears the hounds are at a bay,
Whereat she starts like one that spies an adder
Wreathed up in fatal folds just in his way,
The fear whereof doth make him shake and shudder;   880
   Even so the timorous yelping of the hounds
   Appals her senses, and her spirit confounds.

873 twined] Q (twin'd); twine Q7

865 **myrtle** an evergreen plant with sweetly
   scented flowers, sacred to Venus
866–7 **Musing . . . love** wondering why it is
   that so much of the morning has passed
   and yet she hears nothing of her lover
869 **chant it bay**, bark (*OED* 1c). *It* is an
   indefinite object (Abbott §226).
870 **coasteth** runs in such a way as to out-
   flank ('*Hawking and Hunting*. Not to fly or
   run straight at; to keep at a distance; esp.
   to fly or run from the straight course so
   as to cut off the chased animal when it
   doubles' (*OED* 10)). So mark which
   way an hare bendeth at the first, and
   coast before her to meet her', Turbervile,
   174.
873 **twined** Q1 reads 'twin'd'. Q7 emends to
   'twine'. On the movement between past
   and historic present, see l. 317 and n. This
   may simply be a variant spelling for the
   sake of rhyme; compare *Lucrece* l. 1544 n.
874 **strict** tight
875 **milch-doe** a female deer who is feeding
   young
876 **brake** a thicket of brushwood or briars

877 **By this** by this time
   at a bay (a) the prolonged barking of dogs
   when they encounter the hunted animal;
   (b) the moment when the hunted animal
   turns to face its pursuers. The latter sense
   is perhaps less likely to be meant here,
   since Turbervile (158) says 'A great boar
   . . . will seldom keep hounds at a bay'.
   Venus infers that a boar is being hunted
   from the length of time for which the
   hounds are stationary at l. 885 below,
   which may indicate that she knows little
   about hunting boars.
878–80 The simile derives from Virgil's
   Aeneid (Phaer 2.374–7): 'foot he back-
   ward drew, | As one that unbethought
   hath lapped some snake among the
   briars | To tread, and quickly starting
   back with trembling fear retires, | When
   swoll'n with angry teen he seeth his blue
   neck bent upright'.
879 **Wreathed** coiled
882 **Appals** makes faint
   spirit is monosyllabic, as in Sonnets 56.8,
   74.8, 80.2, 85.7, 86.5, 98.3, 144.4.

For now she knows it is no gentle chase,
But the blunt boar, rough bear, or lion proud,
Because the cry remaineth in one place,   885
Where fearfully the dogs exclaim aloud;
  Finding their enemy to be so cursed,
  They all strain court'sy who shall cope him first.

This dismal cry rings sadly in her ear,
Through which it enters to surprise her heart,   890
Who, overcome by doubt and bloodless fear,
With cold-pale weakness numbs each feeling part,
  Like soldiers, when their captain once doth yield,
  They basely fly, and dare not stay the field.

Thus stands she in a trembling ecstasy,   895
Till cheering up her senses all dismayed
She tells them 'tis a causeless fantasy,
And childish error that they are afraid;
  Bids them leave quaking, bids them fear no more—
  And with that word she spied the hunted boar,   900

Whose frothy mouth bepainted all with red,
Like milk and blood being mingled both together,
A second fear through all her sinews spread,

883–4 recalls Golding 10.623–7: 'But with the sturdy boar | And ravening wolf, and bear-whelps armed with ugly paws, and eke [also] | The cruel lions which delight in blood, and slaughter seek, | She meddled not. And of these same she warnèd also thee, | Adonis, for to shun them, if thou wouldst have warnèd be'.

883 chase animal hunted (*OED* s.v. 'chase' *n.* 1, 4a)

887 cursed savage (*OED* 4b: a sense common among huntsmen)

888 strain court'sy 'to insist too much on, be over-punctilious in, the observance of; to stand upon ceremony' (*OED* s.v. 'courtesy' 1b). The dogs politely defer to each other because they are so reluctant to attack their prey, as in the proverb 'At an ill passage honour thy companion' (Dent P89). The phrase *strain court'sy* is used by Turbervile (188) of dogs who 'would not refuse the wild boar, nor the wolf, yet they would strain courtesy at a fox'.
cope encounter (as in battle; compare *Lucrece* l. 99)

889 dismal ill-omened, fateful (from the Latin *dies mali*, day of ill)

890 surprise 'assail or attack suddenly and without warning' (*OED* 2a). The heart is presented as a *captain* (893) at the centre of a citadel besieged by enemies. Compare ll. 1033–50 below.

891 Who This is always preferred by Shakespeare as the relative pronoun for personifications. See Abbott §264 and l. 956.

894 stay the field stand firm in battle

895 ecstasy a state of passionate paralysis; literally 'standing outside herself'

897 causeless fantasy Compare l. 597: the poem increasingly comes to focus on the relationships between emotions and the imagination.

901 The last previous mention of *red* is at the description of Adonis chafing Venus's cheek at l. 468: the colour comes back with a bloody vengeance at this point.

903 sinews possibly 'nerves'

Which madly hurries her she knows not whither.
  This way she runs, and now she will no further,   905
  But back retires to rate the boar for murther.

A thousand spleens bear her a thousand ways;
She treads the path that she untreads again.
Her more than haste is mated with delays,
Like the proceedings of a drunken brain,   910
  Full of respects, yet naught at all respecting,
  In hand with all things, naught at all effecting.

Here kennelled in a brake she finds a hound,
And asks the weary caitiff for his master;
And there another licking of his wound,   915
'Gainst venomed sores the only sovereign plaster,
  And here she meets another, sadly scowling,
  To whom she speaks, and he replies with howling.

When he hath ceased his ill-resounding noise
Another flap-mouthed mourner, black and grim,   920
Against the welkin volleys out his voice;
Another and another answer him,
  Clapping their proud tails to the ground below,
  Shaking their scratched ears, bleeding as they go.

Look how the world's poor people are amazèd   925
At apparitions, signs and prodigies,

---

906 **retires** returns (*OED* 4); compare *Lucrece* l. 962.
  rate berate
907 **spleens** whimsies, fits of passion. The spleen was a contrary organ, being regarded as the seat of both melancholy and mirth.
908 **untreads** retraces
909 **mated with** thwarted by (as when one player 'checkmates' another in chess). It was proverbial that 'The more haste the less speed' (Dent H198); hence Venus's *more than haste* is completely arrested.
911 **Full . . . respecting** 'having an air of circumstantial gravity, but actually not thinking of anything'. *Respects* probably means here 'a consideration; a fact or motive which assists in, or leads to, the formation of a decision; an end or aim' (*OED* 14a).

912 **In hand with** preoccupied with
914 **caitiff** wretch
916 **venomed** infected
  sovereign plaster uniquely effective cure. Compare l. 28 n. A *plaster* can be a paste or potion, or, figuratively, any form of cure for a wound.
920 **flap-mouthed** describes the loose, floppy jowls of a bloodhound.
921 **welkin** sky (only in poetic and literary uses by the sixteenth century)
  volleys hurls out (like shot from a cannon)
923 **Clapping** probably means here 'fixing firmly' (*OED* 10a): the hounds lower their once *proud* tails to the ground, rather than wagging them.
926 **prodigies** an extraordinary event or thing from which omens are deduced

Whereon with fearful eyes they long have gazèd,
Infusing them with dreadful prophecies;
    So she at these sad signs draws up her breath,
    And, sighing it again, exclaims on death: 930

'Hard-favoured tyrant, ugly, meagre, lean;
Hateful divorce of love,' thus chides she Death,
'Grim-grinning ghost, earth's worm, what dost thou mean
To stifle beauty, and to steal his breath?
    Who, when he lived, his breath and beauty set   935
    Gloss on the rose, smell to the violet.

'If he be dead—O no, it cannot be,
Seeing his beauty thou shouldst strike at it.
O yes, it may: thou hast no eyes to see,
But hatefully at random dost thou hit.   940
    Thy mark is feeble age, but thy false dart
    Mistakes that aim, and cleaves an infant's heart.

'Hadst thou but bid beware, then he had spoke,
And hearing him, thy power had lost his power.
The destinies will curse thee for this stroke: 945
They bid thee crop a weed; thou pluck'st a flower.
    Love's golden arrow at him should have fled,
    And not Death's ebon dart to strike him dead.

---

928 **Infusing** filling them with. The verb is often used to describe the moment when God grants grace; *prophecies* too is often used in this period of those who preach their personally inspired interpretations of scripture: the populace makes a virtual religion from the portents.

930 **exclaims on** cries out against. Compare l. 160 and n.

931–54 In Giovanni Tarchagnota, *L'Adone* (Venice, 1550), Venus makes a similar complaint against death, st. 43–59, although Shakespeare is unlikely to have known this work directly.

931 **Hard-favoured** harsh-featured (and so likely to be harsh in deed). Compare l. 133 and n.

932 **divorce** that which causes the dissolution (*OED* 3; first cited usage in this sense)

933 **earth's worm** the lowest thing on earth, no more than a worm

939 **no eyes** The Death's head is a skull, with sockets empty of eyes.

940 **at random** The sense 'haphazardly' is emerging, but a technical sense from gunnery 'at more than point blank range' (*OED* 5b) is called out by *mark*, *dart*, and *aim*: the idea is that Death is shooting from too great a distance, and so misses his proper aim.

941 **mark** target
dart could be a spear, javelin, or arrow in this period.

944 **had lost** would have lost
his its

947–8 Cupid was sometimes presented as carrying a deadly arrow by sonneteers in the period: he is urged in *FQ* 1. Prol. 3 to 'Lay now thy deadly Heben [ebony] bow apart'.

948 **ebon** made of ebony, black

'Dost thou drink tears that thou provok'st such weeping?
What may a heavy groan advantage thee? 950
Why hast thou cast into eternal sleeping
Those eyes that taught all other eyes to see?
    Now nature cares not for thy mortal vigour.
    Since her best work is ruined with thy rigour.'

Here overcome as one full of despair 955
She vailed her eyelids, who like sluices stopped
The crystal tide that from her two cheeks fair
In the sweet channel of her bosom dropped;
    But through the flood-gates breaks the silver rain,
    And with his strong course opens them again. 960

O how her eyes and tears did lend and borrow:
Her eye seen in the tears, tears in her eye,
Both crystals, where they viewed each other's sorrow,
Sorrow, that friendly sighs sought still to dry,
    But like a stormy day, now wind, now rain, 965
    Sighs dry her cheeks; tears make them wet again.

Variable passions throng her constant woe,
As striving who should best become her grief.
All entertained, each passion labours so
That every present sorrow seemeth chief; 970
    But none is best. Then join they all together,
    Like many clouds, consulting for foul weather.

---

950 **advantage** profit
953 **mortal vigour** deadly energy
954 **rigour** pitilessness
956 **vailed** lowered. See l. 314 n. Compare *Hero and Leander* l. 159: Hero is 'Veiled to the ground, vailing her eyelids close'.
956 **who** which (as usually for a personification; see l. 891 n.).
    sluices is usually glossed as 'floodgates', although the context also supports 'A channel, drain, or small stream, esp. one carrying off overflow or surplus water' (*OED* 2).
960 **his** refers to the *silver rain* of Venus's tears.
962 **Her . . . tears** The conceit is that the crystal sphere of the teardrop contains a miniature image of the eye.

963 **crystals** clear, glass-like, and reflective
963–4 **sorrow, | Sorrow** *Epizeuxis* (emphatic repetition of a word with none in between) is often used as a rhetorical indicator of great passion in Shakespeare.
967 **throng** press around (like courtiers or suitors)
968 **striving** contending
    become suit with
969–70 Each woe is given access to Venus's heart, and each is so powerful that the one which she is presently entertaining always seems the strongest.
971 **join they** they join themselves
972 **consulting for** contriving. The courtier-like passions form a conspiracy against their mistress.

By this, far off she hears some huntsman hallow.
A nurse's song ne'er pleased her babe so well:
The dire imagination she did follow   975
This sound of hope doth labour to expel,
    For now reviving joy bids her rejoice,
    And flatters her it is Adonis' voice.

Whereat her tears began to turn their tide,
Being prisoned in her eye like pearls in glass;   980
Yet sometimes falls an orient drop beside,
Which her cheek melts, as scorning it should pass
    To wash the foul face of the sluttish ground,
    Who is but drunken when she seemeth drowned.

O hard-believing love, how strange it seems   985
Not to believe, and yet too credulous!
Thy weal and woe are both of them extremes:
Despair and hope makes thee ridiculous.

973 **By this** by this time
    hallow Hunting cries were distinct for each phase of the action, and a knowledgeable listener could tell from them exactly what was happening in the chase. It is likely that Q's 'hallow', reproduced here, accurately reflects the cry to mark the end of the hunt. The final division of spoils to the dogs after the kill was often marked by a cry of 'List hallow, hyke hallow, hyke' (Turbervile, 175). Many editors collapse the very precise distinction between this and the cry of horsemanship in l. 284.

974 **nurse's song** Compare *Titus* 2.3.27–9: 'Whiles hounds and horns and sweet melodious birds | Be unto us as is a nurse's song | Of lullaby to bring her babe asleep'.

975 **The dire . . . follow** the sinister train of thought with which she was preoccupied

977 **reviving** (a) which comes back to life (intransitive); (b) which brings her back to life (transitive)

978 **flatters** falsely persuades (continuing the conceit of the passions as courtiers)

979 **turn their tide** ebb

980 **pearls in glass** The embedding of precious substances in glass is also described in Golding 4.438–9: 'As if a man an ivory image or a lily white | Should overlay or close with glass'. Tear-shaped pearls (fantastically valuable in the period) were

worn by the nobility as earrings, but were not set in glass. The image is a fantasy fusion of extremely costly materials and miraculous artifice.

981 **orient drop** tears like pearls. Jewels of high quality were often referred to as *orient* in the period (*OED* s.v. 'orient' *adj.* 2). The tear is also *orient* in that it is arising (*OED* 3) from the eye.
    beside The odd tear slips out from its prison 'by the side so as to miss' (*OED* 6, citing this passage as the last example).

982 **melts** works as both 'thaw' (turning the pearl to liquid) and 'cause to disappear' (*OED* 10, as at l. 1166 below), which would explain why the tears never reach the ground.

984 **Who is . . . drowned** The earth is compared to a woman, who seems *drowned* in tears, but is actually just drunk.

985–6 Love is sceptical (*hard-believing*) and credulous at the same time. The paradox works in relation to this particular point in the story if Venus is directly addressed by the vocative *love*: Venus is *too credulous* in that she wants not to believe the truth, that Adonis is dead.

987 It was proverbial that 'A woman either loves or hates to extremes' (Dent W651).

988 **makes** Two singular nouns are often followed by a singular verb in Shakespeare (Abbott §336).

The one doth flatter thee in thoughts unlikely.
In likely thoughts the other kills thee quickly.   990

Now she unweaves the web that she hath wrought:
Adonis lives, and Death is not to blame;
It was not she that called him all to naught.
Now she adds honours to his hateful name:
    She clepes him king of graves, and grave for kings,   995
    Imperious supreme of all mortal things.

'No, no', quoth she, 'Sweet Death I did but jest.
Yet pardon me: I felt a kind of fear
When as I met the boar, that bloody beast
Which knows no pity but is still severe.   1000
    Then, gentle shadow, (truth I must confess)
    I railed on thee, fearing my love's decease.

' 'Tis not my fault; the boar provoked my tongue.
Be wreaked on him (invisible commander),
'Tis he, foul creature, that hath done thee wrong.   1005
I did but act; he's author of thy slander.
    Grief hath two tongues, and never woman yet
    Could rule them both, without ten women's wit.'

Thus, hoping that Adonis is alive,
Her rash suspect she doth extenuate,   1010

---

989 **The one** is hope; *the other* is despair. The structure is chiastic.
unlikely improbable
990 **likely** probable. That lovers are victims of the shortfall between evidence and belief is a theme which preoccupies the later Shakespeare, notably in *Othello*.
991 **web** weaving
993 **called . . . naught** vehemently abused him, said that he was a complete nothing. The phrase was quite common in the period (*OED* s.v. 'naught' 1d and 'all' *adv.* 12).
995 **clepes** calls. The verb was archaic by 1590, and was often used in formal poetic invocations.
996 **supreme** ruler. The accent is on the first syllable.
999 **When** as when
1000 **still** always (*OED* 3a)
1001 **shadow** phantom, ghost
1002 **railed on** abused, cried out against
   decease Q reads 'decess', which may reflect

Shakespeare's uncertainty over the pronunciation of long 'e' (Kökeritz, 201–2).
1003 **provoked** carries a stronger force of 'to urge on', and can sometimes mean 'incite to evil', as in *As You Like It* 1.3.109: 'Beauty provoketh thieves sooner than gold'.
1004 **Be wreaked** be avenged
1006 **I did . . . slander** Venus's argument would have sounded desperate to its early readers: the court of Star Chamber tended to penalize those who repeated slanders as well as those who authored them, although usually the penalties were less severe.
1007 **hath two tongues** Compare the proverb 'Grief hath two tongues' (meaning 'to say and unsay', Dent G446.1).
1008 **wit** intelligence
1010 **suspect** suspicion (of death). Accented on the second syllable. On the transformation of one grammatical form into another, see l. 830 n.
1010 **extenuate** attempt to excuse

And, that his beauty may the better thrive,
With Death she humbly doth insinuate.
    Tells him of trophies, statues, tombs, and stories
    His victories, his triumphs, and his glories.

'O Jove,' quoth she, 'How much a fool was I   1015
To be of such a weak and silly mind
To wail his death who lives, and must not die
Till mutual overthrow of mortal kind?
    For he being dead, with him is beauty slain,
    And beauty dead, black chaos comes again.   1020

'Fie, fie, fond love, thou art as full of fear
As one with treasure laden, hemmed with thieves.
Trifles unwitnessèd with eye or ear
Thy coward heart with false bethinking grieves.'
    Even at this word she hears a merry horn,   1025
    Whereat she leaps, that was but late forlorn.

As falcons to the lure, away she flies.
The grass stoops not, she treads on it so light,

1013 stories] MALONE; ~, Q; ~. Q16

1012 **insinuate** flatteringly attempt to win round

1013 **stories** relates. The verb is also used in *Lucrece* l. 106. Q treats it as a noun and punctuates 'stories,'. Tales and memorials are one of the chief consolations against death in this period: compare Richard II's intention to speak of 'graves, of worms, of epitaphs', 3.2.141.

1018 **mutual overthrow** common death, universal destruction

1019–20 Since Adonis embodies beauty, and the world is dependent on beauty, his death will bring chaos again. Spenser's Garden of Adonis in *FQ* 3.6.36 describes a world generated by a formless chaos in which Adonis is the guarantor of the continuity of form. The account of chaos in Golding 1.5–9 also influences Shakespeare here: 'Before the sea and land were made, and heaven that all doth hide. | In all the world one only face of nature did abide, | Which Chaos hight, a huge rude heap, and nothing else but even | A heavy lump and clott'red clod of seeds together driven, | Of things at strife among themselves, for want of order due'. And in Golding 1.379–80 Earth complains to Jove: 'If sea and land do go to wrack, and heaven itself do burn | To old confusèd Chaos then of force we must return'. Venus's hyperbole anticipates Othello's 'and when I love thee not, | Chaos is come again', 3.3.92–3.

1021 Compare the proverb 'Love is full of fear' (Dent L507).

1022 **hemmed** surrounded

1023 **unwitnessèd with** unconfirmed by

1024 **bethinking** imagining

1026 **leaps** for joy, as in Sonnet 98.4

1027 **lure** Falcons are attracted back to their keepers by a cluster of feathers tied to a string. The metaphorical sense 'an enticing trap' is active in this context.

1028 **stoops not** does not bend. The passage may recall Virgil's description of Camilla, the amazon who runs so lightly that she does not touch the corn in *Aen.* 7.808–9; it also makes the grieving Venus enact her boast of lightness at ll. 145–56.

And in her haste unfortunately spies
The foul boar's conquest on her fair delight. 1030
   Which seen, her eyes are murdered with the view:
   Like stars ashamed of day themselves withdrew,

Or as the snail, whose tender horns being hit,
Shrinks backward in his shelly cave with pain,
And, there all smothered up, in shade doth sit, 1035
Long after fearing to creep forth again.
   So at his bloody view her eyes are fled
   Into the deep-dark cabins of her head,

Where they resign their office, and their light
To the disposing of her troubled brain, 1040
Who bids them still consort with ugly night,
And never wound the heart with looks again,
   Who, like a king perplexèd in his throne,
   By their suggestion gives a deadly groan,

Whereat each tributary subject quakes, 1045
As when the wind imprisoned in the ground,
Struggling for passage, earth's foundation shakes,
Which with cold terror doth men's minds confound.
   This mutiny each part doth so surprise
   That from their dark beds once more leap her eyes, 1050

And, being opened, threw unwilling light
Upon the wide wound that the boar had trenched

1031 are] Q; as Q3

1029 **unfortunately** ill-fatedly
1031 **are murdered** Q3 reads 'as murdered', which would create a parenthetical simile within a simile. The reading is adopted by Oxford, but not here, since Q1 makes good sense.
1032 **ashamed of day** ashamed to be seen in daylight
1033–4 Compare *L.L.L.* 4.3.313–4: 'Love's feeling is more soft and sensible | Than are the tender horns of cockled snails'.
1034 **shelly cave** The phrase was imitated in Richard Carew's burlesque account of how the snail got his shell, *A Herring's Tale* (1598), l. 228.
1035 **smothered up** covered up closely (*OED* 6b)

1038 **cabins** i.e. her eye-sockets, but recalling also the lair of l. 637.
1039–41 The eyes are implicitly compared to insubordinate inferiors, who are compelled to resign their function, until they are goaded back into action by the chaos which they themselves have caused.
1043 **perplexèd** confused, disturbed
1044 **suggestion** incitement to evil or rebellion. Compare l. 651 and n.
1046–7 Earthquakes were generally believed to be the product of accumulations of wind beneath the earth's surface, after Aristotle, *Meteorology* 2.8.
1051 **threw . . . light** For the belief that eyes emitted rays of light, see l. 487 n.
1052 **trenched** cut into. Both *trench* (as a noun) and *flank* had their present military

In his soft flank, whose wonted lily white
With purple tears that his wound wept was drenched.
No flower was nigh, no grass, herb, leaf or weed   1055
But stole his blood, and seemed with him to bleed.

This solemn sympathy poor Venus noteth.
Over one shoulder doth she hang her head.
Dumbly she passions, frantically she doteth;
She thinks he could not die, he is not dead.   1060
Her voice is stopped, her joints forget to bow,
Her eyes are mad that they have wept till now.

Upon his hurt she looks so steadfastly
That her sight, dazzling, makes the wound seem three.
And then she reprehends her mangling eye,   1065
That makes more gashes where no breach should be.
His face seems twain, each several limb is doubled;
For oft the eye mistakes, the brain being troubled.

'My tongue cannot express my grief for one,
And yet,' quoth she, 'behold two Adons dead.   1070
My sighs are blown away, my salt tears gone;
Mine eyes are turned to fire, my heart to lead.

1054 was] Q7; had Q

associations by the 1590s: the war of love has hit home to its victim.

1054 **purple tears** crimson blood. On *purple*, see l. 1 n. Compare Thomas Lodge, *Scylla's Metamorphosis* ll. 121–32: 'He that hath seen the sweet Arcadian boy | Wiping the purple from his forcèd wound | . . . | And Venus starting at her love-mate's cry, | Forcing her birds to haste her chariot on; | And full of grief at last with piteous eye | Seeing where all pale with death he lay alone . . .'.
was drenched Q reads 'had drencht', which Q7 emends. The error is likely to have resulted from a memory of *had trenched* in l. 1052.

1055–6 Compare Venus's dream at ll. 665–6.
1056 **But which** did not
1057 **sympathy** Objects were believed to have occult affinities with each other, which made them respond to each other: so a deadly wound on the body of a murder victim would bleed in the presence of the murder weapon. This sense is played off against the human meaning 'compassion': the landscape responds both with arcane *sympathy* to Adonis's death, and with human compassion.

1059 **Dumbly she passions** she silently grieves. There is a paradox here, since the verb *passion* in Shakespeare usually describes spoken complaint, as in 'Ariadne, passioning | For Theseus' perjury', *Two Gentlemen*, 4.4.164–5.
doteth talks or acts insanely
1061 **bow** bend
1062 **Her eyes . . . now** Her eyes are furious that they have ever wept before this, the only real cause of grief.
1064 **dazzling** losing the capacity to see clearly, blurring with tears (*OED* 1)
1065 **mangling eye** The eye makes more wounds than there in fact are, and so mangles the body.
1067 **twain** divided in two, double

Heavy heart's lead, melt at mine eyes' red fire:
So shall I die by drops of hot desire.

'Alas, poor world, what treasure hast thou lost,　　　　1075
What face remains alive that's worth the viewing?
Whose tongue is music now? What canst thou boast
Of things long since, or any thing ensuing?
　　The flowers are sweet, their colours fresh and trim,
　　But true sweet beauty lived and died with him.　　　1080

'Bonnet nor veil henceforth no creature wear,
Nor sun, nor wind will ever strive to kiss you,
Having no fair to lose, you need not fear.
The sun doth scorn you, and the wind doth hiss you;
　　But when Adonis lived, sun and sharp air　　　　1085
　　Lurked like two thieves to rob him of his fair.

'And therefore would he put his bonnet on,
Under whose brim the gaudy sun would peep.
The wind would blow it off, and, being gone,
Play with his locks. Then would Adonis weep,　　　　1090
　　And straight in pity of his tender years
　　They both would strive who first should dry his tears.

'To see his face the lion walked along
Behind some hedge, because he would not fear him.
To recreate himself when he hath sung　　　　1095
The tiger would be tame, and gently hear him.
　　If he had spoke, the wolf would leave his prey
　　And never fright the silly lamb that day.

1095 sung] Q (song)

1073 This passage anticipates King Lear's
'mine own tears | do scald like molten
lead', *King Lear* (Folio), 4.6.40–1.
1074 **drops** OED does not record sense 4,
'A medicinal preparation to be taken or
administered in drops', before the eigh-
teenth century, but the sense seems active
here. See *A Lover's Complaint* l. 300 n.
1078 **ensuing** to come in the future
1079 **trim** fine. Schmidt notes that the word
is 'mostly used with irony'.

1083 **fair** beauty
1085 **sharp** pinching, biting, rough
1088 **gaudy** garishly showy
1092 **strive** contend
1094 **fear** frighten
1095 **recreate** entertain
sung Q reads 'song', probably in order
to retain at least an eye-rhyme. It was
a recognized variant form of 'sung'
in the period, which is modernized
here

'When he beheld his shadow in the brook
The fishes spread on it their golden gills.   1100
When he was by, the birds such pleasure took
That some would sing, some other in their bills
　　Would bring him mulberries and ripe-red cherries:
　　He fed them with his sight; they him with berries.

'But this foul, grim, and urchin-snouted boar,   1105
Whose downward eye still looketh for a grave,
Ne'er saw the beauteous livery that he wore:
Witness the entertainment that he gave.
　　If he did see his face, why then I know
　　He thought to kiss him, and hath killed him so.   1110

' 'Tis true, 'tis true, thus was Adonis slain:
He ran upon the boar with his sharp spear,
Who would not whet his teeth at him again,
But by a kiss thought to persuade him there,
　　And, nuzzling in his flank, the loving swine   1115
　　Sheathed unaware the tusk in his soft groin.

1113 would] Q2; did Q   1116 the] Q; his Q2

1099 **shadow** reflection. Another echo of the
Narcissus story, recalling both l. 162
above and Golding 3.519–24: 'For as he
drank, he chanced to spy the image of his
face, | The which he did immediately with
fervent love embrace. | He feeds a hope
without cause why. For like a foolish
noddy | He thinks the shadow that he
sees, to be a lively body: | Astraughted
[distraught] like an image made of marble
stone he lies, | There gazing on his
shadow still with fixèd staring eyes'.

1100 **spread** displayed, unfurled. The verb is
generally used to describe the unfurling of
flags or rich cloths in Shakespeare, so the
fishes offer their gills as rich adornments
of Adonis's image.

1104 **sight** appearance

1105 **urchin-snouted** having a long sharp
nose like a hedgehog

1106 **downward** inclined downward (*OED
adj.* 1, citing this passage)

1107 **livery** outward appearance, a sense
transferred from *OED* 2a, 'A suit of
clothes, formerly sometimes a badge
or cognizance (e.g. a collar or hood),
bestowed by a person upon his retainers
or servants and serving as a token by

which they may be recognized'. This
sense is brought out by *entertainment* in
the next line.

1108 **entertainment** reception (with an iron-
ical play on 'friendly welcome'). *Entertain-
ment* is also the sustenance given as a
right to household retainers (*OED* 2b).
Livery in the line above activates this
sense: the boar has failed to notice that
Adonis is a member of the household and
so has churlishly failed to offer him the
entertainment which is his due.

1110–16 Theocritus's *Lament for Adonis*
describes how Venus sent for the boar,
who defended himself by saying, 'I mind-
ed not to kill, | But as an image still, | I
him beheld for love, | Which made me
forward shove, | His thigh that naked
was, | Thinking to kiss alas', *Six Idyllia . . .
Chosen out of the right famous Sicilian Poet
Theocritus* (Oxford, 1588; repr. 1883), 39.

1113 **would** Q2's reading makes better sense
of the boar's action than Q's blank 'did'.
whet See l. 617 n.

1114 **persuade him** persuade him to stay

1115 **nuzzling** By 1593 the word still had the
sense 'To burrow or dig with the nose'
(*OED* 1), and was commonly used of

'Had I been toothed like him I must confess
With kissing him I should have killed him first;
But he is dead, and never did he bless
My youth with his. The more am I accursed.'   1120
    With this she falleth in the place she stood,
    And stains her face with his congealèd blood.

She looks upon his lips, and they are pale;
She takes him by the hand, and that is cold;
She whispers in his ears a heavy tale,   1125
As if they heard the woeful words she told;
    She lifts the coffer-lids that close his eyes,
    Where, lo, two lamps burnt out in darkness lies.

Two glasses where herself herself beheld
A thousand times, and now no more reflect,   1130
Their virtue lost wherein they late excelled,
And every beauty robbed of his effect.
    'Wonder of time,' quoth she, 'this is my spite,
    That, thou being dead, the day should yet be light.

'Since thou art dead, lo, here I prophesy,   1135
Sorrow on love hereafter shall attend.
It shall be waited on with jealousy,
Find sweet beginning but unsavoury end;

swine. The cosy sense 'To nestle, to lie snug in bed' (*OED* 4) had emerged by 1601. The word is therefore just on the cusp between boarish aggression and loving warmth.

1119–20 **bless . . . his** He never gave me the gift of his youth. To 'bless with' in the sense 'to make happy with some gift' becomes a fashionable phrase in the 1590s (*OED* s.v. 'bless' *v.* 7b); it does not yet appear to be used in the sense 'to bless with a child', although that sense seems to be pressing to emerge here.

1127 **coffer-lids** eyelids. *Coffer* probably refers to a box in which treasure is kept (*OED* 1), but the slightly archaic sense 'coffin' (*OED* 3, last cited in 1550) is reanimated by the context.

1128 **lies** The plural subject *lamps* takes a singular verb because of the proximity of *darkness*. Compare l. 705 n. and l. 840 n.

1129 **glasses** mirrors. See l. 119 n.

1130 **and** and which

1131 **virtue** particular power, efficacy

1132 **his effect** its operation, consequence; but also 'outward manifestation' (*OED* 3a)

1133 **spite** cause of anguish

1135–64 Venus's prophecy turns the poem into an etiology, or story about the origins of a phenomenon. Epyllia from this period frequently include passages of this kind, such as the account of how scholars come to be poor in *Hero and Leander* ll. 386–482.

1137 **waited on with** attended by. Compare the proverb 'Love is never without jealousy' (Dent L510).

1138 **unsavoury** unpleasant tasting (playing on *sweet*: love is a feast that turns sour). It was proverbial that 'Love is sweet in the beginning but sour in the ending' (Dent L513).

Ne'er settled equally, but high or low,
That all love's pleasure shall not match his woe.　　　　1140

'It shall be fickle, false, and full of fraud,
Bud and be blasted in a breathing-while;
The bottom poison, and the top o'erstrawed
With sweets, that shall the truest sight beguile.
　　The strongest body shall it make most weak,　　　　1145
　　Strike the wise dumb, and teach the fool to speak.

'It shall be sparing and too full of riot,
Teaching decrepit age to tread the measures.
The staring ruffian shall it keep in quiet,
Pluck down the rich, enrich the poor with treasures.　　　　1150
　　It shall be raging mad, and silly mild,
　　Make the young old, the old become a child.

'It shall suspect where is no cause of fear;
It shall not fear where it should most mistrust;
It shall be merciful, and too severe,　　　　1155
And most deceiving when it seems most just.
　　Perverse it shall be, where it shows most toward,
　　Put fear to valour, courage to the coward.

'It shall be cause of war and dire events,
And set dissension 'twixt the son and sire;　　　　1160
Subject and servile to all discontents,
As dry combustious matter is to fire.

1139 **Ne'er . . . low** It will swing between elation and misery, and never achieve equipoise.

1140 **That** so that

1142 **be blasted** be caused to wither by malignant wind (*OED* 7). The verb is often used of tender flowers.
in a breathing-while in the time it takes to breathe

1143 **o'erstrawed** sprinkled over. That love was a sweet poison is a commonplace of Petrarchan poetry, to which Venus condemns all lovers: William Alexander, 'Then from her eyes so sweet a poison rained', *Aurora* (1604), Song 7.

1144 **truest** most accurate

1145 **strike . . . dumb** Venus predicts one of the clichés of the sonnet tradition: compare R. Lynch, *Diella* (1596), 13.3–4: 'I know I shall be stricken dumb (my dear) | With doubt of your unpitiful reply'.

1147 **riot** unruly festivity

1148 **tread the measures** dance

1149 **staring** bold-faced

1150 **Pluck down** bring down (usually used in contexts where the proud are being humiliated)

1151 **silly** inoffensively

1153 **where is** where there is

1157 **Perverse** obstinate, stubborn
toward co-operative

1158 It was proverbial that 'Love makes cowards courageous' (Dent D216).

1161 **Subject** stressed on the second syllable
discontents unhappinesses; also malcontents (*OED* s.v. 'discontent' *n.*[2] B).

234

Sith in his prime death doth my love destroy
They that love best their loves shall not enjoy.'

By this the boy that by her side lay killed   1165
Was melted like a vapour from her sight,
And in his blood that on the ground lay spilled
A purple flower sprung up, chequered with white,
      Resembling well his pale cheeks, and the blood
      Which in round drops upon their whiteness stood.   1170

She bows her head the new-sprung flower to smell,
Comparing it to her Adonis' breath,
And says within her bosom it shall dwell.
Since he himself is reft from her by death.
      She crops the stalk, and in the breach appears   1175
      Green-dropping sap, which she compares to tears.

'Poor flower,' quoth she, 'this was thy father's guise,
Sweet issue of a more sweet-smelling sire,
For every little grief to wet his eyes.
To grow unto himself was his desire,   1180
      And so 'tis thine; but know it is as good
      To wither in my breast as in his blood.

'Here was thy father's bed, here in my breast.
Thou art the next of blood and 'tis thy right.

1166 **melted** evaporated. The insubstantiality of this metamorphosis derives from Golding 10.855–7: 'This said, she sprinkled nectar on the blood, which through the power | Thereof did swell like bubbles sheer that rise in weather clear ' On water'. Shakespeare's text, like Golding's, would have read 'sicut fulvo perlucida caelo | surgere bulla solent' (as transpicuous bubbles arise in tawny yellow skies); modern editions tend to replace 'caelo' (sky) by 'caeno' (mud).

1168 **A purple . . . white** Elizabethan flower metamorphoses usually result in fantasy flowers, as does the metamorphosis at the end of Clapham's *Narcissus* ll. 255–9. The flower may be a kind of anemone, to which it is compared in *Met.* 10.734–9. John Gerard, *The Herbal* (1597), 309, describes an anemone that 'hath small leaves very much snipped or jagged, almost like unto camomile, or Adonisflower: among which riseth up a stalk . . .

and at the top of the stalk cometh forth a fair and beautiful flower, compact of seven leaves, and sometimes eight, of a violet colour tending to purple'. He also describes the fritillary (which he terms Lilio-narcissus variegatus) as 'chequered . . . most strangely . . . one square is of a greenish yellow colour, the other purple' (122). *Chequered* can mean simply 'variegated' in this period (*OED* 2a). Q's spelling 'checkred' keeps a red flush on the bloom.

1175 **crops** plucks (the word is sometimes used to imply premature destruction, as in Richard III's description of himself as one 'that cropped the golden prime of this sweet prince', 1.2.234).
      breach broken part of the stalk

1177 **guise** manner

1180 **To grow . . . desire** Compare l. 166 and n.

1182 **in his blood** in his progeny

1184 **next of blood** next of kin

Lo, in this hollow cradle take thy rest: 1185
My throbbing heart shall rock thee day and night.
    There shall not be one minute in an hour
    Wherein I will not kiss my sweet love's flower.'

Thus weary of the world, away she hies,
And yokes her silver doves, by whose swift aid   1190
Their mistress, mounted through the empty skies
In her light chariot, quickly is conveyed,
    Holding their course to Paphos, where their queen
    Means to immure herself and not be seen.

FINIS

1193 **Paphos** is the city in Cyprus sacred to Venus.
1194 **immure** to enclose herself as within a fort or prison. *Means to* may imply either a strong intention, or a vow which she does not intend to keep.

Lucrece

TO THE RIGHT HONOURABLE
Henry Wriothesley, Earl of Southampton
and Baron of Titchfield.

The love I dedicate to your Lordship is without end, whereof this pamphlet without beginning is but a super- 5
fluous moiety. The warrant I have of your honourable disposition, not the worth of my untutored lines, makes it assured of acceptance. What I have done is yours, what I have to do is yours, being part in all I have, devoted yours. Were my worth greater my duty would show greater; 10
meantime, as it is, it is bound to your Lordship. To whom I wish long life still lengthened with all happiness.

Your Lordship's in all duty,

William Shakespeare.

DEDICATION

2 **Henry Wriothesley** On Southampton, see Introduction, pp. 10–15.

4 **love** does not necessarily imply deep personal affection (though it could do). It is often used of an author's affection for his patron.

5 **pamphlet** paper-covered book containing a single work. The modesty of the dedication is pointed: *Lucrece* may be the 'graver labour' promised in the dedication to *Venus*, but Shakespeare leaves open the possibility that there is something yet more substantial to come.
without beginning The poem does not begin with the debate over the chastity of the Roman warriors' wives which is described in the Argument, but plunges its readers *in medias res*. It also lacks any

invocation or proem. The absence of such preliminary matter was a regular feature of erotic narrative poems, but the way Shakespeare draws attention to it may remind his readers of the formal invocations and proems found in epic poems, and modestly establish the contrast with his own slighter work.

6 **moiety** part (often suggesting an inferior or smaller part, as in Sonnet 46.12 n.)
warrant guarantee (possibly suggesting that Southampton had rewarded Shakespeare for *Venus*)

8 **What I have done** presumably refers to *Venus*.

10 **show greater** i.e. he would have produced a longer and more magnificent poem

The Argument

Lucius Tarquinius (for his excessive pride surnamed Superbus) after he had caused his own father-in-law Servius Tullius to be cruelly murdered, and, contrary to the Roman laws and customs not requiring or staying for the people's suffrages, had possessed himself of the kingdom, went accompanied with his sons and other noblemen of Rome to besiege Ardea; during which siege the principal men of the army meeting one evening at the tent of Sextus Tarquinius, the king's son, in their discourses after supper everyone commended the virtues of his own wife. Among whom Collatinus extolled the

5

10

THE ARGUMENT

For Shakespeare's authorship of this summary of Livy, Painter, and Ovid, see Introduction, pp. 45–50. The argument reminds its readers of the historical, narrative, and political context of the poem which follows, as well as establishing Shakespeare's scholarly credentials for composing a brief epic on events from Roman history (it also has a formal precedent in the digest by Florus which was printed at the start of most Renaissance editions of Livy). It may well have been written, as Bush suggests, 150, after the composition of the poem and after Shakespeare had reread Painter's paraphrase of Livy. But, as the notes below illustrate, the imagery of the argument frequently anticipates the concerns of the poem.

1 **Lucius Tarquinius** was the last legendary King of Rome (534–510 BC). He was believed to be the son of Tarquinius Priscus (some authorities believed him to have been his grandson). He began his reign by refusing to bury his predecessor Servius Tullius and by executing his supporters. These actions won him the name of 'Superbus', the proud. 'He had indeed no right to the throne but might, since he was ruling neither by popular decree nor senatorial sanction' (Livy 1.49.3).

3 **Servius Tullius** The sixth king of Rome (c.578–535 BC) was traditionally believed to have been murdered by Tarquinius Superbus at the instigation of his own daughter Tullia. She drove her chariot over her father's body (Livy 1.48.5–7). Servius is thought to have planned to abdicate to enable the liberation of Rome from kingship (Livy 1.46.8–9).

4 **requiring** requesting (as a favour) (OED 5a)

5 **people's suffrages** Monarchy in early Rome was notionally elective rather than hereditary, and usually alternated with a period of interregnum.

7 **Ardea** a city of the Rutuli, a Latin people. It was of some wealth and independence, about 40 km south of Rome, and served as a port for Latium. The siege was long and slow (Livy 1.57.4).

9 **Sextus Tarquinius** the third son (or, according to Dionysius, the first son) of Lucius Tarquinius and the chief protagonist of Shakespeare's poem. After the exile of the Tarquinii he was slain by the Gabii, whom he had previously betrayed.

11 **Collatinus** Tarquinius Collatinus was great-nephew of Tarquinius Priscus, the fifth king of Rome. After the exile of the kings he and Junius Brutus became the first consuls of Rome; the historical Collatinus was then exiled by Brutus.

incomparable chastity of his wife Lucretia. In that pleas-
ant humour they all posted to Rome, and intending by
their secret and sudden arrival to make trial of that
which everyone had before avouched, only Collatinus   15
finds his wife (though it were late in the night) spinning
amongst her maids. The other ladies were all found danc-
ing and revelling, or in several disports. Whereupon the
noblemen yielded Collatinus the victory, and his wife the
fame. At that time Sextus Tarquinius, being inflamed   20
with Lucrece' beauty, yet smothering his passions for
the present, departed with the rest back to the camp.
From whence he shortly after privily withdrew himself,
and was (according to his estate) royally entertained
and lodged by Lucrece at Collatium. The same night   25
he treacherously stealeth into her chamber, violently
ravished her, and early in the morning speedeth away.
Lucrece in this lamentable plight hastily dispatcheth
messengers, one to Rome for her father, another to the
camp for Collatine. They came, the one accompanied   30
with Junius Brutus, the other with Publius Valerius; and

12 **Lucretia** Lucrece. She is known from the
   Latin sources only as the wife of Collati-
   nus, whose rape by Sextus Tarquinius led
   to the exile of the kings from Rome.

13 **posted** rode swiftly. Compare *all in post*, l. 1.

14 **make trial** test

16 **spinning** As she is in *Fasti* 2.741–2 and
   Livy 1.57.9.

18 **several disports** various entertainments.
   Disports may have erotic overtones, as in
   Othello 1.3.271, 'that my disports corrupt
   and taint my business'.

20 **fame** honour, renown. The darker conse-
   quences of relying on public acclaim to
   manifest virtue (*fame* can mean 'evil
   repute, infamy', *OED* 4) emerge later in
   the poem.

20–1 **inflamed . . . smothering** Compare ll.
   4–5 below. *Smothering* means both
   'repressing' (*OED* 2c) and 'suffocating
   with smoke' (*OED* 1a).

24 **estate** status, rank

25 **Collatium** is more correctly Collatia (pro-
   bably modern Lunghezza), a village taken
   under Roman control by Tarquinius
   Priscus (Livy 1.28.1). It lies about 16 km
   east of Rome. It was described by Ovid's

Renaissance commentators as near
Rome, and Shakespeare treats it as effec-
tively being a part of the city.

29 **messengers** In the poem only one messen-
   ger is sent (l. 1334), which has been used
   to deny Shakespeare's authorship of the
   Argument: in fact Livy is vague here:
   Lucrece 'dispatched the same messenger
   to her father in Rome and to her husband
   in Ardea' (Livy 1.58.5); Painter has it that
   'Lucrece sent a post to Rome to her father,
   and another to Ardea to her husband',
   Bullough, 198.

31 **Junius Brutus** After the accession of Tar-
   quin, his nephew Lucius Junius Brutus
   'deliberately assumed the appearance of
   stupidity' (Livy 1.56.7) in order to avoid
   execution. 'Brutus' means 'dullard'. He
   abandoned the deceit after the rape of
   Lucrece, and became one of the first
   consuls of the new Republic. He is sup-
   posed to have died in 509 BC in a battle
   against the Tarquinii. He was frequently
   paired with the later Brutus who assas-
   sinated Julius Caesar as an exemplary
   liberator of Rome. Greek historians
   emphasized his descent from the

finding Lucrece attired in mourning habit, demanded the
cause of her sorrow. She first taking an oath of them for
her revenge, revealed the actor, and whole manner of
his dealing, and withal suddenly stabbed herself. Which   35
done, with one consent they all vowed to root out the
whole hated family of the Tarquins; and, bearing the
dead body to Rome, Brutus acquainted the people with
the doer and manner of the vile deed, with a bitter invec-
tive against the tyranny of the King. Wherewith the peo-   40
ple were so moved that, with one consent and a general
acclamation, the Tarquins were all exiled, and the state
government changed from kings to consuls.

colonists who founded Rome with Aeneas
(Dionysius of Halicarnassus, 4.68.1; this
view of Brutus may well have been
known to Shakespeare since it is quoted
in the Latin commentary on Ovid by
Marsus, 142).

32 **mourning habit** In *LGW* ll. 1830–1
Lucrece is 'In habit swich [such] as
women used tho | Unto the buryinge of
hire [their] frendes go'. In Dionysius's ver-
sion of the story (which is quoted exten-
sively in Marsus's edition, 148) Lucretia
goes to Rome 'veste lugubri' (in mourning
garment). This is the most probable
source of the detail.

33 **first** It is only in Shakespeare's version
that she extracts the oath *before* she
names Tarquin, so in this respect the
argument is entirely in accord with the
story as Shakespeare tells it. Compare
ll. 1688–94.
38 **body to Rome** See ll. 1850–1 n.
43 **changed from kings to consuls** Ovid
relates the story of Lucretia on the
'regifugium' (the day celebrating the ban-
ishment of the kings, 24 February): it
begins 'nunc mihi dicenda est regis fuga'
('Now I must tell of the flight of the king',
Fasti 2.685), and ends, 'dies regnis illa
suprema fuit' ('that was the last day of
kingly rule', *Fasti* 2.852).

The Rape of Lucrece

From the besiegèd Ardea all in post,
Borne by the trustless wings of false desire,
Lust-breathèd Tarquin leaves the Roman host,
And to Collatium bears the lightless fire,
Which, in pale embers hid, lurks to aspire   5
    And girdle with embracing flames the waist
    Of Collatine's fair love, Lucrece the chaste.

Haply that name of 'chaste' unhapply set
This bateless edge on his keen appetite,
When Collatine unwisely did not let   10
To praise the clear unmatchèd red and white,
Which triumphed in that sky of his delight,
    Where mortal stars as bright as heaven's beauties
    With pure aspects did him peculiar duties.

THE RAPE OF LUCRECE

1 Ardea (accented on the first syllable, to make it sound like 'ardour'). See Argument, l. 7 n.
all in post in great haste. Compare Painter, 'whereupon they rode to Rome in post', Bullough, 197.

2 trustless (a) untrustworthy; (b) unbelieving (since Tarquin does not believe the report of Lucrece's chastity)

3 Lust-breathèd animated by lust (animals are described as 'well-breathed', in the sense of 'fit or lively')

4 lightless giving no light; smouldering. Compare ll. 674 and 1555.

5 aspire rise up. Compare Ovid: 'interea iuvenis furiales regius ignis | concipit' ('meanwhile the royal youth conceived a furious flame of passion', *Fasti* 2.761).

6 girdle encircle. There is a conscious irony here: girdles were traditionally associated with chastity.

7 Lucrece is usually accented on the first syllable. The accent appears to fall on the second syllable only in this line.

8 Haply perhaps; by chance. Livy says, 'cum forma tum spectata castitas incitat' ('not only her beauty but her proved

chastity as well, provoked him', Livy 1.57.10). This detail is not in Painter. Compare Ovid: 'verba placent et vox, et quod corrumpere non est' ('her words pleased him and her voice, and the fact that she was incorruptible', *Fasti* 2.765).

9 bateless which cannot be abated (hence 'not to be blunted'). First citation in *OED*.

10 let forbear, cease. The classical sources do not blame Collatine so explicitly.

11 clear (a) 'brightly shining' (*OED* 1); (b) 'Unspotted, unsullied; free from fault, offence, or guilt; innocent' (*OED* 15 a); (c) manifestly
unmatchèd unrivalled (often used in military contexts; hence *triumphed* in the following line)
red and white i.e. her complexion. Compare *Venus* ll. 10, 21.

12 triumphed . . . delight shone victoriously in her face

13 mortal stars i.e. Lucrece's eyes. The senses of *mortal* 'subject to death' and 'causing death' lurk here.

14 pure aspects (a) a chaste gaze (*OED* s.v. 'aspect' 1); (b) the *aspects* of the stars are their positions in relation to each other,

243

For he, the night before in Tarquin's tent,   15
Unlocked the treasure of his happy state,
What priceless wealth the heavens had him lent
In the possession of his beauteous mate,
Reck'ning his fortune at such high proud rate
    That kings might be espousèd to more fame,   20
    But king nor peer to such a peerless dame.

O happiness enjoyed but of a few,
And if possessed as soon decayed and done
As is the morning's silver melting dew
Against the golden splendour of the sun,   25
An expired date cancelled ere well begun.
    Honour and beauty in the owner's arms
    Are weakly fortressed from a world of harms.

Beauty itself doth of itself persuade
The eyes of men without an orator.   30
What needeth then apology be made

21 peer] Q; prince Q2   24 morning's] QB; morning QA (Malone 34, Yale)   31 apology] QA
(Malone 34, Yale); apologies QB

which can be described as 'wicked' or
'bad' or 'friendly' depending on the astro-
logical influence they portend. *Aspects* is
stressed on the second syllable.

14 **peculiar** private, particular. The Latin
sense of 'that which is singularly one's
own property' is strong here. The exclu-
sivity promised by the adjective, though,
is blurred by the slight uncertainty over
the masculine pronouns in this stanza:
his in l. 9 refers to Tarquin, whose desire
to possess Lucrece contaminates the pos-
sessive pronoun in l. 12. *Him* in l. 14 clear-
ly refers to Collatine, but the exclusivity
of marital possession has already been
qualified.

16 **treasure** probably 'treasure-house' or
'treasure chest' (*OED* 3). Compare Sonnet
136.5; and see ll. 1056–7.

17 **lent** granted temporary possession of. *Pos-
session* in l. 18 (re-echoed in *possessed*, l.
23) underscores the point that Collatine
does not permanently own Lucrece, since
to 'possess' means 'to enjoy the use of'
rather than 'to have complete ownership
over'. See Sonnet *18*.10 n., and l. 1794 n.

19 **Reck'ning ... rate** counting ... price. This

continues the financial imagery of
treasure.

19 **proud** glorious (with a suggestion of excess)

20 **espousèd** married (rather than simply
'engaged to be married')

23 **possessed** See l. 17 n., and compare
Sonnet 129.9.
   done destroyed. Compare *Venus* l. 749.

25 **Against** exposed to (*OED* 1b)

26 **An expired ... begun** The impermanent
possession of happiness (ll. 17–18 and n.)
is like a lease granting temporary owner-
ship which is invalidated before its term
has begun. Compare Sonnet *18*.4 and n.
Expired is stressed on the first syllable.

27 **owner's** primarily refers to Collatine, but
may also include Lucrece. These early
stanzas insistently play on the question of
who owns Lucrece.

28 **fortressed** The image of the besieged town
runs through the poem: compare ll. 1 and
463–9.

30 **without an orator** Compare ll. 268,
563–4, 1322–3, 1463. On the ineffective-
ness of other forms of rhetoric in the
poem, see Introduction, pp. 51–3.

31 **apology** formal rhetorical defences (as in a
court)

To set forth that which is so singular?
Or why is Collatine the publisher
　　Of that rich jewel he should keep unknown
　　From thievish ears, because it is his own?　　　　　　35

Perchance his boast of Lucrece' sov'reignty
Suggested this proud issue of a king;
For by our ears our hearts oft tainted be.
Perchance that envy of so rich a thing,
Braving compare, disdainfully did sting　　　　　　40
　　His high-pitched thoughts that meaner men should vaunt
　　That golden hap which their superiors want.

But some untimely thought did instigate
His all too timeless speed, if none of those:
His honour, his affairs, his friends, his state,　　　　　45
Neglected all, with swift intent he goes
To quench the coal which in his liver glows.
　　O rash false heat, wrapped in repentant cold,
　　Thy hasty spring still blasts and ne'er grows old.

48 repentant] Q; repentance Q3

32 **set forth** (a) express in words (*OED* s.v. 'set' 144f(a)); (b) ornament (*OED* 144g); also, in anticipation of *publisher* in l. 33, 'publish' (*OED* 144d)
　singular (a) private (*OED* 8a) (b) rare (*OED* 11)
33 **publisher** the person who makes it public. The sense 'one who publishes a book or literary work' (*OED* 2) is not found by *OED* before the 1650s, but the usage here in conjunction with *set forth*, l. 32, anticipates that sense. Compare l. 1852.
34 **rich jewel** Compare Sonnet 65.9–10.
36 **sov'reignty** pre-eminence; perhaps with a play on 'his absolute control over Lucrece'
37 **Suggested** incited to evil. (The verb is often used of the promptings by the devil, as in *Richard II* 3.4.76–7: 'What Eve, what serpent hath suggested thee | To make a second fall of cursèd man?'). Compare *Venus* l. 651 and Sonnet 144.2.
　issue child
40 **Braving compare** challenging comparison
41 **vaunt** boast. Both *high-pitched thoughts*

and *vaunt* evoke military trials of honour, in which keen-spirited warriors exchange boasts.
42 **golden hap** rich good fortune
43 **untimely** unseasonable. The word has strong destructive associations in the period: miscarriages and abortions are described as 'untimely' (*OED* 1b), as is the premature destruction or cropping of flowers or fruit (*OED* 1a; 2a).
44 **timeless** brief. The antithesis with *untimely* prompts the unusual usage, but the word also reinforces the impression of Tarquin's destructive haste, since *timeless* more usually means 'premature', 'unseasonable'. It may also suggest 'remembered throughout time', as in *Titus* 2.3.265: 'the complot of this timeless tragedy' (Donaldson, privately).
47 **liver** The liver was believed to be the source of anger and sexual desire.
48 **blasts** withers. The conceit is of a premature, *untimely*, spring which runs on too fast and so is destroyed by late frosts. Compare ll. 330–3, 604, 869.

When at Collatium this false lord arrived   50
Well was he welcomed by the Roman dame,
Within whose face beauty and virtue strived
Which of them both should underprop her fame.
When Virtue bragged, Beauty would blush for shame;
    When Beauty boasted blushes, in despite   55
    Virtue would stain that o'er with silver white.

But Beauty, in that white intitulèd
From Venus' doves, doth challenge that fair field;
Then Virtue claims from Beauty Beauty's red,
Which Virtue gave the golden age to gild   60

50 Collatium] QA (Malone 34, Yale); Collatia QB 56 o'er] Q (ore); *or* MALONE 57–8 entitulèd, . . . doves,] GILDON; ~, . . . ~, Q

50 **Collatium** The press variant 'Collatia' is technically the correct form of the name of the town. The correction is not consistently adopted in Qb (compare l. 4) and so is not adopted here.
  arrived Q reads 'arriued' and 'striued' at l. 52, which would usually imply that the final '-ed' is pronounced. For the non-syllabic -ed form after 'u' and 'w', see *Venus* l. 366 n.
53 **underprop** support, sustain (like pillars)
56 **stain** (a) deprive it of colour (*OED* 1a); (b) 'throw into the shade by superior beauty or excellence' (*OED* 1b); with a deliberate paradoxical play on (c) 'Of the blood: To suffuse with colour' (*OED* 3c) and (d) 'To defile or corrupt morally; to taint with guilt or vice' (*OED* 5a). The usage reverses a practice in heraldry whereby a *stain* or tincture sanguine (red) may be used as an 'abatement', which indicates a blot on the honour of those who bear the arms (see l. 206 n.). This creates a deliberate paradox: a symptom of chaste shame (a red blush) resembles a stain of abatement.
  o'er Q's regular spelling 'ore' may pun on metallic 'ore'. Malone suggests reading 'or', finding a play on the heraldic term for gold. The pun is active, though emendation is unnecessary: l. 60 below makes it clear that red and gold are thought of as colours which occupy a similar range, and, as Wyndham notes, *silver* and *white* were frequently interchangeable in heraldic writings (as they are in l. 1012 below), and were taken as symbols of innocence. The effect is of complex layer-

ing of colour on colour, the silver-white of virtue spreading across the reddish gold of her blushes.
57–8 **in that . . . doves** 'having a legal title to (*intitulèd*) whiteness, which derives from the fact that Venus's doves are white . . .'. The imagery of publication earlier in the poem may activate the secondary sense in *intitulèd*, 'inscribed as the author or dedicatee of the volume' (*OED* 1b and c). The word may have caught Shakespeare's eye in [Anthony Chute], *Beauty Dishonoured written under the title of Shore's Wife* (1593), in which Shore's wife complains that her husband has destroyed her quiet life by publicizing her beauty ('thou . . . Intitul'dst my name to my beauty's glory', ll. 486–8).
58 **challenge** 'To assert her title to' (*OED* 5); with a play on 'to summon someone to a duel'
  field (a) heraldic colour ('The surface of an escutcheon or shield on which the "charge" is displayed' (*OED* 13a)); (b) field of combat
59–63 Virtue mounts a counter-claim that she is entitled to red because it is the colour of shame.
60 **golden age** In *Met.* 1, the first and most perfect age of the world: 'Then sprang up first the golden age, which of itself maintained | The truth and right of every thing unforced and unconstrained. | There was no fear of punishment, there was no threat'ning law | In brazen tables nailèd up, to keep the folk in awe' (Golding 1.103–6).

Their silver cheeks, and called it then their shield,
   Teaching them thus to use it in the fight,
   When shame assailed, the red should fence the white.

This heraldry in Lucrece' face was seen,
Argued by Beauty's red and Virtue's white;   65
Of either's colour was the other queen,
Proving from world's minority their right;
Yet their ambition makes them still to fight,
   The sov'reignty of either being so great
   That oft they interchange each other's seat.   70

This silent war of lilies and of roses,
Which Tarquin viewed in her fair face's field,
In their pure ranks his traitor eye encloses,
Where, lest between them both it should be killed,
The coward-captive vanquishèd doth yield   75
   To those two armies that would let him go,
   Rather than triumph in so false a foe.

Now thinks he that her husband's shallow tongue,
The niggard prodigal that praised her so,
In that high task hath done her beauty wrong,   80

77 in] C; o'er SEWELL

61 **shield** protection; also, with a specific
heraldic force, 'insignia'
63 **fence** 'To screen, shield, protect the body,
or a part of it' (*OED* 2a). The verb is
regularly used of armour. The secondary
sense, 'To use the sword scientifically either
for offence or defence' (*OED* 1b), keeps a
sub-current of strife alive beneath the
apparent co-operation of red and white.
64 **heraldry** heraldic symbolism
65 **Argued** expressed. The description has
evoked military and judicial contests, so
the word registers a residual element of
discord.
66 ..i.e. each claimed ownership of the other's
colour.
67 **world's minority** the origins of the world
(*the golden age* of l. 60).
69 **sov'reignty** Wyndham detects a heraldic
sense: 'the dignity attached to certain dis-
positions of heraldic bearings'.
70 **seat** throne, chair of office (*OED* 8a and b)

71 Compare *Venus* ll. 345–7. The whiteness of
lilies and the redness of roses was prover-
bial (Dent L296, R177).
72 **field** This adds to the heraldic *field*, and to
the *field* of battle evoked in l. 58, the sense
of an area of open land in which plants
grow.
73 **ranks** plays on 'row' (as of trees, *OED* 1a)
and 'line of soldiers' (*OED* 3).
encloses 'Of an army, a number of per-
sons, etc.: To surround, hem in on all
sides' (*OED* 6). Tarquin's *traitor eye* is sur-
rounded by the red and white forces of
Lucrece's beauty.
75 **vanquishèd doth yield** accepts complete
defeat
76 **would** wished to; would rather
79 **niggard prodigal** Collatine is ungenerous
(*niggard*) in that he has not sung his wife's
praises to the full, and spendthrift (*prodi-
gal*) in that he has revealed her beauties
at all.

Which far exceeds his barren skill to show.
Therefore that praise which Collatine doth owe
   Enchanted Tarquin answers with surmise,
   In silent wonder of still-gazing eyes.

This earthly saint adorèd by this devil   85
Little suspecteth the false worshipper:
For unstained thoughts do seldom dream on evil,
Birds never limed no secret bushes fear.
So, guiltless, she securely gives good cheer
   And reverent welcome to her princely guest,   90
   Whose inward ill no outward harm expressed.

For that he coloured with his high estate,
Hiding base sin in pleats of majesty,

---

93 pleats] Q; plaits MALONE

---

81 **barren skill** Poets often modestly emphasized their barrenness in relation to the riches of the objects of their praise. See the Dedication to *Venus* l. 13 and Sonnet 83.4.

82 **doth owe** still needs to pay. *Owe* frequently means 'possess' in Shakespeare, leading Malone to take *that praise* as 'that object of praise' which Collatine possesses. This reading is awkward, though not impossible.

83 **answers** pays. *Answers* is used to mean 'discharge a debt' (*OED* 7c), as in *1 Henry IV* 1.3.182–3: 'this proud king, who studies day and night | To answer all the debt he owes to you'.
   surmise thoughts; silent wonder. The word has sinister associations: it is used of false or unproven allegations in actions for slander (*OED* 1; 2) and of uncertain beliefs and suspicions.

85 **adorèd** worshipped as a deity (with a suggestion of idolatry). *OED* cites *Richard III* (*c.*1594) as the first usage of the verb 'adore' in the sense 'to regard [a person] with the utmost affection'.

87–8 These lines are marked with quotation marks in Q to show that they are memorable *sententiae*, which a reader might learn by heart or transcribe into a commonplace book. Lines 460, 528, 530, 560, 831, 832, 853, 867–8, 1109–18, 1125, 1127, 1216, and 1687 are also marked in this way. Puttenham, 235–6: 'In weighty

causes and for great purposes, wise persuaders use grave and weighty speeches, specially in matter of advice or counsel . . . by the Latin he is called *sententia*: we may call him *sage sayer*.' The less weighty *Venus* contains no similar marks. Given that the printer of *Lucrece* and *Venus* was the same, it is likely these markings are authorial rather than the work of a compositor.

87 **unstained** pure, uncorrupted
   dream on have any conception of (*OED* 5)

88 **limed** Birds were trapped when they settled on twigs which had been covered with a sticky substance called 'bird-lime'. See *3 Henry VI* (*True Tragedy*) 5.6.13–14: 'The bird that hath been limèd in a bush | With trembling wings misdoubteth every bush.' The thought is appropriately proverbial for a line marked as a *sententia*: cf. Dent B394.

89 **securely** 'without care or misgiving' (*OED* 1, citing *Titus* as the first usage), but quite definitely not 'in safety'. (Cf. Jonson, *Forest* (1614) 11, l. 116: 'Man may securely sin, but safely never'.)
   good cheer a merry greeting

91 **ill** wickedness

92 **For that he coloured** 'For he speciously disguised his inner designs.' *That* refers back to *inward will.*

93 **base** socially and morally low
   pleats folds (as an opulent garment offers layers of cloth under which to conceal

That nothing in him seemed inordinate,
Save sometime too much wonder of his eye,   95
Which having all, all could not satisfy;
  But, poorly rich, so wanteth in his store
  That, cloyed with much, he pineth still for more.

But she that never coped with stranger eyes
Could pick no meaning from their parling looks,   100
Nor read the subtle shining secrecies,
Writ in the glassy margins of such books.
She touched no unknown baits, nor feared no hooks,
  Nor could she moralize his wanton sight
  More than his eyes were opened to the light.   105

He stories to her ears her husband's fame,
Won in the fields of fruitful Italy,
And decks with praises Collatine's high name,

objects); also associated with deception in *Lear* (Quarto) Scene 1.27 : 'Time shall unfold what pleated cunning hides.'

94 That so that
  inordinate intemperate; disorderly
95 sometime The form without terminal 's' is used throughout the poem (ll. 331, 530, 1105–6, 1786).
97 wanteth in his store feels lack despite his abundance. Compare *Venus* ll. 19–20.
98 pineth starves; also longs for. That 'much would have more' was proverbial (Dent M1287). Compare l. 115.
99 coped encountered (as in a battle, *OED v.* 2), as in *Venus* l. 838. *OED* cites as first usage in sense 5: 'To meet with; to come into contact, touch, or relation with; to have to do with'. For early readers these metaphorical senses would be secondary; the word's association with military encounters would develop the growing association between Lucrece and a town under siege.
100 parling speaking (first cited usage in *OED*); also 'To treat, discuss terms; esp. to hold a parley (with an enemy or opponent)' (*OED* s.v. 'parley' *v.* 2).
101 subtle shining secrecies complex private thoughts which glow in the eye
102 glassy margins The *margin* is *glassy* because it metaphorically represents the eye, which was thought to show the hidden qualities of a person as a margin

glosses the sense of a text: as Lady Capulet says of Paris: 'And what obscured in this fair volume lies | Find written in the margin of his eyes', *Romeo* 1.3.87–8.
103 touched no unknown baits means primarily that Lucrece is a fish who has had no contact with the wiles of fishermen. Secondary senses include 'she apprehended no trick to catch her' (*OED* s.v. 'touch' 17a: 'to apprehend'), and 'she had never slept with anyone who was not her husband' (*OED* s.v. 'touch' 2a: 'to have sexual contact with').
104 moralize give a moral interpretation to (texts are often given moral significance by a commentary in the period)
105 More . . . light Lucrece can see in Tarquin's eyes nothing except what is explicitly revealed.
106 stories relates like a historian. Other usages in the period do not suggest that the word implies deceptiveness, although it seems to do so in this context (compare Gower, *Confessio Amantis* 7.4928–37, where Tarquin weaves 'tales feigned in his wise' of Lucrece's husband).
108 decks 'clothes in rich or ornamental garments' (*OED* 2a), taking on pejorative senses by 1600, which may be emerging here. The description of Tarquin's actions is finely tuned: it hints at meanings which are not quite fully available either to Lucrece or to the readers of the poem in 1594.

Made glorious by his manly chivalry,
With bruisèd arms and wreaths of victory.   110
    Her joy with heaved-up hand she doth express,
    And wordless so greets heaven for his success.

Far from the purpose of his coming thither
He makes excuses for his being there.
No cloudy show of stormy blust'ring weather   115
Doth yet in his fair welkin once appear,
Till sable night, mother of dread and fear,
    Upon the world dim darkness doth display,
    And in her vaulty prison stows the day.

For then is Tarquin brought unto his bed,   120
Intending weariness with heavy sprite;
For after supper long he questionèd
With modest Lucrece, and wore out the night.
Now leaden slumber with life's strength doth fight,
    And every one to rest themselves betake,   125
    Save thieves, and cares, and troubled minds that wake.

As one of which doth Tarquin lie revolving
The sundry dangers of his will's obtaining;

125 themselves betake] QB; himself betakes QA (Malone 34, Yale)   126 wake] QB; wakes QA (Malone 34, Yale)

110 **bruisèd arms** dented armour. The line contains the same two traditional elements of a triumph as 'Now are our brows bound with victorious wreaths, | Our bruisèd arms hung up for monuments', *Richard III* 1.1.5–6.
111 **heaved-up** raised (not necessarily suggesting effort; see *Venus* l. 351 and n.). Q reads 'heaued up', with a non-syllabic '-ed'. Compare *Venus* l. 366 n. Compare also the gesture at l. 638.
113–15 **thither . . . weather** is probably a perfect rhyme in Shakespeare's English, in which 'i' can be lowered to 'e' (Kökeritz, 212).
116 **welkin** sky; so here 'face'
119 **vaulty** vaulted; quite frequently used of the sky in the period
121 **Intending** pretending, claiming (*OED* 22: the majority of examples in this sense

are from Shakespeare, who uses the word idiosyncratically)
121 **heavy sprite** weary spirit
122 **questionèd** conversed with
123 **wore out** passed. Compare *Venus* l. 841.
125 **themselves** Shakespeare often takes indefinite pronouns (here *every one*) to imply more than one person; Sisson, i.208 prefers the reading of the unrevised state of Q 'himself betakes'.
127–441 Nothing in Ovid or any other source corresponds to this section of the poem: its focus on the psychology of Tarquin's action is completely Shakespearian.
127–33 The stanza contains only feminine rhymes, on which see Sonnet 20.1 n.
127 **revolving** turning over in his mind (perhaps with a suggestion that he is tossing and turning)
128 **will's** On the sexual senses, see Sonnet 135.1 and n.

Yet ever to obtain his will resolving.
Though weak-built hopes persuade him to abstaining,   130
Despair to gain doth traffic oft for gaining,
    And when great treasure is the meed proposèd,
    Though death be adjunct, there's no death supposèd.

Those that much covet are with gain so fond
That what they have not—that which they possess—   135
They scatter and unloose it from their bond,
And so by hoping more they have but less,
Or gaining more, the profit of excess
    Is but to surfeit, and such griefs sustain,
    That they prove bankrupt in this poor-rich gain.   140

The aim of all is but to nurse the life
With honour, wealth, and ease in waning age;

---

129 resolving.] Q; ~∧ Q4   130 abstaining,] Q7; ~∧ Q   135 —that which . . . possess—] This edition; , ~ ~ . . . ~∧ Q; that of Q6; (~ ~ . . . ~) MALONE

130 **weak-built hopes** the fact that his hopes are ungrounded

13 **traffic** (a) 'To carry on trade, to trade, to buy and sell' (*OED* 1); (b) 'To have dealings of an illicit or secret character; to deal, intrigue, conspire' (*OED* 2b)

132 **meed** reward (archaic by 1594)

133 **adjunct** inseparably joined (as a consequence)
supposèd believed to exist

134 **fond** foolish

135–6 **That . . . bond** 'That they squander things that they do not really own, that is their possessions.' The phrase is difficult because it is founded on the idea that 'the miser is further from possessing what he has than what he has not', a thought which derives from the school text of Publilius Syrus ('Tam avaro deest quod habet, quam quod non habet', cited in Baldwin, 117) This text would have been known to most of Shakespeare's readers. *That which they possess* is a parenthesis of explanation—'i.e. what they actually do have'. This edition has set it off by dashes (following Malone's parentheses) to indicate this. Q punctuates 'what they haue not, that which they possess | They scatter . . .'. Other emendations of the phrase and punctuation (see collation) do not improve its sense. *Bond* plays on both 'secure ownership' and 'that which binds

something together' like a sheaf of corn or a faggot of wood. The possessions are both materially dispersed and lost to ownership.

137 **hoping more** i.e. hoping for more through gambling their possessions on future gains

133–40 **the profit . . . gain** 'The benefit of having too much is simply to overindulge (*surfeit*), and to endure the hardships which follow from overindulgence; this results in such sickness, diseases, and sorrows (*griefs*) that overabundance leads only to poverty.' The argument depends on the fact that *surfeit* means an overindulgence that disturbs the natural balance of the body, and so leads to illness or sickness. *Excess* means both 'intemperance in eating or drinking' (*OED* 5b) and 'income through usury' (*OED* 6c). *Sustain* may play on a uniquely Shakespearian usage. 'to supply (a person's need)' (*OED* 6e), otherwise found only in *Twelfth Night* 4.2.125–8: 'I'll be with you again, | In a trice, | Like to the old vice | Your need to sustain'; hence the *griefs* are presented as rapacious dependants feeding on the overindulgent miser.

141–2 Compare *Macbeth* 5.3.26–8: 'that which should accompany old age, | As honour, love, obedience, troops of friends, | I must not look to have'.

And in this aim there is such thwarting strife
That one for all, or all for one we gage—
As life for honour in fell battle's rage,   145
   Honour for wealth, and oft that wealth doth cost
   The death of all, and altogether lost.

So that, in vent'ring ill, we leave to be
The things we are for that which we expect;
And this ambitious foul infirmity,   150
In having much, torments us with defect
Of that we have; so then we do neglect
   The thing we have, and, all for want of wit,
   Make something nothing, by augmenting it.

Such hazard now must doting Tarquin make,   155
Pawning his honour to obtain his lust,
And for himself himself he must forsake.
Then where is truth if there be no self-trust?
When shall he think to find a stranger just,
   When he himself himself confounds, betrays   160
   To sland'rous tongues and wretched hateful days?

Now stole upon the time the dead of night,
When heavy sleep had closed up mortal eyes.

---

143 **thwarting strife** self-opposing struggles

144 **gage** wager

145 **fell** deadly, fierce

147 **of all** (a) of all the desirable things of life (*life, honour, wealth*); (b) all people

148 **vent'ring ill** (a) taking an ill-judged risk; (b) embarking on sin
leave to be cease to be

149 **expect** hope for

150 **ambitious foul infirmity** the vile weakness of ambition

151 **defect** the insufficiency (stressed on the second syllable)

153 **wit** understanding, reason

154 'We make what we have appear to be nothing by attempting to increase it.' Two arguments fuse: that excess generates sickness and poverty, and that the more we have the more we desire, and so what we do have seems continually to diminish.

155 **hazard** gamble. The word derives from a dice-game, and Shakespearian usages often allude to this; here *pawning* continues the image of a gamble, since it can mean 'wager'.

157 **himself himself** For the double reflexive pronoun, see l. 160 and *Venus* l. 161. Here the doubling implicitly contrasts Tarquin's appetites (*lust*) with his honour.

159 **just** 'Faithful or honourable in one's social relations' (*OED* 2b, citing *Caeser* 3.2.86 as the first usage in this sense)

160 **confounds** destroys, abashes. Compare ll. 250, 290, 1202, 1489, where the sense 'mingles together confusedly' emerges (*OED* 6: compare *Richard II* 4.1.131–2: 'Tumultuous wars | Shall kin with kin, and kind with kind confound.')

162–8 A set-piece description of a time of day was known as a *chronographia* ('time-painting'). This passage shows some influence from Virgil's *Aeneid* 4.522–8, the most famous classical example of the topos. Compare *Macbeth* 2.1.49–56: 'Now o'er the one half-world | Nature seems dead, and wicked dreams abuse | The curtained sleep. Witchcraft celebrates | Pale Hecate's offerings, and withered murder, | Alarumed by his sentinel the wolf, | Whose howl's his watch, thus with his

No comfortable star did lend his light,
No noise but owls' and wolves' death-boding cries.   165
Now serves the season that they may surprise
　　The silly lambs; pure thoughts are dead and still,
　　While lust and murder wakes to stain and kill.

And now this lustful lord leapt from his bed,
Throwing his mantle rudely o'er his arm,   170
Is madly tossed between desire and dread:
Th' one sweetly flatters, th' other feareth harm;
But honest fear, bewitched with lust's foul charm,
　　Doth too too oft betake him to retire,
　　Beaten away by brainsick rude desire.   175

His falchion on a flint he softly smiteth,
That from the cold stone sparks of fire do fly,
Whereat a waxen torch forthwith he lighteth,
Which must be lodestar to his lustful eye,
And to the flame thus speaks advisedly: 180
　　'As from this cold flint I enforced this fire,
　　So Lucrece must I force to my desire.'

---

165 owls' and wolves'] Q (Owles, & wolues)

---

stealthy pace, | With Tarquin's ravishing
strides, towards his design | Moves like a
ghost.'

164 **comfortable** comforting, benevolent
165 Owls' cries were believed to be portents
　　of ill-fortune (cf. Dent R33).
166 **season** time
167 **silly** guileless, unfortunate. Compare
　　Venus l. 1098.
168 **wakes** Shakespeare often uses the singu-
　　lar form of a verb when it follows two sin-
　　gular subjects (Abbott §336), especially as
　　here when they are virtually synonymous
　　(Partridge, *Grammar*, 51).
170 **mantle** cloak
　　rudely (a) violently; (b) in an uncultivated
　　manner
173 **charm** magic spell or potion. The sense of
　　'fascinating beauty' does not emerge until
　　the end of the seventeenth century, but
　　may be anticipated here.
174 **him** himself (i.e. *fear*)

174 **retire** withdraw (like a timid warrior in
　　battle)
175 **brainsick** mad
　　rude (a) violent; (b) low-born, uncultivated
176 **falchion** a broad sword with the blade on
　　the convex side (pronounced 'falshion',
　　but sometimes with a sufficiently hard
　　'ch' to enable a pun on 'falcon', as in
　　l. 506 below)
179 **lodestar** guiding star
180 **advisedly** 'deliberately, leisurely' (*OED*
　　3). There may be an ironic echo of the
　　Solemnization of Matrimony in the
　　Book of Common Prayer: marriage 'is not
　　by any to be enterprised, nor taken
　　in hand, unadvisedly, lightly, or wan-
　　tonly, to satisfy men's carnal lusts and
　　appetites, like brute beasts that have
　　no understanding; but reverently, dis-
　　creetly, advisedly, soberly, and in the fear
　　of God'.
181 Compare the proverb 'In coldest flint
　　there is hot fire' (Dent F371).

Here, pale with fear, he doth premeditate
The dangers of his loathsome enterprise,
And in his inward mind he doth debate   185
What following sorrow may on this arise.
Then, looking scornfully, he doth despise
     His naked armour of still-slaughtered lust,
     And justly thus controls his thoughts unjust:

'Fair torch, burn out thy light, and lend it not   190
To darken her whose light excelleth thine;
And die, unhallowed thoughts, before you blot
With your uncleanness that which is divine.
Offer pure incense to so pure a shrine.
     Let fair humanity abhor the deed   195
     That spots and stains love's modest snow-white weed.

'O shame to knighthood, and to shining arms;
O foul dishonour to my household's grave;

---

188 still-slaughtered] Q (still slaughtered)

184 **enterprise** could be used of daring military adventures

185 **inward mind** conscience

188 **His . . . lust** His only armour is lust, and lust is no defence (hence is *naked*) since it is always destroyed (*still-slaughtered*) the moment it is satisfied. The fact that he is despising this armour suggests two quite contrary things: (a) that he will abandon his *enterprise* because it clothes him in such squalid armour; (b) that he will seek like an extremely brave warrior to abandon his armour and proceed with his *enterprise* unprotected. *Naked* may hint that Tarquin is actually nude here, although in most pictorial representations of the rape he is fully clad.

190–245 Tarquin's soliloquy anticipates that of Brutus before the assassination of Caesar: 'Between the acting of a dreadful thing | And the first motion, all the interim is | Like a phantasma or a hideous dream. | The genius and the mortal instruments | Are then in counsel, and the state of man, | Like to a little kingdom, suffers then | The nature of an insurrection', *Caesar* 2.1.63–9.

192 **unhallowed** The sense 'wicked' (*OED* 2) was only just beginning to emerge in the 1590s from the earlier and stronger sense

'not formally hallowed or consecrated' (*OED* 1). The language that follows (*divine, incense, shrine*) sustains this religious ambience.

196 **weed** garment (i.e. chastity, the proper attire of love)

197 **knighthood** still connoted a set of values of courtesy and sexual probity by 1594. Compare Chaucer's narrator's interjection in *LGW* ll. 1822–3: 'Whi hastow don dispit to chevalrye? | Whi hastow don this lady vilanye?' It was 'the office and duty of every knight and gentleman', according to William Segar, *The Book of Honour and Arms* (1602), 60, 'to eschew riot and detest intemperancy' and 'to eschew dishonest pleasures and endeavour to do good unto others'. Segar's book explicitly seeks to ground Elizabethan conceptions of knighthood on historical Roman example. The thought here would not have seemed anachronistic to Shakespeare's contemporaries.

198 **household's grave** Family vaults were regularly emblazoned with the arms of illustrious ancestors. For a comparable transposition of such a family grave to a Roman setting, see *Titus* 1.1.346–87, in which Titus regards the burial of Mutius in the family grave as a dishonour to his house.

O impious act including all foul harms—
A martial man to be soft fancy's slave.   200
True valour still a true respect should have;
    Then my digression is so vile, so base,
    That it will live engraven in my face.

'Yea, though I die, the scandal will survive,
And be an eyesore in my golden coat.   205
Some loathsome dash the herald will contrive
To cipher me how fondly I did dote,
That my posterity, shamed with the note,
    Shall curse my bones, and hold it for no sin
    To wish that I their father had not been.   210

'What win I if I gain the thing I seek?
A dream, a breath, a froth of fleeting joy.
Who buys a minute's mirth to wail a week,
Or sells eternity to get a toy?
For one sweet grape who will the vine destroy.   215
    Or what fond beggar, but to touch the crown,
    Would with the sceptre straight be strucken down?

199 **including** encompassing
200 **soft fancy's slave** subordinate to the whimsies of love
201 **true respect** (a) due circumspection, a careful regard for what is good; (b) respect and admiration from others
202 **digression** 'moral deviation' (*OED* 1b; rare in this sense)
203 **engraven** Tarquin believes that his face, like that of Lucrece in ll. 64 and 807–8, will bear the heraldic mark of his moral nature.
204 **scandal** The sense 'damage to reputation' is just emerging in this period (and *OED* attributes to Shakespeare the emergence of this sense); the earlier sense, Discredit to religion occasioned by the conduct of a religious person', would have been live to many readers, and would reinforce the language of religious defilement in ll. 192–6 above.
205 **golden coat** rich coat of arms. Gold figures prominently in royal coats of arms.
206 **loathsome dash** Acts of dishonour were registered in coats of arms by 'marks of abatement', or more correctly 'rebatements of honour'. A reversed ines-

cutcheon sanguine (an inverted small red shield) occupying the central point of the escutcheon of arms was in theory used to indicate a rapist. In practice rebatements of honour are rarely found in escutcheons, and there is much dispute as to whether they were ever used.
207 **cipher me** represent to me by a sign. This is a rare use of the old dative form (compare l. 977). On *cipher* compare l. 196.
fondly foolishly
208 **note** mark, reminder
209 **hold it for no sin** think it justifiable. The fifth commandment is 'Honour thy father and thy mother'.
211–14 Compare both *Fasti* 2.811: 'Quid victor, gaudes?' ('Why are you rejoicing in your victory?') and Mark 8: 36: 'For what shall it profit a man, though he should win the whole world, if he lose his soul?' Compare Sonnet 129.12.
212 **froth** 'something insubstantial and of little worth' (*OED* 2a, citing this as the earliest example)
214 **toy** thing of nothing, an amorous fancy
217 **straight** immediately

'If Collatinus dream of my intent,
Will he not wake, and in a desp'rate rage
Post hither, this vile purpose to prevent?   220
This siege that hath engirt his marriage,
This blur to youth, this sorrow to the sage,
    This dying virtue, this surviving shame,
    Whose crime will bear an ever-during blame.

'O what excuse can my invention make   225
When thou shalt charge me with so black a deed?
Will not my tongue be mute, my frail joints shake,
Mine eyes forgo their light, my false heart bleed?
The guilt being great, the fear doth still exceed,
    And extreme fear can neither fight nor fly,   230
    But, coward-like, with trembling terror die.

'Had Collatinus killed my son or sire,
Or lain in ambush to betray my life,
Or were he not my dear friend, this desire
Might have excuse to work upon his wife,   235
As in revenge or quittal of such strife.
    But as he is my kinsman, my dear friend,
    The shame and fault finds no excuse nor end.

'Shameful it is: ay, if the fact be known,
Hateful it is. There is no hate in loving.   240

---

220 **prevent** arrive beforehand in order to forestall

221 **engirt** surrounded. See *Venus* l. 364 for the military associations of the verb.

   marriage is trisyllabic here

222 **blur** blemish or stain

223 **dying virtue** Both Tarquin's and Lucrece's virtue will be killed if he proceeds with the rape.

224 **ever-during** permanently enduring

225 **invention** in rhetoric the ability to find out matter for a speech, hence here the ability to produce plausible arguments in his own defence

226 **thou** Collatine is suddenly imagined as being present, as Tarquin's *invention* starts into life.

228 **forgo their light** Eyes were often thought to emit rays of light which enabled them to see. See *Venus* l. 487 and n.

229 **doth still exceed** is still greater

230 **extreme** The accent is on the first syllable. Compare Sonnet 129.4 and 10.

235 **work upon** meddle with, seduce. Compare Sonnet 124.10 n.

236 **quittal** requital, payment (rare)

237 **kinsman** Collatine was also a member of the *gens* of the Tarquinii, see Argument l. 11 n. Compare *Macbeth* 1.7.13: 'as I am his kinsman and his subject'.

238 **finds** The tense is present, not future: Tarquin's penitent imaginings precede the actual rape.

239 **fact** 'Thing done or performed' (*OED* 1), as at l. 349.

240–3 On the associations of feminine rhymes in this period see Sonnet 20.1 n.

I'll beg her love; but she is not her own.
The worst is but denial and reproving.
My will is strong past reason's weak removing:
　　Who fears a sentence or an old man's saw
　　Shall by a painted cloth be kept in awe.'　　　　　　245

Thus graceless holds he disputation
'Tween frozen conscience and hot burning will,
And with good thoughts makes dispensation,
Urging the worser sense for vantage still,
Which in a moment doth confound and kill　　　　　　250
　　All pure effects, and doth so far proceed
　　That what is vile shows like a virtuous deed.

251 effects] Q; affects *conj.* Steevens

241 **not her own** (since she is married)

242 **reproving** reproof

243 **past reason's weak removing** beyond the feeble powers of reason to move or dissuade. *Remove* can be used of a siege (*OED* 1b and 2c). It can also mean 'to relieve or free one from, some feeling, quality, condition, etc., esp. one of a bad or detrimental kind' (*OED* 4a) and 'to move or persuade' (*OED* 8a). All of these senses are active.

244 **sentence** proverbial remark. See ll. 87–8 n. There is also a pun on the sense 'judgement'.

　　saw nugget of wisdom

245 **painted cloth** Households too poor to afford tapestries might have painted fabric wall hangings which illustrated biblical or moral tales. These might have a moral *sentence* written beneath them. The story of Lucretia was herself to become a source for subsequent pictorial representation: Sir John Wallop wrote to Henry VIII in 1540 of François I's gallery at Fontainebleau: 'And in diverse places of the same gallery many fair tables of stories set in very finely wrought, as Lucretia and other', PRO State Papers, SP 1/163, fos. 231ᵛ–232ʳ. Compare the painting described below, ll. 1366 ff.

246 **graceless** Senses range from (a) impious (lacking Christian grace); (b) merciless (*OED* 3); (c) 'Wanting a sense of decency or propriety' (*OED* 1b); and perhaps (d) lacking in the ornaments or graces of rhetoric.

246 **disputation** a formal debate in which two parties defend a thesis or debate over a theme, and argue pro and contra. Thomas Wilson's *Logic* (1553), 60ᵛ: 'That is called a disputation or reasoning of matters, when certain persons debate a cause together, and one taketh part contrary unto another'. The poem rings on this word at ll. 822 and 1101. Compare *Venus* ll. 422 n. and 806 n.

248 **makes dispensation** dispenses with. The religious associations of *dispensation* in the period suggest a secondary sense: like a Pope he makes a *dispensation* to his own advantage with all appearance of good intentions (*with good thoughts*).

249 **worser sense** A common attack on the art of rhetoric was that it could make the worse cause appear the better.

　　for vantage to gain a better position

251 **effects** actions; feelings. Q's reading might be modernized as 'affects', but the form *effects* may be used here to suggest that Tarquin is quashing not simply pure emotions but also pure consequences (*OED* s.v. 'effect' 1a) which might result from his remorse. See *Venus* l. 605.

　　proceed continue. The word can refer to legal proceedings or to chains of argument.

252 **vile . . . virtuous** Thomas Wilson describes how the orator can through *amplificatio* make a vice seem like a virtue: this occurs 'when we give vices the names of virtues: as when I call him that is a cruel or merciless man, somewhat sore in

Quoth he: 'She took me kindly by the hand,
And gazed for tidings in my eager eyes,
Fearing some hard news from the warlike band   255
Where her belovèd Collatinus lies.
O how her fear did make her colour rise!
    First red as roses that on lawn we lay,
    Then white as lawn, the roses took away.

'And how her hand in my hand being locked   260
Forced it to tremble with her loyal fear,
Which struck her sad, and then it faster rocked,
Until her husband's welfare she did hear.
Whereat she smilèd with so sweet a cheer
    That had Narcissus seen her as she stood   265
    Self-love had never drowned him in the flood.

'Why hunt I then for colour or excuses?
All orators are dumb when Beauty pleadeth;
Poor wretches have remorse in poor abuses;
Love thrives not in the heart that shadows dreadeth: 270
Affection is my captain and he leadeth,
    And, when his gaudy banner is displayed,
    The coward fights, and will not be dismayed.

'Then, childish fear, avaunt; debating, die.
Respect and reason wait on wrinkled age: 275

judgement. When I call a natural fool, a plain simple man' (Wilson, 121).

253 **kindly** like a kinsman (which Tarquin uses to smuggle in the sense 'in a friendly manner' and 'as if she liked me').
hand On the erotic associations of touching hands, see Sonnet *128*.6 n.

255 **hard** harsh

258 **lawn** fine linen. Compare *Venus* l. 590.

259 **took** having been taken

261 **it** Tarquin's hand (although Tarquin is keen to present the two hands together in something like harmony through his repeated pronoun *it*).

262 **Which** her fear (with the faintest hint that it is her anxious trembling which makes her sad, as though Tarquin is surreptitiously imagining her to be responding to the potential eroticism of the moment when they clasp hands)

262 **struck** Q's 'strooke' may reflect Shakespeare's pronunciation.
it Lucrece's hand

265-6 On the variant of the Narcissus myth in which he drowns himself, see *Venus* l. 162 n.

267 **colour** (a) pretext; (b) a rhetorical ornamentation (which might mask the true nature of an action). The darker senses come through at ll. 92 and 476.

269 **Poor wretches . . . abuses** 'Only worthless creatures feel remorse, and then only for trivial transgressions.'

270 **shadows** insubstantial nothings

271 **Affection** passion, as at *Venus* l. 387 and n.

273 **The coward** i.e. even the coward. Compare the proverb 'Love makes cowards courageous' (Dent D216).
dismayed paralysed with fear. The word is also used by Spenser to mean 'defeated'.

274 **avaunt** be gone

My heart shall never countermand mine eye.
Sad pause and deep regard beseems the sage;
My part is youth, and beats these from the stage.
    Desire my pilot is, beauty my prize:
    Then who fears sinking where such treasure lies?'   280

As corn o'er-grown by weeds, so heedful fear
Is almost choked by unresisted lust.
Away he steals with open-listening ear,
Full of foul hope, and full of fond mistrust,
Both which, as servitors to the unjust,   285
    So cross him with their opposite persuasion
    That now he vows a league, and now invasion.

Within his thought her heavenly image sits,
And in the self-same seat sits Collatine;
That eye which looks on her confounds his wits;   290
That eye which him beholds, as more divine,
Unto a view so false will not incline,
    But with a pure appeal seeks to the heart,
    Which once corrupted takes the worser part,

---

276 **countermand** give a contradictory order which overrides that given by the eye

277 **Sad pause** grave hesitation. *Sad* is often used in conjunction with 'wise' in this period to mean 'grave, serious' (*OED* 4a). **deep regard** careful consideration

279 **pilot** navigator of a ship
prize is frequently used of the booty won by merchant venturers, or of the winnings of gamblers, and continues the fusion of gambling with mercantile imagery which surrounds Tarquin.

281 **corn ... weeds** Compare the proverb 'The weeds overgrow the corn' (Dent W242). **heedful** watchful, cautious

282 **unresisted** irresistible

283 **he** Just for a moment the pronoun drifts between *lust* and Tarquin.
ear, Q ends the line with a comma, which creates a double syntax: Tarquin is nervously listening out for the slightest sound, and is *full of foul hope*; but as the sentence unfolds to describe how *foul hope* and *fond mistrust* fill him with persuasion it is tempting to remove the comma and take *full* with *ear*. Tarquin listens at once to sounds outside him and rival persuasions within him.

285 **servitors . . . unjust** helpers in his wickedness. On *just* see l. 159 n.

286 **cross** thwart (*OED* 14a), perhaps with a suggestion that he is caught at the point of intersection between rival arguments

287 **league** peace treaty

290 **confounds his wits** overwhelms his reason

292 **view** (a) sight; (b) opinion (*OED* 10a, a sense just emerging in this period)
incline (a) tend towards (in belief); (b) bow (with a faint suggestion of idolatrous worship of a mere *view* or appearance)

293 **pure appeal** The eye that looks on Collatine attempts to make legal appeal to the heart based purely on the nature of the case.

294 **once corrupted** already corrupted (although this way of putting it suggests that the eye that looks on Lucrece has just managed to suborn the judge before the eye which looks on Tarquin has a chance to state its case)
worser As at l. 249 persuasion makes the *worser* case appear the better.

And therein heartens up his servile powers,   295
Who, flattered by their leader's jocund show,
Stuff up his lust, as minutes fill up hours,
And as their captain, so their pride doth grow,
Paying more slavish tribute than they owe.
   By reprobate desire thus madly led,   300
   The Roman lord marcheth to Lucrece' bed.

The locks between her chamber and his will
Each one by him enforced retires his ward;
But as they open they all rate his ill,
Which drives the creeping thief to some regard: 305
The threshold grates the door to have him heard;
   Night-wand'ring weasels shriek to see him there.
   They fright him, yet he still pursues his fear.

295 The growing energy of the heart forces a rare cross-stanzaic enjambment (Q ends l. 294 with a full stop, which is likely to reflect compositorial rather than authorial habits of punctuation; compare ll. 427–8).
  heartens up encourages (using the verb which is best suited to the heart)
  servile powers inferior faculties; the passions
296 **Who** is frequently used by Shakespeare as a relative pronoun for things, especially when they are personified (Abbott §264); compare ll. 447, 1740, 1805).
  jocund show cheerful appearance
297 **Stuff up** cram full (and perhaps also 'make turgid'); but also the verb *stuff* continues the military images which surround it, since it can mean 'to supply or furnish (a person) with arms, provisions, money' (*OED* 2a) and 'to arm and equip (a soldier)' (*OED* 2b)
  as minutes . . . hours i.e. completely. The image suggests a growing erection: as the minute hand approaches the hour it rises towards the vertical—as Mercutio puts it, 'the bawdy hand of the dial is now upon the prick of noon', *Romeo* 2.3.104–5.
298 **as their captain** the heart swells with excitement
  pride can mean 'sexual excitement'.
299 **Paying . . . owe** The inferior faculties are presented as vassals of the heart, who pay tribute which exceeds that demanded by their ruler, and perhaps even goes beyond

what they possess. It suggests a wild generosity in the body politic, which overwhelms the heart with the unexpected riches of lust.
300 **reprobate** is a strong term of moral condemnation, ranging from 'morally corrupt' (*OED* 2) to 'abandoned by God' (*OED* 3).
302 **chamber** The word is repeated at ll. 337, 365, and 1626. The intimacy of the violation is represented in terms of domestic geography: a private chamber was in this period a particularly intimate place of retreat, as Cressida knows: 'My lord, come you again into my chamber. | You smile and mock me, as if I meant naughtily', *Troilus* 4.2.39–40.
303 **retires** withdraws
  his its
  ward (a) act of guarding; (b) 'Each of the ridges projecting from the inside plate of a lock' (*OED* 24a). The word can also mean 'garrison' (*OED* 12), which maintains the metaphor of a city under siege.
304 **rate** berate, scold (i.e. they creak)
  ill wrongdoing
305 **regard** heed, caution
306 **The threshold . . . heard** The threshold rubs audibly on the door as though it is determined that Tarquin be heard.
307 **Night-wand'ring weasels** In Alciati's *Emblemata* (Leyden, 1593), emblem 126, weasels are presented as ill-omened beasts. In antiquity domesticated weasels were used to control household pests, as Shakespeare might have known from

As each unwilling portal yields him way,
Through little vents and crannies of the place 310
The wind wars with his torch to make him stay,
And blows the smoke of it into his face,
Extinguishing his conduct in this case;
    But his hot heart, which fond desire doth scorch,
    Puffs forth another wind that fires the torch, 315

And, being lighted, by the light he spies
Lucretia's glove, wherein her needle sticks.
He takes it from the rushes where it lies,
And, gripping it, the needle his finger pricks,
As who should say, 'This glove to wanton tricks 320
    Is not inured; return again in haste:
    Thou seest our mistress' ornaments are chaste.'

But all these poor forbiddings could not stay him.
He in the worst sense consters their denial:
The doors, the wind, the glove that did delay him 325
He takes for accidental things of trial,
Or as those bars which stop the hourly dial,

319 needle] Q; neeld MALONE

Aesop, *Fabulae* (Lyons, 1571), 250–2. See Donald Engels, *Classical Cats: The Rise and Fall of the Sacred Cat* (London and New York, 1999), 66–70.

311 **make him stay** hinder his progress
313 **conduct** guide
    case matter. (Elsewhere: legal case; plight, misfortune (*OED* 1; archaic by 1594).)
317 **Lucretia's** The full Latin form of the name is used in the Argument, here, and at l. 510. The form 'Lucrece's' would scan, but does not occur in the poem, in which 'Lucrece' serves as the possessive form.
318 **rushes** were regularly used as floor coverings
319 **needle** is presumably elided with *his* for the sake of scansion. Malone suggested it was pronounced 'neeld', but this conflicts with the pronunciation in l. 317 above.
320 **As who should say** like one who, as in *Venus* l. 280.
321 **inured** accustomed to

323 **stay** hinder, delay. On the association between feminine rhymes and moments of passion, see Sonnet 20.1 n.
324 **worst sense** Compare ll. 249 and 294. Tarquin hardens from *worser* to *worst* as the rape approaches.
    consters construes, interprets (stressed on the first syllable)
326 **accidental . . . trial** chance occurrences designed to test his endurance (rather than true signs of the lawlessness of his action)
327 **those bars which stop** The lines on the clock face which mark off the minutes do not of course make contact with the hands or slow their movement; hence *stop* probably anticipates *OED* 41, 'furnish with punctuation marks' (first cited from 1776). Early modern clocks, however, moved with regular jolts rather than a smooth movement, which could give the impression that the divisions on the clock's face were delaying the motion of the hands.

Who with a ling'ring stay his course doth let,
Till every minute pays the hour his debt.

'So, so', quoth he, 'these lets attend the time   330
Like little frosts that sometime threat the spring,
To add a more rejoicing to the prime,
And give the sneapèd birds more cause to sing.
Pain pays the income of each precious thing:
    Huge rocks, high winds, strong pirates, shelves, and sands   335
    The merchant fears, ere rich at home he lands.'

Now is he come unto the chamber door
That shuts him from the heaven of his thought,
Which with a yielding latch, and with no more,
Hath barred him from the blessèd thing he sought.   340
So from himself impiety hath wrought
    That for his prey to pray he doth begin,
    As if the heavens should countenance his sin.

But in the midst of his unfruitful prayer,
Having solicited th' eternal power   345
That his foul thoughts might compass his fair fair,
And they would stand auspicious to the hour—

328 **ling'ring stay** slow delay
    let hinder
329 **Till . . . debt** This line contrasts with
    the eagerness of the inferior faculties to
    pay what they owe to the heart in l. 299
    above: the passions gallop eagerly on,
    but as Tarquin moves towards Lucrece
    time slows to a grudging crawl.
330 **lets** hindrances
    attend the time accompany this period
    (like a group of retainers)
332 **prime** early spring
333 **sneapèd** nipped with frost (first cited
    usage of the form in *OED*)
334 **pays** pays for
    income entrance fee; beginning. Most
    eds. gloss as 'harvest' or 'maturation', for
    which *OED* cites first usages from 1635.
    Given that spring frosts are referred to
    earlier in the stanza, and that Tarquin is
    at the very start of his venture, *OED* may
    be right to cite this passage as an illustra-
    tion of the sense 'Coming in, entrance,
    arrival, advent; beginning (of a period of
    time, or an action)' (*OED* 1a). *Pain pays*

suggests there is a play on *OED* 'income'
3, 'A fee paid on coming in or entering;
entry-money, entrance-fee', which many
early readers, especially the theatre-goers
among them, might have taken as the pri-
mary sense (cf. John Gee in 1624: 'The
third abatement of the honour and con-
tinuance of this scenical company is that
they *make their spectators pay too dear for
their income*', *Allusion Book*, i.327).
335 **shelves** sandbanks
338 **thought** imagination
341 **So from . . . wrought** wickedness had
    made him so unlike himself
343 **countenance** favour
346 **compass** The senses 'achieve', 'encircle',
    and 'embrace' collaborate with the sense
    'contrive, devise, machinate'.
347 **they** the heavens. A slippage from singu-
    lar to plural pronouns in addresses to
    deities is common. It occurs also in
    Richard III 1.3.214–16: 'If heaven have
    any grievous plague in store | Exceeding
    those that I can wish on thee | O let them
    keep it till thy sins be ripe'. This cannot be

Even there he starts. Quoth he: 'I must deflower;
  The powers to whom I pray abhor this fact.
  How can they then assist me in the act?   350

'Then Love and Fortune be my gods, my guide.
  My will is backed with resolution:
  Thoughts are but dreams till their effects be tried;
  The blackest sin is cleared with absolution.
  Against love's fire, fear's frost hath dissolution.   355
    The eye of heaven is out, and misty night
    Covers the shame that follows sweet delight.'

This said, his guilty hand plucked up the latch,
  And with his knee the door he opens wide.
  The dove sleeps fast that this night owl will catch: 360
  Thus treason works ere traitors be espied.
  Who sees the lurking serpent steps aside;

352 resolution] Q; dauntless resolution CAPELL; constant resolution *conj.* Taylor   354 The blackest] Q; Blacke Q6

the result of the Act to Restrain Abuses of Players, as Prince suggests, since this prohibition did not take effect until 27 May 1606. It is the result of an awkward elision of the pagan pantheon and a Christian god.

347 **stand auspicious** remain looking kindly on. This pre-dates the first cited usage of *auspicious* in OED, from *All's Well*, and is itself pre-dated by a usage in George Peele's *The Honour of the Garter* (1593). There is a faint sexual innuendo in *stand*.

348 **starts** jolts

351 **Love and Fortune** (as opposed to *the powers* above). That 'Fortune favours the bold' was proverbial (Dent F601). Compare Ovid: 'audentes forsque deusque iuvat' ('god and chance help the brave', *Fasti* 2.782). Marsus's gloss on Ovid at this point says, 'hence that proverb "Fortune favours the brave", and that other, "Love makes a man daring" ' (Marsus, 146).

352 **backed** supported. This line appears to be one foot short, and since Q5 (which alters l. 354 to make it correspond in length) attempts have been made to regularize. It is likely however that *resolution* is

to be pronounced as five syllables and that l. 354 is an alexandrine. The metrical irregularity provides opportunities for dramatic readings which evoke Tarquin's state of mind, but may result from the omission of a word such as 'constant' before *resolution*. The phrase 'constant resolution' occurs in *Henry V* 2.4.35.

353 **Thoughts . . . tried** Compare Bacon's Essay 'Of Great Place' (first printed 1621): 'For good thoughts, (though God accept them,) yet towards men, are little better than good dreams; except they be put in act', *Essays*, ed. M. Kiernan (Oxford, 1985), 34.

354 **absolution** remission of sins. The word does not necessarily carry a Roman Catholic resonance, since it is used in the general confession in the Book of Common Prayer: see l. 714 n.

355 **hath dissolution** melts

356 **heaven** is monosyllabic (compare the more leisurely bisyllabic pronunciation at l. 338).

359 **knee** The anatomical detail creates a parallel between the entering of the chamber and the rape itself.

360 **fast** combines 'deeply (asleep)', 'securely', 'settled', stable'.

But she, sound sleeping, fearing no such thing,
Lies at the mercy of his mortal sting.

Into the chamber wickedly he stalks, 365
And gazeth on her yet unstainèd bed.
The curtains being close, about he walks,
Rolling his greedy eye-balls in his head.
By their high treason is his heart misled,
  Which gives the watchword to his hand full soon 370
  To draw the cloud that hides the silver moon.

Look as the fair and fiery-pointed sun,
Rushing from forth a cloud, bereaves our sight;
Even so, the curtain drawn, his eyes begun
To wink, being blinded with a greater light. 375
Whether it is that she reflects so bright
  That dazzleth them, or else some shame supposed;
  But blind they are, and keep themselves enclosed.

O had they in that darksome prison died
Then had they seen the period of their ill. 380
Then Collatine again, by Lucrece' side,
In his clear bed might have reposèd still.
But they must ope this blessèd league to kill,
  And holy-thoughted Lucrece to their sight
  Must sell her joy, her life, her world's delight. 385

364 **mortal sting** deadly lust. The serpent
   suggests Satanic temptations.
365 **stalks** advances stealthily like a hunter.
   Compare *LGW* l. 1781: 'And in the nyght
   ful thefly gan he stalke'.
367 **close** closed
369 **high treason** The inferior faculties have
   so far only assisted the heart in its insur-
   rection; now they become outright rebels.
   It was an act of 'petty treason' for a wife
   to have an adulterous affair; it was high
   treason for a subject to violate his alle-
   giance to the King. This included violat-
   ing the wife of the King.
370 **watchword** the signal to begin an attack
   (*OED* 2)
371 **the cloud is** the hanging which sur-
   rounds Lucrece's bed.
372 **Look as** just as. See *Venus* l. 67 n.
373 **bereaves** takes away
375 **wink** close. See *Venus* ll. 90, 121.

375 **greater light** greater than the light
   which they themselves emitted. For the
   belief that the eye emitted light, see *Venus*
   l. 487 n.
376 **reflects** Lucrece is imagined as a mirror
   so clear that it reflects light back with
   greater intensity.
377 **shame supposed** imagined shame
379 **darksome prison** i.e. under the eyelids.
   Compare the 'deep, dark cabins' of *Venus*
   l. 1038.
380 **period** final day, end
382 **clear** (a) free of stain; (b) famous (for its
   chastity). The dazzling beauty of Lucrece
   is also registered in this word, which can
   mean 'shining, cloudless'.
383 **they** Tarquin's eyes
   league marriage (figured here as a mili-
   tary treaty for mutual protection)
385 **sell** The many images of trade used so far
   in the poem disturbingly bring out the

Her lily hand her rosy cheek lies under,
Coz'ning the pillow of a lawful kiss;
Who therefore angry seems to part in sunder,
Swelling on either side to want his bliss,
Between whose hills her head entombèd is;   390
   Where, like a virtuous monument, she lies,
   To be admired of lewd unhallowed eyes.

Without the bed her other fair hand was,
On the green coverlet, whose perfect white
Showed like an April daisy on the grass,   395
With pearly sweat resembling dew of night.
Her eyes, like marigolds, had sheathed their light,
   And canopied in darkness sweetly lay
   Till they might open to adorn the day.

Her hair, like golden threads, played with her breath: 400
O modest wantons, wanton modesty!
Showing life's triumph in the map of death,
And death's dim look in life's mortality.
Each in her sleep themselves so beautify
   As if between them twain there were no strife,   405
   But that life lived in death, and death in life.

modern sense of 'give up for a price'; earlier senses include 'to give up (a person) treacherously to his enemies' (*OED* 2a), and 'to hand over (something, esp. food, a gift) voluntarily or in response to a demand or request' (*OED* 1). These senses exculpate Lucrece (she gives her chastity up in response to a demand); but the verb raises other more awkward possibilities of betrayal for profit.

386–95 This description circulated in manuscript copies after the printing of *Lucrece* (e.g. BL MS Add. 27406, fo. 74). On the version in Suckling's *Fragmenta Aurea* (1646), 29–30, see Introduction, pp. 44–5. Lines 386–413 were also printed in *England's Parnassus* (1600). It is noteworthy that later readers identified so strongly with the predatory gaze of Tarquin.

387 Coz'ning cheating

388 in sunder asunder, in two

389 want his lack its

391 virtuous monument Effigies on the tombs of virtuous wives often portrayed their subjects asleep with their head on a

pillow beside their husbands.

392 lewd lecherous, unchaste; the juxtaposition with *unhallowed* (see l. 192 n.) may bring out a play on its etymological sense, obsolete by 1594, of 'lay, not in holy orders'.
unhallowed See l. 192 n.

393 Without outside

394 whose i.e. the hand's

397 marigolds were believed to follow the movement of the sun and close at night. See Sonnet 25.6 n.

398 canopied by the eyelid and lash, as in the closely analogous moment when Jachimo inspects the sleeping Innogen, *Cymbeline* 2.2.19–22: 'The flame o' th' taper | Bows toward her, and would underpeep her lids, | To see th' enclosèd lights, now canopied | Under these windows, white and azure-laced | With blue of heaven's own tinct'.

402 map representation

403 life's mortality the mortal term of life

405 twain two (sometimes with a suggestion of discord or division; on which see Sonnet 36.1).

Her breasts, like ivory globes circled with blue,
A pair of maiden worlds unconquerèd:
Save of their lord no bearing yoke they knew,
And him by oath they truly honourèd.   410
These worlds in Tarquin new ambition bred,
　　Who like a foul usurper went about
　　From this fair throne to heave the owner out.

What could he see, but mightily he noted?
What did he note, but strongly he desirèd?   415
What he beheld, on that he firmly doted,
And in his will his wilful eye he tirèd.
With more than admiration he admirèd
　　Her azure veins, her alabaster skin,
　　Her coral lips, her snow-white dimpled chin.   420

---

407 **ivory** i.e. smooth and white (cf. Dent I109). Globes from this period were not made of ivory, but usually of papier-maché which was polished and glazed to a hard white surface before 'gores' or sections of a map were pasted over it. The material is mentioned here as part of a deliberate attempt to present Lucrece through the eyes of Tarquin as a commodity made of valuable materials.

408–9 Compare *Hero and Leander* ll. 756–61: 'For though the rising iv'ry mount he scaled, | Which is with azure circling lines empaled, | Much like a globe (a globe may I term this, | By which love sails to regions full of bliss), | Yet strive with Sisyphus he toiled in vain'.

408 **maiden worlds** i.e. Lucrece had had no contact with any man except her husband. Compare *Fasti* 2.804: 'tunc primum externa pectora tacta manu' (her breast then for the first time touched by a hand which was not that of her husband). *Maiden* may be used of a castle or a town which has not been taken by the enemy (*OED* 5a).

411–13 The conjunction of the new world and the old here creates a number of shifts of perspective. For Tarquin Lucrece is a new world, awaiting conquest, and has no king; for the narrator, however, the realm she represents already has a legitimate king (Collatine). These lines also uncomfortably remind readers of the eventual banishment of the Tarquinii,

while presenting regicide and usurpation as a crime.

414 **noted** observed

417 **in . . . tirèd** 'in his lust he exhausted his lustful eye'. *Tirèd* may play on the sense (*OED v.* 2) from falconry 'to feed full'. There might be an additional pun on *OED v.* 3, meaning 'to arm' or 'attire', recalling the earlier reference to *his naked armour of still-slaughtered lust*, l. 188.

419 **azure** is originally a blue pigment made from ground lapis lazuli, which retained its association with value even when cheaper forms of the pigment were introduced based on the mineral azurite; *alabaster* is a smooth white mineral often used in funerary monuments, and frequently compared to the whiteness of skin (cf. Dent A95.2). Patrons and viewers of works of art in this period were extremely sensitive to the value of the materials from which they were made. The description of Lucrece makes her appear to be an artefact of extraordinary value. For a similarly sinister usage of *alabaster* when a male is looking at a sleeping female see *Othello* 5.2.5. Othello describes the skin of Desdemona, whom he is about to murder, as 'smooth as monumental alabaster.'

420 **coral** is a traditional epithet for red lips. See Sonnet *130.2* and compare Dent C648.1. It was a material of extreme rarity in this period, and (intriguingly given the context here) was believed to ward off evil.

As the grim lion fawneth o'er his prey,
Sharp hunger by the conquest satisfied,
So o'er this sleeping soul doth Tarquin stay,
His rage of lust by gazing qualified.
Slaked, not suppressed; for standing by her side,   425
 His eye, which late this mutiny restrains,
 Unto a greater uproar tempts his veins,

And they, like straggling slaves for pillage fighting,
Obdurate vassals fell exploits effecting,
In bloody death and ravishment delighting,   430
Nor children's tears nor mothers' groans respecting,
Swell in their pride, the onset still expecting.
 Anon his beating heart, alarum striking,
 Gives the hot charge, and bids them do their liking.

His drumming heart cheers up his burning eye;   435
His eye commends the leading to his hand;
His hand as proud of such a dignity,
Smoking with pride, marched on to make his stand
On her bare breast, the heart of all her land,

425 Slaked] Q (Slakt)

421 **fawneth o'er** shows delight with
422 **Sharp** keen
424 **rage** can be used of any passionate frenzy, not simply of anger.
 qualified tempered, partially abated
425 **Slaked** diminished. This is sometimes modernized as 'slacked'. The orthography of these two words was not distinct in this period: it suggests an appetite which is both partially satisfied and 'slackened', the latter perhaps (playing on *standing*) suggesting partial tetumescence.
427–8 On cross-stanzaic enjambment, see l. 295 n. On feminine rhymes, see Sonnet 20.1 n.
427 **uproar** insurrection or serious outbreak of disorder (a much stronger term in 1590 than now)
428 **straggling slaves** the lowest rank of soldiers who have abandoned the discipline of their formations, and who attempt to pick off booty or stray members of enemy forces
 pillage plunder, booty
429 **Obdurate** unfeeling (*vassals* were so low

in the social order that they were thought to lack humane emotions). The accent is on the second syllable, as in *Venus* l. 199.
430 **ravishment** rape or plunder. The simile re-enacts its tenor.
431 **respecting** regarding, considering
432 **Swell in their pride** Compare l. 297 and n.
 onset first attack. Compare Sonnet 90.11.
433 **alarum** the call to attack (here the heart pounds out a martial drumbeat as a signal)
435 **cheers up** urges on, encourages
436 **commends the leading** entrusts the leadership
437 **as** as if
438 **Smoking with pride** burning with sexual anticipation. For smoking bodies as indicators of passion or sexual arousal, see *Venus* l. 555. For the sexual senses of *pride* see l. 298 n.
 stand 'A holding one's ground against an opponent or enemy; a halt (of moving troops) to give battle or repel an attack' (*OED* 4a), with a play on the sense 'erection'.

Whose ranks of blue veins as his hand did scale   440
Left their round turrets destitute and pale.

They, must'ring to the quiet cabinet
Where their dear governess and lady lies,
Do tell her she is dreadfully beset,
And fright her with confusion of their cries.   445
She, much amazed, breaks ope her locked up eyes,
    Who, peeping forth this tumult to behold,
    Are by his flaming torch dimmed and controlled.

Imagine her as one in dead of night,
From forth dull sleep by dreadful fancy waking,   450
That thinks she hath beheld some ghastly sprite,
Whose grim aspect sets every joint a-shaking.
What terror 'tis! But she in worser taking,
    From sleep disturbèd, heedfully doth view
    The sight which makes supposèd terror true.   455

Wrapped and confounded in a thousand fears,
Like to a new-killed bird she trembling lies.
She dares not look, yet winking there appears
Quick-shifting antics, ugly in her eyes.

442 **must'ring** 'Of an army, etc.: To come
together for inspection, exercise, or prepa-
ration for service' (*OED* 2c)
    cabinet the private inner chamber in
which a lady or gentleman would read
letters, do accounts, or take advice from
their secretary; here probably equivalent
to 'mind'. Compare *Venus* ll. 1043–50.
443 **governess** is the feminine form of 'gover-
nor'; i.e. the ruler or viceroy of a region
or garrison town (*OED* s.v. 'governor' 3a).
444 **beset** besieged
446 **She, much amazed** 'The allegorical
"lady" of the body, the heart, changes
into Lucrece herself, waking in alarm.
The effect of this turn from figurative to
actual description is rather like the experi-
ence of waking from a dream state into
reality' (Lever).
    locked up The eyes are presented figura-
tively as windows which have had protec-
tive covers battened down over them.
447 **Who** which. See l. 296 n.
    tumult riot, insurrection (*OED* 1b)
448 **dimmed** As Lucrece had earlier out-
shone the eye-beams of Tarquin (l. 375),

so here his torch outshines the light
emitted by her eyes.
448 **controlled** overwhelmed
451 **ghastly sprite** terrifying spirit
453 **taking** (a) agitation; (b) plight
457 Compare Ovid: 'sed tremit, ut quondam
stabulis deprensa relictis | parva sub
infesto cum iacet agna lupo' ('But she
trembled as a tiny lamb, caught straying
from the fold, lies below a ravening wolf',
Fasti 2.799–800).
458 **winking** while her eyes are closed
459 **Quick-shifting antics** rapidly shifting
images. *Antics* could be grotesque images
or dances in a pageant or masque. They
are sometimes associated with the harm-
ful dreams generated by love. In Spenser's
FQ 3.11.51 the heroine Britomart goes
into the castle of the enchanter Busirane
and sees walls of gold 'Wrought with
wilde Antickes, which their follies playd, |
In the rich metall, as they liuing were: | A
thousand monstrous formes therein were
made, | Such as false loue doth oft vpon
him weare, | For loue in thousand mon-
strous formes doth oft appeare'.

Such shadows are the weak brain's forgeries, 460
 Who, angry that the eyes fly from their lights,
 In darkness daunts them with more dreadful sights.

His hand that yet remains upon her breast
(Rude ram to batter such an ivory wall)
May feel her heart (poor citizen) distressed, 465
Wounding itself to death, rise up and fall,
Beating her bulk, that his hand shakes withal.
 This moves in him more rage and lesser pity
 To make the breach and enter this sweet city.

First, like a trumpet doth his tongue begin 470
To sound a parley to his heartless foe,
Who o'er the white sheet peers her whiter chin
The reason of this rash alarm to know,
Which he by dumb demeanour seeks to show.
 But she, with vehement prayers, urgeth still 475
 Under what colour he commits this ill.

Thus he replies: 'The colour in thy face—
That even for anger makes the lily pale,
And the red rose blush at her own disgrace—
Shall plead for me and tell my loving tale. 480
Under that colour am I come to scale

---

460 **shadows** dreams, delusions. This line is marked in Q as a *sententia*. See ll. 87–8 n.

461 **Who** which (i.e. the *shadows*). See l. 447 n. **their lights** the eyes' power of vision (that is, the eyes give up their duty of seeing)

464 **ram** battering ram. The whole stanza recalls the literal siege of Ardea, with which the poem opens.
 ivory wall The primary connotation is whiteness (cf. Dent I109), but preciousness and fragility are also implied: cf. *FQ* 2.12.43–4: 'The gate was wrought of substaunce light, | Rather for pleasure, then for battery or fight. | Yt framed was of precious yuory'.

466 **Wounding … death** The heart is dashing itself against the walls of the chest.

467 **bulk** body (*OED* 2a). The additional sense 'dead body' (*OED* 2b) continues the force of *Wounding itself to death*.
 withal with it

469 **breach** 'a gap in a fortification made by battery' (*OED* 7c, pre-dating the first cited usage from *2 Henry IV* 2.4.49)

471 **sound a parley** A wish to negotiate terms for peace or exchange of prisoners (*parley*) was indicated by sounding drums or (as here) by a blast on the trumpet. Contrast Ovid 'insæat amans hostis precibus pretioque minisque' ('her enemy-lover stands over her with prayers and threats', *Fast.* 2.805).
 heartless spiritless, disheartened (*OED* 2); the sense 'destitute of feeling' appears not to be found before the nineteenth century.

472 **white sheets** The surrounding metaphors may indicate that Lucrece is peering out like troops from behind a white flag, which was regularly used as a signal of a wish to parley or surrender.

473 **alarm** can mean 'sudden attack' (*OED* 11) as well as 'call to arms' (*OED* 1).

475 **urgeth** insistently asks

Thy never-conquered fort: the fault is thine,
For those thine eyes betray thee unto mine.

'Thus I forestall thee, if thou mean to chide:
Thy beauty hath ensnared thee to this night,   485
Where thou with patience must my will abide,
My will that marks thee for my earth's delight,
Which I to conquer sought with all my might;
 But as reproof and reason beat it dead,
 By thy bright beauty was it newly bred.   490

'I see what crosses my attempt will bring;
I know what thorns the growing rose defends;
I think the honey guarded with a sting;
All this beforehand counsel comprehends,
But will is deaf, and hears no heedful friends,   490
 Only he hath an eye to gaze on beauty,
 And dotes on what he looks, 'gainst law or duty.

'I have debated, even in my soul,
What wrong, what shame, what sorrow I shall breed.
But nothing can affection's course control,   500

495 will] Q (Will)

483 **For . . . mine** the beauty of your eyes has
 made my eyes desire you
485 **ensnared . . . night** led to your being
 caught as you are tonight
486 **will abide** endure my lust; with a pun on
 'await my wishes', as a servant or a sub-
 ject would the wishes of a monarch (*OED*
 s.v. 'abide' *v.* 15)
488 **Which** i.e. *My will*
489 **reproof** shame, reproach
490 **newly bred** revived anew
491 **crosses** obstacles, trials
492 **defends** The singular form is probably
 used because of the proximity of the
 singular *growing rose*, although noun
 phrases such as *what thorns* could
 take a singular subject in Shakespeare
 (Abbott §333 and §337). The thorni-
 ness of roses was proverbial (cf. Dent
 R182).
493 **think** here probably both 'call to
 mind that' and 'believe as a fact that'
 (the search for further synonyms for
 know presses these extended senses out
 of the word). Compare the proverb

'Honey is sweet but the bee stings' (Tilley
H553).
494 **counsel** deliberation. The word has a
 particular force in the period, since the
 ideal monarch was supposed to take
 counsel of his peers (*heedful friends*),
 rather than relying simply on his own will
 or passions in determining laws or in
 making judgements.
 will is capitalized in Q.
496 **Only he hath** he only has. Tarquin is
 deliberately simplifying the more complex
 internal debate which he has already
 undergone, in which one eye saw Lucrece
 and the other Collatine. See ll. 288–94.
497 **on what he looks** on what he looks on.
 In relative clauses the second use of the
 preposition is frequently suppressed by
 Shakespeare (Abbott §394).
500 **affection's course** the change of
 ungovernable passion. *Affection* is im-
 plicitly compared to a runaway horse
 here, following a tradition which derives
 ultimately from the chariot in Plato's
 Phaedrus 253d; see *Venus* l. 263–70 n.

Or stop the headlong fury of his speed.
I know repentant tears ensue the deed,
    Reproach, disdain, and deadly enmity,
    Yet strive I to embrace mine infamy.'

This said, he shakes aloft his Roman blade,   505
Which, like a falcon tow'ring in the skies,
Coucheth the fowl below with his wings' shade,
Whose crookèd beak threats if he mount he dies;
So under his insulting falchion lies
    Harmless Lucretia, marking what he tells   510
    With trembling fear, as fowl hear falcons' bells.

'Lucrece,' quoth he, 'this night I must enjoy thee.
If thou deny, then force must work my way:
For in thy bed I purpose to destroy thee.
That done, some worthless slave of thine I'll slay,   515
To kill thine honour with thy life's decay,
    And in thy dead arms do I mean to place him,
    Swearing I slew him seeing thee embrace him.

'So thy surviving husband shall remain
The scornful mark of every open eye;   520

---

502 **ensue** follow
506 **falcon** For the pun on *falchion*, see *l*. 176 n.
507 **Coucheth** 'causes to crouch' (*OED* 2; first cited usage in this sense)
508 **Whose** i.e. the falcon's
crookèd curved (the falchion is a curved sword)
threats threatens that
if he mount (a) if the fowl (he) ceases to crouch and flies into the air (*mount OED* 1); with a secondary sense which reflects back on the literal scene of imminent rape; (b) if the falcon (*he*) mounts as though to have intercourse ('mount' *OED* 10 and Partridge) then the fowl dies.
509 **insulting** vaunting, bragging of its conquest
511 **bells** Bells were attached to the jesses of falcons as part of their training: 'so much the greater ought your bells to be, by how much more you see your hawks giddy-headed', George Turbervile, *The Book of Falconry or Hawking* (1575), 148. The object was to frighten off surrounding birds so that the hawk would obey the fal-

coner and come to his lure. The detail suggests Tarquin is being compared to a young, headstrong bird.
514 **destroy** kill
515 **slave of thine** corresponds to Ovid's 'interimam famulum' ('I shall kill a household slave', *Fasti* 2.809). Chaucer's Tarquin threatens, 'I shal in the stable slen thy knave, | And ley hym in thy bed, and loude crye | That I the fynde in swich avouterye', *LGW* ll. 1807–9. Painter's Tarquin threatens to kill one of his own slaves. There is no definite sign that Shakespeare had Chaucer before him as he wrote, however, since a 'famulus' is one of the household retinue, and it is implicit in Ovid that Tarquin has one of Lucrece's slaves in mind. In Thomas Cooper's *Thesaurus Linguae Romanae et Britannicae* (1565), sig. L2ᵛ, Tarquin 'menaced present death, unless she would condescend unto his pleasure, adding moreover that he would kill one of her servants and lay him in bed with her'.
520 **scornful mark** object of scorn, via 'mark' *OED* 7a, 'a target, butt'

Thy kinsmen hang their heads at this disdain;
Thy issue blurred with nameless bastardy;
And thou, the author of their obloquy,
  Shalt have thy trespass cited up in rhymes,
  And sung by children in succeeding times.   525

'But if thou yield, I rest thy secret friend:
The fault unknown is as a thought unacted.
A little harm done to a great good end,
For lawful policy remains enacted.
The pois'nous simple sometime is compacted   530
  In a pure compound; being so applied
  His venom in effect is purified.

'Then, for thy husband and thy children's sake,
Tender my suit. Bequeath not to their lot
The shame that from them no device can take,   535
The blemish that will never be forgot—
Worse than a slavish wipe or birth-hour's blot:

522 **blurred** stained. Compare l. 222.
nameless Bastards were legally *nullius filius*, the son of nobody.
524 **cited up** recalled as an example. Compare *Richard III* 1.4.14–16: 'And cited up a thousand heavy times, | During the wars of York and Lancaster, | That had befall'n us.'
526 **rest** remain
526 **friend** can be used in the period as a euphemism for lover. See Sonnet *104*.1 n.
528, 530 are marked as memorable *sententiae* in Q. See ll. 87–8 n. The thought of 527 also became proverbial, but probably only after Shakespeare (Dent S477, F104.1).
528–9 'A small wrong done to achieve a great end becomes enshrined as law.' *Policy* has pejorative overtones in the period (it can mean 'merely expedient action') which give a darker undercurrent to Tarquin's sentence. Cf. Dent E112: 'The end justifies the means'.
530 **simple** 'A medicine or medicament composed or concocted of only one constituent, esp. of one herb or plant' (*OED* 6)
compacted compounded, mixed with other elements
531 **pure compound** beneficial mixture. Tarquin is attempting to exploit the moral associations of *pure*, but as a result pro-

duces an oxymoron: a *compound* is by definition adulterated.
531 **applied** either 'combined', or 'brought into contact with the surface of the skin'
532 **His** its
534 **Tender** receive favourably (last cited usage in this sense in *OED* s.v. 'tender' *v.* 2); with a play on 'receive tenderly', 'have tender regard for'
535 **device** stratagem, means (with a secondary hint at the heraldic 'devices' so prominent in ll. 204–10)
537 **slavish wipe** probably a mark or scar left by a lash (*OED* s.v. 'wipe' *n.* 2b; only cited example); perhaps, as Malone suggested, an allusion to the brand with which slaves were marked. On the branding of slaves in the sixteenth century, see Sonnet *111*.5 n. **birth-hour's blot** birthmark. Wyndham's suggestion that it refers to a heraldic symbol of illegitimacy is improbable: the point of Tarquin's argument is to distinguish hereditary marks of bastardy from natural accidents with no moral significance, such as scars and birthmarks. In any case 'marks of difference' for bastardy were not intended to display the irregularity of the bearer's birth, but to indicate that he is not the heir to the title (J. Franklyn and John Tanner, *An Encyclopedic Dictionary of Heraldry* (Oxford, 1970), 30).

For marks descried in men's nativity
Are Nature's faults, not their own infamy.'

Here, with a cockatrice' dead-killing eye,   540
He rouseth up himself, and makes a pause,
While she the picture of pure piety,
Like a white hind under the gripe's sharp claws,
Pleads in a wilderness where are no laws,
  To the rough beast that knows no gentle right,   545
  Nor aught obeys but his foul appetite.

But when a black-faced cloud the world doth threat,
In his dim mist th' aspiring mountains hiding,
From earth's dark womb some gentle gust doth get,
Which blows these pitchy vapours from their biding,   550
Hind'ring their present fall by this dividing;

550 blows] MALONE; blow Q

538 **descried** perceived
    men's nativity the moment of birth
    (rather than in the astrological conjunc-
    tions which occur at the time of birth)
539 **infamy** source of shame
540 **cockatrice** a serpent-like mythical being,
    often identified with the basilisk, whose
    stare could (proverbially) kill (Dent
    C496.2). By 1599 *OED* records that the
    word could be used to mean 'prostitute', a
    sense which may flavour the usage in this
    erotic context.
541 **rouseth up** (like a serpent about to strike,
    or like an erection)
543 **hind** doe. John Manwood, *A Treatise and
    Discourse of the Laws of the Forest* (1598),
    fo. 25ᵛ, notes that the word *hind* is proper-
    ly used of a doe of three years or more.
    gripe The word is generally used of a
    vulture (compare *vulture-olly* in l. 556),
    but can also mean 'griffin', which would
    fit the immediate setting of mythological
    animals. The image of a hind grasped by
    a griffin also combines two creatures
    which figure in heraldry, creating a
    visual, quasi-heraldic, image of Lucrece's
    fate which is in keeping with the imagery
    of the poem so far. The fact that *gripe* is
    also used as a variant spelling of 'grip'
    gives an additional edge of violence.

544 **Pleads** At the corresponding point in
    Ovid Lucrece gives way: 'succubuit famae
    victa puella metu' ('the girl gave way,
    overcome by the fear of infamy', *Fasti*
    2.810); in Livy 'her resolute modesty
    was overcome by his victorious lust'
    1.58.5 (modern texts emend to 'velut vi',
    'as if by force', here; early modern texts
    did not); Chaucer has her faint (*LGW*
    ll. 1812–18).
545 **gentle** showing the mildness and civility
    expected of someone who is well-born
548 **aspiring** soaring (with a faint hint of
    pride)
549 **get** breed. Winds were believed to be bred
    in the earth. See *Venus* ll. 1046–7 n.
550 **Which blows** Q's 'blow' may be authori-
    al, with the indefinite *some gentle gust*
    being regarded as a plural. The setting of
    this line in Q, however, is extremely com-
    pressed and may indicate a compositor
    dropped an 's' out.
    pitchy black as pitch (tar)
    biding usual home
551 **present fall** immediate shower of rain
    (*OED* s.v. 'fall' *n.* 1d; first cited usage in
    this sense)
    dividing (a) by separating the clouds from
    the mountains; (b) by breaking up the
    clouds from each other

So his unhallowed haste her words delays,
And moody Pluto winks while Orpheus plays.

Yet, foul night-waking cat, he doth but dally,
While in his hold-fast foot the weak mouse panteth;   555
Her sad behaviour feeds his vulture folly,
A swallowing gulf that even in plenty wanteth.
His ear her prayers admits, but his heart granteth
  No penetrable entrance to her plaining:
  Tears harden lust, though marble wear with raining.   560

Her pity-pleading eyes are sadly fixèd
In the remorseless wrinkles of his face.
Her modest eloquence with sighs is mixèd,
Which to her oratory adds more grace.
She puts the period often from his place,   565
  And midst the sentence so her accent breaks
  That twice she doth begin ere once she speaks.

552 **unhallowed** See l. 192 n.
  words is the subject of *delays*.
553 **moody Pluto** The god of the Roman underworld is traditionally melancholy and irascible (*moody*), but in *Met.* 10 he is so moved by the song of the bard Orpheus ('the bloodless ghosts shed tears', Golding 10.43), who is seeking the return of his wife Eurydice from the underworld, that he permits her to return. The allusion is appropriate: in Virgil's version of the Orpheus myth (*Georgics* 4.457–9) Eurydice is fleeing from a would-be rapist when she is bitten by a snake, and in Ovid's version of the story Orpheus reminds Pluto that he has 'raped' (that is, 'abducted') Proserpina (Golding, 10.28–9: 'If fame that flies about │ Of former rape report not wrong, Love coupled also you').
554–5 The pleasure of cats in playing with their prey was proverbial (Dent C127).
554 **dally** delay; play with (with a suggestion of flirting or trifling with someone)
555 **hold-fast** which grips hard and long
556 **vulture folly** predatory mad desire
557 **wanteth** feels a devouring sense of lack. For the idea that desire famishes the appetite it feeds, see *Venus* ll. 19–20 n.
559 **penetrable entrance** way in. Prince notes that *penetrable* is also associated with pity

in *Hamlet* 3.4.34–5: 'And let me wring your heart; for so I shall │ If it be made of penetrable stuff'.
559 **plaining** complaint. The word is often used of the efforts of female eloquence to fight off male aggression or to lament its consequences. Lucrece's plaints are not here even audible to the reader, who is made to participate in Tarquin's obdurate deafness.
560 Marked as a *sententia* in Q. See ll. 87–8 n. It was proverbial that 'constant dropping will wear the stone' (Dent D618). See *Venus* l. 200 n.
562 **remorseless** pitiless
564 **grace** 'Pronuntiatio', or the way of delivering a speech in tone and pacing, was thought to add to the power of words to move. Compare *Astrophil and Stella* 58, which debates whether written words or 'pronouncing grace' produce the greater effect.
565 **period** full stop
  his its
566 **accent** speech. This detail may come from Marsus's commentary on the final phase of Ovid's tale when Lucretia is unable to tell her family what has happened to her: 'she began to speak and in mid-flow she stopped her voice' ('incipit effari, mediaque in voce resistit', Marsus, 148).

She conjures him by high almighty Jove,
By knighthood, gentry, and sweet friendship's oath;
By her untimely tears, her husband's love;   570
By holy human law, and common troth;
By heaven and earth, and all the power of both,
    That to his borrowed bed he make retire,
    And stoop to honour, not to foul desire.

Quoth she: 'Reward not hospitality   575
With such black payment as thou hast pretended;
Mud not the fountain that gave drink to thee;
Mar not the thing that cannot be amended;
End thy ill aim, before thy shoot be ended:
    He is no woodman that doth bend his bow   580
    To strike a poor unseasonable doe.

'My husband is thy friend; for his sake spare me.
Thyself art mighty; for thine own sake leave me;
Myself a weakling; do not then ensnare me.
Thou look'st not like deceit; do not deceive me.   585
My sighs like whirlwinds labour hence to heave thee:

568 Much is made in Renaissance commentaries of Lucretia's silence in *Fasti* 2.801 (Marsus, 147: 'Nullae vires erant Lucretiae ad loquendum, ob pavorem, nec erat sibi mens ulla'; 'Lucretia had no strength to speak, because of her fear, nor could she think'); Shakespeare's decision to make her argue against Tarquin would have come as a shock to many early readers, and would have drawn attention to the practical ineffectiveness of her rhetoric.

569 **gentry** good breeding, gentleness of manners, courtesy

571 **troth** fidelity, honesty

573 **make retire** return. *Retire* as a noun can have the military sense 'retreat' (*OED* 3).

574 **stoop** to (a) bow as in a gesture of submission to honour (which completes the secondary sense of *retire* in l. 573 above, as Tarquin retreats and then yields); (b) lower himself to *foul desire* (*OED* 2c)

576 **pretended** proposed, offered

577 **Mud not . . . thee** became proverbial (Dent D345). Compare Sonnet 35.2, and l. 1707.

579 **ill aim** (a) wicked design; (2) inaccurate shot at the target

580 **woodman** huntsman. Foresters are frequently associated in Elizabethan literature with ungovernable lust, as in *FQ* 3.1.17.

581 **unseasonable** out of season for hunting. Lucrece, finding herself in *a wilderness where are no laws*, l. 544, desperately appeals in vain to the laws of the forest. The 'fence month', in which deer could not be hunted in forests, extended from fifteen days before midsummer until fifteen days after it. This was instituted 'So that, as those wild beasts, that are already come to their season and perfection, for the service and use of man to be taken away, there may again be others, to grow up in their places', John Manwood, *A Treatise and Discourse of the Laws of the Forest* (1598), fo. 72ᵛ. Violation of it was a serious crime.

584 **ensnare** carries the literal force of 'catch in a trap like an animal', although as *OED* suggests the sense is here being extended to the later figurative sense 'to entrap morally'.

586 **labour** combines 'exert themselves strenuously' with a sinister trace of 'to endure the pangs of labour', as though the sighs seek violently to expel Tarquin from Lucrece's body.
heave throw

If ever man were moved with woman's moans,
Be movèd with my tears, my sighs, my groans.

'All which together like a troubled ocean
Beat at thy rocky and wreck-threatening heart,   590
To soften it with their continual motion;
For stones dissolved to water do convert.
O if no harder than a stone thou art,
    Melt at my tears and be compassionate:
    Soft pity enters at an iron gate.   595

'In Tarquin's likeness I did entertain thee;
Hast thou put on his shape to do him shame?
To all the host of heaven I complain me:
Thou wrong'st his honour, wound'st his princely name.
Thou art not what thou seem'st, and if the same,   600
    Thou seem'st not what thou art, a god, a king;
    For kings like gods should govern everything.

'How will thy shame be seeded in thine age,
When thus thy vices bud before thy spring?
If in thy hope thou dar'st do such outrage,   605
What dar'st thou not when once thou art a king?

590 **wreck-threatening** which threatens shipwreck
591–2 Compare l. 560 n. Even the hardest hearts proverbially melt (Dent H310.1).
597 i.e. 'are you an evil spirit which has impersonated Tarquin?' This begins a string of rhetorical questions (*interrogationes*), of which Peacham, sig. L3ʳ, says, 'sometimes it is used for vehemency'.
598 **complain me** The reflexive form is rare and archaic by 1594, and occurs most frequently in ballads and songs of female complaint.
600 **if the same** if you are what you appear to be
601 Compare the proverb 'Kings are gods on earth' (Dent G275. 1).
602 **govern** 'control' rather than simply 'enjoy supremacy over'. A governor is originally a 'helmsman' (Latin *gubernator*), or one who directs and regulates. It was a commonplace in political theory of the period that 'As God is not touched

with any affections or passions, but ruleth and governeth all things perfectly by his providence: so after his example a prince laying aside the perturbations of his soul must follow reason only in all his doings', Pierre de la Primaudaye, *The French Academy*, trans. Thomas Bowles (1589), 611–12. *Everything* carries the force 'all things, even yourself and your desires'. Although this line is a *sententia* it is not simply absolutist in its force, and can be connected with the poem's general unease about what happens in a monarchy when the king is overwhelmed with passion.
603 **be seeded** bear fruit, produce further offspring. The phrase unites Lucrece's horror at the thought she might be the person to bear Tarquin's offspring with a distant allusion to the parable of the Sower (Luke 8: 5–15).
605 **in thy hope** in your expectations as an heir

O, be remembered, no outrageous thing
   From vassal actors can be wiped away;
   Then kings' misdeeds cannot be hid in clay.

'This deed will make thee only loved for fear, 610
But happy monarchs still are feared for love.
With foul offenders thou perforce must bear,
When they in thee the like offences prove.
If but for fear of this, thy will remove.
   For princes are the glass, the school, the book, 615
   Where subjects' eyes do learn, do read, do look.

'And wilt thou be the school where lust shall learn?
Must he in thee read lectures of such shame?
Wilt thou be glass wherein it shall discern
Authority for sin, warrant for blame 620

---

607 **be remembered** recall to mind (still current in literary texts from the 590s, but falling out of use shortly thereafter)

608 **vassal actors** from low-born people who do a deed

609 **Then . . . clay** 'Then it is *a fortiori* unlikely that the sins of rulers can simply be buried in oblivion and forgotten.' The visibility of the deeds of princes was a standard topos on treatises on the education of a monarch: so Primaudaye, *The French Academy*, 611: 'He must be given to understand that his life is in the face of all the world, that he can do nothing that will be hid'.

610 **only loved** loved only. Volumes of advice for princes in the period regularly argued that it is better to be loved than feared, after Cicero, *De Officiis* 2.7.23; so Guevara's *Dial of Princes*, trans. Thomas North (1557), sig. m1ʳ: 'O it is a goodly matter for a prince to be beloved of his subjects, and a goodly thing also for the Realm, to be fearful of their king'. Guevara later notes (sig. m6ᵛ) that 'if the miserable Tarquin [Guevara confuses him with his father, Tarquinius Superbus] had been beloved in Rome he had never been deprived of the Realm, for committing adultery with Lucretia'.

612–13 'You will have to show tolerance towards (*bear with*) vicious criminals since they will be able to show that you

have offended in the same way.' Compare the proverb 'He that will blame another must be blameless himself' (Dent F107), and *Measure* 2.2.181–2: 'Thieves for their robbery have authority | When judges steal themselves.'

614 **but only**
   thy will remove change your lustful intention

615 **glass mirror** (from which examples of conduct are taken)

615–16 Compare *2 Henry IV* 2.3.31–2: 'He was the mark and glass, copy and book, | That fashioned others.' Lucrece again uses the standard arguments of a Renaissance prince-book, that monarchs should make their actions exemplary: as a work printed by Field in 1594 put it, 'everyone fashioneth himself after the example of the king', Justus Lipsius, *Six Books of Politics or Civil Doctrine*, trans. William Jones (1594), 26.

618 **lectures** lessons which are read

620 **Authority** (a) prior example; (b) a document which grants privileges
   warrant for blame a document which safeguards or authorizes wicked actions. A *warrant* could be specifically 'A writing issued by the sovereign, an officer of state, or an administrative body, authorizing those to whom it is addressed to perform some act' (*OED* 9a).

To privilege dishonour in thy name?
　　Thou back'st reproach against long-living laud,
　　And mak'st fair reputation but a bawd.

'Hast thou command? By him that gave it thee,
From a pure heart command thy rebel will.　　　　　　　625
Draw not thy sword to guard iniquity,
For it was lent thee all that brood to kill.
Thy princely office how canst thou fulfil,
　　When patterned by thy fault foul sin may say
　　He learned to sin, and thou didst teach the way?　　　630

'Think but how vile a spectacle it were
To view thy present trespass in another:
Men's faults do seldom to themselves appear;
Their own transgressions partially they smother.
This guilt would seem death-worthy in thy brother:　　　635
　　O, how are they wrapped in with infamies,
　　That from their own misdeeds askance their eyes?

'To thee, to thee, my heaved-up hands appeal,
Not to seducing lust, thy rash relier.

639 lust . . . relier] Q; lust . . . reply Q6; lust's outrageous fire GILDON 1714

621 **privilege** give immunity from prosecution to (i.e. *Blame* is like a minor court functionary who is allowed in Tarquin's *name* not to prosecute *Dishonour*). Again this implies an abuse of specific royal powers: privileges were granted in the Queen's *name* to exercise specific freedoms such as the printing of books of music, or the manufacture of certain types of goods.
622 **back'st** support (the sense 'bet on' suggested by Roe is not otherwise found before the 1690s)
　　laud praise
624 **him** God (the mental landscape is clearly that of the sixteenth century)
627 **brood** i.e. that of iniquity. (The breeding of evil once again emerges through Lucrece's language.)
628 **princely office** regal duty. 'Prince' and 'King' were used synonymously in this period. *Office* refers to a set of reciprocal duties to kin and country, rather than simply to a constitutional role.
629 **patterned by** shown a precedent by
632 **trespass** sin, as in the Lord's Prayer 'forgive us our trespasses'

634 **partially** with partiality to themselves
634 **smother** (a) conceal, hush up; (b) suffocate, do away with
636 **wrapped in with** enveloped by. The unusual use of two prepositions with *wrap* suggests unholy collaboration. The verb evokes (a) beleaguered contamination with sin ('to surround, encompass, or beset with, some (esp. prejudicial) condition of things, as sin, trouble, sorrow' (*OED* 4a)); (b) deception ('To involve or enfold (a subject or matter) so as to obscure or disguise the true or full nature of it' (*OED* 5a); (c) stifling and threatening enclosure ('To invest, environ, or beset (a person, etc.); to encompass in some condition' (*OED* 6a).
637 **askance** turn aside (the only cited example in *OED* of the verb, formed by enallage. See *Venus* l. 830 n.)
638 **heaved-up** Compare the gesture of joy at l. 111.
639 **rash relier** 'your headstrong dependant'. Editors have had difficulty with the phrase, as the collation shows. It is sometimes glossed 'lust, which you rashly rely

I sue for exiled majesty's repeal: 640
Let him return, and flatt'ring thoughts retire.
His true respect will prison false desire,
    And wipe the dim mist from thy doting eyne,
    That thou shalt see thy state, and pity mine.'

'Have done,' quoth he. 'My uncontrollèd tide   645
Turns not, but swells the higher by this let.
Small lights are soon blown out; huge fires abide,
And with the wind in greater fury fret.
The petty streams, that pay a daily debt
    To their salt sovereign, with their fresh falls' haste   650
    Add to his flow, but alter not his taste.'

'Thou art,' quoth she, 'a sea, a sovereign king,
And, lo, there falls into thy boundless flood
Black lust, dishonour, shame, misgoverning,

---

650 sovereign, . . . haste͏ₐ| DYCE; ~ₐ . . . ~, Q   650 falls'| Q (fals)

---

on' (Prince). Since this is the first cited usage of *relier* in *OED* and the only usage in Shakespeare it is not possible to be sure, but the sense 'rash lust' which relies on you' is grammatically more natural: Lucrece appeals directly to Tarquin—*To thee, to thee*—not to the inferior and volatile passion of lust which depends upon its overlord Tarquin to sustain it. *Relier* might therefore derive from a sense of the verb 'rely' active in the 1590s: 'to be a vassal or subject of another' (*OED* 4b), or from the usual Shakespearian sense of 'to depend upon with full trust or confidence' (*OED* 5). Lust then would be *rash* not by virtue of its ill-advised relience on Tarquin (as Schmidt suggests), but because of its intrinsic wildness which qualifies its loyalty to its overlord. Wyndham suggests that *relier* may be a variant form of *rallier*, one who gathers troops together.

640 **repeal** 'Recall, as from banishment' (*OED* 1); i.e. 'bring back the gentleness which is true majesty'. The line anticipates the exile of the Tarquinii to which the Argument has drawn the reader's attention.

641 **flatt'ring thoughts** A standard way of alleging corruption in the government of the realm without impugning the authority of the monarch was to claim that he was misled by flatterers or bad counsellors.

643 **eyne** eyes (the archaic plural form is used to preserve the rhyme)

644 **state** (a) condition; (b) high rank, with its accompanying obligations to be virtuous

645-6 Compare the proverb 'The stream stopped swells the higher' (Dent S929).

647-8 Compare the proverb 'The wind puts out small lights but enrages great fires' (Dent W448a).

647 **lights** flames; torches (like that which Tarquin is still carrying)

648 **fret** move in agitation (like the sea, which is what makes the transition to the image in the following line). The word can also be used of the consuming destructive energy of the passions (*OED* 3b), or *fury*.

649 **petty** minor

650 **salt sovereign** i.e. the sea. The streams contribute to the bulk of the sea without qualifying its bitterness, as Lucrece's tearful persuasions arouse Tarquin further without altering his intention. The conceit of the sea as a monarch to which streams pay tribute is common in the 1590s.

Who seek to stain the ocean of thy blood. 655
If all these petty ills shall change thy good
    Thy sea within a puddle's womb is hersèd,
    And not the puddle in thy sea dispersèd.

'So shall these slaves be king, and thou their slave,
Thou, nobly base; they, basely dignified; 660
Thou their fair life, and they thy fouler grave;
Thou loathèd in their shame; they in thy pride.
The lesser thing should not the greater hide:
    The cedar stoops not to the base shrub's foot,
    But low shrubs wither at the cedar's root. 665

'So let thy thoughts, low vassals to thy state—'
'No more,' quoth he: 'By heaven I will not hear thee.
Yield to my love; if not, enforcèd hate
Instead of love's coy touch shall rudely tear thee.
That done, despitefully I mean to bear thee 670
    Unto the base bed of some rascal groom
    To be thy partner in this shameful doom.'

This said, he sets his foot upon the light,
For light and lust are deadly enemies.

---

655 **Who** which (this form of the pronoun need not imply a personification allegory, since it is a regular neuter form; see l. 296 n.)
blood implies both 'passions' and 'bloodline'.

656 **good** goodness

657, 658 **puddle** These were fouler than they are today (with no sewers, no road sweepers, and with horses and citizens enriching them with ordure), and could be used as emblems of moral turpitude (*OED* 2a). Lucrece's argument is that if the passions can contaminate Tarquin then his regal grandeur is in fact foul and of small scale already.
hearsèd entombed (with the implication that it is both mortal and of small scale)

659 **slaves** the *petty ills*, the passions which ought to be subordinated to the reason

662 **Thou . . . pride** 'You are hated for the shame which is really theirs, they glory in the pride which is properly yours.' The antithetical structure of the line implies a

verb antithetical to *loathèd* in its second half.

664–5 **cedar** is the tree of kings. Lucrece may here be inverting a proverb about the dangers of high position: 'High cedars fall when low shrubs remain' (Dent C208).

664 **stoops** See l. 574 n.

666 **state**—Lucrece is forced to break off her sentence before it is finished. When done deliberately in rhetoric this was known as 'aposiopesis', and was often presented as a figure by which to 'indicate passion or anger' (Quintilian 9.2.54), as well as sorrow (Peacham, sig. N1ᵛ). Here it is the passions of her audience rather than those of the orator which break off the sentence. Compare ll. 1534 and 1717.

667 **heaven** is monosyllabic.

668 **enforcèd hate** hateful force

669 **coy** tentative, reserved

670 **despitefully** with complete contempt for you; shamefully

671 **rascal** one who completely lacks rank or status

Shame folded up in blind concealing night,   675
When most unseen, then most doth tyrannize.
The wolf hath seized his prey; the poor lamb cries,
   Till with her own white fleece her voice controlled
   Entombs her outcry in her lips' sweet fold.

For with the nightly linen that she wears   680
He pens her piteous clamours in her head,
Cooling his hot face in the chastest tears
That ever modest eyes with sorrow shed.
O that prone lust should stain so pure a bed!
   The spots whereof, could weeping purify,   685
   Her tears should drop on them perpetually.

But she hath lost a dearer thing than life,
And he hath won what he would lose again.
This forcèd league doth force a further strife;
This momentary joy breeds months of pain;   690
This hot desire converts to cold disdain.

677 seized] Q (ceazd)   684 prone] Q; proud Q4; foul Q6

675 **folded up** enveloped (possibly 'blind-folded'). Compare *Venus* l. 822.

677 **seized his prey** Q's 'ceazd his pray' allows for a secondary, harshly incongruous, reading: 'ceased his pray[er]'. Compare Chaucer's 'Right as a wolf that fynt a lomb aloon, | To whom shall she compleyne, or make moon?' (*LGW* ll. 1798–9) and *Fasti* 2.800: 'parva sub infesto cum iacet agna lupo' ('a poor lamb that lies beneath the ravening wolf').

678 **white fleece** literally her sheets, *nightly linen* (l. 680), which Tarquin uses to muffle her cries

679 **fold** (a) sheepfold; (b) the lips are compared to a fold of fabric doubled over

680 **nightly linen** Since Elizabethans usually slept naked this probably refers to sheets rather than to a nightgown (although commentators have haggled over this). Partridge, *Gramma-*, 58, suggests 'cloth worn round the head' and compares *Merry Wives* 4.2.73.

684 **prone** (a) eager, headstrong (*OED* 7); (b) lying down, horizontal

686 **should** would

687–8 **lost . . . won** The simple antithesis is knocked off balance by the radical incommensurability of what she has lost (the permanent possessions of virtue and reputation) and he has won (a moment of sexual pleasure). There may be a distant echo of Ovid's 'Quid, victor, gaudes? haec te victoria perdet' (*Fasti* 2.811): 'why do you rejoice in your victory? This victory is your undoing.' Compare l. 730.

689 **forcèd league** the enforced truce; with a play on *league* meaning 'marriage', as in l. 383

683–700 For a comparable treatment of the self-defeating effects of lust, see Sonnet 129. Compare the proverb 'What is sweet in the mouth is oft sour in the maw (stomach)' (Dent M1265).

690 **breeds . . . pain** acts as a reminder of the ten months (as it was usually thought of in this period) between conception and the pain of birth

691 **converts** turns into (often used in the period, as here, to suggest a change of something into its diametrical opposite)

Pure chastity is rifled of her store,
And lust, the thief, far poorer than before.

Look as the full-fed hound, or gorgèd hawk,
Unapt for tender smell, or speedy flight,   695
Make slow pursuit, or altogether balk
The prey wherein by nature they delight;
So surfeit-taking Tarquin fares this night:
    His taste delicious, in digestion souring,
    Devours his will that lived by foul devouring.   700

O deeper sin than bottomless conceit
Can comprehend in still imagination!
Drunken desire must vomit his receipt
Ere he can see his own abomination:
While Lust is in his pride no exclamation   705
    Can curb his heat, or rein his rash desire,
    Till like a jade, self-will himself doth tire.

And then with lank and lean discoloured cheek,
With heavy eye, knit brow, and strengthless pace,
Feeble desire all recreant, poor and meek,   710
Like to a bankrupt beggar wails his case.
The flesh being proud, desire doth fight with grace:

712 proud] Q; prov'd Q4

692 **rifled** plundered. The word could be used
of the unscrupulous sacking and despoil-
ing of a city.
695 **Unapt** unsuitable
    tender sensitive (*OED* cites this passage as
    the last usage in sense 10a, 'Having a
    delicate or finely sensitive perception of
    smell'). Prince suggests 'delicate or weak
    smell' which a hound would need a keen
    appetite to follow. The analogy with
    speedy flight, however, suggests that *tender
    smell* refers to the abilities of the hound
    rather than to the qualities of the thing
    pursued.
696 **balk** let slip
699–700 'The initially delicious taste sours
    as he digests, and eventually destroys the
    very appetite of lust that prompted it.'
701 **bottomless conceit** infinite imagination
702 **still imagination** silent contemplation.
    Still may also suggest 'continuous' by
    extension of its adverbial usage.
703 **receipt** that which he has received

704 **abomination** Q's spelling 'abhomina-
tion' recalls the contemporary (false)
etymology of the word from 'ab homine',
that which is alien to the nature of
humanity; so both 'his transformation
into something unlike a man' and 'act
that gives rise to a sense of disgust and
defilement'.
705 **exclamation** vehement reproach, outcry
706 **curb . . . rein** The metaphors allude to
the tradition of presenting desire as an
uncontrollable horse. See l. 500 n.
707 **jade** a broken-down and worthless horse
(used by extension of a prostitute)
    self-will persistent sexual self-indulgence
708 **lank and lean** a common doublet, mean-
ing 'thin and withered'
710 **recreant** like a defeated soldier
711 **wails his case** laments his misfortune.
Compare Sonnet 29.1–2.
712 **The flesh . . . grace** The conjunction of
these terms creates a strong theological
resonance: *flesh* is St Paul's term for fallen

For there it revels, and when that decays
The guilty rebel for remission prays.

So fares it with this faultful lord of Rome, 715
Who this accomplishment so hotly chasèd;
For now against himself he sounds this doom,
That through the length of times he stands disgracèd.
Besides, his soul's fair temple is defacèd,
    To whose weak ruins muster troops of cares, 720
    To ask the spotted princess how she fares.

She says her subjects with foul insurrection
Have battered down her consecrated wall,
And by their mortal fault brought in subjection
Her immortality, and made her thrall 725
To living death and pain perpetual,

mankind before it has received, and while
it resists the acceptance of, God's *grace*.
Proud suggests both the chief deadly sin
and 'sexual arousal'.

713 **there** in the flesh
    that the flesh
714 **for remission prays** begs for forgiveness.
Remission is the word most frequently
used of the forgiveness of sins, as in the
general confession in the Book of Com-
mon Prayer: 'The Almighty and merciful
Lord grant you absolution and remission
of all your sins, true repentance, amend-
ment of life, and the grace and consola-
tion of his Holy Spirit'.
715 **faultful** faulty, culpable. Q spells 'fault-
full', which may be a compositorial quirk
(this is only the second cited usage in
OED, so a compositor may have felt awk-
ward with the word), but may suggest a
sense 'full up, engorged with sins' and
bring back the imagery of self-disgusted
over-eating from ll. 699–703.
716 **accomplishment** aim, achievement
717 **sounds . . . doom** proclaims this judge-
ment (*sounds* gives an overtone of the last
trump)
718 **length of times** full duration of all
periods of history
719 **temple** of the body, with an allusion to
'Know ye not that ye are the Temple of
God, and that the spirit of God dwelleth in
you?', 1 Corinthians 3: 16. Compare also
Erasmus in 'The Godly Feast': 'No less

choice is the speech of Socrates in Plato:
"the human soul is placed in the body as if
in a garrison which it must not abandon
except by the commander's order, or
remain in longer than suits him who
stationed him there" ', *The Colloquies*, ed.
Craig R. Thompson (Chicago, 1965), 67.
720–8 Tarquin's soul is presented as a female
ruler of a town under siege, whose defile-
ment is described in terms which could
be used of Lucrece. This establishes a
shocking affinity between the supposed
victor and his victim. The passage recalls
Lucrece's mental processes in ll. 442–8
above, even to the point of echoing the
verb *muster* (l. 442).
721 **spotted princess** defiled ruler (Tarquin's
soul)
722 **subjects** i.e. the passions
723 **consecrated** sanctified; continues the
image of the *temple* from l. 719 and gains
intensity from the earlier references to
Tarquin as *unhallowed* at ll. 192, 392, 552.
724 **mortal** (a) deadly; (b) characteristic of a
fallen being
726 **pain perpetual** The poem keeps the pos-
sibility of perpetual damnation in play
while also allowing for more appropri-
ately pagan forms of punishment. So this
phrase suggests that (a) Tarquin may be
damned in hell; (b) his future reputation
and that of his heirs will be marked for
ever as a result of his crime; (c) he will feel
the misery of his violation as long as he
lives.

Which in her prescience she controllèd still,
But her foresight could not forestall their will.

Ev'n in this thought through the dark night he stealeth,
A captive victor that hath lost in gain,   730
Bearing away the wound that nothing healeth,
The scar that will despite of cure remain,
Leaving his spoil perplexed in greater pain.
    She bears the load of lust he left behind,
    And he the burden of a guilty mind.   735

He, like a thievish dog creeps sadly thence;
She, like a wearied lamb lies panting there.
He scowls and hates himself for his offence;
She, desperate, with her nails her flesh doth tear.
He faintly flies, sweating with guilty fear;   740
    She stays exclaiming on the direful night.
    He runs and chides his vanished loathed delight.

He thence departs, a heavy convertite;
She there remains a hopeless castaway.
He in his speed looks for the morning light;   745

727–8 'The soul by virtue of her powers of anticipation governed her subjects, the passions, but her foreknowledge could not prevent their impassioned rebellion.'

727 **Which** i.e. her subjects, the passions

730 **captive victor** For the possible Ovidian origins of this paradox, see l. 687–8 n.

732 **scar** 'Though the wound be healed yet the scar remains' was proverbial (Dent W929).

733 **Leaving his spoil** is a paradox: spoils are normally valuable things which are captured and taken away from a city which has been sacked. Here Lucrece is left behind and only the wounds of shame are removed. There may be a play on the verb *spoil* in the sense 'to mar or vitiate completely or seriously' (*OED* 11a).

734 **load of lust** (a) burden of guilt; (b) mass of semen. *Bears* and *burden* are frequently used of childbearing (*OED* s.v. 'burden' 4a). They suggest that Lucrece is pregnant with Tarquin's child, and he with guilt. Tarquin does not carry out his

threat to kill her, which increases the atmosphere of guilt: it either implies that Lucrece did consent to him under duress in order to save Collatine's family from disgrace, or that he is so overburdened by guilt that he cannot carry out his threat.

739 Compare Lucrece's later attempt to tear the image of Sinon, l. 1564.

740 **faintly** timidly (*OED* 2)

741 **exclaiming on** blaming; protesting against
    direful dreadful

743–1589 There is no equivalent for this section of the poem in Ovid or Livy, in which Lucretia simply summons her husband and her father.

743 **convertite** penitent (technically 'A professed convert to a religious faith' (*OED* 1), but the word is only first recorded from 1592, so has some flexibility)

744 **castaway** (a) someone who has been abandoned (by Tarquin); (b) a lost soul, reprobate from God (*OED* B). See Sonnet *80*.13.

She prays she never may behold the day.
'For day,' quoth she, 'Night's scapes doth open lay,
    And my true eyes have never practised how
    To cloak offences with a cunning brow.

'They think not but that every eye can see   750
The same disgrace which they themselves behold,
And therefore would they still in darkness be,
To have their unseen sin remain untold;
For they their guilt with weeping will unfold,
    And grave, like water that doth eat in steel.   755
    Upon my cheeks what helpless shame I feel.'

Here she exclaims against repose and rest,
And bids her eyes hereafter still be blind.
She wakes her heart by beating on her breast,
And bids it leap from thence, where it may find   760
Some purer chest to close so pure a mind.
    Frantic with grief thus breathes she forth her spite,
    Against the unseen secrecy of night:

'O comfort-killing Night, image of hell,
Dim register and notary of shame,   765
Black stage for tragedies and murders fell,

---

755 in] Q; e'en *conj.* Taylor

746 This line ironically recalls the traditional *aubade* in which a lover tries to stop the arrival of day in order to prolong the joys of the night. See e.g. Ovid, *Amores* 1.13.
747 **scapes** 'A transgression due to thoughtlessness; also, with different notion, a breaking out from moral restraint, an outrageous sin; often applied to a breach of chastity' (*OED* 2). Compare the proverb 'What is done by night appears by day' (Dent N179).
748 **true eyes** On the simple virtue of Lucrece's eyes, see ll. 99–105.
752 **would they** they wished that they would
754 **unfold** relate
755 **grave** engrave, etch
    like water . . . steel *Aqua fortis* (nitric acid) is the particular kind of water *that* might wear steel away—although ordinary water might do so over a long period.

757 **exclaims against** accuses. Compare l. 741 n.
761 **chest** (a) breast; (b) coffer
    close enclose
762 **spite** outrage, injury, harm (*OED* 1); sometimes with an undercurrent of 'A strong feeling of (contempt,) hatred or ill-will' (*OED* 2a)
764–70 The complaint is similar to that in *FQ* 3.4.55, 58.
765 **register** 'A book or volume in which regular entry is made of particulars or details of any kind' (*OED* 1)
    notary scribe
766 **Black stage** Malone supposed that 'the stage was hung with black when tragedies were performed'. The evidence for this is slight, however, so this may be nothing more than a metaphor, although compare *1 Henry VI* 1.1.1.

Vast sin-concealing chaos, nurse of blame,
Blind muffled bawd, dark harbour for defame,
   Grim cave of death, whisp'ring conspirator
   With close-tongued treason and the ravisher.   770

'O hateful, vaporous, and foggy Night,
Since thou art guilty of my cureless crime,
Muster thy mists to meet the eastern light,
Make war against proportioned course of time;
Or if thou wilt permit the sun to climb   775
   His wonted height, yet, ere he go to bed,
   Knit poisonous clouds about his golden head.

'With rotten damps ravish the morning air;
Let their exhaled unwholesome breaths make sick
The life of purity, the supreme fair,   780
Ere he arrive his weary noontide prick,
And let thy musty vapours march so thick
   That in their smoky ranks his smothered light
   May set at noon, and make perpetual night.

'Were Tarquin night, as he is but night's child,   785
The silver-shining queen he would distain;

782 musty] Q; misty Q3

767 **Blame** 'Blameworthiness, culpability; fault' (*OED* 3)
768 **blind muffled bawd** a pimp so heavily disguised as to be invisible. *Muffled* means 'Wrapped or covered up, esp. about the face, for the purpose of concealment or disguise' (*OED* 1; first cited usage) and *blind* means 'dark, obscure' (*OED* 6a).
   harbour shelter, lodging (*OED* 1; used especially of places found by undesirable guests or homeless people)
   defame slander
770 **close-tongued** secretive. Those who plot treason keep their plots *close*, or secret.
774 **proportioned . . . time** the regular passage of the hours. There is a painful reminiscence here of the lover in Ovid's *Amores* 1.13, who urges the dawn not to break in order to prolong his night of bliss; Lucrece wishes night to continue in order to hide her shame.
777 **Knit** join together in a dense clump
778 **ravish** seize or spoil; with an evident reflection on Lucrece's own condition

779 **exhaled** Damp and mist were believed to be breathed out of the earth.
780 **life of purity** (a) the animating principle (*OED* s.v. 'life' 5a) of goodness, the sun; (b) a mode of life founded on virtue
781 **arrive** arrive at
   noontide prick the dot of noon; the point at which the hands of a sundial are vertical, as in *3 Henry VI* (*True Tragedy*) 1.4.34–5: 'Now Phaëton hath tumbled from his car, | And made an evening at the noontide prick'.
782 **musty** damp, foetid. Q3–9 simplify to 'misty'.
   thick densely (the adverbial usage is rare in Shakespeare's period)
785 **but night's child** i.e. merely an offshoot of the true wickedness of night
786 **silver-shining queen** the moon; Diana, goddess of the moon, was also goddess of chastity
   distain (a) defile; (b) dim the brightness of

Her twinkling handmaids too (by him defiled)
Through night's black bosom should not peep again.
So should I have co-partners in my pain,
    And fellowship in woe doth woe assuage,   790
    As palmers' chat makes short their pilgrimage.

'Where now I have no-one to blush with me,
To cross their arms and hang their heads with mine,
To mask their brows and hide their infamy;
But I alone, alone must sit and pine,   795
Seasoning the earth with showers of silver brine,
    Mingling my talk with tears, my grief with groans,
    Poor wasting monuments of lasting moans.

'O Night, thou furnace of foul reeking smoke!
Let not the jealous day behold that face,   800
Which underneath thy black all-hiding cloak
Immodestly lies martyred with disgrace.
Keep still possession of thy gloomy place,
    That all the faults which in thy reign are made
    May likewise be sepulchred in thy shade.   805

'Make me not object to the tell-tale day;
The light will show charactered in my brow

---

791 palmers' chat makes] Q; palmers that make Q4   791 their] Q5 the Q4

---

787 **twinkling handmaids** the stars. Elizabeth I was particularly concerned with the chastity of her maids of honour, and in 1592 banished Sir Walter Ralegh from the court for his secret marriage to Elizabeth Throckmorton.

790 **And . . . assuage** Compare the proverb 'It is good to have company in misery' (Dent C571).

791 **palmers'** Pilgrims who had returned from the Holy Land would carry a palm-leaf. Compare the proverb 'Good company makes short miles' (Dent C566).

792 **Where** whereas (Abbott §134).

793 **cross their arms** Crossing the arms was a conventional expression of love melancholy on the Elizabethan stage, as Mote's parody reveals in *L.L.L.* 3.1.15–18: 'with your hat penthouse-like o'er the shop of your eyes, with your arms crossed on your thin-belly doublet like a rabbit on a spit'.

794 **mask their brows** conceal their expression; possibly also with an allusion to the habit onstage of signifying grief by pulling one's hat down over one's face, as in *Macbeth* 4.3.209

796 **Seasoning** salting. Compare *A Lover's Complaint* l. 18.

798 **wasting monuments** The phrase evokes (a) 'wasted reminders'; (b) 'memorials which are perpetually wasting away'; (c) 'efforts of memory which deplete the one who remembers'. The image may develop the repeated references to water wearing away the permanence of steel and stone (at ll. 592, 755, 959).

799 **reeking smoke** is a virtual tautology, since *reeking* means 'smoking' rather than 'stinking' in this period, but the word's associations with recently spilled blood give it a sinister edge. See Sonnet 130.8 n.

802 **martyred** keeps holiness to the fore, although it can simply mean 'cruelly slaughtered'.

287

The story of sweet chastity's decay,
The impious breach of holy wedlock vow.
Yea, the illiterate that know not how   810
  To cipher what is writ in learnèd books
  Will quote my loathsome trespass in my looks.

'The nurse to still her child will tell my story,
And fright her crying babe with Tarquin's name;
The orator to deck his oratory   815
Will couple my reproach to Tarquin's shame.
Feast-finding minstrels, tuning my defame,
  Will tie the hearers to attend each line,
  How Tarquin wrongèd me, I Collatine.

'Let my good name, that senseless reputation,   820
For Collatine's dear love be kept unspotted.
If that be made a theme for disputation
The branches of another root are rotted,
And undeserved reproach to him allotted,

---

809 wedlock] Q; wedlocks Q3   812 quote] Q (cote)

803 **place** habitual place of abode; almost 'seat, throne'

805 **sepulchred** entombed. The earliest cited forms of the verb in *OED* are from Shakespeare. Stressed on the second syllable.

806 **object** exposed to the view of (a participular adjective)

807 **charactered** enscribed. The emphasis is on the second syllable.

809 **The ... vow** The breach is Tarquin's, but the way of putting it transfers the shame to Lucrece: she, not Tarquin, has made the *vow*.

811 **cipher** interpret. The verb is also used at ll. 207 and 1396.

812 **quote** Q's form 'cote' is an archaic spelling of 'quote' (*OED* s.v. 'cote' *v.* 3), meaning 'To take mental note of; to notice, observe, mark, scrutinize' (*OED* 5b); but there might just also be a play on 'coat' in the heraldic sense of 'coat of arms', especially since the previous use of *cipher* in the poem (l. 207) has a heraldic setting.

813–18 express the horror of a literate person who knows that she will enter the store of popular and learned exemplary fables as an example of sin. The passage

has points of similarity with Cleopatra's fear that in the future 'I shall see ¦ Some squeaking Cleopatra boy my greatness ¦ I'th' posture of a whore' (*Antony* 5.2.215–17), but lacks the queenly fear that the medium in which she will be recorded alone will vulgarize her: Lucrece is horrified above all by the moral associations of her tale in the future. Compare Livy 1.58.10: 'nor in the time to come shall ever unchaste woman live through the example of Lucretia'.

815 **deck** adorn

816 **couple** link. Lucrece's language after the rape is persistently riven with secondary sexual senses: *OED* 3a, 'To join in wedlock or sexual union'.

817 **Feast-finding** roving minstrels who move from house to house performing at feasts **tuning my defame** turning my infamy into harmony

819 **I Collatine** (and the singers will claim that) I wronged Collatine

820 **senseless reputation** (a) reputation for lacking sensuality or lust; (b) reputation which in fact has no reason behind it

822 **theme for disputation** See l. 246 n.

823 **another root** (of Collatine's family tree)

288

That is as clear from this attaint of mine   825
As I, ere this, was pure to Collatine.

'O unseen shame, invisible disgrace!
O unfelt sore, crest-wounding private scar!
Reproach is stamped in Collatinus' face,
And Tarquin's eye may read the mot afar: 830
How he in peace is wounded, not in war.
    Alas, how many bear such shameful blows,
    Which not themselves but he that gives them knows.

'If, Collatine, thine honour lay in me,
From me by strong assault it is bereft: 835
My honey lost, and I, a drone-like bee,
Have no perfection of my summer left,
But robbed and ransacked by injurious theft.
    In thy weak hive a wand'ring wasp hath crept,
    And sucked the honey which thy chaste bee kept.   840

'Yet am I guilty of thy honour's wrack;
Yet for thy honour did I entertain him.
Coming from thee I could not put him back,
For it had been dishonour to disdain him.
Besides, of weariness he did complain him,   845
    And talked of virtue—O unlooked-for evil
    When virtue is profaned in such a devil.

'Why should the worm intrude the maiden bud?
Or hateful cuckoos hatch in sparrows' nests?

825 **attaint** stain, dishonour. See *Venus* l. 741 and Sonnet 82.2.
828 **crest-wounding** marring the family crest. On heraldic marks of shame, see l. 206 n.
829 **Reproach** shame (with perhaps a secondary sense of 'shameful rebuke of me')
830 **mot** a family motto or saying which accompanies a coat of arms (a very recent introduction to English)
831–2 These lines are marked in Q as *sententiae*. See ll. 87–8 n.
835 **bereft** taken away by force
836 **drone-like** Drones are male bees which defend the Queen. Since they eat but do not gather honey, they are often treated as types of worthless idlers (as in Dent D612.1: 'To eat honey like a drone').

837 **perfection** honey, the sweetest production of summer
841 **wrack** ruin
843 **put him back** repulse him (*OED* s.v. 'put' 40a). Compare *P. Pilgrim* 18.24. Lucrece's argument awkwardly combines the moment when she welcomed Tarquin as her husband's friend and the moment when she was unable to repulse his attack.
844 **disdain** (a) not to welcome him; (b) to resist his advances
847 **profaned** desecrated
848 **intrude** enter forcibly (5a; the only cited example in *OED*). The transitive use of a normally intransitive verb compounds the physical with a linguistic violation.

Or toads infect fair founts with venom mud?   850
Or tyrant folly lurk in gentle breasts?
Or kings be breakers of their own behests?
    But no perfection is so absolute
    That some impurity doth not pollute.

'The agèd man that coffers up his gold   855
Is plagued with cramps, and gouts, and painful fits,
And scarce hath eyes his treasure to behold,
But like still-pining Tantalus he sits,
And useless barns the harvest of his wits,
    Having no other pleasure of his gain   860
    But torment that it cannot cure his pain.

'So then he hath it when he cannot use it,
And leaves it to be mastered by his young,
Who, in their pride, do presently abuse it:
Their father was too weak, and they too strong   865
To hold their cursèd-blessèd fortune long.
    The sweets we wish for turn to loathèd sours
    Even in the moment that we call them ours.

'Unruly blasts wait on the tender spring;
Unwholesome weeds take root with precious flowers;   870
The adder hisses where the sweet birds sing;

---

871 hisses] Q; hisseth Q3

850 **founts** fountain (the first cited example of this poetic form in *OED*). Compare l. 577 n. For the association between inchastity and toads, see *Othello* 4.2.59–63.

851 **folly** lustfulness (*OED* 3a)

852 **behests** commands, injunctions

853 **absolute** perfect. This line is marked in Q as a *sententia*. See l. 87–8 n.

858 **still-pining Tantalus** Tantalus is 'permanently starving' since in the underworld fruit is suspended above him which rises up as he attempts to reach it. Tantalus was presented as a miser by Erasmus in the *Adagia*; Baldwin, 134–5. See *Venus* l. 599 n.

859 **barns** puts in a barn (the first cited example of the verb in *OED*, formed by enallage. See *Venus* l. 830). Baldwin, 135, compares a note in the 1560 Geneva Bible on Luke 12: 15: 'Christ condemneth the arrogancy of the rich worldlings, who as though they had God locked up in their coffers and barns, set their whole felicity in their goods'.

863 **mastered** possessed (*OED* 3; first cited occurrence)

864 **in their pride** (a) through their arrogance; (b) in their prime

866 **hold** retain ownership of (*OED* 6a)

867 **sours** sour things (the usage is quite common in the sixteenth century). Compare the proverb 'After sweet the sour comes' (Dent S1034.1). This line and the next are marked in Q as *sententiae*. See ll. 87–8 n.

869 **wait on** lie in wait for (*OED* s.v. 'wait' 14b); with perhaps a hint of 'attend (as servants)' (*OED* 14j), which is turned to sinister treachery by the primary sense. Compare Sonnet *18*.3.

What virtue breeds iniquity devours.
We have no good that we can say is ours,
　But ill-annexèd Opportunity
　Or kills his life, or else his quality.　　　　　875

'O Opportunity, thy guilt is great:
'Tis thou that execut'st the traitor's treason;
Thou sets the wolf where he the lamb may get;
Whoever plots the sin, thou point'st the season.
'Tis thou that spurn'st at right, at law, at reason,　　875 880
　And in thy shady cell, where none may spy him,
　Sits sin to seize the souls that wander by him.

'Thou mak'st the vestal violate her oath;
Thou blow'st the fire when temperance is thawed;
Thou smother'st honesty, thou murd'rest troth,　　885
Thou foul abettor, thou notorious bawd.
Thou plantest scandal, and displacest laud,
　Thou ravisher, thou traitor, thou false thief:
　Thy honey turns to gall, thy joy to grief.

'Thy secret pleasure turns to open shame;　　890
Thy private feasting to a public fast;
Thy smoothing titles to a ragged name;

879 point'st] Q (poinst); points Q5　883 mak'st] Q (makest)　884 blow'st] Q (blowest)

874 **ill-annexèd** added in a destructive way
Opportunity has here a technical sense,
'occasion for performing wrong'. In the
emblematic tradition 'Occasion' is the
word usually given to the circumstances
which enable sin to happen, as in *FQ*
2.4.4–13.

875 **Or ... or either ... or**
quality the distinctive excellence by virtue
of which a thing is itself. The emerging
sense 'Nobility, high birth, rank' (*OED*
4a) may also be in play: Lucrece has just
been describing the destruction of Colla-
tine's family dignity.

876 This sententious line is not marked in Q,
but in a British Library copy of Q1 a
seventeenth-century hand has written
'not[e] this' in the margin.

879 **point'st** appoint. Q reads 'poinst' for the
sake of euphony.

880 **spurn'st at** show contempt (originally by
kicking with the foot)

881 **cell** small isolated dwelling. In Spenser
the word often suggests an unwholesome
solitude in which an allegorical personifi-
cation lurks to entrap the unwary.

883–4 **mak'st** and *blow'st* are not elided by
the otherwise alert compositor of Q.

886 The idea that 'opportunity was whore-
dom's bawd' was proverbial (Dent O70).

887 **plantest** 'To establish or set up (a person
or thing) in some position or state' (*OED*
5c). That is, *scandal* (ill-repute/ecclesiasti-
cal corruption; see l. 204 n.) is put in the
position or office which properly belongs
to *laud* (praiseworthiness).

889 **honey ... gall** proverbial: 'No honey
without gall' (Dent H556; cf. Dent
H551.1).

892 **smoothing** flattering

Thy sugared tongue to bitter wormwood taste;
Thy violent vanities can never last.
    How comes it then, vile Opportunity,   895
    Being so bad, such numbers seek for thee?

'When wilt thou be the humble suppliant's friend
And bring him where his suit may be obtainèd?
When wilt thou sort an hour great strifes to end?
Or free that soul which wretchedness hath chainèd?   900
Give physic to the sick, ease to the painèd?
    The poor, lame, blind, halt, creep, cry out for thee,
    But they ne'er meet with Opportunity.

'The patient dies while the physician sleeps;
The orphan pines while the oppressor feeds.   905
Justice is feasting while the widow weeps,
Advice is sporting while infection breeds.
Thou grant'st no time for charitable deeds.
    Wrath, envy, treason, rape, and murder's rages,
    Thy heinous hours wait on them as their pages.   910

'When truth and virtue have to do with thee
A thousand crosses keep them from thy aid:
They buy thy help, but sin ne'er gives a fee.
He gratis comes, and thou art well appaid
As well to hear as grant what he hath said.   915
    My Collatine would else have come to me
    When Tarquin did, but he was stayed by thee.

---

893 **wormwood** The plant *Artemisia absinthium* became proverbial for its bitter taste. The leaves and tops were used as a tonic.

894 **vanities** empty delights, pointless pursuits. Compare the proverb 'Nothing violent can be permanent' (Dent N321).

899 **sort** 'To choose or select (time, opportunity, etc.) as fitting or suitable' (*OED* 14a). To 'sort an opportunity' in this sense was an idiom in the period. Compare 1 *Henry VI* 2.3.26: 'I'll sort some other time to visit you.'

901 **physic** medical treatment

902 **halt** is either a verb ('limp') or an adjective ('the lame, crippled').

907 **Advice** is used here specifically of medical counsel (*OED* 5).
sporting entertaining itself, at leisure. The

infection could carry a reminder of the plague which raged in London in 1592–4.

910 **heinous** hateful

911 **have to do** have dealings

914 **appaid** (a) satisfied; with a play on (b) 'repaid, requited, rewarded' (*OED* 2, predating the first cited usage of 1598)

915 **hear as grant** The image is of Opportunity as a corrupt judge who *hears* ('To listen to judicially in a court of law', *OED* 6) a case from Sin, and *grants* it as soon as it is heard.

917 **stayed** prevented; playing on the technical legal sense 'To stop, arrest, delay, prevent (an action or process, something which is begun or intended)' (*OED* 25). The undercurrent of a legal allegory leads naturally to the verdict *Guilty thou art* in the next stanza.

'Guilty thou art of murder, and of theft;
Guilty of perjury, and subornation;
Guilty of treason, forgery and shift;   920
Guilty of incest, that abomination,
An accessary by thine inclination
   To all sins past and all that are to come,
   From the creation to the general doom.

'Misshapen Time, copesmate of ugly Night,   925
Swift subtle post, carrier of grisly care,
Eater of youth, false slave to false delight,
Base watch of woes, sin's packhorse, virtue's snare,
Thou nursest all, and murd'rest all that are.
   O hear me then, injurious shifting Time,   930
   Be guilty of my death, since of my crime.

'Why hath thy servant Opportunity
Betrayed the hours thou gav'st me to repose?
Cancelled my fortunes, and enchainèd me
To endless date of never-ending woes?   935

919 **subornation** (a) bribery; (b) paying a witness to commit perjury

920 **shift** fraudulent behaviour the word is less technically precise than the other terms, but there is no well-known crime which rhymes with *theft*)

922 **accessary** one who assists in a crime whilst not being the primary person responsible. Stressed on the first syllable. **inclination** natural predisposition; perhaps also (continuing the judicial metaphors) 'bias in favour of'

924 **general doom** Last Judgement. Compare 'the general all-ending day', *Richard III* 3.1.78.

925 **copesmate** (a) (neutrally) 'a partner or colleague in power, office, etc.; an associate, companion, comrade'; (b) (pejoratively) 'an accomplice in cheating; a confederate at cards, dice, or the like' (*OED* 3a)

926 **subtle** (a) cunning (*OED* 10); (b) thin as air, ungraspably fine
post 'From the beginning of the 16th c., applied to men with horses stationed or appointed in places at suitable distances along the post-roads, the duty of each being to ride with, or forward with all speed to the next stage' (*OED* 1a).

927 **Eater of youth** *edax rerum*, eater of things, *Met.* 15.234 (Golding 15.258–9, 'Thou time the eater up of things, and age of spiteful teen, | Destroy all things').

928 **Base watch of woes** Time is compared to a watchman who brings bad tidings.
packhorse literally a horse who carries heavy burdens, hence used of someone who does a superior's dirty work for them, as in *Richard III* 1.3.122: 'I was a packhorse in his great affairs'.

929 **nursest** as a mother does a child)

930 **shifting** (a) cheating, evasive, deceptive; (b) perpetually mobile

931 **my crime** appears to indicate that Lucrece has taken responsibility for Tarquin's *crime*, but the whole line means 'be found responsible for my death as you are responsible for what [appears to be] my crime, but which is in fact yours'.

934–5 **Cancelled . . . woes?** Time has dissolved Lucrece's temporary lease on good fortune, and has inextricably bound her to perpetual grief. *Cancelled* means 'To deface or obliterate (writing), properly by drawing lines across it lattice-wise; to cross out, strike out. Of legal documents, deeds, etc.: To annul, render void or invalid by so marking' (*OED* 1). Compare

Time's office is to fine the hate of foes,
    To eat up errors by opinion bred,
    Not spend the dowry of a lawful bed.

'Time's glory is to calm contending kings,
To unmask falsehood, and bring truth to light,   940
To stamp the seal of time in agèd things,
To wake the morn, and sentinel the night,
To wrong the wronger till he render right,
    To ruinate proud buildings with thy hours,
    And smear with dust their glitt'ring golden towers;   945

'To fill with worm-holes stately monuments,
To feed oblivion with decay of things,
To blot old books, and alter their contents,
To pluck the quills from ancient ravens' wings,
To dry the old oaks' sap, and cherish springs,   950

---

937 errors] Q; errour Q3   950 oaks'] Q (oakes)   950 cherish] Q; perish *conj.* Johnson; blemish OXFORD (*conj.* Taylor)

l. 1729 and n. *Endless date* means 'having no fixed term of expiry'. For similar uses of *date* see Sonnets 14.14, 18.4, 30.6, 124.10 and nn.

936 **fine** (a) finish (*OED v.*[1] 3); (b) penalize, impose a fine on (*OED v.*[2] 8, a sense reinforced by *office*, which suggests that Time is presented as a constable or magistrate); (c) refine, purify (*OED v.*[3], a sense favoured by Malone)

937 **opinion** popular misconceptions

940 **and bring truth to light** Truth is traditionally 'the daughter of time', as in the proverb 'Time brings the truth to light' (Dent T324).

941 **stamp . . . things** give value and authority to things of antiquity. Time is represented as a king or nobleman whose seal gives authority to documents or coins on which it appears.

942 **sentinel** keep guard over (the first cited example of the verb in *OED*, formed by enallage. See *Venus* l. 830 n.)

943 **wrong . . . render right** inflict harm on the wrongdoer until he rectifies his wrong. *OED* does not support Malone's view that *wrong* means 'punish by the compunctious visitings of conscience'.

944 **ruinate** reduce to ruins (often used of violent destruction by an army rather

than of slow decay). Compare Sonnet 10.7.

945 **smear with dust** Compare Sonnet 55.4.

946 **worm-holes** Presumably the monuments are of wood. These are the first worm-holes to find their way into *OED*.

948 **alter their contents** change what is in them, either by making them illegible or by destroying parts of them. *Quills* in the next line may subliminally suggest that Time is a corrupt scribe who modifies old manuscripts. *Contents* is stressed on the second syllable. Compare Spenser's lament for the supposed loss of the end of Chaucer's *Squire's Tale*, *FQ* 4.2.33: 'But wicked Time that all good thoughts doth waste, | And workes of noblest wits to nought out weare, | That famous moniment hath quite defaste, | And robd the world of threasure endlesse deare, | The which mote haue enriched all vs heare. | O cursed Eld the cankerworme of writs, | How may these rimes, so rude as doth appeare, | Hope to endure, sith workes of heauenly wits | Are quite deuourd, and brought to nought by little bits?'

949 **ancient ravens** Ravens were believed to live three times as long as human beings. See 'Let the bird of loudest lay' l. 17 and n.

950 **cherish springs** 'nurture mere cuttings,

To spoil antiquities of hammered steel,
And turn the giddy round of Fortune's wheel;

'To show the beldam daughters of her daughter,
To make the child a man, the man a child,
To slay the tiger that doth live by slaughter,   955
To tame the unicorn and lion wild,
To mock the subtle in themselves beguiled,
 To cheer the ploughman with increaseful crops,
 And waste huge stones with little water-drops.

'Why work'st thou mischief in thy pilgrimage,   960
Unless thou couldst return to make amends?
One poor retiring minute in an age
Would purchase thee a thousand thousand friends,
Lending him wit that to bad debtors lends.
 O this dread night, wouldst thou one hour come back, 965
 I could prevent this storm, and shun thy wrack.

suckers or young shoots' (*OED* s.v. 'spring' *n.*[1] 9); since this sense is frequent *c.*1560–*c.*1650 it is more likely than 'stream' which disturbs the expectation of the line's antithetical structure, and has prompted many editors to emend (see collation). The line if interpreted in this way does not need emendation. It emphasizes the wilfulness of Time (he destroys the venerable trunk and advances the upstart new growth), as well as making a transition to the next stanza, which treats 'the decays *and* the repairs of time' (Prince).

953 **beldam** an old woman; sometimes more specifically, as probably here, 'a grandmother' (*OED* 1)

954 **man a child** has both a destructive sense, since 'Old fools are babes again', *Lear* (Quarto) 3.19, or 'Old men are twice children' (Dent M570), and a recuperative one: to make (supplied) the *man* have a *child*.

956 **tame the unicorn** Topsell notes (sig. 3S6ʳ): 'It is a beast of an untamable nature . . . Except they be taken before they be two years old they will never be tamed.' Time therefore achieves the all but impossible. Unicorns are also proverbially strong (Numbers 23: 22

and 24: 8). The marginal note in the Geneva version of Job 39: 12 reads: 'Is it possible to make the unicorn tame? Signifying that if man cannot rule a creature, that it is much more impossible that he should appoint the wisdom of God, whereby he governeth all the world.'

957 **To mock . . . beguiled** (a) Time derides the efforts of the treacherous (*OED* 'subtle' 10) who are entrapped by their own cunning; (b) Time derides the sophisticated (*OED* 'subtle' 9) who have charmed themselves with their own sophistications.

958 **increaseful** fertile (earliest of only two examples in *OED*)

959 **waste** wear away; dissolve. For the proverbial origins of this line see l. 560 n.

962 **retiring** returning (*OED* 4); compare *Venus* l. 906.

964 **Lending . . . lends** The idea here is that hindsight would prevent folly: Time allows someone who has made a bad debt to see the folly of what he has done.

966 **prevent** (a) anticipate; (b) prevent from happening
shun thy wrack avoid the shipwreck which you have brought to me

'Thou ceaseless lackey to Eternity,
With some mischance cross Tarquin in his flight.
Devise extremes beyond extremity
To make him curse this cursèd crimeful night: 970
Let ghastly shadows his lewd eyes affright,
    And the dire thought of his committed evil
    Shape every bush a hideous shapeless devil.

'Disturb his hours of rest with restless trances;
Afflict him in his bed with bedrid groans.   975
Let there bechance him pitiful mischances,
To make him moan, but pity not his moans.
Stone him with hardened hearts harder than stones,
    And let mild women to him lose their mildness,
    Wilder to him than tigers in their wildness.   980

'Let him have time to tear his curlèd hair;
Let him have time against himself to rave;
Let him have time of Time's help to despair;
Let him have time to live a loathèd slave;
Let him have time a beggar's orts to crave,   985
    And time to see one that by alms doth live
    Disdain to him disdainèd scraps to give.

'Let him have time to see his friends his foes,
And merry fools to mock at him resort;

---

975 bedrid] Q (bedread)

967 **ceaseless lackey** primarily 'endlessly running footman' (*OED* s.v. 'lackey' 1), who runs on to eternity alongside a coach; also 'permanent toady' (*OED* 1b)
968 Compare Lucrece's curses with Queen Margaret's in *Richard III* 1.3.214–30.
970 **crimeful** full of crimes (first of only three citations in *OED*)
973 Compare *Dream* 5.1.21–2: 'Or in the night, imagining some fear, | How easy is a bush supposed a bear' and Dent B738: 'He thinks every bush a bear'.
974 **trances** the bewildered state between sleeping and waking (*OED* 3a); also perhaps playing on the sense 'A state of extreme apprehension or dread' (*OED* 1), which was slightly archaic by 1594
975 **bedrid** bedridden (i.e. the sickness makes him bedridden). Q's spelling 'bedread' in this context of sickness and bad dreams

also might suggest the rare form 'bedread', or 'dreaded'.
977 **make him moan** 'to make causes of grief for him' (*him* is dative). To 'make moan' is a set phrase in which *moan* is a noun rather than a verb: this is a vengeful transformation of the phrase in which someone else is compelled to make moan.
978 **Stone him** To *stone* can be to put someone to death by pelting them with stones. Compare the proverb 'A heart as hard as a stone' (Dent H311).
981 **curlèd** may imply that Tarquin has used curling tongs, as Roe suggests, but until the emergence of the word 'curly' (in the late eighteenth century) there was no means of distinguishing between naturally and artificially curled hair.
985 **orts** scraps, leftovers
986 **one . . . live** a beggar

Let him have time to mark how slow time goes   990
In time of sorrow, and how swift and short
His time of folly, and his time of sport.
    And ever let his unrecalling crime
    Have time to wail th' abusing of his time.

'O Time, thou tutor both to good and bad,   995
Teach me to curse him that thou taught'st this ill.
At his own shadow let the thief run mad;
Himself himself seek every hour to kill:
Such wretched hands such wretched blood should spill;
    For who so base would such an office have   1000
    As sland'rous deathsman to so base a slave.

'The baser is he, coming from a king,
To shame his hope with deeds degenerate.
The mightier man the mightier is the thing
That makes him honoured, or begets him hate: 1005
For greatest scandal waits on greatest state.
    The moon being clouded presently is missed,
    But little stars may hide them when they list.

'The crow may bathe his coal-black wings in mire,
And unperceived fly with the filth away;   1010
But if the like the snow-white swan desire,
The stain upon his silver down will stay.

992 folly ... sport lust ... merry-making. The thought here is proverbial: 'Hours of pleasure are short' (Dent H747); 'Hours of sorrow are long' (Dent H747.1).

993 unrecalling irrevocable. This is the only cited example in *OED*. Shakespeare sometimes uses '-ing' as a suffix denoting a passive participle (Abbott §372).

997 Being afraid of one's own shadow was a near-proverbial example of fear from *c.*1550 (Dent S261).

999 wretched despicable (*OED* 4)

1000 who so ... have who is so contemptible that he would take on the duties of ...

1001 sland'rous deathsman shameful executioner. In *Measure* 4.2 the convicted bawd Pompey is compelled to become an executioner in order to win remission of his imprisonment: the profession of executioner was close to being criminal, hence is *sland'rous*.

1003 shame his hope destroy the expectations people had of him by virtue of his birth. On this sense of *hope* see l. 605 n.

degenerate which shame his *genus*, or family. Most humanist prince-books presented true nobility as a set of moral qualities which had to be renewed in each generation, and from which each generation could decline.

1005 begets him produces for himself; with a play on the biological sense. Tarquin is *degenerate* and so *begets* only loathing.

1007 presently immediately

1008 them themselves

list please, like. Compare Sonnet 94.13–14.

1009 mire slimy mud

1010 unperceived The epithet is transferred from the *filth* to the crow.

1012 silver white. See l. 56 n.

Poor grooms are sightless night, kings glorious day;
   Gnats are unnoted whereso'er they fly,
   But eagles gazed upon with every eye.   1015

'Out, idle words, servants to shallow fools,
Unprofitable sounds, weak arbitrators,
Busy yourselves in skill-contending schools:
Debate, where leisure serves, with dull debaters.
To trembling clients be you mediators;   1020
   For me, I force not argument a straw,
   Since that my case is past the help of law.

'In vain I rail at Opportunity,
At Time, at Tarquin, and uncheerful Night;
In vain I cavil with mine infamy;   1025
In vain I spurn at my confirmed despite:
This helpless smoke of words doth me no right.
   The remedy indeed to do me good
   Is to let forth my foul defilèd blood.

'Poor hand, why quiver'st thou at this decree?   1030
Honour thyself to rid me of this shame;
For, if I die, my honour lives in thee,
But if I live thou liv'st in my defame.

1013 **sightless** invisible (i.e. their crimes are invisibly obscure)

1016 **Out** Away with you!
shallow lacking in depth of character (first cited usage in *OED* for this sense)

1017 **arbitrators** judges

1018 **skill-contending schools** A routine part of education in schools and universities was the formal display of rhetorical expertise through formal competitive speaking.

1019 **where leisure serves** where there is enough leisure to do so

1021 **force . . . a straw** regard argument as of no significance. *Force* means 'attach force or importance to' (*OED* 14a; becoming obsolete by 1600). *Straws* were proverbial for worthlessness from *c.*1489 (Dent S918).

1025 **cavil with** raise frivolous objections to (like a tricksy lawyer)

1026 **confirmed despite** shame which has been ratified and made irreversible. *Con-* firmed in conjunction with *cavil* in the previous line has the sense 'To make valid by formal authoritative assent' (*OED* 2), often used of legal documents and decisions. It is too late for an appeal.

1027 **helpless** affording no help (*OED* 3; a distinctively Shakespearian usage. See *Venus* l. 604, and ll. 756 and 1056.
smoke of words worthless obfuscation. Rhetoric is often referred to as 'sweet smoke' (as in *L.L.L.* 3.1.61), a usage which is here made negative.

1028 **remedy** playing on (a) medical cure (*OED* 1); (b) legal redress (*OED* 3)

1029 **Is to . . . blood** Bloodletting (here turned into a method of suicide) was used as a cure for many minor ailments.

1030 **decree** final legal judgement

1033 **liv'st in my defame** persist while I am in a condition of infamy. *Liv'st in* might just carry the rare sense 'feed on' (*OED* 2a), although Shakespeare elsewhere favours the forms 'live by' and 'live upon'.

Since thou couldst not defend thy loyal dame,
    And wast afeard to scratch her wicked foe,   1035
    Kill both thyself and her for yielding so.'

This said, from her betumbled couch she starteth,
To find some desp'rate instrument of death;
But this, no slaughterhouse, no tool imparteth
To make more vent for passage of her breath,   1040
Which thronging through her lips so vanisheth
    As smoke from Etna, that in air consumes,
    Or that which from dischargèd cannon fumes.

'In vain,' quoth she, 'I live, and seek in vain
Some happy mean to end a hapless life.   1045
I feared by Tarquin's falchion to be slain,
Yet for the self-same purpose seek a knife;
But when I feared I was a loyal wife:
    So am I now—O no, that cannot be;
    Of that true type hath Tarquin rifled me.   1050

'O that is gone for which I sought to live,
And therefore now I need not fear to die.
To clear this spot by death (at least) I give
A badge of fame to Slander's livery,

1037 betumbled] Q (betombled)

1037 **betumbled** disordered (only cited example in *OED*). 'Tumble' can have the sense 'to have sex with', as in *Hamlet* 4.5.62–3: ' "before you tumbled me | You promised me to wed" '. Q's 'betombled' suggests that a violated bed has a natural affinity with the tomb.

1039 **no**   **slaughterhouse**   being no slaughterhouse *imparteth provides*

1042 **Etna** The association of the volcano with evanescence may derive from a distant recollection of Shakespeare's favourite passage of Ovid: Golding 15.375–9: describes how the flames of Etna will eventually consume themselves. **consume** vanishes. *OED* records a sense 'cause to evaporate' (*OED* 1b) for the transitive verb; this sense may extend to this intransitive usage.

1045 **mean** means

1050 **true type** ideal name. *Type* means (a)

symbol, representation; (b) 'A distinguishing mark or sign; a stamp' (*OED* 3, citing 3 *Henry VI (True Tragedy)*, 1.4.122: 'Thy father bears the type of King of Naples').

1053 **To clear** by clearing

1054 **badge . . . livery** Although Lucrece has become a subordinate of Slander, and wears his *livery* (the clothing of one of his retainers), she will at least by committing suicide add to that livery a symbol of good repute. Retainers might wear both the livery and the *badge* of their master, which would be a small device (such as a boar) which had no necessary connection with the arms of the magnate to whom it belonged. Sometimes those in the *livery* of an overlord would wear the badge appropriate to their own locality. So here Lucrece attempts to qualify her subservience to Slander by wearing the *badge* of another secondary master, Fame.

A dying life to living infamy: 1055
   Poor helpless help, the treasure stol'n away
   To burn the guiltless casket where it lay.

'Well, well, dear Collatine, thou shalt not know
The stainèd taste of violated troth:
I will not wrong thy true affection so,   1060
To flatter thee with an infringèd oath.
This bastard graff shall never come to growth:
   He shall not boast who did thy stock pollute,
   That thou art doting father of his fruit.

'Nor shall he smile at thee in secret thought,   1065
Nor laugh with his companions at thy state;
But thou shalt know thy int'rest was not bought
Basely with gold, but stol'n from forth thy gate.
For me, I am the mistress of my fate,
   And with my trespass never will dispense,   1070
   Till life to death acquit my forced offence.

1055 **A dying life** an immortal reputation acquired through dying
   living infamy (a) the disrepute which would pursue me if I stayed alive; (b) the disrepute which will live for ever
1057 **guiltless casket** the body (which is both innocent ('guiltless') and worthless ('giltless')). *Caskets,* or small containers for jewels, miniature portraits, and occasionally private letters, were often richly ornamented and made of valuable materials. The fact that Lucrece voices an objection to suicide here has been seen as a mark of confusion which 'seems to reflect Shakespeare's own uncertainty about the moral import of the story' (Lever; compare Donaldson, 48–9). This misses the dramatic point: her impetus wavers at the end of this stanza, and she has to pull herself round at the start of the next with *Well, well* and by remembering the harm done to Collatine if she lived.
1061 **flatter . . . oath** Collatine might believe the child to be his; Lucrece will not deceive (*flatter*) him by pretending her *oath* of chastity has not been broken.
1062 **bastard graff** illegitimate offspring. A *graff* is a slip or shoot inserted into the bark of a mature plant. For the association between grafting and the contamination of stock, see *Richard III* 3.7.127–9: 'Her royal stock graft with ignoble plants,

| And almost shouldered in the swallowing gulf | Of dark forgetfulness, and deep oblivion'. For the idea that this process produces illegitimate offspring see *Winter's Tale* 4.4.79–108. Pregnancy has run through Lucrece's earlier language (see l. 734 n.), but becomes here the chief ground for her suicide. In early modern England conception was believed to imply consent: 'rape is the carnal abusing of a woman against her will. But if the woman conceive upon any carnal abusing of her, that is no rape, for she cannot conceive unless she consent', Henry Finch, *Law, or a Discourse thereof in four Books* (1627), 204.
1063 **stock** plays on (a) trunk of a mature tree (into which a slip or shoot is engrafted); (b) a line of descent (*OED* 3c).
1064 **doting** (a) loving; (b) foolishly self-deceiving
1067 **int'rest** your title to ownership over (your offspring)
1069 **For me** as for me
1070 **trespass** sin. See l. 632 n.
   dispense grant mercy to, make a special case for (as also in ll. 1279 and 1704)
1071 **Till life . . . offence** The line is a miniature allegory: Life will discharge the debt (*OED* s.v. 'acquit' 4; first cited example) which is owed to Death on account of Lucrece's involuntary crime.

'I will not poison thee with my attaint,
Nor fold my fault in cleanly coined excuses;
My sable ground of sin I will not paint
To hide the truth of this false night's abuses.   1075
My tongue shall utter all; mine eyes, like sluices,
 As from a mountain spring that feeds a dale,
 Shall gush pure streams to purge my impure tale.'

By this, lamenting Philomel had ended
The well-tuned warble of her nightly sorrow,   1080
And solemn night with slow sad gait descended
To ugly hell, when, lo, the blushing morrow
Lends light to all fair eyes that light will borrow:
 But cloudy Lucrece shames herself to see,
 And therefore still in night would cloistered be.   1085

Revealing day through every cranny spies,
And seems to point her out where she sits weeping.
To whom she sobbing speaks: 'O eye of eyes,
Why pry'st thou through my window? Leave thy peeping,
Mock with thy tickling beams eyes that are sleeping.   1090
 Brand not my forehead with thy piercing light,
 For day hath naught to do what's done by night.'

1073 **fold** wrap up. Compare l. 675 n.
cleanly coined artfully manufactured, with perhaps a suggestion of artful forgery
1074 **sable ground** black base colour (*ground* is the background colour of a shield or *impresa*)
1076 **sluices** is usually glossed 'floodgates', although the context suggests rather 'A channel, drain, or small stream, esp. one carrying off overflow or surplus water' (*OED* 2). Compare *Venus* l. 956 and n.
1079 **Philomel** the nightingale. Philomela was raped and had her tongue cut out by her brother-in-law Tereus. She revealed her story to her sister by weaving a tapestry which depicted it. After feeding his children to Tereus in revenge she was metamorphosed into a nightingale. See *Met.* 6.424–676. Her tale underlies Shakespeare's *Titus*, which was composed *c.* 1592.
1084 **shames** feels shame (the intransitive form is quite common up to 1650; compare l. 1143)

1085 **cloistered** shut up (as though in a nunnery). The verb enters the language in the 1590s
1086–92 This stanza ironically inverts an *aubade*, in which a lover urges day not to break in order to prolong the pleasures of the night.
1087 **point her out** Being pointed at carries a burden of shame and accusation with it: compare *Othello* 4.2.55–7: 'To make me | The fixèd figure for the time of scorn | To point his slow and moving finger at'.
1089 **peeping** The verbal noun is first recorded from 1593 in *OED*.
1090 **tickling** The sun playfully tickles sleepers until they awake.
1091 **Brand** Branding on the forehead was a punishment for perjury in this period; see Sonnet 111.5 n. The allusion to the practice follows on naturally from Lucrece's insistence that she will not lie to Collatine.
1092 **to do** to do with. Shakespeare sometimes omits prepositions where the verb is clearly transitive (Abbott §200). Partridge

Thus cavils she with everything she sees:
True grief is fond and testy as a child,
Who, wayward once, his mood with naught agrees. 1095
Old woes, not infant sorrows, bear them mild:
Continuance tames the one, the other wild,
   Like an unpractised swimmer plunging still,
   With too much labour drowns for want of skill.

So she, deep drenchèd in a sea of care, 1100
Holds disputation with each thing she views,
And to herself all sorrow doth compare.
No object but her passion's strength renews,
And as one shifts, another straight ensues.
   Sometime her grief is dumb and hath no words; 1105
   Sometime 'tis mad and too much talk affords.

The little birds, that tune their morning's joy,
Make her moans mad with their sweet melody:
For mirth doth search the bottom of annoy.
Sad souls are slain in merry company. 1110
Grief best is pleased with grief's society:
   True sorrow, then, is feelingly sufficed
   When with like semblance it is sympathized.

'Tis double death to drown in ken of shore;
He ten times pines, that pines beholding food; 1115

notes that to 'do naught with' can mean
'to have sexual intercourse with', as in
Richard III 1.1.100.

1094 **fond and testy** foolishly touchy; petu-
lant and irritable
1095 **wayward once** after one act of
wilfulness
1096 **bear them** bear themselves
1097 **Continuance** persistence (in suffering)
1098 **plunging** ducking under water; heav-
ing up and down like a ship in heavy seas
(*OED* 7a)
1099 **want of skill** lack of competence
1100 **drenchèd** immersed (the sense
'drowned' is still active in this period). To
˙e 'drowned in a sea of troubles' was a
common sixteenth-century poetic image,
which verged on the proverbial (Dent
S177.1).
1101 **Holds disputation** See l. 246 n.

1103 **No object . . . renews** i.e. every object
she sees intensifies her grief
1109 **mirth . . . annoy** Happiness probes the
wounds ('search', *OED* 8) of sorrow (*annoy*)
to their very depths. Compare *Titus*
2.3.262: 'Now to the bottom dost thou
search my wound.' Lines 1109–18 are
marked as *sententiae* in Q. See ll. 87–8 n.
1111 Compare l. 790 and n.
1112 **feelingly sufficed** emotionally satisfied
1113 **When . . . sympathized** 'when it is pre-
sented with an expression of emotion
which resembles it'. *Semblance* means
both 'resemblance' (as in l. 1246) and
'a person's appearance or demeanour,
expressive of his thoughts, feelings' (*OED*
3): *like semblance* therefore is not simply
tautologous, but means 'an appearance of
grief so like it as to be virtually identical to
it'.
1114 **in ken** within sight

To see the salve doth make the wound ache more;
Great grief grieves most at that would do it good;
Deep woes roll forward like a gentle flood,
    Who being stopped, the bounding banks o'erflows:
    Grief dallied with nor law nor limit knows.   1120

'You mocking birds,' quoth she, 'your tunes entomb
Within your hollow-swelling feathered breasts,
And in my hearing be you mute and dumb:
My restless discord loves no stops nor rests.
A woeful hostess brooks not merry guests.   1125
    Relish your nimble notes to pleasing ears:
    Distress likes dumps when time is kept with tears.

'Come, Philomel, that sing'st of ravishment:
Make thy sad grove in my dishevelled hair.
As the dank earth weeps at thy languishment,   1130
So I at each sad strain will strain a tear,
And with deep groans the diapason bear:

1116 **salve** remedy; perhaps ointment

1117 **that would** that that would. Shakespeare frequently omits a relative 'that' after a demonstrative 'that' (Abbott §244).

1118–20 Compare the proverb 'The stream stopped swells the higher' (Dent S929).

1119 Who which. See l. 296 n.

1120 **dallied with** (a) trifled or flirted with; (b) delayed (*OED* 5)

1124 **stops nor rests** hindrances nor intervals; playing on the secondary sense for *stop* ('The closing of a finger-hole or ventage in the tube of a wind instrument so as to alter the pitch' (*OED* 15a)), and for *rests* ('An interval of silence occurring in one or more parts during a movement' (*OED* 7a)). The music Lucrece is making is unusually harsh by Elizabethan standards, since, as Thomas Morley notes, 'Some rests also (as the minim and crotchet rests) were devised to avoid the harshness of some discord or the following of two perfect concords together' (Morley, 118).

1125 **brooks** tolerates. This line is marked in Q as a *sententia*. See ll. 87–8 n.

1126 **Relish** (a) make pleasant; (b) ornament with grace notes (this sense is not recorded by *OED*, but the context strongly suggests a play on 'relish' *n.*², a musical

term of art meaning 'A grace, ornament, or embellishment'; compare *Two Gentlemen* 2.1.19: 'to relish a love-song, like a robin redbreast').

1127 **dumps** 'A mournful or plaintive melody or song' (*OED* 3). Compare *Two Gentlemen* 3.2.83–4: 'To their instruments | Tune a deploring dump.' This line is marked in Q as a *sententia*. See ll. 87–8 n.

1129 **dishevelled** is used twice in *LGW*: at ll. 1720 and 1829. It is only used elsewhere by Shakespeare at *Venus* l. 147.

1130 **languishment** depression or affliction of spirits, sadness. Spenser associated the word with love melancholy and sympathetic mourning, as in *The Ruins of Time* ll. 159–60: 'Yet it is comfort in great languishment, | To be bemoanèd with compassion kind'.

1131 **strain . . . strain** The sense moves from 'musical theme' to 'wring out'. The rhetorical figure of *antanaclasis*, in which the same word is used in two quite different grammatical forms and senses, is used to turn all melodies (*strains* can be happy) to melancholy.

1132 **diapason** a bass line of music which produces a precise octave consonance with the main melody (first cited example for this sense in *OED*)

For burden-wise I'll hum on Tarquin still,
While thou on Tereus descants better skill.

'And whiles against a thorn thou bear'st thy part,   1135
To keep thy sharp woes waking, wretched I
To imitate thee well, against my heart
Will fix a sharp knife to affright mine eye,
Who if it wink shall thereon fall and die.
    These means, as frets upon an instrument,   1140
    Shall tune our heart-strings to true languishment.

'And for, poor bird, thou sing'st not in the day,
As shaming any eye should thee behold,
Some dark deep desert seated from the way,
That knows not parching heat, nor freezing cold,   1145
Will we find out: and there we will unfold,
    To creatures stern, sad tunes to change their kinds:
    Since men prove beasts, let beasts bear gentle minds.

As the poor frighted deer that stands at gaze,
Wildly determining which way to fly,   1150

1145 not] Q; nor Q6

1133 **burden-wise** A 'bourdon' is a bass or undersong, which might be repeated in a chorus or when the main line of the melody pauses. The form 'burden' is used here (for the first time, according to *OED*) in order to keep in play the additional associations of *burden*: 'a load of blame, sin, sorrow' (*OED* 2a) and 'That which is borne in the womb; a child' (*OED* 4a).

1134 **descants** A *descant* is 'A melodious accompaniment to a simple musical theme (the plainsong), sung or played, and often merely extemporized, above it, and thus forming an air to its bass' (*OED* 1). The expected form 'descant'st' is avoided for euphony (Abbott §340).
better skill with greater skill. The preposition is omitted (Abbott §202). Wyndham notes this may refer to the greater artistry of the higher part (that of the nightingale) in the harmony.

1135 **against a thorn** The nightingale was believed to keep itself awake in order to sing of its sorrows by bruising its breast on a thorn. See *P. Pilgrim* 20.9–10. Compare Thomas Lodge, *Scylla's Metamorphosis* ll. 89–90: 'pricks do make birds sing, | But pricks in ladies' bosoms often sting'. The

image was near-proverbial (Dent N183).
bear'st thy part keep up your performance

1139 **Who** which. See l. 296 n. The antecedent is likely to be the *heart*, although *it* refers to the eye.
wink closes, looks away; perhaps also 'flinches away from'. See *Venus* l. 90 n.

1140 **means** methods, resources; perhaps a pun on *OED n.*[1] 'A lament, complaint', and possibly also on the musical sense 'A middle or intermediate part in any harmonized composition or performance, esp. the tenor and alto' (*OED n.*[2] 2a)
frets Ridges which mark and regulate the notes on a lute (*OED n.*[3]), punning on *n.*[3] 3: 'agitation of mind; a ruffled condition of temper; irritation, passion, vexation'.

1143 **As shaming** as if ashamed that. For the intransitive usage, see l. 1084.

1144 **desert** abandoned spot
seated from situated away from ('seat' in the passive is often used of the location of dwellings, *OED* 5a)

1147 **stern** merciless, cruel (*OED* 3)
kinds natures

1149 **at gaze** is used especially of the dazed and bewildered stance of deer when they are unsure what to do (*OED* 3b).

Or one encompassed with a winding maze,
That cannot tread the way out readily;
So with herself is she in mutiny,
   To live or die, which of the twain were better
   When life is shamed and death reproach's debtor.   1155

'To kill myself,' quoth she, 'Alack what were it
But with my body my poor soul's pollution?
They that lose half with greater patience bear it
Than they whose whole is swallowed in confusion.
That mother tries a merciless conclusion,   1160
   Who, having two sweet babes, when death takes one
   Will slay the other, and be nurse to none.

'My body or my soul, which was the dearer,
When the one pure, the other made divine?
Whose love of either to myself was nearer   1165
When both were kept for heaven and Collatine?
Ay me, the bark pilled from the lofty pine,
   His leaves will wither and his sap decay;
   So must my soul, her bark being pilled away.

'Her house is sacked, her quiet interrupted,   1170
Her mansion battered by the enemy;

1169 pilled] ç (pild); peeled OXFORD

1151 **encompassed with** surrounded by
1153 **in mutiny** in a state of discord (*OED* 2),
with a memory of the insubordinate
rebellion of the inferior faculties described
in l. 426 above.
1155 **When life . . . debtor** i.e. to live would
be to remain an object of shame, but
to commit suicide would give rise to
reproach
1156–7 The idea that suicide would extend
Tarquin's contamination of her body to
include her soul strikes a Christian note.
Early readers are unlikely to have felt this
as any kind of anachronism.
1158 **half** i.e. they lose just the purity of their
body without also forgoing that of their
soul
1159 **confusion** destruction (*OED* 1)
1160 **tries . . . conclusion** tests out a merciless
experiment. Compare *Antony* 5.2.349–
50: 'She hath pursued conclusions infi-
nite | Of easy ways to die'.
1164 **When . . . divine** The body was created

pure, and its purity was matched by the
divinity of the soul.
1165 **Whose . . . nearer** Which did I love
more? (*Whose* means 'of which', Abbott
§264. The semi-personification prompts
the usage.)
1167, 1169 **pilled** stripped away (used specifi-
cally of bark, skin, or rind). The repetition
of the word in exactly the same sense is
unusual for this poem, in which repeti-
tions tend to advance or alter sense.
Oxford's emendation of the second occur-
rence of the word to 'peeled' provides the
right sort of chiming reminder of the ear-
lier usage. The alternative is to accept that
this is unusually slack writing.
1169 **bark** i.e. the body
1170–3 These lines establish a strong ana-
logy between Lucrece and Tarquin as he is
described in ll. 719–20.
1171 **mansion** dwelling-place (with no impli-
cation of grandeur; the word can be used
of a room within a *house*)

305

Her sacred temple spotted, spoiled, corrupted,
Grossly engirt with daring infamy.
Then let it not be called impiety
    If in this blemished fort I make some hole   1175
    Through which I may convey this troubled soul.

'Yet die I will not, till my Collatine
Have heard the cause of my untimely death,
That he may vow, in that sad hour of mine,
Revenge on him that made me stop my breath.   1180
My stainèd blood to Tarquin I'll bequeath,
    Which by him tainted shall for him be spent,
    And as his due writ in my testament.

'My honour I'll bequeath unto the knife
That wounds my body so dishonourèd: 1185
'Tis honour to deprive dishonoured life;
The one will live, the other being dead.
So of shame's ashes shall my fame be bred;
    For in my death I murder shameful scorn;
    My shame so dead, mine honour is new born.   1190

'Dear lord of that dear jewel I have lost,
What legacy shall I bequeath to thee?

1182 by] QB; for QA (Malone 34, Malone 886 and Sion)   1190 mine] Q; my Q4

1172 **spoiled** pillaged, despoiled (perhaps anticipating the emergent sense 'mar'; see l. 733 n. and Sonnet *146*.2 n.
1173 **engirt** surrounded. See l. 221 n.
1175 The justification of suicide rests on the idea that Lucrece's soul is a captive in a defiled fort; to breach the walls secretly would not enable the foe to enter, but would allow the captive to leave (*convey* can imply secrecy (*OED* 6)). Compare Sonnet *145*.
1181 **I'll bequeath** Cruelly appropriate legacies are a recognizable literary topos; see Donne, 'The Will'. Formulae for wills in the sixteenth century regularly open with a bequest of the testator's body to the earth and of his or her soul to God (which is how Shakespeare's own will began). Lucrece's will is, however, a rhetorical performance rather than a legally effective instrument, since a married woman could only make testaments of goods and

chattels with the consent of her husband, and the testaments of suicides were deemed void. See Henry Swinburne, *A Briefe Treatise of Testaments and Last Wills* (1590), fos. 47ᵛ–48ʳ and 58ᵛ.
1182 **tainted** sullied; made guilty
1183 **his due** that to which he has a legal right
    testament Technically the 'will' disposes of land, and the *testament* of personal property.
1186 **deprive** 'to take away (a possession)' (*OED* 5, citing this passage). Compare l. 1752 and the proverb 'It is better to die with honour than to live with shame' (Dent H576).
1187 **The one** i.e. the honour due to the knife for having killed Lucrece
1188 **shame's ashes** The Phoenix is reborn from its own ashes. See Sonnet *19*.4 n.
1190 **so dead** having died in this way

My resolution, love, shall be thy boast,
By whose example thou revenged mayst be.
How Tarquin must be used, read it in me: 1195
 Myself thy friend will kill myself thy foe,
 And for my sake serve thou false Tarquin so.

'This brief abridgement of my will I make:
My soul and body to the skies and ground;
My resolution, husband, do thou take;   1200
Mine honour be the knife's that makes my wound;
My shame be his that did my fame confound;
 And all my fame that lives disbursèd be
 To those that live and think no shame of me.

'Thou, Collatine, shalt oversee this will—   1205
How was I overseen that thou shalt see it?
My blood shall wash the slander of mine ill.
My life's foul deed my life's fair end shall free it.
Faint not, faint heart, but stoutly say "So be it":
 Yield to my hand, my hand shall conquer thee;   1210
 Thou dead, both die, and both shall victors be.'

1193 resolution, love,] Q3: $\sim_\wedge \sim_\wedge$ Q 1200 resolution, husband,] MALONE *(conj.* Capell); $\sim_\wedge$
$\sim_\wedge$ Q

1193 **thy boast** your cause of pride (*OED* 3c; first cited example for this sense). Collatine's willingness to *boast* of Lucrece is of course the origin of her rape. See ll. 36–7.

1194 **example** Lucrece wishes to become a positive example for Collatine, which he can read (l. 1195) and imitate. This avoids the fate she imagined for herself as an example of wickedness in ll. 813–26.

1195 **used** treated, dealt with

1197 **so** i.e. not just 'kill him' (which would destroy the point of the paradoxes of *friend* killing *foe*) but 'kill Tarquin, who is both your *friend* (as l. 234 shows) and your *foe*'.

1198 **abridgement** summary. (Wills do not appear in practice to have been concluded in this way.)

1203 **disbursèd** The expenses arising from the implementation of a will (legal expenses and payments of the deceased's debts) were often referred to as 'disbursements': see Thomas Wentworth, *The Office and Duty of Executors* (1640), sigs. Aaa1ᵛ–2ʳ.

1205 **oversee** execute (a will). Overseers were rarely in fact synonymous with executors: the identification is made here in order to support the pun on *overseen* in l. 1206. They were sometimes appointed to assist and advise the executors of the will (*OED* s.v. 'overseer' 1b): 'nor hath such coadjutor, or an overseer any power to administer or intermeddle otherwise, than to counsel, persuade, and advise', Wentworth, *Duty of Executors*, sigs. C2a–b. The overseers of Philip Henslowe's will were to resolve 'any ambiguity doubt or question' about the will (E. A. J. Honigmann, ed., *Playhouse Wills, 1558–1642* (Manchester, 1993), 102). Shakespeare himself was aware of the legal distinction: he appointed both executors (his son-in-law John Hall and his daughter Susanna) and overseers (Thomas Russell and Francis Collins), Honigmann, *Wills*, 108.

1208 **free** it absolve. On the grammatically superfluous 'it', see Abbott §417.

1209 **Faint not** do not lose your resolve

This plot of death when sadly she had laid,
And wiped the brinish pearl from her bright eyes,
With untuned tongue she hoarsely calls her maid,
Whose swift obedience to her mistress hies: 1215
For fleet-winged duty with thought's feathers flies.
    Poor Lucrece' cheeks unto her maid seem so
    As winter meads when sun doth melt their snow.

Her mistress she doth give demure good-morrow,
With soft, slow tongue, true mark of modesty,   1220
And sorts a sad look to her lady's sorrow
(For why her face wore sorrow's livery),
But durst not ask of her audaciously
    Why her two suns were cloud-eclipsèd so,
    Nor why her fair cheeks over-washed with woe.   1225

But as the earth doth weep, the sun being set,
Each flower moistened like a melting eye;
Even so the maid with swelling drops gan wet
Her circled eyne enforced by sympathy
Of those fair suns set in her mistress' sky,   1230
    Who in a salt-waved ocean quench their light,
    Which makes the maid weep like the dewy night.

1229 enforced,] Q4; ~, Q

1213 **brinish pearl** salty tears. Compare *A Lover's Complaint* l. 17 n.
1214 **untuned** discordant, harsh
    maid None of Shakespeare's sources gives Lucretia a maid.
1215 **hies** goes
1216 **For . . . flies** Marked in Q as a *sententia*. See ll. 87–8 n. Thought was proverbially swift (Dent T240).
1218 **meads** meadows
1219 **demure** sober
1221 **sorts** adapts, suits
1222 **For why** for which reason (*OED* s.v. 'why' VI. 8b), rather than 'because', as it is usually glossed (see Schmidt s.v. 'for'). *Her face* refers to the maid rather than to Lucrece.
    sorrow's livery The maid, as a retainer of the household, puts on the appearance appropriate to a servant of Sorrow. On *livery*, see l. 1054 n.
1223 **audaciously** boldly (the word is first cited from *L.L.L.* 5.2.104; here it antici-

pates the sense 'presumptuously' which *OED* dates to 1611)
1228 **gan** began to (archaic/poetic by 1590, as was *eyne* for 'eyes' in the following line). The maid's grief jolts the register of the poem into an archaic mode—a fact which is suggestive in connection with the conscious archaism of Shakespeare's plaintful heroine in *A Lover's Complaint*.
1229 **circled eyne** Presumably the maid's eyes are swollen with weeping, and have puffy circles around them. It is possible that the tears are encircling the eye, as in l. 1587 below. On the archaic form *eyne* see l. 643 n.
    sympathy See l. 1113 n. The *sympathy* here is meteorological as well as emotional: it is a constraining affinity (*enforced by*) which forces the maid to respond to her mistress as the ocean is moved by the influence of the planets.
1231 **quench** extinguish

A pretty while these pretty creatures stand,
Like ivory conduits coral cisterns filling.
One justly weeps; the other takes in hand 1235
No cause but company of her drops' spilling.
Their gentle sex to weep are often willing,
  Grieving themselves to guess at others' smarts,
  And then they drown their eyes, or break their hearts.

For men have marble, women waxen minds, 1240
And therefore are they formed as marble will:
The weak oppressed, th' impression of strange kinds
Is formed in them by force, by fraud, or skill.
Then call them not the authors of their ill,
  No more than wax shall be accounted evil 1245
  Wherein is stamped the semblance of a devil.

Their smoothness, like a goodly champaign plain,
Lays open all the little worms that creep;
In men, as in a rough-grown grove, remain
Cave-keeping evils that obscurely sleep. 1250

1236 drops'] Q (drops)

1233 **pretty ... pretty** fairly long ... beautiful. On the figure of *antanaclasis*, see l. 1131 n.
1234 **Like ... filling** The two are compared to an elaborate fountain in which tributary streams (*conduits*) of ivory fill central reservoirs (*cisterns*) of coral. The white of the eye turns into the red of *coral* as they weep. Compare *Hero and Leander* ll. 295–8: 'and as she spake, | For from those two tralucent cisterns brake | A stream of liquid pearl, which down her face | Made milk-white paths'.
1235 **justly** 'with good reason' (Schmidt, 2)
1235–6 **takes . . . cause** acknowledges no reason
1237 **gentle sex** The phrase was beginning to establish itself as a set phrase for 'womankind'.
1238 **Grieving . . . smarts** They themselves feel sorrow since they intuit the sufferings of others (with a hint of the sense 'putting on a show of grief in order to find out why others are sorrowful').
1240 **women waxen minds** Caxton's *Game and Play of the Chess* expresses this commonplace, ed. William E. A. Axon (1883), 123–4: 'For the women been likened unto soft wax or soft air and therefore she is called *mulier* which is as much to say in Latin as *mollis aer*. And in English "soft air". And it happeth oft times that the nature of them that been soft and mole taketh sooner impression than the nature of men that is rude and strong.' Compare *Cymbeline* 5.6.437–54. The commonplace here, though, is used to exculpate women by emphasizing the violence of the male.
1241 **will** i.e. as marble desires it (the waxen minds of women bear the impression of hard marble)
1242 **The weak oppressed** The weak being oppressed . . .
  strange kinds alien natures
1243 **skill** cleverness. The context suggests a pejorative sense ('tricksy cunning') which is not found elsewhere. The poet may have needed a rhyme.
1247 **champaign** flat open land; often land which has not been cultivated or enclosed into fields. Stressed on the first syllable.
1248 **Lays open** exposes to the view
1250 **Cave-keeping** cave-dwelling. *OED* records no non-Shakespearian examples. Compare *Cymbeline* 4.2.300: 'I thought I was a cavekeeper'.
  obscurely hidden from the eye; in darkness

Through crystal walls each little mote will peep;
    Though men can cover crimes with bold, stern looks,
    Poor women's faces are their own faults' books.

No man inveigh against the withered flower,
But chide rough winter that the flower hath killed;   1255
Not that devoured, but that which doth devour
Is worthy blame. O let it not be held
Poor women's faults that they are so fulfilled
    With men's abuses: those proud lords, to blame,
    Make weak-made women tenants to their shame.   1260

The precedent whereof in Lucrece view,
Assailed by night with circumstances strong
Of present death, and shame that might ensue
By that her death to do her husband wrong.
Such danger to resistance did belong   1265
    That dying fear through all her body spread,
    And who cannot abuse a body dead?   –

By this mild patience bid fair Lucrece speak
To the poor counterfeit of her complaining:

1257 held] Q (hild) 1258 fulfilled] Q; full filled GILDON 1714; full-filled OXFORD 1263
ensue‸] MALONE (*conj.* Capell); ~. Q; ~, Q3

1251 **mote** speck. (The *crystal walls* are the faces or eyes of women.)
1253 Compare the inscrutability of Tarquin at ll. 101–2.
1254 No man let no man
1255 **rough winter** Compare the 'rough winds' of Sonnet *18*.3.
1257 **held** Q's 'hild' is a regular sixteenth-century spelling of 'held', and may reflect Warwickshire dialect pronunciation (Kökeritz, 188).
1258 **fulfilled** filled up to the full (*OED* 1). Oxford's 'full-filled' conveys the suggestion that women carry the burden of men's lust (compare *the load of lust*, l. 734), but is unnecessary given that Q reads 'fulfild' and that the sense is common in the period.
1259 **abuses** ill-usage, with perhaps a sexual overtone (*OED* 6 and Partridge). Compare *Venus* l. 792.
    lords the owners of property, as distinct from *tenants* (*OED* 2d)
    to blame either parenthetically '(to their

shame)' or 'lords *of* blame'. The latter would be very unusual.
1260 **tenants** enjoy temporary possession of land from a *lord* on condition of making payments or offering services.
1261 **precedent** example, pattern
1262 **strong** which gave a strong likelihood
1263 **present** imminent
1266 **dying fear** paralysing fear; perhaps too 'fear of death'. The uncertainty in the sense here reflects an uncertainty in the action of the poem: did Lucrece pass out when Tarquin assaulted her, as Chaucer's Lucretia does ('And in a swogh [swoon] she lay, and wex [became] so ded | Men myghte smyten of hire arm or hed', *LGW* ll. 1816–17)? Was she too afraid of infamy to resist him as she is in Livy and Ovid? Or was she physically unable to resist him because she was paralysed with terror?
1268 **bid** bade
1269 **poor counterfeit** i.e. the maid, who is imitating Lucrece's grief

'My girl,' quoth she, 'on what occasion break   1270
Those tears from thee, that down thy cheeks are raining?
If thou dost weep for grief of my sustaining,
    Know, gentle wench, it small avails my mood:
    If tears could help, mine own would do me good.

'But tell me, girl, when went' (and there she stayed   1275
Till after a deep groan) 'Tarquin from hence?'
'Madam, ere I was up,' replied the maid,
'The more to blame my sluggard negligence.
Yet with the fault I thus far can dispense:
    Myself was stirring ere the break of day,   1280
    And ere I rose was Tarquin gone away.

'But, lady, if your maid may be so bold,
She would request to know your heaviness.'
'O peace,' quoth Lucrece. 'if it should be told
The repetition cannot make it less;   1285
For more it is than I can well express,
    And that deep torture may be called a hell
    When more is felt than one hath power to tell.

'Go get me hither paper, ink, and pen—
Yet save that labour, for I have them here.   1290
(What should I say?) One of my husband's men
Bid thou be ready, by and by, to bear
A letter to my lord, my love, my dear.
    Bid him with speed prepare to carry it:
    The cause craves haste, and it will soon be writ.'   1295

Her maid is gone, and she prepares to write,
First hovering o'er the paper with her quill.
Conceit and grief an eager combat fight:
What wit sets down is blotted straight with will.

1299 straight] Q; still Q3

1272 **my sustaining** which I am supporting
1273 **small avails** is little help to
1279 **fault** The word has had a weighty moral
    sense for Lucrece throughout the early
    part of the poem, ll. 629, 715, 724, 1073,
    etc.; here it dwindles to a domestic failing
    in a manner that evokes the different
    mental realms of the two women.

1283 **know your heaviness** understand the
    reasons for your sorrow
1285 **repetition** recital, narration (*OED* 3;
    first cited from *Richard III*)
1298 **Conceit** thought (about how best to
    phrase the letter)
1299 **What wit . . . will** As she forms a
    mannered literary expression (*wit*) her

This is too curious good; this blunt and ill.   1300
   Much like a press of people at a door
   Throng her inventions which shall go before.

At last she thus begins: 'Thou worthy lord
Of that unworthy wife that greeteth thee,
Health to thy person; next, vouchsafe t' afford   1305
(If ever, love, thy Lucrece thou wilt see)
Some present speed to come and visit me.
   So I commend me, from our house in grief:
   My woes are tedious, though my words are brief.'

Here folds she up the tenor of her woe,   1310
Her certain sorrow writ uncertainly.
By this short schedule Collatine may know
Her grief, but not her grief's true quality.
She dares not thereof make discovery
   Lest he should hold it her own gross abuse   1315
   Ere she with blood had stained her stained excuse.

Besides the life and feeling of her passion,
She hoards to spend, when he is by to hear her,

1306 love] Q; live *MS conj. in Q4* (Malone 327)   1310 tenor] Q (tenure)   1316 stained . . .
stained] Q; stained . . . strain'd SEWELL; stained . . . stain's OXFORD (*conj.* Taylor)

passions (*will*) prompt her to cross it out.
She produces a figure rhetoricians called
'aporia², 'when we show that we doubt
either where to begin for the multitude of
things, or what to say or do, in some
strange and doubtful matter' (Peacham,
sig. Mı").

1300 **curious good** corresponds to *wit*: too
mannered, over-artful.
1301 **press** crowd (*OED* 1a)
1302 **which . . . before** striving which
shall enter first (or have precedence in
rank)
1305 **vouchsafe t' afford** graciously consent
to give
1308 **commend . . . house** 'From our house
at . . .' is a formulaic ending to letters in
the period.
1310 **tenor** (a) an exact copy of a legal state-
ment by a witness (*OED* 1b; also Wynd-
ham); (b) quality, nature (*OED* 3a); (c)
general drift of (*OED* 1a). Q's 'tenure' is

a common sixteenth-century spelling of
tenor.
1311 **uncertainly** 'not so as to convey certain
knowledge' (Schmidt)
1312 **schedule** note (probably pronounced
'sedule', as in Q's spelling 'Cedule'). Since
letters in this period often went astray or
were read by spies they frequently con-
tained only brief warnings of matters of
greater import, and appealed to the
reader either to come to the writer to
obtain full information, or to ask the
bearer for more detail.
1313 **quality** occasion, nature (*OED* 8b)
1314 **make discovery** disclose
1315 **abuse** Compare l. 1259 n.
1316 **stained excuse** Her excuse is contami-
nated by the crime which it attempts to
excuse. It is tempting to emend to 'stain's
excuse', but Q unemended does reflect a
recurrent preoccupation in the poem with
the ways in which Lucrece is involuntarily
contaminated by Tarquin's crime.

When sighs, and groans, and tears may grace the fashion
Of her disgrace, the better so to clear her   1320
From that suspicion which the world might bear her.
  To shun this blot, she would not blot the letter
  With words, till action might become them better.

To see sad sights moves more than hear them told,
For then the eye interprets to the ear   1325
The heavy motion that it doth behold,
When every part, a part of woe doth bear.
  'Tis but a part of sorrow that we hear:
  Deep sounds make lesser noise than shallow fords,
  And sorrow ebbs, being blown with wind of words.   1330

Her letter now is sealed, and on it writ
'At Ardea to my lord with more than haste'.
The post attends, and she delivers it,
Charging the sour-faced groom to hie as fast
  As lagging fowls before the northern blast.   1335

1335 blast] QB; blasts QA (Malone 34, 886 and Sion)

1319 **grace** add rhetorical ornaments to
  fashion (a) appearance; (b) the shaping forth
1322 **blot** disgrace
1323 **action** formalized gesture (as in *Hamlet* 3.2.17–18: 'Suit the action to the word, the word to the action'). An orator went through five stages: *inventio*, or finding out matter; *dispositio*, or placing it in order; *elocutio*, or clothing the matter in words; *memoria*, or committing it to memory; and *pronuntiatio*, or expressive delivery. *Actio* (or *gestus*) was a subdivision of this last, in which the orator used gesture to increase the effect of his speech. As Quintilian notes (11.3.65), 'there are many things which we can express without the assistance of words'.
1324 Throughout the period there were formalized debates as to the relative superiority of the sister arts of poetry and painting. See Sonnet 16.10 n.
1326 **heavy motion** grave emotion. *Motion* can also mean 'puppet show', which were in this period often on serious or biblical topics. This would tie in with *part* in the following line.
1327 **part . . . part** theatrical role . . . portion.

On the figure of *antanaclasis*, see l. 1151 n.
1329 **Deep sounds** (a) deep waters (playing on *OED* 'sound' *n.*[1] II.4: 'strait, inlet of the sea'); (b) low notes. It was proverbial that 'shallow waters make the greatest sound' (Dent W130).
1330 **ebbs** diminishes. For the proverbial belief that sorrow dwindles the more it is expressed see *Venus* l. 331 n.
1331 **or it** Addresses were written on the outside of the folded and sealed sheet of a letter. Here the poem seems almost to fold back on itself, as the address recalls its first line.
1334 **sour-faced groom** peevish-looking servant. Compounds of *-faced* in Shakespeare describe a permanent feature rather than a volatile expression: so 'lean-faced envy' in *2 Henry VI (Contention)* 3.2.319, 'paper-faced villain' in *2 Henry IV* 5.4.10, 'smooth-faced wooers' in *L.L.L.* 5.2.815; although the 'cream-faced loon' in *Macbeth* 5.3.11 is simply showing his fear. Lucrece's groom just looks *sour* by nature, rather than as a result of his response to Lucrece.
1335 **lagging** loitering (the wind forces them along despite their natural slowness)

Speed more than speed but dull and slow she deems:
Extremity still urgeth such extremes.

The homely villein curtsies to her low,
And, blushing on her with a steadfast eye,
Receives the scroll without or yea or no,   1340
And forth with bashful innocence doth hie.
But they whose guilt within their bosoms lie
    Imagine every eye beholds their blame:
    For Lucrece thought he blushed to see her shame,

When, silly groom, God wot, it was defect   1345
Of spirit, life, and bold audacity:
Such harmless creatures have a true respect
To talk in deeds, while others saucily
Promise more speed, but do it leisurely.
    Even so this pattern of the worn-out age   1350
    Pawned honest looks, but laid no words to gage.

His kindled duty kindled her mistrust,
That two red fires in both their faces blazèd.
She thought he blushed, as knowing Tarquin's lust,
And blushing with him wistly on him gazèd.   1355
Her earnest eye did make him more amazèd:
    The more she saw the blood his cheeks replenish
    The more she thought he spied in her some blemish.

1338 curtsies] Q (cursies)   1350 this pattern of the] Q (most copies); the patterne of this Q
(British Library C.21.c.45, Folger-Devonshire, Huntington, Rosenbach)

1337 **Extremity** extreme suffering or urgency
1338 **homely villein** rough-mannered ser-
vant. *Villain* derives from 'villein', a feudal
serf, and can be used in this period simply
to describe someone's class without
implying wickedness.
curtsies Both men and women were regu-
larly said to curtsy in this period. Q's
'cursies' is a common sixteenth-century
spelling which is modernized here.
1339 **blushing** looking on her with a blush
(exploiting the archaic sense 'to glance
at', *OED* 2)
1342 **bosoms lie** The proximity of *bosoms*
prompts the plural form of the verb.
1345 **wot** knows

1347 **true respect** proper concern. Compare
ll. 201 n.
1348 **talk in deeds** 'Few words and many
deeds' is proverbial (Tilley W797). Com-
pare its rhetorically sophisticated equiva-
lent in l. 1323.
saucily presumptuously (especially used
of remarks by inferiors to their social
superiors)
1350 **pattern** example (i.e. the groom)
1351 **Pawned** gave as a security (for his
obedience)
to gage as a pledge
1353 **That** with the result that
1355 **wistly** intently. See *Venus* l. 343.
1356 **amazèd** abashed, confused

But long she thinks till he return again
And yet the duteous vassal scarce is gone;   1360
The weary time she cannot entertain,
For now 'tis stale to sigh, to weep, and groan:
So woe hath wearied woe, moan tired moan,
    That she her plaints a little while doth stay,
    Pausing for means to mourn some newer way.   1365

At last she calls to mind where hangs a piece
Of skilful painting, made for Priam's Troy,
Before the which is drawn the power of Greece,

1359 **long she thinks** it seems a long time; she eagerly awaits (*OED* s.v. 'think' *n.*[1] 3 and 'think' *n.*[2] 10c). Originally the phrase used the obsolete verb 'think', which means 'to seem', and which normally takes the dative (as in 'methinks' or 'it seems to me'). By the 1590s it was usual to use the phrase, as here, with the nominative.

1361 **entertain** occupy, while away (*OED* 9b)

1362 **stale** wearisome. The word is often used in Shakespeare of immaterial things that have lost their freshness.

1364 **stay** pause

1366–1568 The *piece of skilful painting* presents an elaborate and illusionistic alternative to the simple moralized stories of the *painted cloth* referred to in l. 245. The description explores the ways in which an artistic representation can harmonize with and be affected by the emotions of an observer. This concern with the relations between emotion and semblance has already been explored in the exchange between Lucrece and her maid. The description is an exercise in ecphrasis (or the verbal description of a work of art), and engages with debates about the relative merits of poetry and painting (for which see Sonnet 16.10 n). It may owe something to Samuel Daniel's *Complaint of Rosamond* (1592), which includes a similar extended description of mythological scenes on a casket (ll. 372–92), and perhaps to Sackville's Induction to *The Mirror for Magistrates*, in which there is an extensive ecphrasis of the siege of Troy, which is represented on the shield of Mars in the Underworld. Arguments as to whether this depiction is a tapestry or a

painting are beside the point (although the references to *each dry drop* in l. 1375 and *painter* in l. 1390 tip the balance decisively in favour of a painting): the focus is on how words relate to visual images, and how both relate to human emotions and experiences, rather than on the precise medium of representation. The chief source is the moment when Virgil's Aeneas sees a depiction of the sack of Troy in Venus's Temple (*Aen.* 1.453 ff.): in Phaer's translation, Aeneas 'wondered at the precious things the craftsmen there had wrought: | He seeth among them all the gests of Troy, and stories all, | And wars that with their fame had filled all kingdoms great and small. | King Priam and Atridas twain, and wroth to both Achille' (Phaer 1.430–3). The episode brings to a climax the images of siege and battery which have run through the poem so far, and gives Shakespeare's second narrative poem epic resonances, since it implicitly establishes an analogy between the heroine Lucrece and Virgil's Aeneas. There are notable similarities between the pathetic portrait of Hecuba and the Player King's speech in *Hamlet* 2.2.422–520, which, like Lucrece's *skilful painting*, provides an archaic parallel for Hamlet's emotions.

1367 **made for** representing

1368 **the which** The redundant use of the definite article before the relative *which* was archaic by the 1590s.
drawn (a) assembled (*OED* 29a), as in *K. John* 4.2.118: 'That such an army could be drawn in France'; (b) depicted. The pun elides the act of depiction and the activities which are depicted.

For Helen's rape the city to destroy,
Threat'ning cloud-kissing Ilion with annoy,   1370
   Which the conceited painter drew so proud,
   As heaven (it seemed) to kiss the turrets bowed.

A thousand lamentable objects there,
In scorn of Nature, Art gave lifeless life;
Many a dry drop seemed a weeping tear,   1375
Shed for the slaughtered husband by the wife.
The red blood reeked to show the painter's strife,
   And dying eyes gleamed forth their ashy lights,
   Like dying coals burnt out in tedious nights.

There might you see the labouring pioneer,   1380
Begrimed with sweat, and smearèd all with dust;
And from the tow'rs of Troy there would appear
The very eyes of men through loop-holes thrust,
Gazing upon the Greeks with little lust:
   Such sweet observance in this work was had,   1385
   That one might see those far off eyes look sad.

In great commanders grace and majesty
You might behold, triumphing in their faces;
In youth quick bearing and dexterity,

1374 lifeless] Q (liuelesse)

1369 **rape** (a) forcible removal; (b) sexual violation. The word is used only here and in l. 909. It is never used directly of Lucrece except in the running-titles at the head of each page of Q.

1370 **cloud-kissing Ilion** The towers of Troy (otherwise known as Ilium or, more rarely, Ilion) were proverbially high, as in Marlowe's 'topless towers of Ilium' (*Dr Faustus* A Text 5.1.92).

1371 **conceited** artful, with a play on *proud*. Throughout the poem artifice is placed just on the boundaries of moral defect, as in ll. 1296–1302 and 1423.

1372 **As** that (Abbott §109). Compare l. 1420.

1374 **lifeless** inanimate. Compare *Venus* l. 211. The secondary sense 'dead' implies that art can reanimate scenes and people long since dead.

1375 **dry drop** (of paint)

1377 **strife** (a) effort (*OED* 4; pre-dating the first cited example from *All's Well*); (b) a secondary suggestion via the more usual sense 'contention, struggle' that the painter is actually participating in the battle he depicts. *Strife* is often used to describe the emulous competition between art and nature, as in *Venus* l. 291.

1380 **pioneer** 'One of a body of foot-soldiers who march with or in advance of an army or regiment, having spades, pickaxes, etc. to dig trenches, repair roads' (*OED* 1)

1383 **loop-holes** 'A narrow vertical opening, usually widening inwards, cut in a wall or other defence, to allow of the passage of missiles' (*OED* 1)

1384 **lust** relish

1385 **observance** attention to detail

1388 **triumphing** gloriously apparent (compare l. 12 and n.). The word is stressed on the second syllable.

And here and there the painter interlaces 1390
Pale cowards marching on with trembling paces,
    Which heartless peasants did so well resemble,
    That one would swear he saw them quake and tremble.

In Ajax and Ulysses, O what art
Of physiognomy might one behold! 1395
The face of either ciphered either's heart;
Their face their manners most expressly told.
In Ajax' eyes blunt rage and rigour rolled;
    But the mild glance that sly Ulysses lent
    Showed deep regard and smiling government. 1400

There, pleading, might you see grave Nestor stand,
As 'twere encouraging the Greeks to fight,
Making such sober action with his hand
That it beguiled attention, charmed the sight.
In speech it seemed his beard, all silver-white, 1405
    Wagged up and down, and from his lips did fly
    Thin winding breath, which purled up to the sky.

1391 paces,] Q6; ~. Q   1399 sly] Q; she Q4

1390 **interlaces** artfully interweaves
1393 **he** 'One' is regularly masculine in
    sixteenth-century English; here, however,
    the pronoun opens a gap between the
    abstract, ideal observer and the female
    Lucrece.
1394–1400 The descriptions of the wrathful
    Ajax and the sly Ulysses draw on the tra-
    ditional attributes of the two heroes, but
    there may be some debt to Golding's epis-
    tle to his translation of *Met*. ll. 248–53:
    'Ulysses doth express | The image of dis-
    cretion, wit, and great advisedness. | And
    Ajax on the other side doth represent a
    man | Stout, heady, ireful, halt of mind,
    and such a one as can | Abide to suffer no
    repulse'. The juxtaposition of the two
    heroes recalls *Met*. 13, in which Ajax and
    Ulysses debate their rival claims for the
    arms of Achilles in the clearest set-pieces
    of rhetorical disputation in classical lit-
    erature: the description of the power of
    painting is inconspicuously leading back
    to the power of oratory
1395 **physiognomy** 'The art of judging char-
    acter and disposition from the features of
    the face' (*OED* 1)

1396 **ciphered** expressed. See l. 207 n.
    either's his own
1397 **manners** moral character, disposition
    expressly distinctly
1398 **rigour** harshness, obduracy
1399 **sly Ulysses** This epithet is also found in
    Golding 13 58, 115, and 913, although
    Ovid himself does not give the hero any
    distinguishing epithet (Phaer favours
    'false Ulysses').
1400 **smiling government** affable leadership
1403 **action** expressive gesture. See l. 1323 n.
1406 **Wagged** moved. Editors have found a
    colloquial or comic effect here (Prince,
    Roe), but the verb was regularly used of
    repeated slight motions of the body, and
    did not come to be reserved for the fore-
    fingers of grandmothers, the tongues of
    fools, and the tails of happy dogs until
    c.1700.
1407 **purled** curled (like smoke or a rivulet;
    OED v.² 2, first cited usage in this sense). If
    the **painting** is thought to be a tapestry
    there may be some play on *OED* v.¹
    'To embroider with gold or silver
    thread' (such thread often took the form
    of a tightly wound spiral).

About him were a press of gaping faces,
Which seemed to swallow up his sound advice,
All jointly list'ning, but with several graces,   1410
As if some mermaid did their ears entice;
Some high, some low, the painter was so nice.
 The scalps of many, almost hid behind,
 To jump up higher seemed to mock the mind.

Here one man's hand leaned on another's head,   1415
His nose being shadowed by his neighbour's ear;
Here one being thronged bears back, all boll'n and red;
Another, smothered, seems to pelt and swear,
And in their rage such signs of rage they bear
 As, but for loss of Nestor's golden words,   1420
 It seemed they would debate with angry swords.

For much imaginary work was there,
Conceit deceitful, so compact, so kind,
That for Achilles' image stood his spear,
Gripped in an armèd hand, himself behind   1425
Was left unseen, save to the eye of mind:

1409 **sound** The pun on 'worthy' and 'audible' shifts back from praise of painting to praise of oratory.

1410 **several graces** quite distinct postures (and each was beautiful)

1411 **mermaid** On the charms of mermaids' voices, see *Venus* l. 429 n.

1412 **Some high, some low** (both in social status and physical position)
nice precise

1414 **mock the mind** deceive. Viewers know that they are not actually higher, but are deceived by the perspective: compare *Winter's Tale* 5.3.68: 'As we are mocked with art.'

1417 **thronged** pressed back
boll'n swollen up (archaic by 1594)

1418 **pelt** strike out repeatedly. *OED* gives this as the first citation for sense 6, 'To throw out angry words', but offers no other examples before 1630.

1420 **As . . . loss** as if, but for the fear that they would lose . . .

1421 **debate** fight (a sense slightly archaic by 1594)

1422–8 Compare the description of a painting of the siege of Thebes in Philostratus's *Imagines* 1.4 (ed. with an English transla-

tion by A. Fairbanks (Cambridge, Mass., and London, 1931), 16–17): 'some [soldiers] are seen in full figure, others with the legs hidden, others from the waist up, then only the busts of some, heads only, helmets only, and finally just spear-points'. This work was required reading at St John's College, Oxford, where Thomas Jenkins, principal master at Stratford Grammar School, was a student. French and Latin translations of the Greek were available.

1422 **imaginary work** both 'a work of the artist's imagination' and 'a work which stimulates the imagination of the viewer'. Compare *Henry V* 1.0.17–18: 'And let us . . . on your imaginary forces work'.

1423 **Conceit deceitful** a work of art so intricate that it tricks the eye. Compare the use of *conceited* in l. 1371 and n.
compact made up of a complex intermingling of elements
kind natural

1424 **spear** Achilles's spear was sufficiently well-known to stand by metonymy for his physical presence. See e.g. *2 Henry VI (Contention)* 5.1.100.

A hand, a foot, a face, a leg, a head
Stood for the whole to be imaginèd.

And from the walls of strong-besiegèd Troy,
When their brave hope, bold Hector, marched to field,   1430
Stood many Trojan mothers, sharing joy
To see their youthful sons bright weapons wield,
And to their hope they such odd action yield
    That through their light joy seemèd to appear
    (Like bright things stained) a kind of heavy fear.   1435

And from the strand of Dardan where they fought,
To Simois' reedy banks the red blood ran,
Whose waves to imitate the battle sought,
With swelling ridges, and their ranks began
To break upon the gallèd shore, and then   1440
    Retire again, till meeting greater ranks
    They join, and shoot their foam at Simois' banks.

To this well-painted piece is Lucrece come,
To find a face where all distress is stelled.
Many she sees, where cares have carvèd some,   1445
But none where all distress and dolour dwelled;
Till she despairing Hecuba beheld,

1436 strand] Q (strond)   1440 then] Q (than)

1429 **strong-besiegèd** heavily besieged. Q does not hyphenate here.
1430 **Hector** the eldest son of King Priam of Troy, and the greatest warrior of the Trojans. His death and the restoration of his body conclude Homer's *Iliad*.
1433 **such . . . yield** they make such unusual gestures to express their hope. On *actions* see l. 1323 n.
1434 **light** cheerful
1436 **strand of Dardan** the sea-shore of Troy. Dardania was an alternative name for Troas, the country in which Troy was situated, and derives from its first founder King Dardanus. Shakespeare probably uses it because 'Dardanius' is the epithet most frequently used by Virgil to mean 'Trojan', and its anglicized form occurs frequently in Phaer's translation of the *Aeneid*. Q's 'strond' is an archaic spelling which is modernized here.
1437 **Simois** a river which flowed from Mount Ida and joined the Scamander in

the plain of Troy. It is often associated with the death of warriors in Virgil: 'where Hector fierce lieth under Achilles' lance | King Sarpedon and many a lord, now blissful was their chance? | Whose bodies with their arms and shields in Simois' waters sinks', Phaer 1.95–7.
1439 **ridges** crests
1440 **gallèd** chafed, worn; perhaps also influenced by *OED* v.[1] 5: 'To harass or annoy in warfare'
1440 **then** Q reads 'than' (an archaic spelling by 1594) for the sake of rhyme.
1444 **stelled** portrayed. See Sonnet 24.1 n.
1445 **carvèd some** engraved some *distress*
1447 **despairing** The participle dangles sympathetically between Hecuba and Lucrece. Through the figure of *prosopopoeia* an orator invents suitable words for a person or thing, 'and sometime they raise as it were the dead again, and cause them to complain or to witness that they knew' (Peacham, sig. O3r).

Staring on Priam's wounds with her old eyes,
Which bleeding under Pyrrhus' proud foot lies.

In her the painter had anatomized   1450
Time's ruin, beauty's wrack, and grim care's reign.
Her cheeks with chaps and wrinkles were disguised:
Of what she was no semblance did remain.
Her blue blood changed to black in every vein,
   Wanting the spring that those shrunk pipes had fed,   1455
   Showed life imprisoned in a body dead.

On this sad shadow Lucrece spends her eyes,
And shapes her sorrow to the beldam's woes,
Who nothing wants to answer her but cries,
And bitter words to ban her cruel foes.   1460
The painter was no god to lend her those;
   And therefore Lucrece swears he did her wrong,
   To give her so much grief, and not a tongue.

'Poor instrument', quoth she, 'without a sound,
I'll tune thy woes with my lamenting tongue,   1465
And drop sweet balm in Priam's painted wound,

1452 chaps] Q (chops)

1447 **Hecuba** the wife of King Priam, whose
misery at witnessing the death of her
husband and the destruction of her city
forms the subject of Euripides' *Trojan
Women* and *Hecuba*, as well as the sub-
stance of the First Player's speech in
Hamlet 2.2.504–20

1449 **Which** Priam's wounds substitute for
his body as the description adopts
Hecuba's viewpoint.
  Pyrrhus kills Priam in the *Aeneid* with-
out this ritual gesture of victory: ' "Now
die," and (as he spake that word) from
the altar self he drew | Him trembling
there, and deep him through his sons'
blood did imbrue. | And with his left
hand wrapped his locks, with right
hand through his side | His glist'ring
sword outdrawn, he did hard to the hilts
to glide' (Phaer 2.555–8). In Marlowe's
Dido Queen of Carthage 2.1.242, however,
he is described as 'treading upon his
breast'.

1450 **anatomized** laid bare, minutely
explored the inner workings of
1451 **ruin** destructive influence (*OED* 8)
1452 **chaps** cracks. Q's 'chops' is the pre-
ferred Shakespearian spelling. See Sonnet
62.10 n.
1454 **blue blood** is purely descriptive of
colour: *OED* does not record the sense
'noble' before the nineteenth century.
1455 **spring** stream (i.e. Priam)
  shrunk pipes i.e. her veins
1457 **shadow** representation; also 'an at-
tenuated remnant' (*OED* 5g)
1460 **ban** curse
1461 **lend** give. As *OED* notes (s.v. *v*.² 2a), the
object of the verb (here *words*) 'usually
denotes something which though capable
of being bestowed by the subject is not in
his possession'.
1465 **tune** give musical expression to (imply-
ing that she will adapt her voice to suit the
lamentations of Hecuba)
1466 **balm** ointment (usually aromatic;
hence *sweet*)

And rail on Pyrrhus that hath done him wrong,
And with my tears quench Troy that burns so long.
   And with my knife scratch out the angry eyes
   Of all the Greeks that are thine enemies.   1470

'Show me the strumpet that began this stir
That with my nails her beauty I may tear:
Thy heat of lust, fond Paris, did incur
This load of wrath that burning Troy doth bear;
Thy eye kindled the fire that burneth here,   1475
   And here in Troy, for trespass of thine eye,
   The sire, the son, the dame, and daughter die.

'Why should the private pleasure of some one
Become the public plague of many moe?
Let sin alone committed light alone   1480
Upon his head that hath transgressèd so.
Let guiltless souls be freed from guilty woe:
   For one's offence why should so many fall,
   To plague a private sin in general?

1475 Thy] Q; Thine COLLIER

1467 **rail on** abuse
1468 **quench** Troy put out the fire which raged through Troy at its destruction
1471 **the strumpet** i.e. Helen, whose abduction by Paris initiated the Trojan war. The sequence of Lucrece's observations of the painting up to this point closely follows the order of narration in Virgil's *Aeneid*. After the death of Priam and the burning of Troy in Book 2, Aeneas finds Helen skulking away in the midst of the falling city: 'Dame Helen I might see to sit, bright burnings gave me light | Wherever I went, the ways I past, all thing was set in sight. | She fearing her the Trojans' wrath, for Troy destroyed to wreak, | Greeks' torments, and her husband's force whose wedlock she did break, | The plague of Troy, and of her country monster most untame: | There sat she with her hated head, by the altars hid for shame' (Phaer 2.574–9).
1474 **load of wrath** Compare the *load of Lust* with which Tarquin leaves Lucrece in l. 734.

1475 **Thy eye** The anomalous form (the norm is 'thine eye') may indicate the scornful emphasis of accusation, or may be used simply to reinforce the symmetry with *Thy heat*, as in Sonnet 47.5 and n.
1479 **plague** calamity (often with its origins in divine displeasure). Plague raged in London through 1592–4. Preachers frequently argued that it was the consequence of sin. See F. P. Wilson, *The Plague in Shakespeare's London* (Oxford, 1927), 2–4.
moe more (the form is often used of number; here it is used for rhyme, in l. 1615 it is used for assonance)
1480 **light** descend upon the head of (as a punishment)
1482 **guilty woe** the misery suitable to one who has done wrong (with a glance at Lucrece's own state: 'the misery of feeling responsible for something which is not in fact their fault')
1484 **To plague . . . general** to make a general punishment as a result of one person's crime

'Lo, here weeps Hecuba, here Priam dies,   1485
Here manly Hector faints, here Troilus sounds,
Here friend by friend in bloody channel lies,
And friend to friend gives unadvisèd wounds,
And one man's lust these many lives confounds.
    Had doting Priam checked his son's desire   1490
    Troy had been bright with fame, and not with fire.'

Here feelingly she weeps Troy's painted woes;
For sorrow, like a heavy hanging bell,
Once set on ringing with his own weight goes;
Then little strength rings out the doleful knell.   1495
So Lucrece, set a-work, sad tales doth tell
    To pencilled pensiveness, and coloured sorrow;
    She lends them words, and she their looks doth borrow.

She throws her eyes about the painting round,
And who she finds forlorn she doth lament: 1500
At last she sees a wretched image bound,

1486 **manly Hector** should not technically be fainting if the picture is of the sack of Troy since he was already dead, but the scene encompasses the whole history of the siege.
sounds swoons. Again there may be an allusion to events before the sack of Troy, since Troilus is chiefly famous for having loved and lost Cressida. *Sound* is often used of the swoons of lovers.

1487 **bloody channel** either 'stream of blood' or 'gutter which is running with blood' (*OED* s.v. 'channel' *n.*[1] 3a)

1488 **unadvisèd** unintended

1490 **checked** (a) restrained; (b) rebuked (*OED* 11). There may be a reminder here that Tarquin is the son of a king who has failed to control his conduct.

1492 **feelingly** with emotion (*OED* 3; first cited usage in this sense). The word also suggests that she had herself experienced the emotions which she is sympathetically lamenting (*OED* 4: 'By or from actual personal feeling').

1494 **on ringing** a-ringing (Abbott §180)

1495 **knell** is used especially when bells are rung to mark or memorialize a death. See Sonnet 71.2 n.

1496 **a-work** to work (Abbott §24)

1497 **pencilled pensiveness** painted sorrow. The 'pencil' was frequently used as a metonymy for the art of painting: see Sonnet 16.10 n.
coloured painted. The verb has strong negative associations with deception and misrepresentation; so 'mere images of sorrow'.

1498 **looks** appearance, expressions

1499 **about . . . round** all over

1500 **who** whoever

1501 **wretched image bound** the image of a miserable prisoner. This is Sinon, the Greek who in *Aen.* 2.57–198 pretended to have been abandoned by his allies, and who persuaded the Trojans to admit into their city the wooden horse which contained the Greek warriors. The comparison between Tarquin and Sinon (developed in ll. 1541–61) derives from an earlier episode in the career of Tarquinius Sextus. His father Tarquinius pretended to have abandoned the war against the Gabii, and left Sextus behind to pretend, as Sinon does in the *Aeneid*, that he had been cast out by his own side. He then became general of the Gabii and betrayed them (*Fasti* 2.690–710; Livy 1.53–4). Marsus's annotations make the comparison between Tarquin and Sinon explicit (Marsus, 141; Constantius also quotes *Aen.* 2.196, when Aeneas describes how the Trojans were deceived by Sinon, Marsus, 140).

That piteous looks to Phrygian shepherds lent
His face though full of cares, yet showed content.
  Onward to Troy with the blunt swains he goes,
  So mild that patience seemed to scorn his woes.   1505

In him the painter laboured with his skill
To hide deceit, and give the harmless show
An humble gait, calm looks, eyes wailing still,
A brow unbent that seemed to welcome woe,
Cheeks neither red, nor pale, but mingled so   1510
  That blushing red no guilty instance gave,
  Nor ashy pale the fear that false hearts have.

But, like a constant and confirmèd devil,
He entertained a show so seeming just,
And therein so ensconced his secret evil,
That jealousy itself could not mistrust   1515
False creeping Craft and Perjury should thrust
  Into so bright a day such black-faced storms,
  Or blot with hell-born sin such saint-like forms.

The well-skilled workman this mild image drew   1520
For perjured Sinon, whose enchanting story
The credulous old Priam after slew,
Whose words like wild-fire burnt the shining glory

1507 deceit] Q; conceit Q4   1508 wailing] Q; vailing Anon. *conj.* in CAMBRIDGE

1502 **piteous looks** Compare Phaer 2.64: 'And with his eyes on Trojan men did look with piteous mood'.
Phrygian Trojan
1503 **showed content** appeared satisfied (Sinon wishes to be captured in order to be able to deceive the Trojans)
1504 **blunt swains** simple shepherds (who had captured him)
1505 **So . . . woes** with such equanimity that it seemed his patience took no heed of his sufferings. Roe takes *his* as a neuter pronoun agreeing with *patience*, but it seems more probable that it here refers to Sinon.
1507 **harmless show** i.e. the painting
1508 **An humble** 'An' before an aspirate is rare in Shakespeare.
wailing Given that this is the only citation for *OED* 1c ('of the eyes: to weep') the anonymous emendation to 'vailing' (i.e. 'lowering'; see collation) is attractive. Compare *Venus* l. 956.

1509 **unbent** not cast-down or furrowed by anxiety
1511 **guilty instance** evidence of guilt (*OED* s.v. 'instance' 7)
1513 **confirmed** hardened, inveterate; playing on the ecclesiastical sense 'having received the rite of confirmation'
1514 **entertained** a show put on an appearance
1515 **ensconced** sheltered within a fortification or 'sconce' (*OED* 2)
1516 **jealousy** suspicion (*OED* 5)
mistrust suspect that (*OED* 3a)
1517 **thrust** insinuate (*OED* 7b)
1521 **Sinon** The 'i' is long, as in 'sigh'. For his history, see l. 1501 n.
enchanting bewitching
1523 **wild-fire** explosively burning incendiary matter. This combination of sulphur, naphtha, and pitch was used in warfare and would burn even under water. It is analogous to the ancient Greek fire.

Of rich-built Ilium, that the skies were sorry,
  And little stars shot from their fixèd places   1525
  When their glass fell, wherein they viewed their faces.

This picture she advisedly perused,
And chid the painter for his wondrous skill,
Saying some shape in Sinon's was abused:
So fair a form lodged not a mind so ill.   1530
And still on him she gazed, and gazing still
  Such signs of truth in his plain face she spied
  That she concludes the picture was belied.

'It cannot be', quoth she, 'that so much guile—'
She would have said 'can lurk in such a look',   1535
But Tarquin's shape came in her mind the while,
And from her tongue 'can lurk' from 'cannot' took.
'It cannot be' she in that sense forsook,
  And turned it thus: 'It cannot be, I find,
  But such a face should bear a wicked mind.   1540

'For even as subtle Sinon here is painted,
So sober-sad, so weary, and so mild
(As if with grief or travail he had fainted)
To me came Tarquin armèd to beguild

1544 armèd to beguild] Q; armed; so beguiled MALONE; armèd; too beguiled COLLIER

Compare Marlowe's *Dido Queen of Carthage* 2.1.216–18: 'And after him his band of Myrmidons, | With balls of wild-fire in their murdering paws | Which made the funeral flame that burnt fair Troy'.

1524 **that** with the result that. The stars sympathetically respond to the catastrophe.

1525 **fixèd places** The fixed stars were believed to occupy the eighth sphere in the cosmos, and were still popularly believed to be immutable. The collapse of the seemingly immutable Troy therefore prompts their fall.

1526 **glass** mirror; ideal pattern

1529 **Saying . . . abused** some other (innocent) person had been mistakenly represented as Sinon

1530 Compare the proverb 'A fair face must have good conditions' (Dent F5).

1533 **was belied** told a lie

1534 **guile—** On the rhetorical figure of aposiopesis, see l. 666 n.

1536 **the while** meanwhile

1537 Compare Sonnet 145.13.

1538 **forsook** gave up, abandoned

1539 **turned it** changed the sense

1543 **travail** labour

1544 **armèd to beguild** 'armed (like Sinon) to trick'. Q's 'begild' is probably a form of 'beguile' with a redundant final 'd'. This creates a pun on 'gild', or 'give a superficial covering to'. Compare *Venus* l. 873. Oxford (following Collier) reads, 'Tarquin armèd, too beguiled | With outward honesty'. This requires 'beguiled' to mean 'concealed or disguised by guile' (*OED* b, citing Heywood's translation of *Hercules Furens* (1581): 'He his beguilèd hooks doth bait'). An alternative modernization, which would preserve the 'beguile/ begild' ambiguity, is 'Tarquin armèd, too begild | With outward honesty'. Here 'begild' functions as a variant form of 'begilt' (the past participle 'begild' is found in the form 'beguiled' in the 1590s).

With outward honesty, but yet defiled   1545
    With inward vice: as Priam him did cherish
    So did I Tarquin; so my Troy did perish.

'Look, look how list'ning Priam wets his eyes
To see those borrowed tears that Sinon sheds.
Priam, why art thou old and yet not wise?   1550
For every tear he falls a Trojan bleeds;
His eye drops fire, no water thence proceeds.
    Those round clear pearls of his that move thy pity
    Are balls of quenchless fire to burn thy city.

'Such devils steal effects from lightless hell,   1555
For Sinon in his fire doth quake with cold,
And in that cold hot burning fire doth dwell:
These contraries such unity do hold
Only to flatter fools and make them bold;
    So Priam's trust false Sinon's tears doth flatter,   1560
    That he finds means to burn his Troy with water.'

Here all enraged such passion her assails
That patience is quite beaten from her breast.
She tears the senseless Sinon with her nails,
Comparing him to that unhappy guest   1565

1546 vice:] Q5; ~, Q   1549 sheds] Q (sheeds)

The sense would then be 'too gilded with a show of honesty [for his true nature to appear]'. Against modernizing Q's 'to' as 'too' lie (a) the awkward placing of the caesura it necessitates; (b) the fact that *armèd* becomes a lamely hanging epithet. Q's *Armèd to beguild* is in keeping with the experimental compression of the poem's language, and so is followed here. Compare the crux at Sonnet 28.12 n.

1546 **him** i.e. Sinon
    cherish entertain kindly as a guest (*OED* 3, citing *1 Henry IV* 3.3.172–3: 'Look to thy servants, cherish thy guests.') The primary sense, 'To hold dear, treat with tenderness and affection', registers Lucrece's guilty suspicion that she may have shown too much warmth to Tarquin.
1549 **borrowed** counterfeit
1549 **sheds** For the rhyme compare Sonnet 34.13–14 and n.

1554 **balls . . . fire** The tears are like *wild-fire*, l. 1523 n.
1555 **effects** appearances (more usually as a symptom of emotions (*OED* 3a); here extended to imply falsehood)
1558 **such . . . hold** form such an appearance of harmonious allegiance among themselves
1560 **doth flatter** The singular form probably derives from the fact that the plural *tears* belong to a singular subject, Sinon.
1561 **That he . . . water** i.e. the wet tears are the origin of the flames which engulf Troy. *He* refers to Sinon; *his* to Priam. *Water* was pronounced with a flatter vowel than in modern southern English (Kökeritz, 187).
1554 **senseless** insentient (used of the picture'; also perhaps 'callously unfeeling' (which applies to the man it represents)
1565 **unhappy** 'causing misfortune or trouble' (*OED* 1)

Whose deed hath made herself herself detest.
   At last she smilingly with this gives o'er:
   'Fool, fool', quoth she, 'his wounds will not be sore.'

Thus ebbs and flows the current of her sorrow,
And time doth weary time with her complaining.   1570
She looks for night, and then she longs for morrow,
And both she thinks too long with her remaining.
Short time seems long in sorrow's sharp sustaining:
   Though woe be heavy, yet it seldom sleeps,
   And they that watch see time how slow it creeps.   1575

Which all this time hath overslipped her thought
That she with painted images hath spent,
Being from the feeling of her own grief brought
By deep surmise of others' detriment,
Losing her woes in shows of discontent: 1580
   It easeth some, though none it ever curèd,
   To think their dolour others have endurèd.

But now the mindful messenger come back
Brings home his lord and other company,
Who finds his Lucrece clad in mourning black,   1585
And round about her tear-distainèd eye
Blue circles streamed, like rainbows in the sky.
   These water-galls in her dim element
   Foretell new storms to those already spent.

1566 **herself herself** The first use of the pronoun is emphatic, the second reflexive.

1567 **with this gives o'er** ceases, with this remark

1568 **sore** grievous

1573 **Short . . . sustaining** while one is enduring sorrow short periods seem long

1574 **heavy** oppressive; playing on *OED* 28, ' "Weighed down" by sleep'

1575 **watch** stay awake

1576 **Which** i.e. *woe*
overslipped passed by unnoticed (*OED* 3, citing this passage)

1579 **surmise** imagination, meditation. The other senses of the word, 'suspicion, conjecture, allegation', flavour its use here, since Lucrece has been both entertaining hypotheses about the sufferings of others, and making allegations about Sinon's wrongdoing.

1580 **shows** i.e. the picture

1581–2 Compare ll. 1111–13, and the proverb 'I am not the first and shall not be the last' (Dent F295).

1585 **mourning black** The detail may derive from Ovid: 'quae luctus causa, requirunt | cui paret exuvias?' (' "what is the cause of your grief", they asked, "whose funeral are you preparing?" ', *Fasti* 2.817–18); compare *LGW* ll. 1830–1: 'In habit swich as women used tho | Unto the buryinge of hire frendes go'.

1587 **Blue circles** See l. 1229 n.

1588 **water-galls** 'A secondary or imperfectly-formed rainbow; also applied to various other phenomena in the clouds that are believed to portend rain' (*OED* 2; first cited usage)
dim element overcast sky. This use of *element* was a poetic cliché by *Twelfth*

Which when her sad-beholding husband saw 1590
Amazedly in her sad face he stares:
Her eyes, though sod in tears, looked red and raw,
Her lively colour killed with deadly cares.
He hath no power to ask her how she fares.
   Both stood like old acquaintance in a trance, 1595
   Met far from home, word'ring each other's chance.

At last he takes her by the bloodless hand
And thus begins: 'What uncouth ill event
Hath thee befall'n, that thou dost trembling stand?
Sweet love, what spite hath thy fair colour spent? 1600
Why art thou thus attired in discontent?
   Unmask, dear dear, this moody heaviness,
   And tell thy grief, that we may give redress.'

Three times with sighs she gives her sorrow fire,
Ere once she can discharge one word of woe. 1605
At length, addressed to answer his desire,
She modestly prepares to let them know
Her honour is ta'en prisoner by the foe,
   While Collatine and his consorted lords
   With sad attention long to hear her words. 1610

And now this pale swan in her wat'ry nest
Begins the sad dirge of her certain ending:
'Few words', quoth she, 'shall fit the trespass best,

Night 3.1.57–8: 'out o' my welkin—I might say "element" but the word is overworn.'

1592 **sod** sodden. There is an awkward pun on the sense 'boiled' which gives rise to *red and raw* in the later part of the line.

1595 **acquaintance** acquaintances. The collective noun could be either singular or plural in this period.

1596 **wond'ring . . . chance** (a) amazed at their chance meeting; (b) speculating about each other's fortune in the world

1598 **uncouth** strange unknown

1602 **moody heaviness** deep melancholy

1603 **grief** both 'sorrow' and 'hurt, harm, cause of sorrow'

1604–5 **Three times . . . discharge** Early-modern firearms had to be lit before

they would *discharge*. The image is presumably that of an artilleryman who has to blow on a smouldering wick before he applies it to the fuse of a firearm. For the triple repetition, common in heroic narrative, compare Ovid: 'ter conata loqui' ('three times she tried to speak', *Fasti* 2.823).

1606 **addressed** prepared; the context activates a pun on *OED* 5, 'to aim (a missile)'

1609 **consorted** associated; fellows in a military league

1611 **swan** The bird was believed to sing only immediately before its death, as in *Othello* 5.2.254–5 and Dent S1028.

1612 **dirge** The word derives from 'dirige', the first word in the antiphon at Matins in the Office of the Dead.

1613 **fit . . . best** be suitable for this crime. On *trespass* see l. 632 n.

Where no excuse can give the fault amending.
In me moe woes than words are now depending, 1615
   And my laments would be drawn out too long
   To tell them all with one poor tirèd tongue.

'Then be this all the task it hath to say:
Dear husband, in the interest of thy bed
A stranger came, and on that pillow lay 1620
Where thou wast wont to rest thy weary head,
And what wrong else may be imaginèd
   By foul enforcement might be done to me,
   From that (alas) thy Lucrece is not free.

'For in the dreadful dead of dark midnight, 1625
With shining falchion in my chamber came
A creeping creature with a flaming light,
And softly cried "Awake, thou Roman dame,
And entertain my love, else lasting shame
   On thee and thine this night I will inflict, 1630
   If thou my love's desire do contradict.

' "For some hard-favoured groom of thine", quoth he,
"Unless thou yoke thy liking to my will,
I'll murder straight, and then I'll slaughter thee,
And swear I found you where you did fulfil 1635
The loathsome act of lust, and so did kill
   The lechers in their deed. This act will be
   My fame, and thy perpetual infamy."

'With this I did begin to start and cry,
And then against my heart he set his sword, 1640
Swearing, unless I took all patiently,
I should not live to speak another word.

1614 **give . . . amending** make atonement for the crime

1615 **depending** impending (the verb was used of legal judgements which were awaiting final resolution (*OED* 7))

1617 **To tell** if I were to tell

1619 **in the interest of thy bed** i.e. Tarquin violated your right or title over your marital bed

1623 **enforcement** use of force

1629 **entertain** receive. As in the use of *cherish* (l. 1546 and n.), the language of hospitality is given a taint of corruption.

1631 **contradict** forbid; speak against (*OED* 1)

1632 **hard-favoured groom** coarse-featured servant. Compare *Venus* l. 133.

1633 **yoke** join; submit
liking wishes; although *OED* notes the sense 'Sensuality, sexual desire, lust' (2b) in this period

1635 **fulfil** complete

So should my shame still rest upon record,
    And never be forgot in mighty Rome
    Th' adulterate death of Lucrece, and her groom.   1645

'Mine enemy was strong, my poor self weak
(And far the weaker with so strong a fear).
My bloody judge forbade my tongue to speak:
No rightful plea might plead for justice there.
His scarlet Lust came evidence to swear   1650
    That my poor beauty had purloined his eyes,
    And when the judge is robbed the prisoner dies.

'O teach me how to make mine own excuse,
Or (at the least) this refuge let me find:
Though my gross blood be stained with this abuse,   1655
Immaculate and spotless is my mind.
That was not forced, that never was inclined
    To accessary yieldings, but still pure
    Doth in her poisoned closet yet endure.'

1648 forbade] Q (forbod)   1652 robbed] Q (rob'd)

1643 **rest upon record** remain in written testimony. On *record,* stressed on the second syllable, see Sonnet 55.8 n.

1645 **adulterate** adulterous (first cited in *OED* from *Errors*)

1648 Compare Lucrece's account of her silence at l. 1266 and n.
forbade Q's 'forbod' is a regular variant form in the sixteenth century, which is modernized here.

1650 **scarlet Lust** The scarlet woman of Revelation 17: 4 ('And the woman was arrayed in purple and scarlet, and gilded with gold, and precious stones, and pearls, and had a cup of gold in her hand, full of abominations, and filthiness of her fornication') links the colour with sexual crimes; *OED* s.v. 'scarlet' 3 ('Official or ceremonial costume of scarlet, as the uniform of a soldier, the gown or robe of a doctor of divinity or law, a judge, a cardinal, etc.') is extended by metonymy in the early seventeenth century to mean 'judge'.
evidence to swear This marks radical corruption: a judge may not make a sworn affidavit of evidence in an English court of law in a case over which he is presiding.

1652 **robbed** Q's rob'd may suggest a pun on 'robed': if the same person is robed in the *scarlet* of a judge and is also *robbed,* then the prisoner will be condemned. Robbery—openly and forcibly taking property belonging to another—carried the death penalty without benefit of clergy (Sokol, 326).

1654 **refuge** plea, pretext (*OED* 4c)

1655-6 Compare Livy 1.58.7: 'Yet my body only has been violated; my heart is guiltless'.

1655 **abuse** violation, defilement

1658 **accessary yieldings** consent to complicity in the crime

1659 **closet** a small room used for conducting intimate or private work; compare the *cabinet* in l. 442. Its space was notionally private, as Angel Day, *The English Secretary* (first printed 1586; 1625 edn.), 103, notes: 'The closet in every house, as it is a reposement of secrets, so is it only . . . at the owner's, and no other's commandment'.

Lo, here the hopeless merchant of this loss,   1660
With head declined and voice dammed up with woe,
With sad set eyes and wreathèd arms across,
From lips new waxen pale, begins to blow
The grief away, that stops his answer so.
  But, wretched as he is, he strives in vain: 1665
  What he breathes out, his breath drinks up again.

As through an arch, the violent roaring tide
Outruns the eye that doth behold his haste,
Yet in the eddy boundeth in his pride
Back to the strait that forced him on so fast,   1670
In rage sent out, recalled in rage being past:
  Even so his sighs. His sorrows make a saw,
  To push grief on, and back the same grief draw.

Which speechless woe of his poor she attendeth,
And his untimely frenzy thus awaketh: 1675
'Dear lord, thy sorrow to my sorrow lendeth
Another power: no flood by raining slaketh.
My woe too sensible thy passion maketh,
  More feeling-painful. Let it then suffice
  To drown on woe, one pair of weeping eyes.   1680

1661 declined] Q; inclined Q2 1662 wreathèd] DYCE 1866 (*conj.* Walker); wretched Q
1680 on] Q; one Q3; in *conj.* Malone

1660 **hopeless ... loss** i.e. Collatine, who has
  lost Lucrece after boasting of her and has
  lost hope of regaining her. The image
  associates him with Tarquin in ll. 131–3.
1662 **wreathèd** Q's 'wretched' is likely to
  derive from a misreading: crossed, or
  wreathèd, arms are a traditional sign of
  love-melancholy, as in *L.L.L.* 4.3.131–4:
  'Longueville | Did . . . never lay his
  wreathèd arms athwart | His loving
  bosom, to keep down his heart'.
1663 **new waxen** recently grown
1664 **stops** carries a physical force: 'blocks in'
1667–70 Furnivall thought this passage
  might derive from observations of London
  Bridge; Spurgeon relates to Clopton Bridge
  at Stratford. The latter is very unlikely,
  since the river here is clearly tidal.
1669 **eddy** 'The water that by some interrup-
  tion in its course, runs contrary to the
  direction of the tide or current' (*OED*)

1669 **boundeth in his pride** (a) restricts his
  swelling majesty; (b) leaps in his full
  vigour. The double sense of *boundeth*
  (*OED v.*[1] 'confine within bounds' and *v.*[2]
  2 'leap') captures the effect of a river
  growing stronger through constraint.
1670 **strait** narrow place or constrained
  waterway
1672 **saw** His grief is pushed painfully forward
  and backward in the motion of a saw.
1675 **frenzy** madness; here presumably a
  trance-like state. It is *untimely* since
  Collatine should be taking action.
1678 **sensible** acutely felt (*OED* 6, citing this
  as the first example in this sense)
1679 **feeling-painful** sensitive to its pain
  (more capable of feeling, and so more
  responsive to pain)
1680 **on woe** in woe. Many editors follow Q3
  ('one woe'), but the simple repetition
  seems compositorial rather than Shake-

'And for my sake, when I might charm thee so,
(For she that was thy Lucrece now attend me)
Be suddenly revengèd on my foe—
Thine, mine, his own. Suppose thou dost defend me
From what is past, the help that thou shalt lend me   1685
   Comes all too late: yet let the traitor die,
   For sparing justice feeds iniquity.

'But ere I name him, you fair lords', quoth she,
Speaking to those that came with Collatine,
'Shall plight your honourable faiths to me,   1690
With swift pursuit to venge this wrong of mine:
For 'tis a meritorious fair design
   To chase injustice with revengeful arms.
   Knights by their oaths should right poor ladies' harms.'

At this request, with noble disposition,   1695
Each present lord began to promise aid,
As bound in knighthood to her imposition,
Longing to hear the hateful foe bewrayed.
But she, that yet her sad task hath not said,
   The protestation stops: 'O speak', quoth she,   1700
   'How may this forcèd stain be wiped from me?

spearian. *One* and *on* were more alike in pronunciation than they are now, and the early Shakespeare elsewhere plays on this fact: *Two Gentlemen* 2.1.1–3: '*Speed*: Sir, your glove. *Val*: Not mine. My gloves are on. *Speed*: Why then, this may be yours, for this is but one.'

1681–2 Lucrece is appealing to Collatine not in her present state as a wife whose *gross blood is stained with this abuse*, but on behalf of her former self: hence *when I might* means 'at that time when I was able to charm you'.

1682 **she** her (Abbott §211 speculates that ' "she" seemed more like an uninflected noun than "he" ').

1683 **suddenly** immediately

1684 **defend** is poised between 'vindicate' and 'use force to protect me'.

1687 **For . . . iniquity** Compare *Romeo* 3.1.196: 'Mercy but murders, pardoning those that kill.' The line is marked as a *sententia*

in C. See ll. 87–8 n. The thought is proverbial: 'Pardon makes offenders' (Dent P50).

1638–91 Only in Shakespeare's version does her audience agree to the oath before she names Tarquin. Compare Livy 1.58.7: 'But pledge your right hands and your words that the adulterer shall not go unpunished'; she then names Tarquin before they swear vengeance.

1694 **Knights . . . harms** William Segar also identified the Roman rank of *equites* with that of knighthood (*Honour Military and Civil* (1602), 74).

1697 **imposition** the vow she imposed on them, 'The action of imposing or laying as a burden, duty, charge, or task' (*OED* 4, giving this as the first cited example of the sense)

1698 **bewrayed** exposed, revealed

1700 **protestation** formal public declaration of an oath (by Collatine's attendants)

'What is the quality of my offence,
Being constrained with dreadful circumstance?
May my pure mind with the foul act dispense,
My low-declinèd honour to advance?   1705
May any terms acquit me from this chance?
    The poisoned fountain clears itself again,
    And why not I from this compellèd stain?'

With this they all at once began to say
Her body's stain her mind untainted clears,   1710
While, with a joyless smile, she turns away
The face, that map which deep impression bears
Of hard misfortune, carved in it with tears.
    'No, no', quoth she, 'No dame hereafter living
    By my excuse shall claim excuse's giving.'   1715

Here, with a sigh as if her heart would break,
She throws forth Tarquin's name: 'He, he', she says,
But more than 'he' her poor tongue could not speak,
Till, after many accents and delays,
Untimely breathings, sick and short assays,   1720
    She utters this: 'He, he, fair lords, 'tis he
    That guides this hand to give this wound to me.'

1702 my] Q; mine Q3   1712 The] Her HUDSON 1881 (*conj.* Walker)   1713 in it] MALONE (*conj.*
Capell); it in Q

1702 **quality** nature. See l. 875 n.
1706 **terms** arguments
    chance misfortune (*OED* 2)
1707 Compare l. 577 n. The metaphor may
    appear to suggest an incongruous hope
    that Lucrece can be purified (Donaldson,
    privately), and Lucrece's audience take it
    in that sense; however she is thinking of
    the *fountain* (l. 1734) of blood that will
    purify her body.
1710 **clears** purifies; with a pun on *OED* 9a:
    'acquits'
1712 **map** picture, or 'detailed representation
    in epitome' (*OED* 2a); although the word
    may imply a precise relationship between
    Lucrece's face and a representation of
    rough terrain. Compare *Twelfth Night*
    3.2.74–5: 'He does smile his face into
    more lines than is in the new map with
    the augmentation of the Indies'.
1714–15 Compare Livy: 'nor in time to come
    shall ever unchaste woman live through

the example of Lucretia' (1.58.10); cf.
Painter: 'for no unchaste or ill woman
shall hereafter impute no dishonest act
to Lucrece' (Bullough, 198).
1715 **By my . . . giving** will claim that they
    should be excused by citing the fact that I
    was excused
1716 Lucrece's hesitation derives from Ovid,
    Fasti 2.827: 'quaeque potest, narrat. resta-
    bant ultima: flevit' ('what she can say she
    relates. The rest remained. She wept').
1717–18 On the figure of aposiopesis, see
    l. 666 n.
1719 **accents** expressive sounds
1720 **sick** 'Deeply affected by some strong
    feeling' (*OED* 4a)
    assays attempts (to speak). Compare
    Ovid, *Fasti* 2.825–6: ' "eloquar," inquit,
    | "eloquar infelix dedecus ipsa meum?" '
    (' "shall I relate," she said, "shall I myself
    relate, unhappy creature that I am, my
    own disgrace?" ').

Even here she sheathèd in her harmless breast
A harmful knife, that thence her soul unsheathèd.
That blow did bail it from the deep unrest   1725
Of that polluted prison where it breathèd.
Her contrite sighs unto the clouds bequeathèd
    Her wingèd sprite, and through her wounds doth fly
    Life's lasting date, from cancelled destiny.

Stone-still, astonished with this deadly deed,   1730
Stood Collatine, and all his lordly crew,
Till Lucrece' father, that beholds her bleed,
Himself on her self-slaughtered body threw,
And from the purple fountain Brutus drew
    The murd'rous knife, and, as it left the place,   1735
    Her blood in poor revenge held it in chase,

And, bubbling from her breast, it doth divide
In two slow rivers, that the crimson blood
Circles her body in on every side,
Who, like a late-sacked island, vastly stood   1740
Bare and unpeopled in this fearful flood.
    Some of her blood still pure and red remained,
    And some looked black, and that false Tarquin stained.

1729 Life's] Q (Liues)   1743 stained] Q; sham'd Q5 (Huntington)

1723 **harmless** innocent (*OED* 3). Shakespeare omits the detail in Ovid (*Fasti* 2.833–4) and Chaucer (*LGW* ll. 1856–60) that Lucretia makes sure that her clothing preserves her modesty even as she falls in death.

1725 **bail** release (by the offering of a security)

1727 Compare Lucrece's testament at l. 1199.

1729 **Life's . . . destiny** eternal life, which escapes from the temporary *cancelled* bond which tied her to her human fate. On *cancelled* see ll. 934–5 n. This line marks the inversion of the fear Lucrece had expressed in those lines, that she would be permanently bound to receive endless woes.

1730 **astonished** plays on 'stone-still', as in *FQ* 2.6.31.9: 'Wherewith astonisht, still he stood, as senselesse stone'.

1732 In *Fasti* 2.835 ff. both Lucretius and Collatine fall on Lucrece's body.

1733 **self-slaughtered** First cited example in *OED*. Compare *Hamlet* 1.2.131–2. The word 'suicide' is not found before *c*.1650. The more usual alternative in this period was 'self-murder'.

1734 **purple** may connote nobility. See *Venus* l. 1 n.

1736 **held it in chase** pursued it

1738 **that** so that

1740 **late-sacked island** For dwellers in the island of Britain this image might have 'held a peculiar horror' (Linda Woodbridge, *Palisading the Elizabethan Body Politic*, *Texas Studies in Literature and Language* 33 (1991), 327).
vastly 'In a waste or desolate manner' (*OED* citing this as the first usage and the only one in this sense). The Latin *vastus* from which it derives can mean 'desolate as the result of destruction', and is used in this sense in Livy (*OLD* 1c).

1743 **false Tarquin stained** Tarquin is both subject and object of *stained*: he both stained the blood and is stained by the defilement he has caused.

About the mourning and congealèd face
Of that black blood a wat'ry rigol goes,   1745
Which seems to weep upon the tainted place,
And ever since, as pitying Lucrece' woes,
Corrupted blood some watery token shows,
    And blood untainted still doth red abide,
    Blushing at that which is so putrefied.   1750

'Daughter, dear daughter', old Lucretius cries,
'That life was mine which thou hast here deprived.
If in the child the father's image lies,
Where shall I live now Lucrece is unlived?
Thou wast not to this end from me derived.   1755
    If children predecease progenitors
    We are their offspring, and they none of ours.

'Poor broken glass, I often did behold
In thy sweet semblance my old age new born,
But now that fair fresh mirror, dim and old,   1760
Shows me a bare-boned death by time outworn.
O from thy cheeks my image thou hast torn,
    And shivered all the beauty of my glass,
    That I no more can see what once I was.

'O Time, cease thou thy course and last no longer,   1765
If they surcease to be that should survive.
Shall rotten death make conquest of the stronger,
And leave the falt'ring feeble souls alive?
The old bees die, the young possess their hive;

1765 last] Q; hast Q4   1766 they] Q; thou Q4

1745 **wat'ry rigol** a circle of watery matter which had separated out from the congealed blood (as serum does in fact separate from clotted blood). First cited instance of *rigol* in *OED*.

1747–8 This is the only brief etiological fiction in the poem. Compare *Venus* ll. 1135–64 n. The sense is that the blood of the pure remains red, as though blushing at the foulness of the defiled blood, which has turned black.

1752 **deprivèd** taken away. See l. 1186 n.

1754 **unlivèd** deprived of life (first cited example in *OED*)

1755 **to this end** (a) for this reason; (b) for this kind of death

1756 **predecease** die before (first cited example in *OED*). The exceptional grief of Lucretius prompts a string of verbal innovations.

1761 **death** death's head or *memento mori*. Lucretius changes from a *mirror* in which Lucrece sees his own features to a *mirror* in the metaphorical sense of 'exemplary image' of his future.

1763 **shivered** shattered
1766 **surcease** cease

Then live, sweet Lucrece, live again and see   1770
Thy father die, and not thy father thee.'

By this starts Collatine as from a dream,
And bids Lucretius give his sorrow place,
And then in key-cold Lucrece' bleeding stream
He falls, and bathes the pale fear in his face,   1775
And counterfeits to die with her a space,
    Till manly shame bids him possess his breath,
    And live to be revengèd on her death.

The deep vexation of his inward soul
Hath served a dumb arrest upon his tongue,   1780
Who, mad that sorrow should his use control,
Or keep him from heart-easing words so long,
Begins to talk; but through his lips do throng
    Weak words, so thick come in his poor heart's aid
    That no man could distinguish what he said.   1785

Yet sometime 'Tarquin' was pronouncèd plain,
But through his teeth, as if the name he tore.
This windy tempest, till it blow up rain,
Held back his sorrow's tide to make it more.
At last it rains, and busy winds give o'er.   1790
    Then son and father weep with equal strife,
    Who should weep most, for daughter, or for wife.

The one doth call her his, the other his,
Yet neither may possess the claim they lay.

1773 **give . . . place** i.e. acknowledge his greater claim to grief. There is a faint anticipation here of Hamlet's battle with Laertes in grieving for Ophelia, *Hamlet* 5.1.244–90.

1774 **key-cold** cold as steel, as in *Richard III* 1.2.5: 'Poor key-cold figure of a holy king'. Keys were proverbially cold (Tilley K23).

1776 **counterfeits . . . space** imitates death with her for a while (i.e. he faints or lies immobile with passion)

1780 **served . . . arrest** i.e. has forced him, as though by warrant, to be dumb. However, on *arrest* as a 'pause or cessation', see Sonnet 74.1 n.

1784 **so thick come** which come in such thronging crowds. To speak *thick* in this period could mean to talk indistinctly

(*OED* s.v. 'thick' *adv.* 4, quoting 2 *Henry IV* 2.3.24–5: 'Speaking thick, which nature made his blemish, | Became the accents of the valiant').

1788 **till . . . rain** until it produced rain with its gusts. For the belief that high winds precede the stillness of a rainstorm, see *Venus* l. 458 n, and the proverb 'Small rain allays great winds' (Dent R16).

1791 **strife** competition

1794 **possess . . . lay** enjoy possession of that to which they lay claim. As *interest* makes clear in l. 1797 the two are presented as offering legal arguments for their right to possess Lucrece. As Donaldson notes, 49, 'One of the central themes in *The Rape of Lucrece* is that of the precariousness of all forms of possession, material and

The father says 'She's mine.' 'O mine she is',   1795
Replies her husband, 'Do not take away
My sorrow's interest; let no mourner say
   He weeps for her, for she was only mine,
   And only must be wailed by Collatine.'

'O', quoth Lucretius, 'I did give that life   1800
Which she too early and too late hath spilled.'
'Woe, woe', quoth Collatine, 'She was my wife:
I owed her, and 'tis mine that she hath killed.'
'My daughter' and 'My wife' with clamours filled
   The dispersed air, who, holding Lucrece' life,   1805
   Answered their cries, 'My daughter and my wife.'

Brutus, who plucked the knife from Lucrece' side,
Seeing such emulation in their woe,
Began to clothe his wit in state and pride,
Burying in Lucrece' wound his folly's show.   1810
He with the Romans was esteemèd so
   As silly jeering idiots are with kings,
   For sportive words, and utt'ring foolish things.

But now he throws that shallow habit by,
Wherein deep policy did him disguise,   1815

1812 silly] Q ('seelie)

immaterial'. It is the air which finally claims her (l. 1806).

1795 'She's mine . . . is' The absence of speech marks in Q makes the two rival claims to ownership dissolve into one. It is not certain who utters 'O mine she is'.

1797 sorrow's interest my title to ownership of sorrow

1801 too late (a) too late to prevent her rape; (b) too recently (as in 3 *Henry VI (True Tragedy)* 2.5.92–3: 'O boy, thy father gave thee life too soon, | And hath bereft thee of thy life too late!')
spilled destroyed (the verb was slightly archaic by 1594)

1803 owed owned. See l. 1794 n.
'tis mine . . . killed that which she has killed belongs to me

1805 dispersed scattered. The epithet is transferred from the *clamours* to the *air*.

1805 who which

1806 A version of the echo song which is a

favourite topos of the genre. See *Venus* ll. 829–41 n. The air re-echoes the possessive cries of father and husband with good reason: since it is *holding Lucrece' life* it can claim ownership of her more fully than they do (*OED* s.v. 'hold' *v.* 6a: 'to own, have as property').

1808 emulation effort to outdo each other

1809 Began . . . pride Brutus had formerly been known as a fool; now he begins to give his intelligence an appearance of dignity and self-esteem (*state and pride*). Compare *Henry V* 2.4.37–8: 'the Roman Brutus, | Covering discretion with a coat of folly'. Marsus's edition of Ovid (149) notes that he acquired the cognomen 'Brutus' for his apparent stupidity ('brutus' means 'dullard').

1810 Burying is only two syllables here.
folly's show appearance of foolishness

1813 sportive high-spirited, jesting (a vogue-word in the 1590s)

1814 habit (a) outward demeanour; (b) clothing

And armed his long-hid wits advisedly,
To check the tears in Collatinus' eyes.
'Thou wrongèd lord of Rome,' quoth he, 'arise.
   Let my unsounded self, supposed a fool,
   Now set thy long experienced wit to school.   1820

'Why, Collatine, is woe the cure for woe?
Do wounds help wounds, or grief help grievous deeds?
Is it revenge to give thyself a blow
For his foul act, by whom thy fair wife bleeds?
Such childish humour from weak minds proceeds: 1825
   Thy wretched wife mistook the matter so,
   To slay herself that should have slain her foe.

'Courageous Roman, do not steep thy heart
In such relenting dew of lamentations;
But kneel with me and help to bear thy part,
To rouse our Roman gods with invocations,   1830
That they will suffer these abominations,
   Since Rome herself in them doth stand disgracèd,
   By our strong arms from forth her fair streets chasèd.

'Now, by the Capitol that we adore,   1835
And by this chaste blood so unjustly stainèd,
By heaven's fair sun that breeds the fat earth's store,
By all our country rights in Rome maintainèd,

1822 help] Q; heal *conj.* Walker   1832 abominations,] Q3; ~. Q   1838 rights] Q; rites Q3

1819 **unsounded** unfathomed (like water which has not been sounded by a piece of lead sinking to its bottom, continuing from *shallow* and *deep* above)
1821–9 Brutus's role here follows Livy 1.59.4: 'They were moved, not only by the father's sorrow, but by the fact that it was Brutus who chid their tears and idle lamentations and urged them to take up the sword, as befitted men and Romans.'
1821 Why Come now! For the thought here, compare Harington's translation of *Orlando Furioso* (1591) 11.41: 'By tears no good the deed is done, | And sharp revenge assuageth malice chief.'
1822 **grievous** flagrantly wicked
1825 **childish humour** childlike fancy or whim. (Compare Painter: 'childish lamentations', Bullough, 199.)

1826 **so** in the same way
1829 **relenting** which softens
1834 **chased** to be chased (Abbott §382)
1835 **Capitol** the smallest of the hills of Rome, and the site of the temple (begun by the Tarquinii) dedicated to Jupiter Optimus Maximus, Juno, and Minerva. It was also the location for the assassination of Caesar by the later Brutus.
1835 Compare Livy 1.59.1: 'By this blood, most chaste until a prince wronged it, I swear'; Painter: 'I swear by the chaste blood of this body here dead', Bullough, 198.
1837 **fat** fertile (*OED* 9a)
1838 **country rights** national proprieties (*country* is an uninflected possessive). Q3 reads 'rites', which would suit the context of an appeal to the gods.

And by chaste Lucrece' soul that late complainèd
    Her wrongs to us, and by this bloody knife,   1840
    We will revenge the death of this true wife.'

This said, he struck his hand upon his breast,
And kissed the fatal knife to end his vow;
And to his protestation urged the rest,
Who, wond'ring at him, did his words allow.   1845
Then jointly to the ground their knees they bow,
    And that deep vow which Brutus made before
    He doth again repeat, and that they swore.

When they had sworn to this advisèd doom,
They did conclude to bear dead Lucrece thence,   1850
To show her bleeding body thorough Rome,
And so to publish Tarquin's foul offence;
Which being done, with speedy diligence,
    The Romans plausibly did give consent
    To Tarquin's everlasting banishment.   1855

FINIS

1855 Tarquin's] Q (Tarqvins)

1839 **complainèd** complained of (the transitive form of the verb is rare by 1590)

1842–8 Compare Livy 1.59.2: 'The knife he then passed to Collatinus, and from him to Lucretius and Valerius. They were dumbfounded at this miracle . . . As he bade them, so they swore.' Painter: 'Then he delivered the knife to Collatinus, Lucretius and Valerius, who marvelled at the strangeness of his words; and from whence he should conceive that determination. They all swore that oath' (Bullough, 199).

1845 **allow** approve

1849 **advisèd doom** considered verdict

1850 **conclude** decide (*OED* 12), with perhaps a hint of the legal sense (*OED* 3b), 'to bind to a particular course of action'

1850–1 In *LGW* ll. 1866–8 Lucrece is displayed in Rome. Chaucer's heroine does not have to be transported there, however. In Livy she is displayed in the market-place of Collatia. The version of the story in Barnabe Googe's *Proverbs of Sir John Lopes de Mendoza* (1579), fo. 60ᵛ, however, concludes with the removal of the body to Rome and its public display.

1852 **publish** make public (echoing *publisher* from l. 33)

1854 **plausibly** with applause, approvingly. See the Argument, ll. 40–3.
    consent The echo of the Argument's 'with one consent' is a strong piece of evidence for the consistency of political outlook of poem and Argument.

1855 **Tarquin's . . . banishment** Q's 'Tarqvins' may indicate the singular or plural form. The poem ends by dwelling on the punishment of Tarquin, rather than the constitutional change from monarchy to republic which resulted from the rape of Lucrece, and which is noted in the Argument. Some commentators have taken this as a sign that Shakespeare wished to play down the political overtones of the story. The genre of the work, however, focuses on the passions of individuals and on the ways in which the government of passion reflects on government of the state. For this reason the final emphasis on the punishment of Tarquin is not surprising, nor necessarily indicative of Shakespeare's wish to depoliticize the story.

The Passionate Pilgrim

I

When my love swears that she is made of truth,
I do believe her (though I know she lies),
That she might think me some untutored youth,
Unskilful in the world's false forgeries.
Thus vainly thinking that she thinks me young,   5
Although I know my years be past the best:
I, smiling, credit her false-speaking tongue,
Outfacing faults in love with love's ill rest.
But wherefore says my love that she is young?
And wherefore say not I that I am old?   10
O, love's best habit is a soothing tongue,
And age (in love) loves not to have years told.
　　Therefore I'll lie with love, and love with me,
　　Since that our faults in love thus smothered be.

For an alternative version, see Sonnet 138　4 Unskilful ... forgeries] o　; Vnlearned ... subtilties Q
6 I know my yeares be] o1; she knowes my dayes are Q; I know my yeres are FOL9　7 I, smil-
ing] o1; Simply I Q　8 Outfacing ... rest] o1; On both sides thus is simple truth supprest Q　9
my ... young] o1; she not she is vniust Q　11 habit ... tongue] o2; habit's in a soothing toung
o1; habit is in seeming trust Q; habit is a smoothinge tongue FOL9　12 to have] o1; t'haue Q
13 love ... me] o1; I lye with her, and she with me Q　14 Since ... smother'd be] o1; And in
our faults by lyes we flattered be Q

THE PASSIONATE PILGRIM
The title probably alludes to the sonnet exchanged between Romeo and Juliet in 1.5.94–9. Romeo says, 'My lips, two blushing pilgrims, ready stand | To smooth that rough touch with a tender kiss', to which Juliet replies, 'Good pilgrim, you do wrong your hand too much, | Which mannerly devotion shows in this. | For saints have hands that pilgrims' hands do touch, | And palm to palm is holy palmers' kiss.' *Romeo* was first printed in 1597, two years before this volume appeared.

POEM I

A variant version of Sonnet 138. Roe (following Brooke) argues that it is a memorial reconstruction. It is, however, quite possible that it is a mistranscribed or poorly remembered version of an early draft of 138, since some of its variants have parallels in other works by Shakespeare. These are discussed below. For detailed notes see Sonnet 138. It presents an emotionally simpler scenario than 138: here the falsity of the lovers seems to be limited to lying about their respective ages. A manuscript copy is found in Folger MS V.a.339, fo. 197ᵛ.

4 **Unskilful ... forgeries** The differences from Q here may be Shakespearian: *forgeries* is used in works from the 1590s to refer to the delusions of the mind, especially of those in love (e.g. *Dream* 2.1.81 and *Lucrece* l. 460); the pleonasm of *false forgeries* is comparable with 'false perjury', *L.L.L.* 4.3.59 (reproduced as 3.3 below).

6 **I know** seems likely to be a memorial simplification of Sonnet 138's 'she knows'; alternatively the complexity of the 1609 version ('I know that she knows that what I say is false') came to Shakespeare later in the process of composition.

8 **Outfacing ... rest** 'putting a brave face on the deceptions of love with the uneasy show of calm which lovers do put on'

9 **But ... young** Compare Sonnet 138.9, in which the woman refuses to confess that she is 'unjust'.

11 **soothing** flattering

12 **told** (a) publicly related; (b) counted

14 **smothered** (a) silenced; (b) killed. Compare *Lucrece* l. 634.

2

Two loves I have, of comfort and despair,
That like two spirits do suggest me still:
My better angel is a man (right fair);
My worser spirit a woman (coloured ill).
To win me soon to hell, my female evil   5
Tempteth my better angel from my side,
And would corrupt my saint to be a devil,
Wooing his purity with her fair pride.
And whether that my angel be turned fiend
Suspect I may, yet not directly tell: 10
For being both to me, both to each, friend,
I guess one angel in another's hell:
    The truth I shall not know, but live in doubt,
    Till my bad angel fire my good one out.

For an alternative version, see Sonnet 144 2 That| O1; Which Q 3, 4 My] O1; The Q 6 side]
O1; sight Q 8 fair] O1; foul Q 11 For . . . to me] O1; But . . . from me Q 13 The truth . . .
know] O1; Yet this shal I nere Q

POEM 2

    A variant version of Sonnet *144*. The dif-
ferences from 1609 are less significant
than those of the previous poem, and
may be no more than corruptions by a
copyist. For full notes see Sonnet *144*.

8 **fair** This could be an earlier less violently
    hostile authorial version of Sonnet *144*'s
    'foul'.

11 **to me** reads like a simplification of *144*'s
    'from me'.

3

Did not the heavenly rhetoric of thine eye,
'Gainst whom the world could not hold argument,
Persuade my heart to this false perjury?
Vows for thee broke deserve not punishment.
A woman I forswore, but I will prove,   5
Thou being a goddess, I forswore not thee:
My vow was earthly; thou a heavenly love.
Thy grace being gained cures all disgrace in me.
My vow was breath, and breath a vapour is;
Then thou, fair sun that on this earth doth shine,   10
Exhale this vapour vow. In thee it is; ·
If broken then it is no fault of mine.
    If by me broke, what fool is not so wise
    To break an oath, to win a paradise?

2 could not] 01; cannot LLL   9 My vow was] 01; Vowes are but LLL   10 that...this...doth]
01; which...my...dost LLL   11 Exhale] 02; Exhalt 01; Exhalst LLL   14 break] 01; loose LLL

POEM 3

A version of Longueville's sonnet to
Maria in *L.L.L.* 4.3.57–70. The variants
offer no definitive indication of the source
of Jaggard's text. The modifications of
pronouns suggest programmatic modifi-
cation rather than simply memorial
scrambling or poor typesetting of the
1598 quarto of *L.L.L.* The modifications
are likely to be those of Jaggard or his
source rather than Shakespeare's.

2 **whom** which (Abbott §264)
  hold argument argue so as to win
5 **A woman** In *L.L.L.* this is Maria. The
  argument is that although he was
  unfaithful to a mortal, Maria is a goddess;

hence his loyalty to her gives grace to his
shameful action.
9 **vapour** a mist or fog exhaled from the
  earth (which can be burnt away by the
  sun). Proverbial: 'Words are but wind'
  (Tilley W833).
10 **this earth** i.e. my mortal body (a reading
  clarified by *L.L.L.*: 'my earth')
11 **Exhale** draw up (a rare usage; *OED* 4).
  01 reads 'Exhalt', which may derive
  from a mistranscription of 'Exhalst' in
  the Quarto of *L.L.L.* or indicate a com-
  positorial misreading of 'exhale' in the
  copy.
  In thee it is i.e. you, as the sun, have
  sucked up the vow

4

Sweet Cytherea, sitting by a brook
With young Adonis, lovely, fresh and green,
Did court the lad with many a lovely look,
Such looks as none could look but beauty's queen.
She told him stories to delight his ears;   5
She showed him favours to allure his eye.
To win his heart she touched him here and there:
Touches so soft still conquer chastity.
But whether unripe years did want conceit,
Or he refused to take her figured proffer,   10
The tender nibbler would not touch the bait,
But smile and jest at every gentle offer:
    Then fell she on her back, fair queen, and toward.
    He rose and ran away, ah, fool too froward.

1 Sweet] O1; ffaire FOL11 4 could] O1; can FOL11 5 ears] O1; eare FOL11; *a final 's' is
deleted in* FOL9 8 soft] O1; sought FOL9 10 refused] O1; did scorne FOL11 her] O2; his O1
11 touch] O1; take FOL11 12 smile . . . jest] O1; blusht . . . smild FOL11 13 queen] O1; *omit-
ted* FOL11 14 rose] O1; blusht FOL11 ah] O1; O FOL11

POEM 4

The attribution of this poem is uncertain:
a version exists in a manuscript miscel-
lany from the 1630s and 1640s, Folger MS
V.a.339, fo. 197^r, the commonplace book
of Joseph Hall, where it follows Poem 6.
Here the poem is attributed to 'W.S'. in
what is probably the hand of J. P. Collier
(on Collier's forged additions to this
manuscript, see Giles E. Dawson, 'John
Payne Collier's Great Forgery', *Studies in
Bibliography* 24 (1971), 1–26). Another
copy is in a commonplace book compiled
*c.*1620–30, Folger MS V.b.43, fo. 22^r.
Here it immediately follows Poem 11 and
is entitled 'Second part'. This supports
an attribution to Griffin, who is almost
certainly the author of 11.

1 **Cytherea** Venus. The name is derived from
Cythera, an island on the coast of the
Peloponnese sacred to Venus. It is used
elsewhere by Shakespeare (e.g. in *Shrew*
Induction 2.50), although not in *Venus*.

2 **fresh and green** youthful. (Compare
Sonnet 104.8, although this repetitious
sequence of epithets does not seem
Shakespearian.)

3 **lovely** amorous

5–7 **ears . . . eye . . . touched** The sequence
suggests a banquet of sense; on which see
Venus ll. 433–50 and n.

6 **favours** probably here 'love tokens'
(gloves, ribbons, etc.), but there may
also be a hint that she is revealing
parts of her body to him as a mark of
favour

9 **want conceit** lack understanding

10 **figured proffer** coded signal that she
would give herself to him

13 Compare *Venus* l. 814.
toward willing; yielding. Compare *Venus*
l. 1157.

14 **froward** obstinate, contrary. The 'toward/
froward' rhyme also occurs three times
in *Shrew* (1.1.68–9, 4.6.79–80, and
5.2.187–8).

5

If love make me forsworn, how shall I swear to love?
O, never faith could hold, if not to beauty vowed.
Though to myself forsworn, to thee I'll constant prove:
Those thoughts to me like oaks, to thee like osiers bowed.
Study his bias leaves and makes his book thine eyes,   5
Where all those pleasures live that art can comprehend.
If knowledge be the mark, to know thee shall suffice:
Well-learnèd is that tongue that well can thee commend;
All ignorant that soul that sees thee without wonder,
Which is to me some praise, that I thy parts admire.   10
Thine eye Jove's lightning seems; thy voice his dreadful
    thunder,
Which (not to anger bent) is music and sweet fire.
   Celestial as thou art, O, do not love that wrong,
   To sing heaven's praise with such an earthly tongue.

2 O] o1; Ah LLL 3 constant] o1; feythfull LLL 4 like] o1; were LLL 6 can] o1; would LLL
11 Thine] o1 (Thin); Thy LLL seems] o1; beares LLL 13 do . . . wrong] o1; pardon love this
wrong LLL 14 To sing] o1; That singes LLL

POEM 5
   A version of *L.L.L.* 4.2.106–19.

4 i.e. My thoughts seem to me rigid as oaks,
but to you they bend like willows (*osiers*
were proverbial for pliancy because they
were used in basket-weaving).
5 **Study . . . eyes** The student (*Study*) leaves
his natural course (*bias*) in order to dwell
on your eyes.
6 **art** i.e. study

7 **mark** goal, aim
10 **Which . . . praise** which is to my
credit
   that because (Abbott §284)
12 **(not . . . bent)** when it is not being used to
express his anger
13 **do not love that wrong** *L.L.L.* reads
'pardon, love, this wrong'. The reading
here suggests an attempt to win a lady
from her devotions.

6

Scarce had the sun dried up the dewy morn,
And scarce the herd gone to the hedge for shade,
When Cytherea (all for love forlorn)
A longing tarriance for Adonis made,
Under an osier growing by a brook,   5
A brook where Adon used to cool his spleen.
Hot was the day; she hotter, that did look
For his approach, that often there had been.
Anon he comes and throws his mantle by,
And stood stark naked on the brook's green brim.   10
The sun looked on the world with glorious eye,
Yet not so wistly as this queen on him.
    He spying her bounced in whereas he stood.
    'O Jove,' quoth she, 'why was not I a flood?'

3 for] FOL9; in 02   12 this] 02; the FOL9   14 O] 02; ah FOL9

POEM 6

A version exists in Folger MS V.a.339, fo.
197ʳ, where it precedes 4 and is attributed
to 'W.S.' in what is probably the hand of J.
P. Collier. On this MS, see headnote to *P.
Pilgrim* 4. There is a general resemblance
to *Shrew* Induction 2.48–52: 'Dost thou
love pictures? We will fetch thee straight |
Adonis painted by a running brook, |
And Cytherea all in sedges hid, | Which
seem to move and wanton with her
breath | Even as the waving sedges play
wi'th' wind.' This parallel may suggest
Shakespearian authorship (see also n. to
Poem 4.14), although it is most probable
that this poem is a Shakespearian pas-
tiche by Bartholomew Griffin, and is part
of a group of Venus sonnets omitted from
his *Fidessa*.

1 Compare *Venus* l. 1 (the opening of which
   was much imitated in the 1590s).

4 **tarriance** delay. The only other usage
   in Shakespeare is in *Two Gentlemen*
   2.7.90.
6 **Adon** The contracted form is also used in
   Venus l. 769.
   spleen is used more for rhyme (and means
   'hot body') than to recall its associations
   with lust and anger (neither of which is
   appropriate to the notoriously lustless
   Adonis).
12 **wistly** attentively, yearningly (compare
   Venus l. 343 and *Lucrece* l. 1355).
   queen may register 'quean', or prostitute.
13 **bounced** leapt nimbly (in an age before
   rubber balls this would sound less absurd
   than it does now). It sometimes connotes
   an aggressive or destructive assault, and
   in the period is often used to describe the
   action of waves.
   whereas where
14 **flood** river

7

Fair is my love, but not so fair as fickle;
Mild as a dove, but neither true nor trusty;
Brighter than glass, and yet as glass is brittle;
Softer than wax, and yet as iron rusty:
    A lily pale with damask dye to grace her,   5
    None fairer, nor none falser to deface her.

Her lips to mine how often hath she joinèd,
Between each kiss her oaths of true love swearing.
How many tales to please me hath she coinèd,
Dreading my love, the loss whereof still fearing.   10
    Yet in the midst of all her pure protestings
    Her faith, her oaths, her tears and all were jestings.

She burnt with love as straw with fire flameth;
She burnt out love as soon as straw out-burneth;
She framed the love, and yet she foiled the framing;   15
She bade love last, and yet she fell a-turning.
    Was this a lover, or a lecher, whether?
    Bad in the best, though excellent in neither.

7 joinèd] O2; Ioynd FOL9   9 coinèd] O2; Coynd FO_9   11 midst] O3; mids O2

POEM 7
There is a version in Folger MS V.a.339, fo. 197ᵛ which is attributed to 'W.S.' in what is probably the hand of J. P. Collier. The MS shows remarkably few variants from the printed text. The poem could have been written by almost any competent poet at work between 1575 and 1599.

3 **brittle** The spelling 'brickle' (common in the period) would have made this rhyme.

5–6 i.e. she has skin as white as lilies with cheeks the red of damask roses (on which see Sonnet 130.5 n.); no one is lovelier than her, but she is discredited/made ugly (*deface*) by her infidelity, which also cannot be equalled.

10 **Dreading** being fearful about

13 **straw** was proverbial for burning fiercely for a very short time. (Cf. Dent F255 and Tilley F270.)

15 **framed** made, contrived. (Roe suggests 'made a setting for'; this sense of 'frame' is not recorded before the eighteenth century.)

18 **Bad ... neither** i.e. she was bad as a lover (*the best*), but she did not excel even as a lecher.

8

If music and sweet poetry agree,
As they must needs (the sister and the brother)
Then must the love be great 'twixt thee and me,
Because thou lov'st the one, and I the other.
Dowland to thee is dear, whose heavenly touch   5
Upon the lute doth ravish human sense;
Spenser to me, whose deep conceit is such
As passing all conceit needs no defence.
Thou lov'st to hear the sweet melodious sound
That Phoebus' lute (the queen of music) makes;   10
And I in deep delight am chiefly drowned

POEM 8

This poem is by Richard Barnfield. It was printed in 1598 by Jaggard's brother as the first poem in *Poems in Diverse Humours* (1598), which is part of *The Encomion of Lady Pecunia, or the praise of Money* (STC 1485). There are no significant variations between the two texts, which may suggest that Jaggard used the printed version for his copy-text here. Barnfield was an imitator of Shakespeare; he is also notable for having printed the most openly homoerotic collection of love lyrics in the sixteenth century, *The Affectionate Shepherd* (1594). These aspects of Barnfield's oeuvre might have prompted Jaggard to present his poem as Shakespeare's. The poem was omitted from the second edition of *Lady Pecunia*, which Collier took to indicate Barnfield's recognition that the poem was Shakespeare's. This is more likely to have been a 'publisher's convenience', probably dictated by the price of the book' (Barnfield, *Poems*, ed. Edward Arber (Birmingham, 1883), p. xxii), than an indication that Jaggard or Barnfield genuinely believed it to be by Shakespeare. Other poems manifestly by Barnfield are omitted from the 1605 edition.

3 **thee and me** The setting of the poem in this collection of heterosexual love poems makes a reader naturally suppose the addressee to be feminine. In *Poems in Diverse Humours* it is addressed to 'Master R.L.', who is usually thought to be Richard Lynch, the author of the sonnet sequence *Diella*.

5 **Dowland** John Dowland (?1563–?1626), lutenist and composer. The allusion is highly fashionable: some of Dowland's works first appeared without his permission in Barley's *New Book of Tablature* (1596), and in 1597 appeared the authorized *First Book of Songs or Airs*.
heavenly touch delicate manner of playing

7 **Spenser** Edmund Spenser (?1552–99) was as much a fashionable figure as Dowland: the second instalment of *The Faerie Queene* appeared in 1596.

7–8 **conceit . . . conceit** This plays on Spenser's own description of the allegorical method of *The Faerie Queene* as a 'dark conceit': so, 'his deep thought is beyond comprehension'.

10 **Phoebus' lute** Phoebus Apollo, god of music, is traditionally presented carrying a lyre, of which the Elizabethan equivalent is a lute.
queen of music must refer to the lute (since Phoebus is male).

When as himself to singing he betakes.
One god is god of both (as poets feign)
One knight loves both, and both in thee remain.

12 **singing** i.e. when he uses words

13 **god** Apollo, god of music and poetry

14 **One knight** appears to be a private allusion to a patron. Grosart suggested Sir George Carey, to whom Dowland dedicated his *First Book of Airs* (1597) and to whose wife Spenser dedicated *Muiopotmos*. This is enticing, since by March 1597 Carey was Lord Chamberlain and patron of Shakespeare's company. However, if the identification is correct the poem must have been composed before 23 July 1596, when Carey became second Lord Hunsdon (after this date to call him 'knight' would be inappropriate). This would date the poem before the appearance of the Dowland volume and before Carey became patron of the Lord Chamberlain's Men. It seems unlikely that Barnfield would have printed in 1598 a poem which praised Hunsdon by an inferior title; hence the identification must be regarded as improbable.

9

Fair was the morn when the fair queen of love,

.　　　.　　　.　　　.　　　.　　　.

Paler for sorrow than her milk-white dove,
For Adon's sake, a youngster proud and wild,
Her stand she takes upon a steep-up hill.　　　　　　5
Anon Adonis comes with horn and hounds;
She, silly queen, with more than love's good will,
Forbade the boy he should not pass those grounds.
'Once,' quoth she, 'did I see a fair sweet youth
Here in these brakes deep wounded with a boar,　　　10
Deep in the thigh, a spectacle of ruth.
See in my thigh,' quoth she, 'here was the sore.'
　　She showèd hers; he saw more wounds than one,
　　And blushing fled, and left her all alone.

POEM 9

This is the only known version of this sonnet, which is formally defective (it appears to lack l. 2). On the attribution of the Venus Sonnets see Introduction, pp. 79–80.

1 **queen of love** Venus
4 **Adon's** On the contracted form see Poem 6.6 n.
5 **stand** 'The standing-place from which a hunter or sportsman may shoot game' (*OED* 13)
　　steep-up Compare Sonnet 7.5.
7 **silly** unfortunate
10 **brakes** thickets; pubic hair. Compare *Venus* ll. 229–34.
13 **wounds more than one** i.e. the imagined wound suffered by her previous lover and her vagina

10

Sweet rose, fair flower, untimely plucked, soon vaded,
Plucked in the bud, and vaded in the spring;
Bright orient pearl, alack too timely shaded,
Fair creature killed too soon by Death's sharp sting,
    Like a green plum that hangs upon a tree,   5
    And falls (through wind) before the fall should be.

I weep for thee, and yet no cause I have;
For why thou left'st me nothing in thy will.
And yet thou left'st me more than I did crave,
For why I cravèd nothing of thee still.   10
    O yes, dear friend, I pardon crave of thee:
    Thy discontent thou didst bequeath to me.

6 falls] O2 (fals)   8, 9 left'st] O2 (lefts)

POEM 10

No other versions have been found and
there is no evidence about the authorship
of the poem apart from its appearance in
The Passionate Pilgrim, in which it was
probably included because it shares the
stanzaic form of *Venus*.

1 **vaded** faded. Compare Sonnet 54.14.
3 **orient pearl** Pearls from the Indian sea
were unusually beautiful. *Orient* also
plays on 'sunrise'.

3 **timely** early
4 **Death's sharp sting** echoes 'oh death,
where is thy sting', 1 Corinthians
15:55.
8 **For why** because
left'st O reads 'lefts'. This is Shakespeare's
preferred second-person-singular form of
verbs ending in 't' (Abbott §340).
11 **pardon crave** forgive me, I did receive a
bequest from you (which was your
unhappiness)

11

Venus with Adonis sitting by her
Under a myrtle shade began to woo him.
She told the youngling how god Mars did try her,
And as he fell to her, she fell to him.
'Even thus,' quoth she, 'the warlike god embraced me.'   5
· And then she clipped Adonis in her arms;
'Even thus,' quoth she, 'the warlike god unlaced me,'
As if the boy should use like loving charms.
'Even thus,' quoth she, 'he seizèd on my lips,'
And with her lips on his did act the seizure.   10
And as she fetchèd breath, away he skips,
And would not take her meaning nor her pleasure.
 Ah, that I had my lady at this bay,
 To kiss and clip me till I run away.

1 Venus with] O2; Venus, and yong *Fidessa*, FOL11; Venus, & FOL9   3 god] O2; great FOL11   4 she fell] O2; so fell she *Fidessa*, FOL11   5 warlike] O2; wanton *Fidessa*   6 clipped] O2; clasp'd *Fidessa*; tooke FOL11   7 Even] O2; & FOL9   warlike] O2; lusty FOL11   9–12 Even . . . pleasure.] O2; But he a wayward boy refusde her offer, | And ran away, the beautious Queene neglecting: | Shewing both folly to abuse her proffer, | And all his sex of cowardise detecting. *Fidessa*   9 Even] O2; then FOL9   11 And] O2; But FOL11   fetchèd] O2; tooke hir FOL11   13 Ah, . . . this] O2; Oh . . . that *Fidessa*, FOL11   lady] O2; mistris *Fidessa*, FOL9, FOL11   14 kiss . . . me] O2; clipp & kisse hir FOL11   run] O2; ranne *Fidessa*, FOL11

POEM 11

This is almost certainly by Bartholomew Griffin since a version appears in his *Fidessa* (1596). Versions also exist in Folger MS V.b.43, fo. 21ᵛ, a commonplace book of 34 folio leaves compiled *c.*1630, and in Folger MS V.a.339, fo. 197ᵛ, in which the poem is attributed to 'W.S.' in what is probably the hand of J. P. Collier. Lines 9–12 differ markedly from the version in *Fidessa*. This may indicate authorial revision, or that the poem was used as a theme for variations among a group of poets (which could conceivably have included Shakespeare).

1 A scribe or compositor has omitted a syllable from this line, which in Folger MS V.b.43 and *Fidessa* contains eleven syllables (including the hypermetrical feminine ending of the line). See collation. Griffin uses feminine rhymes more frequently than Shakespeare (although see Sonnet *20.*1 n.)

2 **myrtle** is the plant traditionally associated with Venus.

4 **fell** *to* means 'assailed' the first time it occurs and 'sexually succumbed' the second time.

6 **clipped** embraced

7 **unlaced me** Unlacing the stays (of the corset) was the height of erotic excitement.

9 **seizèd** conveys as much 'took possession of' (*OED* 1) as 'physically grasped'.

12 **take** understand

13 **at this bay** Probably 'in full and enthusiastic pursuit like a dog who has cornered the deer' (*OED* 2) rather than 'like a hunted animal which has been cornered'. He wants to be pursued like Adonis.

12

Crabbèd age and youth cannot live together:
Youth is full of pleasance, Age is full of care;
Youth like summer morn, Age like winter weather;
Youth like summer brave, Age like winter bare;
Youth is full of sport, Age's breath is short;   5
Youth is nimble, Age is lame;
Youth is hot and bold, Age is weak and cold,
Youth is wild and Age is tame.
    Age I do abhor thee, Youth I do adore thee,
      O my love, my love is young.   10
    Age I do defy thee. Oh, sweet shepherd, hie thee,
      For methinks thou stays too long.

2 pleasance] O2; pleasure DELONEY   3 summer ... winter] O2; summers ... winters DELONEY
4 Youth ... weather] O2; *omitted* DELONEY   12 stays] O2; stay'st DELONEY

POEM 12

This is the first surviving printing of the first stanza of 'A Maiden's Choice twixt Age and Youth', which was printed in Thomas Deloney's *Garland of Good Will*, the earliest surviving edition of which appeared in 1628 (the work was entered 5 March 1593 and was in circulation by 1596, since Nashe refers to it in *Have With You to Saffron Walden*, Nashe, iii.84). On 1 March 1601–2 Dekker's work was transferred to Thomas Pavier, a close associate of Jaggard. The implied dramatic setting of the poem (a woman chooses between an old and a young lover) made it popular onstage: Beaumont and Fletcher, *The Woman's Prize* 4.1.32 alludes to it ('Hast thou forgot the Ballad, crabbed Age ...?'), as does Rowley's *Match at Midnight* (1633), sig. I2ᵛ. The poem may conceivably be connected with 'A Pleasant New Ballad Called the Maiden's Choice' entered in the Stationers' Register on 26 August 1591. There are no grounds for the attribution to Shakespeare beyond its inclusion in Jaggard's volume. It was probably included because a later part of the poem alludes to Adonis: 'Lo where he appears | like to young Adonis, | Ready to set on fire, | the chastest heart alive'. The remaining stanzas are reprinted in Rollins 1, 548–9.

1 **Crabbèd** bad tempered
4 **brave** finely dressed (as trees are decked with leaves in summer); compare Sonnet 15.8.
11 **hie thee** come quickly
12 **stays** is used for 'stay'st'. Compare Poem 10.8 n.

353

13

Beauty is but a vain and doubtful good,
A shining gloss that vadeth suddenly,
A flower that dies when first it gins to bud,
A brittle glass that's broken presently,
    A doubtful good, a gloss, a glass, a flower,   5
    Lost, vaded, broken, dead within an hour.

And as goods lost are seld or never found,
As vaded gloss no rubbing will refresh,
As flowers dead lie withered on the ground,
As broken glass no cement can redress,   10
    So beauty blemished once, for ever lost,
    In spite of physic, painting, pain and cost.

9 withered] 02 (withered; *i.e. witherèd*)   10 cement] 02 (symant)

POEM 13

No other version is known. The attribution is uncertain. There are no specifically Shakespearian features, and the poem contains one word not otherwise found among Shakespeare's early rare words; see note on l. 10. Versions purporting to derive from 'a corrected MS' were printed in *The Gentleman's Magazine* Nov. 1750, 521 and Jan. 1760, 39. The variants in these texts are clearly eighteenth-century sophistications and have not been collated.

2 **gloss** superficial lustre. (The association with evanescence is not clearly matched in any usage of the word in works certainly attributed to Shakespeare.)
4 **presently** immediately
10 **cement** is here (as usually in the period) accented on the first syllable. The word is not otherwise found in the Shakespearian canon before *Coriolanus* (*c*.1608).
12 **physic** medicine
    pain labour, effort

14

Good night, good rest, ah, neither be my share.
She bade goodnight that kept my rest away,
And daffed me to a cabin hanged with care,
To descant on the doubts of my decay.
   'Farewell', quoth she, 'and come again tomorrow.'   5
   Fare well I could not, for I supped with sorrow.

Yet at my parting sweetly did she smile,
In scorn or friendship, nill I conster whether:
'T may be she joyed to jest at my exile,
'T may be again to make me wander thither.   10
   Wander—a word for shadows like myself,
   As take the pain but cannot pluck the pelf.

Lord, how mine eyes throw gazes to the East.
My heart doth charge the watch, the morning rise
Doth cite each moving sense from idle rest,   15
Not daring trust the office of mine eyes.

---

14 the watch,] O2; them watch *conj* Pooler

POEM 14

No other version is known. The attribution is uncertain. The allusions to Philomel might have made attribution to the author of *Lucrece* plausible to the volume's first readership. Malone divided the poem after l. 12.

1 **Good . . . rest** (a) I bid you goodnight (i.e. farewell), good rest; (b) both 'good night' and 'sleep well'.

3 **daffed** me thrust me aside. Compare *Much Ado* 5.1.78 and *1 Henry IV* 4.1.96.
  cabin the traditional location for a spurned lover, as in *Twelfth Night* 1.5.257. Compare *Venus* l. 637.

4 **descant** elaborate, enlarge upon, with perhaps a suggestion of melancholy singing, as at *Lucrece* l. 1134.
  decay death, destruction

8 **nill I conster whether** I could not/will not determine which

11 **shadows** people of no substance; also used of actors

12 **pluck the pelf** take the rewards. *Pelf* otherwise occurs in the Shakespearian canon in the consciously archaic chorus of Gower, *Pericles* Scene 5.35, and in Apemantus's grace in *Timon* 1.2.62, which is also marked off from the surrounding dialogue by clear lexical idiosyncrasies.

14 **charge** 'blame' (*OED* 15a); perhaps with a secondary sense 'impose duties on' (*OED* 13a and b). The heart is acting as a governor of the body who is waking the other senses to augment the lookout provided by the eye. O's comma after *watch* (followed here) might permit the gloss 'My heart urges the watch and the morning to rise [and] urges each sense to wake up, not daring to trust the eyes alone'. This makes *My heart* the grammatical subject of the whole sentence. Pooler's conjecture 'doth urge them [i.e. the eyes] watch' has the same effect.

15 **cite** summon, arouse

While Philomela sits and sings, I sit and mark,
And wish her lays were tunèd like the lark.

For she doth welcome daylight with her ditty,
And drives away dark dreaming night: 20
The night so packed, I post unto my pretty.
Heart hath his hope, and eyes their wishèd sight,
    Sorrow changed to solace, and solace mixed with sorrow,
    For why she sighed, and bade me come tomorrow.

Were I with her the night would post too soon,   25
But now are minutes added to the hours.
To spite me now each minute seems a moon,
Yet not for me, shine sun to succour flowers.
    Pack night, peep day. Good day of night now borrow
    Short night tonight, and length thyself tomorrow.   30

27 moon] MALONE 1790 (*conj.* Steevens); an houre O2

17 **Philomela** the nightingale. Compare *Lucrece* ll. 1128–48.
19 **she** i.e. the lark
21 **packed** sent packing
  post hasten
  pretty The only other substantive usage of this word in the Shakespearian canon is in *Winter's Tale* (*c.*1609) 3.3.47.

27 **moon** month. O2's 'hour' does not rhyme.
30 He is urging the night to be short tonight (when he is absent from her) and long tomorrow (when he hopes he will be with her).

Sonnets to Sundry Notes of Music

15

It was a lording's daughter, the fairest one of three,
That likèd of her master, as well as well might be;
Till looking on an Englishman, the fairest that eye could see,
    Her fancy fell a-turning
Long was the combat doubtful, that love with love did fight   5
To leave the master loveless, or kill the gallant knight;
To put in practice either, alas it was a spite
    Unto the silly damsel.
But one must be refusèd: more mickle was the pain,
That nothing could be used to turn them both to gain,   10
For of the two the trusty knight was wounded with disdain,
    Alas she could not help it.
Thus art with arms contending was victor of the day,
Which by a gift of learning did bear the maid away.
Then, lullaby, the learnèd man hath got the lady gay,   15
    For now my song is ended.

3 that] O2; *omitted* O3

SONNETS TO SUNDRY NOTES OF MUSIC
    This section of *The Passionate Pilgrim* is introduced by a separate title-page. It is possible that the poems which follow were known to have musical settings which are now lost. The new title-page may indicate that Jaggard did not wish to attribute the following poems to Shakespeare (in which case Poem 16 from *L.L.L.*, is anomalous). See Introduction, pp. 75–6

POEM 15
    No other version is known. The attribution is uncertain. There are no stylistic, metrical, or lexical features of the poem which suggest Shakespeare's authorship.

1 **lording's** a diminutive form of 'lord', frequently used in popular ballads
2 **master** schoolmaster. The poem engages in a traditional dispute between a soldier and a clerk, in which (writers having a predisposition towards clerks) the learned man usually emerges victorious.
7 **spite** source of unhappiness
9 **more mickle** more great
10 **nothing . . . gain** no scheme could be adopted to enjoy both of them
11 **wounded with disdain** i.e. rejected
15 **lullaby** goodnight

16

On a day (alack the day)
Love whose month was ever May
Spied a blossom passing fair,
Playing in the wanton air.
Through the velvet leaves the wind   5
All unseen gan passage find,
That the lover (sick to death)
Wished himself the heavens' breath.
'Air,' quoth he, 'thy cheeks may blow;
Air, would I might triumph so;   10
But (alas) my hand hath sworn
Ne'er to pluck thee from thy thorn,
Vow (alack) for youth unmeet,
Youth, so apt to pluck a sweet.
Thou, for whom Jove would swear   15
Juno but an Ethiope were,
And deny himself for Jove,
Turning mortal for thy love.

2 was] O1; is LLL   6 gan] O1; can LLL   7 lover] O1; Sheepheard EH   8 Wished] O1; Wish LLL
11 alas . . . hath] O1; alacke . . . is LLL   12 thorn] EH; throne O1, LLL   14 *Two additional lines
follow in* LLL: 'Do not call it sinne in me, | That am forsworne for thee:—'

POEM 16

Dumaine's 'sonnet' from *L.L.L.*
4.3.99–118 is reprinted in *England's Heli-
con* (ed. Rollins 1, 55) with some minor
variants. It is the only one of the three
poems from *The Passionate Pilgrim* re-
printed in *England's Helicon* to be attrib-
uted to Shakespeare. The trochaic
seven-syllable lines anticipate the form of
'Let the bird of loudest lay'.

3 **passing** exceptionally
4 **wanton** playful (with an undertone of
sexual licence)
7 **That** so that (Abbott §283)
8 **Wished . . . breath** (as the lover in Sonnet
128 wishes to become the keys of the vir-
ginal or harpsichord)
9 **Air** plays on the highly fashionable sense
'melody', for which the first cited usage in
OED is *Dream* 1.1.183. After the publica-
tion of Dowland's *First Book of Songs or
Airs* (1597; see Poem 8.5 and n.) the word
could mean 'solo song accompanied by

the lute'. This sense is active here, since
the poem is grouped along with 'Sonnets
to Sundry Notes of Music'.
12 **thorn** O and *L.L.L.* read 'throne', pre-
sumably as a result of contamination
with the set phrase 'pluck us from our
throne'.
13 **unmeet** unsuitable
14 The two lines which follow in *L.L.L.* ('Do
not call it sin in me | That I am forsworn
for thee') are cut because they allude to
the dramatic setting of the lyric in the
play: Dumaine has sworn to forgo love,
and is now smitten with desire. This
leaves *Thou* in this version hanging.
16 **Ethiope** dark-skinned woman; considered
unattractive in the poetic conventions of
the period and frequently used as a nega-
tive contrast to fairness ('Silvia . . . Shows
Julia but a swarthy Ethiope', *Two Gentle-
men* 2.6.25–6).
17 **And . . . Jove** i.e. deny his identity as king
of the gods

17

My flocks feed not, my ewes breed not,
My rams speed not, all is amiss;
Love is dying, faith's defying,
Heart's denying, causer of this.
All my merry jigs are quite forgot,   5
All my lady's love is lost (God wot),
Where her faith was firmly fixèd in love
There a 'nay' is placed without remove.
  One silly cross wrought all my loss,
  Oh frowning Fortune, cursèd fickle dame,   10
  For now I see inconstancy
  More in women than in men remain.

1 flocks feed ... breed] O1; flocke feedes ... breeds HARL.   2 speed ... amiss] O1; speedes not in
their bais HARL.   3 Love is dying] O1; Loue is denying EH   faith's defying] O1; fayth defying
HARL.; Faith is defying EH   4 Heart's denying] O1; Harts renying O2; her denyinge HARL.;
Harts renying EH   5 my] O1; our WEELKES   quite] O1; cleane HARL.   6 lady's love is] O1;
layes of Loue are HARL.   7 her] O1; my HARL.; our WEELKES   faith was ... fixed in] O1; ioyes
were firmly linkt by HARL.   8 a 'nay' is] O1; annoyes are HARL.; ennoy is WEELKES   9 one
silly] O1; our seely WEELKES   cross ... my] O1; poore crosse hath wrought me this HARL.   10
frowning ... cursèd fickle] O1; fickle ... cruell cursed HARL.   11 For ... see] O1; Now you may
see that HAEL.   12 More ... remain] O1; In women more then I my selfe haue found HARL.
men remain] O1; many men to be WEELKES   12 women] O1; wowen O2

POEM 17

The attribution is uncertain. First printed
as the second song in three parts in
Thomas Weelkes, *Madrigals to 3, 4, 5, and
6 voices* (London 1597), sigs. B1ᵛ–B2ʳ,
without attribution; reprinted, in a text
which is likely to derive from O2 of *The
Passionate Pilgrim*, in *England's Helicon*,
where it is attributed to 'Ignoto'; a version
also exists (without attribution) in BL
Harleian MS 6910, fo. 156ʳ, a verse miscel-
lany from the period 1596–1601 which
is in general sparing but accurate with
attributions. The poem was attributed to
Richard Barnfield by Grosart (*Complete
Poems of Richard Barnfield* (Roxburgh
Club, 1876), 197), since in *England's Heli-
con* it is followed by 'As it fell upon a day'
(Poem 20 below, which appears in Barn-
field's *Poems in Diverse Humours*), which
is entitled 'Another of the same shep-
herd's'. The 'same shepherd' is more
likely to refer to the anonymous author of
the poem as it appears in *The Passionate
Pilgrim* than to Barnfield, however. The
lack of attribution to Shakespeare of this
and Poem 20 in *England's Helicon* is,
however, reasonably weighty negative
evidence.

2 **speed** flourish

3 **defying** lacking in faith (the intransitive
usage is rare)

4 **Heart's . . . this** Her denial of me is the
source of all my miseries.

5 **jigs** These were short entertainments,
often involving rustic characters who
sang and danced, which were frequently
performed after theatrical performances
up to the early years of the seventeenth
century. They may have been based on
popular rural pastimes which remained
unrecorded. See Charles Read Baskervill,
The Elizabethan Jig and Related Song Drama
(Chicago, 1929).

6 **wot** knows

8 **without remove** irremovably

9 **cross** piece of ill fortune (perhaps 'blunder
on my part')

In black mourn I, all fears scorn I;
Love hath forlorn me, living in thrall:
Heart is bleeding, all help needing,   15
O cruel speeding, fraughted with gall.
My shepherd's pipe can sound no deal,
My wether's bell rings doleful knell,
My curtal dog that wont to have played
Plays not at all, but seems afraid.   20
  With sighs so deep, procures to weep,
  In howling wise, to see my doleful plight.
  How sighs resound through heartless ground,
  Like thousand vanquished men in bloody fight.

Clear wells spring not, sweet birds sing not,   25
Green plants bring not forth their dye;
Herds stand weeping, flocks all sleeping,
Nymphs back peeping fearfully.
All our pleasure known to us poor swains,
All our merry meetings on the plains,   30
All our evening sport from us is fled,
All our love is lost, for love is dead.

13 fears] OI; feare WEELKES   14 Love . . . living] OI; lo how forlorne I, live HARL.   15 help]
OI; helps HARL.   16 cruel] OI; cursed HARL.   fraughted] OI; fraught HARL., WEELKES   17
can] OI; will HARL.   deal] OI; *omitted* HARL. *An 'x' in a later hand marks the omission*   18 bell
rings] OI; ringe a HARL.   19 curtal dog] (curtaile) OI; curtail'd Dogge HARL.   that wont to]
OI; wch would HARL.   20 afraid] OI; dismayd HARL.   21 With . . . procures] OI; My . . . pro-
cures WEELKES; My sights so deepe, doth cause him HARL.; Which . . . procure *conj.* Sisson   22
In howling wise] OI; With houling noyse HARL., WEELKES   see . . . doleful] OI; wayle . . . woe-
full HARL.   23 How . . . heartless ground] OI; how . . . harcklesse ground WEELKES; My shrikes
resoundes, throughe Arcadia groundes HARL.   24 Like] HARL.; Like a OI   thousand . . .
bloody] OI; thousands . . . deadly HARL.   26 Green plants bring not forth their dye] OI; Greene
palmes bring not foorth yor dye HARL.; Lowde bells ring not, cherefully WEELKES   27 Herds]
OI; Herd OXFORD   stand] WEELKES; stands OI   flocks all] OI; Ecchoes HARL.   28 back peep-
ing] EH; blacke peeping OI; back creping WEELKES   fearefully] OI; pittyfully HARL.   29 our
pleasure] OI; the pleasures HARL.   31 sport . . . us is] OI; sports . . . greenes are HARL.   32 our
love is] OI; alas is HARL.; our loues are WEELKES   for love] OI; now Dolus HARL.

14 **in thrall** as a slave
16 **speeding** outcome, lot (often a favourable
   outcome; here emphatically not)
   fraughted laden
17 **no deal** not at all
18 **wether** ram (often a castrated ram)
19 **curtal** with a docked tail
21 **procures** causes
23 **heartless ground** desolate landscape
   (*resound* creates a play on the relatively

new musical sense of *ground*, 'The plain-
song or melody on which a descant is
raised' (*OED* 6c), and provides an oppor-
tunity for expressive effects in the setting)
26 **dye** colour (i.e. they do not flower)
28 **back peeping** is feeble even by the
   standards of this poem, but is preferable
   to O's 'black peeping' or the Harleian
   MS's tautological 'look peeping' (see
   collation).

Farewell, sweet love, thy like ne'er was
For sweet content, the cause of all my woe.
Poor Corydon must live alone: 35
Other help for him I see that there is none.

33–6] OI; *omitted* HARL.   33 love, thy] OI; lasse, the WEELKES   34 For] EH; For a OI   woe] OI; moane EH   36 see ... is] OI; know ther's WEELKES

35 **Corydon** the name of the shepherd who in Virgil's Eclogue 2 laments the loss of his male lover Alexis

18

When as thine eye hath chose the dame,
And stalled the deer that thou shouldst strike,
Let reason rule things worthy blame,
As well as fancy, partial might.
    Take counsel of some wiser head,   5
    Neither too young, nor yet unwed.

And when thou com'st thy tale to tell,
Smooth not thy tongue with filèd talk,
Lest she some subtle practice smell—
A cripple soon can find a halt—   10
    But plainly say thou lov'st her well,
    And set her person forth to sale.

And to her will frame all thy ways:
Spare not to spend, and chiefly there

1 as] O1; y^t FOL1, FOL9 2 shouldst] O1; wouldest FOL1; wouldst FOL9 4 fancy, partial might] O1; fancye parcyall like FOL1; partiall fancie like FOL9; fancy, partial wight Capell 5 Take] O1; aske FOL9 wiser] O1; other FOL1, FOL9 6 too young] O1; unwise FOL1, FOL9 unwed] O1; unwayde FOL1 8 Smooth] O1; whett FOL1, FOL9 10 find] O1; spie FOL9 a halt] O1; one haulte FOL1 11 say] O1; *omitted* FOL9 12 her person . . . sale] O1; thy person . . . sell FOL1; thy body . . . sell FOL9 13–24] *order as in* O1, FOL1, FOL9; *these lines follow 25–36 in* O2 13 And to] O1; unto FOL9

POEM 18

No other printed version is known and there are no grounds for the attribution to Shakespeare beyond the inclusion of the poem in *The Passionate Pilgrim*. There is a manuscript version in Folger MS V.a.89, p. 25^{r–v}. This MS is roughly contemporary with *The Passionate Pilgrim*, and contains poems by Sidney, Dyer, Vavasor, and John Bentley. Another version is in Folger MS V.a.339, fo. 185^v. These show significant variants from the *Passionate Pilgrim* text (see collation). If they are authorial they give no indication of who the author might be.

2 **stalled** brought to a standstill (used specifically though rarely of beasts of the chase, *OED* 10)
4 **fancy, partial might** The general sense is that reason should control the mind, including the whimsical (*partial*) power (*might*) of fancy. The text as it stands makes poor sense. It is tempting to emend

with Pooler to 'fancy's partial might' (i.e. fancy's arbitrary power). The collation shows that the MS tradition is no clearer.
6 **nor yet unwed** i.e. take as your adviser someone who is married
8 **filèd** rhetorically polished (and hence deceptive)
10 **halt** limp (first cited usage). The line means that someone who habitually deceives people will be able to spot someone who is doing the same thing. Proverbial: 'It is hard (ill) halting before a cripple' (Tilley H60).
12 **sale** praise it as though you were trying to sell it. Compare Sonnet 21.14, which also associates praising with selling.
13–24 The order of the stanzas given here follows that of O1 and the Folger MSS. O2 positions these two stanzas after ll. 25–36.
14 **spend** (a) money on gifts; (b) words on praise; with perhaps a faint underpresence of the sexual sense of *spend* (on which see Sonnet 149.7 n.)

Where thy desert may merit praise   15
By ringing in thy lady's ear.
   The strongest castle, tower, and town,
   The golden bullet beats it down.

Serve always with assurèd trust,
And in thy suit be humble true,   20
Unless thy lady prove unjust
Press never thou to choose a new.
   When time shall serve, be thou not slack
   To proffer, though she put thee back.

What though her frowning brows be bent,   25
Her cloudy looks will calm ere night,
And then too late she will repent,
That thus dissembled her delight,
   And twice desire ere it be day,
   That which with scorn she put away.   30

What though she strive to try her strength
And ban and brawl, and say thee nay,
Her feeble force will yield at length,
When craft hath taught her thus to say
   'Had women been so strong as men,   35
   In faith, you had not had it then.'

15 desert may merit] O1; expenses may sound thy FOL1; expence may sound thy FOL9   16 in thy lady's] O1; allwayes in her FOL1; in in her FOL9   17 castle, tower] O1; towres fort FOL9 and] O1; or FOL1, FOL9   18 bullet beats it] O1 bullett hathe beat FOL1; bullet beateth FOL9   20 humble] O1; ever FOL9   21 Unless] O1; untill FOL1   22 Press] O1; seek FOL1   choose] O1; change FOL1, FOL9   a new] O1; for newe FOL9   23 shall . . . be thou] O1; doth . . . then be FOL1; doth . . . thee be FOL9   24 thee] O1; it FOL1, FOL9, C3   25 though . . . frowning] O1; if she frowne wth FOL9   26 calm ere] O1 (calme yer); cleare ere FOL1; calme at FOL9   27 And . . . will] O1; And she perhappes will sone FOL1; when 't perhaps shee will FOL9   28 thus] O1; she FOL1; so FOL9   29 twice] O1; thrice FOL9   ere it] O1 (yer it) it ere FOL9   30 which with] O1; wth suche FOL1, FOL9   31 though . . . her] O1; i^t . . . thy FOL9   32 ban] O1; chide FOL1 say] O1; sweare FOL9   34 When] O1; & FOL1, FOL9   hath taught] O1; will cause FOL9   35 so] O1; as FOL1, FOL9   36 In faith] O1; by cock FOL9   had it] O1; got it FOL1   37–42] *order as O1; FOL1 and FOL9 place these lines after O1's l. 48*

16 **ringing** (a) pouring out words; (b) jingling coins
18 **golden bullet** (a) money; (b) words
21 **unjust** unfaithful (compare Sonnet 138.9)
23 **slack** remiss; with a pun on the sexual sense 'flaccid' (compare *Lucrece* l. 425 and n.)
24 **put thee back** resists you
30 **put away** refused
32 **ban** curse. Compare *Lucrece* l. 1460. **brawl** wrangle

The wiles and guiles that women work,
Dissembled with an outward show;
The tricks and toys that in them lurk,
The cock that treads them shall not know.   40
   Have you not heard it said full oft
   'A woman's "nay" doth stand for naught'?

Think women still to strive with men
To sin, and never for to saint.
There is no heaven: be holy then   45
When time with age shall them attain.
   Were kisses all the joys in bed
   One woman would another wed.

But soft, enough; too much I fear,
Lest that my mistress hear my song.   50
She will not stick to round me on the ear,
To teach my tongue to be so long.
   Yet will she blush, here be it said,
   To hear her secrets so bewrayed.

37 The . . . women work] O1; The . . . in them lurkes FOL1; A thousand wiles in wantons lurkes FOL9   39 that . . . lurk] O1; & meanes to worke FOL1; the meanes to worke FOL9   40 shall] O1; doth FOL9   41 have you] O1; hast y^u FOL9   it] O1; that FOL1   43 still to strive] O1; love to matche FOL1; seeke [think *deleted*] to match FOL9   44 To . . . saint] O1; and not to liue soe like a sainte FOL1; to liue in sinne & not to saint FOL9   45 There] O1; here FOL1, FOL9   be holy then] FOL9; (by holy then) O1; they holy then FOL1   46 When . . . them] O1; beginne when age doth them FOL1; till time shall thee wth age FOL9   47 kisses] O1; kyssinge FOL1, FOL9   49 But soft] O1; Nowe hoe FOL1; ho now FOL9   too much, I fear] O1; & more I feare FOL9   50 Lest . . . mistress] O1; for if my ladye FOL1; for if my m^{rs} FOL9   hear my] O1; hear this FOL1; hard this FOL9   51 she will] O1; she would FOL9   round me on the ear] O1; ringe my eare FOL1; warme my eare FOL9; round me in th'ear GILDON 1714   53 will] O1; would FOL1, FOL9   blush] O1; smile FOL9   54 so] O1; thus FOL1, FOL9

39 **toys** fancies
40 **cock that treads them** *Tread* means 'Of the male bird: To copulate with (the hen)' (*OED* 8a). Compare Chaucer's *Nun's Priest's Tale*, *Riverside Chaucer*, 3rd edn., ed. Larry D. Benson (Oxford, 1988), ll. 3177–8: 'He fethered Pertelote twenty tyme, | And trad hire eke as ofte, ere it was pryme'. *Cock* has its modern slang sense 'penis'.
42 Gruesomely misogynist, but proverbial: 'A woman says nay and means aye' (Tilley W660). The proverb here puns on 'nothing', which can be used of the female sexual organs (as in Sonnet 20.12), and the locker-room crudity of the line might even have invited a raised

eyebrow over 'stand', which can mean 'get an erection'.
43–4 **Think . . . saint** Believe me, women try to overgo men in sinning, but never in being good.
45 **There is no heaven** Probably *there* refers to 'in women', rather than marking a general statement of atheism (although the world-weariness of the poem so far does not resist the emergence of this sense).
46 **When . . . attaint** So don't try to be chaste until women are old and ugly.
49 **soft** sshh!
51 **stick** scruple, hesitate
round usually means 'whisper'; here the context suggests 'clout'
54 **bewrayed** betrayed, made public

19

Live with me and be my love,
And we will all the pleasures prove
That hills and valleys, dales and fields,
And all the craggy mountains yield.

There will we sit upon the rocks,   5
And see the shepherds feed their flocks,
By shallow rivers, by whose falls
Melodious birds sing madrigals.

There will I make thee a bed of roses,
With a thousand fragrant posies,   10
A cap of flowers and a kirtle
Embroidered all with leaves of myrtle.

A belt of straw and ivy buds,
With coral clasps and amber studs,

1 Live] O2; Come live EH   3 hills and valleys, dales and fields] O2; Vallies, groues, hills and fieldes EH   4 and . . . craggy] O2; Woods, or steeple EH   mountains yield] O2; mountaine yeeldes EH   5 There will we] O2; And wee will EH   6 And see] O2; Seeing EH   7 by] O2; to EH   falls] O2; tales O3   8 sing] O2; sings EH   9 There will I] O2; And I will EH   a bed] O2; beds EH   10 With . . . posies] O2 (poses); And . . . poesies EH   12] O2; EH *includes an additional stanza here:* A gowne made of the finest wooll, | Which from our pretty Lambes we pull, | Fayre lined slippers for the cold: | With buckles of the purest gold.

Sir Hugh Evans sings fragments of Christopher Marlowe's 'Come live with me' as he waits for Dr Caius (*Merry Wives* (probably first performed 1597) 3.1.16–25). This may have influenced Jaggard in his attribution of this version to Shakespeare, or it may have made him feel his readers would find the attribution convincing. A longer version of the poem is attributed to Marlowe in *England's Helicon* (1600), and it had an extensive afterlife in manuscript miscellanies. Gill (212) suggests that this version 'may have been an early draft for the poem as it appears fully in *England's Helicon*'. The final stanza printed here is from 'The Nymph's Reply', commonly attributed to Sir Walter Ralegh. The omission of the final five stanzas of the 'The Nymph's Reply' here

is probably the consequence of pressures of space: at this point in O2 the compositor had to abandon his earlier practice of setting poems only on the recto of each page in order to keep the volume within four sheets folded to make thirty-two pages.

8 **madrigals** The vogue for madrigals, polyphonic settings of short poems often on amorous subjects, began in 1588 with the publication of Nicholas Yonge's *Musica Transalpina: Madrigals translate of four, five and six parts*. This continues one of a number of allusions to fashionable musical forms in the volume. See notes to Poems 8.5, 16.9, 17.23.

11 **kirtle** skirt (it can also be a shirt or tunic)

And if these pleasures may thee move,   15
Then live with me, and be my love.

Love's Answer

If that the world and love were young,
And truth in every shepherd's tongue,
These pretty pleasures might me move
To live with thee and be thy love.   20

16] O2; EH *includes an additional stanza here*: The Sheepheards Swaines shall daunce & sing, | For thy delight each May-morning, | If these delights thy minde may moue; | Then liue with mee, and be my loue   Then] O2; Come EH   17 Love's Answer] O2; The Nimphs reply to the Sheepheard EH   17 that] O2; all EH   20 thy] O2; my O3; EH *includes five additional stanzas here*

20

As it fell upon a day,
In the merry month of May,
Sitting in a pleasant shade,
Which a grove of myrtles made,
Beasts did leap, and birds did sing,   5
Trees did grow, and plants did spring.
Every thing did banish moan,
Save the nightingale alone.
She (poor bird) as all forlorn
Leaned her breast up till a thorn,   10
And there sung the doleful'st ditty
That to hear it was great pity.
'Fie, fie, fie', now would she cry;
'Tereu, Tereu' by and by:
That to hear her so complain   15
Scarce I could from tears refrain,
For her griefs so lively shown
Made me think upon mine own.
'Ah,' thought I, 'thou mourn'st in vain,
None takes pity on thy pain: 20
Senseless trees, they cannot hear thee;
Ruthless bears, they will not cheer thee.
King Pandion, he is dead,

10 up till] O2; against EH   22 bears] O2; beasts EH

POEM 20

Richard Barnfield's poem first appeared in *Poems in Diverse Humours*, a group of poems which follow *The Encomion of Lady Pecunia, or the praise of Money* (STC 1485), which was printed by Jaggard's brother in 1598, where it is entitled 'An Ode'. The text in *The Passionate Pilgrim* shows no significant variations from the earlier printed version, and is likely to have been set from printed copy. The poem is omitted from the second edition of *Poems in Diverse Humours*. See Poem 8 headnote. An abbreviated form of the poem was subsequently printed in *England's Helicon*. The superficial resemblance between the first two lines and Poem 16.1–2, combined with the nightingale in ll. 8–30 (compare *Lucrece* ll. 1128–48), may have made the attribution to Shakespeare convincing to early readers, as would its seven-syllable trochaic lines (as used in Poem 16 and, later, in 'Let the bird of loudest lay').

7 moan] complaint
10 up till] up against
14 Tereu This is the vocative form of Tereus, the brother-in-law of Philomela. He raped her. She metamorphosed into a nightingale. See *Lucrece* l. 1079 n.
23 King Pandion Philomela's father. After the rape of Philomela 'The sorrow of this

All thy friends are lapped in lead.
All thy fellow birds do sing,   25
Careless of thy sorrowing.
Whilst as fickle Fortune smiled
Thou and I were both beguiled.
Everyone that flatters thee
Is no friend in misery.   30
Words are easy, like the wind;
Faithful friends are hard to find.
Every man will be thy friend,
Whilst thou hast wherewith to spend,
But if store of crowns be scant   35
No man will supply thy want.
If that one be prodigal,
"Bountiful" they will him call,
And with such-like flattering:
"Pity but he were a king."   40
If he be addict to vice,
Quickly him they will entice.
If to women he be bent
They have at commandement;
But if Fortune once do frown,   45
Then farewell his great renown:
They that fawned on him before
Use his company no more.
He that is thy friend indeed,
He will help thee in thy need.   50
If thou sorrow, he will weep;
If thou wake, he cannot sleep.

26] 02; *after this line* EH *reads* 'Euen so poore bird like thee, | None a-liue will pitty mee'   27–56]
02; *omitted from* EH

great mischance did stop Pandion's
breath | Before his time, and long ere age
determined had his death' (Golding
6.844–5).

24 **lapped in lead** buried in lead coffins
31 **Words . . . wind** proverbial (Tilley W833)
37–8 **prodigal,** | **"Bountiful"** The figure of
paradiastole substitutes a word for a vice

with a near-equivalent virtue (Quintilian
9.3.65).
40 **Pity but he were a king** what a shame he
is not a king
41 **addict** given over to. Stressed on the sec-
ond syllable.
43 **commandement** at their disposal. The
medial 'e' is pronounced here to stop the
line limping.

    Thus of every grief in heart
    He with thee doth bear a part.
    These are certain signs to know   55
    Faithful friend from flatt'ring foe.'

54 **bear a part** participates in your suffering

'Let the bird of loudest lay'

'Let the bird of loudest lay'

Let the bird of loudest lay,
On the sole Arabian tree,
Herald sad and trumpet be:
To whose sound chaste wings obey.

But thou, shrieking harbinger,   5
Foul precurrer of the fiend,
Augur of the fever's end,
To this troop come thou not near.

From this session interdict
Every foul of tyrant wing,   10
Save the eagle, feathered king:
Keep the obsequy so strict.

The poem—first printed in a group of poems by various authors, including Marston, Chapman, and Jonson, appended to Robert Chester's *Love's Martyr* (1601)—is signed 'William Shake-speare'. See Introduction, pp. 82–90.

1 **the bird of loudest lay** This is presumably 'any bird, so long as it has a loud voice'. The reference to the *sole Arabian tree*, however, the traditional resort of the Phoenix (as in *Tempest* 3.3.23), may imply that the Phoenix is meant: Shakespeare is likely to have known from grammar school Lactantius's poem *De Ave Phoenice*, which refers to the 'wonderful voice' (l. 46) of the phoenix. Compare also William Smith's *Chloris* (1596), sonnet 23, ll. 5–8: 'And on a lofty tow'ring cedar tree, | With heavenly substance, she herself consumes. | From whence she young again appears to be | Out of the cinders of her peerless plumes'. The fact that the bird is not named here, however, is significant: it leaves readers uncertain whether a second Phoenix has sprung from the death of the Phoenix and the Turtle (= turtle dove) in order to act as herald in its own obsequies. Other birds have been proposed, including the crane and the cock.

3 **trumpet** trumpeter (*OED* 4a)

5 **shrieking harbinger** presumably the owl, on which there is a passage in Chester's poem: 'The filthy messenger of ill to come | The sluggish owl is, and to danger some' (ed. Grosart, 129).

6 **precurrer** precursor (only example in *OED*)

7 **Augur of the fever's end** prophet of the end of illness (in death or cure)

9 **session** sitting (as of a court). *OED* suggests that it is only in Scotland that the word is used of an ecclesiastical gathering, but this sense seems appropriate here.
interdict prohibit (sometimes used in a specifically ecclesiastical sense, *OED* 3: 'To cut off authoritatively from religious offices or privileges', which fits the ritual setting here). The owl is presumably the subject of this verb.

11 **feathered king** The eagle is traditionally regarded as king of the birds, as in Chester (ed. Grosart, 126): 'The princely eagle of all birds the King, | For none but she can gaze against the sun'.

12 **obsequy** commemorative rites at the grave (with perhaps a suggestion through its etymology of 'those that follow in the funeral procession')

Let the priest in surplice white,
That defunctive music can,
Be the death-divining swan,   15
Lest the requiem lack his right.

And thou, treble-dated crow,
That thy sable gender mak'st
With the breath thou giv'st and tak'st,
'Mongst our mourners shalt thou go.   20

Here the anthem doth commence:
Love and Constancy is dead,
Phoenix and the Turtle fled,
In a mutual flame from hence.

So they loved as love in twain,   25
Had the essence but in one,
Two distincts, division none:
Number there in love was slain.

---

12 **strict** rigorously observed; perhaps also 'limited in number'

13 **surplice** is a loose overgarment of linen, worn by all but the hotter sort of Protestant clergy in the Elizabethan period.

14 **defunctive music can** skilled in the music of death (first citation of *defunctive* in *OED*)

15 **death-divining** The swan was believed to sing once only, before its own death.

16 **requiem** the first word of the Introit in the Mass for the Dead, 'Requiem æternam dona eis, Domine'
lack his right fails to receive its due (the swan's presence is necessary to give the rite its full force). *Right* plays on 'rite'.

17 **treble-dated crow** Pliny quotes a passage of Hesiod to support the view that the crow lives nine times as long as a man, i.180.

18 **sable gender mak'st** Crows were believed to generate their black offspring (*sable gender*) not by sexual reproduction, but by touching beaks and exchanging breath. This form of chaste union makes them a suitable audience to the chaste love of the Phoenix and the Turtle. According to Pliny i.276 'the common sort are of opinion, that [ravens] conceive and engender at the bill, or lay their eggs by it', but Pliny cites Aristotle to the effect that this is not so.

21 **anthem** a passage of scripture set to music. The Book of Common Prayer service for the burial of the dead begins: 'All stand while one or more of the following anthems are sung or said: I am the resurrection and the life, saith the Lord; he that believeth in me, though he were dead, yet shall he live; and whosoever liveth and believeth in me shall never die'.

26 **essence** The theological sense, 'A synonym of "substance", as denoting that in respect of which the three persons in the Trinity are one' (*OED* 4b), is active. The vocabulary used at this stage of the poem would have had clear associations with the mystery of the Trinity, as is illustrated by Hooker's *Laws of Ecclesiastical Polity*, 5.56.2: 'And sith they are all but one God in number, one indivisible essence or substance, their distinction cannot possibly admit separation'.

27 **distincts** distinguishable entities which are essentially one (*OED* cites only this use of the noun). Thomas Aquinas allows that the term 'distinction' could be used to describe the separateness of the persons of the Trinity: 'we must not, in speaking of God, use the words "diversity" and "difference" lest we

Hearts remote, yet not asunder;
Distance and no space was seen   30
'Twixt this Turtle and his queen;
But in them it were a wonder.

So between them love did shine
That the Turtle saw his right
Flaming in the Phoenix' sight;   35
Either was the other's mine.

Property was thus appalled
That the self was not the same:
Single natures, double name,
Neither two nor one was called.   40

Reason in itself confounded
Saw division grow together;

39] Single natures, double name, Q (Single Natures double name)

should compromise the unity of nature we can, however, use the word "distinction" [*distinctio*] on account of relative oppositions . . . we must avoid "separation" [*separatio*] and "division" [*divisio*] as implying a whole divided into parts', *Summa Theologiae* (London and New York, n.d.), vi.89 (1a.31.2).

27 **division none** no possibility of breaking them down into their constituent parts. *Division* was a term of art from logic: 'As definition doth declare what a thing is, so a division showeth how many things are contained in the same', Thomas Wilson, *The Rule of Reason* (1563), fos. 14ᵛ–15ʳ.

28 **Number** the abstract principle that entities have separated existence and so can be counted.

29 **remote** separate
asunder in two parts. The force of the word here derives partly from its one use in the Book of Common Prayer at the end of the Solemnization of Matrimony: 'Those whom God has joined together let no one put asunder'.

31 **his queen** Turtle doves are usually presented as feminine, as in John Maplet, *A Green Forest* (1567), sig. P3ʳ: 'And as for the Turtle Dove, her best praise is in keeping undefiled wedlock (and losing her mate) for her constant widowhoode'. In

Chester's poem, however, the turtle dove is male.

32 **But . . . wonder** in any other less remarkable birds it would have been a miracle

34 **his right** that which he owned

36 **Either was the other's mine** (a) each bird belonged to the other, such was the mutuality of their love; (b) each of them was a source of riches for the other

37 **Property** (a) the abstract principle of ownership; (b) the principle that particular qualities inhere in one entity alone. As Wilson puts it in *The Rule of Reason*, fo. 6ʳ, property is 'a natural proneness and manner of doing, which agreeth to one kind and the same only and that evermore'. The pair of birds consequently threaten the logical principle that entities are distinct.

41 **Reason in itself confounded** The pair contradict the foundational premises on which reason bases its account of experience. The presence of Reason as a commentator on the fate of the two birds may owe something to Chester's poem, in which a Pelican makes the final comments on the immolation of the Phoenix and the Turtle.

42 **division** The general sense is 'things which appear separate', but there is also a play on the logical sense, 'the action of separating into kinds or classes'.

To themselves yet either neither,
Simple were so well compounded,

That it cried 'How true a twain   45
Seemeth this concordant one:
Love hath reason, Reason none,
If what parts can so remain.'

Whereupon it made this threne
To the Phoenix and the dove,   50
Co-supremes and stars of love,
As chorus to their tragic scene.

Threnos

Beauty, Truth, and Rarity,
Grace in all simplicity,
Here enclosed, in cinders lie.   55

Death is now the Phoenix' nest,
And the Turtle's loyal breast
To eternity doth rest.

Leaving no posterity,
'Twas not their infirmity: 60
It was married chastity.

43 **To . . . neither** each was its own being (*To themselves*), but neither of them was simply itself nor the other.

44 **Simple . . . compounded** 'Simples' are pure ingredients which are mixed to make 'compounds'.

46 **concordant one** Harmony is also used as an image for an ideal married union in Sonnet 8.13–14. A single sound or entity cannot of course be said to be in concord with itself. This is Reason's problem.

48 **parts can so remain** if that which is separate can none the less remain so together

49 **threne** lamentation

51 **co-supremes** joint rulers (earliest cited usage in *OED*)

52.1 *Threnos* lamentation. This is the earliest cited usage in *OED*; it is pre-dated by Peacham (1593), 66, in which it is defined

as 'a form of speech by which the orator lamenteth some person or people for the misery they suffer'. This title is preceded by a page-break in *Love's Martyr* (sigs. Z3ᵛ–Z4ʳ). The appearance of two separate poems which this offers reinforces the paradox of two entities in a single nature described in l. 40.

59–61 'The fact that they left no children was not the result of any physical weakness or incapacity, but was the expression of the chastity of their marriage.' There is a faint secondary suggestion that *married chastity* might itself be an *infirmity*. *Leaving no posterity* contradicts both the traditional view of the Phoenix (it dies and then is reborn from fire) and Chester's poem, which ends with the birth of a new Phoenix.

Truth may seem, but cannot be;
Beauty brag, but 'tis not she:
Truth and Beauty burièd be.

To this urn let those repair   65
That are either true or fair:
For these dead birds sigh a prayer.

62 **may seem** i.e. may seem to be true, but
Truth died with the Phoenix and the
Turtle

63 **Beauty brag** Beauty may boast of being
beautiful, but she does not represent the
reality of beauty.

Shakespeare's Sonnets

DEDICATION

The dedication resembles a Roman inscription, in which capitalized words were separated by full stops, and in which main verbs were often delayed until the final line. Thorpe and Eld produced no other dedicatory epistle of similar appearance. The Latin dedication to Ben Jonson of Marston's *Malcontent* (1604), published by William Apsley, one of the tradesmen involved in the publication of Q, has a similar layout ('BENIAMINI IONSONIO | POETAE | ELEGANTISSIMO | GRAVISSIMO'), although without points between its words. Thorpe's close associate Edward Blount printed *Ben Jonson His Part of King James his Royall and Magnificent Entertainment* (1604), which includes a lengthy Latin dedicatory inscription to James and his son Prince Henry (sig. D3ᵃ). This includes lapidary stops ('D.I.O.M. | BRITANNIARVM. IMP.' . . .). Katherine Duncan-Jones, 'Was the 1609 Shake-Speare's Sonnets Really Unauthorized?', *RES* NS 34 (1983), 151–71, has proposed the dedication to Jonson's *Volpone* (printed for Thorpe in 1605) as an analogue, although the absence of full stops and its use of three different sizes of type differentiates it from this dedication. The Latinate delay of the verb, however ('BEN. IONSON | THE GRATEFULL ACKNOWLEDGER | DEDICATES | BOTH IT, AND HIMSELFE.'), suggests that Thorpe and Eld were attempting to produce a dedicatory format which linked the Sonnets with the classical learning of Ben Jonson and his circle. The typographical form of the dedication makes a claim that the book that follows will be a learned work which confers eternal life on the people it is about, despite its careful reluctance to reveal who they are.

I ONLIE.BEGETTER (a) sole originator; (b) sole procurer (of the manuscript). On these alternatives hangs a multiplicity of consequences and questions: if sense (a) the assumption is that the publication has the blessing and collaboration of Shakespeare (or that Thorpe was intimately acquainted with the genesis of the poems). If so, then is 'Mr W.H.' to be iden-

tified with the friend of Sonnets 1–126? Or with a patron to whom the poems are flatteringly addressed as their sole creator? If (b) then the sonnets are assumed to have reached Thorpe through an intermediary, and hence the authority of the volume is called into question, and Mr W.H. loses any connection with the subjects of the sonnets. For a consideration of these questions, see the Introduction, pp. 98–103.

3 Mʳ.W.H. See Introduction, pp. 100–1. The initials may be used to generate excitingly multiple hypotheses about the identities of the persons referred to: cf. George Gascoigne's *A Hundred Sundry Flowers* (1573): 'F.I., whom the reader may name Freeman Jones, for the better understanding of the same' (sig. A3ᵃ).

4 THAT.ETERNITIE the eternity referred to by the poet in e.g. *18, 19, 60, 63, 101*.

10 ADVENTVRER Thomas Thorpe, as publisher of the volume, put up the capital for paper required to produce the book, and did so with no guarantee of return. He was therefore like a merchant adventurer (*OED* 4, 'One who undertakes, or shares in, commercial adventures or enterprises', citing this as the first usage). Precedent for the comparison between publisher and merchant who 'adventures' can be found in the prefatory matter to Gascoigne's *A Hundred Sundry Flowers* (1573), 201 ('This I have adventured, for thy contentation (learned reader)') and 204.

11–12 SETTING. | FORTH Printing (*OED* s.v. 'set' 144e); also continuing the image of merchant adventurers via 144b(a), 'To send out (soldiers, etc.) for service; hence, to equip, fit out (men, a fleet, a voyage)'. The phrase was relatively common in preliminary matter.

14 T.T. Thomas Thorpe, who usually signed his name in prefatory material either 'T. Th.' or 'Th. Th.'. He is the subject of the verb 'wisheth'. Some have suggested that he could also be its object with Mr W.H. its subject. This is unlikely, since the piece is clearly a publisher's dedication, and Thorpe is cited as the publisher on the title-page.

TO.THE.ONLIE.BEGETTER.OF.
THESE.INSVING.SONNETS.
M^r.W.H. ALL.HAPPINESSE.
AND.THAT.ETERNITIE.
PROMISED.   5
BY.
OVR.EVER-LIVING.POET.
WISHETH.
THE.WELL-WISHING.
ADVENTVRER.IN.   10
SETTING.
FORTH.

T.T.

Sonnets 1–17 urge a young man to marry. They are frequently indebted to Erasmus's 'Epistle to persuade a young man to marriage' which Shakespeare probably read in Wilson, 39–63. The epistle makes analogies between having children, tilling the earth for cultivation, grafting old trees to ensure new stock, and perpetuating one's fame for posterity, all of which are elements in this mini-sequence. Relevant extracts are quoted in the notes.

1 increase 'The multiplication of a family or race of men or animals' (*OED* 2b), stressed on the second syllable. A faint play on the sense 'profit' (*OED* 4) reminds us that this is a poem to a potential patron.

2 That so that
   beauty's rose the prime of beauty; compare *Antony* 3.13.19–20: 'Tell him he wears the rose | Of youth upon him'. Q italicizes 'rose'. Southamptonites have claimed that Henry Wriothesley's name could be pronounced 'Rosely', and that a biographical allusion is meant. Q italicizes thirty-five words, of which seventeen are proper names; the rest appear to mark phrases which the compositor found unusual or difficult. The metaphor *beauty's rose* (the fragile vehicle of beauty) was probably enough to make compositor A reach for his italics.

3 But as the riper but while the older (roses)

4 tender heir might bear his gentle offspring might (a) carry his memory; (b) bear his resemblance. *Tender heir* may play on the false etymology which derived the Latin 'mulier' (woman) from 'mollis aer', meaning 'soft air' (for which, see *Cymbeline* 5.6.448–54), and *Lucrece* l. 1240 n.). The pun makes the generations mingle: a wife *bears* (gives birth to) a son at the same time as an *heir* reproduces his father's manner.

5 contracted (a) betrothed, affianced (*OED* 2, as in *1 Henry IV*, 4.2.15–18: 'I . . . enquire me out contracted bachelors, such as had been asked twice on the banns'); (b) 'shrunken' (*OED* 5a)

6 Feed'st . . . fuel The friend is accused of burning up the substance of his own life in an echo of Ovid's Narcissus, 'uror amore mei: flammas moveoque feroque' ('I am burned by love of myself: I produce and am consumed by flames', *Met.* 3.464).

6 self-substantial which derives from your own substance. *OED* cites only this example. It may hint at a play on 'substance' in the sense of 'family property' which the friend wastes on himself rather than leaving to an heir.

7 Making . . . lies Narcissus's cry 'inopem me copia fecit' ('my very abundance (of contact with what I love) makes me poor') was one of the most frequently quoted phrases from the *Met.* (3.466). Cf. *Venus* l. 19–20 n.

10 only herald chief forerunner. Like an early rose, the friend is presented as one who precedes the arrival of spring in its full panoply.

11 content (a) happiness (*OED n.* 2, 1); (b) that which you contain, the children who are hidden within you (*OED n.* 1, I). Stressed (as usually before the nineteenth century) on the second syllable.

12 tender churl *tender* ranges through 'soft' (used of plants, *OED* 3b), 'young' (*OED* 4), 'effeminate' (*OED* 3a), 'sensitive'. *Churl* connotes low social status; it can mean 'bondsman', and 'One who is sordid, "hard", or stingy in money-matters; a niggard' (*OED* 6). The conjunction of niggards and churls is also found in Coverdale's translation of Isaiah 32: 5: 'Then shall the niggard be no more called gentle, nor the churl liberal'. The phrase praises and wounds the aristocratic friend at once: although he is *tender* his lack of an heir is an ignoble meanness.
   niggarding 'To act in a niggardly fashion' (*OED* 'niggard', *v.* 1. *intr.*, citing this as the first occurrence); also 'To put off *with* a small amount of something; to treat in a niggardly fashion' (*OED* 2) as in *Caesar* 4.2.281–2: 'Nature must obey necessity, | Which we will niggard with a little rest'.

14 the world's due what you owe to the world: children
   by the grave and thee The *world's due* is destroyed once by his self-absorption, and once by death. Compare *Venus* ll. 757–60.

I

From fairest creatures we desire increase,
That thereby beauty's rose might never die,
But as the riper should by time decease,
His tender heir might bear his memory:
But thou, contracted to thine own bright eyes,   5
Feed'st thy light's flame with self-substantial fuel,
Making a famine where abundance lies,
Thy self thy foe, to thy sweet self too cruel.
Thou that art now the world's fresh ornament,
And only herald to the gaudy spring,   10
Within thine own bud buriest thy content,
And, tender churl, mak'st waste in niggarding:
 Pity the world, or else this glutton be,
 To eat the world's due, by the grave and thee.

0.1] MALONE; *unnumbered in* Q 2 rose] Q (*Rose*)

Seventeenth-century manuscripts preserve versions of this sonnet which may represent an early draft. See 'Spes Altera' printed here at the end of the sequence. The MS tradition is collated with the variant version.

1 **forty** is used to mean 'many', as in the biblical 'forty days and forty nights' (e.g. Genesis 7: 4)

2 **field** (a) plot of agricultural land (ploughed by time). The violent action of *besiege* suggests also (b) battlefield (*OED* 6a); the association with *livery* activates the sense (c) from heraldry 'The surface of an escutcheon or shield on which the "charge" is displayed' (*OED* 13a).

4 **tattered weed** (a) ragged garment (instead of fine *livery*); (b) drooping wild plant torn out of beauty's *field*. Q reads 'totter'd', a variant spelling of *tattered*, which is usually used of clothing, as in *1 Henry IV*, 4.2.34–5: 'a hundred and fifty tattered prodigals, lately come from swine-keeping'. MS versions read 'rotten weeds', lending support to (b), for which otherwise *tattered* would be an unusual epithet.

5–8 allude to the story of the prodigal son (Matthew 25: 24–30).

6 **lusty** (a) vigorous (*OED* 5); (b) sexually active, lustful (*OED* 4)

8 **all-eating** (a) all-consuming; (b) universally destructive, alluding back to 1.14
thriftless 'wasteful, improvident, spend-thrift' (*OED* 3). The word is used in *Richard II* 5.3.66–7 with a similar sense of intergenerational wastage: 'he shall spend mine honour with his shame; | As thriftless sons their scraping fathers' gold'.

9 **use** active deployment, with return; the negative associations of usury are muted here. On the Elizabethan law of usury, see 6.8 n.

10 '**This . . .** Q does not mark direct speech; contemporary readers might have included l. 12 in the speech, making *thine* into an address by an embarrassed son to his father (as in *1 Henry IV* 3.2.129–59, in which Prince Harry too speaks of the final reckoning up of an account), or, as Seymour-Smith suggests, to the world.

11 **sum my count** tot up my accounts
old excuse (a) the excuse I make when I am old; (b) the excuse I habitually make

12 **succession** 'according to the customary or legal principle by which one succeeds another in an inheritance, an office, etc. by inherited right' (*OED* 5b(a), citing this passage); also 'proving your son to be yours in perpetuity, rather than by gift or conquest'

14 **thy blood warm** Old people were believed to become cold and dry, while youths were believed to be hot and moist. The blood of a son was supposed to be the same as that of his father. Hence 'to see your own blood vigorously alive in your son'.

2

When forty winters shall besiege thy brow,
And dig deep trenches in thy beauty's field,
Thy youth's proud livery so gazed on now
Will be a tattered weed of small worth held:
Then, being asked where all thy beauty lies,   5
Where all the treasure of thy lusty days,
To say within thine own deep-sunken eyes
Were an all-eating shame, and thriftless praise.
How much more praise deserved thy beauty's use
If thou couldst answer 'This fair child of mine   10
Shall sum my count, and make my old excuse',
Proving his beauty by succession thine.
   This were to be new made when thou art old,
   And see thy blood warm when thou feel'st it cold.

4 tattered] Q (totter'd); tattered JOHN'S 9 deserved] Q; deserves JOHN'S 10–11 answer 'This . . . excuse'] MALONE 1790 *italic* (*conj.* Capell); ~ ̬ ~~ ̬ Q: say that, this faire . . . excuse JOHN'S 11 my old] Q; thy old JOHN'S

1 **glass** mirror; often a source of admonition (as in the popular collection *A Mirror for Magistrates*, which warned those in high estate how best to govern) or as an emblem of vanity. Compare *Lucrece* ll. 1758–64.

2 **another** another face. Q reads 'an other', extending the sense to 'an other person, someone completely new'.

3 **fresh repair** (a) appearance of newness; (b) recently renovated state

4 **beguile** cheat (charmingly)
unbless some mother deprive a woman of motherhood. *Unbless* is the first cited usage in *OED*.

5 **uneared** unploughed, untilled. Ploughing also carries sexual overtones in *Antony* 2.2.233–4: 'She made great Caesar lay his sword to bed. | He ploughed her, and she cropped.'

6 **husbandry** 'tillage or cultivation of the soil' (*OED* 2); with a pun on a sense not recognized by *OED* of 'your being her husband'. The pun is also active in *Measure* 1.4.42–3: 'even so her plenteous womb | Expresseth his full tilth and husbandry', and in Louis Le Roy, *Of the Interchangeable Course or Variety of Things*, trans. R[obert] A[shley] (1594), 130ᵛ: 'The husbandman hateth the fruitless ground, and the husband a wife that is barren.'

7 **fond** infatuated, foolish, silly

8 **posterity** the emergence of future generations. Cf. *Venus* ll. 757–60.

10 **Calls back** The expected sense 'recall, remember' is not cited in *OED* before 1850, although it must be in play here;

the physical sense 'summons back into being' is, though, very strong. For the idea that a child is a mirror to its father see *Lucrece* ll. 1758–64. Compare Erasmus: 'Old age cometh upon us all, will we or nill we, and this way nature provided for us, that we should wax young again in our children . . . For what man can be grieved that he is old when he seeth his own countenance, which he had being a child, to appear lively in his son?' (Wilson, 56). Erasmus says little about mothers, however: the suggestion that the friend resembles his mother anticipates the androgyny of 20.2.

10 **April** proverbially fresh (Dent A310)

11 **windows of thine age** aged eyes; eyes clouded with age. There may also be an allusion to lattice windows, criss-crossed with lead, as in *A Lover's Complaint* l. 14.

12 **Despite of wrinkles** *Batman upon Bartholomew* (1582), fos. 18ᵛ–19ʳ, records that 'the sight of old men is not sharp, because their skins are rivelled [wrinkled]' which is a rough paraphrase of Aristotle: 'the reason why old people do not have keen vision is that the skin in the eyes, like that elsewhere, gets wrinkled and thicker with age' (*De Generatione Animalium* 780a, 31–3). The lines exploit an analogy between the wrinkled surface of an aged eye and the irregularity of Elizabethan glass.

13 **rememb'red** Q's spelling, 'remembred', embeds the word 'bred' in remembering.

14 **image** (a) physical appearance (as reflected in a mirror); (b) embodiment (such as a child)

3

Look in thy glass and tell the face thou viewest
Now is the time that face should form another,
Whose fresh repair if now thou not renewest
Thou dost beguile the world, unbless some mother.
For where is she so fair whose uneared womb   5
Disdains the tillage of thy husbandry?
Or who is he so fond will be the tomb
Of his self-love to stop posterity?
Thou art thy mother's glass, and she in thee
Calls back the lovely April of her prime;   10
So thou through windows of thine age shalt see,
Despite of wrinkles, this thy golden time.
   But if thou live rememb'red not to be,
   Die single, and thine image dies with thee.

1 **Unthrifty** (a) improvident, prodigal;
(b) unprofitable. An archaic sense,
'unchaste, wanton, profligate' (*OED* 3),
may be in play. *Spend* can mean 'ejacu-
late', and *Spend | Upon thyself* suggests
masturbation. *Unthrifty loveliness* begins
a string of oxymorons which dominate
the poem (*beauteous niggard, profitless
usurer*).

4 **frank** 'not in serfdom or slavery' (*OED* 1)

5 **niggard** miser

7 **Profitless . . . use** A moneylender who
makes no profit, the friend uses up
nature's loan rather than using it to gen-
erate interest (or children).

8 **sum of sums** total made up of the sum of
lesser sums, pointing back to the debt to
nature of 2.11

9 **traffic** (a) 'bargaining; trade' (*OED* 2a);
(b) 'Sexual commerce; (sexual) inter-
course' (Partridge), which revives the
suggestions of masturbation from the
poem's opening.

12 **acceptable** is stressed on the first syllable.
audit final reckoning (an image brought
back at *126*.11). Underlying the whole
sonnet is a preoccupation with preserv-
ing noble household, its wealth, material
structures, and bloodlines. Here the
friend is implicitly compared to a steward
called upon to give an account of the
wealth of a household, or an executor
required to sum up the assets of a
deceased person. Failure to provide an
acceptable audit in this period could result
in imprisonment (Sokol, 17).

13 **unused** not put out to loan for profit.
See 6.8 n.

14 **executor** 'A person appointed by a testa-
tor to execute or carry into effect his will
after his decease' (*OED* 3); in this case a
son.

4

Unthrifty loveliness, why dost thou spend
Upon thyself thy beauty's legacy?
Nature's bequest gives nothing, but doth lend.
And being frank she lends to those are free:
Then, beauteous niggard, why dost thou abuse   5
The bounteous largess given thee to give?
Profitless usurer, why dost thou use
So great a sum of sums yet canst not live?
For having traffic with thyself alone
Thou of thyself thy sweet self dost deceive.   10
Then how, when nature calls thee to be gone,
What acceptable audit canst thou leave?
    Thy unused beauty must be tombed with thee,
    Which usèd lives th' executor to be.

12 audit] Q (*Audit*)

1 **hours** two syllables (Q reads 'howers')
frame make, construct (a building). The
noun is often used in the period to
describe the human body. Cf. *Venus* ll.
729–31.

2 **dwell** linger (also perhaps 'live in', since
frame can mean 'to construct a building')

4 **un-fair** 'To deprive of fairness or beauty.'
OED cites only this example of the transi-
tive verb; the verbal innovation makes
shocking the suddenness with which
the gentle hours turn into destructive
tyrants.

5 **Time** Q is sporadic in capitalizing personi-
fications, capitalizing *Summer* but not
time. These irregularities are almost
certainly compositorial rather than
authorial. This edition capitalizes nouns
when it clarifies the outlines of a personi-
fication allegory. Q's irregularity in this
respect does indicate, however, that barri-
ers between outright personifications and
what are simply rather energetic nouns
were not clearly marked in early modern
printed texts.
leads . . . on Initially Time appears to be
leading a dance of the hours, until the
sinister associations of *lead on* emerge:
'to entice or beguile into going to greater
lengths' (*OED* s.v. 'lead' 20a).

6 **confounds** defeats utterly

7 **checked** stopped up. Also used to describe
the death of plants at 15.6.

8 **o'ersnowed** is used by Shakespeare only
here.
bareness blank leaflessness; as in 97.4.
'Barrenness' may also be implicit in Q's
'barenes'.

9 **distillation** the product of distillation
(*OED* 4b), hence rose or other scent. *OED*
shows Shakespeare's usage here (and in
Merry Wives 3.5.104: 'And then, to be
stopped in, like a strong distillation') to be
unusual: the word more often refers
to the process rather than its outcome.

10 **liquid prisoner** The constraint of perfume
into a bottle qualifies the attractions of
immortality.

11 **Beauty's . . . bereft** The beautiful scent
which is the chief effect of beauty would
die with the petals of the rose. *With*
means 'at the same time as' but also
almost suggests that beauty is the
means by which *beauty's effects* are
destroyed.

12 **Nor it . . . was** leaving us with neither
beauty nor any means of recalling it. The
poem excels at evoking bareness: here *it*
could refer back to *beauty's effect* as well as
to *beauty*, depriving us of all.

14 **Lose** Q reads 'Leese', a regular variant
form of 'lose' in the seventeenth century,
although it occurs in Shakespeare only
here. Q's spelling may suggest the imper-
manence of 'lease' (anticipating *13*.5) and
the dregs or deposits left behind by distilla-
tion ('lees').
substance Primarily 'essential character',
but given the concern of these sonnets
with the preservation of an estate 'Posses-
sions, goods, estate' (*OED* 16a) may
also be in play. Opposition between
show and *substance* was proverbial (Dent
S408).
still echoes *distilled*, and gains additional
permanence from the echo.

5

Those hours, that with gentle work did frame
The lovely gaze where every eye doth dwell,
Will play the tyrants to the very same,
And that un-fair which fairly doth excel:
For never-resting Time leads summer on   5
To hideous winter, and confounds him there,
Sap checked with frost and lusty leaves quite gone,
Beauty o'er-snowed and bareness everywhere.
Then, were not summer's distillation left
A liquid prisoner pent in walls of glass,   10
Beauty's effect with beauty were bereft,
Nor it nor no remembrance what it was.
    But flowers distilled, though they with winter meet,
    Lose but their show; their substance still lives sweet.

8 bareness] Q (barenes); barenesse BENSON; Barrenness GILDON   14 Lose] Q (Leese)

1 **ragged hand** In sixteenth-century usage usually 'rough', hence 'savage', rather than 'tattered'. The usage may be underwritten by a personification of Winter jagged with frost, hence 'having a broken jagged outline or surface' (*OED* 2). *Hand* can mean 'handwriting'; here winter may be marking the features of the friend with rough lines. Cf. the usage in E.C.'s *Emaricdulfe* (1595) 22.9: 'Smile on these rough-hewed lines, these ragged words'.
deface (a) 'To mar the face, features, or appearance of' (*OED* 1); (b) 'To blot out, obliterate, efface (writing, marks)' (*OED* 3).

3 **vial** a container for perfume; hence a woman

5–6 **That use . . . loan** that practice of lending money out for interest is not forbidden where those who pay the loan happily consent to it. *Happies* is the *OED*'s first cited usage of 'happy' as a transitive verb.

7 **That's for . . . thee** glosses the previous line: that is, when you, for your own benefit, have a child who resembles you.

8 **ten for one** ten children in exchange for you, who are only one. The maximum legal rate of interest according to the statutes 13 Eliz. cap. 8 and 39 Eliz. cap. 18 was 10 per cent; childbirth here becomes an exercise in venture capital.

10 **refigured** re-embodied; perhaps 'remultiplied' (although this stretches the recorded senses). The multiplication of ten by ten occurs, inevitably, in the tenth line.

12 **posterity** By about 1600 this word was acquiring its modern sense, 'All succeeding generations (collectively)' (*OED* 2b). The revised version of Drayton's *Idea* (1619) 17.9 responds to this usage: 'posteritie' is used to replace 'after-worlds' from the version of 1594.

13 **self-willed** (a) obstinate; (b) self-obsessed; with possibly a pun on 'bequeathed to yourself' (as in will and testament). Q's 'selfe-wild' may suggest 'do not be savage to yourself', although see 17.2 n.

14 **conquest** (a) something overcome by death; (b) 'property acquired other than by inheritance' (*OED* 6a), a sense which interacts with *self-willed* and *heir*. In early modern England property could be held by inheritance, by gift, or else by 'conquest', a category used to cover many other means of acquiring property.

6

Then let not winter's ragged hand deface
In thee thy summer ere thou be distilled:
Make sweet some vial; treasure thou some place
With beauty's treasure ere it be self-killed:
That use is not forbidden usury   5
Which happies those that pay the willing loan;
That's for thyself to breed another thee,
Or ten times happier be it ten for one:
Ten times thyself were happier than thou art,
If ten of thine ten times refigured thee.   10
Then what could death do if thou shouldst depart,
Leaving thee living in posterity?
   Be not self-willed, for thou art much too fair
   To be death's conquest and make worms thine heir.

1 ragged] Q (wragged)   4 beauty's] GILDON 1714; beautits Q; beauties BENSON   13 self-willed] Q (selfe-wild)

This sonnet echoes elements in *Met.* 15.184–227, probably via Golding 15.243–51: 'The child new-born lies void of strength. Within a season though | He waxing four-footed learns like savage beasts to go. | Then somewhat faltering, and as yet not firm of foot, he stands | By getting somewhat for to help his sinews in his hands. | From that time growing strong and swift, he passeth forth the space | Of youth: and also wearing out his middle age apace, | Through drooping age's steepy path he runneth out his race. | This age doth undermine the strength of former years, and throws | It down.'

2 **under-eye** (a) inferior eye (person); (b) mortal eye, i.e. 'creature which lives beneath the sun'

3 **homage** 'In *Feudal Law*, Formal and public acknowledgement of allegiance, wherein a tenant or vassal declared himself the man of the king or the lord of whom he held, and bound himself *to his service*' (*OED* 1); hence reinforcing *under-eye* (a).

5 **having** refers to the sun rather than to the worshippers beneath him. For a moment the activities of the sun subside into the past tense, before they are revived into the vigour of the present by their continuing appeal to *mortal looks* in l. 7.
steep-up precipitous

6 **Resembling . . . age** like a fit youth at the peak of his prime. The sonnet appears to use a tripartite division of the ages of man, which are related to the stages of the sun's course. In such schemes *youth* (corresponding to the Latin *iuventus*) can include men as old as 49. *Middle age* is more likely to mean that the youth is in his prime or central age than that he is approaching his decline, since by 1600 middle age had not acquired its current associations with ageing corpulence. See J. A. Burrow, *The Ages of Man: A Study in Medieval Writing and Thought* (Oxford, 1986), 57. The phrase could be used of an older generation by a younger in

Shakespeare, however: in *Winter's Tale* 4.4.106–8 Perdita says to the disguised Polixenes: 'These are flowers | Of middle summer, and I think they are given | To men of middle age'; she clearly means to distinguish herself from his generation. *Yet* in l. 7 augments the uncertainty: it means primarily 'even now', but its possible concessive sense ('despite this') suggests that having reached the top of the hill the friend is just about to decline: as these various senses come into play the sun slips from prime to decline before one's eyes.

8 **Attending on** (a) watching; (b) attending like servants

9 **highmost pitch** utmost peak
car chariot. *OED* 1b: 'From 16th to 19th c. chiefly poetic, with associations of dignity, solemnity, or splendour; applied also to the fabled chariot of Phaëthon or the sun'.

11 **fore** before. The form is a recognized variant of 'before', although even in the sixteenth century it was sometimes printed ''fore'.
converted turned away. Cf. *Timon* 1.2.141: 'Men shut their doors against a setting sun' and Dent (S979) 'The rising, not the setting, sun is worshipped by most men'.

12 **tract** course. In this context it may also evoke a variety of limited temporal or physical extents: 'A stretch or extent of territory' (*OED* 3a); 'The drawing out . . . or lapse of time' (*OED n.*³ I.1a); also 3b, 'Protraction (of time), deferring, putting off, dilatory proceeding, delay', and 3c, 'A space or extent of time'.

13 **outgoing** To 'go out' can mean 'to die', hence 'reaching your end during what should be your prime'. Also 'outstripping yourself'. The suggestion is that the friend is burning himself out.

14 **get a son** beget a son. The word 'sun' is not used in this poem; the pressure to name *the gracious light* is only released by the pun on 'son'.

7

Lo in the orient when the gracious light
Lifts up his burning head, each under-eye
Doth homage to his new-appearing sight,
Serving with looks his sacred majesty;
And having climbed the steep-up heavenly hill,   5
Resembling strong youth in his middle age,
Yet mortal looks adore his beauty still,
Attending on his golden pilgrimage:
But when from highmost pitch, with weary car,
Like feeble age he reeleth from the day,   10
The eyes (fore duteous) now converted are
From his low tract and look another way:
   So thou, thyself outgoing in thy noon,
   Unlooked on diest unless thou get a son.

1 **Music to hear** (a) when there is music to hear; (b) you, who are music to listen to

2 **Sweets** BL Add. MS 15226, which is divided into stanzas as though for a song setting, reads 'Sweet', a vocative which Kerrigan suggests might be authorial (443), but which is more likely to be the result of misreading a scribal abbreviation for terminal 'es'.

3–4 **Why lov'st . . . annoy** Why do you love that which you listen to without any sign of joy—or are you glad to hear things which make you sad? The paradox of enjoying the sadness of music is a commonplace of the period, from Jacques's 'I can suck melancholy out of a song as a weasel sucks eggs' (*As You Like It* 2.5.11–12) to John Dowland's motto *Semper Dowland semper dolens* ('always Dowland always doleful').

4 **receiv'st** 'to attend, listen, or give heed to' (*OED* 1d)

5 **true concord** perfect harmony (also thought to reflect the harmonies of the heavens and of the state)

6 **unions** married refers to the harmonies of a polyphonic setting of a song. *Union* is also used by Shakespeare to mean 'marriage' (*OED* 5) in *K. John* 2.1.447–8: 'This union shall do more than battery can | To our fast-closèd gates'.

7 **sweetly chide thee** mellifluously rebuke you

7–8 **confounds | In singleness** destroys (a) by being a bachelor; (b) by refusing to blend your voice into the harmony

8 **parts . . . bear** (a) lines of the song which you should sing; (b) personal attributes which you should reproduce; (c) roles (in a family) which you should play

9–10 **Mark how . . . ordering** The metaphor probably refers to a lute in which strings are tuned in unison (*by mutual ordering*) in order to enable them to resonate in sympathy with each other. *Strike* is the verb regularly used to mean 'pluck the strings of a lute'; its extension to mean 'resonate, or cause to sound' is warranted by *OED* 30b, 'To produce (music, a sound, note) by touching a string or playing upon an instrument'.

11 **sire** father

14 **'Thou . . . none'** unmarried you shall amount to nothing (Q does not use quotation marks). *Prove* means 'turn out to be' (*OED* 8). The line alludes to the proverb 'One is no number' (Dent O54, and see 136.8 n.), which has its origins in Aristotle's *Metaphysics* 1088a, 6. Marlowe's Leander uses the proverb as part of his persuasion of Hero (*Hero and Leander* l. 255); shortly before, in ll. 229–30, he uses an argument from harmony: 'Like untuned strings all women are, | Which long time lie untouched will harshly jar'. This suggests that the whole passage was running through Shakespeare's memory.

8

Music to hear, why hear'st thou music sadly?
Sweets with sweets war not, joy delights in joy:
Why lov'st thou that which thou receiv'st not gladly,
Or else receiv'st with pleasure thine annoy?
If the true concord of well-tunèd sounds   5
By unions married do offend thine ear,
They do but sweetly chide thee, who confounds
In singleness the parts that thou shouldst bear.
Mark how one string, sweet husband to another,
Strikes each in each by mutual ordering;   10
Resembling sire, and child, and happy mother,
Who all in one, one pleasing note do sing:
   Whose speechless song being many, seeming one,
   Sings this to thee, 'Thou single wilt prove none.'

Title in BL2 reads: 'In laudem musice et opprobrium contemptoris eiusdem'   2 Sweets] Q;
Sweete BL2   6 thine] Q; thy BL2   8 the parts that] Q; a parte, which BL2   10 in] Q; on BL2
11 sire, and child] Q; Childe, and Syer BL2   12 Who] Q; which BL2   one pleasing note do] Q;
this single note dothe BL2   14 'Thou . . . none.'] MALONE; ˌ~ . . . ~·ˌ Q   wilt] Q; shalt BL2

3 **issueless** childless
hap chance

4 **makeless** 'Mateless; wifeless, husband-less, widowed' (*OED* 2)

6 **form** both the non-technical 'appear-ance', 'likeness', and possibly also 'In the Scholastic philosophy: The essential determinant principle of a thing . . . the essential creative quality' (*OED* 4a)

7 **private** particular; possibly 'deprived, bereft, dispossessed' (*OED* 'private', *ppl. a.*, for which no instance is cited after 1573)

8 **By** by means of

9–10 **unthrift** 'a spendthrift, prodigal' (*OED* 3). The sense is 'whatever a prodigal spends in the world is simply redistributed to a new owner (*his* functions as a neuter pronoun); but the beautiful man com-pletely destroys the beauty which he wastes'.

12 **unused . . . it** if it is not put out to usury the person who wastes it (*user*) also destroys it

14 **murd'rous shame** shameful murder (with a suggestion of auto-eroticism)

9

Is it for fear to wet a widow's eye
That thou consum'st thyself in single life?
Ah, if thou issueless shalt hap to die
The world will wail thee like a makeless wife.
The world will be thy widow and still weep   5
That thou no form of thee hast left behind,
When every private widow well may keep,
By children's eyes, her husband's shape in mind.
Look what an unthrift in the world doth spend
Shifts but his place, for still the world enjoys it;   10
But beauty's waste hath in the world an end,
And kept unused the user so destroys it:
   No love toward others in that bosom sits
   That on himself such murd'rous shame commits.

1 **For shame** (a) Shame on you! (b) out of a sense of shame. Q has no punctuation after this phrase, although editors often add an exclamation mark.

3 **Grant, if thou wilt** accept (if you must) that. . . .

6 **stick'st** hesitate or scruple (*OED* 15)

7–8 **Seeking . . . desire** The *roof* is the body, but also the literal roof over his family's heads. Compare Erasmus's letter on marriage: 'it lieth in your hands to keep that house from decay, whereof [you are] lineally descended' (Wilson, 51). The poet's voice here becomes almost that of an aged family counsellor rebuking a friend for destroying the fabric of his household.

9 **O . . . mind** O change your attitudes (to reproduction), so that I can revise what I think of you. This is the first time the first-person pronoun occurs in the sequence.

10 **Shall hate . . . love?** The friend's *hate* is implicit in his refusal to have a child; his *beauteous roof* asks for a gentler inhabitant to suit it.

11 **kind** willing to acknowledge the emotional ties of kinship

13 **Make thee another self** have a child; perhaps also 'transform your moral character'
love of me This is the first suggestion of a personal relationship between poet and addressee.

14 **thine** both the possessive form of 'thy', and 'Those who are thine; thy people, family, or kindred' (*OED* 5b)

10

For shame deny that thou bear'st love to any,
Who for thyself art so unprovident.
Grant, if thou wilt, thou art beloved of many,
But that thou none lov'st is most evident:
For thou art so possessed with murd'rous hate   5
That 'gainst thyself thou stick'st not to conspire,
Seeking that beauteous roof to ruinate,
Which to repair should be thy chief desire.
O, change thy thought, that I may change my mind:
Shall hate be fairer lodged than gentle love?   10
Be as thy presence is, gracious and kind,
Or to thyself at least kind-hearted prove:
   Make thee another self for love of me,
   That beauty still may live in thine or thee.

1–2 'For all that you diminish yourself by sexual reproduction, by an equal amount you will grow again in your child.' *Departest* must mean 'give up', as in the phrase 'depart with', *OED* 12b: 'To part with; to give up, surrender', as in *K. John* 2.1.563–4: 'John . . . Hath willingly departed with a part'. Sexual intercourse was believed to shorten a man's life.

2, 4 thine As in 10.14 the play on 'thine' as the possessive form of 'thy', and 'Those who are thine; thy people, family, or kindred' (*OED* 5b) enables Shakespeare to suggest that a loss of what is the friend's property—his semen—remains his in the form of his future kin. So 'the blood of yours which you expend as semen you may still call yours, and yours in a richer, familial sense, when it produces your children'.

3 youngly (a) 'early in life' (*OED* 1); (b) with youthful vigour

4 when . . . convertest when you have left youth behind

5 Herein if you follow this course

6 Without this if you do not follow this course

7 so as you are

8 threescore . . . away i.e. everyone would die within a single generation. The same argument is used in Wilson, 60.

9 store resources for the future, with perhaps an agricultural flavour via *OED* 2, 'Live stock' (as kept for breeding)

11 Look whom . . . more Nature gives more (including more offspring) to those who are already well endowed with qualities. *The* does not need to be emended to *thee*, as it is in many editions, following Sewell. The proposition is a general one which includes the friend in its compass.

13 seal the stamp with which she seals documents

14 copy 'The original writing, work of art, etc. from which a copy is made' (*OED* 8a). *Copy* derives from the Latin *copia*, fullness or abundance, a sense (*OED* 1a) which was common in the sixteenth century, which would here allude back to Nature's *bounty*, and give an organic strength to the mechanical process of reproduction.

II

As fast as thou shalt wane, so fast thou grow'st
In one of thine, from that which thou departest,
And that fresh blood which youngly thou bestow'st
Thou mayst call thine, when thou from youth convertest.
Herein lives wisdom, beauty, and increase;   5
Without this, folly, age, and cold decay.
If all were minded so the times should cease,
And threescore year would make the world away.
Let those whom Nature hath not made for store,
Harsh, featureless, and rude, barrenly perish.   10
Look whom she best endowed she gave the more,
Which bounteous gift thou shouldst in bounty cherish.
   She carved thee for her seal, and meant thereby
   Thou shouldst print more, not let that copy die.

8 year] Q; yeares BENSON   11 the] Q; thee SEWELL

1 **count** 'count the strokes of the clock'. The twelve hours in the day figure strongly in this twelfth sonnet.

2 **brave** fine, splendid, beautiful (Schmidt, 3). Most usages of the word in the Sonnets associate it with courageous resistance to insurmountable forces (as at 12.14, 15.8).

3 **past prime** (a) past its best; (b) when spring is over (*OED* 7; cf. 97.7)

4 **all silvered o'er** Q reads 'or silver'd ore with white', a reading Rollins defends: ' "or" can be the heraldic term for gold, which is here conceived as being covered over with silver'. This ingenious defence of Q is hard to reconcile with the fact that Shakespeare says the curls were *sable* (black) to begin with, not gold. Malone's 'all silvered o'er' is, as Sisson notes, i.209–10, suspiciously alike 'all girded up' (l. 7). Stanley Wells, 'New Readings in Shakespeare's Sonnets', in J. P. Vander Motten, ed., *Elizabethan and Modern Studies* (Ghent, 1985), 319–20, suggests 'ensilvered', which requires only a misreading of two letters, an error of the kind which occurs several times in the passage attributed to Shakespeare in *Sir Thomas More*. 'Ensilvered' is, however, not cited by *OED* after 1382. Malone's emendation remains the most plausible.

5 **barren** Unusual in the sense of 'bare of leaves'; its usual sense 'bare of fruit' recalls the chill landscape of infertility, the *bareness everywhere* of 5.8.

6 **canopy** *OED*'s first cited usage as a verb, 'To cover with, or as with, a canopy'
herd flock

7 **girded up** 'To surround as with a belt; to tie firmly or confine' (*OED* 5 *transf.* and *fig.* a; first cited usage)

8 **bier** in earliest uses 'A framework for carrying; a handbarrow; a litter, a stretcher' (*OED* 1), with also the more usual sense of 'The movable stand on which a corpse, whether in a coffin or not, is placed before burial' (*OED* 2). The combination of senses turns harvest into a funeral, as the friend turns opportunities for reproduction into self-love.

9 **do I question make** speculate about

10 **among the wastes of time must go** is a phrase so rich in its evocation of empty destruction that it defies glossing: (a) you must be counted among the things ruined by time; (b) you must travel in the regions devastated by time (*OED* 3, citing the 1611 Bible, Isaiah 61: 4: 'They shall build the old wastes, they shall raise up the former desolations'); (c) you must mingle with the trifles that squander time pointlessly (with a chiming reminiscence of the admonitory clock in *Twelfth Night* 3.1.129: '*Clock strikes*. The clock upbraids me with the waste of time.')

11 **sweets and beauties** Vendler notes that sweetness in the Sonnets tends to connote permanent inner virtue, while beauty is frequently presented as fragile and external.
do themselves forsake change, leave their beauty and sweetness behind

13 **Time's scythe** Time is given a scythe and often an hourglass in Renaissance emblem books.

14 **breed** offspring. *Breed* is a noun, but there is just a hint of a desperate imperative.
brave challenge, defy (*OED* 1). The verb carries over some of the despairingly vain resistance of the *brave day* from l. 2.

12

When I do count the clock that tells the time,
And see the brave day sunk in hideous night;
When I behold the violet past prime,
And sable curls all silvered o'er with white;
When lofty trees I see barren of leaves,   5
Which erst from heat did canopy the herd,
And summer's green all girded up in sheaves,
Borne on the bier with white and bristly beard:
Then of thy beauty do I question make,
That thou among the wastes of time must go,   10
Since sweets and beauties do themselves forsake,
And die as fast as they see others grow,
   And nothing 'gainst Time's scythe can make defence
   Save breed to brave him when he takes thee hence.

4 all silvered o'er] MALONE; or siluer'd ore Q; are silver'd o'er GILDON 1714; o'er-silver'd all
conj. Verity; ensilvered o'er OXFORD (*conj.* Wells); o'er-silvered are *conj.* G. B. Evans

1 **yourself** Q always prints 'yourself' as two words. Here Q's spelling seems emphatic: 'your true self, existing beyond the constraints of time'. This is the first sonnet to address the friend as 'you' rather than 'thou'. The shift may mark an increase in intimacy: 'you' is the normal form of address between educated Elizabethans, and by the mid-1590s 'thou' might seem poetic. Euphony plays its part in the shift, too (try reading the poem aloud with *thou* substituted for *you*).

love 'This poem marks the momentous instant in which the speaker first uses vocatives of love' (Vendler).

1–2 **but . . . live** But you cannot outlive your short time on earth. *No longer yours* implies temporary ownership over the mansion of the body, anticipating the short leasehold over beauty described in ll. 5–6.

3 **this coming end** death, which is just about to occur

5 **lease** To hold in *lease* is to enjoy the temporary possession and use of something for a fixed period. In Shakespeare this usually connotes impermanence.

6 **determination** is the technical legal word for the expiry of a lease, which might terminate on the death of the last male heir: 'the cessation of an estate or interest of any kind' (*OED* 1b). '*Law*. (esp. in *Conveyancing*)'.

7 **Yourself** Q reads 'You selfe'. See note on l. 1 above.

8 **sweet issue . . . bear** (a) dear children should resemble your form; (b) dear children would bear children which resembled you. On *form* see 9.6 n.

9 **house** On the importance of sustaining the fabric and lifeblood of a noble house, see 10.7–8 n. Here a well-managed house is figured initially as a literal protection from the *stormy gusts* of l. 11, and then grows to become a dynastic unit which offers protection against the *barren rage of death's eternal cold*, l. 12.

12 **barren rage** destructive anger which robs the world of fertility. *Rage* can also mean 'sexual desire'. *Barren* has gradually accumulated the sinister weight it carries here from the faint trace of the word in Q's 'barenes' in 5.8, through 11.10 and 12.5.

13 **unthrifts** See 9.9 and n. Q punctuates: 'O none but unthrifts, deare my love you know, | You had a Father, let your Son say so'. This admits two possible interpretations: (a) 'O none but spendthrifts allow the decay of so fair a mansion. Dear my love you know you had a father: let your son say so too'; (b) 'You know that none but the spendthrift allows the decay of so fair a mansion. You had a father: make a son who can say so too.' The punctuation in this edition follows the latter on the grounds that the former is too commonplace a thought to warrant the strenuous enjambment required to make it possible. It also cuts across the idiom of the period: Justice Shallow says 'To her, coz! Oh boy, thou hadst a father!' (*Merry Wives* 3.4.35–6) when he is urging Slender to woo Anne Page. The set phrase for egging on young men to woo, 'You had a father', is broken if Q's comma is not hardened.

13

O that you were yourself; but, love, you are
No longer yours than you yourself here live.
Against this coming end you should prepare,
And your sweet semblance to some other give.
So should that beauty which you hold in lease   5
Find no determination; then you were
Yourself again after your self's decease,
When your sweet issue your sweet form should bear.
Who lets so fair a house fall to decay,
Which husbandry in honour might uphold   10
Against the stormy gusts of winter's day
And barren rage of death's eternal cold?
　　O none but unthrifts. dear my love, you know:
　　You had a father, let your son say so.

7 Yourself] BENSON; You selfe] Q   13 unthrifts,] Q; unthrifts: GILDON 1714; unthrifts!
KEREIGAN   know:] INGRAM AND REDPATH; know, Q; know GILDON 1714; know. BOSWELL

2 **methinks** it seems to me
astronomy knowledge of how the stars influence human affairs; astrology

4 **Of plagues . . . quality** There was an insatiable appetite in the period for books which professed to predict the weather or the progress of disease. The popular handbook *The Calendar of Shepherds* offered pages of predictions of this kind.

5 **Nor can . . . tell** 'nor am I able to enumerate the minute particularities of future events'

6 **Pointing** The usual gloss is 'appointing', although this would imply a belief that a star-gazer could control rather than merely predict the future; hence one might prefer *OED* 'point' 2: 'To mark with, or indicate by, pricks or dots; to jot down, note, write, describe', which fits the imagery of minute cataloguing established by *tell*.

8 **predict** prediction. *OED* cites only this example. So: 'by frequent predictions which I find in the stars'.

10 **constant stars** unmoving guides; morally reliable beauties. Compare Sidney's *Astrophil and Stella* 26.14, in which the poet opposes the scepticism of others about astrology by claiming that he is influenced 'By only those two stars in Stella's face'.

11 **As** i.e. as the proposition that

12 **If from . . . convert** provided that you shall turn away from your preoccupation with yourself in order to breed. On *store* see 11.9 n.

14 **doom** 'Final fate, destruction, ruin, death' (*OED* 4b)
date 'The limit, term, or end of a period of time, or of the duration of something' (*OED* 5)

14

Not from the stars do I my judgement pluck,
And yet methinks I have astronomy,
But not to tell of good or evil luck,
Of plagues, of dearths, or seasons' quality;
Nor can I fortune to brief minutes tell,   5
Pointing to each his thunder, rain, and wind,
Or say with princes if it shall go well
By oft predict that I in heaven find.
But from thine eyes my knowledge I derive,
And, constant stars, in them I read such art   10
As truth and beauty shall together thrive
If from thyself to store thou wouldst convert:
    Or else of thee this I prognosticate,
    Thy end is truth's and beauty's doom and date.

5 minutes] Q (mynuits) 6 Pointing] Q; 'Pointing *conj.* Walker 8 oft] Q; aught DUNCAN-
JONES; ought GILDON 1714

1–9 When . . . When . . . Then The meditative structure of the sonnet, moving inevitably from general observation to the particular case of the friend, closely parallels that of *12*, but it broadens outwards from the violets and trees of the earlier poem to absorb the astronomical breadth of *14*.

1 consider initially 'look at', but by l. 2 'consider that'. As Kerrigan finely puts it, 'the great sweep of the first line records the grandeur of a world suddenly shown to be vulnerable at the turn into line 2'.

3 this huge stage . . . shows 'All the world's a stage' (*As You Like It* 2.7.139) was a Renaissance commonplace (Dent W882) deriving ultimately, via scores of intermediaries, from John of Salisbury to Palingenius, from Lucian. *Totus mundus agit histrionem* ('all the world plays the actor') may have been the motto of Shakespeare's Globe theatre.

4 influence 'The supposed flowing or streaming from the stars or heavens of an etherial fluid acting upon the character and destiny of men' (*OED* 2a *spec.* in *Astrol.*)
comment Schmidt's gloss 'to discourse, reason' is too bland. The stars are a critically learned audience which 'make comments or remarks (*on, upon*). (Often implying unfavourable remarks)' (*OED* 4a). This sense continues the metaphor of the *stage* from l. 3. Also perhaps 'make remarks deriving from arcane wisdom', as in *Two Gentlemen* 2.1.38–40: 'not an eye that sees you but is a physician to comment on your malady'.

6 Cheerèd encouraged. The sense 'To salute with "cheers" or shouts of applause' (*OED* 8) is not found before the late eighteenth century, although the metaphor of stars as audience may indicate that this sense is struggling to emerge.
checked Cf. 5.7 n.

7 Vaunt 'To boast or brag; to use boastful, bragging, or vainglorious language. Fairly common *c.*1600' (*OED* 1 *intr.*)

8 wear . . . memory The young men wear out their proud clothes, their elevated status, and their exhilarated condition all at once, and wear them out to the point that they are erased from memory.

9 conceit . . . stay 'then the perception of this continual change . . .'. *Conceit* also suggests that the fashionable vitality described above is 'absurdly far-fetched'. *Stay* is used in *OED* sense 6c: 'Continuance in a state, duration'. The phrase *unconstant stay* is deliberately unsettling, since 'stay' is more usually employed *c.*1600 to describe a state of stability or a place of rest.

10 rich in youth full of youth and enriched by youth. The echo of *you* in *youth* plangently records a desire that the relationship between the two be intrinsic rather than transient: 'you-th is you-ness in this adoring pun' (Vendler). It suggests too that Shakespeare could switch between 'thou' and 'you' in order to pun.

11 time . . . decay Time and Decay either discuss how they can best together bring youth to an end, or they haggle over who should be the agent of the friend's destruction. *Debateth* may carry the sense, slightly archaic by 1609, of 'fight with'. See *Lucrece* l. 1421 n.

12 sullied 'Soiled, polluted (*lit.* and *fig.*); made gloomy or dull' (*OED*, citing this passage)

13 in war is a standard but less common alternative for 'at war'. It is chosen here because it is so pointedly not '*in* love'.

14 engraft I renovate and eternize you through poetry. To *engraft* is 'to insert (a scion of one tree) as a graft *into* or *upon* (another)' (*OED* 1) in order to renovate it, 'even as a young graff [grafted shoot] buddeth out when the old tree is cut down' (Wilson, 56). The metaphor suggests that the friend provides slips (or small shoots) which are then inserted into the bark of an established tree in order to create further living examples of the parent plant. The poet is the skilled artist who accomplishes this. Cf. 'You see, sweet maid, we marry | A gentler scion to the wildest stock, | And make conceive a bark of baser kind | By bud of nobler race' (*Winter's Tale* 4.4.92–5). There may also be a pun on 'graphein', the Greek verb to write. This is the first hint in the sequence that writing can immortalize even someone who is reluctant to eternize himself by having children.

15

When I consider every thing that grows
Holds in perfection but a little moment;
That this huge stage presenteth naught but shows,
Whereon the stars in secret influence comment;
When I perceive that men as plants increase,   5
Cheerèd and checked even by the selfsame sky,
Vaunt in their youthful sap, at height decrease,
And wear their brave state out of memory;
Then the conceit of this inconstant stay
Sets you most rich in youth before my sight,   10
Where wasteful time debateth with decay
To change your day of youth to sullied night,
    And, all in war with Time for love of you,
    As he takes from you, I engraft you new.

1 **But wherefore** but why (abruptly continuing the argument of *15*)

3 **fortify** make yourself strong; perhaps, 'build ramparts against Time'

4 **blessèd** continues the association between childbearing and happy good fortune established by *unbless* (*3.4*).
barren rhyme is the first explicit mention of poetry in the sequence. It shockingly denies the vitality implicitly granted to verse by *engraft* in *15.14*, and links poetry with one of the most negatively charged adjectives in the early part of the sequence (see *13.12* n.)

5 **top** zenith

6 **unset** 'Not furnished with plants', *OED* 5c, citing only this example, in which Shakespeare has extended sense 5b, 'Not planted, self-seeded', to mean 'not yet subjected to human husbandry', hence 'unmarried women'.

7 **With virtuous . . . flowers** who chastely desire to bear your children. The comparison of a bride to a garden is a Renaissance commonplace, deriving ultimately from the Song of Solomon 4: 12: 'My sister my spouse is as a garden inclosed, as a spring shut up, and a fountain sealed up'.

8 **Much liker** more similar to you
counterfeit is possible in the neutral sense 'An imitation or representation in painting, sculpture, etc.' (*OED* 3), but 'A false or spurious imitation' (*OED* 1) initiates the interest in the inadequacies of art explored further in *24*.

9 **lines of life** (a) bloodlines which perpetuate (*OED* 24a); (b) outlines or living depictions of the friend in the form of his children; (c) lines of verse which confer immortality (*OED* 23e), this despite the *barren rhyme* of l. 4; (d) limits imposed on human life (*OED* s.v. 'line' 1g: 'The thread fabled to be spun by the Fates, determining the duration of a person's life'). The phrase is echoed by Hugh Holland's *Prefatory Verses* in the First Folio: 'Though his line of life went soon about, | The life yet of his lines shall never out'.
repair Cf. *3.3* and *10.8*.

10 **pencil** and *pen* are traditionally opposed as representatives of fine art and poetry respectively in a formalized debate about the rival merits of the sister arts known in the Renaissance as a 'paragone' (for an example of which, see *Timon* 1.1.1–95). Hence 'neither the painters of this age nor my amateurish pen can represent either your inward or outward being to the life'. Q reads 'this (Times pensel or my pupill pen)', in which 'this' presumably refers to 'this sonnet', as in *18.14*. It would be odd for the poet to identify his 'pen' (which writes) with time's 'pencil' (which draws). Q could be defended, since the phrase *the lines of life* has implicitly already made such an identification: *lines* there unites pictorial outlines with lines of verse. Parallels for treating the descriptive pen as an illustrator's pencil can also be found in Canzon 2 of the anonymous *Zepheria* (1594): 'Though be thou limned in these discoloured lines, | Delicious model of my spirit's portrait, | Though be thou sable pencilled, these designs | Shadow not beauty but a sorrow's extract'. None the less the chiastic relation between *pencil* and *pen* on the one hand and 'inward *worth*' and 'outward fair' on the other makes one expect an opposition between the pen, which describes the inward, and the pencil, which depicts the outward, and such an opposition is achieved by removing Q's parenthesis.

12 **in eyes of men** (a) before men's eyes; (b) in the opinion of the world

13 **To give away** to marry, or to lose semen in sex. Compare the Solemnization of Matrimony in the Book of Common Prayer: 'who giveth this woman to be married to this man?'
keeps your self still 'eternally keeps yourself alive (through having children)'

14 **must** will be able to (Abbott §314)
drawn i.e. reproduced in children. Quibbles on 'pen' and penis are quite common in the period, as in Graziano's threat 'Well, do you so. Let me not take him then, | For if I do I'll mar the young clerk's pen' (*Merchant* 5.1.236–7).

16

But wherefore do not you a mightier way
Make war upon this bloody tyrant Time,
And fortify yourself in your decay
With means more blessèd than my barren rhyme?
Now stand you on the top of happy hours,   5
And many maiden gardens, yet unset,
With virtuous wish would bear your living flowers,
Much liker than your painted counterfeit:
So should the lines of life that life repair,
Which this time's pencil or my pupil pen   10
Neither in inward worth nor outward fair
Can make you live yourself in eyes of men:
   To give away yourself keeps your self still.
   And you must live drawn by your own sweet skill.

10 this time's pencil or my pupil pen] GILDON 1714; this (Times pensel or my pupill pen) Q; this, Time's pencil, or my pupil pen MALONE

1–2 **will . . . were** Subjunctive constructions were loose in this period. A contemporary reader would not have felt any lack of co-ordination between the moods of the indicative *will* and the subjunctive *were*. There is consequently no need to tinker with the punctuation of Q. (Ingram and Redpath follow Tucker in putting a question mark after l. 1 and dashes at the ends of 2 and 4 to mark what they consider to be a parenthesis. This is at the cost of an awkward disruption to the relative movements of syntactic units and quatrain.)

2 **filled** is spelled 'fild' in Q on three occasions (here, at *63*.3, and at *86*.13, set by compositors B and A respectively) and 'fil'd' once (*85*.4). This spelling may bring with it a pun on 'filed', or 'given a final artistic polish'. Before one assumes authorial artistry here, however, one should note that the character-strings 'lld' and 'll'd' do not occur in Q. Its compositors evidently would not double the final consonant of a verb's stem before a final contracted 'ed'; hence the only available form of 'filled' with a syncopated final 'ed' is 'fild' or 'fil'd' (cf. the forms 'self wilde' *6.13*; 'selfe kil'd' *6.4*; 'distil'd' *5.13*, *6.2*, *119.2*; comparable too are 'miscalde' *66.11* and 'cal'd' *105.1*). Given this limitation it is noteworthy that the only occurrence in Q of 'fil'd', rather than 'fild', is at *85*.4, at a point where it is clear that 'filing' (polishing) rather than 'filling' is the primary action described ('And precious phrase by all the Muses fil'd'). It seems the compositors distinguished 'filled' and 'filed' by inserting an apostrophe in the contracted form of the latter. In which case the secondary sense 'filed' is not active here, and the anguish of a modernizing editor described by Katherine Duncan-Jones in 'Filling the Unforgiving Minute: Modernising SHAKE-SPEARES SONNETS (1609)', *Essays in Criticism* 45 (1995), 199–207 would not have been shared by early modern readers.

deserts 'Meritoriousness, excellence' (*OED* 1b), probably pronounced 'desarts' to rhyme with 'parts' (cf. Q's spelling 'desart' at *49*.10)

3–4 **Though . . . parts** 'although heaven knows my verse is a dead monument which obscures your vitality and shows less than half of your abilities and attributes'. *Parts* means both 'an act (usually with qualification expresssing praise or blame)' (*OED* 11), and 'A personal quality or attribute, natural or acquired, esp. of

an intellectual kind' (*OED* 12), both of which might figure on a 'monument'.

5 **write the beauty** 'A direct object declares the poet's radical ambition: not to write about but inscribe beauty on the page' (Kerrigan). The sense 'To score, outline, or draw the figure of (something); to incise' (*OED* s.v. 'write' 1a) is recorded as late as 1590, but only in the consciously archaic world of *FQ* (2.8.43: 'Guyons shield . . . | Whereon the Faery Queenes pourtract was writ').

6 **in fresh numbers number** 'in innovative verse enumerate'. *Fresh*, though, carries a breath of vitality from its earlier uses in the sequence (e.g. *1.9*, *11.3*).

7 **This poet** The word 'poet' could be used as a term of abuse in the period, meaning 'fantastical or absurd person', as in Ben Jonson, *Works*, ed. C. H. Herford and Percy and Evelyn Simpson, 11 vols. (Oxford, 1925–53), viii.572: 'He is upbraidingly called a *Poet*, as if it were a most contemptible nick-name'; 'Commonly whoso is studious in the art [of poetry] . . . they call him in disdain a "fantastical", and a light-headed or fantastical man (by conversion) they call a "poet"', Puttenham, 18.

8 **touches** (a) 'distinguishing qualities, characteristics, traits' (*OED* 18a); (b) 'touching a surface with the proper tool in painting, drawing, writing, carving, etc.' (*OED* 10a). The noun is associated by Shakespeare with the ravishingly real, as in *Timon* 1.1.37–8: 'It [a picture] tutors nature. Artificial strife | Lives in these touches livelier than life'.

9 **papers** poetic compositions are regularly referred to as 'papers' *c*.1600, especially those which were written for manuscript circulation in a small coterie, as in Daniel's *Delia* (1592) 39: 'O be not grieved that these my papers should | Bewray unto the world how fair thou art', and 48.5–6: 'For God forbid I should my papers blot, | With mercenary lines, with servile pen'. Petrarch too refers to his poems as *carte*, papers.

10 **of less . . . tongue** more talkative than honest. Cf. 'Old men and far travellers may lie by authority' (Dent M567).

11 **true rights** (a) praise which is accurate and deserved by you; (b) (punning on 'rites') rituals of worship which you deserve

poet's rage 'Poetic or prophetic enthusiasm or inspiration' (*OED* s.v. 'rage' 8; first cited instance), with a suggestion of

17

Who will believe my verse in time to come
If it were filled with your most high deserts?
Though yet, heaven knows, it is but as a tomb
Which hides your life, and shows not half your parts.
If I could write the beauty of your eyes,   5
And in fresh numbers number all your graces,
The age to come would say 'This poet lies:
Such heavenly touches ne'er touched earthly faces.'
So should my papers (yellowed with their age)
Be scorned, like old men of less truth than tongue,   10
And your true rights be termed a poet's rage,
And stretchèd metre of an antique song.
    But were some child of yours alive that time,
    You should live twice, in it, and in my rhyme.

2 filled] Q (fild)   7–8 'This . . . faces.'] COLLIER; ˏ~ . . . ~ˏ Q   12 metre] Q (miter)

madness, as in Chapman's *Iliad* 1.66: 'His prophetic rage | Given by Apollo'.

12 **stretchèd metre . . . song** 'irregular metre of an ancient (and "mad", via the frequent pun on "antique" and "antic") song'. *OED* quotes this passage as the first citation under 'stretched' 4a: 'Of language, ideas, prerogative, etc.: Strained beyond natural or proper limits'. This is itself a stretched point, since the earliest subsequent citation is not until 1674. It is more likely that the term alludes to perceived metrical defects in earlier versification. Uncertainty over the pronunciation (particularly of final 'e') of Middle English verse led to a frequent belief *c.* 1600 that it was metrically irregular. Here that uncertainty is projected onto Shakespeare's future readers. Cf. Daniel's *Delia*, 46.1–2: 'Let others sing of Knights and Palladines, | In aged accents, and untimely words'. *Antique* is stressed on the first syllable.

14 **rhyme** verse. By 1590 *rhyme* could be used as a term of contempt, opposed to 'poem', so there is a modest shrug here to counterpoise the optimism. Cf. *rhymers* at 38.10.

1 **a summer's day** was proverbially perfect (cf. Dent S967).

2 **temperate** (a) moderate, even-tempered; (b) 'neither too hot nor too cold; of mild and equable temperature' (*OED* 3a)

4 **lease** temporary period of legal possession, limited by a *date*, or period of expiry. See *13*.5 and 6 nn.

6 **complexion** (a) 'Countenance, face' (*OED* 4c); (b) 'Colour, visible aspect, look, appearance' (*OED* 5 *transf.*), as in *Richard II* 3.2.190–1: 'Men judge by the complexion of the sky | The state and inclination of the day.'

7 **fair from . . . declines** every beautiful thing loses its beauty; playing on the 'fairness' of the sun's *gold complexion*.

8 **untrimmed** 'deprived of trimness or elegance; stripped of ornament' (*OED* 1; first cited usage). Cf. *K. John* 3.1.134–5: 'the devil tempts thee here | In likeness of a new untrimmèd bride', where it has been suggested that the term means 'undevirginated' (Partridge) or 'recently divested of her wedding-gown' (Schmidt). 'Deprived of the ornaments of youth' would fit both contexts, as well as tallying with the influential passage from Revelation 21: 2: 'And I John saw the holy city new Jerusalem come down from God out of heaven, prepared as a bride trimmed for her husband.'

10 **lose possession . . . ow'st** Nor will you lose control over the beauty which you own absolutely and for ever. This contrasts with the impermanent *lease* of l. 4 above, and does so by emphatically linking *possession* with ownership. These terms are not synonymous in law. *Possession* (especially when applied to land or property) means occupancy or enjoyment of a piece of property in a manner which brings with it the right to exercise control over it, but it does not necessarily imply ownership; hence to enjoy something fully one must have both ownership and permanent possession of it.

11 **wand'rest . . . shade** alluding to Psalm 23: 4: 'Yea, though I should walk through the valley of the shadow of death, I will fear no evil: for thou art with me: thy rod and thy staff, they comfort me'.

12 **eternal lines** 'enduring lines of verse' and 'perpetual genealogical descent'; see *16*.9 note.

to time thou grow'st you become a living part of time. To *grow to* is 'to be an organic or integral part of' (*OED* 3b), as in *2 Henry IV* 1.2.85–90: '*Ser.* I pray you, sir, then set your knighthood and your soldiership aside . . . *Fal.* I lay aside that which grows to me?' See *Venus* l. 540. The addressee of the poem is like a shoot grafted into time's substance, and continues to live through either the poet's *lines* or his own bloodline.

14 **this** 'this sonnet'

18

Shall I compare thee to a summer's day?
Thou art more lovely and more temperate:
Rough winds do shake the darling buds of May,
And summer's lease hath all too short a date;
Sometime too hot the eye of heaven shines,   5
And often is his gold complexion dimmed,
And every fair from fair sometime declines,
By chance or nature's changing course untrimmed:
But thy eternal summer shall not fade,
Nor lose possession of that fair thou ow'st;   10
Nor shall Death brag thou wand'rest in his shade,
When in eternal lines to time thou grow'st.
  So long as men can breathe or eyes can see,
  So long lives this, and this gives life to thee.

1 **Devouring Time** renders Ovid's *tempus edax rerum* ('time the devourer of things'), *Met.* 15.234 (proverbial; cf. Dent T326).

paws *c.*1600 were sharper than they are now: 'The foot of a beast having claws or nails' (*OED* 1a), and in Shakespeare equivalent to 'claws', as in 'The lion, moved with pity, did endure | To have his princely paws pared all away', *Titus* 2.3.151–2.

3 **keen** sharp

4 **phoenix** 'A mythical bird, of gorgeous plumage, fabled to be the only one of its kind, and to live five or six hundred years in the Arabian desert, after which it burnt itself to ashes on a funeral pile of aromatic twigs ignited by the sun and fanned by its own wings, but only to emerge from its ashes with renewed youth, to live through another cycle of years' (*OED*). Time therefore destroys even the indestructible; although Shakespeare's readers would know that the Phoenix was immortal, and so might anticipate the ending of the poem.

in her blood both literally and 'in her prime, full vigour' (*OED* s.v. 'blood' 7)

5 **fleet'st** fly by. It is often emended, for the sake of a perfect rhyme, to 'fleets'.

6 **swift-footed Time** The thought was proverbial (Dent T327).

7 **fading sweets** perishable beauties. *Fading* is often used on the boundary between 'the diminution of some sensual delight' (usually colour, but here perhaps smell)

and simple transience, or 'perishing'. Cf. *18.9, 73.6, 146.6.*

10 **Nor . . . no** The multiple negatives reinforce each other for emphasis, as regularly in Shakespeare.

antique (a) ancient; (b) 'antic', or mad. Stressed on the first syllable. The epithet associates the destructive artistry of Time with the *antique song* which describes the poet's own verse in *17.12*.

11 **untainted** 'Not affected by any physical taint', i.e. unmarked (*OED* 2; first cited usage). *Course* (galloping career) may activate an allusion to a hit or 'taint' in tilting (*OED* s.v. 'taint' *n.* 1a), although no other negative form of the verb is recorded.

12 **pattern** 'the archetype; that which is to be copied; an exemplar' (*OED* 1a). Hence 'leave him unsullied as an ideal example of beauty for later ages'. *Succeeding* may just carry a continued suggestion from the 'reproduction' group of 'those who succeed him, his heirs'; but at this stage of the sequence literary reproduction is beginning to oust the biological.

13 **do thy worst** a common phrase in challenges or gestures of proud but vain defiance (cf. Dent W914)

14 **ever live** Some would emend to 'live ever' for metrical smoothness; but the pressure exerted on *ever* by the slight metrical irregularity is surely deliberate, as *ever* (two syllables here, as against the usual one) labours to cover both 'live for ever' and 'live young for ever'.

19

Devouring Time, blunt thou the lion's paws,
And make the earth devour her own sweet brood,
Pluck the keen teeth from the fierce tiger's jaws,
And burn the long-lived phoenix in her blood,
Make glad and sorry seasons as thou fleet'st,   5
And do whate'er thou wilt, swift-footed Time,
To the wide world and all her fading sweets:
But I forbid thee one most heinous crime,
O carve not with thy hours my love's fair brow,
Nor draw no lines there with thine antique pen.   10
Him in thy course untainted do allow
For beauty's pattern to succeeding men.
    Yet do thy worst, old Time: despite thy wrong,
    My love shall in my verse ever live young.

3 jaws] Q (yawes)   5 fleet'st] Q; fleets DYCE   14 ever live] Q; live ever *conj.* Nicholson in Cambridge 1893

1 **painted** (a) drawn, depicted; (b) made up. The poem, about a womanly man, contains only feminine rhymes (the technical term for a hypermetrical line with an additional unstressed final syllable was first used in England by Samuel Daniel *c.*1603). Feminine rhymes often occur at sexually suggestive moments, as in *Hero and Leander* ll. 555–8.

2 **master mistress** is an unprecedented phrase, often hyphenated by modern editors. Q, however, reads 'Master Mistris' which is more readily glossed as 'sovereign mistress' than its modernized equivalent. Critics debate whether it has a homosexual connotation ('both my patron and my sexual mistress'), whether it refers to the femininity of the friend's appearance, or whether it simply highlights the way in which the friend occupies the role in the sequence more usually taken by a mistress. The poet's disavowal of sexual interest in the friend in the couplet of this sonnet may neutralize any sexual charge from the phrase (as Malone coolly claims: 'Such addresses to men, however indelicate, were customary in our author's time, and neither imported criminality, nor were esteemed indecorous'), but a frisson of homoerotic pleasure was one of the joys expected by readers of late Elizabethan and Jacobean sonnet sequences, and even the couplet is fruitfully ambiguous (see Introduction, p. 130). Many glosses overlook that he is described as *the master mistress of my passion,* that is either the object of my passionate love, or the person who directs and controls my passions. The sonnet is as much concerned with the power of the friend to influence others as it is with his sexuality. *Passion,* as Dowden suggested, 'may be used in the old sense of *love-poem,* common in Watson'.
acquainted 'Quaint' is slang for the female sexual organs in this period, giving a glancing sexual pun.

4 **With . . . fashion** The mutability of women is a commonplace of the period, attributed in Thomas Wright, *The Passions of the Mind in General* (dedicated to the Earl of Southampton in 1601) to 'a lack of prudence and judgement in their determinations', ed. W. W. Newbold, The Renaissance Imagination 15 (New York and London, 1986), 119.

5 **rolling** to glance at lovers

6 **Gilding . . . gazeth** To *gild* in Shakespeare is seldom simply a good thing; so both 'turning what it looks at to gold' and 'giving a superficial glitter to whatever it glances at'. The parallel between the false *rolling* of women's eyes and the *gilding* performed by the friend's eye is not accidental, and anticipates the *concerns* later in the sequence with his ability to falsify appearances of value.

7 **hue . . . hues** (a) 'a man whose beauty enthralls all others'; (b) continuing the theme of l. 1, 'a man in form, who is able by nature to adopt the perfect colouring of any complexion, including that of a woman'; (c) continuing the imagery of *gilding,* 'a man in form, who is able to control all appearances and to make all succumb to him'; (d) 'he is so comely that all complexions (blushing or turning pale) lie in his power' (Kerrigan, after Beeching). *Hue* moves from 'Form, shape, figure' (*OED* 1a) through 'External appearance of the face and skin, complexion' (*OED* 2), to 'Colour' (*OED* 3a). Baldwin, 165, cites Hoby's translation of Castiglione's *Book of the Courtier* (1561): a courtier will have 'a certain grace and (as they say) a hue', which he glosses as 'noble grace'. That passage illustrates that 'hue' in the sixteenth century could be used to evoke an elegant *je ne sçais quoi,* the equivalent of Castiglione's notoriously untranslatable *sprezzatura.* Q reads 'Hews', and its italics (on which see 1.2 n.) have spawned a generation of creatures: on the fevered workings of earlier editors' imaginations, see the admirably cool summary in Rollins 2, ii.180–5. Some are not quite fevered enough, however, and seek to emend *a man in* to 'a maiden' or 'a native'; for which neutered versions see collation.

8 **Which** can be used as either masculine or neuter relative pronoun in Shakespeare; hence 'a man who attracts the eyes of men and amazes the souls of women', or 'of a hue which . . .'.
amazeth 'To overwhelm with wonder, to astound or greatly astonish' (*OED* 4). Cf. *Venus* ll. 633–4.

9 **for a woman** (a) you were originally intended to be a woman; (b) you were made to belong to a woman. Sense (b) points back to the 'reproduction' sonnets; (a) points forward to the less certain gender relations of the later sonnets to the friend.

10 **fell a-doting** became besotted with you

11 **addition** primarily 'by addition of a penis'. Also, though, possibly alluding to the friend's high social status via the defini-

20

A woman's face with nature's own hand painted,
Hast thou, the master mistress of my passion;
A woman's gentle heart, but not acquainted
With shifting change as is false women's fashion;
An eye more bright than theirs, less false in rolling,   5
Gilding the object whereupon it gazeth;
A man in hue, all hues in his controlling,
Which steals men's eyes and women's souls amazeth.
And for a woman wert thou first created,
Till Nature as she wrought thee fell a-doting,   10
And by addition me of thee defeated,
By adding one thing to my purpose nothing.
　　But since she pricked thee out for women's pleasure,
　　Mine be thy love, and thy love's use their treasure.

2 master mistress] Q (Master Mistris); master-mistress MALONE (*conj.* Capell)　7 man in] Q;
maiden *conj.* Beeching; native *conj.* Mackail in Beeching; maid in *conj.* Tannenbaum in Rollins
2 hues] MALONE; *Hews* Q; hears *conj.* Pooler

tions 'Something annexed to a man's name, to show his rank' (*OED* 4) and '(*Heraldic*) Something added to a coat of arms, as a mark of honour' (*OED* 5', citing *Troilus* 4.7.24–5 'I came to kill thee, cousin, and bear hence | A great addition earnèd in thy death'.

11 defeated 'To do (a person) out *of* (something expected, or naturally coming to him); to disappoint, defraud, cheat' (*OED* 7)

12 one thing a penis (perhaps also high rank)
nothing of no significance to me, playing on 'thing' meaning 'sexual organs' (Partridge)

13 pricked thee out (a) selected you from a list (*CED* 15); (b) sketched your outline; (c) equipped you with a penis. 'Prick' was common slang for a penis in the 1590s. The pun on senses (a) and (b) occurs in 2 *Henry IV* 3.2.105–83, and also in Ben Jonson's *Cynthia's Revels* 5.2.79: 'Why did the ladies prick out me?'

14 thy love's use their treasure (a) they have the physical act of love; (b) they enjoy the interest on the capital of love which the poet still owns; (c) they win the ability to multiply your image (alluding to the association between sexual reproduction and usury already explored in the sequence). See Introduction, p. 130.

1 **So ... that Muse** I am not in the same case as that poet

2 **painted beauty** (a) excessively made-up woman; (b) mere secondary depiction. Sense (a) is brought to prominence by *stirred* which means both 'inspired' and 'stimulated out of torpor'.

3 **heaven . . . use** Presumably this implies that the poet is using something potentially sacred as a mere rhetorical ornament in a comparison such as those in l. 6 below. By 1600 excess of rhetorical *ornament* in verse was subjected to several attacks, notably that in Sir Philip Sidney's *Apology for Poetry* (first printed 1595), ed. G. Shepherd (Manchester, 1973), 138: 'So is that honey-flowing matron eloquence apparelled, or rather disguised, in courtesan-like painted affectation'. It is unlikely that this attack is directed against a specific 'rival poet'.

4 **rehearse** *OED* does not record a sense 'compare', which is what is required here; also perhaps 'endless repetition'.

5 **couplement of proud compare** a comparison which proudly favours the charms of his own mistress over others. *Couplement* means 'a uniting of two things in a comparison' or 'The act of coupling' (*OED* s.v. 'couplement' 1, citing this passage), with perhaps a hint at the rare sense (2b): 'Of verses: A couplet or stanza'. *Proud* is often used of the activities of rival poets in the sequence to suggest both 'boldness' and 'excessive arrogance'.

6 **sun . . . gems** are traditional instances of hyperbole. Nashe satirizes the Earl of Surrey by saying 'his tongue thrust the stars out of heaven and eclipsed the sun and moon with comparisons', Nashe, ii.270. Thomas Howard satirizes the hyperbole of

Jacobean courtiers in similar terms, *Nugae Antiquae*, ed. Henry Harington, 2 vols. (1804), i.396: 'Will you say that the moon shineth all summer? That the stars are bright jewels fit for Carr's ears?'

8 **in this huge rondure hems** encloses in the vast expanse of the sky. *Rondure* is 'a circle or round object; roundness, hence the sphere of the earth as delimited by the sky' (*OED* 1; first cited usage).

9 **O let me ... write** let me, faithful in love as I am, merely write the unornamented truth

10 **fair** beautiful; playing on 'fair complexioned'

11 **mother's child** Throughout the poem there is no explicit indicator of the gender of the beloved: *child* can be boy or girl. The play on *fair* links the poem closely with a number of the later Sonnets (e.g. *127*, *131*) to the mistress, and those associations intensify the sexual uncertainties initiated by the previous poem.

12 **gold candles** stars

13 **hearsay** oral testimony rather than truth, making an implicit opposition between the private 'writing' of Shakespeare and the public report of the imagined other poets

14 **I will not . . . sell** Cf. Berowne in *L.L.L.* 4.3.237–9: 'Fie, painted rhetoric! O, she needs it not. | To things of sale a seller's praise belongs', and Dent P546. The sonnet is aware that its protestations of plainness are themselves familiar tropes, and declares the fact in its consciously declamatory style. This is the first poem in the sequence in which the poet declaims to an audience which is larger than the friend.

21

So is it not with me as with that Muse,
Stirred by a painted beauty to his verse,
Who heaven itself for ornament doth use,
And every fair with his fair doth rehearse,
Making a couplement of proud compare   5
With sun and moon, with earth, and sea's rich gems,
With April's first-born flowers, and all things rare
That heaven's air in this huge rondure hems.
O let me, true in love, but truly write,
And then, believe me, my love is as fair   10
As any mother's child, though not so bright
As those gold candles fixed in heaven's air:
　　Let them say more that like of hearsay well:
　　I will not praise, that purpose not to sell.

5 couplement] Q; Complement GILDON

1 **old** Convention made sonneteers age rapidly: Daniel at 29, Barnfield at 20, Drayton at 31 all complain of their age. Cf. *62.9, 73, 138.5.*

2 **of one date** last as long as each other

3 **time's furrows** wrinkles. Cf. *2.2.* Q's 'forrwes' might conceivably be a misreading of 'sorrows', since long 'ſ' can readily be misread as 'f' by a compositor. It is likely the MS made a graphical pun on these two forms.

4 **Then . . . expiate** then I hope that death will end my days. *Expiate* is not cited before 1594. The unusual usage here ('finish', Schmidt) may derive from a slight misunderstanding of Marlowe's lines in *Dido Queen of Carthage* 5.2.316–17: 'Cursèd Iarbas, die to expiate | The grief that tires upon thine inward soul!'

5–7 The exchanging of hearts between lovers is a Petrarchan commonplace, as in *L.L.L.* 5.2.809: 'My heart is in thy breast.' Here the friend's beauty becomes the decorous covering (*seemly raiment*) for the poet's heart, which resides in the beloved's bosom. Compare the proverb 'The lover is not where he lives but where he loves' (Dent L565).

8 **elder** is a variant of 'older' (slightly antiquated by 1600)

10 **will** will be wary

11 **chary** 'carefully, tenderly' (*OED* 8 *quasi-adv.*)

13 **Presume not on** do not presumptuously lay claim to. This is a very rare usage of 'presume' (cf. *OED* 3b and 5).

22

My glass shall not persuade me I am old,
So long as youth and thou are of one date,
But when in thee time's furrows I behold,
Then look I death my days should expiate.
For all that beauty that doth cover thee   5
Is but the seemly raiment of my heart,
Which in thy breast doth live, as thine in me.
How can I then be elder than thou art?
O therefore, love, be of thyself so wary
As I, not for myself, but for thee will,   10
Bearing thy heart which I will keep so chary
As tender nurse her babe from faring ill.
   Presume not on thy heart when mine is slain:
   Thou gav'st me thine not to give back again.

3 furrows] Q (forrwes); Sorrows GILDON   4 expiate] Q; expirate *con*. Steevens in Malone

1 **unperfect** who does not properly know his lines. (*OED* cites this passage only). 'Perfect' is often used by Shakespeare to mean 'knowing one's lines', as in *L.L.L.* 5.2.555–6: 'I hope I was perfect. I made a little fault in "great" ', and *Venus* ll. 407–8.

2 **with his . . . part** is made to forget his part by stage fright

3 **replete with** full of; here almost 'stuffed to bursting with'. Cf. *113.13*.

5 **for fear of trust** (a) afraid to trust myself; (b) fearful of the responsibility laid on me; perhaps also (c) for fear of not being believed

6 **The perfect . . . rite** the formalities due to love, and remembered exactly. Q's 'right' could be read as both 'ritual' and 'those things which are due to love as a right'. *Perfect* recalls *unperfect* from l. 1.

7 **decay** deteriorate, weaken (*OED* 1)

8 **O'ercharged** overburdened (like an overladen ship)

9 **books** Notebooks, loose sheets of writing, single paged documents all could be called *books*. Here presumably it means 'these sonnets', although some have extended it to include *Venus* and *Lucrece*. Sewell's emendation to *looks* at least has the virtue of drawing attention to the deliberate unexpectedness of *books*. Sonneteers regularly oppose the dumb eloquence of the gaze to their tongue-tied addresses to their mistresses (e.g. Griffin, *Fidessa* 45); that cliché is deliberately avoided here.

10 **dumb presagers** silent witnesses which go before. *OED* defines *presager* as 'One who or that which presages or portends', which does not quite fit this context (although it is noteworthy that it would if *books* were emended to 'looks'). The word is a new one in the 1590s, and Shakespeare seems to be using it as a near synonym for 'ambassador', rather than exploiting its associations with understanding of the future.

11 **plead** legal sense: 'To address the court as an advocate' (*OED* 2a)

12 **More . . . expressed** to a greater degree than a tongue that has uttered a greater love in more words. The second *more* is a noun: 'more love'; the first and third are adjectives.

13 **love** was near-proverbially silent (Dent L165).

14 **fine wit** sharp intelligence. Q's compositor was thrown by the play on *with* and *wit*: 'To heare wit eies belongs to loves fine wiht'.

23

As an unperfect actor on the stage,
Who with his fear is put besides his part,
Or some fierce thing replete with too much rage,
Whose strength's abundance weakens his own heart;
So I, for fear of trust, forget to say   5
The perfect ceremony of love's rite,
And in mine own love's strength seem to decay,
O'er-charged with burden of mine own love's might:
O let my books be then the eloquence
And dumb presagers of my speaking breast,   10
Who plead for love, and look for recompense,
More than that tongue that more hath more expressed.
    O learn to read what silent love hath writ:
    To hear with eyes belongs to love's fine wit.

6 love's rite] Q (loues right)   9 books] Q; looks SEWELL   14 with . . . wit] BENSON; wit
. . . wiht Q

1 **stelled** a recently introduced term of art from painting, meaning 'To portray, delineate' (*OED* 3, citing R. Haydocke's 1598 translation of *Lomazzo* i.16: 'Before you begin to stell, delineate and trick out the proportion of a man, you ought to know his true quantity and stature', and this passage). See *Lucrece* l. 1444. Q reads 'steeld', which may be a compositor's response to an unknown word, or which may anticipate later Sonnets' concern with the permanence of steel (65.8, 120.4).

2 **table** notebook. Cf. *122.1* and *Hamlet* 1.5.107–9: 'My tables, | My tables—meet it is I set it down | That one may smile and smile and be a villain.'

3 **frame** (a) 'A structure, fabric, or engine constructed of parts fitted together (including an easel)' (*OED* 7a); (b) 'the human body, with reference to its make, build, or constitution' (*OED* 9a; as in 59.10); (c) 'That in which something, *esp.* a picture, pane of glass, etc. is set' (*OED* 12a). This passage is the first citation for the last of these senses. Early readers would have favoured sense (a) over sense (c).

4 **perspective** either (a) 'and the art of creating an effect of depth is the painter's highest skill', or (b) 'the art of deliberate distortion is a painter's highest skill'. The latter suits what follows, since it implies that the viewer must work his way through the distorted representations created by the painter to arrive at a 'true image'. Stressed 'pèrspective'. The emergent technical sense of *perspective* ('The art of delineating solid objects upon a plane surface so that the drawing produces the same impression of apparent relative positions and magnitudes, or of distance, as do the actual objects when viewed from a particular point' (*OED* 3a)) works alongside the more common sense, 'A picture or figure constructed so as to produce some fantastic effect; e.g. appearing distorted or confused from one particular point of view, or presenting totally different aspects from different points' (*OED* 4b).

5–8 The conceit of the beloved's picture hanging in the bosom of the lover is a common one, as in Constable's *Diana* 1.5: 'Thine eye, the glass where I behold my heart; | Mine eye, the window through the which thine eye | May see my heart; and there thyself espy | In bloody colours how thou painted art'.

5 **you** The shift from *thy* in l. 2 may indicate a general reference ('one'). It may just be an inconsistency.

7 **shop** workshop (*OED* 3a)

9 **good turns** favours. Compare the proverb 'One good turn deserves another' (Dent T616).

10–12 **Mine eyes . . . thee** The two lovers see each other reflected in each other's eyes, a commonplace which is given a twist of Shakespearian self-consciousness: he not only looks at himself in his love's eyes; he looks at himself looking. *Perspective* here takes on an additional sense: etymologically it means 'looking through', and a desire for moral perspicuousness emerges at the end of the poem.

13 **this cunning want** lack this skill

14 **They . . . heart** The eyes can only present outward appearance, and cannot depict the heart. The note of doubt here (what is the lover thinking?) anticipates later poems.

24

Mine eye hath played the painter and hath stelled
Thy beauty's form in table of my heart;
My body is the frame wherein 'tis held,
And perspective it is best painter's art,
For through the painter must you see his skill   5
To find where your true image pictured lies,
Which in my bosom's shop is hanging still,
That hath his windows glazèd with thine eyes.
Now see what good turns eyes for eyes have done:
Mine eyes have drawn thy shape, and thine for me   10
Are windows to my breast, wherethrough the sun
Delights to peep, to gaze therein on thee.
    Yet eyes this cunning want to grace their art:
    They draw but what they see, know not the heart.

1 stelled] Q (steeld)

1 **in favour . . . stars** whose stars are favourable. *Stars* means 'A person's fortune, rank, or destiny, disposition or temperament, viewed as determined by the stars' (*OED* 2c).

3 **of** from

4 **Unlooked for** ignored, overlooked
joy in . . . most take my delight in my love, the object which I most honour. *Honour* shifts from 'public acclaim' (l. 2) to 'privately worship'.

6 **marigold** *OED* notes that 'The property possessed by the flower of opening when the sun shines (whence the L. name *solsequium*, F. *souci*) was often referred to by writers of the 16–17th c'.

7 **And in . . . burièd** (a) when left to themselves their glory is shut up inside them (as *marigolds* hide their petals in the dark); (b) their flaunting conceit, self-centred, dies with them. *Pride* means 'That of which any person or body of persons is proud' (*OED* 5a), and 'Magnificence, splendour' (*OED* 6a), both with strong overtones of disapproval.

8 **frown** i.e. when the sun ceases to shine or they lose the approval of their monarch

9 **painful** painstaking (*OED* 5); and, perhaps, 'full of pain'
might Q's 'worth' does not rhyme, unless *quite* in l. 11 is emended to 'forth'. Many editors adopt Malone's 'fight', which produces an alliteration too harsh even for this military context. Capell's 'might' is more likely to have been misread as

'worth', since an initial minim error on the 'm' could have led a scribe or compositor to mistake the remainder of the word.

10 **foiled** defeated

11 **razèd quite** completely erased

14 **remove** primarily 'shift place', hence 'be unfaithful' (as in 116.4); but 'remove' is often used in moral or medical contexts in this period: 'to relieve or free one from, some feeling, quality, condition, etc., esp. one of a bad or detrimental kind' (*OED* 4a). Cf. Donne, *Satire* 2.5–9 (*c.*1595–1600): 'Though poetry indeed be such a sin | As I think that brings dearths, and Spaniards in, | Though like the pestilence and old fashioned love, | Riddlingly it catch men; and doth *remove* | Never, till it be starved out'. This meaning qualifies the optimism of the couplet's primary sense ('I am happy in that I love in a manner which is not subject to change') by suggesting that the poet has the tenacity of a disease.

beloved . . . removed is a full rhyme in Shakespearian English. Q customarily elides where terminal 'ed' is not syllabic; here, however, it reads 'beloued' and 'remoued', so it is possible that the rhymes should be pronounced 'belovèd' and 'removèd' (but see *Venus* l. 366 n.). The compositor may have confused the participle 'beloved' with the noun 'belovèd' (i.e. the object of someone's devotion) and fleshed out 'removed' accordingly.

25

Let those who are in favour with their stars
Of public honour and proud titles boast,
Whilst I, whom fortune of such triumph bars,
Unlooked for joy in that I honour most.
Great princes' favourites their fair leaves spread   5
But as the marigold at the sun's eye,
And in themselves their pride lies burièd,
For at a frown they in their glory die.
The painful warrior famousèd for might
After a thousand victories, once foiled   10
Is from the book of honour razèd quite,
And all the rest forgot for which he toiled:
    Then happy I that love and am beloved
    Where I may not remove, nor be removed.

9 might] CAPELL; worth Q; fight MALONE (*conj.* Theobald) 11 razèd quite] Q (rased quite);
razèd forth COLLIER 1878 (*conj.* Theobald)

1 **vassalage** A vassal is 'In the feudal system, one holding lands from a superior on conditions of homage and allegiance' (*OED* I). The language of vassalage is often used in dedications in this period to suggest the complete subjection of the poet to the merits of the patron. Comparisons are often made between this sonnet and the dedication to *Lucrece*, often with a view to identifying the friend with the Earl of Southampton. A large body of convention unites the two works, however, rather than a specific individual. This is the first poem since 20 in which the addressee is specified as a male.

3 **ambassage** 'The message conveyed by an ambassador' (*OED* 2, citing this passage). The sonnet is the first to be presented as an epistle, although an epistolary distance between author and addressee may be inferred from *books* in 23.9.

4–8 **To witness . . . bestow** it 'to show my sense of obligation rather than to display my skill—and my obligation is so great that my weak invention could only diminish it, since I could never hope to find adequate words to express it. My only hope is that some benevolent wish of yours will give substance and livelihood to its naked poverty.'

10 **Points on** directs its influence towards me. Cf. *14*.6.
   fair aspect benign influence. *Aspect* (stressed aspèct) carries the astrological sense 'The relative positions of the heavenly bodies as they appear to an observer on the earth's surface at a given time, which has good or bad influence over human affairs' (*OED* 4).

11 **puts apparel on** The poet's inarticulate love is presented as a ragged vagrant, who is endowed with clothing by his star, or fortune. This continues the feudal imagery of the poem's opening: the poet is clad as a retainer in the livery of his

lord. Players were notionally the liveried servants of noblemen in the period after 1572.

12 **thy** Q reads 'their'. Sisson and Ingram and Redpath argue for its retention here. Since it is extremely hard to find an antecedent for the plural pronoun I follow Capell's emendation. The same error occurs at *27*.10, *35*.8, *37*.7, *43*.11, *45*.12, *46*.3, *46*.8, *46*.13, *46*.14, *69*.5, *70*.6, *128*.11, *128*.14, and may occur at *41*.11 and *85*.3. It is usually made by compositor B, although *35*.8 and *37*.7 were set by compositor A. Malone suggested that the copy contained two letter abbreviations for the personal pronoun in which 'they' and 'thy' looked alike. Another strong possibility must be that the copy for Q was revised, with 'your' being in some places overwritten with 'thy' (or vice versa), and then misread by the compositor as 'their'. Hand D in *Sir Thomas More*, usually accepted as Shakespeare's, writes 'their' at Addition 2 l. 136 and then corrects it to 'yo''. Compare the inconsistent pronouns in 24 above, which could be taken as evidence of partial revision, and *70*.1 n. The absence of such errors between *70* and *128* may indicate that the copy for that section was in a different hand.
   sweet respect benign regard or care, possibly pressing also for 'esteem' (Schmidt, 6).

14 The proverbial phrase 'He dares not show his head' was sometimes used of those who feared arrest for debt, which may underlie the use of the phrase here (Dent H246).
   prove try out, test. Vendler comments: 'The truest mark of infatuation is the pretense in the couplet that *prove me* rhymes with *love me*'. In all probability the phrases were a perfect rhyme in Shakespeare's English (Kökeritz, 244), as at *32*.13–14.

26

Lord of my love, to whom in vassalage
Thy merit hath my duty strongly knit,
To thee I send this written ambassage
To witness duty, not to show my wit;
Duty so great, which wit so poor as mine   5
May make seem bare, in wanting words to show it,
But that I hope some good conceit of thine
In thy soul's thought (all naked) will bestow it,
Till whatsoever star that guides my moving
Points on me graciously with fair aspect,   10
And puts apparel on my tattered loving
To show me worthy of thy sweet respect.
    Then may I dare to boast how I do love thee;
    Till then, not show my head where thou mayst prove me.

11 tattered] Q (tottered)   12 thy] MALONE (*conj.* Capell); their Q

2 **travail** Q's 'trauaill' can mean either 'travail' (labour) or 'travel'. Since the pun is worked so strongly here Q's form has been retained.

4 **expirèd** ended, with perhaps an allusion to the widespread view of sleep as a little death

5 **from far** far away from you

6 **Intend** (a) 'proceed on (a journey, etc.)' (*OED* 6); (b) 'have in the mind as a fixed purpose' (*OED* 18); (c) 'To turn one's thoughts to' (*OED* 12)

6 **zealous** is frequently used of enthusiastic religious devotion in the period, so it reinforces the devotedness of a *pilgrimage*.

8 **which** such as. It is a darkness so intense that it resembles the nothingness seen by the blind.

9 **Save** except
imaginary sight sight enabled by the

faculty of imagination. Imagination is the faculty 'whereby the soul beholdeth the likeness of bodily things when they be absent', *Batman upon Bartholomew* (1582), fo. 14ʳ.

10 **thy** Q reads 'their'. See 26.12 n.
shadow 'An unreal appearance; a delusive semblance or image; a vain and unsubstantial object of pursuit. Often contrasted with *substance*' (*OED* 6 *fig.* a). The *shadow*, dark though it is, has a mental brilliance since it is the image of the beloved, whose beauty makes even a *shadow* shine through the night.

11–12 **Which . . . beauteous** Cf. *Romeo* 1.5.44–5: 'It seems she hangs upon the cheek of night | As a rich jewel in an Ethiope's ear'.

14 **For . . . for** (a) on account of; (b) 'to the comfort of'

27

Weary with toil, I haste me to my bed,
The dear repose for limbs with travail tirèd,
But then begins a journey in my head
To work my mind, when body's work's expirèd.
For then my thoughts (from far, where I abide)   5
Intend a zealous pilgrimage to thee,
And keep my drooping eyelids open wide,
Looking on darkness which the blind do see;
Save that my soul's imaginary sight
Presents thy shadow to my sightless view,   10
Which like a jewel (hung in ghastly night)
Makes black Night beauteous, and her old face new.
   Lo, thus by day my limbs, by night my mind,
   For thee, and for myself, no quiet find.

2 travail] Q; travel GILDON 1714   tirèd] Q; tir'd MALONE 1790   4 expirèd] Q; expir'd
MALONE 1790   10 thy] MALONE (conj. Capell); their Q

1 **return in happy plight** come back (from the journey described in *27*) in a fortunate state

3 **day's oppression** the oppressive travel and labour of the daytime

5 **either's** each other's

6 **Do in . . . me** agree to form a partnership to oppress me

7 **The one . . . the other** are day and night respectively.

9 **to please him** Some editors mark this off by commas. Q's lack of punctuation doubles the flattery: both 'I tell the day, in order to please him, that . . .', and 'I tell the day that you are bright only to please him'.

11 **So flatter I** in a similar way I please (with a touch of deceit)
swart-complexioned dark-faced, with a suggestion of malignity

12 **twire** peep out; '*intr.* To look narrowly or covertly; to peer; to peep. Also *fig.* of a light, etc'. (*OED* 1; first cited usage)
gild'st the even give a glitter to the evening. Q reads 'guil'st th' eauen'. This could be modernized as 'guilest th' heaven', meaning 'beguile or charm the skies'. 'Gild'st' makes the friend's presence a more obvious substitute for the stars. For a similar moment where Shakespeare seems to have collapsed together guile and gilding see *Lucrece* l. 1544 and n.

14 **length** Many editors emend to 'strength'. As Kerrigan notes, this makes the couplet excessively predictable. The couplet works by using repetition to evoke endless labour (*day . . . daily*), whilst offsetting the dangerously mimetic tedium so generated by a daring interchange of length and intensity.

28

How can I then return in happy plight,
That am debarred the benefit of rest,
When day's oppression is not eased by night,
But day by night and night by day oppressed?
And each (though enemies to either's reign)   5
Do in consent shake hands to torture me,
The one by toil, the other to complain
How far I toil, still farther off from thee.
I tell the day to please him thou art bright,
And dost him grace when clouds do blot the heaven;   10
So flatter I the swart-complexioned night,
When sparkling stars twire not thou gild'st the even.
  But day doth daily draw my sorrows longer,
  And night doth nightly make grief's length seem stronger.

5 either's] Q (ethers); others BENSON; other's GILDON 1714   12 gild'st the even] MALONE; guil st th'eauen Q   13–14 longer . . . length . . . stronger] Q; longer . . . strength . . . stronger CAPELL; stronger . . . length . . . longer *conj.* Capell in Malone

This and the following sonnet (linked in a cycle of woe by their opening word) make use of the conventions of complaint: the lover is isolated and apparently deprived of all means of comfort until thoughts of the friend dispel his gloom.

1 **in disgrace** out of favour
Fortune is capitalized as in Q.
men's eyes the opinions of the many

3 **bootless** fruitless, vain

5 **one more rich in hope** (a) someone with better prospects of material success; (b) someone blessed by having a greater capacity for hope

6 **Featured** having his (beautiful) looks
like him, like him The repetition of the end of one clause at the start of the next (*anadiplosis*) locks the poet into his desire to resemble others.

7 **scope** mental range (*OED* s.v. 'scope' *n.*[2] 6a; first cited usage); perhaps also 'The subject, theme, argument chosen for treatment' (*OED* 3a); and 'opportunity or liberty to act' (*OED* 7a); hence the poet envies both the potential skill ('art') and freedom of others as well as their actual range of achievement.

10 **Haply** by chance (and also 'happily')

11 **(Like . . . arising)** The parentheses are placed as in Q. Many editors extend them to include *From sullen earth* on the grounds that it is a lark rather than an abstract *state* which arises from the *sullen* (i.e. heavy, dark, melancholy) earth. *Earth*, however, can convey the sense of 'mortal nature' in this period. As punctuated here the phrase suggests a sudden uplifting of the spirit from its clayey lodging, which none the less still retains its grip on the poet: he sings hymns at heaven's gate, but *from* a position on earth.

12 **sings** The sound of the word is anticipated in 'despi*sing*' and 'ari*sing*', making the poem at this point 'fairly carol' (Vendler).

14 **kings** Q does not use possessive apostrophes, so its form 'kings' also encompasses the possessive plural 'kings''.

29

When in disgrace with Fortune and men's eyes
I all alone beweep my outcast state,
And trouble deaf heaven with my bootless cries,
And look upon myself and curse my fate,
Wishing me like to one more rich in hope,   5
Featured like him, like him with friends possessed,
Desiring this man's art, and that man's scope,
With what I most enjoy contented least;
Yet in these thoughts myself almost despising,
Haply I think on thee, and then my state   10
(Like to the lark at break of day arising)
From sullen ëarth sings hymns at heaven's gate.
    For thy sweet love remembered such wealth brings
    That then I scorn to change my state with kings.

11–12 (Like . . . arising) . . . earth] Q: (~ . . . ~ ~) MALONE; ~ . . . ~ ~, GILDON 1714   13
remembered] Q (remembred)   14 kings] Q; kings' OXFORD (*conf.* Wells)

1 **When** The repetition of the first word of the previous sonnet takes us back to the gloomy isolation evoked at its opening, cancelling the joyous leap of the *lark at break of day arising* of *29*.11. It introduces the figure of *anamnesis*, 'a form of speech by which the speaker calling to remembrance matters past, doth make recital of them. Sometimes *matters of sorrow*', Peacham (1593), 76.

sessions 'A continuous series of sittings or meetings of a court' (*OED* 3a). Sonnets rooted in legal imagery were common, as in the anonymous *Zepheria*, Canzon 20: 'How often hath my pen, mine heart's solicitor | Instructed thee in breviate of my case?' The style, always tending to self-parody, was parodied in the *Gulling Sonnets* (*c.*1594) of Sir John Davies, especially 7.1–2: 'Into the Middle Temple of my heart | The wanton Cupid did himself admit . . .'. The transformation of the topos here into the gloomy inner meditation of the poet depends partly on the complaint-based solitude evoked in Sonnets *26*–*9*, and partly on the delicate way in which the literal scene of a courtroom is subordinated to the inner landscape of lament.

2 **summon** continues the precise legal terminology ('To cite by authority to attend at a place named, *esp.* to appear before a court or judge to answer a charge or to give evidence' (*OED* 2)), but not obtrusively, allowing for a more neutral sense, 'call to mind'.

remembrance of things past echoes Wisdom 11: 10: 'For their grief was double with mourning, and the remembrance of things past'.

4 **And with . . . waste** and I waste my precious time freshly bewailing past sorrows. Modernization delimits the possible senses of Q's 'And with old woes new waile my deare times waste', in which both 'waile' and 'waste' could function as either noun or verb, and in which either 'woes' or 'times' could be a possessive form. The line could be equally well be modernized as 'And with old woes' new wail (noun) my dear times waste (verb)':

actions and nouns fuse in the continuing waste of sorrow. Equally possible is 'times'' rather than 'time's'. *Dear* functions as both 'costly' (taken with *waste*) and 'beloved' (taken with *time's*). *Waste* means both 'destruction' and 'pointless expenditure'.

5, 9 **Then can** The repeated phrase establishes the presence of ancient and ineradicable grief: it means both 'at those times I am able', but it also embeds the speaker in re-enactment of the past through the archaic use of *can* to mean 'begin' (*OED* n. 2, beloved of Spenser, and found in *L.L.L.* 4.3.104).

6 **dateless** 'having no determined time of expiry'; hence 'endless'

7 **cancelled** 'Of legal documents, deeds, etc.: To annul, render void or invalid by striking across' (*OED* 1a). A presiding metaphor in this sonnet is that of a debt which has been discharged, but which retains its effect.

8 **sight** (a) things once seen; (b) sighs (archaic spelling)

9 **fore-gone** in the past (with perhaps a knowingly masochistic acknowledgement that it is hard to forgo, or renounce, grieving)

10 **heavily** sadly
tell o'er (a) relate through again; (b) sum up (anticipating *account* in the next line)

11 **fore-bemoanèd** already lamented. This is the only cited instance in *OED*.

13 **(dear friend)** This is the first time the addressee of the sonnets is called 'friend'. The word is often used of lovers or mistresses in erotic writing from the period (see *104*.1 n.). *Dear* carries a suggestion of costliness, hinting that the friend is at once a source of restoration and of loss.

14 **losses are restored** the accounts are made good; friends lost in the past come back, the waste of time is rectified. *Restored* means 'to make return or restitution of (anything previously taken away or lost)' (*OED* 1), and the financial sense is prominent given its conjunction with *pay* and *account*.

30

When to the sessions of sweet silent thought
I summon up remembrance of things past,
I sigh the lack of many a thing I sought,
And with old woes new wail my dear time's waste;
Then can I drown an eye (unused to flow)   5
For precious friends hid in death's dateless night,
And weep afresh love's long-since-cancelled woe,
And moan th' expense of many a vanished sight;
Then can I grieve at grievances fore-gone,
And heavily from woe to woe tell o'er   10
The sad account of fore-bemoanèd moan,
Which I new pay as if not paid before.
    But if the while I think on thee (dear friend)
    All losses are restored, and sorrows end.

8 sight] Q; sigh *conj.* Malone

1 **endearèd with** (a) loved by; (b) 'rendered more costly by' (*OED* 2), playing on the familiar conceit whereby a lover acquires the heart of the beloved. The sonnet continues from 30 the metaphors of past debts made good through the friend. The dominant mood here is of a triumph over death through the friend, but there is also a faint suggestion (anticipating the jealousies later in the sequence) that the poet has lost all his former lovers and thinks they are dead because they have switched their affections to the friend.

3 **loving parts** all the attributes which make people love

5 **many** a is pronounced as two syllables.
obsequious 'Through association with obsequy²: Dutiful in performing funeral obsequies or manifesting regard for the dead; proper to obsequies' (*OED* 1b). Three syllables.

7 **interest** continues the financial conceit of 'endearèd'; hence (a) 'Right or title to a share in something' (*OED* 1c); (b) return owing to those who lend capital. Cf. *Richard III* 2.2.47–8: 'Ah, so much interest have I in thy sorrow | As I had title in thy noble husband.'

8 **there** i.e. in your bosom. Most editors follow Gildon's emendation to 'thee', on the grounds that it is easy to misread 'thee' as 'there', and that 'there' is 'comparatively flat' (G. B. Evans). Q makes good sense, however. The referent of 'there' is clearly the friend's bosom, which in Q is referred to in each of the first two quatrains as 'there' (cf. l. 3). This prepares for the dramatic shift to *Thou* at the start of the third quatrain.

9 **live** is a dramatic surprise: after *grave* and *buried* one expects 'lie'. Whilst that deadly word is cancelled out, it also remains at the back of the reader's mind, hinting that there is something at once resurrective and vampiric in the way the beloved makes life from buried former loves.

10 **trophies** In Roman triumphs the arms of the conquered are hung from a tree as 'trophies'. So *OED* 1: 'A structure erected (originally on the field of battle, later in any public place) as a memorial of a victory in war, consisting of arms or other spoils taken from the enemy, hung upon a tree, pillar, etc. and dedicated to some divinity'.

11 **all their parts of me** all of me; the qualities and physical elements of me which they had won in the battle of love

12 **That** that which, i.e. the parts of the poet given by former lovers to the friend

13–14 **Their . . . me** The friend is presented as final embodiment of all the remembered images of the poet's former lovers. He consequently enjoys possession of all the parts of the poet which his former lovers had obtained, and so possesses the poet completely.

31

Thy bosom is endearèd with all hearts
Which I by lacking have supposèd dead,
And there reigns Love and all Love's loving parts,
And all those friends which I thought burièd.
How many a holy and obsequious tear   5
Hath dear religious love stol'n from mine eye,
As interest of the dead, which now appear
But things removed that hidden in there lie?
Thou art the grave where buried love doth live,
Hung with the trophies of my lovers gone,   10
Who all their parts of me to thee did give;
That due of many, now is thine alone.
   Their images I loved I view in thee,
   And thou (all they) hast all the all of me.

8 there] *q*; thee GILDON

The death of former lovers imagined in the previous poem is now extended to include the death of the poet too. Verse is here no longer intrinsically the agent of immortality: it needs to be read affectionately by its addressee in order to have permanent value. A copy of the poem, which dates from *c*.1650, exists in Folger MS V.a.162, fo. 26ʳ.

1 **well-contented day** 'the day when I am content to die'. 'Day' can refer to a point at which a debt becomes due (*OED* 12), a sense active here through the idea of death as the moment when one pays one's last debt to nature. 'Content' too can mean 'To satisfy (a person) by full payment' (*OED* 4).

3 **by fortune** by chance
resurvey is unusual in the sense 'to read again'. It may imply deliberative reading, as in Shakespeare's only other usage: 'I have but with a cursitory eye | O'erglanced the articles. Pleaseth your grace | To appoint some of your council presently | To sit with us once more, with better heed | To re-survey them', *Henry V* 5.2.77–8.

4 **These poor ... lover**, Q's punctuation 'resurvey: | These poore rude lines of thy deceased Louer' is defended by William Empson, *Seven Types of Ambiguity* rev. edn. (1953), 51, on the grounds that 'Line 4 is isolated between colons, carries the whole weight of the pathos'; it is as if the Sonnet 'was making a quotation from a tombstone'.

5 **the bett'ring of the time** the superior productions of the present. *OED* cites this passage to support the definition 2: 'The

process of becoming better; improvement, progress in a right direction', which seems less likely.

6 **outstripped** is a vogue-word in the 1590s, meaning 'To excel, surpass, get ahead of, or leave behind, in any kind of competition, or in any respect in which things may be compared' (*OED* 2).

7 **Reserve** keep, preserve. Compare 85.3, where the same word is used of treasured writings.

8 **the height** the high achievement
happier more fortunate

9 **vouchsafe me but** condescend to grant me just this one

10–14 'Had ... love.' Q does not mark direct speech by quotation marks. This imagined future voice of the friend would have seemed extraordinarily prophetic to many readers in 1609, who were reading a sequence which both harked back to and *outstripped* the vogue for sonnet sequences in the 1590s.

11 **a dearer birth than this** (a) a better poem than this sonnet; (b) a poem of richer, more aristocratic lineage

12 **To march ... equipage** worthy of joining a company of better poets. 'Equipage' here is said by *OED* to mean (2) 'The state or condition of being equipped; equipment'. It is more likely to anticipate the slightly later sense (*OED* 9): 'Formal state or order; ceremonious display; the "style" of a domestic establishment, etc.'. Had the poet lived later he would have been capable of producing poems of a *dearer birth*, which could hold their own in the company of the higher born.

13 **better prove** turn out now to be better

32

If thou survive my well-contented day,
When that churl Death my bones with dust shall cover,
And shalt by fortune once more resurvey
These poor, rude lines of thy deceasèd lover,
Compare them with the bett'ring of the time,   5
And, though they be outstripped by every pen,
Reserve them for my love, not for their rhyme,
Exceeded by the height of happier men.
O then vouchsafe me but this loving thought:
'Had my friend's Muse grown with this growing age,   10
A dearer birth than this his love had brought,
To march in ranks of better equipage:
    But since he died, and poets better prove,
    Theirs for their style I'll read, his for his love.'

8 height, Q; high FOL5   10–14 'Had . . . love.'] MALONE (*italics*); ~ . . . ~., Q 11 birth] Q; love FOL5

1 **Full** very

2 **Flatter . . . eye** There is a paradox in a
sovereign flattering his subordinates; the
idea is that the morning, like a gracious
monarch, elevates the mountains by
deigning to gaze at them.

4 **Gilding . . . alchemy** The sun is also pre-
sented as an alchemist, capable of trans-
muting base metals to gold, in *K. John*
3.1.3–6: 'To solemnize this day, the glori-
ous sun | Stays in his course and plays the
alchemist, | Turning with splendour of
his precious eye | The meagre cloddy
earth to glittering gold.' See also *Venus* ll.
856–8.

5 **Anon** soon

basest (a) lowest born; (b) the meanest of
substance; (c) possibly 'darkest' (*OED* 5:
the cited instances are all from medical
contexts, and the sense is not recorded in
Schmidt. Kerrigan cites 'the base Indian'
from *Othello* 5.2.356 to support the sense,
but the epithet there may well not refer to
colour).

5–6 **Anon . . . face** The marked reminiscence
of Prince Harry in *1 Henry IV* (*c.* 1598), the
heir to the throne who wishes tempo-
rarily to mix with low-born companions,
supports other evidence which places
Sonnets 1–60 in the mid-to-late 1590s
(see Introduction, pp. 104–5): *1 Henry IV*
1.2.194–200: 'Yet herein will I imitate the
sun, | Who doth permit the base conta-
gious clouds | To smother up his beauty
from the world, | That when he please
again to be himself, | Being wanted he
may be more wondered at | By breaking
through the foul and ugly mists | Of
vapours that did seem to strangle him'. In
both passages the sun is presented as an
active agent which allows the clouds to
dull its glitter.

6 **rack** 'Clouds, or a mass of cloud, driven
before the wind in the upper air' (*OED*

3a); with a play on 'wrack', or 'ignomin-
ious destruction'

7 **forlorn** is stressed on the first syllable.

11 **out alack** is an exclamation of despair.
Some editors make the two words into
separate exclamations or add punctua-
tion between them, but this runs against
the majority of usages in early modern
literature.

12 **region cloud** 'the clouds of the air'.
'Region' can mean 'A separate part or
division of the world or universe, as the
air, heaven, etc.' (*OED* 3a), as it does in
Hamlet 2.2.488–9: 'anon the dreadful
thunder | Doth rend the region'. The
usage may be archaic, since the *Hamlet*
passage is from the player's archaizing
speech on Hecuba. Here it is used in the
uninflected genitive form.

14 **Suns . . . staineth** 'Mortal rulers may per-
fectly well pollute their region when the
heavenly sun does so too.' *Stain* may
mean physically to pollute with some-
thing, or morally to corrupt, and can
also be used 'Of the sun, etc.: To deprive
(feebler luminaries) of their lustre. Also
fig. of a person or thing: To throw into
the shade by superior beauty or excel-
lence; to eclipse' (*OED* 1b). The context
implies the unparalleled sense 'allow
others to dim *their* brightness'. The inno-
cent meteorological accidents that cover
the sun at the start of the poem, though,
have turned into moral contaminations,
in which the sun itself (and by impli-
cation the friend) plays its part. Q's 'stain-
teh', combined with the repetition of
'stain', may indicate textual corruption,
although the repetition may serve to
heighten the pressure put on the word
by the poet's desire not to say explic-
itly that the presence of clouds darkening
the lover's brightness is the friend's
fault.

33

Full many a glorious morning have I seen
Flatter the mountain tops with sovereign eye,
Kissing with golden face the meadows green,
Gilding pale streams with heavenly alchemy,
Anon permit the basest clouds to ride   5
With ugly rack on his celestial face,
And from the forlorn world his visage hide,
Stealing unseen to west with this disgrace:
Even so my sun one early morn did shine
With all triumphant splendour on my brow;   10
But out alack, he was but one hour mine,
The region cloud hath masked him from me now.
   Yet him for this my love no whit disdaineth:
   Suns of the world may stain, when heaven's sun staineth.

8 west] Q; rest *conj.* Steevens in Malone 11 But out alack,] Q; ~, ~, ~! GILDON 1714; ~~!~!
KNIGHT; ~, ~, ~! DOWDEN; out alas FOL4 14 staineth] BENSON; stainteh Q

447

1–2 **Why . . . cloak** Cf. 'Although the sun shines, leave not thy cloak at home' (Dent S968). A *cloak* is the sixteenth-century equivalent of an overcoat.

3 **base clouds** See 33.5 n. Here the sun does not collude with the clouds as it does in 33 but is reluctant to allow his glory to be obscured.

4 **brav'ry** finery, fineness. *O'ertake* hints at a literal scenario in which a group of retainers who surround a lord pass by the poet, keeping him from view and fouling his journey.

7 **salve** 'A healing ointment for application to wounds or sores' (*OED* 1a). The sun simply dries the poet's tears rather than curing their cause. The image of the all-powerful sun is broken off before the conclusion of the octave and is supplanted by a vocabulary of wounds and sin, as though it is impossible to sustain the laudatory image of the friend with which the poem began, and as though the friend remains on the surface level, drying tears as the sun dries the rain, rather than recognizing the full extent of the wrong he has committed.

8 **disgrace** suggests a spiritual rather than a material hurt. The *disgrace* concerned could be the ignominy suffered by the poet or the ungracious conduct of the friend, or both.

9 **shame . . . physic** 'nor can your public repentance cure my pain'. *Grief* means both 'a bodily injury or ailment . . . a dis-

ease, sickness' (*OED* 5a) and 'mental pain, distress, or sorrow' (*OED* 7a).

12 **cross** Q's 'loss' is probably the result of eyeskip by the compositor. To 'bear one's cross' is a set phrase meaning 'to endure one's allotted suffering patiently'. It derives from Matthew 10: 38: 'And he that taketh not his cross, and followeth after me, is not worthy of me.'

13 **Ah** The exclamation occurs at *67.1, 90.5, 104.9*. Only here is it at the start of the couplet. It always expresses ruefully resistant yielding to the inevitable.

pearl was believed to have medicinal properties, but the suggestion that the lover is buying forgiveness with tokens of value is strong here. Throughout the poem the friend is responding to the poet's complaint, first by drying his tears and then finally by weeping. The tears at the end do mark a kind of recognition of the friend's guilt, since they show that he is willing to identify himself not just with the sovereign sun, but also with the clouds that produce rain (or tears).

sheds Q's 'sheeds' is likely to reflect contemporary (Warwickshire) pronunciation. For a similar rhyme, see *Lucrece* l. 1549.

14 **rich** valuable

ransom 'To atone or pay for, to expiate' (*OED* 1d); with perhaps a suggestion that the tears *merely* make financial restitution rather than full atonement for the wrong

34

Why didst thou promise such a beauteous day,
And make me travel forth without my cloak,
To let base clouds o'ertake me in my way,
Hiding thy brav'ry in their rotten smoke?
'Tis not enough that through the cloud thou break   5
To dry the rain on my storm-beaten face,
For no man well of such a salve can speak
That heals the wound and cures not the disgrace;
Nor can thy shame give physic to my grief:
Though thou repent, yet I have still the loss.   10
Th' offender's sorrow lends but weak relief
To him that bears the strong offence's cross.
   Ah, but those tears are pearl which thy love sheds,
   And they are rich, and ransom all ill deeds.

2 travel] Q (trauaile)   12 cross] MALONE (*conj.* Capell); losse Q   13 sheds] Q (sheeds)

1 **No more** no longer

2 **Roses have thorns** Compare the proverb
'No rose without a thorn' (Dent R182).
mud strongly pejorative, used in *OED*
sense 2 *fig.* a, 'As a type of what is
worthless or polluting'. Compare *Lucrece*
l. 577.

3 **stain** obscure. See 33.14 n.

4 **canker** 'A caterpillar, or any insect larva,
which destroys the buds and leaves of
plants; a canker-worm' (*OED* 4), here
used as a type of that which defiles beau-
ty. 'The canker soonest eats the fairest
rose' (Dent C56).

5 **All men make faults** turns the passive
conception of fallibility embedded in the
proverb 'Every man has his faults' (Dent
M126) into an active principle. To 'make
fault' is a standard idiom for 'to be in the
wrong', as in *Antony* 2.5.74: 'I have made
no fault.'
even 'Euen' occurs 22 times in the Son-
nets. It is disyllabic only four times (here,
39.5, 41.11, and 48.13). These cases all
occur in the group *1–60*, which was prob-
ably composed in the mid-to-late 1590s,
and they all mark a very strong rhetorical
emphasis.

5 **in this** (a) by doing this, that is . . . ; (b) in
this poem

6 **Authorizing . . . compare** 'giving your sin
a validity and authority through making
comparisons', like those in ll. 1–4. *Autho-
rizing* is stressed on the second syllable. A
rose cannot be blamed for having thorns,
nor can silver fountains be blamed for
their mud, so the comparisons make the
addressee's sins appear to be involuntary.
This line makes implicit the hints in 33
and 34 that the poet is fully aware that he
is vainly seeking to exonerate the friend by
comparing him to natural phenomena
such as the sun.

7 **salving . . . amiss** 'in curing your fault'.
To 'salve' may imply palliation rather
than cure, as it may mean 'To anoint
(a wound, wounded part) with salve or
healing unguent' (*OED* 1a). Compare
34.7.

8 **Excusing . . . are** 'providing your sins with
excuses which are even greater than the
sins themselves require'. Q reads 'their'
twice (see collation). For the 'their' for
'thy' error, see 26.12 n. Some editors read
'thy' and 'their', and refer 'their' back to
the inanimate objects of the first quat-
rain: so, 'Exculpating your sins to a
greater extent than the sins of inanimate
objects (cankers in roses and so on)
extend', or to *all men*. G. B. Evans suggests
emending 'Excusing' to 'Accusing' as
well as emending both 'their's to 'thy's.
This makes the line easy to gloss ('con-
demning your sins more than they
deserve'), but misses the point of the
poem, which is that the poet is corrupting
himself, and by extension his art, in his
excessive efforts to exculpate his friend.

9 **For to . . . sense** I provide arguments
to support your fleshly failing. 'Sense'
means 'the rational faculties' (*OED* 10b),
but its usage here is deliberately con-
taminated by 'The faculties of corporeal
sensation considered as channels for
gratifying the desire for pleasure and the
lusts of the flesh' (*OED* 4a). A sweet
flavour of 'incense' may waft from the
phrase.

10 **Thy adverse . . . advocate** 'your opponent,
who should be pleading against you, is in
fact pleading for you'. *Party, advocate,
plea,* and *commence* evoke a courtroom
scene.

13 **accessary** 'In *Law*: He who is not the chief
actor in the offence, nor present at its per-
formance, but in some way concerned
therein, either before or after the fact
committed' (*OED* 1). Stressed on the first
syllable. The poet is an *accessary* after the
fact through his efforts to exculpate the
lover.

14 **sourly** 'churlishly (in action), bitterly (in
effect)' (Kerrigan). The paradox depends
on a legal distinction between theft and
robbery. A *thief* steals furtively, and so
might be *sweet*; robbery, however, is the
open and forcible taking of property
which belongs to another.

35

No more be grieved at that which thou hast done:
Roses have thorns, and silver fountains mud,
Clouds and eclipses stain both moon and sun,
And loathsome canker lives in sweetest bud.
All men make faults, and even I in this,   5
Authorizing thy trespass with compare,
Myself corrupting salving thy amiss,
Excusing thy sins more than thy sins are:
For to thy sensual fault I bring in sense—
Thy adverse party is thy advocate—   10
And 'gainst myself a lawful plea commence:
Such civil war is in my love and hate
     That I an accessary needs must be
     To that sweet thief which sourly robs from me.

8 thy . . . thy] MALONE (conj. Capell); their . . . their Q; thy . . . their WYNDHAM; their . . . thy
BULLEN; thee . . . thy conj. Beeching; these . . . these DUNCAN-JONES   9–10 in sense— . . .
advocate—] MALONE (brackets); in sence, . . . Aduocate, Q; Incense, . . . Advocate GILDON 1714

1 **Let me confess** Coming as it does immediately after the previous sonnet's recognition that the poet's techniques of praise have been self-deceiving, this phrase might be taken as a recognition that the love must end. It may also introduce a rhetorical supposition, rather than a reluctant acceptance. So 'Suppose I do recognise . . .' more than 'I must acknowledge . . .'.

twain 'two separate people'. *OED* cites this as the first instance of 3a: 'disunited, estranged, at variance', as also in *Troilus* 3 1.98–9: 'No, she'll none of him. They two are twain', and Drayton's *Idea* (1619) 9.9–10: 'Thus talking idly in this Bedlam fit. | Reason and I (you must conceive) are twain'.

3 **So . . . blots** 'In those circumstances the moral stains that already reside chiefly in me will be borne exclusively by me without your help.' *Blots* means 'a moral stain; a disgrace, fault, blemish' (*OED* 2 *fig.* a); possibly also suggesting tears. Q's punctuation (followed here) allows *Without thy help* to point backwards to *with me remain* as well as forwards. This creates the impression that separation will simply reinforce what is already the case, that the poet bears the weight of shame.

5 **one respect** 'one mutual regard'. In logical contexts 'respect' can be used to suggest that without a relationship to each other two entities do not exist, which is a

piquant suggestion here. Also note *OED* 16a: 'Deferential regard or esteem felt or shown towards a person or thing', a sense which is developed in the couplet.

6 **separable spite** 'a malicious force which parts us'. *OED* cites only this passage s.v. 'separable' 2: '? Capable of separating'. The usage derives from Shakespeare's habit of reversing adjective and abstract noun, as in *composèd wonder* (59.10).

7–8 **Which . . . delight** 'which, although it does not affect the unity of our love for each other, does cause us to spend hours apart'. *Love* in l. 7 refers to the emotion; in l. 8 it suggests physical proximity.

9–10 **I may . . . shame** 'I am permanently prevented from greeting you in public, in case my publicly recognized guilt should adversely affect your reputation.' *Acknowledge* 'To recognize (one) to be what he claims; to own the claims or authority of' (*OED* 2b).

11–12 **Nor thou . . . name** 'nor can you grace me with a public show of recognition, without accordingly detracting from the status of your name'

13–14 **But . . . report** 'But do not lessen your honour by acknowledging me: I love in such a way that, since you are mine, your reputation is also my reputation', hence if the friend diminishes his own honourable standing he also detracts from that of the poet. This couplet is duplicated in 96.13–14, q.v.

36

Let me confess that we two must be twain,
Although our undivided loves are one:
So shall those blots that do with me remain,
Without thy help by me be borne alone.
In our two loves there is but one respect,   5
Though in our lives a separable spite,
Which, though it alter not love's sole effect,
Yet doth it steal sweet hours from love's delight.
I may not evermore acknowledge thee,
Lest my bewailèd guilt should do thee shame,   10
Nor thou with public kindness honour me,
Unless thou take that honour from thy name:
   But do not so; I love thee in such sort
   As thou being mine, mine is thy good report.

Sonnets 37 and 38 appear to disrupt a sequence of poems on separation and estrangement which is resumed in 39. They may, as Vendler (191) suggests, be earlier work inserted slightly awkwardly into the sequence. Given that 36 ends with a couplet that is repeated in 96 there may well have been some irregularity in the MS at this point. However, these two poems do continue the wounded selflessness of the end of 36, in which the poet takes a surrogate delight in the successes of the friend, and they prepare for the suggestion in 39 that praise of the friend is in fact self-praise.

3 **made lame . . . spite** To be *made lame* by Fortune is to suffer material disadvantages as a result of chance misfortunes, as in *Lear* (Quarto) Scene 20.213: 'A most poor man made lame by fortune's blows'. Many earlier editors combined this passage with 89.3 to make Shakespeare lame indeed, even after Malone's sage words in 1790: 'If the words are to be understood literally we must then suppose that . . . [he] was also *poor* and *despised*, for neither of which suppositions there is the smallest ground'.

4 **of** from

5 **wit** intelligence

7 **Entitled . . . sit** with due entitlement sit like kings among your excellent qualities.

This is the easiest solution to a crux which has generated more than its due of commentary. Q reads 'Intitled in their parts, do crowned sit'. Some editors follow Q's 'their', and interpret 'entitled by their own good qualities'. Others, following a less than lucid note by Wyndham, find an allusion to heraldry in which the *parts* each find their respective places in an escutcheon. On the their/thy error, see 26.12 n.

8 **I make . . . store** 'like a gardener I graft my love on to the rich supply of your virtues, from which it draws life and nourishment'

10 **Whilst . . . give** 'while the image of your virtues gives body and sustenance to my poverty'. *Shadow* may also mean 'protective shade'. Since *shadow* is normally the subsidiary product of a *substance* the line paradoxically suggests that the mere image of the friend's virtues can give life to the poet. The suggested emendation of 'this' to 'thy' in the Bodley-Caldecott copy appears to be in a nineteenth-century hand.

11 **abundance** (a) store (of qualities); (b) generosity

12 **part** mere portion

13 **Look what** whatever

14 **This . . . me** Since the poet is grafted onto the *store* of the friend, then any increase in it will also benefit him.

37

As a decrepit father takes delight
To see his active child do deeds of youth,
So I, made lame by Fortune's dearest spite,
Take all my comfort of thy worth and truth.
For whether beauty, birth, or wealth, or wit,   5
Or any of these all, or all, or more,
Entitled in thy parts do crownèd sit,
I make my love engrafted to this store.
So then I am not lame, poor, nor despised,
Whilst that this shadow doth such substance give   10
That I in thy abundance am sufficed,
And by a part of all thy glory live.
　　Look what is best, that best I wish in thee;
　　This wish I have, then ten times happy me.

7 thy] MALONE (*conj.* Capell); their Q　10 this] Q; thy *MS conj. in Bodley-Caldecott*

1 **want . . . invent** lack subject matter to write about. The context pushes *invent* away from its usual sense in sixteenth-century rhetoric, 'to find out (pre-existing) matter for a poem' (corresponding to the Latin *inventio*), to the emergent sense, 'To compose as a work of imagination or literary art' (*OED* 1b).

3 **argument** 'subject for a poem' (*OED* 6), as in Prince Harry's dry comment to Falstaff (*1 Henry IV* 2.5.284–5): 'and the argument shall be thy running away'.

4 **vulgar paper** writing open to the public view; perhaps 'printed poem'. See 17.9 n.
rehearse repeat

6 **stand against thy sight** The standard gloss 'meets your eye' is too flat. To *stand against* usually means in Shakespeare 'to oppose, to offer resistance' (Schmidt, 7a; *OED* 67); hence perhaps 'withstand the rigour of your scrutiny'.

7 **dumb** silent, inarticulate, dull-spirited

8 **invention** 'the faculty for finding out matter for a poem' (*OED* 1d): 'Rhet. The finding out or selection of topics to be treated, or arguments to be used'.
thou . . . light The friend is so remarkable that he illuminates and ignites the powers of composition.

9 **tenth Muse** Drayton also added his love to the orthodox total of nine muses (as well as to the nine worthies and the nine orders of angels) in *Idea's Mirror* (1594), sonnet 8. The reason for this may well be that although there is a muse for lyric love poetry (Erato) there is no muse for panegyric. The thought was near-proverbial (Dent T91.1).

10 **rhymers** is said with a sneer. It is often opposed to 'poet' in the period and means 'mere rhymester'.

11 **bring forth** The association of poetic composition and birth is also common in the period, as in 76.8.

12 **Eternal numbers** everlasting verses
outlive long date which will endure even beyond the longest possible term of expiry

13 **curious** 'difficult to satisfy; particular; nice, fastidious' (*OED* 2)

14 **pain** trouble; but the whole phrase recalls 36.4, which releases the sense 'physical anguish'
thine . . . praise (a) you, as the person who inspires my verse, shall deserve all the acclaim; (b) the poems will relate your praises.

38

How can my Muse want subject to invent,
While thou dost breathe, that pour'st into my verse
Thine own sweet argument, too excellent
For every vulgar paper to rehearse?
O give thyself the thanks if aught in me   5
Worthy perusal stand against thy sight,
For who's so dumb that cannot write to thee,
When thou thyself dost give invention light?
Be thou the tenth Muse, ten times more in worth
Than those old nine which rhymers invocate;   10
And he that calls on thee, let him bring forth
Eternal numbers to outlive long date.
   If my slight Muse do please these curious days,
   The pain be mine, but thine shall be the praise.

This poem appears to continue the argument of 36, on which see the headnote to 37. It attempts to find a justification for separation on the grounds that it enables the poet to praise the friend without seeming also to praise himself. It plays on the proverbial phrase 'A friend is one's second self' (Dent F696), which was frequently cited in philosophical discussions of friendship: 'a friend is a second self, and that whosoever would take upon him this title in regard of another, he must transform himself into his nature whom he purposeth to love', Pierre de la Primaudaye, *The French Academy*, trans. Thomas Bowles (1589), 131.

1 **worth** (a) value; (b) merit; (c) value to me **manners** 'Good "manners", customs, or way of living' (*OED* 3d). The first two lines mean 'How can I praise you with due modesty when you are both the larger and the better part of me?'

3–4 **What can . . . thee?** 'How can my own praise add to what is myself, and what else is it to praise you than to praise myself?' Underlying these lines is an assumption that lover and beloved are one flesh, which may have its roots in Ephesians 5: 28–31, 'He that loveth his wife loveth himself: for no man ever yet hated his own flesh, but nourisheth and cherisheth it, even as the Lord the Church', a passage which figures prominently in the Solemnization of Matrimony in the Book of Common Prayer.

5 **Even for this . . . divided** 'for this reason let us live apart'. *Divided* has strong pejorative associations in Shakespeare, as in *OED* 1a: 'Split, cut, or broken into pieces; incomplete, imperfect', 3: 'Separated in opinion or interest; discordant, at variance; split into parties or factions', and *Richard III* 1.4.233: 'He little thought of this divided friendship'. These bitter associations are compounded by the emphatic disyllabic use of 'even' (on which see

35.5 n.), which here occurs, uniquely in the Sonnets, at the start of the line, forcing a trochaic inverted first foot.

6 **lose name of single one** (a) lose the reputation of being a union of two people into one; (b) stop being open to description as a single love, rather than two

8 **That due . . . alone** 'return to your exclusive ownership the praise that we have hitherto shared'. In other words if the poet and the friend separate the poet will then be able to praise the friend as he deserves without being accused of self-flattery.

10 **sour** bitter. The word (and its derivate adverb) is prominent at this stage in the sequence: the only other occurrences are at 35.14 and 41.8.

11 **entertain the time** while away the time. Cf. *Lucrece* l. 1361.

12 **Which time . . . deceive** 'You, absence, beguilingly charm away that time and those thoughts.' Many editors follow Malone in emending *dost* to 'doth', which takes *love* as its subject ('love, which sweetly beguiles time and thoughts'). Others favour Capell's 'do', which either takes *time and thoughts* as its subject and *which* as a relative pronoun ('all of which time and thoughts sweetly beguile'), or else takes *thoughts of love* as its subject. In Q's favour is that it allows the negative associations of *deceive* to emerge: *absence* encourages lovers to indulge in the false satisfaction of merely thinking time away by imagining the beloved.

13–14 **And that . . . remain** 'were it not for the fact that you teach me, on my own here, to become two people by praising my absent love'. The act of praising the friend makes him present. Note, however, the negative associations of *twain* elsewhere, as in 36.1, where it means 'two separate people'. This makes the optimism of the couplet seem forced, and compounds the sinister associations of *deceive* in l. 12.

39

O, how thy worth with manners may I sing,
When thou art all the better part of me?
What can mine own praise to mine own self bring,
And what is 't but mine own when I praise thee?
Even for this, let us divided live,⁣ 5
And our dear love lose name of single one,
That by this separation I may give
That due to thee which thou deserv'st alone.
O absence, what a torment wouldst thou prove,
Were it not thy sour leisure gave sweet leave 10
To entertain the time with thoughts of love,
Which time and thoughts so sweetly dost deceive;
   And that thou teachest how to make one twain,
   By praising him here who doth hence remain.

12 dos⁣ Q; doth MALONE; do CAPELL

1 **my loves** is pitched throughout the sonnet deliberately and dangerously between 'feelings of love' and 'lovers'. Sonnets 40–3 imply that the friend has taken away a lover from the poet, which anticipates the betrayals explored in a number of sonnets between *133* and *152*.

4 **All mine . . . more** 'All my true love was yours before you received this additional love (or lover).' The promise 'With all my worldly goods I thee endow' of the marriage service is not far away from the chime on *mine* and *thine*.

5–6 **Then . . . usest** (a) if you take my lover in the place of my love, I cannot rebuke you, since you are making good use of my love (and my lover); (b) if you take my lover because she is another recipient of my love, I cannot rebuke you. . . . 'The coolly reasonable "I can't blame you for your conduct because you did it for love of me" (compare *42*.6) is undercut by a sardonic "I can't blame you for sexually enjoying my *mistress*" ' (Kerrigan).

7–8 **But yet . . . refusest** These are very obscure lines. Presumably their gist is that the poet *will* blame the friend if he is simply stealing his lover in order to try him or her out, rather than keeping her or him for permanent use and (implicitly) multiplication. He will blame him the more because such sensuous sampling runs counter to the promptings of the friend's better self (*what thyself refusest*). *This self* is the poet (part of the friend's self through their fusion of identities), which yields the additional possible suggestion that the friend is granting sexual favours

to the poet's *love* which he is denying to the poet himself. *Thyself* is usually glossed 'your true self', but could as well be a simple reflexive. *Refusest* means primarily 'reject' (Schmidt, 3), although it may draw on *OED* 6: 'to cast off (a person); to divorce (a wife)', as in *Much Ado* 4.1.186: 'Refuse me, hate me, torture me to death'. *Wilful* means 'stubborn, perverse and lustful'. Some editors emend *this self* to *thyself*; however, this mutes the opposition between the self which deceives and the 'true' self which resists sensual allurements, and which is implicitly identified with the poet. Ingram and Redpath propose that Q's 'thy selfe' in l. 8 may result from compositorial eyeskip and propose the emendation 'thy sense' (meaning 'your rational powers'). This proposal warrants serious attention: the play on *sense* which would result, meaning at once 'rationality' and 'sensuality', has a parallel in 35.9.

9 **gentle** kindly; perhaps also 'well-born'. A plea of mitigation is implicitly made in the move from *robbery* (forcible and open removal of property) to *thief* (one who only surreptitiously removes property).

10 **steal thee . . . poverty** steal for yourself the little I have. On the ethical dative (steal for yourself), see Abbott § 220.

13 **Lascivious grace** (a) libidinous elegance; (b) lustful generosity. *Grace* is usually used in the vocative in addresses to members of the nobility, so a further sense of 'lustful nobleman' is vestigially registered.

40

Take all my loves, my love, yea, take them all:
What hast thou then more than thou hadst before?
No love, my love, that thou mayst true love call:
All mine was thine before thou hadst this more.
Then if for my love thou my love receivest,   5
I cannot blame thee, for my love thou usest;
But yet be blamed, if thou this self deceivest
By wilful taste of what thyself refusest.
I do forgive thy robb'ry, gentle thief,
Although thou steal thee all my poverty;   10
And yet love knows it is a greater grief
To bear love's wrong than hate's known injury.
    Lascivious grace, in whom all ill well shows,
    Kill me with spites, yet we must not be foes.

7 this self] Q; thy self GILDON   8 thyself] Q; thy sense *conj.* Ingram and Redpath

1 **pretty wrongs** wicked or unfair actions made beautiful by the fact that they are committed by the friend
liberty (a) freedom; (b) 'Unrestrained action, conduct, or expression; freedom of behaviour or speech, beyond what is granted or recognized as proper; licence' (*OED* 5a)

2 **sometime** sometimes

3 **befits** suits; also with a sarcastic tone, 'is entirely appropriate to'. The plural subject with a singular verb is not unusual in the period.

5 **Gentle** puns on 'well-born' (*OED* 1a), and 'noble, generous, courteous' (*OED* 3a), and 'kind, tender' (*OED* 8). The friend is noble, of good character (therefore inviting suitors), and as yielding as a woman. This is reinforced by the echo of the proverb 'She is a woman, therefore to be won' (cf. *1 Henry VI* 5.5.35 and *Titus* 2.1.83–4), and by the *parison* (repeated syntactic structure) of ll. 4 and 5.

8 **he** Many editors emend to 'she'. The bitterness of Q's 'he', though, is right: the woman initiates an encounter from which she emerges the loser. The suggestion of blame directed at the friend for his active part in prevailing suits the sourness of this sonnet. On *sourly*, see 39.10 n.

9 **thou mightst . . . forbear** at least you might abstain from corrupting the central place of my love. *Seat* means 'place of occupation', with a suggestion of sexual ownership, as in *Othello* 2.1.294–5: 'I do suspect the lusty Moor | Hath leaped into my seat'. There may be a bawdy sense in play, via *OED* 9a: 'The sitting part of the body; the posteriors', first cited 1607; but such a direct suggestion of buggery would make it exceptional in the Sonnets.

11 **Who** which (beauty and youth are almost personified)
their riot uncontrolled dissipation. Conceivably 'their' should be amended to 'thy'. See 26.12 n.
even On this emphatic disyllabic use of 'even', see 35.5 n. above.

12 **truth** 'troth', or vow

13–14 **Hers . . . me** 'You break her vow to me because your beauty has led her to abandon me, and you break your vow to me because your beauty has made you false to me.' *Beauty* becomes an autonomous force independent of the friend as the poet labours to exculpate him, but the shift from *temptation* in l. 4 (where the friend is its passive victim) to *tempting* in l. 13 (where the friend is using his beauty in order to tempt) does not simply let him off the hook. *Tempting* could be consonant with either 'thou' or *beauty*; *being false* similarly struggles to attribute to *beauty* a betrayal which is actually that of the friend.

462

41

Those pretty wrongs that liberty commits,
When I am sometime absent from thy heart,
Thy beauty and thy years full well befits,
For still temptation follows where thou art.
Gentle thou art, and therefore to be won;   5
Beauteous thou art, therefore to be assailèd.
And when a woman woos what woman's son
Will sourly leave her till he have prevailèd?
Ay me, but yet thou mightst my seat forbear,
And chide thy beauty and thy straying youth,   10
Who lead thee in their riot even there
Where thou art forced to break a two-fold truth:
    Hers, by thy beauty tempting her to thee,
    Thine, by thy beauty being false to me.

6 assailèd] Q; assail'd MALONE   8 he] Q; she MALONE   prevailèd] Q; prevail'd MALONE   9 mightst BENSON; mighst Q

1 **all my grief** (a) entirely a source of grief to me; (b) the entirety of my suffering—there is more

2 **dearly** (a) affectionately, fondly; (b) at a high price; at great cost

3 **of my wailing chief** the main cause of my complaint

4 **that touches . . . nearly** which strikes closer to my heart (than the loss of her)

5 **Loving offenders** is both a vocative ('You loving criminals'), and perhaps too a participle clause, 'Since I love you offenders'. As at the end of the previous sonnet slippery participles are letting the poet blame and love at once.

7 **And for . . . abuse me** 'And she in a similar way loves you (and so *abuses* me) because she knows that I love you.' Abuse means (a) 'to injure, wrong, or hurt' (*OED* 5); (b) 'To make a wrong use of anyone's confidence; to impose upon, cheat, or deceive (a person)' (*OED* 4a).

8 **Suff'ring** allowing. The participle could agree with either 'she' or 'me'.
approve 'To put to the proof or test of experience; to try, test' (*OED* 8). Here with an undertone of 'try out sexually'.

9, 10 **lose . . . losing** Q reads 'loose' and 'loosing', which might be modernized as 'loosing' and so give the poet the consolation of having voluntarily relinquished his loves.

9 **my love's the mistress's.** The idiom vainly tries to wrest some consolation in loss from the secondary sense 'my affection for you'. At this point the poem ceases to address the friend in the second person.

10 **found** recovered

11 **and** is possibly the archaic form (corresponding to 'an') meaning 'if'.
both twain the one as well as the other. On the negative associations of *twain*, see 36.1 n.

12 **cross** (a) 'A trial or affliction viewed in its Christian aspect, to be borne for Christ's sake with Christian patience' (*OED* 10a); (b) 'annoyance; misfortune, adversity; sometimes (under the influence of the verb) anything that thwarts or crosses' (*OED* 10b). Cf. 34.12 n.

13 **are one** Compare the proverb 'A friend is one's second self' (Dent F696).

14 **Sweet flatt'ry** 'Gratifying deception, delusion' (Schmidt). *OED* cites only this passage and *Othello* 4.1.128 in this sense (2 *fig.*), which is forced from *flatt'ry* by the peculiar self-deceptions involved in jealous love. The unity of poet and friend, so elaborately argued for in *39*, is now presented as delusion to which the poet must cling in order to preserve a semblance of contentment.

42

That thou hast her, it is not all my grief,
And yet it may be said I loved her dearly;
That she hath thee is of my wailing chief,
A loss in love that touches me more nearly.
Loving offenders, thus I will excuse ye: 5
Thou dost love her, because thou know'st I love her,
And for my sake even so doth she abuse me,
Suff'ring my friend for my sake to approve her.
If I lose thee, my loss is my love's gain;
And, losing her, my friend hath found that loss: 10
Both find each other, and I lose both twain,
And both for my sake lay on me this cross.
  But here's the joy: my friend and I are one.
  Sweet flatt'ry! Then she loves but me alone.

9–11 lose . . . losing . . . lose] 𝑄 (loose . . . loosing . . . loose)

The poem arches back across the preceding sonnets of separation and loss to recall the simpler absences brought about by travel in *28*. The group up to *48* deals in simpler antithetical concepts and more straightforward amorous relationships than *29–42*.

1 **wink** sleep (*OED* 3)

2 **unrespected** 'Unregarded, unnoticed' (*OED* 1), citing Griffin's *Fidessa* (1596) 37: 'Whilst I . . . do sit in heavy plight, | Wailing alone my unrespected love'. Possibly also 'of no importance'.

4 **darkly bright** able to see more clearly in the dark
bright in dark directed directed piercingly towards their object, although it is night

5 **whose shadow . . . bright** 'whose mere appearance in a dream can make darkness shine'. On *shadow* see *27*.10 n.

6–8 **How . . . so?** 'How delightfully would

your real presence (with its far greater brightness) shine out in the day, when your imagined presence shines so brightly to eyes which are shut.' *Thy shadow's form* is the substance which gives rise to the imaginary resemblance.

11 **thy** Q reads 'their'. On this error, see *26*.12 n.
imperfect 'not fully real'; also, perhaps, given the concern of this part of the sequence with the failings of the friend, 'Positively faulty, vicious, evil' (*OED* 3)

12 **heavy** deep. The word is often associated with sleep, and can mean 'slow, sluggish, dull' (Schmidt, 5), 'weary, drowsy, sleepy' (Schmidt, 6).
stay remain with (although Schmidt proposes 'be in the same place as')

14 **show thee me** show you to me. The reverse reading is possible ('show me to you'), but nothing in the preceding poem encourages it.

43

When most I wink, then do mine eyes best see,
For all the day they view things unrespected,
But when I sleep, in dreams they look on thee,
And, darkly bright, are bright in dark directed.
Then thou, whose shadow shadows doth make bright,   5
How would thy shadow's form form happy show,
To the clear day with thy much clearer light,
When to unseeing eyes thy shade shines so?
How would (I say) mine eyes be blessèd made
By looking on thee in the living day,   10
When in dead night thy fair imperfect shade
Through heavy sleep or sightless eyes doth stay?
   All days are nights to see till I see thee,
   And nights bright days when dreams do show thee me.

11 thy⟩ MALONE (*conj.* Capell); their Q

1 **dull** (a) 'insensible . . . senseless, inanimate' (*OED* 2a); (b) 'depressed' (*OED* 4), as in *Errors* 5.1.79–80: 'Sweet recreation barred, what doth ensue | But moody and dull melancholy?'

2 **Injurious** harmful; with a suggestion of 'malicious wrongdoing'
stop my way prevent my movement, bar my passage to you

4 **limits** distant regions
stay 'To reside or sojourn in a place for a longer or shorter period' (*OED* 8)

5 **No matter then** it would not matter if

7–8 **For . . . be** The speed of thought is proverbial (Dent T240). Compare the Chorus to *Henry V* 3. Pr. 1–3: 'Thus with imagined wing our swift scene flies | In motion of no less celerity | Than that of thought.'

9 **thought ... thought** *Epanalepsis* (repetition of the same word at the beginning and end of a clause) combines with *antanaclasis* (repetition of a word in different senses) to create a deadlocked loop of thought.

11 **But that . . . wrought** 'However, being completely constituted of earth and water . . .'. The human body was thought to be composed of two heavy elements (earth and water) and two lighter and more nimble elements (air and fire). The relative balance of these elements varied with mood, health, personal constitution, season, and age. To be composed of *earth and water* is to be slow both physically and mentally. The Dauphin's horse (or Bourbon's horse in Oxford) illustrates the opposite qualities: 'It is a beast for Perseus. He is pure air and fire, and the dull elements of earth and water never appear in him, but only in patient stillness while his rider mounts him' (*Henry V* 3.7.20–3).

12 **attend time's leisure** wait on the whim of time, like a retainer awaiting the command of a lord

13 **Receiving . . . so slow** obtaining nothing from the slow and heavy elements of earth and water

14 **badges of either's woe** tokens of the woe of earth and water. In *2 Henry IV* 4.2.99–102 there is a hint that *badges* for Shakespeare at the end of the 1590s could mean 'physical manifestations of an inner balance of humours' as well as 'heraldic emblems': 'The second property of your excellent sherry is the warming of the blood, which, before cold and settled, left the liver white and pale, which is the badge of pusillanimity and cowardice'.

468

44

If the dull substance of my flesh were thought,
Injurious distance should not stop my way;
For then, despite of space, I would be brought
From limits far remote, where thou dost stay.
No matter then although my foot did stand   5
Upon the farthest earth removed from thee,
For nimble thought can jump both sea and land
As soon as think the place where he would be.
But ah, thought kills me that I am not thought,
To leap large lengths of miles when thou art gone,   10
But that, so much of earth and water wrought,
I must attend time's leisure with my moan,
   Receiving naught by elements so slow
   But heavy tears, badges of either's woe.

13 naught] GILDON; naughts Q

1 **other two** i.e. the elements of air and fire
slight 'Lacking in solid or substantial qualities' (*OED* 3b)
purging purifying

3 **The first . . . desire** The identification of thought with air and love with fire is common.

4 **present-absent . . . slide** these are so volatile that they are not here at once. Cf. the 'absent presence' of Stella with which Sidney's Astrophil is left at the end of *Astrophil and Stella* (106.1).

5 **quicker** both 'more rapid' and 'more vital'. (Old age was believed to be accompanied by a diminution in air and fire in the body, which caused the system to slow down.)

6 **embassy** Early modern embassies tended to be missions to foreign rulers designed to achieve a particular point of policy such as a dynastic marriage or treaty (permanent resident ambassadors were beginning to emerge *c*.1600, as Shakespeare recognizes in *Measure* 3.1.54–6).

7 **being made of four** i.e. four elements. See 44.11 n.

8 **melancholy** is traditionally associated with the element of earth, with old age, and with death. Three syllables here.

9 **life's composition** (a) the compound of elements which is necessary for life (*OED* 2); (b) life's 'combination of personal qualities that make any one what he is' (*OED* 16b). Q's reading 'liues composition' probably reflects contemporary pronunciation, in which a medial fricative could be voiced before a possessive (Partridge, 116).
recurèd made whole again, returned to a healthy balance.

10 **those swift messengers** i.e. air and fire.

12 **thy** Q reads 'their' which is just possible (referring to the new health of the elements), but is probably another 'their' for 'thy' error; on which see 26.12 n.

14 **I send . . . sad** The ambassadors air and fire are sent off once more, which brings back a melancholy state. The couplet introduces the new suggestion that the poet is actually in control of when fire and air are sent on their embassies, rather than a passive victim of their wish to be with the friend.

45

The other two, slight air and purging fire,
Are both with thee, wherever I abide:
The first my thought, the other my desire,
These present-absent with sweet motion slide.
For when these quicker elements are gone   5
In tender embassy of love to thee,
My life, being made of four, with two alone
Sinks down to death, oppressed with melancholy,
Until life's composition be recurèd
By those swift messengers returned from thee,   10
Who even but now come back again assurèd
Of thy fair health, recounting it to me.
    This told, I joy; but then, no longer glad,
    I send them back again and straight grow sad.

5 For] Q; Forth *conj.* Tucker; So INGRAM AND REDPATH   9 recurèd] Q; recured BOSWELL
11 assurèd] Q; assured BOSWELL   12 thy] GILDON 1714; their Q

Debates between the eye and the heart are quite common in sonnet sequences: Drayton's *Idea* (1619) 33 begins: 'Whilst yet mine eyes do surfeit with delight, | My woeful heart, imprisoned in my breast, | Wisheth to be transformèd to my sight'; Watson's *Tears of Fancy* (1593) 20 begins: 'My heart accused mine eyes and was offended, | Vowing the cause was in mine eyes' aspiring'.

2 **conquest** See 6.14 n. The eye and heart plead their claim for the friend as in action for partition of a piece of property over which they both claim ownership.

3, 8, 13-14 **thy** Q reads 'their'. See 26.12 n.

3 **bar** prohibit, drawing on 'To arrest or stop (a person) by ground of legal objection from enforcing some claim' (*OED* 5 *Law* a)

4 **My heart . . . right** My heart wishes to deny my eye the liberty to see the friend's picture. To enjoy the *freedom of* something is to be granted specific rights to enjoy it (as when one is granted the freedom of a city or a guild).

5 **thou in . . . lie** i.e. that the friend's image resides in him

6 **closet** private inner chamber, or a small private chest; often used as a metaphor for private inner space. See *Lucrece* 1659 n.

9 **'cide** decide. This is the received modernization of Q's 'side', which could alternatively mean 'To assign to one of two sides or parties' (*OED* s.v. 'side' *v.* 5). Since *OED* cites only this passage the definition lacks firm support.

   impanellèd the technical term for 'to enrol or constitute (a body of jurors)'

10 **quest** 'An official or judicial inquiry' (*OED* s.v. 'quest' *n.*[1] 1)

   tenants 'One who holds a piece of land, a house, etc., by lease for a term of years or a set time' (*OED* 2). The *tenants to the heart* therefore temporarily hold their land from him, as from a superior, and so cannot be expected to be impartial.

12 **moiety** 'A half, one of two equal parts: a. in legal or quasi-legal use' (*OED* 1); but usually in Shakespeare 'one of two parts (not necessarily equal)' (*OED* 2a). A 'moiety' in this sense may be strikingly unequal to the other part, as when Hotspur complains in *1 Henry IV* 3.1.93-4: 'Methinks my moiety north from Burton here | In quantity equals not one of yours.' It can even shrink to the point of becoming 'a small part; a lesser share, portion, or quantity' (*OED* 2 b), as in the dedication to *Lucrece* l. 5. The jury of thoughts shows its bias by allocating the less valuable, outward part of the friend to the eye.

46

Mine eye and heart are at a mortal war
How to divide the conquest of thy sight.
Mine eye my heart thy picture's sight would bar;
My heart, mine eye the freedom of that right.
My heart doth plead that thou in him dost lie   5
(A closet never pierced with crystal eyes),
But the defendant doth that plea deny,
And says in him thy fair appearance lies.
To 'cide this title is impanellèd
A quest of thoughts, all tenants to the heart,   10
And by their verdict is determinèd
The clear eye's moiety, and the dear heart's part.
    As thus: mine eye's due is thy outward part,
    And my heart's right thy inward love of heart.

3, 8 thy] MALONE (*conj.* Capell); their Q   4 freedom] BENSON; freeedome Q   9 'cide] Q (side)
13, 14 thy] MALONE (*conj.* Capell); their Q; thine MALONE 1790

1 **a league is took** a treaty of alliance is established

2 **And each . . . other** Compare the proverb 'One good turn deserves another' (Dent T616).

4 **Or** or when

smother suffocate

5 **my eye** is an anomalous form, where one would expect 'mine eye'. It is used to retain symmetry with *my love's* earlier in the line and *my heart* in the next line. Compare *Lucrece* l. 1475.

6 **painted banquet** illusory feast, possibly alluding to the widely invoked tale of the artist Zeuxis who painted grapes so vividly that birds pecked vainly at

them. Compare *Venus* ll. 601–2 and n.

8 **in . . . part** joins my heart in thinking of love

9–10 **So either . . . me** 'so either your picture or my love for you makes it as though you are present to me even when you are away'

10 **are** Q's reading is retained here. 'Are' rather than 'art' is sometimes used as the second-person-singular form of the verb 'to be' before consonants.

11–12 **For thou . . . thee** 'since you cannot go further than my thoughts, which are always accompanied by me, and which always follow you'

47

Betwixt mine eye and heart a league is took,
And each doth good turns now unto the other.
When that mine eye is famished for a look,
Or heart in love with sighs himself doth smother,
With my love's picture then my eye doth feast,   5
And to the painted banquet bids my heart.
Another time mine eye is my heart's guest,
And in his thoughts of love doth share a part.
So either by thy picture or my love,
Thyself away are present still with me;   10
For thou not farther than my thoughts canst move,
And I am still with them, and they with thee;
   Or if they sleep, thy picture in my sight
   Awakes my heart, to heart's and eye's delight.

10 self] Q (*Rosenbach copy only*); selfe Q   are] Q; art MALONE (*conj.* Capell)   11 not] BENSON; nor Q; no CAPELL

1 **took my way** set off on my journey

2 **bars** Like a miser, the poet locks away everything in a safe-room.

thrust 'To press (objects) into a confined space; also, to fill (a space) densely; to crowd, cram' (*OED* 3c)

4 **wards** either 'Guardianship, keeping, control' (*OED* 2a) or (as l. 9 implies) 'that which secures a door; a bolt' (Schmidt, 7). It is impossible here to separate physical security from dependable guardianship.

trust? Q's question mark is retained, although in early modern usage it could indicate an exclamation. This edition retains question marks at the end of rhetorical questions (as here), since such questions are very often subsequently assailed by the doubts which they seek emphatically to exclude (as happens in the next quatrain here). Exclamation marks are used sparingly, and only late on, in Q (*92.12, 95.4, 123.1, 126.10*,

148.1), and almost always to mark what are unequivocally exclamations ('No!' or 'O me!').

5 **to whom** (a) in comparison with whom; (b) for whom, in whose estimation

6 **grief** source of pain or anxiety

10 **Save ... art** 'except where you are not in fact (though I think you are)'

11 **gentle closure** the lovingly mild confine. *Closure* means 'Bound, limit, circuit' (*OED* 1b), and can imply physical constriction, as it does in *Richard III* 3.3.10: 'Within the guilty closure of thy walls'. Compare *Venus* l. 782.

12 **come and part** come and go; although 'part' is often used in love poetry of the period to mean 'separate'

13 **even** On this emphatic disyllabic use of 'even', see 35.5 n.

14 **For ... dear** For even truth becomes a thief for so rich a reward. Compare *Venus* l. 724, and the proverb 'The prey entices the thief' (Dent P570).

48

How careful was I, when I took my way,
Each trifle under truest bars to thrust,
That to my use it might unusèd stay
From hands of falsehood, in sure wards of trust?
But thou, to whom my jewels trifles are,   5
Most worthy comfort, now my greatest grief,
Thou best of dearest, and mine only care,
Art left the prey of every vulgar thief.
Thee have I not locked up in any chest,
Save where thou art not, though I feel thou art,   10
Within the gentle closure of my breast,
From whence at pleasure thou mayst come and part;
　And even thence thou wilt be stol'n, I fear:
　For truth proves thievish for a prize so dear.

1 **Against that time** in preparation for that time. Cf. l. 9 below and n., and 63.1 and n. That both this poem and 63 begin with an effort to resist the effects of time is significant: 49 (seven times seven) was a minor climacteric or point of crisis in the body's development; 63 (seven times nine) was the 'grand climacteric'. As G. B. Evans suggests, the poem seems out of place in a group which chiefly concerns travel; but its numerological appropriateness offsets that effect.

2 **defects** is accented on the second syllable

3 **Whenas** 'at the time when'; an archaism or poeticism by 1609
cast . . . sum 'calculated his final total'. *Cast* means 'To count or reckon, so as to ascertain the sum of various numbers, orig. by means of counters' (*OED* 37). An unlikely secondary sense is 'squandered his last penny', unlikely because it conflicts with *that audit* in the following line.

4 **Called . . . respects** 'summoned to that final calculation of debts by learned and respectable advisers'. *Advised respects*, however, leaves it deliberately uncertain as to whether the friend has been called to make an audit of his love by senior advisers or by his own sense of propriety (*OED* s.v. 'respect' 14a: 'a consideration; a fact or motive which assists in, or leads to, the formation of a decision; an end or aim'), so one could gloss 'by well-informed consideration'.

5 **strangely pass** 'pass by me like a stranger'. *Strangely* means 'In an unfriendly or unfavourable manner; with cold or distant bearing' (*OED* 2). Cf. 89.8 and 110.6.

7–8 **When love . . . gravity** 'When love, transformed from how it is now, shall present strong and severe arguments against knowing me'; or 'find reasons for a premature appearance of gravity'. *Settled* can convey the sense of 'having acquired maturity' in Shakespeare (*OED* 1b), as when Isabella describes Angelo in *Measure* 3.1.88–9 as one 'Whose *settled* visage and deliberate word | Nips youth i' th' head'.

9 **Against that time** in fearful anticipation of that time
ensconce 'To shelter within or behind a fortification' (*OED* 2). Cf. *Lucrece* l. 1515.

10 **Within . . . desert** inside the knowledge of my own merit. Q's 'desart' makes the rhyme with 'part' complete.

11 **uprear** 'raise up, elevate, erect' (*OED* 1), often used in military contexts. Here the poet's *hand* is presented as a loyal defender of the friend's *lawful reasons*, or just arguments.

13–14 **To leave . . . cause** 'You have the strength of law on the side of ceasing to love me, since I can present no legally binding reason why you should love.' The poet is again seen as pleading in a law court against his own interests, as in 35.10 above.

49

Against that time (if ever that time come)
When I shall see thee frown on my defects,
Whenas thy love hath cast his utmost sum,
Called to that audit by advised respects;
Against that time when thou shalt strangely pass,   5
And scarcely greet me with that sun, thine eye,
When love, converted from the thing it was,
Shall reasons find of settled gravity;
Against that time do I ensconce me here,
Within the knowledge of mine own desert,   10
And this my hand against myself uprear
To guard the lawful reasons on thy part.
   To leave poor me thou hast the strength of laws,
   Since why to love I can allege no cause.

1 **heavy** adverbial, meaning 'slowly, slug-gishly; laboriously' (*OED* 2). It also may reflect the character of the horse which bears the poet. Horses were believed, like all living things, to have an individual temperament based on the relative dominance of the four humours in their bodies: as Thomas Blundeville puts it, 'And if the earth have sovereignty [in the temperament of a horse], then he is black of colour, or a mouse dun, and therewith fearful, faint-hearted, dull and heavy', *The Order of Dieting Horses* (1593), fo. 3ᵃ. The ideal horse is hot, moist, and dominated by the humour of blood.

2–4 **When . . . friend** when the only rest and repose which my destination offers me after my laborious journey is the thought that each mile I have travelled has taken me further from my friend (which is no rest at all)

2 **travel's** Q's 'trauels' excludes the other-wise frequent pun on 'travail' or labour

4 **'Thus . . . friend'** Q does not use inverted commas to mark direct speech.

5 **tirèd** (a) exhausted; (b) attired. The description could suit either horse or rider.

6 **dully** Q's 'duly' is best modernized in this way, given that 'dull' was a semi-techni-cal term for the temperament of a horse in the period. See note to l. 1 above, and compare *dull bearer* in 51.2.

7 **instinct** stressed on the second syllable

8 **being made . . . thee** since it was being made away from you

10 **That** which; i.e. the *bloody spur*

11 **heavily** sadly. Cf. l. 1.

12 **sharp** painful; also conveying the physical pain inflicted by the *sharp* spurs

14 **my joy** (a) my happiness; (b) the cause of my joy, i.e. the friend

50

How heavy do I journey on the way,
When what I seek (my weary travel's end)
Doth teach that ease and that repose to say
'Thus far the miles are measured from thy friend.'
The beast that bears me, tirèd with my woe,   5
Plods dully on, to bear that weight in me,
As if by some instinct the wretch did know
His rider loved not speed being made from thee.
The bloody spur cannot provoke him on
That sometimes anger thrusts into his hide,   10
Which heavily he answers with a groan
More sharp to me than spurring to his side,
    For that same groan doth put this in my mind:
    My grief lies onward, and my joy behind.

4 'Thus . . . friend.'] MALONE (*italic*); ^ ‐ . . . ‐·^ Q   6 dully] Q (duly)

1 **slow offence** offence of slowness
2 **dull bearer** the horse described in *50*. See note to *50*.1
3-4 **'From . . . need'** The editorial tradition here slavishly follows Malone and does not mark these lines as direct speech. Consistency with 51.4 demands that they should be.
4 **posting** 'Speedy travelling: hastening, haste, hurry' (*OED* 2)
5-6 **O . . . slow** 'What excuse for his slowness will my horse give on the return journey when the fastest possible speed will seem slow?' *Swift extremity* means 'extreme swiftness'.
7 **though** even if I were
8 **In wingèd . . . know** even travelling at the speed of the wind I shall feel as if I am not moving
10 **perfect'st** Q represents the superlative form metaplasmically as 'perfects'. The modernization creates an awkward-sounding line which it is likely the poet deliberately avoided.
11 **Shall weigh** take no account of. Q's 'Shall naigh' is a notorious crux. It can be glossed if the punctuation is emended to make 'no dull flesh' into a parenthesis: 'desire—no dull flesh but an impulse of the spirit—will neigh like a carnal horse as an expression of sexual impatience'. The association of the passions with horses goes back to Plato's *Phaedrus*. See *Venus* ll. 259–324 n. Some commentators see it as a paradox worthy of the *Sonnets* that desire in seeking to transcend its carnal vehicle ('no dull flesh') should become at that very moment carnal and horse-like by neighing with delight. Others see it as nonsense. Stanley Wells, 'New Readings in Shakespeare's Sonnets', in J. P. Vander Motten, ed., *Elizabethan and Modern Studies* (Ghent, 1985), 320, argues for Taylor's 'shall reign' (i.e. rein), an emendation which supposes simple minim error from the compositor. Since the flesh is *dull* the poet will have no need to rein it in. MacDonald P. Jackson, 'How Many Horses has Sonnet 51? Textual and Literary Criticism in Shakespeare's Sonnets', *English Language Notes* 27/3

(1990), 10–19 argues for 'waigh' (weigh), as Bray had earlier done. This requires of compositor B, the less reliable of Q's two compositors, a simple minim error combined with an over-sensitivity to the horsey flavour of the sonnet. Jackson's reading requires no additional alteration to Q's punctuation in order to mean 'desire shall weigh (i.e. take account of) no dull flesh such as his horse in his progress to his friend'. Cf. *108*.10. 'Weigh' has the heaviness which Shakespeare elsewhere associates with flesh, and Hand D in *Sir Thomas More* (probably that of Shakespeare) also uses the form 'waigh'. Jackson's strong case is marred only by his claim that 'naigh' is not an accepted spelling of 'neigh' in this period. Joshua Sylvester's translation of Du Bartas's *Divine Weekes and Workes*, The First Part of the Third Day of the Second Week (1606), ll. 1143–4 reads: 'For, those that first these two bright Starrs survaide | Wilde Stalion-like, after their bewties naigh'd', ed. Susan Snyder, 2 vols. (Oxford, 1979). 'Weigh' is none the less the most convincing solution to the crux.
11 **dull . . . race** No mortal flesh will impede his heated flight. If Q's 'neigh' is accepted in l. 11 the phrase could also mean 'there is no heavy flesh in his fiery bloodline'. Horses dominated by choler and the element of fire were believed to be the ideal short sprinters, since they were 'hot and fiery, and seldom of any great strength', Blundeville, *The Order of Dieting Horses*, fo. 3ʳ.
12 **love** affection; possibly also Cupid
jade nag
13-14 **'Since . . . go'** 'Since he left you with a resistant slowness, I will charge back to you, and allow him free rein.' *Run* here means 'To ride on horseback at a quick pace' (*OED* 6a). The poet, *mounted on the wind*, probably does not propose to race his horse home, but allows this potentially absurd image to emerge in order to bear witness to his eagerness. These lines are not traditionally marked as direct speech, but consistency requires that they should be.

51

Thus can my love excuse the slow offence
Of my dull bearer, when from thee I speed:
'From where thou art, why should I haste me thence?
Till I return, of posting is no need.'
O what excuse will my poor beast then find   5
When swift extremity can seem but slow?
Then should I spur, though mounted on the wind:
In wingèd speed no motion shall I know.
Then can no horse with my desire keep pace;
Therefore desire (of perfect'st love being made)   10
Shall weigh no dull flesh in his fiery race,
But love, for love, thus shall excuse my jade:
   'Since from thee going he went wilful slow,
   Towards thee I'll run, and give him leave to go.'

3–4 'From . . . need.'] This edition; ‿ ... ‿‿ Q   10 perfect'st] DYCE 1857; perfects Q; perfect
GILDON   11 weigh] BRAY (*conj.* C. C. M. Smith); naigh Q; Faign OXFORD (*conj.* Taylor)   13–14
'Since . . . go.'] DOWDEN; ‿‿ ... ‿‿ Q

1 **So am I** I am just like
  blessèd 'Bringing, or accompanied by,
  blessing or happiness' (*OED* 4a)
4 **For** for fear of
  seldom pleasure a pleasure which is
  stronger for being infrequently enjoyed.
  Compare the proverb 'A seldom use of
  pleasures maketh the same the more
  pleasant' (Dent P417).
5 **feasts** carries more religious associations
  than it does now: 'religious anniversaries'
  (*OED* 1), rather than 'sumptuous meals'
  (*OED* 2). The sonnet echoes Prince
  Harry's soliloquy in *1 Henry IV* 1.2.201–
  4: 'If all the year were playing holidays, |
  To sport would be as tedious as to work; |
  But when they seldom come, they wished-
  for come, | And nothing pleaseth but rare
  accidents.' He goes on to compare his
  future reformation to a jewel which glit-
  ters more brightly for having a foil to
  highlight its brilliance.
  rare (a) infrequent; (b) valuable
7 **thinly placèd** sparsely distributed
8 **captain jewels . . . carcanet** 'principal
  jewels in a necklace or coronet'
9–11 **So is . . . blest** 'So the time that keeps

you from me is like a chest or wardrobe
which conceals a rich garment in order
that the day on which it is removed will be
truly special.' There is a pun on *keeps*,
meaning both 'delays' and 'retains
securely': although time delays (*keeps*)
the friend it does not *keep* him locked away
safely in the poet's chest. The pun
attempts to turn a forced separation into a
willed moderation of contact, and the
strain of this wishful thinking shows all
too clearly.
12 **unfolding** develops the simile of the
  wardrobe, and means both 'To open or
  unwrap the folds of' (*OED* 1), and 'to dis-
  play' (*OED* 3).
  imprisoned pride means 'concealed prize
  possession'. A 'wardrobe' in this period is
  a room set apart specifically for the stor-
  age of rich clothes or armour; hence the
  whole sonnet depends on the poet's imag-
  ining himself having the accoutrements
  of the *rich*.
13–14 **Blessèd . . . hope** 'You are blessed
  because you are of such worth that to
  have you is to triumph, and not to have
  you is to long for you.'

52

So am I as the rich, whose blessèd key
Can bring him to his sweet up-lockèd treasure,
The which he will not ev'ry hour survey
For blunting the fine point of seldom pleasure.
Therefore are feasts so solemn and so rare,   5
Since, seldom coming, in the long year set
Like stones of worth they thinly placèd are,
Or captain jewels in the carcanet.
So is the time that keeps you as my chest,
Or as the wardrobe which the robe doth hide   10
To make some special instant special blest,
By new unfolding his imprisoned pride.
    Blessèd are you whose worthiness gives scope,
    Being had, to triumph; being lacked, to hope.

2 **strange shadows** could be (a) attendants ('parasite, toady' (*OED* 8)); (b) supernatural presences; (c) representations or images of the friend. The sonnet moves between senses (a) and (b) in its first quatrain, and settles on sense (c) by l. 10.
tend wait upon you as attendant or servant (*OED* 4a)

3–4 **Since . . . lend** 'All people have only one reflected image, but you, although you are a single being, can adopt the appearance of anyone.' *Every one* could alternatively be modernized as 'everyone'.

5–6 **Describe . . . you** 'the verbal representation of Adonis is simply a poor imitation of you'. *Counterfeit* means 'imitation, forgery' (*OED* 1). This section of the poem has close parallels with Orlando's poem on Rosalind in *As You Like It* 3.2.141–9: 'Nature presently distilled | Helen's cheek, but not her heart, | Cleopatra's majesty, | Atalanta's better part, | Sad Lucretia's modesty. | Thus Rosalind of many parts | By heavenly synod was devised | Of many faces, eyes, and hearts | To have the touches dearest prized'. Compare also Richard Barnfield's *Cynthia* (1595), Sonnet 17, a poem of high erotic charge about a male subject: 'Cherry-lipped Adonis in his snowy shape, | Might not compare with his pure ivory white'.

7–8 **On Helen's . . . new** 'Add all the arts of beautification to the already beautiful face of Helen of Troy, and she will represent you, dressed afresh in Greek costume.' *Painted new* means both (neutrally) 'represented afresh' and (with a slight pejorative edge) 'newly made up'. Adonis was a reluctant lover, and the abduction of Helen of Troy caused the Trojan war: neither are happy precedents for love.

9 **foison** 'Plentiful crop or harvest' (*OED* 1b)

10 **The one . . . show** 'the spring is merely an image of your beauty'

11 **The other . . . appear** 'the bountiful harvest seems like your generosity'

12 **know** recognize

13–14 **In all . . . heart** (a) 'You are represented in every outward beauty; but you are like none, and none are like you, for constancy in love'; (b) 'You have share in every form of noble elegance that there is, but you are unparalleled for constancy'; (c) 'You are as lovely as can be, but you do not admire anyone for their constancy, nor does anyone admire you for your constancy'. *Grace* ranges from 'external beauty', through 'elegant refinement of manner (connoting aristocratic ease)', to 'willingness to grant favours'. *Like* functions as an adjective, but also possibly as verb.

53

What is your substance, whereof are you made,
That millions of strange shadows on you tend?
Since every one hath, every one, one shade,
And you, but one, can every shadow lend.
Describe Adonis, and the counterfeit   5
Is poorly imitated after you.
On Helen's cheek all art of beauty set,
And you in Grecian tires are painted new.
Speak of the spring and foison of the year,
The one doth shadow of your beauty show,   10
The other as your bounty doth appear,
And you in every blessèd shape we know.
   In all external grace you have some part,
   But you like none, none you, for constant heart.

2 **By** as a result of
  truth fidelity
3 **deem** consider, judge
5 **canker-blooms** the (scentless) dog-roses; or just possibly *OED* 5b: 'A local name for the common wild poppy'. See Katherine Duncan-Jones, 'Deep-dyed Canker Blooms: Botanical Reference in Shakespeare's Sonnet 54', *RES* 46 (1995), 521–5. Poppies are richly coloured (as dog-roses are not) but lack scent. In these respects they would suit the context; but it is hard to believe Shakespeare thought poppies *hang on such thorns*, and this sense of *canker* was found chiefly in East Anglia.
  dye colour. Both this and *tincture* impose on the world of nature the threat of artificial colouring, which anticipates the transformation of natural rose to man-made perfume in l. 12.
6 **tincture** 'Hue, colour: esp. as communicated (naturally or artificially) by a colouring matter or dye, or by something that stains; a tinge, tint' (*OED* 2a)
7 **Hang on such thorns** Dog-roses are suspended above thorns similar to those of cultivated roses.
  wantonly 'Frolicsomely, sportively' (*OED* 1b); a rebuke to the friend may be teased out of 'Lewdly, lasciviously; voluptuously' (*OED* 1a)

8 **maskèd** concealed. The petals of unopened rosebuds are concealed beneath a whorl of leaf-like calyxes.
9 **But, for . . . show** but since the sole value of dog-roses lies in their appearance (rather than also in their sweet smell)
11–12 **Sweet roses . . . made** Cultivated roses with a rich scent do not just die; their sweet-smelling dead blooms are made into *sweetest perfumes*.
13 **And so of you** and the same is true of you
14 **When that shall . . . truth** 'When your beauty shall pass away my verse will preserve the essence of your truthfulness (as a parfumier preserves the scent of a rose).' *Vade* is often used as a variant form of *fade* in this period. It is retained here since it marks a shift from *fade* ('lose colour') in l. 10 above towards the stronger sense 'lose vitality' (*OED* 3), exploiting the derivation of *vade* from the Latin 'vadere', to go, pass away.
14 **by verse** Capell's emendation to 'my verse' is attractive, since *OED* cites only transitive uses of 'distils'. Q's reading, however, implies that the friend's truth has a sufficient potency to distil itself into poetry without the assistance of the poet; as such it is a more gracious piece of flattery. 'My verse', however, would anticipate the confidence of the following poem.

54

O how much more doth beauty beauteous seem
By that sweet ornament which truth doth give.
The rose looks fair, but fairer we it deem
For that sweet odour which doth in it live.
The canker-blooms have full as deep a dye   5
As the perfumèd tincture of the roses,
Hang on such thorns, and play as wantonly
When summer's breath their maskèd buds discloses;
But, for their virtue only is their show,
They live unwooed, and unrespected fade,   10
Die to themselves. Sweet roses do not so;
Of their sweet deaths are sweetest odours made:
    And so of you, beauteous and lovely youth:
    When that shall vade, by verse distils your truth.

14 vade] Q; fade GILDON   by] Q; my MALONE (*conj.* Capell)

1–2 **Not marble . . . rhyme** Horace, *Odes* 3.30.1–9 and *Met.* 15.871–9 are the chief precedents for this confident affirmation of the power of verse to immortalize. Golding 15.983–95: 'Now have I brought a work to end which neither Jove's fierce wrath, | Nor sword, nor fire, nor fretting age with all the force it hath | Are able to abolish quite. Let come that fatal hour | Which (saving of this brittle flesh) hath over me no power, | And at his pleasure make an end of mine uncertain time. | Yet shall the better part of me assurèd be | to climb | Aloft above the starry sky. And all the world shall never | Be able for to quench my name. For look how far so ever | The Roman Empire by the right of conquest shall extend, | So far shall all folk read this work. And time without all end | (If poets as by prophecy about the truth may aim) | My life shall everlastingly be lengthened still by fame'. This poem differs from its predecessors in two respects: (a) The poet immortalizes not himself, as Horace and Ovid do, but the friend, whose literary afterlife gives him enough vitality to *pace forth* (l. 10); (b) Horace and Ovid both make the life of their verse coextensive with the sway of the Roman Empire in time and space; Shakespeare promises endurance in all lands (*all posterity*, l. 11) until Judgement Day (the *ending doom*, l. 12). This poem also notably fails to record any of the friend's achievements or actions. It is the poem's tenacity of remembrance rather than the deeds of the friend which is celebrated.

1 **monuments** 'A monument is a thing erected, made or written, for a memorial of some remarkable action, fit to be transferred to future posterities. And thus generally taken, all religious Foundations, all sumptuous and magnificent structures, Cities, Towns, Towers, Castles, Pillars, Pyramids, Crosses, Obelisks, Amphitheatres, Statues and the like, as well as Tombs and Sepulchres, are called Monuments', John Weever, *Ancient Funerall Monuments* (1631), 1.

2 **pow'rful** Q marks this as disyllabic by spelling it 'powrefull'. 'Power' is usually monosyllabic and usually spelt 'powre' in Q. The only exception is 65.2, when 'power' rhymes with 'flower' in what may be a feminine rhyme.

3 **contents** 'The sum or substance of what is contained in a document; tenor, purport'; hence 'in the matter of these poems' (*OED* 3a); here, as normally

before the nineteenth century, accented 'contènt'.

4 **besmeared with sluttish time** Most editors gloss 'dirtied over by the filthy servant time', in which *sluttish* is taken to mean 'Of persons: Dirty and untidy in dress and habits' (*OED* 1). 'Besmeared *with*', however, indicates that time is not the agent causing the dirt to spread on the monument, but that it is the substance with which it is besmeared (DuBellay's poems on the *Antiquitez de Rome* frequently refer to the 'poudreuse cendre' (1.1), the dusty cinders, which obscure the lineaments of ancient Rome). *Sluttish* therefore probably means 'Of things: Unclean, dirty, grimy; untidy' (*OED* 2). Compare *Lucrece* ll. 945 and 1381.

6 **broils** tumults; esp. in Shakespeare civil war or internal disturbance
work of masonry stone structures which are the products of a stonemason's labour

7 **Mars his sword** the sword of Mars, god of war
quick rapid; also, perhaps with a deliberate paradox, 'alive'

8 **record** (stressed on the first syllable) is usually a written report in the Sonnets, as at 59.5 and 123.11.

9 **all oblivious enmity** 'all hostilities which destroy records of antiquity'. Wars cause the decay of monuments and therefore bring about oblivion of the past. For the usage of *oblivious* to mean 'bringing about oblivion' see *Macbeth* 5.3.43–7: 'Raze out the written troubles of the brain, | And with some sweet oblivious antidote | Cleanse the fraught bosom of that perilous stuff | Which weighs upon the heart'. Ingram and Redpath's conjecture 'oblivion's enmity' misses this idiosyncratic usage. Many editors hyphenate *all-oblivious-enmity*, which hardens the sense unnecessarily towards 'hostility which destroys everything', and excludes 'all forms of hostility which generate oblivion'.

10 **pace forth** stride out with the measured confidence of a warrior
find room gain admittance

11 **eyes of** opinion of
posterity See 6.12 n.

12 **ending doom** apocalypse; end of the world

13 **the judgement . . . arise** the Last Judgement, in which you will be resurrected in your own body

14 **this** this poem

55

Not marble, nor the gilded monuments
Of princes shall outlive this pow'rful rhyme,
But you shall shine more bright in these contents
Than unswept stone besmeared with sluttish time
When wasteful war shall statues overturn,   5
And broils root out the work of masonry,
Nor Mars his sword, nor war's quick fire shall burn
The living record of your memory.
'Gainst death, and all oblivious enmity
Shall you pace forth, your praise shall still find room,   10
Even in the eyes of all posterity
That wear this world out to the ending doom.
   So, till the judgement that yourself arise,
   You live in this, and dwell in lovers' eyes.

1 monuments] MALONE; monument Q   9 all oblivious] Q; all-oblivious MALONE; all obliv-ion's *conj.* Ingram and Redpath

14 **dwell** in this period has strong connota-tions of permanence (e.g. Jonson's appeal to God in 'To Heaven', l. 15: 'Dwell, dwell here still'); so 'live for ever'.

14 **lovers'** Q's 'louers' allows for either 'lover's' (meaning 'my own') or 'lovers'' (many of them).

1 **love** could be the friend, or the poet's own
fading passion, or Cupid. By its repetition
in l. 5 it is more likely to be an address to
the friend.

2 **blunter** Appetites are still said to be 'keen'
and to need 'whetting', which preserves
a metaphorical association between the
strength of desire and the sharpness
of a knife which was widespread
c. 1600.

3–4 **Which but . . . might** 'which was only
today satisfied by feeding, but which
tomorrow will return to its previous
intensity'

6 **wink with fullness** 'loll shut with feeding',
suggesting the eyes themselves are
glutted

8 **dullness** (a) 'Gloominess of mind or
spirits: now esp. as arising from want of
interest' (*OED* 3); (b) bluntness; (c) the
word can be used of appetite, so 'with a
perpetual lack of hunger'

9 **Let** imagine that, let us suppose that. The
sestet here confesses that the poem does
not address simply the effects of excessive

love and the consequent dulling of
appetite, but actual separation. See *52* for
a similar attempt to turn separation into a
means of reinforcing love.

9 **int'rim** 'period between our meetings'
(with a spatial sense: 'gap between us');
also used of a period of separation
between lovers in Desdemona's 'And I a
heavy interim shall support | By his dear
absence', *Othello* 1.3.258–9. The word is
italicized in Q, which indicates the
compositor regarded it as a strange
importation.

10 **contracted new** recently engaged to be
married; possibly even 'married'

12 **Return of love** is elliptical for 'the return of
the one they love'. It may also mean 'reci-
procation of love', especially given that
the poem urges renewed keenness in love
on the friend.

13 **Or** 'or else call this interim a winter,
which makes the summer more delightful
by variety'. Q reads 'As', which is defend-
ed by Sisson, i.212. He glosses 'As (*who
should*) call it winter'.

56

Sweet love, renew thy force. Be it not said
Thy edge should blunter be than appetite,
Which but today by feeding is allayed,
Tomorrow sharpened in his former might.
So love be thou, although today thou fill   5
Thy hungry eyes, even till they wink with fulness,
Tomorrow see again, and do not kill
The spirit of love with a perpetual dullness.
Let this sad int'rim like the ocean be,
Which parts the shore where two, contracted new,   10
Come daily to the banks, that when they see
Return of love, more blest may be the view,
　　Or call it winter, which being full of care,
　　Makes summer's welcome thrice more wished, more rare.

13 Or] MALONE (*conj.* Capell); As Q; Else PALGRAVE

1 **tend** attend like a servant. See 53.2 n.

2 **hours and times of your desire** (a) the hours when you require my services; (b) the moment-by-moment fluctuations of your whims; possibly also (c) the times when you arbitrarily decide to desire my presence as a lover

3 **precious . . . spend** implies that the poet's time is worthless unless it is 'spent' serving the friend.

4 **require** (a) order; (b) wish

5 **world-without-end hour** endless (alluding to the doxology 'As it was in the beginning, is now, and ever shall be, world without end')

6 **watch the clock** stare at the clock, urging its hands to move; also 'stay awake around the clock'

7–8 **Nor think . . . adieu** both tonally flat ('I do not find separation objectionable when we have parted'), devoted ('I can't even think of our separation with bitterness since you have imposed it'), and ironic: 'Nor do I think that absence is unpleasant provided that you have at least bothered to say goodbye to your humble servant'.

9 **question with** 'To ask questions of; to hold discourse or conversation with; to dispute with' (OED 2)

10 **your affairs suppose** 'imagine what business you are doing'. *Affairs* is more likely to have suggested 'business matters' than 'love affairs' to a contemporary reader, but the context presses it towards amours.

12 **Save . . . those** 'except how happy you make those who are with you'

13 **true** both 'faithful' and 'absolute'. The couplet draws back to view the folly of the relationship in the third person, and in doing so draws out the rueful and reproachful undercurrents of the quatrains.

13–14 **that . . . anything** (a) 'that although you do anything which your power enables you to do'; (b) 'that he thinks there is no evil in your will whatever you do'. *Will* means (a) power; (b) power of volition; (c) (as often in Shakespeare) 'sexual licence'. Q capitalizes 'Will', which may indicate a pun on the male or female sexual organs, as well as anticipating the play on the poet's name in e.g. *136*.

57

Being your slave, what should I do but tend
Upon the hours and times of your desire?
I have no precious time at all to spend,
Nor services to do, till you require.
Nor dare I chide the world-without-end hour   5
Whilst I (my sovereign) watch the clock for you,
Nor think the bitterness of absence sour
When you have bid your servant once adieu.
Nor dare I question with my jealous thought
Where you may be, or your affairs suppose,   10
But like a sad slave stay and think of naught,
Save where you are how happy you make those.
   So true a fool is love, that in your will,
   Though you do anything, he thinks no ill.

13 will] Q (*Will*)

1 **That god** Love, or possibly Cupid

2 **in thought ... pleasure** 'that I should even in imagination seek to regulate your times for recreation (or possibly sexual enjoyment)'. *Control* can mean both 'regulate' and *OED* 1. *trans.*, 'To check or verify, and hence to regulate (payments, receipts, or accounts generally)'. This anticipates *th'account of hours.*

3 **crave** By *c.* 1600 this word is usually used by an inferior begging a favour from a superior, but can also mean 'To long or yearn for, to desire earnestly' (*OED* 5). It therefore expresses both the poet's sense of subordination, and his insubordinate desire.

4 **vassal** feudal servant

bound could imply an informal obligation, or that the poet is actually the bondsman of the lover.

stay await

5 **at your beck** 'absolutely subject to your control'. *Beck* means 'The slightest indication of will or command' (*OED* 2).

6 **imprisoned absence** 'liberty' for the friend is imprisoning for the poet

7 **patience-tame to sufferance** trained to patient endurance of hardships. *Sufferance* means both 'suffering' (*OED* 4) and 'Patient endurance, forbearance, long-suffering' (*OED* 1). Both senses need to be in play: the suffering referred to in l. 5 does not vanish with the acquisition of the virtue of patient endurance; rather it is physically registered within the word '*sufferance*'. Q's punctuation diminishes this effect: 'patience tame, to sufferance bide each check' creates a near-tautology. If 'patience tame' is taken as a compound adjective (frequently unhyphenated in Q) then 'sufferance' must mean 'patient endurance': 'Let me, tame as patience itself, endure to the point of patient endurance, every unresponsive coldness'. This neutralizes the pain implicit in *sufferance*. Some editors punctuate 'And patience, tame to . . .' (i.e. 'and let

patience, inured to hardship . . .'). This introduces an additional grammatical subject which diminishes the intensive focus on 'I' and 'you' in the sonnet, and also allows the poem to drift into abstraction at its centre.

7 **bide each check** endure each rebuff

8 **injury** carries more of a legal (and etymologically exact) sense than a physical: 'wrongdoing, illegality', more than 'causing pain'.

9 **where you list** wherever you like. Q's *where* may represent a contracted form of 'wherever'.

charter (a) 'A written document delivered by the sovereign or legislature: a. granting privileges to, or recognizing rights of, the people, or of certain classes or individuals' (*OED* 1); hence (as usually in Shakespeare) (b) 'Privilege; immunity; publicly conceded right' (*OED* 3). The authority imputed to the friend extends as the sonnet progresses, until he becomes an absolute law-giver.

10–11 **privilege ... will** grant your own time a special freedom to do exactly what it likes

12 **Yourself ... crime** both 'to pardon yourself for crimes which you have committed', and 'to pardon yourself for crimes which you commit against yourself'

13 **I am to wait** I have to wait, in the sense 'defer one's departure until something happens' (*OED* 7), and 'To be in readiness to receive orders; hence, to be in attendance as a servant' (*OED* 9a)

14 **Not blame ... well** (a) 'Not to criticize your wishes and commands, be they good or bad' (in which *pleasure* is neutralized of all pejorative sense via its usual usage in Shakespeare to describe what a superior wishes of a servant); (b) 'Not to condemn your (sexual) freedoms be they good or bad' (in which *pleasure* becomes viciously charged). The 'hell/well' rhyme produces a sinister half-rhyme with the couplet of the previous sonnet.

58

That god forbid, that made me first your slave,
I should in thought control your times of pleasure,
Or at your hand th' account of hours to crave,
Being your vassal bound to stay your leisure.
O let me suffer (being at your beck)   5
Th' imprisoned absence of your liberty,
And, patience-tame to sufferance, bide each check
Without accusing you of injury.
Be where you list, your charter is so strong
That you yourself may privilege your time   10
To what you will: to you it doth belong
Yourself to pardon of self-doing crime.
   I am to wait, though waiting so be hell,
   Not blame your pleasure be it ill or well.

7 patience-tame] INGRAM AND REDPATH; ~, ~, Q; ~, ~, GILDON 1714; ~, ~, CAPELL   10–11 time | To] Q; time: | Do MALONE

1 **nothing new** This sonnet engages with a widespread debate in the Renaissance as to whether time proceeded circularly, and so periodically revived past customs and past political systems, or in a linear manner which allowed for innovatory departures from the ancient world. It is influenced by the discourse of Pythagoras in *Met.* 15.75–478, which presents the universe as a grand process of flux. Ecclesiastes 1: 9–10 provides biblical precedent for a belief that all things recur: 'What is it that hath been? that that shall be: and what is it that hath been done? that which shall be done: and there *is* no new thing under the sun.' Compare the defence of *new* inventions found in Louis Le Roy, *Of the Interchangeable Course or Variety of Things*, trans. R[obert] A[shley] (1594): 'Is it not then an abusing of study, and of learning, to dwell continually among the ancients, and not to endeavour to bring forth new inventions, agreeable to the manners and affairs of this time?' (128ᵛ).

3 **invention** See 38.8 n. Cf. Le Roy, 129ᵛ: 'So must learning also be provided for, by seeking of new inventions, instead of those that are lost, by changing what is not well.'

4 **The second . . . child?** 'bring to birth a literary production which has already been produced by another writer'. Associations between childbirth and writing are common in the late sixteenth century, as when Samuel Daniel cries, 'Go, wailing verse, the infants of my love, | Minerva-like brought forth without a mother', *Delia* (1592) 2.1–2.

5 **record** is stressed on the second syllable. Here, as usually in the Sonnets, written records are meant. See 55.8.

8 **Since mind . . . done** 'since the first time human experiences were recorded in writing'. *Mind* is probably used here with an archaic flavour to mean 'memory' (*OED* 1), a sense which Shakespeare otherwise only uses in phrases such as 'to have in mind'.

10 **composèd wonder . . . frame** this harmoniously constructed miracle of your form. *Composèd* may pun on the idea of the friend's body as a literary composition. *Frame* too is often used of both the human body and poetic artefacts, as in 'Now ginnes that goodly frame of Temperaunce | Fayrely to rise', *FQ* 2.12.1.

11 **mended** improved, set to rights

12 **revolution be the same** the cyclical recurrence of events and the heavenly bodies has returned us to exactly the same state as before

14 **subjects worse** (a) inferior topics; (b) inferior people. The meiosis, or deliberate diminution of the poet's object of praise, gives a double twist to the poem: the friend is praised for his singular eminence over ancient examples, but *worse* revives the suspicion of the poetry of praise aired in 35 and hints at 'they were even worse than you'.

59

If there be nothing new, but that which is
Hath been before, how are our brains beguiled,
Which, labouring for invention, bear amiss
The second burden of a former child?
O that record could with a backward look,   5
Even of five hundred courses of the sun,
Show me your image in some antique book,
Since mind at first in character was done,
That I might see what the old world could say
To this composèd wonder of your frame;   10
Whether we are mended, or whe'er better they,
Or whether revolution be the same.
    O, sure I am the wits of former days
    To subjects worse have given admiring praise.

11 whe'er] Q (where)

The sixtieth sonnet is concerned with the passage of minutes. Spenser's *Amoretti* 60 is also rich in references to the passage of the years. See René Graziani, 'The Numbering of Shakespeare's Sonnets: 12, 60, and 126', *Shakespeare Quarterly* 35 (1984), 79–82. It is indebted to *Met.* 15.178–85; Golding (15.197–206): 'In all the world there is not that that standeth at a stay. | Things ebb and flow: and every shape is made to pass away. | The time itself continually is fleeting like a brook. | For neither brook nor lightsome time can tarry still. But look | As every wave drives other forth, and that that comes behind | Both thrusteth and is thrust itself: Even so the times by kind | Do fly and follow both at once, and evermore renew. | For that that was before is left, and straight there doth ensue | Another that was never erst. Each twinkling of an eye | Doth change'.

1 **Like as** just as
  towards is monosyllabic.

2 **minutes** Q's 'minuites' may deliberately evoke both 'minutes' and, via the French 'minuit', 'midnights'.
  end plays on 'goal' and 'death', as though the minutes are eager to die.

4 **sequent** 'forming an unbroken series or course; consecutive' (*OED* 3b: earliest citation). The usage also anticipates *OED* 3a: 'Following one another in succession or in a series; successive'. Shakespeare is importing 'sequuntur' from Ovid's Latin, *Met.* 15.183 ('tempora sic fugiunt pariter pariterque sequuntur'). See Introduction, pp. 112–14.
  contend The sense 'To strive in rivalry with another, for an object; to compete, vie' (*OED* 4) is first recorded in 1589.

5 **Nativity** the newborn child. The astrological sense ('Birth considered astrologically; a horoscope' (*OED* 4)) is also present, anticipating the *crooked eclipses* later in the poem.

5 **main of light** expanse of light. First citation of 'main' in the sense 'a broad expanse' (*OED* 5b); also 'The high sea, the open ocean' (*OED* 5a), a sense activated by the *waves* of l. 1.

7 **Crookèd eclipses** malign astrological conjunctions

8 **confound** ruin, destroy

9 **transfix the flourish set on youth** 'destroy the ornament of beauty which belongs to youth'. It is difficult to say exactly how the phrase means this. *Transfix* is said by Schmidt to mean 'remove', but he cites only this instance. All other instances imply stabbing, either literally or metaphorically. Shakespeare is probably extending its physical and metaphorical sense, 'To pierce through (esp. with pain, grief, or other emotion)' (*OED* 1b *fig.*), in order to anticipate *delves*: Time subjects youth to such violent pangs of emotion, and to such physical shocks, that its bloom passes away. *Flourish* means both 'vital liveliness' and 'beautiful ornament'. The senses run through *OED* 1, 'the blossom or mass of flowers on a fruit-tree', to 2b *fig.*, 'prosperity, vigour; the "bloom" (of youth)', and thence to 3: 'Ostentatious embellishment; gloss, varnish'.

10 **delves the parallels** The lines on the brow are imagined as being parallel to each other, like furrows ploughed into the earth.

11 **Feeds on . . . truth** feeds on the delicacies produced by the constant perfection of nature

12 **but** except

13 **in hope** which only exist in my hopeful anticipation
  stand echoes, anxiously perhaps, *nothing stands* in the previous line (a figure of repetition called *ploce*), striving to give verse a monumental immobility which can counter the inevitability of destruction. That it then rhymes with the *cruel hand* of time suggests that the couplet is aware of how fragile its optimism is.

60

Like as the waves make towards the pebbled shore,
So do our minutes hasten to their end,
Each changing place with that which goes before,
In sequent toil all forwards do contend.
Nativity, once in the main of light,   5
Crawls to maturity, wherewith being crowned
Crookèd eclipses 'gainst his glory fight,
And Time that gave doth now his gift confound.
Time doth transfix the flourish set on youth,
And delves the parallels in beauty's brow,   10
Feeds on the rarities of nature's truth,
And nothing stands but for his scythe to mow.
   And yet to times in hope my verse shall stand,
   Praising thy worth, despite his cruel hand.

2 minutes] Q (minuites)

1 **will** wish, often with overtones of sexual desire. The association of the word with the commands of a superior to an inferior (as in 'What's thy will, Sir?') grows as the poet metamorphoses into the addressee's *watchman* in l. 12.

image mental picture

4 **shadows** both 'patches of shade which appear to look like you' and 'mental images', or even 'ghosts', which anticipates the *spirit* in l. 5.

mock my sight 'make me wrongly believe that you are there, and so taunt me'

5 **spirit** ghostly presence

7 **shames** shameful actions

8 **scope and tenure** (a) the focus and object; (b) the legal domain controlled by your jealousy. Most editors modernize Q's 'tenure' as 'tenor', since the two were alternative forms *c.*1600 (as is indicated by *Lucrece* l. 1310 and textual notes). However, 'tenure' has the sense of 'property which falls within the jurisdiction of a governor' and therefore meshes with the Sonnets' recurrent interest in the nature and extent of the friend's legal control over the poet. So 'You pry into my deeds in order to find out my shameful actions, which fall within the judicial control of your jealousy'. This is reinforced by a rare (sixteenth-century

Anglo-Irish) sense of *scope* (*OED* 10): 'A tract (of land); esp. a piece of land belonging to an individual owner'.

10 **my love** my affection; but also 'you, the object of my affection', who is imagined to be present in spirit. Four first-person pronouns in two lines emphasize that the poet was merely fantasizing that the friend was jealously spying on him through dreams. The octet . wistfully imagines that the friend is collaborating with the poet's jealous fantasies; the sestet ruthlessly shows that he is not.

11 **defeat** thwart

12 **watchman** both (a) 'One who keeps vigil ... a guardian' (*OED* 3), and more technically (b) 'a constable of the watch who ... patrolled the streets by night to safeguard life and property' (*OED* 4). The pun occurs in *Much Ado* 3.3.38–9: 'Why, you speak like an ancient and most quiet watchman, for I cannot see how sleeping should offend'. Compare the proverb 'One good friend watches for another', which is recorded from 1611 (Dent F716).

13 **watch** (a) keep lookout to protect your property; (b) stay awake; (c) keep watch to see if you are coming

wake (a) stay awake; (b) stay up revelling (*OED* 1d), as in *Hamlet* 1.4.9: 'The King doth wake tonight and takes his rouse'.

61

Is it thy will thy image should keep open
My heavy eyelids to the weary night?
Dost thou desire my slumbers should be broken,
While shadows like to thee do mock my sight?
Is it thy spirit that thou send'st from thee   5
So far from home into my deeds to pry,
To find out shames and idle hours in me,
The scope and tenure of thy jealousy?
O no, thy love, though much, is not so great:
It is my love that keeps mine eye awake,   10
Mine own true love that doth my rest defeat,
To play the watchman ever for thy sake.
 For thee watch I, whilst thou dost wake elsewhere,
 From me far off, with others all too near.

8 tenure] Q; tenour MALONE (*conj.* Capell)

1 **possesseth** occupies. The verb can be used of evil spirits (*OED* 5a) and of diseases (*OED* 1c), which would anticipate *remedy* in l. 3.

4 **grounded** firmly fixed or established. Suggests both foundations and nutritious soil, as in *FQ* 4.5.1: 'Friendship . . . | Without regard of good, dyes like ill grounded seeds'.

5 **Methinks** it seems to me

6 **true** well-formed

no truth of such account (a) no perfect shape so valuable; (b) no integrity or fidelity so valuable

7 **for myself** (a) by myself; (b) to satisfy myself

define 'To frame or give a precise description or definition' (*OED* 6c. *intr. or absol.*)

8 **other** others. The form is a relic of the Middle English plural 'othere'.

9 **glass** mirror

10 **Beated** a regular alternative form of 'beaten'

chapped 'Fissured; cracked; chapped' (*OED* 1). Q reads 'chopt'. The modernized

text here loses the violence generated by the conjunction with *beated*; not to modernize, however, would overemphasize the physicality so lightly registered in Q.

10 **tanned** 'That has been rendered brown or tawny, esp. by exposure to the sun; sunburnt' (*OED* 2a). To be *tanned* in this period was not considered attractive. This complements *chapped* (which suggests that the poet has been repeatedly exposed to frosts) by implying repeated exposure to the sun.

11 **quite contrary I read** I interpret in quite the opposite sense

12 **Self . . . iniquity** To love oneself to such a degree would indeed be a sin.

13 **for** in the stead of. Compare the proverb 'A friend is one's second self' (Dent F696).

14 **Painting . . . days** describing (or making up) my old age with your youthful beauty. For other sonneteers who followed the convention that they should be ageing, see *22.1* n. For the idea that praise of the friend is a form of self-praise, see *39*.

62

Sin of self-love possesseth all mine eye,
And all my soul, and all my every part;
And for this sin there is no remedy,
It is so grounded inward in my heart.
Methinks no face so gracious is as mine,　　　　　　5
No shape so true, no truth of such account,
And for myself mine own worth do define
As I all other in all worths surmount.
But when my glass shows me myself indeed,
Beated and chapped with tanned antiquity,　　　　　10
Mine own self-love quite contrary I read;
Self so self-loving were iniquity:
　　'Tis thee (my self) that for myself I praise,
　　Painting my age with beauty of thy days.

7 for] Q; so HUDSON 1881 (*conj*. Lettsom in Walker)　do] Q; so *conj*. Walker　10 Beated] Q;
'Bated MALONE; batter'd *conj*. Malone; blasted *conj*. Steevens in Malone; beaten, *conj*. Collier
chapped] Q (chopt)

Graziani, 'Numbering' (see headnote to Sonnet 60), notes that the 'grand climacteric', or main crisis in the development of the human body, was believed to occur in one's 63rd year. See headnote to 49. This sonnet marks the midpoint of the 126 poems addressed to the friend.

1 **Against** To secure me against the time when. 'In resistance to, in defence or protection from' (*OED* 13a).

2 **injurious** unjustly harmful. See 44.2 and n.

crushed and o'erworn 'broken down and worn to pieces by Time'. The metaphor suggests at once fallen masonry and clothing which is creased, its pile crushed and worn out. Compare *outworn* in 64.2.

3 **filled** See note to 17.2 above.

5 **travelled** Q's 'trauaild' suggests 'laboured' as well as 'journeyed'.

5 **steepy** both 'a precipitous journey' and 'the very depths of night'

9 **For** against

fortify '*intr.* To erect fortifications; to establish a position of defence' (*OED* 9)

10 **confounding** destructive, thwarting

11 **That** so that

memory probably a material record; but the notion that age physically slices away the memory gives a graphic explanation of the absent-mindedness of old age. The surrounding organic imagery (*spring . . . still green*) gives to age's knife something of the renovatory power of a pruning implement.

12 **though . . . life** although he cuts (understood) my lover's life

14 **still green** a set phrase, meaning, 'permanently alive and fresh', 'Full of vitality; not withered or worn out. b. of immaterial things, *esp.* the memory of a person or event' (*OED* s.v. 'green' 6).

63

Against my love shall be as I am now,
With Time's injurious hand crushed and o'er-worn,
When hours have drained his blood and filled his brow
With lines and wrinkles, when his youthful morn
Hath travelled on to age's steepy night,   5
And all those beauties whereof now he's king
Are vanishing, or vanished out of sight,
Stealing away the treasure of his spring:
For such a time do I now fortify
Against confounding age's cruel knife,   10
That he shall never cut from memory
My sweet love's beauty, though my lover's life.
  His beauty shall in these black lines be seen,
  And they shall live, and he in them, still green.

3 filled] Q (fild); filed *conj.* Kerrigan   5 travelled] Q (trauaild)

1 **fell** cruel, ruthless
2 **rich proud cost** lavish, showy extravagant things
  outworn 'Worn out, as clothes' (*OED*). Given the high cost of clothing in Shakespeare's age, it is likely that clothes are here on the poet's mind, although the word could also be used of inscriptions, as it is in Robert Sanderson's *Sermons* (1624), i.226: 'In old marbles and coins and out-worn inscriptions'.
3 **When sometime . . . razed** primarily 'When I see formerly high towers demolished to the ground', rather than the relatively lame 'When I from time to time see . . .'
4 **brass eternal slave** Here *eternal* could function either adjectivally or adverbially: 'immortal brass is a slave' or 'brass is eternally a slave'.
  mortal rage (a) deadly destructiveness; (b) the passions of the merely mortal
6 **Advantage on** advantage over. Compare *Venus* l. 405.
  kingdom The example of the erosion of the sea is often used in legal arguments in the period about the nature and limits of human jurisdiction (hence *kingdom*), as well as an instance of mutability. The two themes interpenetrate as here in *FQ* 5.4.1–21, where two brothers Amidas and Bracidas argue over ownership of a chest lost at sea by 'tract of time, that all things doth decay'. There is also an allusion to *Met.* 15.262–3; Golding 15. 287–9: 'Even so have places oftentimes exchangèd their estate, | For I have seen it sea which was substantial ground alate [formerly], | Again where sea was, I have seen the same become dry land'.

8 **Increasing . . . with store** As one side loses so the other gains, and as the one gains so the other loses. The dark vision of the poem's end is foreshadowed in the asymmetry which hides under the apparent balance of this line: *loss is increased* rather than diminished by *store*.
9 **interchange of state** At the most abstract level this means 'exchange of relative conditions'. 'Interchange' can also mean both 'vicissitude' and the exchange of reciprocal gifts (especially between aristocrats), and 'state' can extend through 'the body politic' (*OED* 29a) through to the legal sense of 'right or title to property' (*OED* 34). The phrase therefore also encompasses 'vicissitudes in political life' and 'exchanges of ownership of heritable possessions', senses activated by the comparison of sea and earth to kingdoms in the preceding lines. It may echo Golding's 'exchangèd their estate' from the passage quoted in the note to l. 6.
10 **state . . . decay** 'existence itself brought to nothing'. 'Confound' can mean 'To demolish, smash' (*OED* 1d), and 'To waste, consume, spend' (*OED* 1e). The political sense of 'state' may well be active here: so, 'commonwealths brought to nothing'.
11 **Ruin . . . ruminate** The internal semi-rhyme draws attention to the fact that the letters which make up *ruin* are hidden within *ruminate*. This anticipates the couplet's conclusion that thought and death are inextricable.
13 **which** The antecedent is *thought*, but its proximity to *death* makes thought and death become momentarily united.

64

When I have seen by Time's fell hand defacèd
The rich proud cost of outworn buried age,
When sometime lofty towers I see down razèd
And brass eternal slave to mortal rage;
When I have seen the hungry ocean gain   5
Advantage on the kingdom of the shore,
And the firm soil win of the wat'ry main,
Increasing store with loss, and loss with store;
When I have seen such interchange of state,
Or state itself confounded to decay,   10
Ruin hath taught me thus to ruminate,
That Time will come and take my love away.
    This thought is as a death, which cannot choose
    But weep to have that which it fears to lose

14 lose] Q (loose)

1 **Since** since there is neither

2 **o'ersways** combines physical and legal supremacy: 'To exercise sway over, rule over, govern' (*OED* 1); and 'In reference to physical qualities: To overpower by superior strength or intensity' (*OED* 1c).

3 **rage** destructive energy
hold a plea successfully present a legal suit

4 **action** combines the general sense of 'power to move' with the specific legal sense 'legal process; the right to raise such process' (*OED* 7a).

5 **hold out** 'To maintain resistance, remain unsubdued; to continue, endure, persist, last' (*OED* s.v. 'hold' 41j), with a strong military flavour

6 **wrackful** destructive
batt'ring The days are like battering rams.

7 **impregnable** invincible, proof against attack

8 **but time decays?** but time destroys (the gates)

10 **Shall . . . lie hid?** The friend is the treasured possession of Time, which cannot be prevented from returning to his coffers. Malone and Theobald found the idea of hiding something from a *chest* objectionable, hence their emendation to 'quest'. Time, though, simply wants to have his possession, the friend, locked away securely, as the poet had done in 52.

12 **spoil** continues the metaphor of sieging, via *OED* 1: 'Goods, esp. such as are valuable, taken from an enemy or captured city in time of war'.

14 **my love** my beloved, although the sense 'my affection' cannot be excluded

65

Since brass, nor stone, nor earth, nor boundless sea,
But sad mortality o'ersways their power,
How with this rage shall beauty hold a plea,
Whose action is no stronger than a flower?
O how shall summer's honey breath hold out   5
Against the wrackful siege of batt'ring days,
When rocks impregnable are not so stout,
Nor gates of steel so strong, but time decays?
O fearful meditation; where, alack,
Shall Time's best jewel from Time's chest lie hid?   10
Or what strong hand can hold his swift foot back,
Or who his spoil of beauty can forbid?
   O none, unless this miracle have might,
   That in black ink my love may still shine bright.

10 chest] Q; quest *conj*. Theobald in Malone   12 Or . . . of] MALONE; Or . . . Or Q; Or . . . o'er CAPELL.

1 **all these** points forward to the list which follows. Q capitalizes the personifications sporadically (Nothing, Folly, Truth, Simplicity are capitalized; faith, honour, virtue, perfection, strength, art, captive good are not). The poem reads more like a survey of abstract ills than a personification allegory, so the capitals have all been removed. There is a general resemblance to *Lucrece* ll. 848–924 and to *Hamlet* 3.1.72–84.

2 **desert a beggar born** deserving merit (personified) born to be a beggar

3 **needy nothing** beggarly worthlessness (who spends what he does not have on ornaments and trifles). Editors have sometimes suggested the phrase means 'people who have need of nothing'.
trimmed dressed, connoting ornament as in Revelation 21: 2: 'And I John saw the holy city new Jerusalem come down from God out of heaven, prepared as a bride trimmed for her husband'.

4 **purest . . . forsworn** *Faith* ranges from 'personal oaths' to 'religious beliefs' which are repudiated or broken.

5 **gilded here** suggests 'splendid'; but its usual Shakespearian sense 'superficially attractive' makes the line double-edged.
misplaced denied the place that is its due

6 **strumpeted** either 'given the reputation of a whore' or 'forcibly turned into a whore'

8 **limping sway** a crippled authority. The idea is of legal power which is not matched by physical strength, via 'sovereign power or authority; dominion, rule' (*OED* s.v. 'sway' 6a). 'Limping sway' may have had political resonances to early readers, since James I had suffered an injury in childhood which made his walk ungainly. Complaints about the disregard of merit are common in the Jacobean period, as are lists of generalized abuses linked by anaphora. See e.g. Drayton's 'The Owl' ll. 1219–25. Art judiciously makes itself tongue-tied here by refusing to make specific references to particular abuses, but the timbre of the poem points to a date after 1603.

8 **disablèd** is pronounced as four syllables. Liquids 'are frequently pronounced as though an extra vowel were introduced between them and the preceding consonant', Abbott §477.

9 **art . . . authority** learning and literature is either (a) suppressed or censored by the powers that be; or (b) inhibited by the authority of the ancients. Efforts at censorship in the period were more frequently directed against the stage than other media.

10 **doctor-like** 'Doctor' in this period is not necessarily limited to medical practitioners, but could include all those deemed sufficiently competent to teach in a particular area of study.

11 **simple truth** plain, true speech

12 **captive . . . ill** goodness is the prisoner and servant of a dominant wickedness. The context suggests *OED* II for *attending*: 'To watch over, wait upon, with service, accompany as servant'. The image conveys the idea of a high-ranking officer imprisoned and made to serve a person of lower rank.

13 **Tired with all these** The repetition of the first line (*epimone*) closes the sonnet off without allowing it to progress forwards.

14 **to die** if I die

66

Tired with all these, for restful death I cry:
As to behold desert a beggar born,
And needy nothing trimmed in jollity,
And purest faith unhapp'ly forsworn,
And gilded honour shamefully misplaced, 5
And maiden virtue rudely strumpeted,
And right perfection wrongfully disgraced,
And strength by limping sway disablèd,
And art made tongue-tied by authority,
And folly (doctor-like) controlling skill, 10
And simple truth miscalled simplicity,
And captive good attending captain ill.
   Tired with all these, from these would I be gone,
   Save that to die I leave my love alone.

1–4 The opening question combines two distinct points of view: (a) a lament for the conduct of the friend: why should such a perfect creature spend time with worthless people? This requires the emphasis in reading the first line to be placed on *infection*, and carries a rebuke. As the poem progresses on to increasingly abstract concerns it is overwritten with (b) a lament for the times: why should such a perfect being exist in a corrupted world which is so unworthy of his perfection? This shifts the emphasis of l. 1 from *infection* to *he* ('who of all people deserves a better world'), and follows on from the satirical attack on present abuses in the previous poem.

1 **infection** carries more of a moral than a physical charge in this period: 'Moral contamination; vitiation of character or habits by evil influences' (*OED* 6). Also, perhaps anticipating *impiety* in l. 2, 'Corruption of faith or loyalty by heretical or seditious principles' (*OED* 7).
live is rhymed with *achieve* only here and in the Epilogue to *Henry V* (1599), which may indicate a date for this poem at the very end of the 1590s.

2 **grace** perhaps 'lend a gloss of elegance to'

3 **advantage** social advancement and material benefit

4 **lace** 'To mark as with (gold or silver) lace or embroidery' (*OED* 6a). This may take from the noun 'lace' (5a: 'Ornamental braid used for trimming men's coats') a connotation of 'tricking oneself out with unmerited ornaments of worth'.

5 **Why should . . . cheek** 'Why should others use make-up artificially to recreate the natural beauty of his face?' Recent editors have tended to exclude references here to 'painting' in the sense of 'pictorial representation', but the poem allows both forms of artifice to coexist and attacks them both at once.

6 **And steal . . . hue** and take a lifeless appearance of beauty from his fresh and living complexion. *Seeming* emends Q's 'seeing': it is likely the compositor missed a tilde over the second 'e' in his copy.

7 **poor beauty** refers probably to the secondary artificial beauty of those who paint. Alternatively it may be personified: 'Why should poor old Beauty bother with mere painted roses?'
indirectly seek Beauty proceeds obliquely, looking for charms in artificial representations rather than in the friend himself.

8 **Roses of shadow** unreal images of roses (either in make-up or in pictorial representations)
his rose is true the hue of his cheeks is real and unfeigned (and he is faithful)

9 **Why should he live** broadens to despair the initial question *wherefore with infection should he live* to mean 'why should he even remain alive now that nature has been deprived of true vitality by his exceptional beauty?'

10 **Beggared** deprived of. The word refers to 'Nature'.
blush course with a lively flush

11 **For she . . . his** Nature's only store of beauty and vitality is the friend.

12 **proud of many** while she boasts of many offspring (who are in fact derivative offspring of the friend). The sense is not very good here, but all emendations so far proposed are unsatisfactory. Capell modernized Q's 'proud' as 'proved', which might weakly mean 'tested out by' if Shakespeare had ever used the form 'proved of' anywhere else (which he does not), or be an abbreviated form of 'approved' if Shakespeare had ever used that form elsewhere (which he does not).

13–14 The couplet marks a final effort not to criticize the friend as one who lives with *infection* by claiming that Nature retains him as a reminder of her past glory.

14 **these last** these most recent times; also perhaps 'these final days of the world', alluding to recurrent millenarian fears that the end of the world was nigh

67

Ah, wherefore with infection should he live,
And with his presence grace impiety,
That sin by him advantage should achieve
And lace itself with his society?
Why should false painting imitate his cheek,   5
And steal dead seeming of his living hue?
Why should poor beauty indirectly seek
Roses of shadow, since his rose is true?
Why should he live, now Nature bankrupt is,
Beggared of blood to blush through lively veins,   10
For she hath no exchequer now but his,
And proud of many, lives upon his gains?
    O him she stores to show what wealth she had
    In days long since, before these last so bad.

6 seeming] MALONE (*conj.* Capell); seeing Q   12 proud] Q; prov'd CAPELL

A manuscript copy is in Folger MS V.a.148, Pt. 1, fo. 22ᵛ.

1 **Thus** builds on the conclusion to the previous poem.

1, 13 **map** 'A detailed representation in epitome; a circumstantial account of a state of things. Very common in the 17th c.' (*OED* †2a *fig.*); 'The embodiment or incarnation (*of* a virtue, vice, character, etc.); the very picture or image *of*' (*OED* 2b).

days outworn past times, but also suggesting that the past has succumbed to exhaustion and destruction and perhaps subliminally too that nights of revelry have taken their toll on the friend's face (compare 61.13).

3 **bastard signs of fair** make-up, or 'unnatural outward tokens of beauty stolen from others rather than naturally conceived'

born Q's 'borne' allows for both 'given birth to' and 'borne like garments'.

5–7 **Before . . . head** Wigs (popular in the 1580s and 1590s) were sometimes made from the hair of dead people. Cf. Bassanio's similar attack on unnatural ornament in *Merchant* 3.2.92–6: 'So are those crispèd, snaky, golden locks | Which makes such wanton gambols with the wind | Upon supposèd fairness, often known | To be the dowry of a second head, | The skull that bred them in the sepulchre'.

6 **The right of sepulchres** the due possessions of the tomb

8 **Ere . . . gay** 'in days before the hair of the dead made another person beautiful'

9 **holy antique hours** those pious ages past

10 **itself and true** The friend uses no deceptive ornaments, and so is a pattern of the unadorned simplicity of the golden age.

12 **Robbing no old** stealing from no old thing

14 **what beauty was of yore** what beauty (there) was in the past

68

Thus is his cheek the map of days outworn,
When beauty lived and died as flowers do now,
Before these bastard signs of fair were born,
Or durst inhabit on a living brow:
Before the golden tresses of the dead,⠀⠀⠀⠀⠀⠀⠀⠀⠀⠀5
The right of sepulchres, were shorn away,
To live a second life on second head,
Ere beauty's dead fleece made another gay:
In him those holy antique hours are seen
Without all ornament, itself and true,⠀⠀⠀⠀⠀⠀⠀⠀10
Making no summer of another's green,
Robbing no old to dress his beauty new;
⠀⠀And him as for a map doth Nature store,
⠀⠀To show false Art what beauty was of yore.

3 born] (borne) Q⠀⠀7 a second] BENSON; a scond Q

1 **parts** combines 'portions' and 'personal attributes'.

2 **Want** lack
mend improve

3–4 **All tongues . . . commend** Everyone pays you that compliment simply by stating what is obviously the case, so that even your enemies commend you.

3 **due** Q's 'end' does not rhyme, and results either from eyeskip from 'mend' in the previous line or a misreading of what must have been 'due' in the manuscript.

5 **Thy outward** your outward appearance. Q's 'their' for 'thine/thy' is a frequent error. See 26.12. Gildon's 'thy' is slightly more probable here than Malone's 'thine'. Although 'thine' is generally used before a vowel, on two occasions in the Sonnets 'thy' appears followed by a long 'o', once in l. 13 below and also in 87.9: 'Thyself thou gav'st, thy own worth then not knowing'. In these cases the need for symmetrical repetition of 'thy' appears to overrule the requirement for 'thine' before a vowel (as also in *L.L.L.* 4.2.116). Sonnet 146.4 reads 'thy outward'.
outward praise both 'public praise', and perhaps 'merely superficial praise'.

6 **that give . . . own** The friend deserves praise as his due, so he is simply receiving what belongs to him by right when he is praised.

7 **other accents** (a) other words; (b) different emphasis
confound confute, destroy

9 **beauty of thy mind** The poem still retains the expected Neoplatonic identification of external and internal beauty; in this way it manages to displace the odium for criticizing the friend onto the unnamed observers: '*I* know your mind is as beautiful as your body; but what of those lesser creatures who can only know what your mind is like by looking at your deeds?'

10 **in guess . . . deeds** They estimate the qual-
ity of your mind by that of your deeds (which are foul).

11 **churls** ungracious creatures (with an ironically incredulous intonation, since the people referred to are simply making inferences from what they have seen the friend do). The commas surrounding the word (which I take as a parenthetical term of abuse) are not in Q. N. F. Blake has argued that Q's 'churls their thoughts' should be retained as a possessive form (analogous to 'Purchas his Pilgrimage') which means 'churls' thoughts' (*NQ* 243 (1998), 355–7). This use of 'their' as a redundant indication of a genitive form, however, lessens the opposition in the line between *their thoughts* and *their eyes*.

12 **To thy . . . weeds** They add to your glorious outward appearance the sour smell of weeds. Cf. 93.13–14 and 94.13–14.

13 **odour** smell. Editors often follow Tucker in suggesting a secondary sense 'reputation'. This is not found before the nineteenth century, and is certainly not in Shakespeare.

14 **soil** solution. Q reads 'solye'. For emendations, see collation. Those which fit the required sense (to follow on from 'why' some word meaning 'reason' or 'solution' is required) are unfortunately all neologisms. Malone's 'solve' (a noun meaning 'solution') is not otherwise found. Benson, however, evidently felt that 'soyle' was an appropriate word which fitted its context. It was in use as a verb (*OED v.*[2] 3) meaning 'To resolve, clear up, expound, or explain; to answer (a question)'. A noun 'assoil' was also used to mean 'solution' in the 1590s, although the aphetic form is not otherwise recorded. 'Soil' also has secondary associations with earth and contamination which link it with the imagery of the poem, and is also used of sexual contact in *Measure* 5.1.140–1: 'Who is as free from touch or soil with her | As she from one ungot'.

69

Those parts of thee that the world's eye doth view
Want nothing that the thought of hearts can mend:
All tongues (the voice of souls) give thee that due,
Utt'ring bare truth, even so as foes commend.
Thy outward thus with outward praise is crowned,   5
But those same tongues that give thee so thine own
In other accents do this praise confound
By seeing farther than the eye hath shown.
They look into the beauty of thy mind,
And that, in guess, they measure by thy deeds.   10
Then, churls, their thoughts (although their eyes were kind)
To thy fair flower add the rank smell of weeds.
   But why thy odour matcheth not thy show,
   The soil is this, that thou dost common grow.

3 that due] MALONE (*conj.* Capell); that end Q; thy due GILDON 1714   5 Thy] GILDON 1714;
Their Q; Thine MALONE 1790   14 soil] BENSON; solye Q; Toil GILDON; solve MALONE

1 **That thou ... defect** It is through no fault of yours that you will (inevitably) be criticized. *Defect* is stressed on the second syllable, as is *suspect* (ll. 3. 13).

thou art Q reads 'thou are'; the only other occasion in which the Sonnets use 'thou are' is in 22.2, 'So long as youth and thou are of one date', in which the plural subject ('youth and thou') explains the use of 'are'. This slip, combined with the 'their/thy' error in l. 6, suggests that 'you' and 'your' may have been overwritten with 'thou' and 'thy' in the manuscript of this poem. See 26.12 n.

2 **mark** target

was ever yet has always been. Compare the proverb 'Envy shoots at the fairest mark' (Dent E175).

3 **The ornament . . . suspect** Beauty's adornment is suspicion.

4 **crow** a bird of ill-omen. Pliny (i.276) writes of crows and rooks: 'These birds all of them keep much prattling and are full of chat; which most men take for an unlucky sign and presage of ill fortune'.

5 **So provided that**

doth but approve only proves

6 **Thy** Q reads 'Their'. For the 'their/thy' error see 26.12 n.

being wooed of time probably means 'since you are seduced by the nature of these corrupt times' or perhaps 'time is showering all its gifts upon you'. It is hard to see how the phrase can mean 'being led astray by your youthful years' or 'wooed because of your time of life' as many editors wish. Of the many emendations proposed the manuscript suggestion in the Bodley-Caldecott copy, 'woo'd ofttime', is attractively simple. Q is retained as the *difficilior lectio*, but it is so difficult that Bodley may be preferable.

7 **canker ... love** Canker worms proverbially love the fairest blooms. See 35.4 n.

8 **prime** youth, spring

9 **the ambush of young days** Youth is presented as a time in which one could be surprised by enemies.

10 **charged** primarily 'attacked'; also perhaps 'blamed, censured' (*OED* 15a)

11–12 **Yet ... enlarged** 'Yet this praise cannot be so irrefutably strong as to prevent the attacks of envy, which is constantly captured and then freed.' The final image suggests the Blattant Beast of *FQ* 6.12.23–41, which is chained up by Calidore and then breaks free once more.

13–14 **If some ... owe** If some suspicion of wickedness did not cloud your appearance you would be sole monarch over whole kingdoms of lovers. *Suspect* means 'suspicion'. *Owe* means 'own'. The couplet stays on the level of outward appearance (*masked . . . show*) and pointedly avoids reflections on the friend's deeds or moral nature.

70

That thou art blamed shall not be thy defect,
For slander's mark was ever yet the fair.
The ornament of beauty is suspect,
A crow that flies in heaven's sweetest air.
So thou be good, slander doth but approve   5
Thy worth the greater, being wooed of time.
For canker vice the sweetest buds doth love,
And thou present'st a pure unstainèd prime.
Thou hast passed by the ambush of young days,
Either not assailed, or victor, being charged;   10
Yet this thy praise cannot be so thy praise
To tie up envy, evermore enlarged.
    If some suspect of ill masked not thy show
    Then thou alone kingdoms of hearts shouldst owe.

1 art] BENSON; are Q   6 Thy] MALONE (*conj.* Capell); Their Q   wooed of time] Q; woo'd oftime *MS conj. in Bodley-Caldecott*; void of crime *conj.* Malone; woo'd o'th'time *conj.* Ingram and Redpath

The expected term of life is threescore and ten (70) years; as Duncan-Jones notes, the 71st sonnet turns to thoughts of death. A manuscript copy is found in MS Folger V.a.162, fo. 12ᵛ.

1 **No** The intensity of self-denial (*No . . . Nay . . . O if*) in fact makes strong claims to be remembered, linking this sonnet with 57 as a poem in which professed abjection masks an attempt to claim reciprocal love. See Introduction, pp. 121–2.

2 **surly sullen bell** The passing bell was rung to mark the death of a parishioner, and was then rung annually for a fee in remembrance of the dead.

4 **vilest worms** Q's archaic form 'vildest' has greater phonic weight than its modernized equivalent. 'I shall say to corrup-tion, Thou art my father, *and* to the worm, Thou art my mother and my sister', Job 17: 14.

6 **so** both 'in such a way' and 'to such an extent'

7 **in your sweet thoughts** The phrase makes a compensation for oblivion: if the poet is forgotten about he at least has the pleasure of remaining unnoticed in the friend's *sweet thoughts*. That pleasure is, however, immediately qualified by *If*.

8 **make you woe** cause you grief

10 **compounded** mingled with

12 **decay** die

13 **look into** investigate

14 **mock you with me** use your love for me as a means of scorning you; also 'associate you with their already established mockery of me'

71

No longer mourn for me when I am dead
Than you shall hear the surly sullen bell
Give warning to the world that I am fled
From this vile world with vilest worms to dwell:
Nay, if you read this line, remember not   5
The hand that writ it, for I love you so
That I in your sweet thoughts would be forgot,
If thinking on me then should make you woe.
O, if (I say) you look upon this verse
When I (perhaps) compounded am with clay,   10
Do not so much as my poor name rehearse;
But let your love even with my life decay,
    Lest the wise world should look into your moan
    And mock you with me after I am gone.

2 Than] Q (Then)   surly sullen] Q; sullen surly FOL5   8 you] Q; me FOL5

1 **recite** tell (often with a suggestion as now of repeating something learnt by rote from a book). There may be a more formal sense (*OED* 2b *Law*: 'To rehearse or state in a deed or other document (some fact bearing closely upon the matter in hand)'), which would anticipate *prove* in l. 4.

2–3 **love | After my death** Q does not punctuate after *love*, which allows *after my death* to function with both *forget me quite* and (wistfully) with *love*.

4 **prove** show (to the satisfaction of a chillingly dispassionate authority)

6 **To do . . . desert** (a) to praise me more than I deserve; (b) to do more for me than my merits could if left unassisted

7 **hang more praise** The image is of a monument strewn with verses or trophies.

7 **I** is ungrammatical, presumably for the sake of rhyme.

8 **niggard** mean, sparing

9–10 **O, lest . . . untrue** The paradox here is that a love which is *true* (faithful) might lead the friend to lavish false praises on the poet. *Untrue* functions both as an adjective agreeing with *me* and as adverb describing the friend's hypothetical speech of praise.

11 **My name be buried** let my name be buried (subjunctive)

12 **nor . . . nor** neither . . . nor

13 **bring forth** is often used of poetic compositions: so 'my sonnets'.

14 **so should you** (be ashamed)
nothing worth which are without any value (i.e. me)

72

O, lest the world should task you to recite
What merit lived in me that you should love
After my death (dear love) forget me quite,
For you in me can nothing worthy prove;
Unless you would devise some virtuous lie,   5
To do more for me than mine own desert,
And hang more praise upon deceasèd I
Than niggard truth would willingly impart.
O, lest your true love may seem false in this,
That you for love speak well of me untrue,   10
My name be buried where my body is,
And live no more to shame nor me, nor you.
   For I am shamed by that which I bring forth,
   And so should you, to love things nothing worth.

6 To do more for me] Q; To doe for me more *conj.* Taylor in Oxford

2 **or none, or few** Some editors remove Q's comma in order to produce a straight choice ('either none or few'). Q's punctuation creates the effect of a searching eye, which sees first no leaves and then a few reminders of past luxuriance.

3 **against** in anticipation of; also perhaps 'in opposition to'

4 **Bare ruined choirs** Malone's emendation of Q's 'Bare rn'wed quiers' is substantively a modernization of Benson's 'Bare ruin'd quires'. *Choirs* refers to 'That part of a church appropriated to the singers; *spec.* the part eastward of the nave, in which the services are performed' (*OED* 2a). The comparison depends primarily on the fact that singing once went on both in the trees and in the choirs, but may be reinforced by the visual similarity between the silhouette of a bare tree and of the ruined framework of Gothic tracery. Q's 'quiers' may also distantly suggest 'quires' of paper, a sense activated both by *yellow leaves* in l. 2 (cf. *17*.9) and by the disparaging remarks on Shakespeare's own works with which the previous sonnet ends. The passage invites comparison with *Cymbeline* 3.3.42–3: 'Our cage | We make a choir, as doth the prisoned bird'.

4 **where late the sweet birds sang** The phrase applies simultaneously to the trees (once filled with birds) and to the *ruined choirs*, once filled with a singing choir. It is also possible that, on the narrower time-scale implied by *late* (recently), birds used to sing on the ruins. The effect is of both recent and longer-term abandonment.

6 **fadeth** The subject is *such day*, but as sunset also fades in the west *day* may seem for a moment to be a hanging subject, left deprived of the activity of a verb.

7 **Which** The antecedent is *twilight*, but a reader might for a moment see *day*, and even *west*, as possible alternatives. This grammatical uncertainty widens the sway of night, which seems at once to absorb twilight, the day, sunset, and even perhaps the west.

8 **Death's second self** is a conventional representation of sleep.

seals up (a) encloses, as in a coffin, and marks with a seal to prevent unauthorized opening; (b) 'seels up' as a falconer stitches up the eyes of a hawk, as in *Macbeth* 3.2.47–8: 'Come, seeling night, | Scarf up the tender eye of pitiful day'.

12 **Consumed with** choked by (ash). Cf. *1*.5–7. The third quatrain eases the poem towards total darkness: *autumn*, then *twilight*, then the final stages of a day as a fire is allowed to choke itself in ash.

14 **that** the poet; also life

leave forgo; the sense 'depart from' is also in play

73

That time of year thou mayst in me behold
When yellow leaves, or none, or few, do hang
Upon those boughs which shake against the cold,
Bare ruined choirs, where late the sweet birds sang.
In me thou seest the twilight of such day   5
As after sunset fadeth in the west,
Which by and by black night doth take away,
Death's second self, that seals up all in rest.
In me thou seest the glowing of such fire
That on the ashes of his youth doth lie,   10
As the death-bed whereon it must expire,
Consumed with that which it was nourished by.
   This thou perceiv'st, which makes thy love more strong,
   To love that well, which thou must leave ere long.

4 Bare ruined choirs] MALONE; Bare rn'wd quiers Q; Bare ruin'd cuires BENSON; Barren'd of quires CAPELL

1 **contented** Q has no punctuation here. Malone's colon (often adopted) is unnecessary.

when that fell arrest i.e. death. *Fell* means 'cruel, deadly'. 'Arrest' can mean just 'pause or cessation'. The lack of *bail* referred to in l. 2 would have activated the modern sense 'to apprehend someone' *(OED* 8), as in *Hamlet* 5.2.288–9: 'this fell sergeant Death | Is strict in his arrest'.

2 **bail** 'Security given for the release of a prisoner from imprisonment, pending his trial' *(OED* 5)

3 **some interest** some right of ownership or title *(OED* 1a), rather than 'money paid for the use of money lent' *(OED* 10a). The conceit here is that the poet's life has a continuing share in the poems; as the poems pass on after the poet's death to the friend, he retains a partial share of the poet through the poems.

4 **for memorial** (a) as a reminder; (b) as a formal monument

5 **review** 'To survey; to take a survey of' *(OED* 5a). Manuscript poems in the period were often copied into miscellanies and 'improved' by the copyist. This activates the sense 'To look over or through (a book, etc.) in order to correct or improve; to revise' *(OED* 3a), as in Holland's translation of *Plutarch's Moralia* 1274: 'Dionysius had put into his hands a tragedy of his own making, commanding him to review and correct the same'. This would allay the unease of G. B. Evans, who finds the repetition of *review* 'rhetorically flat' and suggests emending to *renew*.

6 **was which was**

consecrate to solemnly devoted to you (like a religious shrine)

7 **The earth can have but earth** echoes the Elizabethan burial service: 'earth to earth, ashes to ashes, dust to dust', which was proverbial (Dent E30).

8 **spirit** monosyllabic. It may mean 'soul' *(OED* 2a), but its opposition to *dregs* suggests that it may also mean 'the sweet volatile essence' (as in *OED* 21a, just becoming active in this period), with perhaps a glance back to the idea of preserving life through the extraction of perfume in 5 and 6.

9 **So then** (a) when I die; (b) therefore. The past tense *(hast lost)* suddenly verifies the argument: the poet presents himself as already dead while he offers his consolation to the friend, which rings out like an echo from the grave.

but only

9–11 **dregs . . . knife** The four noun clauses in apposition here all describe *my body being dead*, which is both the useless remnant of life *(dregs)*, a thing that is preyed upon by worms, and something which is conquered in a cowardly manner by a person of no account *(the coward conquest of a wretch's knife)*. The last phrase is problematic because *coward* functions chiefly as an adjective which is transferred from the *wretch* to his action, but is also used to register contempt for the weakness of the body (a mere coward). Editors have also fruitlessly speculated as to who the *wretch* is (Shakespeare, Marlowe, Death, Time, or an unnamed assassin are the favoured candidates). It seems most likely to be a generic term for 'any worthless person'.

12 **of thee** by you

13 **The worth . . . contains** the real value of the body is the spirit

14 **this** i.e. this poem

74

But be contented when that fell arrest
Without all bail shall carry me away;
My life hath in this line some interest,
Which for memorial still with thee shall stay.
When thou reviewest this, thou dost review   5
The very part was consecrate to thee.
The earth can have but earth, which is his due;
My spirit is thine, the better part of me.
So then thou hast but lost the dregs of life,
The prey of worms, my body being dead,   10
The coward conquest of a wretch's knife,
Too base of thee to be rememberèd.
    The worth of that, is that which it contains,
    And that is this, and this with thee remains.

1 contented] Q; contented: MALONE   5 review] Q; renew *conj.* G. P. Evans   12 rememberèd] Q (remembred)

1 **So . . . life** 'you nourish my thoughts as food nourishes life'

2 **sweet seasoned** gentle and temperate. *Seasoned* carries the senses 'Seasonable, opportune, suitable' (*OED* 1) and 'Flavoured, spiced' (*OED* 2). Some editors read 'sweet-seasoned', meaning both 'tempered with gentleness or sweetness' and perhaps 'of the sweet season' (Pooler).

3 **for the peace of you** in order to obtain the peace afforded by your company

5 **proud as an enjoyer** glorying in his material possession. To have 'enjoyment' of something is in effect to have possession of it.

6 **Doubting** fearing
filching age thievish age in which we live

7 **counting** reckoning. The word bridges the gap between the miser, obsessively counting his money, and the lover's assessment of what is most enjoyable.

8 **bettered . . . pleasure** thinking it better than what I had thought best (that is, privately contemplating you) that everyone should see the source of my delight

10 **clean** is an adverb: completely, utterly.

12 **Save what . . . took** except what is received from you or which must be taken from you (presumably because the friend will not always voluntarily supply it). For the sexual senses of 'have' and 'take' see Partridge, 119 and 197.

13 **pine** starve. Cf. *Lucrece* l. 1115.

14 **Or . . . away** Either feasting on every delight, or with all my source of nourishment absent. *Gluttoning* is the first cited instance in *OED* of the verb.

75

So are you to my thoughts as food to life,
Or as sweet seasoned showers are to the ground;
And for the peace of you I hold such strife
As 'twixt a miser and his wealth is found:
Now proud as an enjoyer, and anon   5
Doubting the filching age will steal his treasure,
Now counting best to be with you alone,
Then bettered that the world may see my pleasure;
Sometime all full with feasting on your sight,
And by and by clean starvèd for a look.   10
Possessing or pursuing, no delight,
Save what is had or must from you be took.
    Thus do I pine and surfeit day by day,
    Or gluttoning on all, or all away.

3 peace] Q; price *or* sake *conj.* Malone

1 **pride** 'ostentatious adornment or orna-
mentation' (*OED* 7). The word, like many
terms used to describe the vitality which
the Sonnets supposedly lack, has pejora-
tive associations. The poem as a whole
plays with the varied connotations of
mutability in the period, both positive
(bringing innovation), and negative
(fickle departures from stable ancient
points of reference).

2 **variation** here 'variety' in a positive
sense. Many sixteenth-century usages of
the word associate it with fickleness or
discord. (The musical sense, 'repetition of
a theme in a new form', is not found
before the nineteenth century.)
quick change 'lively variety'. *Quick* may
suggest 'Living, endowed with life, in con-
trast to what is naturally inanimate' (*OED*
1a) and contrast with *barren* above.

3 **glance** 'To move rapidly, esp. in an oblique
or transverse direction; to dart, shoot; to
spring *aside*' (*OED* 2)

4 **new-found methods** The word 'method'
in the period 1590–1600 was undergoing
significant changes. Emergent senses
include: 'A special form of procedure
adopted in any branch of mental activity'
(*OED* 2a) and 'a way of doing anything,
esp. according to a defined and regular
plan' (*OED* 3a; first cited in *Errors* 2.2.34);
'an author's design or plan' (*OED* 6a, first
cited from *1 Henry VI* 3.1.13: 'the method
of my pen'); 'A regular, systematic
arrangement of literary materials; a
methodical exposition' *OED* 6b). As Put-
tenham put it, 5: 'If Poesy be now an Art
. . . and yet were none, until by studious
persons fashioned and reduced into a
method of rules and precepts'. Shake-

speare describes his verse as lacking inno-
vation in language which draws on recent
literary criticism and displays his own
powers of linguistic innovation.

4 **compounds strange** *OED* suggests 'A
compound word, a verbal compound'
(*OED* 2c). At the end of Jonson's *Poetaster*
Crispinus, a character representing John
Marston, is made to vomit out his polysyl-
labic coinages. Compound epithets were,
however, favourites with Shakespeare.
The phrase plays on 'A compound sub-
stance; *spec.* a compounded drug, as
opposed to "simples" ' (*OED* 2a), exploit-
ing the potentially poisonous effect of
such medicines to suggest that strange
words can kill. Compare *Cymbeline* 1.5.8:
'These most poisonous compounds',
which is *OED*'s first citation of this sense.

5 **all one** constantly the same

6 **noted weed** familiar dress

7 **tell** relate. Q reads 'fel'.

8 **their birth** 'Parentage, lineage, ex-
traction, descent; *esp.* rank, station,
position' (*OED* 5a). The antecedent of
their is *every* word, which is taken as
plural.
where whence

11 **new** afresh

13 **daily new and old** The same sun bursts
forth freshly each day. The triumphal
image makes explicit what the many
linguistic innovations in the poem have
already made implicit: that Shakespeare's
professed old-fashionedness is novelty.

14 **telling what is told** (a) relating what has
already been related; (b) counting what
has been counted before. Sense (b) picks
out the financial register of *spending* in l.
12.

76

Why is my verse so barren of new pride,
So far from variation or quick change?
Why with the time do I not glance aside
To new-found methods, and to compounds strange?
Why write I still all one, ever the same,   5
And keep invention in a noted weed,
That every word doth almost tell my name,
Showing their birth, and where they did proceed?
O know, sweet love, I always write of you,
And you and love are still my argument;   10
So all my best is dressing old words new,
Spending again what is already spent:
   For as the sun is daily new and old,
   So is my love, still telling what is told.

7 tell] MALONE (*conj.* Capell); fel Q; tell LINTOT; sell *conj.* This edition

1 **wear** endure, or wear away. Q reads 'were'. A seventeenth-century reader might have had a glimpse of an accelerated process of ageing ('your mirror will show you how your beauties were') before settling on 'your mirror will show you how your beauties are withstanding the effects of time'.

2 **Thy dial** The possessive pronoun suggests a personal timepiece is meant, rather than a sundial, although the *shady stealth* of l. 7 evokes the movement of the sun's shadow across a dial's face. Shakespeare uses the word in both senses: cf. *3 Henry VI (True Tragedy)* 2.5.24–5: 'To carve out dials quaintly, point by point, | Thereby to see the minutes how they run', and *As You Like It* 2.7.20–3: 'And then he drew a dial from his poke, | And . . . | Says very wisely "It is ten o'clock" '. The word can also be used of large clocks, as in Barnabe Barnes, *Parthenophil and Parthenophe* (1593), 56, which compares each element of the lover to a part of a clock. *Dial* is also used in the period in the title of didactic works, such as Guevara's *Dial of Princes* (trans. North (1557), sig. b1ᵛ), which 'showeth and teacheth us, how we ought to occupy our minds'.
minutes Q's 'mynuits' also suggests 'midnights' via the French 'minuit'. See *60.2*.

3 **vacant leaves** blank sheets. Steevens first suggested that this poem may have been written to accompany the gift of a blank manuscript notebook (cf. *122*). This line then would mean 'you will write your thoughts on these blank pages'.

4 **taste** experience

6 **mouthèd** gaping, open-mouthed (*OED* 2)
give thee memory remind you. The odd locution unites remembering with learning for the first time.

7 **shady stealth** slow-moving shadow; also anticipating *thievish* in l. 8, as Time steals away youth like a thief by night. The

imperceptible motion of a clock's hand was proverbial (Dent D321).

9 **Look what** whatever (as at *9.9*); 'determine' and 'have regard to' also register.

10 **Commit** consign. Table books could be used as an external form of memory in the period, as in Hamlet's 'My tables— meet it is I set it down | That one may smile and smile and be a villain' (1.5.108–9).
waste blanks these empty sheets of paper. Q's 'blacks' might refer to ink, but is hard to reconcile with 'these', a pronoun which seems most naturally to be in concord with the *vacant leaves* referred to above. The manuscript copy probably had a tilde over the 'a', a standard abbreviation for 'an' often misread by compositors, as it was in *Hamlet* Q2 2.2.348, which reads 'black verse' where F1 and Q1 read 'blanke'.

10–12 **thou shalt . . . mind** The exhortation to breed from Sonnets *1–17* has become metaphorical: 'Leave those children (i.e. writings) which were born from your brain, and nurse them for a while, and you will find in them a new resemblance of your mind, as one sees a new resemblance of oneself in one's children, once they have grown up.' *To take a new acquaintance* is the equivalent of 'to make an acquaintance'.

13 **offices** kindly duties. The word evokes the Ciceronian conception of an *officium* which can embrace family responsibilities: the friend is urged to keep a kindly watch on his metaphorical family of thoughts and writings. The couplet also points back to the whole argument of the poem, urging the friend to repeat, as a duty, or as a clerk in holy orders says the *offices* of the dead (*OED* 5), his observations of the passage of time, which will enrich him and his writing.

77

Thy glass will show thee how thy beauties wear,
Thy dial how thy precious minutes waste,
The vacant leaves thy mind's imprint will bear,
And of this book this learning mayst thou taste:
The wrinkles which thy glass will truly show   5
Of mouthèd graves will give thee memory;
Thou by thy dial's shady stealth mayst know
Time's thievish progress to eternity.
Look what thy memory cannot contain,
Commit to these waste blanks, and thou shalt find   10
Those children nursed, delivered from thy brain,
To take a new acquaintance of thy mind.
   These offices, so oft as thou wilt look,
   Shall profit thee, and much enrich thy book.

1 wear] GILDON 1714; were Q   2 minutes] Q (mynuits)   3 The] Q, These CAPELL   6 thee] Q;
the BENSON   10 blanks] MALONE (*conj.* Theobald); blacks Q

Sonnets *78–86* concern a 'rival poet', who has been severally identified with Chapman, Marlowe, Jonson, and a variety of lesser figures. There are moments in the sequence (notably *86*) which appear to attack claims to divine inspiration of a kind which were made more consistently by Chapman than by any other English poet of the period, but on the whole there are insufficient grounds for finally identifying a single rival. Sonnet sequences do occasionally attack scribbling rivals, although never at such length (the anonymous *Zepheria* (1594), Canzon 31: 'Admit he write, my quill hath done as much: | Admit he sigh, that have I done and more'). In the criticism and poetry of the 1590s claims for the value and critical integrity of one's own verse are often made in the form of attacks on usually unnamed and often composite rivals: so Daniel's *Delia* (1592), 46.1–2 defines its own project against that of others, 'Let others sing of Knights and Palladines, | In agèd accents, and untimely words', and Sidney frequently opposes his own art—which he claims is relatively unornamented and the product of passion which has not been learnt by rote from Petrarch—to that of unnamed rivals. The 'rival poet' is probably a similar composite, born out of the need to define and defend one's own writing by opposition to that of another.

1–4 So oft . . . disperse 'I have invoked you as my inspiration so often, and have found you such a benefit to my writing, that every stranger has adopted my practice and circulates their verse under the protection of your patronage.' *Fair assistance* delicately suggests that the friend provides at once material assistance through patronage ('deserved material reward'), elegant critical help, and a beauty which inspires. *Alien* is italicized in Q, probably to indicate that it is a rare word. *OED* cites no other adjectival usage under 1, 'Belonging to another person, place, or family; strange, foreign, not of one's own', after 1382. *Disperse* is used in *OED* sense 4b: 'To distribute, put into circulation (books, coins, articles of commerce); to give currency to', suggesting that the

friend's patronage gives value to poetry issued in his name.

5 on high (a) from the heavens; (b) at high volume

7 added feathers In falconry feathers were added ('imped') onto the wings of birds to replace broken plumage. Alternatively stolen plumage could be used to beautify the ugly: Shakespeare himself was called by Robert Greene 'an upstart crow beautified with our feathers'.

learned's Q's 'learneds' could also represent a metaplasmic superlative form of learned, corresponding to 'learnedest's'. Cf. *51.10* n.

9 compile compose. The word was archaic by 1600 in this sense: later usages tend to mean 'mere gathering together of pre-existing documents'. It suits the humility with which Shakespeare is presenting his own work. The verb is otherwise only used by Shakespeare in *85.2*, another poem which considers rival poets, and *L.L.L.*, a play much concerned with the banging together of derivative Petrarchan poems.

10 influence that which gives it strength and status. There may be an allusion to the *influence* of the stars on the affairs of men, for which see 15.4 n.

11 mend the style improve on the ornament and verbal disposition

12 graces gracèd be are improved by your additional touches of elegance. The musical sense 'to provide with grace notes (trills etc.)' is not cited in *OED* before 1659, but may be anticipated here.

13 thou art all my art you provide the entire substance of my skill (not merely its ornamentation)

advance Both this and *influence* can refer to social or political authority: 'To raise or promote (a person) in rank or office, to prefer' (*OED* 10a). The friend bestows position and authority on an unworthy recipient.

14 learning . . . ignorance Both of these terms had wider and stronger senses in the sixteenth century than they do now: *learning* implies achieved mastery in all the arts and in what we now call sciences; *ignorance* connotes not simple lack of knowledge but lack of all cultivation.

78

So oft have I invoked thee for my Muse
And found such fair assistance in my verse
As every alien pen hath got my use,
And under thee their poesy disperse.
Thine eyes, that taught the dumb on high to sing,   5
And heavy ignorance aloft to fly,
Have added feathers to the learnèd's wing,
And given grace a double majesty.
Yet be most proud of that which I compile,
Whose influence is thine, and born of thee.   10
In others' works thou dost but mend the style,
And arts with thy sweet graces gracèd be:
    But thou art all my art, and dost advance
    As high as learning my rude ignorance.

7 learned's] Q (learneds); learnedst *conj.* Anon. in Cambridge

2 **gentle grace** (a) mild elegance; (b) benign generosity; (c) high-born excellence

3 **decayed** can mean 'dead' (as in 71.12 and 15.11), and 'beaten down by age' (as in 13.9 and 16.3). It combines the poet's fear that his art has been superseded (as in 76) with his anxieties about his own decrepitude (compare 37).

4 **give another place** yield supremacy to another person, as in a formal procession or state entry organized by rank

5 **thy lovely argument** the beautiful subject for verse which is you

7 **thy poet** (i.e. no longer me). For the contemptuous usage of *poet*, see 17.7 n.
of thee . . . invent whatever he finds as a

literary subject in you. *Invent* often implies that the matter found out already exists: *of thee* may therefore have a sense of 'taken from you', which is brought out by *robs* in l. 8.

9 **lends** attributes to, with a play on the financial sense

10 **behaviour** 'Good manners, elegant deportment' (*OED* 1e) as much as the neutral 'way of conducting yourself'

11 **afford** primarily 'offer', but also with a suggestion, crisply emphasized in the couplet, that the poet's imagination is impoverished, possessing only what the friend has previously given him

14 **owes** is obliged to pay you

79

Whilst I alone did call upon thy aid
My verse alone had all thy gentle grace,
But now my gracious numbers are decayed,
And my sick Muse doth give another place.
I grant (sweet love) thy lovely argument   5
Deserves the travail of a worthier pen,
Yet what of thee thy poet doth invent
He robs thee of, and pays it thee again.
He lends thee virtue, and he stole that word
From thy behaviour; beauty doth he give   10
And found it in thy cheek; he can afford
No praise to thee but what in thee doth live.
   Then thank him not for that which he doth say,
   Since what he owes thee, thou thyself dost pay.

2 **better spirit** the 'poet' of the previous sonnet. *Spirit* is monosyllabic.

use continues the financial metaphors of the previous poem: turn a fast buck from usury.

5 **(wide . . . is)** which is as capacious as the sea

7 **saucy barque** presumptuous small boat. *Saucy c.*1600 conveys a strong sense of indecorous disrespect for social rank. Cf. *Troilus* 1.3.41–3: 'Where's then the saucy boat, | Whose weak untimbered sides but even now | Co-rivalled greatness?'

inferior is trisyllabic.

8 **wilfully** (a) 'According to one's own will; at will, freely' (*OED* 2b); (b) 'In a self-willed manner, perversely, obstinately, stubbornly' (*OED* 5).

9 **shallowest help** slightest assistance. In the conceit of the poem Shakespeare's barque is presented as a boat with a very small draught which can exist in the shallows of his patron's favour, whereas the rival poet's vessel can venture onto the *sound-less deep* (l. 10), i.e. the unfathomable depths of the centre of the ocean.

11 **(being wrecked)** (a) since I am already wrecked; (b) when I happen to be wrecked

12 **tall building** high-masted, and presumably also deep in draught

goodly pride rich equipment. *Pride* is used, as often, to confer praise whilst suggesting presumption. See e.g. 76.1.

13 **cast away** abandoned, made masterless; also with a very strong theological sense of 'having been denied God's grace', as (frequently) in the marginal notes to the Geneva Bible. The maritime context here may reflect Jonah 2: 4–5: 'Then I said, I am cast away out of thy sight: yet will I look again toward thine holy Temple. The waters compassed me about unto the soul: the depth closed me round about, and the weeds were wrapped about mine head.'

14 **The worst . . . decay** 'The worst aspect of my story was that (a) my beloved (b) my affection was the source of my ruin.'

80

O, how I faint when I of you do write,
Knowing a better spirit doth use your name,
And in the praise thereof spends all his might
To make me tongue-tied speaking of your fame.
But since your worth (wide as the ocean is)   5
The humble as the proudest sail doth bear,
My saucy barque (inferior far to his)
On your broad main doth wilfully appear.
Your shallowest help will hold me up afloat,
Whilst he upon your soundless deep doth ride;   10
Or (being wrecked) I am a worthless boat,
He of tall building, and of goodly pride.
   Then if he thrive and I be cast away,
   The worst was this, my love was my decay.

11 wrecked] Q (wrackt)

1–2 **Or ... Or** Whether (*OED* sense 3b) ... or.
See Abbott §136. The poem works by
establishing a careful asymmetry beneath
these apparently symmetrical alterna-
tives: there is no suggestion that the
friend will rot, or that he will compose an
epitaph for the poet.

3 **From hence** from this world; possibly
also anticipating the senses of the same
phrase in l. 5 'from this poem' and 'from
henceforth'

4 **in me each part** all the qualities I have.
Just possibly also 'although every aspect
of you will be forgotten by me in death'.

6 **I ... to all the world must die** I must lose at
once my existence and my reputation in
the eyes of the world.

7 **common grave** undistinguished burial.
Bones were in this period jumbled
together in charnel houses (and it was to
avoid this fate that tradition has it Shake-
speare composed the epitaph on his tomb,
'Blessed be the man that spares these
stones, | And cursed be he that moves my
bones'), so also perhaps 'shared with
others'.

8 **entombèd in men's eyes** (a) placed in a
splendid tomb where all can see you; (b)
given a tomb in the eyes of those who read
my poems. Sense (b) anticipates the fol-
lowing quatrain, which puts increasing
emphasis on the revitalizing power of
verse when it is read aloud with *tongue*
and *breath*. It also moves this quatrain
beyond a simple restatement of the oppo-
sition between the poet's fate (oblivion)
and that of the friend (stately epitaphs).

9 **Your ... verse** my verse will be your mon-
ument. A *monument* could be an effigy or
written memorial, not just a stone edifice.
The inversion of the phrase allows for the
momentary reading 'your monument is
all I need for verse', before the remainder
of the sestet moves to consider the
immortality conferred by the constant
rereadings of verse. Milton's poem 'On
Shakespeare', ll. 1–4, takes its departure
from this poem: 'What need my Shake-
speare for his honoured bones | The
labour of an age in pilèd stones, | Or that
his hallowed relics should be hid | Under
a star-ypointing pyramid'.

12 **breathers** a Shakespearian coinage for
'living creatures'

81

Or I shall live your epitaph to make,
Or you survive when I in earth am rotten,
From hence your memory death cannot take,
Although in me each part will be forgotten.
Your name from hence immortal life shall have,   5
Though I (once gone) to all the world must die.
The earth can yield me but a common grave
When you entombèd in men's eyes shall lie:
Your monument shall be my gentle verse,
Which eyes not yet created shall o'er-read,   10
And tongues-to-be your being shall rehearse,
When all the breathers of this world are dead.
   You still shall live (such virtue hath my pen)
   Where breath most breathes, even in the mouths of men.

1 **married** i.e. irrevocably tied, 'forsaking all other' as the Solemnization of Matrimony in the Book of Common Prayer has it. The past tense *wert* hints that the marriage has been irrevocably damaged by the friend's infidelity in accepting the *dedicated words* of other writers.

2 **attaint** dishonour, or the reputation of dishonour, especially sexual dishonour. Shakespeare probably found the word in Daniel's *Complaint of Rosamond* l. 38, which follows the sonnet sequence *Delia*: 'Her legend justifies her foul attaint'. Possibly also 'disease': see *Venus* l. 741 n., where there is a possible link with venereal disease.

o'er-look read; perhaps 'cast a glance at' or 'To look down upon' (*OED* 4)

3 **dedicated words** (a) 'devoted words'; (b) words of praise in a poem dedicated to a particular recipient

4 **their fair subject** It is just possible this should read 'thy fair subject' (i.e. the beautiful subject which is you) given the frequency of the 'their/thy' error in Q, on which see 26.12 n.

5 **fair** (a) beautiful; (b) blond; (c) just, anticipating *finding* in the semi-legal sense in l. 6

6 **Finding . . . praise** in finding (as a jury does) that your merit exceeds my capacity to praise; or perhaps 'lies beyond a boundary past which it is unseemly to praise'

8 **Some . . . days** some more up-to-date production of these times which constantly improve on what has gone before

(compare 32.5). *Stamp* may simply mean 'Character, kind' (*OED* 13e). It might also continue the submerged legal metaphor and mean 'seal of authority'. It can also (although rarely) mean 'printing press' (*OED* 6).

10 **strainèd touches** 'forcedly artificial ornaments'. *OED* cites this as the first instance of 'strained' 5: 'interpreted in a laboured, far-fetched, or non-natural sense'. *Touches* is used in sense 10a: 'a stroke or dash of a brush, pencil, pen, chisel, or the like'.

11 **sympathized** represented; also used by Shakespeare to convey a correspondence between an emotion or object and its representation in *Richard II* 5.1.46–7: 'the senseless brands will sympathize | The heavy accent of thy moving tongue, | And in compassion weep the fire out', and *Lucrece* l. 1113.

12 **plain** exploits the range of senses from 'unornamented' to 'honest'. Often used in the period 1580–1610 to mean 'speech lacking the schemes and tropes of rhetoric and therefore honest'. For the association between make-up and excessive rhetorical ornamentation, see 21.3 n.

13 **gross painting** (a) crude artificial ornaments resembling make-up; (b) bad pictorial representation; (c) excessive rhetorical ornamentation.

14 **need** lack

in thee in applying it to thee; also with a hint of criticism of the friend himself for contaminating himself with flattering misrepresentations.

82

I grant thou wert not married to my Muse,
And therefore mayst without attaint o'er-look
The dedicated words which writers use
Of their fair subject, blessing every book.
Thou art as fair in knowledge as in hue,   5
Finding thy worth a limit past my praise,
And therefore art enforced to seek anew
Some fresher stamp of the time-bettering days.
And do so, love; yet when they have devised
What strainèd touches rhetoric can lend,   10
Thou, truly fair, wert truly sympathized
In true, plain words, by thy true-telling friend.
   And their gross painting might be better used
   Where cheeks need blood: in thee it is abused.

8 the] Q; these OXFORD   time-bettering] Q (ftime‿bettering)

1 **painting need** have need of make-up, continuing the argument of *82.*13–14

2 **to . . . set** added no rhetorical ornamentation to your beauty

4 **barren tender** worthless offer to repay a debt. *Tender* is used in the legal sense 'An offer of money, or the like, in discharge of a debt or liability, *esp.* an offer which thus fulfils the terms of the law and of the liability' (*OED* 1b).

5 **your report** singing your praises. *Report* is used in *OED* sense 3b: 'Testimony *to*, or commendation of, a person or quality'.

6 **extant** (a) still alive; (b) prominent; (c) 'Continuing to exist; that has escaped the ravages of time, still existing' (*OED* 4b). The friend is like a marvel from antiquity which still exists, making efforts by a *modern quill* to represent it inadequate.

7 **modern** is commonly used to imply inferiority of the modern to the ancient, hence Shakespeare's regular use of it to connote 'trite'. A scornful defiance of the 'modern

Laureates of this later age' is also voiced in E.C.'s *Emaricdulfe* (1595), 23.1.

8 **what worth** of that worth which

9 **impute** consider as a sin (*OED* 1a). *OED* 2 *Theol.*, 'To attribute or ascribe (righteousness, guilt, etc.) *to* a person by vicarious substitution', also may register, according to which the friend is regarded as a God who arbitrarily determines the merits and demerits of the poet.

11 **For I . . . being mute** Unlike others who detract from your virtues by reducing them to the level of mere rhetoric, I do not diminish your beauty because I say nothing.

12 **When . . . tomb** whereas others attempt to immortalize you in verse, and only succeed in burying you in a monument of pompous rhetoric. Compare the *monument* of praise built by Shakespeare's verse in *81.*9.

14 **both your poets** presumably refers to Shakespeare plus the rival, but it could conceivably refer to two rivals.

83

I never saw that you did painting need,
And therefore to your fair no painting set.
I found (or thought I found) you did exceed
The barren tender of a poet's debt;
And therefore have I slept in your report,   5
That you yourself being extant well might show
How far a modern quill doth come too short,
Speaking of worth, what worth in you doth grow.
This silence for my sin you did impute,
Which shall be most my glory, being dumb: 10
For I impair not beauty, being mute,
When others would give life, and bring a tomb.
   There lives more life in one of your fair eyes
   Than both your poets can in praise devise.

1 **Who . . . most** what extravagant eulogist. *Which* is a relative pronoun with *Who* as its antecedent.

2 **you,** Some editors end the line with a question mark (often these are used in Q only once after a string of separate questions, e.g. at *8.1–4*). This would turn *whose* in l. 3 from a relative pronoun which refers to the friend into an indefinite pronoun. This emendation is undesirable, since the imagery of ll. 3–4 recalls terms which earlier in the sequence had been applied to the friend (see next note).

3–4 **In . . . grew?** 'within whose boundaries the abundance is enclosed which is the only possible source of someone who might be equal to you in birth'. There is a faint reprise of the procreation sonnets here: the friend jealously guards the one place in which his equal, i.e. his heir, could be found. *Immurèd* connotes imprisonment or protective custody, and is a word which enters the language in the late 1580s. In conjunction with *grew* it may suggest a walled garden or an environment of protective horticulture. Barnabe Barnes uses the word in an allegory which compares his mistress to an enclosed orchard 'Immured in steely walls of chaste desire', *Parthenophil and Parthenophe* Elegy 12.22.

5 **Lean penury** stingy poverty, which refuses to *lend* any of the little it has to the friend

8 **so . . . story.** in this way ennobles his writing. Some editors replace Q's full stop with a comma, taking *So* as anticipating a result clause ('So . . . that') beginning

with *Let*. Q does sometimes punctuate over-strongly at the end of quatrains, but here the unit of sense appears to be completed with *story.*

10 **clear** (a) self-evident; (b) famous (from the Latin *claris*); (c) lustrous, shining

11 **counterpart** mimetic image of the friend. This sense of *counterpart*, 'A person or thing so answering to another as to appear a duplicate or exact copy of it' (*OED* 3 *fig.*), is not acknowledged by *OED* before 1680.
fame his wit make his poetic skill famous. (Transitive uses of 'fame' are rare.)

14 **fond on** fond of, perhaps with a suggestion of 'being foolishly besotted with'. Cf. *Dream* 2.1.265–6: 'Effect it with some care, that he may prove | More fond on her than she upon her love'.
Being . . . worse (a) being excessively eager to be praised, which makes the kind of praise you receive deteriorate in quality (by making it become hyperbolic); (b) being excessively eager to be praised, which devalues the praise you give; (c) being fond of lavishing praise on others, which devalues the praise you give; (d) being fond of lavishing praise on others, which makes the kind of praise you receive deteriorate in quality. In (a) and (b) the friend is presented as unable through vanity to ensure that praise retains its true value; in (c) and (d) he is presented as an indiscriminate critic of works which praise him. *Your praises* is either a subjective genitive ('the praises you give') or an objective genitive ('the praises given to you').

84

Who is it that says most, which can say more
Than this rich praise: that you alone are you,
In whose confine immurèd is the store
Which should example where your equal grew?
Lean penury within that pen doth dwell,   5
That to his subject lends not some small glory,
But he that writes of you, if he can tell
That you are you, so dignifies his story.
Let him but copy what in you is writ,
Not making worse what nature made so clear,   10
And such a counterpart shall fame his wit,
Making his style admirèd everywhere.
    You to your beauteous blessings add a curse,
    Being fond on praise, which makes your praises worse.

1 **in manners** within the bounds of social decorum

2 **comments** 'An expository treatise, an exposition; a commentary' (*OED* 1)

3 **Reserve . . . quill** hoard away their writings in incorruptible gold. *Reserve* means 'To keep for future use or enjoyment' (*OED* 1a). *Character* is used in the sense: 'The style of writing peculiar to any individual; handwriting' (*OED* 4c). These senses make many of the proposed emendations (see collation) unnecessary. Given the frequency with which Q mistakes 'thy' for 'their' (see 26.12 n.), however, it is impossible to exclude the possibility that the copy read 'Reserve thy character', or perhaps 'Reserve your character', which would be in accord with *your praise* in l. 2. These readings would mean 'preserve your nature, or an imprint of you'. It might also widen the sense of *character* to include a form of short sketch of a particular kind of disposition made popular in the early seventeenth century by the vogue for Theophrastus's *Characters*.

filed polished. A term often used in the period for literary artifice. On the unique form in Q, 'fil'd', see 17.2 n.

5 **other** The use of the indefinite 'other' for 'others' is a recognized Elizabethan usage, deriving from the loss of the masculine plural inflection -e in Middle English (Partridge, 117).

6 **unlettered clerk** illiterate cleric in minor orders, who cannot read the lesson, so joins in with 'Amen'. Parish clerks led the responses to the priest in church. Cf. *Richard II* 4.1.163–4: 'God save the King! Will no man say "Amen"? | Am I both priest and clerk? Well then, Amen.'

7 **that able spirit affords** which any able person might offer you. *That* may be a demonstrative pronoun referring to a particular *able spirit*, the rival poet, who is referred to as a *spirit* also at *80.2* and *86.5*.

8 **In polished . . . pen** 'Polite letters' are originally the same as 'polished letters' or those which have been carefully revised, written in fair hand, and smoothed with pumice-stone (hence *filed*). The aim of the sonnet is to imply that style and substance have collapsed together in a uniform glossiness in the work of the rival poet: it is impossible to distinguish the content of the verse from its elegant calligraphy.

10 **most of praise** highest pitch of praise

12 **Though . . . before** as in a formal procession my words are the last and lowliest, but my thoughts are by their strength and value in the vanguard. Q's 'hind-most' re-emphasizes the point: the one who comes *behind* in fact loves *most*.

14 **in effect** in action. Compare the proverb 'The effect speaks, the tongue need not' (Tilley E64).

85

My tongue-tied Muse in manners holds her still,
While comments of your praise, richly compiled,
Reserve their character with golden quill
And precious phrase by all the Muses filed.
I think good thoughts, whilst other write good words,   5
And like unlettered clerk still cry 'Amen'
To every hymn that able spirit affords,
In polished form of well-refinèd pen.
Hearing you praised, I say ' 'Tis so, 'tis true',
And to the most of praise add something more,   10
But that is in my thought, whose love to you
(Though words come hindmost) holds his rank before.
   Then others for the breath of words respect,
   Me for my dumb thoughts, speaking in effect.

3 Reserve their] Q; Preserve their GILDON 1714; Rehearse your *conj.* Anon. in Cambridge; Reserve your *conj.* Anon. in Cambridge 1893   4 filed] Q (fil'd); Filled GILDON   9 ' 'Tis . . . true',] MALONE (*italic*); $_\wedge$ ~ . . . ~$_{\wedge^2}$ Q

1 **proud full sail** Cf. the nautical comparison of *80*.5–14. On the association of poetic rivals with pride, see 76.1 n.

2 **prize** reward; often used of the spoils brought back from voyages by travellers to the new world
all-too-precious In Q's '(all to precious)' the brackets probably indicate a compound adjective rather than a parenthesis.

3 **ripe** matured and ready for birth
inhearse entomb

4 **womb** The shift from the *sail* of l. 1 to the *womb* of l. 4 makes visual sense (both swell; one with wind, the other with new life), a comparison also found in *Dream* 2.1.128–9: 'When we have laughed to see the sails conceive | And grow big-bellied with the wanton wind'.

5 **Was it . . . write** No specific allusion is obvious, but George Chapman claims in *Euthemiae Raptae* (1609), ll. 75–85, to have been inspired by the spirit of Homer to translate his works. For other candidates, see Rollins 2, ii, Appendix 10.
spirit is monosyllabic (cf. *80*.2 and *85*.7), *spirits* disyllabic. *Spirit* ranges in meaning from 'vigour of mind' to 'supernatural agency', or 'daemon'. It is used often in Marlowe's *Dr Faustus* to mean 'devil'. Chapman's translation of the *Iliad* (1598–?1614) exploits this range of senses to the full. See Colin Burrow, *Epic Romance: Homer to Milton* (Oxford, 1993), 206–10. Editors since Ingram and Redpath have sought to de-spiritualize the relationship between the poet and his *spirits* by arguing that the term could refer to a coterie of fellow writers or to the great writers of the past. None of the 24 senses of 'spirit' in the *OED* supports this interpretation.

6 **pitch** 'The height to which a falcon or other bird of prey soars before swooping down on its prey' (*OED* 18a), as in *2 Henry VI (Contention)* 2.1.12: 'And bears his thoughts above his falcon's pitch.'

7 **compeers** 'A companion, associate, comrade, fellow' (*OED* 2). Here either 'literary cronies' or 'spiritual instructors'. The word can be used contemptuously, as in Jonson's *The Alchemist* 4.6.41: 'Your sooty, smoky-bearded compeer'.

8 **astonishèd** stunned into silence

9 **affable familiar ghost** This yokes together the domestic and the spiritual: *affable* means 'friendly, conversible', as can *familiar* (*OED* 7). The phrases 'familiar angel' and 'familiar devil, or spirit', however, refer to supernatural beings supposed to be in association with or under the power of a human agent. A *familiar ghost* need not be sinister, however, and could be something like a guardian angel: Nicholas Udall, in his *Apothegmes of Erasmus* (1542), a work often used in Tudor grammar schools, notes that 'Socrates said that he had a familiar ghost or Angel peculiar and proper to himself, of whom he was by a privy token forbidden if he attempted . . . any unhonest thing' (32).

10 **gulls . . . intelligence** 'tricks him with (false) information'. *Gull* could conceivably mean 'stuff, engorge' (*OED v.*[1] 2). At this point in the sonnet, however, the rival is represented as the gullible receiver of what he fondly imagines to be useful information from the spirit world.

13 **countenance** (a) face; (b) 'Patronage; appearance of favour' (*OED* 8). A similar play is apparent in *1 Henry IV* 1.2.27–9: 'being governed, as the sea is, by our noble and chaste mistress the moon, under whose countenance we steal'.
filled up Q's 'fild up' has been modernized by Malone as 'filed up', or 'polished'. This is unlikely: there is no recognized early modern usage of 'filed up'. See also 17.2 n.

14 **that enfeebled mine** (a) that fact (either my lack of matter or the rival's enjoyment of the friend's patronage) enfeebled my verse; (b) that line (by the rival)

86

Was it the proud full sail of his great verse,
Bound for the prize of all-too-precious you,
That did my ripe thoughts in my brain inhearse,
Making their tomb the womb wherein they grew?
Was it his spirit, by spirits taught to write   5
Above a mortal pitch, that struck me dead?
No, neither he, nor his compeers by night
Giving him aid, my verse astonishèd.
He, nor that affable familiar ghost
Which nightly gulls him with intelligence,   10
As victors of my silence cannot boast:
I was not sick of any fear from thence.
    But, when your countenance filled up his line,
    Then lacked I matter, that enfeebled mine.

13 filled] Q (flld); fil'd MALONE (conj. Steevens)

1 **dear** (a) lovely; (b) expensive
possessing (a) control over or tenure (see
18.10 n. and *OED* s.v. 'possession' 1b:
'*Law*. The visible possibility of exercising
over a thing such control as attaches to
lawful ownership (but which may also
exist apart from lawful ownership))'; (b)
exclusive loving ownership

2 **like enough** likely enough. There is a
sardonic edge here ('and don't you just
know it').
estimate (a) value to me ('The price at
which anything is rated; *fig.* attributed
value' (*OED* 1b)); possibly also (b)
'Repute, reputation' (*OED* 1c).

3 **charter of thy worth** (a) royally sanc-
tioned document establishing the friend's
material value; (b) royally sanctioned
document establishing the friend's special
legal privileges. The friend's *charter* in the
sense 'a document which conveys title to
land', established by agreement between
him and the poet, *gives him releasing*
because the poet can no longer meet its
terms (he is *too dear*, i.e. too costly). The
friend's *charter* in the sense 'privilege,
immunity' gives him the absolute
power to release himself from the quasi-
contractual agreement with the poet
because of his *worth* in the sense of 'high
and privileged status'.
releasing (a) freedom from the obligations
of love; (b) technical legal dispensation
from contractual obligations. The legal
resonances of 'release' in the period
are strong: they range from 'withdraw,
recall, revoke, cancel (a sentence, punish-
ment, condition, etc.)' (*OED* 1), through
'grant remission or discharge of . . . a
debt, tax, tribute' (*OED* 3), to 'surrender,
make over, transfer (land or territory) to
another' (*OED* 4b), the last of which
continues the dominant metaphor of the
quatrain, that of contracts which estab-
lish the tenure of land.

4 **My bonds . . . determinate** (a) my claims
to ownership of you have all expired; (b)
my ties of obligation to you have expired.
These two senses conflict: the poet is
attempting both voluntarily to forgo the
friend, and to suggest that the friend has
dissolved their mutually binding agree-
ment. Depending on which way one reads
the line it either supports or conflicts with
the previous one. *Bonds* means 'a deed, by
which A (known as the *obligor*) binds him-
self, his heirs, executors, or assigns to pay
a certain sum of money to B (known as
the *obligee*), or his heirs, etc. A may bind

himself to this payment absolutely and
unconditionally, in which case the deed is
known as a *single or simple bond* (*simplex
obligatio*): bonds in this form are obsolete.
Or a condition may be attached that the
deed shall be made void by the payment,
by a certain date, of money, rent, etc.
due from A to B, or by some other perfor-
mance or observance, the sum named
being only a penalty to enforce the perfor-
mance of the condition, in which case the
deed is termed a *penal bond*' (*OED* 9a). It is
likely that a penal bond is referred to here,
with the service referred to having been
fulfilled. For Shakespeare's awareness of
this distinction, see *Merchant* 1.3.143–4:
'Go with me to a notary, seal me there |
Your single bond'. *Determinate*, or 'deter-
mine', is used of the expiry of a legal
instrument.

5 **how . . . granting** what claim do I have to
possess you except that which is given to
me by you? The friend is presented as the
overlord from whom Shakespeare receives
his temporary grant of possession (*OED*
s.v. 'hold' 6a).

7 **cause** (a) merit which warrants; (b) ade-
quate grounds for (as in law, having a
cause for an action)

8 **patent** privileged right granted by you
(*patents*—effectively monopolies—to sell
particular goods, such as wines, were
granted in this period as marks of royal
favour, until the 1623 Statutes of
Monopolies abolished the practice)
swerving reverting to you. (The word does
not have particular legal charge.)

9–10 'At the time when you granted the
patent you were unaware of your own
value, or were mistaken about my identity
or worth.' The suggestion is that since the
supposed contract was made in error it
should be dissolved.

11 **upon misprision growing** occurring as a
result of error or oversight

12 **Comes . . . making** reverts back to you on
the making of a properly informed judge-
ment. The sense is clear although the pre-
cise grammatical relations of *making* are
obscure. It functions as a participle agree-
ing with 'you' (understood), or with 'gift',
which is presented metaphorically as a
kind of prodigal son, which makes a
mistake and then returns home. It also
functions as a quasi-compound noun,
'judgement-making'.

13–14 **Thus . . . matter** So I have possessed
you as in a self-deceptive dream: while I
was asleep I dreamed I was a king who

87

Farewell, thou art too dear for my possessing,
And like enough thou know'st thy estimate.
The charter of thy worth gives thee releasing:
My bonds in thee are all determinate.
For how do I hold thee but by thy granting,   5
And for that riches where is my deserving?
The cause of this fair gift in me is wanting,
And so my patent back again is swerving.
Thyself thou gav'st, thy own worth then not knowing,
Or me, to whom thou gav'st it, else mistaking;   10
So thy great gift, upon misprision growing,
Comes home again, on better judgement making.
    Thus have I had thee as a dream doth flatter:
    In sleep a king, but waking no such matter.

owned all, but when I awoke I realized I was no such thing.' There is also a sugges-tion of disillusionment: 'in my dreams *you* were a king'.

1 **set me light** (a) value me at a low rate; (b) regard me as fickle

2 **And . . . scorn** hold my deserts up to public contempt

3 Compare 35.10.

4 **though** both 'even though you are' and 'if (hypothetically) you were to be'. This masks a direct accusation as a piece of speculative hyperbole.

forsworn perjured; used especially of those who have broken vows of love

5 **With . . . acquainted** since I know more about my failings than anyone else

6 **Upon thy part** on your side, to strengthen your case. It is possible to take the phrase with *faults concealed* in the next line: so 'I can tell a story about hidden faults on your side too'.

7 **attainted** (a) tainted, stained; (b) found guilty of a criminal offence. These two senses were associated as a result of a false etymology which derived 'attainder' from French *taindre*, dye or stain.

8 **losing me** Q reads 'loosing', which is the usual spelling of 'losing' (only in 125.6 is the verb spelt 'lose' rather than 'loose'). Here, though, Q's form allows a secondary sense, 'loosing', i.e. 'in setting me free'.

shall occurs where one would normally expect 'shalt', but the use of plural for singular form is not unusual.

10 **bending . . . on** turning towards

12 **double vantage me** do me a double advantage. That is, the poet will benefit twice by slandering himself: once because it will require him to think of the friend (ll. 9–10), and once because any benefit done to the friend will also benefit the poet, since the two lovers are one.

13 **so** (a) so completely; (b) in such a way

14 **That for thy right** (a) in order to assist your case; (b) in order to present you as virtuous (although you are not)

bear all wrong (a) put up with all injustice; (b) take the responsibility for all wrongdoing

88

When thou shalt be disposed to set me light,
And place my merit in the eye of scorn,
Upon thy side against myself I'll fight,
And prove thee virtuous, though thou art forsworn.
With mine own weakness being best acquainted,   5
Upon thy part I can set down a story
Of faults concealed, wherein I am attainted,
That thou in losing me shall win much glory.
And I by this will be a gainer too,
For bending all my loving thoughts on thee: 10
The injuries that to myself I do,
Doing thee vantage, double vantage me.
  Such is my love, to thee I so belong,
  That for thy right myself will bear all wrong.

1 disposed] BENSON; dispode Q   8 losing] Q (loosing)

1 **Say** 'suppose' rather than the ordinary sense. Compare *88*.4 for the equivocation: this first line both imagines a future hypothetical circumstance, and allows the reading 'suppose that the reason why you have forsaken me (as you have done) is some fault in me'.

fault crime or failing

3 **straight will halt** 'immediately will limp'. Some biographical critics have supposed Shakespeare to be lame on the basis of this line and *37*.3; the suggestion is however that the poet will accept whatever the friend says as truth, and act accordingly. *Lame* may play on the sense 'poetically weak': Drayton's *Idea's Mirrour* (1594), 12 7 explores the miracle that 'a cripple hand' is 'made to write, yet lame by kind' as a result of Idea's beauty.

4 **reasons** arguments

6 **To set . . . change** in order to give an appearance of decorous normality to the separation for which you wish

7 **As I'll . . . will** as I will do myself down, knowing what it is you want. *Will* may carry a sexual sense, 'knowing what new thing you lust after'.

8 **acquaintance strangle** suppress all signs of our knowing each other. *Acquaintance* may have a distinctive homosocial resonance: the frontispiece to Richard Brathwait's *The English Gentleman* (1630) presents two men hugging each other as an emblem of acquaintance, and glosses: 'Acquaintance is in two bodies individually incorporated, and no less selfly than sociably united: two twins cannot be more near than these be affectionately dear, which they express in hugging one another'. For the use of *strangle* compare *Winter's Tale* 4.4.47–8: 'Strangle such thoughts as these with anything | That you behold the while'.

strange unfamiliar, as though I do not know you

9 **walks** 'The usual place of walking, the haunt or resort (of a person or animal)' (*OED* 8a). Also perhaps implying absence from the estate of the friend, via 'A place prepared or set apart for walking' (*OED* 9).

11 **too much profane** The uncorrected state of Q reads 'proface'. This is likely to be a misprint, although 'proface' could be used as a 'formula of welcome or good wishes at a dinner or other meal, equivalent to "may it do you good", "may it be to your advantage"' (*OED*), and mean 'excessively eager with my greetings'.

13 **debate** 'Strife, contention, dissension, quarrelling, wrangling; a quarrel' (*OED* 1a)

89

Say that thou didst forsake me for some fault,
And I will comment upon that offence.
Speak of my lameness, and I straight will halt,
Against thy reasons making no defence.
Thou canst not (love) disgrace me half so ill,   5
To set a form upon desirèd change,
As I'll myself disgrace, knowing thy will.
I will acquaintance strangle and look strange,
Be absent from thy walks, and in my tongue
Thy sweet belovèd name no more shall dwell,   10
Lest I (too much profane) should do it wrong,
And haply of our old acquaintance tell.
    For thee, against myself, I'll vow debate;
    For I must ne'er love him whom thou dost hate.

11 profane] QB; proface QA

559

1 **Then** therefore
2 **bent my deeds to cross** determined to oppose me in all that I do
3 **bow** assume a posture of abject submission
4 **drop in for an after-loss** probably 'fall upon me as an additional loss to come at a later date'. 'Drop in' is used in this sense in *Antony* 3.13.164. The sonnet appeals (with the mock bravura of a wounded lover) to the friend to leave now, so that all catastrophes come at once. *Drop in* is unlikely to bear the sense given by *OED* (27b: 'to pay a casual visit'), a usage which became common only at the end of the seventeenth century. If the passage meant 'and (worst of all) do not stop by for a chat' it would be pure bathos.
5–6 **when . . . woe** Once I have endured my present hardships, do not come as the general leading a rearguard attack by an army of sorrow which I had thought was conquered.
7 **Give not . . . morrow** It was proverbial that 'A blustering night [promises] a good morrow', *Lucrece* ll. 1788–90 and Dent N166; cf. 'Next the dark night the glad morrow' (Dent N173.1). If the friend leaves after the 'windy night' he will thwart the expectation of a sunny day following.
8 **To . . . overthrow** to protract an intended destruction
11 **onset** first assault. The noun is often used of military attacks (*OED* 1a). Compare *Lucrece* l. 432.
13 **strains** (a) mental impulses, stresses; (b) types

90

Then hate me when thou wilt, if ever, now,
Now, while the world is bent my deeds to cross,
Join with the spite of Fortune, make me bow,
And do not drop in for an after-loss.
Ah do not, when my heart hath 'scaped this sorrow,   5
Come in the rearward of a conquered woe;
Give not a windy night a rainy morrow
To linger out a purposed overthrow.
If thou wilt leave me, do not leave me last,
When other petty griefs have done their spite.   10
But in the onset come, so shall I taste
At first the very worst of Fortune's might,
    And other strains of woe, which now seem woe,
    Compared with loss of thee, will not seem so.

11 shall] BENSON; stall Q

1–4 **Some . . . Some** The fourfold *anaphora* (repetition at the start of the line) prepares for the strongly contrastive *But* in l. 7.

3 **new-fangled ill** shoddily made, although after the most recent fashion

4 **horse** horses (although many noblemen, such as Bourbon in *Henry V* 3.7.20–3, had a favourite horse)

5 **every humour . . . pleasure** Each type of person has their own peculiar pursuit. *Humour* refers to a person's disposition, as determined by the relative balance of the four humours (blood, phlegm, melancholy, and choler) in their bodies. *Adjunct* is probably used in a quasi-logical sense, 'Something joined to or connected with another, and subordinate to it in position, function, character, or essence' (*OED* 1). It may also anticipate the sense 'A personal addition or enhancement; a quality increasing a man's native worth' (*OED* 3). *OED*'s first cited instance of this sense is from Healey's translation of St Augustine's *City of God* (1610), a work which was being set in Eld's print-shop at roughly the same time as the Sonnets.

7 **particulars** (a) single things; (b) merely personal preferences; limited selfish interests such as those listed in the quatrain

are not my measure (a) are not equal to me; (b) are not the scale of measurement to apply to me; (c) are not the scale of measurement which I use. In the follow-

ing lines (c) is developed: the friend makes all other ways of assessing goods and pleasures seem inadequate.

8 **better** overgo

general best all-encompassing source of delight

9 **better** Q's 'bitter' is a common misprint in the period, occurring (for example) in the 1614 edition of Gorges's translation of Lucan's *Pharsalia* in which Thorpe had a hand. That the friend's high rank is also a source of bitterness is almost certainly a tangy coincidence.

10 **prouder than garments' cost** more grandly impressive than the rich display of garments. For a similar use of *cost*, see 64.2. Although *garments* on its own does not connote expense, clothes (especially the aristocratic cast-offs which found their way into the wardrobes of theatrical companies) were extraordinarily expensive: Edward Alleyn records that a single 'black velvet cloak with sleeves embroidered in silver and gold' cost £20 10*s*. 6*d*. (Andrew Gurr, *The Shakespearean Stage 1574–1642*, 2nd edn. (Cambridge, 1980), 178.)

12 **of all men's pride** the object of every man's envious respect. *Pride* is used in the sense 'That of which any person or body of persons is proud' (*OED* 5a); its conjunction with *boast* and *prouder* brings to it a colour of vainglory.

13 **wretched** unfortunate

91

Some glory in their birth, some in their skill,
Some in their wealth, some in their body's force,
Some in their garments, though new-fangled ill,
Some in their hawks and hounds, some in their horse.
And every humour hath his adjunct pleasure   5
Wherein it finds a joy above the rest;
But these particulars are not my measure,
All these I better in one general best.
Thy love is better than high birth to me,
Richer than wealth, prouder than garments' cost,   10
Of more delight than hawks or horses be:
And, having thee, of all men's pride I boast,
   Wretched in this alone: that thou mayst take
   All this away, and me most wretched make.

9 better] BENSON; bitter Q

1 **But do thy worst** even if you try your hardest. The phrase plays on 'do your best'.
steal thyself away (a) rob me of yourself; (b) sneak furtively away

2 **For term . . . mine** you are contracted to me as long as life lasts. *Assurèd* can mean 'Engaged, covenanted, pledged' (*OED* 3) or, more strongly, 'Engaged for marriage, betrothed' (*OED* 4), as in *Errors* 3.2.145–6: 'this drudge or diviner laid claim to me, called me Dromio, swore I was assured to her'. This sense is reinforced by the echo of the Solemnization of Matrimony from the Book of Common Prayer: 'to have and to hold from this day forward . . . till death us do part'. *Term* is also a word used to describe the period of legal possession of land etc. (*OED* 6).

5 **the worst of wrongs** i.e. the loss of the friend

6 **the least of them** i.e. the slightest hint of coolness will kill him, so he is not dependent on the whims of the friend, since he will die at once if he loses his affection.

8 **humour** (a) whim; (b) mental constitution (see 91.5 n.).

9–10 **Thou . . . lie** You cannot trouble me with your inconstancy, because my life hangs on your change of heart. In other words the poet will not feel the effects of the friend's fickleness, since he will die the moment he is abandoned.

11 **title** 'Legal right to the possession of property' (*OED* 7 *spec. Law* a), referring back to the *term* and the implied contract at the start of the poem. *Happy* means 'fortunate' here, and 'joyful' in the next line. The *title* is *happy* (fortunate) in that the poet can never be unhappy as a result of it: either he lives, and enjoys the favour of the friend, or he dies, and so does not experience the sorrow of his disfavour.

13 **But . . . blot?** What is so beautiful or fortunate that it fears no contamination of its perfection? The line initially refers to the poet's happy state; once the second line of the couplet is read it refers also to the friend. The point of the couplet is that if the friend is secretly, rather than openly, untrue the poet will not find release in death from unhappiness, and will live on like the *deceivèd husband* at the start of the next sonnet.

92

But do thy worst to steal thyself away,
For term of life thou art assurèd mine,
And life no longer than thy love will stay,
For it depends upon that love of thine.
Then need I not to fear the worst of wrongs,   5
When in the least of them my life hath end.
I see a better state to me belongs
Than that which on thy humour doth depend.
Thou canst not vex me with inconstant mind,
Since that my life on thy revolt doth lie.   10
O, what a happy title do I find,
Happy to have thy love, happy to die!
    But what's so blessèd fair that fears no blot?
    Thou mayst be false, and yet I know it not.

1 **So . . . true** In this way I shall live on
believing you to be true. Continues the
argument of 92. *Supposing* straddles the
boundary between the involuntary belief
of one who is deceived ('to believe as a
fact' (*OED* s.v. 'suppose' 1a)) and the vol-
untary act of one who wishes to entertain
a hypothesis ('To assume (without refer-
ence to truth or falsehood) as a basis of
argument' (*OED* s.v. 'suppose' 6)).

2 **so** (a) in this way; (b) in order that. Sense
(b) reinforces the suggestion of *supposing*,
that the poet is deliberately deceiving
himself.

3 **altered new** turned into a new form. The
phrase puts a brave face on deception.

5 **For** since. It looks both forward and back:
it explains why the friend's *looks* are *with
me*, and gives the precondition of *therefore*
in l. 6.

6 **in that** in your eye
change inconstancy, change of heart

8 **moods** bad humour, anger

9 **in** at

11 **heart's workings** the movements of your
emotions

12 **should** follows from *that* in l. 10, but
almost also suggests that the poet is advis-
ing the friend how best to deceive him.

13 **Eve's apple** 'So the woman (seeing that
the tree was good for meat, and that it was
pleasant to the eyes, and a tree to be
desired to get knowledge) took of the fruit
thereof, and did eat, and gave also to her
husband with her and he did eat', Genesis
3: 6. Adam is of course the original
deceivèd husband. Compare the proverb
'An apple may be fair without and bad
within' (Dent A291.1).
grow (a) become; (b) flourish like a spe-
cious fruit on a tree

14 **sweet virtue . . . show** (a) if your beautiful
moral worth does not correspond to your
appearance; (b) if your sweet-tasting
medicinal effect does not match your deli-
cious appearance (*OED* s.v. 'virtue' 9b)

93

So shall I live, supposing thou art true,
Like a deceivèd husband, so love's face
May still seem love to me, though altered new:
Thy looks with me, thy heart in other place.
For there can live no hatred in thine eye,   5
Therefore in that I cannot know thy change.
In many's looks the false heart's history
Is writ in moods and frowns and wrinkles strange;
But heaven in thy creation did decree
That in thy face sweet love should ever dwell.   10
Whate'er thy thoughts, or thy heart's workings be,
Thy looks should nothing thence but sweetness tell.
   How like Eve's apple doth thy beauty grow,
   If thy sweet virtue answer not thy show.

1 **They . . . none** Praise is often given in the period to those who withhold the full effects of their authority, as in Sidney, *Arcadia* (1590), 246: 'the more power he hath to hurt, the more admirable is his praise, that he will not hurt', and Dent H170.

2 **That . . . show** that do not do what it seems likely from their appearance they will do. The initial commonplace is pulled towards duplicitousness by this line: it suggests two positive qualities and one negative: (a) powerful people who do not act with the power which they appear to possess; (b) people who do not act on their emotions but merely show them; (c) people who duplicitously present an outward face which does not correspond to their actions. Sense (c) is likely to spring quickly to a reader's mind as a result of the poem's position in a group of poems which meditate on what it is to be deceived in love.

3 **moving others . . . stone** (a) who retain a laudable immobility as they cause movement in others; (b) who remain unemotional whilst generating emotion in others; (c) who remain insensible and culpably cool whilst they give rise to emotion in others. The next line pushes this description, which is almost that of a Stoic sage who controls his passions, towards the hostility implicit in (c). The effect is of a desperate search for terms of praise with which to describe someone who has caused only pain. The proverbs 'As steadfast as a stone' (Dent S878.2) and 'As cold as any stone' (Dent S876) are also both in play.

4 **to temptation slow** resistant to temptation (hence a good thing); but *slow* can imply culpable deficiency ('constitutionally inert or sluggish' (*OED* 2a))

5 **They rightly . . . graces** (a) people who resist temptation and suppress their passions deservedly come to possess the grace of God (*inherit*: 'To come into possession of, as one's right or divinely assigned portion', often in biblical contexts, as Tyndale's translation of Matthew 25: 34: 'Come ye blessed children of my father, inherit ye the kingdom prepared for you from the beginning of the world'); (b) people who are unsusceptible to passion really are the ones who deserve to receive heavenly beauty (with a sarcastic stress). Here the carefully modulated tonal instability of the poem reaches its climax: the line is a confession, trembling with hard-assumed orthodoxy, of a moral truth in spite of the pain it costs to utter; it also bitterly acknowledges that beauty is often found in the stonily insensible.

6 **husband . . . expense** prevent the squandering of natural beauties

7–8 **They . . . excellence** The opposition is between those who own and are therefore in complete control of the goods of a household (*lords and owners*) and those who are merely administrators of a household economy (*stewards of their excellence*). *Faces* can be neutral in sense: 'The countenance as expressive of feeling or character' (*OED* 6a), although the plural may carry a suggestion that the presentation of emotion is voluntary, as in *Cymbeline* 1.1.13–14: 'they wear their faces to the bent | Of the King's looks'. The word can also suggest shamelessness or hypocrisy: 'Command of countenance, *esp.* with reference to freedom from indications of shame' (*OED* 7a), and 'Outward show; assumed or factitious appearance' (*OED* 10a).

8 **their excellence** The antecedent of *their* could be either *others* or *lords and owners*. The former would suggest that other people only have temporary control over the management of whatever qualities they have, but it would at least grant them some *excellence* of their own. The latter would suggest a greater distinction between the two classes of people: that all other people apart from *the lords and owners of their faces* have nothing at all to call their own, and simply administer, like stewards, an estate which they could never hope to own. This is reinforced by the echo of the phrase 'your excellence' which is often used in addressing social superiors in the period.

9 **flower** The shift from the ethical concerns of the octet to this image makes perhaps the most pronounced *volta* (or turn in the argument between the octet and sestet) in the Sonnets. The shift skirts around the unutterable: that the friend's deeds are unbearably at odds with his face. This suggestion is made in ll. 9–10 by recalling the friend's refusal to breed from earlier in the sequence and then in l. 11 adding *infection* to the sweet flowers with which the friend is habitually associated.

10 **to itself** (a) by itself; (b) for its own benefit

11 **infection** disease, also 'Moral contamination; vitiation of character or habits by evil influences' (*OED* 6)

94

They that have power to hurt and will do none,
That do not do the thing they most do show,
Who, moving others, are themselves as stone,
Unmovèd, cold, and to temptation slow:
They rightly do inherit heaven's graces,   5
And husband nature's riches from expense.
They are the lords and owners of their faces,
Others but stewards of their excellence.
The summer's flower is to the summer sweet,
Though to itself it only live and die,   10
But if that flower with base infection meet,
The basest weed outbraves his dignity:
    For sweetest things turn sourest by their deeds;
    Lilies that fester smell far worse than weeds.

12 **outbraves** surpasses, especially in looks, as in the Preface to Gerard's *Herbal* (1597): 'The lilies of the field outbraved him'.

14 **Lilies . . . weeds** Compare the proverb 'The best things corrupted become the worst' (Dent C668). Lilies were thought to produce a foul smell if handled: 'The lily flower smelleth full sweet, while it is whole and not broken, and stinketh full foul if it be broken and froted [chafed] with hands', *Batman upon Bartholomew* (1582), fo. 300ᵛ. The same line occurs in *Edward III* (1596, containing scenes thought to be by Shakespeare), 2.1.451. Cf. Dent L297.

1 **sweet** sweet-smelling (only)

3 **budding name?** your reputation which is just approaching its prime. The pointing of Q's rhetorical question has been retained in order to differentiate it from the exclamation mark which ends the following line. On exclamation marks in Q see *48*.4 n.

7–8 **Cannot . . . report** Q's punctuation is followed here, although many editors place a semicolon after *praise*. In Q's version the subject of *blesses* is either *Naming* or *tongue* and *but in a kind of praise* qualifies either *blesses* or *dispraise*.

8 **Naming . . . report** simply mentioning the friend's name gives a gloss of praise to a critical account of his doings

9 **mansion** glorious abode (i.e. the friend's body)

11 **blot** On the high moral charge of this word in Shakespeare, see *36*.3 n.

12 **turns to** transforms to. (The subject of the verb is *beauty's veil*.)
   see! Q's exclamation mark may serve to emphasize the carefully limited praise of *that eyes can see*.

13 **large privilege** extensive freedom granted particularly to you

14 **The hardest . . . edge** has a proverbial ring, but has only distant recorded parallels (as 'Iron with often handling is worn to nothing', Dent I92). Compare Nashe, *Christ's Tears over Jerusalem*, Nashe, ii.37: 'No sword but will lose his edge in long striking against stones'. Swords and penises are so commonly associated in the period that there may well be a sexual pun here.

95

How sweet and lovely dost thou make the shame,
Which, like a canker in the fragrant rose,
Doth spot the beauty of thy budding name?
O, in what sweets dost thou thy sins enclose!
That tongue that tells the story of thy days   5
(Making lascivious comments on thy sport)
Cannot dispraise, but in a kind of praise,
Naming thy name blesses an ill report.
O, what a mansion have those vices got,
Which for their habitation chose out thee,   10
Where beauty's veil doth cover every blot,
And all things turns to fair that eyes can see!
   Take heed (dear heart) of this large privilege:
   The hardest knife ill-used doth lose his edge.

7 praise,] Q; ~; MALONE (*conj.* Capell)   8 name‚] MALONE; ~, Q   12 turns] Q; turn SEWELL

2 **Some . . . sport** Some say that your distinctive charm lies in youth and elegant recreation. *Anaphora* (repetition of the same phrase at the start of the line) and *parison* (the use of parallel grammatical structures) create an equivalence between the terms of praise and condemnation which are notionally being distinguished. *Grace* and *gentle* are used frequently of the friend. They both connote aristocratic ease and mild winningness.

3 **of more and less** by both high- and low-born people

4 **that to thee resort** which frequent your company. *Resort* is often used on occasions when the protection or advice of a superior (a king or a God) is sought. The transforming magic of the friend's presence is registered in the syntax: *that* refers either to *graces* or to *faults*.

8 **translated** transformed
for true things deemed are judged to be virtues. This is the only occurrence in Shakespeare of 'to deem *for*'. This form

detracts from the stability of *deem* (which usually means 'to decide with the finality of a judge') by recalling the phrase 'to take for', which usually means 'to *mistake* something for'. Hence almost 'are mistakenly thought to be virtues'.

9 **stern** 'grim, harsh' (*OED* 1d)

10 **If like . . . translate** if he could metamorphose himself into a lamb. A wolf in sheep's clothing is a proverbial example of hypocrisy (Dent W614).

11 **lead away** here 'mislead'

12 **strength . . . state** full unqualified power of your position. Cf. 94.1–2.

13–14 **But do . . . report** The same couplet occurs at the end of 36. It fits less neatly here, and textual corruption or incomplete authorial revision cannot be ruled out. Kerrigan notes that both 36 and this poem end groups of sonnets which are critical of the friend: 'The common couplet makes the two groups rhyme, as it were'.

96

Some say thy fault is youth, some wantonness,
Some say thy grace is youth and gentle sport.
Both grace and faults are loved of more and less:
Thou mak'st faults graces, that to thee resort.
As on the finger of a thronèd queen   5
The basest jewel will be well esteemed,
So are those errors that in thee are seen
To truths translated, and for true things deemed.
How many lambs might the stern wolf betray,
If like a lamb he could his looks translate?   10
How many gazers mightst thou lead away,
If thou wouldst use the strength of all thy state?
   But do not so; I love thee in such sort
   As thou being mine, mine is thy good report.

11 mightst] LINTOT; mighst Q

1 **absence** suggests physical separation. Some editors link the phrase with the emotional estrangements explored in 92–6. Certainly the start of this sonnet opens up a breathing space after the increasingly intense bitterness of the previous group. It promises a fresh start, spring after winter, presence after absence. This hope collapses as the sonnet progresses: *summer* is compressed into *autumn, autumn* recalls the fecundity of the *prime* (spring) only in a posthumous birth, and *winter* recurs in the penultimate word of the poem, which ends with a continuing separation.

2 **thee . . . year** you, who are the chief source of enjoyment in the transient year

4 **bareness everywhere** Cf. 5.8.

5 **time removed** time away from you; also suggesting time which has been lost

6 **teeming** full of fecundity, bountifully fertile

7 **wanton burden** *burden* often means 'offspring in the womb' in Shakespeare. Its conjunction with *wanton* suggests a superabundance which accompanies excessive sexual freedom.

9 **issue** offspring

10 **hope of orphans** The general sense 'little hope at all' is clear, but hard to explain precisely. The phrase may mean (a) the kind of hope, tinged with regret, which is born at the same time as a posthumous child; (b) the kind of hope experienced by an orphan, who could not expect to inherit an estate until his majority, by which time it might have been wasted by his guardian.

10 **unfathered fruit** continues the faint hint presented by *wanton* that to the jaded eyes of the poet the abundance of the year has hints of bastardly begetting.

11 **wait on thee** tend on you, are at your disposal like servants

12 **thou away** with you away

13 **with so . . . cheer** in such a gloomy manner. The apparent paradox of 'dull cheer' would be less apparent to a seventeenth-century reader, to whom *cheer* could mean 'countenance or mood' with no presumption that the mood would be happy.

97

How like a winter hath my absence been
From thee, the pleasure of the fleeting year?
What freezings have I felt, what dark days seen?
What old December's bareness everywhere?
And yet this time removed was summer's time,   5
The teeming autumn big with rich increase,
Bearing the wanton burden of the prime,
Like widowed wombs after their lords' decease:
Yet this abundant issue seemed to me
But hope of orphans and unfathered fruit,   10
For summer and his pleasures wait on thee,
And thou away, the very birds are mute.
   Or if they sing, 'tis with so dull a cheer
   That leaves look pale, dreading the winter's near.

4 bareness] Q; Barrenness GILDON

1 **spring** draws out the absence described in 97 either forwards (to the spring which follows the *autumn* of 97) or backwards (to the spring preceding it). The inversion of the expected seasonal order of these two poems has the effect of imaginatively extending the absence to a whole year, spring to spring, as a reader tries out possibilities.

2 **proud-pied** proudly dressed in parti-coloured clothes. (The flashes of green and blossom in an April woodland are probably meant.)
   trim adornment, array

4 **That** with the result that
   heavy Saturn Saturn is the god of melancholy and old age, whose association with the slower, denser elements and humours makes him *heavy* in the senses of 'weighty' and 'gloomy'. To 'laugh and leap' is a set phrase for mirthful celebration (Dent L92a.1).

5 **nor . . . nor** neither . . . nor
   lays songs. This was a poeticism even by 1600.

6 **Of different . . . hue** of flowers differing in their scent and colour

7 **summer's story** Since 'A sad tale's best for winter' (*Winter's Tale* 2.1.27) a *summer's tale* would be cheery. Cf. 'summer songs', *Winter's Tale* 4.3.11.

8 **proud lap** The lap of earth on which they grow is *proud* of its offspring.

9 **lily's white** Q reads 'Lillies white'. The apostrophe (not regularly used to mark the genitive in this period) is needed in order to point the similarity with the *vermilion in the rose* of the next line.

10 **vermilion** a strong bright red. The word occurs only here in Shakespeare.

11 **but** only, merely
   figures mere representations, poorly rendering their *pattern*, on which see 19.12 n. and compare 53.

13 **you away** with you away

14 **shadow** representation or ghost, as opposed to substance. See 27.10 n.

98

From you have I been absent in the spring,
When proud-pied April (dressed in all his trim)
Hath put a spirit of youth in every thing,
That heavy Saturn laughed and leapt with him.
Yet nor the lays of birds, nor the sweet smell   5
Of different flowers in odour and in hue,
Could make me any summer's story tell,
Or from their proud lap pluck them where they grew.
Nor did I wonder at the lily's white,
Nor praise the deep vermilion in the rose;   10
They were but sweet, but figures of delight
Drawn after you, you pattern of all those.
    Yet seemed it winter still, and, you away,
    As with your shadow I with these did play.

9 lily's] Q (Lillies) 11 were] Q (weare)

The fifteen lines of this sonnet have prompted much adverse commentary. Some find in them early work which was not subsequently revised; others present the poem as a deliberately unconvinced panegyric to the friend. For the latter view, see Gerald Hammond, *The Reader and Shakespeare's Young Man Sonnets* (1984), 144–9; for a refinement, which presents the poem as one which Shakespeare could not 'have wished to bring quite round', see Kerrigan, 32–3. It is close in subject to Petrarch's *Rime Sparse* 127, Henry Constable's *Diana* 1.9, and to Campion's lyric 'There is a garden in her face'. It treats a timeworn theme. Fifteen-line 'sonnets' are found in Barnabe Barnes's *Parthenophil and Parthenophe* (1593) and Bartholomew Griffin's *Fidessa* (1596). It confirms the effect of seasonal and stylistic regression established by the previous poem: *thus did I chide* points to a past spring, and, in its metrical awkwardness, perhaps too to an earlier period of composition. The final *more flowers I noted* suggests that the poem is reluctant to fit into even fifteen lines.

1 **forward** (a) precocious (with a suggestion of presumption); (b) early

2 **'Sweet . . . smells** This line of ten monosyllables is among the least metrically refined in the Sonnets, and may indicate an early date, or that the poem was not finally revised.

3 **purple pride** In Elizabethan and Jacobean English 'purple' extended in range from red to violet. In classical literature purple is associated with imperial power; hence *pride* means more than just an object of visual pride, and suggests almost 'an emblem of glory'.

4 **for complexion** to give it (artificial) colour. 'A colouring preparation applied (by women) to "give a complexion" to the face' (*OED* 6, which cites Pliny ii, sig. A4ᵛ: 'They are called at this day complexions, whereas they be clean contrary; for the complexion is natural, and these altogether artificial').

5 **grossly** (a) crudely (in a way that draws attention to its artifice); (b) impolitely (having rudely taken it from the friend); (c) violently (having spilled his blood in order to beautify yourself)

6 **for thy hand** for having stolen the whiteness from your hand

7 **marjoram** is sweet-smelling and, in its new growth (*buds*), of a golden lightness. This probably is enough to warrant the comparison with the beloved's hair.

8 **on thorns did stand** (a) were placed above thorns; (b) were on tenterhooks. 'To stand on thorns' was a proverbial expression for 'to be in a state of anxiety' (Dent T239).

10 **nor red, nor white** This probably refers to a variegated variety such as 'York and Lancaster', although it may be an elaborate periphrasis for 'pink', since that word was not available as a colour name independent of the flower until 1720. See *130*.5 n.

11 **annexed** added

12 **in pride** at the height of; suggesting also vaunting boastfulness

13 **eat** an archaic form of the past tense, pronounced 'et'

15 **But** except

99

The forward violet thus did I chide:
'Sweet thief, whence didst thou steal thy sweet that smells,
If not from my love's breath? The purple pride,
Which on thy soft cheek for complexion dwells,
In my love's veins thou hast too grossly dyed.'   5
The lily I condemnèd for thy hand,
And buds of marjoram had stol'n thy hair.
The roses fearfully on thorns did stand,
One blushing shame, another white despair,
A third nor red, nor white, had stol'n of both,   10
And to his robb'ry had annexed thy breath;
But for his theft, in pride of all his growth,
A vengeful canker eat him up to death.
    More flowers I noted, yet I none could see
    But sweet or colour it had stol'n from thee.   15

2–5 'Sweet . . . dyed.'] BELL; ⌣ . . . ⌣, Q   3–4 breath? The . . . dwells] GILDON; ~, ~ . . . ~? Q
9 One] SEWELL; Our Q   13 eat] Q (eate), ate BUTLER

3 **Spend'st thou** are you expending, wasting
fury frenzy of poetic inspiration. The phrase 'to spend one's fury' normally means to 'vent one's rage' (as in *2 Henry VI (Contention)* 5.1.26–7: 'And now, like Ajax Telamonius, | On sheep or oxen could I spend my fury'), which allows a secondary sense 'waste your critical anger on worthless trash', i.e. in attacking the works of rivals.

4 **Dark'ning . . . light?** sullying your talent in order to illuminate insignificant themes

5–6 **redeem . . . time** make reparation for time which has been lost. Cf. *1 Henry IV* 1.2.214: 'Redeeming time when men think least I will'. Both passages echo Ephesians 5: 15–16: 'Take heed therefore that ye walk circumspectly, not as fools, but as wise, redeeming the time: for the days are evil'.

6 **gentle numbers** noble verses
idly wastefully, as well as lazily

8 **skill and argument** ability to write and subject matter to write about

9 **resty** usually means 'restive', suggesting ungovernable restlessness; it can also mean 'Disinclined for action or exertion; sluggish, indolent, lazy; inactive' (*OED* 2a), as in Jonson's *Silent Woman* (1609), 1.1.171–2: 'He would grow resty else in his ease. His virtue would rust without action.' This latter sense is likely to be the primary one, given that the poet has spoken of *time so idly spent*.
survey, look at, assess. Q's comma (fol-

lowed here) allows the following line to link either with this or l. 11. This releases the sense 'see whether Time has . . .'.

11 **be a satire to decay** vilify the actions of time as a satirist would. *Satire* is capitalized and italicized in Q, probably because it was new to the compositor (this is one of the earliest citations in *OED* for sense 4, 'satirist'). It may emphasize the frequent association in the period between satirical verses and the savage mythological wood-dwelling creatures known as satyrs. As Puttenham, 31, put it: 'and besides to make their admonitions and reproofs seem graver and of more efficacy, they made wise as if the gods of the woods, whom they called *Satyrs* or *Silvans*, should appear and recite those verses of rebuke'.

12 **spoils** 'acts of plundering' (Schmidt, 3). A secondary sense, 'make people despise things which are subject to Time's power', may be in play, anticipating the appeal to perdurable *fame* in the couplet.

14 So so that
prevent'st outstrip, anticipate. Q reads 'preuenst' which may represent a form of 'prevene', an obsolete term of largely Scottish provenance meaning 'To anticipate, take precautions against (a danger, evil, etc.); hence, to prevent, frustrate, evade' (*OED* s.v. 'prevene' 1a). It is more likely to be a form of 'prevent'st' which avoids a cluster of consonants.
scythe and crookèd knife Both terms probably refer to Time's sickle. *Crookèd* is introduced to connote malice (as at 60.7).

100

Where art thou, Muse, that thou forget'st so long
To speak of that which gives thee all thy might?
Spend'st thou thy fury on some worthless song,
Dark'ning thy pow'r to lend base subjects light?
Return, forgetful Muse, and straight redeem   5
In gentle numbers time so idly spent.
Sing to the ear that doth thy lays esteem,
And gives thy pen both skill and argument.
Rise, resty Muse, my love's sweet face survey,
If Time have any wrinkle graven there;   10
If any, be a satire to decay,
And make Time's spoils despisèd everywhere.
   Give my love fame faster than Time wastes life,
   So thou prevent'st his scythe and crookèd knife.

14 prevent'st] GILDON; preuenst Q; preven'st OXFORD

1 **amends** payment in compensation

2 **truth in beauty dyed** truth suffused in and permeated by beauty. Dyeing in Shakespeare is usually not used as a metaphor for deceitfully superficial colouring, since early modern England prided itself on the durability of its woad-based dyes; cf. *the dyer's hand*, III.7. The potential duplicity of the art of colouring emerges as the sonnet progresses.

3 **on my love depends** (a) (objectively) depend upon my love, the friend, for their existence; (b) (subjectively) depend upon my feeling love in order to exist. The singular ending of the verb after a plural subject is common in Shakespeare.

4 **therein dignified** you (my muse) are rendered worthy by my love

6 **'Truth . . . intermixed'** Compare the proverb 'Truth needs no colours' (excuses or rhetorical ornaments) (Dent T585). Speech-marks do not occur in Q.

colour fixed ingrained hue. *OED* does not record a usage of 'fixed' to refer to the process whereby colour is made stable in dyeing before 1790, but this sense could be anticipated here. The initial stability of the metaphor of colouring here begins to erode via a play on 'colour', meaning both 'hue' and 'Outward appearance, show, aspect, semblance of (something): generally that which serves to conceal or cloak the truth' (*OED* 11a).

7 **lay** 'To put upon a surface in layers; to put or arrange (colours, †a picture) on canvas' (*OED* 41 Art. a)

8 **best is . . . intermixed** The best things are really the best if they are left unadulterated.

11 **gilded tomb** develops the growing suspicion of artificial colour: cf. *Merchant* 2.7.69: 'Gilded tombs do worms infold'.

13 **office** duty

how, Q's comma after *how* is removed by many editors to create a strong enjambment. Q makes good sense: the Muse's *office* is to preserve the friend, and *I teach thee how* is a parenthesis.

14 **seem . . . shows** appear in the future as he looks now. *Seem* and *shows* together suggest appearance *rather than* substance.

101

O truant Muse, what shall be thy amends
For thy neglect of truth in beauty dyed?
Both truth and beauty on my love depends:
So dost thou too, and therein dignified.
Make answer, Muse, wilt thou not haply say   5
'Truth needs no colour with his colour fixed,
Beauty no pencil beauty's truth to lay,
But best is best if never intermixed'?
Because he needs no praise, wilt thou be dumb?
Excuse not silence so, for 't lies in thee   10
To make him much outlive a gilded tomb,
And to be praised of ages yet to be.
    Then do thy office, Muse, I teach thee how,
    To make him seem long hence, as he shows now.

6–8 'Truth . . . intermixed?'] MALONE (*italic*); ˏ~ . . . ~·ˏ Q   11 him] Q; her BENSON   14 him
. . . he] Q; her . . . she BENSON

1 **strengthened** by the passage of time

2 **show** outward appearance; also 'display, parade, ostentation' (Schmidt, 2)

3 **merchandized** made into commercial merchandise. Compare the proverb 'He praises who wishes to sell' (Dent P546).

4 **publish** make public, with a play on the modern sense of 'to distribute in print'

7–8 **Philomel . . . his pipe** Philomela, sister-in-law of Tereus, who raped her and cut out her tongue, is female both when in human form and when she turns into a nightingale. Nightingales sing *in summer's front*, that is at the start of the summer. It is probably the mention of a *pipe* which makes Shakespeare change her sex: for a moment Philomel becomes a character from a pastoral, where pipers are invariably male, and often are allegorical projections of their poets. The nightingale's metamorphosis back into *her* in l. 10 occurs when the context of pious nocturnal unhappiness jogs Shakespeare into remembering her mythological past. Nocturnal hymn-singing tends to be a feminine activity in Shakespearian drama. Many editors emend *his* to *her*; a few brave souls suggest that Shakespeare may have been enough of an ornithologist to have known that only *cock* nightingales sing (and in Petrarch *Rime Sparse* 311, as well as in Barnabe Barnes's

Parthenophil and Parthenophe 57.12–14, it is a male nightingale which laments). The inconsistency illustrates Shakespeare's instinctive association of certain locales with particular genders.

8 **growth of riper days** as summer advances towards the fruitfulness of autumn

10 **hush the night** The night is presented as an enraptured and pious audience moved to silence by the nightingale's *hymns*.

11 **But that** but the reason is that. It is in parallel with *Not that* and introduces the explanation of why the nightingale is quiet later in the year.
   wild music (a) unrestrained song; (b) frolicsome song; (c) the song of wild birds
   burdens suggests the excessive fecundity of late summer. The noun 'burden' can mean 'chorus' (*OED* 10).

12 **common** too frequent; also perhaps with a reminiscence of earlier rebukes to the friend for making himself excessively *common* in the sense 'vulgar, open to the sexual advances of everyone', as at 69.14. There also may be a residue of criticism for the rival poets who continually produce wordy panegyrics which are devalued by their frequency. The whole line has a proverbial ring to it, but no precise parallel has been found.

14 **dull** bore you, blunt your appetite for song

102

My love is strengthened though more weak in seeming;
I love not less, though less the show appear.
That love is merchandized whose rich esteeming
The owner's tongue doth publish everywhere.
Our love was new, and then but in the spring,   5
When I was wont to greet it with my lays,
As Philomel in summer's front doth sing,
And stops his pipe in growth of riper days:
Not that the summer is less pleasant now
Than when her mournful hymns did hush the night,   10
But that wild music burdens every bough,
And sweets grown common lose their dear delight.
   Therefore, like her, I sometime hold my tongue,
   Because I would not dull you with my song.

8 his] Q; her *conj.* Housman in Rollins 2

1 **poverty** poetry of low value, contrasting with the *worth* of the friend

2 **scope** range. See 29.7 n.
pride (a) the object of her pride, the friend; (b) poetic ability.

3–4 **argument all bare . . . beside** simple subject matter is of more value when it is unadorned by eloquence than it is when given what should be the additional worth that comes from being praised by me. On *argument* see 38.3 n. Compare the proverb 'The truth shows best being naked' (Dent T589).

7 **blunt invention** lame creative powers. On *invention* see 38.8 n.

8 **Dulling** (a) taking the edge off (picking out *blunt* from the previous line); (b) making tedious

9–10 **Were it . . . well?** Would it not be a sin to make something worse by attempting to improve it? Cf. *Lear* (Folio) 1.4.325: 'Striving to better, oft we mar what's well' and Dent W260. *Sinful* adds a particular taint

to the proverbial matter of these lines: taken in conjunction with *graces* in l. 12 it implies that the poet is attempting to represent a divine benignity, which can only be contaminated by its representation in his verse.

11 **pass** end, goal

12 **graces and your gifts** refer to qualities residing in the friend ('inexpressible beauties and abilities') and to gifts which are bestowed upon the poet by the friend ('presents and bounties given to the undeserving'). This casts a retrospective light on the *poverty* of the poet and suggests that the poem is a delicately phrased supplication to a patron. *Tell* can mean 'enumerate, count'. Hence ll. 11–12 present two senses: (a) my poems are only aimed at recounting your extraordinary beauty and abilities; (b) my verses are designed to tot up your bounty to me. Sense (b) is delicately pushed to the background.

103

Alack, what poverty my Muse brings forth,
That having such a scope to show her pride
The argument all bare is of more worth
Than when it hath my added praise beside.
O, blame me not if I no more can write!   5
Look in your glass, and there appears a face
That overgoes my blunt invention quite,
Dulling my lines, and doing me disgrace.
Were it not sinful then, striving to mend,
To mar the subject that before was well?   10
For to no other pass my verses tend
Than of your graces and your gifts to tell.
   And more, much more, than in my verse can sit
   Your own glass shows you, when you look in it.

There may be a pause in the sequence here. The previous poem claims that the mirror reveals more than the poet can; this poem dwells on the three winters which have passed since the addressee was seen in youthful glory. A. Kent Hieatt, Charles W. Hieatt, and Anne Lake Prescott, 'When did Shakespeare Write *Sonnets* 1609?', *SP* 88 (1991), 69–109, have suggested that *104–26* show signs of later composition, since they contain a significantly higher proportion of 'late rare words' and a lower proportion of 'early rare words' than those which precede them.

1 **friend** often used of a mistress as well as a friend of the same sex, as in *Willobie His Avisa* Canto 25.19–22: 'The gravest men of former time, | That lived with fame, and happy life, | Have thought it none, or petty crime, | To love a friend besides their wife', or in *Measure* 1.4.29: 'He hath got his friend with child'.
    never can be old Underlying this is a recognition that the friend *is* visibly ageing, or a faint threat that the preservation of his or her former beauty depends increasingly on the imagination of the poet: the chime in the following line on *eye I eyed* links together the poet, perception, and the identity of the friend.

3 **Such seems** The imperfect co-ordination of *as you were* and *Such seems your beauty* creates a disparity between the friend as he was, and his mere appearance of beauty now.
    Three winters cold Sonneteers tended to live life in multiples of three. Horace's declaration in *Epodes* 11.5–6 ('This third December since I ceased to desire Inachia is shaking the leaves from the trees') was imitated by Desportes and Ronsard. There are signs this was not simply a convention, however: Daniel refers in the 1592 text of *Delia* (31.6) to three years of courtship, but extends it to five in 1594. Petrarch regularly punctuates the *Rime Sparse* with allusions to the amount of time which has passed since he first saw Laura's eyes.

6 **process** progression, forward movement

8 **Since ... green** since I first saw you youthful, who are still full of vitality. *Fresh* and *green* continue the botanical imagery of the preceding lines, and suggest that the friend has the power to resist the passing of the seasons.

9–10 **Ah ... perceived** Beauty, like the shadow cast on a sundial, shifts away from its position without any perceptible motion. Compare the proverb 'To move as the dial hand, which is not seen to move' (Dent D321). *Dial* may suggest either a sundial or a watch, on which see *77.2 n*. Since watches usually had only one hand until about 1675 any movement would be very slow. *Steal from his figure* is ambiguous: (a) Beauty creeps away from his (i.e. the friend's) form; (b) Beauty (like the hand of the clock) creeps slowly away from his (i.e. beauty's own) time of perfection; (c) Beauty robs from the perfect form of the friend with the slow imperceptible movement of a clock's hand. Sense (a) is the primary sense, but brings a shockingly abrupt change from second to first person (*you* to *his*) in the mode of address to the friend. Beauty is presented as at once a slowly vanishing quality, and as a thief in league with time, who tiptoes away with the perfection of the friend.

11 **hue** beauty, but see *20.7 n*.
    stand shows no alteration, remains unmoving

12 **and** both the normal modern sense, and 'if'. This continues the uncertainty as to whether the poet can see the friend change: (a) So your beauty is actually changing, despite its appearance of stasis, and my eye *is* capable of deceiving me; (b) So your beauty is actually changing ... if my eye is capable of deceiving me. Sense (b) emerges as the primary sense, since it is presumably *for fear of* his eye's deceiving him that the poet issues his final rebuke to posterity.

13 **unbred** *OED* cites only this passage to support the definition 'unborn'. Sense 2, 'unmannerly, ill-bred', is first cited in 1622, so may be an emergent sense here.

13–14 **thou ... you** The shift from singular to plural marks a movement from an address to a collective *age* to the particular people who constitute it.

104

To me, fair friend, you never can be old,
For as you were when first your eye I eyed,
Such seems your beauty still. Three winters cold
Have from the forests shook three summers' pride,
Three beauteous springs to yellow autumn turned   5
In process of the seasons have I seen,
Three April perfumes in three hot Junes burned,
Since first I saw you fresh, which yet are green.
Ah yet doth beauty, like a dial hand,
Steal from his figure, and no pace perceived;   10
So your sweet hue, which methinks still doth stand,
Hath motion, and mine eye may be deceived.
   For fear of which, hear this thou age unbred:
   Ere you were born was beauty's summer dead.

1 friend] Q; love BENSON   5 autumn] Q (*Autumne*); autumns *conj.* Capell

1 **idolatry** The conceit underlying the sonnet is that the poet has one god only, the friend, who embodies a Trinitarian unity of *Three themes in one.* Hence he is not committing *idolatry* by worshipping several idols. The apparent aim of the poem is to exclude uncertainty both of reference and of meaning—its subject is the friend and its aim is to describe his qualities with a simplicity which approaches tautology (*fair, kind, and true*). This aspiration is necessarily idolatrous, however, since its object is not God but the friend.

2 **show** appear

3 **Since** It is not clear whether this introduces the reason for an accusation of idolatry or a defence against it. Ingram and Redpath prefer the former, but the latter is more likely, since it initiates the poem's deliberate self-deception: 'How can you call me an idolater when I always sing the praises of one person' *is*, as Ingram and Redpath note, a very weak defence against the charge of idolatry if the object of worship is not God: that is the point.

4 **still such . . .** so The Gloria ('Glory be to the Father, and to the Son, and to the Holy Ghost. As it was in the beginning, is now, and ever shall be') is echoed here, and through it, as Booth points out, the 1563 'Homily against Idolatry': 'images in temples and churches be indeed none other but idols, as unto which idolatry hath been, is, and ever will be committed', *Sermons or Homilies* (1833), 120.

5 **Kind . . . kind** *Epanalepsis* (the repetition of a word at either end of a clause or line) reinforces the tautology.

6 **constant** (a) the same; (b) faithful

7 **to constancy confined** restricted to representing constancy; limited to fidelity. The *polyptoton* (repetition of *constant* in a different form) loops back to the previous line.

8 **leaves out difference** (a) excludes other subjects; (b) omits mention of differences between the lovers

9 **'Fair, kind, and true'** These apparently simple terms cover a range of senses: beautiful, just, equitable; friendly, generous, gentle; truthful, faithful, unchanging. Vendler detects here a secular Platonic alternative to the Trinity, which draws on the Platonic triad of the Beautiful, the Good, and the True. However, Nicholas Breton's *Melancholic Humours* (1600) includes a similar list of united virtues, 'Sweet, fair, wise, kind, blessed, true | Blessed be all these in you', which suggests a sonneteer's convention.

11 **invention** ability to write, or to find out words to suit his subject

spent (a) exhausted; (b) deployed

12 **Three themes in one** (a) three subjects in one; (b) three virtues combined into one superior virtue; (c) three virtues combined in one man

scope range of subject matter. See 29.7 and n.

13 Compare the proverb 'Beauty and chastity seldom meet' (Dent B163).

14 **kept seat** resided

105

Let not my love be called idolatry,
Nor my belovèd as an idol show,
Since all alike my songs and praises be
To one, of one, still such, and ever so.
Kind is my love today, tomorrow kind,   5
Still constant in a wondrous excellence;
Therefore my verse, to constancy confined,
One thing expressing, leaves out difference.
'Fair, kind, and true' is all my argument,
'Fair, kind, and true' varying to other words;   1C
And in this change is my invention spent,
Three themes in one, which wondrous scope affords.
    Fair, kind, and true have often lived alone,
    Which three till now never kept seat in one.

9, 10 'Fair, kind, and true'] GLOBE; ͵‾, ‾, ‾ ‾͵ Q

The text is found in two MSS dating from the 1630s: Pierpont Morgan MA 1057, p. 96, and Rosenbach MS 1083/16, p. 256, which are printed as separate and possibly authorial variants in Kerrigan and Oxford. There are no clear Shakespearian analogues for the scribal variants, however: 'all-wasting' is not otherwise used by Shakespeare, and removes the pun on 'waste' which is also found in 12.10. 'Annals' is found elsewhere only in the Roman setting of *Coriolanus* 5.6.114, and suggests a Jacobean sophistication: 'Chronicles' were passé by 1620, and the fashion for Tacitus, the author of 'Annals', was well entrenched. The substitution of 'face' for *hand* in l. 6, combined with the fussy 'or' to round off the list, suggests a memorial reconstruction of the unorthodox blazon in Q (which zooms in from extremities to the ornaments of the face). The other minor variants suggest poor recollection of the Q text rather than an early version, with the exception of the intelligent emendation to Q of 'skill' in l. 12.

1 **chronicle of wasted time** record of past time misspent. *Wasted time* could conceivably be a semipersonification, meaning 'attenuated, skinny Time'.

2 **fairest wights** most beautiful people. Spenser's *Faerie Queene* (1590–1609), in which knights and heroes purporting to derive from British prehistory are praised in a consciously archaic style (and in which *wights* is a frequent term), prompted a number of sonneteers to declare the superiority of their mistresses to ancient beauties, as in Daniel's *Delia* (1592), 46. The posthumous printing of the final instalment of Spenser's poem in 1609, the year of Thorpe's Quarto, would have given the reference to Spenser's *antique pen* added topicality.

5 **blazon** a formal catalogue of the elements of a lady's beauty, as in a heraldic description, which became one of the standard elements in sonnet sequences in the 1590s.

7 **would have** wished to. (The poet turns past prophets into writers who are attempting to write descriptions of the friend. Being deprived of his actual presence, they fall short of representing his *worth*.)

8 **master** 'To have at one's disposal; to own, possess' (*OED* 6). The earliest cited examples of the transitive verb are from Shakespeare, e.g. *Lucrece* l. 863.

9 **praises are but prophecies** 'their praises of past beauties in fact were predictions of your beauties'. Compare the Todd MS of Henry Constable's *Diana* (date uncertain; Constable died in 1613): 'I never will deny | That former poets praise the beauty of their days; | But all those beauties were but figures of thy praise, | And all those poets did of thee but prophesy'.

10 **prefiguring** In biblical exegesis, Old Testament events were supposed to 'prefigure' their true archetypes in the New Testament. In conjunction with *divining* this makes a quasi-theological claim that the friend is the type of all that is beautiful. This connects it thematically with *105*.

11 **for . . . eyes** since they looked only with the eyes of prediction (rather than seeing you in reality)

12 **skill** Random Clod (Randall McLeod), 'Information upon Information', *Text* 5 (1991), 253–8, defends Q's 'still' on the grounds that it is an unlikely compositorial error for 'skill', given that 'st' is a ligature and 'sk' is not. The MSS support 'skill', which is very likely to have been misread by the compositor. Q's reading could be glossed 'And because they only saw you with the eyes of divination, rather than actually seeing you, they still lacked enough (words or ability, supplied) to describe your worth'. The MS reads more easily, which may be a reason to suspect it: Q's reluctance to state even what these past writers lacked could be seen as an expressive hiatus.

14 **wonder** look on with amazement

106

When in the chronicle of wasted time
I see descriptions of the fairest wights,
And beauty making beautiful old rhyme
In praise of ladies dead, and lovely knights;
Then in the blazon of sweet beauty's best,　　　　　　　　5
Of hand, of foot, of lip, of eye, of brow,
I see their antique pen would have expressed
Even such a beauty as you master now.
So all their praises are but prophecies
Of this our time, all you prefiguring,　　　　　　　　10
And, for they looked but with divining eyes,
They had not skill enough your worth to sing.
　　For we, which now behold these present days,
　　Have eyes to wonder, but lack tongues to praise.

1 chronicle of wasted] Q; annals of all-wasting RO 1; Annalls of all wastinge M　2 descriptions] Q, RO 1; discription M　3 rhyme] Q, RO 1; mine M　6 Of hand, of foot] Q; Of face, of hand RO 1; Of face of hands M　of eye] Q, M; or eye RO 1　of brow] Q; or brow RO 1, M　8 Even] Q, RO 1; Eu'n M　9 their] Q, M, RO 1 *mistakenly transcribed as 'these' in* OXFORD　are] Q; were RO 1, M　10 this] Q; these RO 1; those M　time] Q; days RO 1, M　11 looked] Q; saw M; say RO 1　divining] Q, M; deceiving RO 1　12 skill] RO 1, M; still Q; style *conj.* Tucker　your] Q; thy RO 1, M　13 we] Q, M; me RO 1　present] Q, M; pleasant RO 1　14 tongues] Q, M; tongue RO 1

The date of this poem has been much discussed. The *mortal moon* has been seen as an allusion to the Spanish Armada (which was drawn up in a crescent), defeated in 1588 (Hotson); to the eclipse which passed without incident in 1595; to the 'grand climacteric' (63rd year, thought to be particularly perilous) of Queen Elizabeth I, who was regularly associated with Cynthia the goddess of chastity and the moon (1595–6); a serious illness which the Queen was rumoured to have had in 1599–1600; the death of the Queen and the accession of James I in 1603 (although his coronation was delayed until March 1604 as a result of plague). The last is the most likely: *sad augurs* alludes to the many who predicted national catastrophe after the death of the childless Queen, and *olives of endless age* alludes to the frequent efforts of James I and his panegyrists to present his reign as an age of imperial peace. The Jacobean ambience of the poem is reinforced by its position immediately after 106, Shakespeare's most direct allusion to Spenser, whose Elizabethan epic is presented as a thing of the past, and by its echoes of *Antony* (1609), on which see J. M. Nosworthy, 'All Too Short a Date: Internal Evidence in Shakespeare's Sonnets', *Essays in Criticism* 2 (1952), 311–24. For a summary of all the proposed dates (which range from 1579 to 1609) see Rollins 2, i.263–8. A manuscript version from *c.* 1660 entitled 'A Monument' survives in Folger MS V.a.148, Pt. 1, fo. 22.

1 **prophetic soul** intuitions about the future, as in Hamlet's 'O my prophetic soul', 1.5.41. Cf. Dent S666.2.

2 **dreaming on** having fantastical imaginings about

3 **control** The context suggests 'achieve sufficient authority over (the lease) in order to emend it'; *OED* offers only 'To challenge, find fault with, censure, reprehend, object to (a thing)' (3b) and 'to hold sway over, exercise power or authority over' (4). It also gives a specifically Shakespearian usage, 'To overpower, overmaster' (5), as in *Lucrece* l. 678.

4 **Supposed** 'considered to be', with also possibly a technical legal usage of 'suppose', 'To state, allege: esp. formally in an indictment' (*OED* 11); i.e. the poet's limited *lease* of *true love* is formally recognized to terminate at a particular time

4 **confined doom** (a) expiry at a particular time; (b) judgement that will bring with it confinement, or imprisonment. *Confined* is stressed on the first syllable. It can also mean 'stated with precision', as in 2 *Henry IV* 4.1.173, although some editions choose to read 'consigned' in that place (Schmidt).

5 **The mortal . . . endured** See headnote. The reference is probably to the death of Elizabeth I on 24 March 1603. If the poem dates from 1603/4 *endured* must mean 'has suffered, undergone' (a sense implicit in Edgar's 'Men must endure | Their going hence even as their coming hither', *Lear* (Folio) 5.2.9–10); if it refers to a period of illness from which the Queen recovered it means 'passed through alive'.

6 **sad augurs . . . presage** disappointed prophets of doom now confute their own predictions. Cf. *Venus* l. 457.

7 **Incertainties . . . assured** things which appeared uncertain now adopt a regal posture of certainty. There may be an allusion here to the unexpectedly peaceful accession of James I.

8 **olives of endless age** olive branches, symbolizing peace, which will last for ever

9 **drops . . . balmy time** Drops of balm were used in the coronation ceremony. *Balmy* also means 'Deliciously soft and soothing' (*OED* 4 *fig.*).

10 **My love looks fresh** If *My love* is taken to mean 'the person I love' and if this is identified with the friend, and if the friend is the Earl of Southampton, then this could allude to the release of the Earl from the Tower on 10 April 1603, a *confined doom* indeed, or perhaps to his full reinstatement to his title by Parliament on 18 April 1604. A similar chain of hypotheses could equally frailly be tacked to the supposition that it alludes to the release of the Earl of Pembroke from the Fleet prison in March or April 1601. If any link in these chains of supposition were to be found less than rigid then either hypothesis would fall—if indeed they had ever tottered to their feet.

subscribes 'submits, yields' (*OED* 8), with a stronger suggestion of reversing the legal effects of the limited lease referred to in l. 3, via *OED* 8b: 'To submit or subject oneself *to* law or rule'. The etymological association of 'subscribe' with writing one's name *beneath* (*sub-scribere*) is alive in this poem in which a poet seeks to assert the power of his writing over death.

107

Not mine own fears, nor the prophetic soul
Of the wide world, dreaming on things to come,
Can yet the lease of my true love control,
Supposed as forfeit to a confined doom.
The mortal moon hath her eclipse endured,   5
And the sad augurs mock their own presage.
Incertainties now crown themselves assured,
And peace proclaims olives of endless age.
Now with the drops of this most balmy time
My love looks fresh, and death to me subscribes,   10
Since, spite of him, I'll live in this poor rhyme,
While he insults o'er dull and speechless tribes.
   And thou in this shalt find thy monument,
   When tyrants' crests and tombs of brass are spent.

11 **spite** in spite
12 **insults** enjoys arrogant supremacy
dull and speechless tribes peoples who
cannot write verse, and who cannot
therefore conquer death. Louis Le Roy,
*Of the Interchangeable Course or Variety
of Things*, trans. R[obert] A[shley]
(1594), 22ᵛ, writes that 'The Nomads
of great Tartaria, and some savages of

the new-found lands do use no letters
at all'.
13 **in this** in this poem
monument See 51.9 and n.
14 **crests** (a) crested helmets (used to frighten
an enemy, as by the tyrannical sultan in
Tasso's *Gerusalemme Liberata* 9.25); (b)
heraldic devices
spent wasted to nothing

1–2 **What's . . . spirit?** 'What mental resource is there which can be set down in writing which I have not used to represent to you my loyal inner nature?' *True spirit* means both 'loyal nature' and 'my spirit as it actually is'.

3 **new . . . now** Malone's emendation of the 'now' to 'new' shows his love of symmetry rather than Shakespeare's. 'What is there now to add to the list' is perfectly intelligible.

4 **dear merit** loved worth, or expensive desert

5 **sweet boy** the only time this phrase is used in the Sonnets. It is used in Shakespeare by fathers to their sons, and makes great claims to intimacy. The last exchange between Falstaff and Henry V (as Hal has become) runs: 'God save thee, my sweet Boy. *King:* My Lord Chief Justice, speak to that vain man. *Chief Justice:* Have you your wits? Know you what 'tis you speak?', *2 Henry IV* 5.3.43–5. It can carry homosexual overtones, as when Richard Barnfield, *Cynthia* 14.5, calls his Ganymede-like male lover 'sweet boy'. Cf. *Venus* l. 155. These associations may have prompted Benson to one of his bowdlerizations, 'sweet-love'.

7 **no old thing old** seeing even amorous clichés as fresh

thou . . . thine a representatively predictable prayer of those in love, venerably echoing the Song of Solomon 2: 16: 'My beloved is mine, and I am his'.

8 **hallowed** alludes to the Lord's Prayer, 'Our father which art in heaven, hallowed be thy name', Matthew 6: 9.

9 **fresh case** (a) new circumstances; (b) bright new clothes; (c) new argument

10 **Weighs not** See 51.10 n.

11 **Nor . . . place** does not yield priority to wrinkles, which necessarily come with age. To *give place* is to defer to someone's higher status in, for example, seating at table or in a formal procession.

12 **antiquity for aye his page** age (or 'the writings of the ancients') his inferior servant (or 'the page which he reads') for ever (picking up on *give place*) above. The pun on page the young servant and page of paper was popularized by 'The Induction' to Nashe's *Unfortunate Traveller* in which Jack Wilton boasts that 'a proper fellow-page of yours . . . hath bequeathed for waste paper here amongst you certain pages of his misfortunes', Nashe, ii. 207.

13–4 **Finding . . . dead** The first principle of love is alive and well in the pages of antiquity, despite their aged appearance. *There bred* suggests that love is born anew with each reiteration of an old commonplace prayer.

108

What's in the brain that ink may character,
Which hath not figured to thee my true spirit?
What's new to speak, what now to register,
That may express my love, or thy dear merit?
Nothing, sweet boy; but yet, like prayers divine,   5
I must each day say o'er the very same,
Counting no old thing old thou mine, I thine,
Even as when first I hallowed thy fair name.
So that eternal love in love's fresh case
Weighs not the dust and injury of age,   10
Nor gives to necessary wrinkles place,
But makes antiquity for aye his page,
    Finding the first conceit of love there bred,
    Where time and outward form would show it dead.

3 now] Q; new MALONE   5 sweet boy] Q; sweet-love BENSON

2 **my . . . qualify** moderate, diminish my ardour

3 **easy** easily
from myself depart 'abandon my true self' (Ingram and Redpath); or, with extreme literalness, 'step out of my own skin'. Compare the proverb 'The lover is not where he lives but where he loves' (Dent L565).

4 **my soul . . . lie** For the commonplace of lovers exchanging hearts or souls, see 22.5–7.

6 **him that** one that

7 **Just to . . . exchanged** exactly at the appointed moment, unchanged by the passage of time. *Time* is a slippery word here, meaning both a transitory 'moment', and 'period of absence', with overtones too of 'this age'. Hence *not with the time exchanged* suggests also 'I have not taken on the fickleness of this age'.

8 **So that . . . stain** in order that I might bring water (repentant tears) to wash away the moral stain of my absence. Lady

Macbeth's 'a little water clears us of this deed' is a dark analogue of this passage, *Macbeth* 2.2.65. The claim is indeed suspiciously pat, especially from one who has claimed that 'Th' offender's sorrow lends but weak relief | To him that bears the strong offence's cross' (34.11–12).

9–10 **nature . . . blood** Underlying this image is a scene often enacted in morality plays such as *The Castle of Perseverance* in which the vices lay siege to the body. *Frailty* can connote sexual infidelity. *Blood* is a frequent metonym for passionate bodily nature.

11 **preposterously** absurdly; putting that which should come last (*nothing*) ahead of that which should come first (*all thy sum of good*). *Stained* means 'contaminated, blotted by dishonour'.

13 **For nothing . . . call** I regard the whole universe as worthless

14 **Save . . . all** except for you, my rose, who are to me all the universe, despite being only one element in it. Cf. *1*.2.

109

O, never say that I was false of heart,
Though absence seemed my flame to qualify.
As easy might I from myself depart,
As from my soul which in thy breast doth lie:
That is my home of love: if I have ranged,   5
Like him that travels I return again,
Just to the time, not with the time exchanged,
So that myself bring water for my stain.
Never believe, though in my nature reigned
All frailties that besiege all kinds of blood,   10
That it could so preposterously be stained,
To leave for nothing all thy sum of good:
   For nothing this wide universe I call,
   Save thou, my rose; in it thou art my all.

14 rose] Q (Rose)

2 **motley** fool. *OED* cites this as the first usage of the noun in this sense. It also connotes incoherence, since the *motley* worn by a fool is parti-coloured. 'Folly' could be used to mean 'wantonness or promiscuity' (Partridge, 108), as in Othello's 'She turned to folly, and she was a whore' (5.2.141). Some editors detect an allusion to Shakespeare's activities as a player. This is at best a distant reference, since the role of fool was a specialized one which Shakespeare did not play.

3 **Gored** (a) furnished with 'gores' or triangular pieces of cloth (continuing from *motley*); (b) wounded; (c) a 'gore sinister' was a heraldic mark assigned to those who fled from their enemies. Although *OED* does not record a verbal form derived from this sense of the noun, the tincture of disgrace provided by this association is appropriate here.

4 **Made . . . new** repeated old infidelities as the result of new passions. *Affections* could mean 'objects of loving attachment' or 'feeling as opposed to reason; passion, lust' (*OED* 3). *Old offences* might suggest buggery, which was referred to in the period euphemistically as 'old-fashioned love'. Cf. Donne's Satire 2.7.

5 **truth** constancy in love

6 **Askance and strangely** with haughty disregard. *Askance* can also mean 'sidelong', 'out of the corner of one's eye'.

7 **blenches** (a) swervings aside from what is right; (b) sidelong glances. *OED* cites no other examples for this sense. The more usual meaning is 'trick or stratagem'.
gave my . . . youth rejuvenated my affections (Booth's suggested sense 'won me the affections of another friend' is strained but not impossible)

8 **And worse . . . love** and experiments with less satisfactory loves have proved you to be my best love, or the best object of my love

9 **Now all is done** now all that is over
have no end receive from me something which will endure for ever

10 **appetite . . . grind** The metaphor is from the sharpening of knives, which like an appetite need to be whetted against a new object. For the suggestion of sexual misconduct here compare 95.14.

11 **try** both 'to test out the worth and strength of' and 'to subject to trial', with a suggestion of deliberately imposing hardship

13 **heaven** is monosyllabic.

110

Alas 'tis true, I have gone here and there,
And made myself a motley to the view,
Gored mine own thoughts, sold cheap what is most dear,
Made old offences of affections new.
Most true it is that I have looked on truth   5
Askance and strangely; but, by all above,
These blenches gave my heart another youth,
And worse essays proved thee my best of love.
Now all is done, have what shall have no end.
Mine appetite I never more will grind   10
On newer proof, to try an older friend,
A god in love, to whom I am confined.
   Then give me welcome, next my heaven the best,
   Even to thy pure and most most loving breast.

6 Askance] Q (Asconce)

1 **with Fortune chide** blame Fortune (and
not me). Randall McLeod, 'Unemending
Shakespeare's Sonnet 111', *SEL* 21
(1981), 75–96 argues in favour of Q's
'wish'. Since 'sh' is a ligature (single piece
of type) he claims it is unlikely that com-
positor B made a mechanical error in sub-
stituting it for the 't' in his copy-text. He
claims too that Q is intelligible unemend-
ed. 'O for my sake do you wish Fortune
chide' could be read as a bitterly
masochistic command: 'Now that I am
down ask fortune to chide me further,
and do it for me', a command pointedly at
odds with the poet's later urging to 'wish I
were renewed'. Against this reading,
however, is (a) the possibility that the
compositor misread the whole word of his
copy as 'wish' and so used a 'sh' ligature
(as may occur at *106*. 12). (b) It creates a
suggestion that 'The guilty goddess' is the
object of Fortune's chiding rather than a
description of Fortune herself. One does
not need to be a vigorous wielder of
Occam's razor to feel that goddesses
should not be unduly multiplied, especial-
ly if the changing of a letter could make
them vanish. (c) Q's reading leads to an
extremely harsh transition between the
ironical self-subjection of the beginning
('goad Fortune on') and the appeal for
pity in l. 8 ('Pity me then'). Pity is often
associated in the Sonnets with abjection,
however, and such violent shifts of mood
do occur, although rarely before the *volta*
(i.e. as here before l. 9). It is wise always to
be suspicious of eighteenth-century ratio-
nalizations of Q (although Gildon 1710,
the first edition to read 'with', is scarcely
vigorous in his emendations of Benson's
text). In this instance, however, the ratio-
nalization makes appreciably better sense
than the original. McLeod's claim that
Benson was satisfied with 'wish' is not
quite right: Benson emends 'harmfull'
to 'harmless' in l. 2 in order to thrash
some kind of sense out of a text which he
clearly found obscure.

2 **guilty goddess** goddess who is guilty of
(rather than me)

4 **public means . . . public manners** These
phrases mark an opposition between the
methods which the poet/playwright has
to use to earn a living and those of a
leisured aristocrat (cf. *110*. 2). Although
many players were wealthy, they were
frequently associated with low social
orders. A statute of 1572, directed against
'Rogue, vagabonds and sturdy beggars',

required members of theatrical compa-
nies to become the retainers of noblemen,
and linked the theatre with vagrants, tin-
kers, and bearwards.

5 **brand** indelible mark of shame. The prac-
tice of branding criminals continued in
England until 1829. People claiming Ben-
efit of Clergy and found guilty of murder
were branded on the thumb with an 'M'.
Under the Statute of Vagabonds 1547 men
and women who would not work were to
be branded on the breast with a 'V' and
adjudged a slave for two years. Those who
were guilty of perjury were placed in the
pillory and then branded on the forehead
with a 'P'. Compare *112*. 1–2. There may
alternatively be an allusion to the shame
attached to the career of playwright in
this period: Philip Stubbes, *The Anatomy
of Abuses* (1583), sig. L6ᵛ: 'they carrying
the note or brand of God upon their
backs, which way soever they may go, are
to be hissed out of Christian Kingdoms'.

6–7 **subdued | To** brought to subjection
(either physical or spiritual) by

7 **dyer's hand** English dyes of this period
were woad-based, and produced an
indelible stain in those regularly exposed
to them. Shakespeare's father was a
glover, so he may have had practical expe-
rience of this.

8 **renewed** restored. Often 'made spiritually
regenerate' (*OED* 2b), as in the Collect for
Christmas Day in the 1548 Book of Com-
mon Prayer: 'Grant that we . . . may daily
be renewed by thy Holy Spirit'.

10 **Potions of eisel** medicinal drinks based on
vinegar; bitter cures. Vinegar was a fre-
quent ingredient in recommended cures
for the plague, which struck London
severely in 1592–4 and in 1603, both peri-
ods which have been associated with the
composition or revision of the Sonnets.
'Eat sorrel steeped in vinegar, in the
morning fasting', W. P. Barrett, ed., *Pre-
sent Remedies against the Plague* (1933),
sig. A4ᵛ.
  infection fuses the medical imagery
with that of *the dyer's hand*, since its Latin
root *inficere* means literally 'to dip into, to
stain' (Geoffrey Hill, *The Lords of Limit*
(1984), 153).

11 **No bitterness** there is no bitterness

12 **Nor double . . . correction** nor a double act
of penitential atonement designed to cor-
rect what has already been corrected

14 **Even that your pity** The line retains some
of the bitterness of the other cures pro-
posed: *that* may introduce the following

III

O, for my sake do you with Fortune chide,
The guilty goddess of my harmful deeds,
That did not better for my life provide
Than public means which public manners breeds.
Thence comes it that my name receives a brand,   5
And almost thence my nature is subdued
To what it works in, like the dyer's hand.
Pity me then, and wish I were renewed,
Whilst, like a willing patient, I will drink
Potions of eisel 'gainst my strong infection.   10
No bitterness that I will bitter think,
Nor double penance to correct correction.
   Pity me then, dear friend, and, I assure ye,
   Even that your pity is enough to cure me.

1 with] GILDON; wish Q   2 harmful] Q; harmless BENSON   12 to] Q; too *conj.* Kenyon in Rollins 2

clause ('I assure you that . . .') or may be a demonstrative pronoun clinging disparagingly to *your pity*. The latter reading gives it a scorn approaching the Latin *iste*: so 'even that undesirable thing your pity is enough to cure me'.

1 **th' impression** Scandal (or perhaps the *brand* referred to in 111.5) leaves a declivity which the friend's pity fills.

2 **vulgar scandal** (a) public disgrace; (b) base slander

3 **calls me . . . ill** represents me as good or bad

4 So provided that
o'er-green gloss over, render fresh. A coinage. Seymour-Smith suggests 'cover over so as to hide—as a gardener re-turfs an unsightly patch of earth, or as old buildings are covered by ivy', which seems unduly literal: *green* is used to mean 'fresh' or 'young' with no reference to colour in 63.14 and 104.8. Polonius's 'You speak like a green girl', *Hamlet* 1.3.101, suggests a possible sense 'attribute to mere youthfulness'.
allow 'concede merit to'. The primary sense of *allow* is 'praise', but it is often used in contexts which suggest reluctant praise or a partial concession.

7–8 **None . . . wrong** 'There is no one else who means enough to me, nor do I mean enough to anyone alive, either to alter my obdurate senses, or to change right and wrong.' The lines are among the most obscure in the sequence, partly because the poet takes it as read that the friend will understand *None else* to imply 'no one else is so dear to me or means so much to me'. In l. 8 *or* implies an 'either' before *steeled*, and *changes* has as its objects both *steeled sense* and *right and wrong*. The relationship between these two phrases is particularly hard to determine, since it is unclear whether the friend has power to change what is objectively right and wrong, or simply to change the poet's subjective and obdurate sense of what is and is not right. Pooler suggests 'none but you can alter my fixed opinions, whether they are right or wrong'. Although many emendations

have been proposed, Q's uncertainty is expressive: for the poet what is really right and wrong and what he thinks of as being right and wrong have become identified, and the only person of any import in changing his views is the friend.

9 **profound abysm** deep abyss

10 **adder's sense** Adders are proverbially deaf (Dent A32), and were thought to be able to close their ears, as in Psalm 58: 4–5: 'Their poison is even like the poison of a serpent: like the deaf adder *that* stoppeth his ear'.

12 **Mark . . . dispense** (a) notice how I justify my neglect of others' opinion; (b) notice how I gloss over my previous neglect of you; (c) notice how I pass over your former neglect of me. Sense (a) is the primary sense: the other two surface with a painful reminder of earlier stages of the sequence.

13–14 **You are . . . dead** Q's reading here can be glossed: 'You are so powerfully a part of my mental and moral powers that it is to me alone of all the world that you are truly alive'. This almost solipsistic reading of the couplet is contentious, though warranted by a poem in which the poet has sunk himself into a *profound abysm* of neglect of others' opinions. Line 14 is often emended, after Malone, to 'That all the world besides, methinks, they're dead', on the grounds that 'y' is a compositorial misreading of þ (th), used as an abbreviated form of 'they'. This diminishes the solipsism of the poem into an adolescent petulance in its final 'they're dead'. It also weakens the force of *bred* in l. 13: 'you are generated solely by my imagination'. This prepares for the hyperbole of the final line in Q, which in turn prepares for the blindness claimed by the poet at the start of the next sonnet.

112

Your love and pity doth th' impression fill
Which vulgar scandal stamped upon my brow,
For what care I who calls me well or ill,
So you o'er-green my bad, my good allow?
You are my all the world, and I must strive   5
To know my shames and praises from your tongue.
None else to me, nor I to none alive,
That my steeled sense or changes right or wrong.
In so profound abysm I throw all care
Of others' voices, that my adder's sense   10
To critic and to flatterer stoppèd are:
Mark how with my neglect I do dispense.
   You are so strongly in my purpose bred
   That all the world besides me thinks y' are dead.

8 or changes] Q; e'er changes *conj. Malone;* o'erchanges *conj.* Tucker   9 abysm] Q (*Abisme*);
abyss OXFORD   14 besides me thinks y' are dead] Q; besides, me thinks, are dead *conj.* Capell;
besides methinks they are dead MALONE 1790; besides methinks th'are dead G. B. EVANS

1 **mine eye . . . mind** I am so preoccupied with you that I see only with my mind's eye, and my outward vision is entirely suppressed. Compare Pliny, i.334–5: 'It cannot be denied that with the soul we imagine, with the mind we see, and the eyes as vessels and instruments receiving from it that visual power and faculty, send it soon after abroad. Hereupon it cometh that a deep and intentive cogitation blindeth a man so that he seeth not, namely when the sight is retired inward.' The sonnet inverts the common belief that objects were required to bring absent loved ones to mind, as in Thomas Wright's *Passions of the Mind in General*, ed. W. W. Newbold, The Renaissance Imagination 15 (New York and London, 1986), 200: 'for although true friends have always a secret cabinet in their memories to talk in their minds with them whom they love although absent, yet except the memory be revived by some external object oblivion entereth'.

2 **that which . . . about** the eye which shows me where to go

3 **part his function** give up, or decide to share, his office

4 **effectually is out** in effect is blinded

5 **delivers to the heart** In Renaissance psychology sensitive apprehension, such as sight, was received in the brain. Here the heart, which Wright, *Passions of the Mind*, 114, presents as the physical centre for apprehending passions, usurps the function of the mind.

6 **latch** grasp (the word can be used of the power of the senses or mind to apprehend an impression). Q's 'lack' (which does not rhyme) is likely to be a misreading of this unusual word, used by Shakespeare only in *Macbeth* 4.3.194–6: 'I have words | That would be howled out in the desert air | Where hearing should not latch them'.

7 **quick objects . . . part** the mind has no power to control or retain the rapidly varying objects which pass before the eye. *His* is used interchangeably with *its* to refer to the eye. The change of pronoun here, however, prompts a reading in which *his* might momentarily be taken to agree with *mind*, which would imply that the mind has madly lost control over its own *objects*, or 'purposes'.

8 **holds . . . catch** retains images at which it glances

10 **sweet-favour** Q's hyphen probably indicates a compound adjective with 'ed' understood from *deformèd*: so 'sweet favoured' or attractively shaped. Without the hyphen it would mean 'beautiful appearance' (Schmidt, 7). Delius conjectured 'sweet-favoured'. To harden the phrase completely into a compound adjective, however, loses the momentary effect of an antithesis between the beautiful abstraction 'favour' on the one hand and the brutal physicality of 'creature' on the other.

13 **Incapable** 'Unable to take in, receive, contain, hold, or keep' (the first citation for *OED* 1). The eye is so occupied with the friend that it can take in no other image. **replete** full (as with food)

14 **My . . . untrue** My mind is so loyally obsessed with you that it makes my eye incapable of seeing accurately what is before it. Q reads 'maketh mine untrue', which could be glossed 'creates my lack of truth' were it not that 'untrue' is not elsewhere used by Shakespeare to mean 'untruth'. The next sonnet turns to the deficiencies of the *mind*, confirming the impression that the couplet of this sonnet should concern those of the *eye*.

113

Since I left you, mine eye is in my mind,
And that which governs me to go about
Doth part his function, and is partly blind.
Seems seeing, but effectually is out:
For it no form delivers to the heart   5
Of bird, of flower, or shape which it doth latch.
Of his quick objects hath the mind no part,
Nor his own vision holds what it doth catch:
For if it see the rud'st or gentlest sight,
The most sweet-favour or deformèd'st creature.   10
The mountain, or the sea, the day, or night,
The crow, or dove, it shapes them to your feature.
   Incapable of more, replete with you,
   My most true mind thus makes mine eye untrue.

6 bird, of] Q; birds, or BENSON   latch] MALONE 1790 (*conj.* Capell): lack Q   8 catch] Q; take GILDON 1714   10 sweet-favour] Q; sweet-favoured *conj.* Delius   13 more, replete| GILDON; ~ ₍ ~, Q   14 makes mine eye untrue] MALONE (*conj.* Capell): maketh mine vntrue Q; mak'th mine eye untrue *conj.* Lettsom in Dyce 1866

1–3 **Or whether . . . or whether** 'does . . .
or . . .?' *Shall I say* governs both alterna-
tives: so 'Shall I say that my mind, elevat-
ed to kingship by its love for you, drinks in
deadly flattery like a king? Or shall I say
that my eye is correct in seeing as it does,
and in turning monsters and shapeless
things into angels like you, taught this
magic of transformation by your love?'

4 **alchemy** the art of turning base metals to
gold, here loosely 'magic of transforma-
tion'. Used elsewhere to suggest superfi-
cial transformation, as at 33.4, where it is
also associated with flattery.

5 **indigest** 'shapeless, confused; unar-
ranged. (Often with reference to Ovid's
Quem dixere chaos, rudis indigestaque moles,
Met. i.7.)' (OED 1), as in *K. John* 5.7.25–7:
'you are born | To set a form upon that
indigest, | Which he hath left so shapeless
and so rude'.

6 **Such . . . resemble** The praise is put in
such a way as to render both sides of the
comparison unstable: the monsters are
turned to cherubim which resemble the
friend, but there is no guarantee that he is
not also a monster transformed into an
angelic form (which he only *resembles*
outwardly) by the alchemical magic of
the eye.

7 **Creating** The regal context established in

l. 2 suggests *OED* 3: 'to create a peer'. The
eye is presented as a monarch who dubs
all things good that *assemble* around him.
In 1603 James I created 906 knights.

8 **As fast . . . assemble** as rapidly as objects
gather round (a) the beams which the eye
was believed to emit; (b) the rays which
were supposed to emanate from majesty

9 **'tis the first** i.e. the first option set out in ll.
1–4, that the mind is flattered. Via the use
of *creating* in l. 7 the sonnet had already
been drifting towards this alternative.
in my seeing which inheres in how I see;
also perhaps 'as I see the case'

11 **what . . . 'greeing** what is to the mind's
taste. The apostrophe before *greeing* is not
in Q and not strictly necessary, since *gree*
is a recognized aphetic form of *agree*.

12 **to his . . . cup** and laces the brew to suit
the mind's palate

13–14 **If . . . begin** The eye is presented here
as both cook and chief taster, preparing
the view of the world to suit the mind's
preferences. So if the cup (the misrepre-
sentation of the world in the shape of the
friend) turns out to be poisoned, the eye
commits a *lesser sin* than it might other-
wise do because it lovingly tastes the cup
first. It therefore dies (committing suicide)
before it has a chance to perform the
greater sin of regicide.

114

Or whether doth my mind, being crowned with you,
Drink up the monarch's plague this flattery,
Or whether shall I say mine eye saith true,
And that your love taught it this alchemy?
To make of monsters, and things indigest,   5
Such cherubins as your sweet self resemble,
Creating every bad a perfect best
As fast as objects to his beams assemble?
O, 'tis the first, 'tis flatt'ry in my seeing,
And my great mind most kingly drinks it up.   10
Mine eye well knows what with his gust is 'greeing,
And to his palate doth prepare the cup.
    If it be poisoned, 'tis the lesser sin,
    That mine eye loves it and doth first begin.

11 'greeing] Q (greeing)

1–14 The sense of this very difficult sonnet is: 'I lied when in the past I said I could not love you more completely: I said that because I did not then understand that things could grow as well as decline. Given that I was so afraid of time in those former days why should I not say "Now I love you best"? I was trying to celebrate the momentary triumph of love over time and to regard the present moment as the best and crowning moment of love, and to forget about the rest of time's destructive activity. But now I know that love is a baby which continues to grow, therefore I should not say "Now I love you best".'

2 **Even those** those very ones

4 **clearer** *'clear fire*, a fire in full combustion without flame or smoke' (*OED* 1a)

5–9 Modern editions follow Q's 'divert' in l. 8. This makes the second quatrain ungrammatical and disconnected from the argument of the poem, a fact frequently noted and deplored. Capell's emendation of Q's 'divert' to *diverts* solves this problem: it makes *diverts* the main verb of the quatrain, with *reckoning time* as its subject, rather than leaving it as a further verb agreeing with the (plural) *millioned accidents* of time. It is likely that the compositor was beguiled into repeating the plural forms which have preceded this verb, and missing the final 's' before *strong*. The whole quatrain then becomes a grammatically complete explanation of how the poet came to see that his love would change to become stronger: he is one of the *strong minds* which are diverted to accommodate the changeability of time, and he comes to appreciate that *the course of altering things* can include growth as well as decay. The second quatrain works in two ways, both as a description of all the things which in the past made him desperately try to claim his love was perfect and therefore outside time's power, *and* as an account of how the poet has come to change his mind about his love.

5 **reckoning time** 'time who brings all to their reckoning'. If Q's 'Divert' is followed in l. 8, as in the majority of modern editions, *reckoning* functions first confidently as a participle agreeing with *I*, with 'time' as its object: 'considering, or counting up time, like an authoritative assessor'; then as a participular adjective agreeing with time. Then, with the apparent absence of a main verb for 'time' by l. 9, and with the participle *fearing* which agrees with *I*, the first interpretation returns. The constantly shifting efforts of a reader to hold Q's syntax in check could be argued to imitate the continuing processes of change which are the poem's theme. They are much more likely to result from a misprint in l. 8 of Q. See note to ll. 5–9.

5 **millioned** numbered by the million; possibly a dialect form of 'million'. First cited usage in *OED*.
  accidents literally 'things which fall', hence chance events which drop between vows and their fulfilment

7 **Tan** make weather-beaten and suntanned, and hence unattractive
  sharp'st intents the most eager intentions

8 **Diverts . . . things** makes even confident minds consider the mutability of things, diverting their strength (like a river) into a new *course*. This functions in two ways: it describes how the poet in the past began to think about change and so to insist on the full perfection of his love; (secondarily) it made him begin to realize that things grow as well as decline. See note on ll. 5–9 above.

11 **certain o'er incertainty** 'attempting to establish one point of certainty in a world of universal uncertainty'. Q's 'certaine ore in-certainty' suggests also 'excessively certain in my certainty'.

12 **Crowning . . . rest** making my present certainty a king, whilst the past and future were matters of uncertain fear. The symmetry of the present participles *crowning* and *doubting* unites certainty and fear as the previous line had paradoxically combined certainty and uncertainty.

13–14 **Love . . . grow** But Love, like Cupid, is a baby which was growing in the past and which continues to grow now; that is why I should not have said 'Now I love you best', because that would be to call a baby full grown, but it is of the essence of babies to keep growing. *Then* is temporal ('at that time') in l. 10, and logical ('therefore') in l. 13. *Still* implies that love's growth continues both in past and present.

115

Those lines that I before have writ do lie,
Even those that said I could not love you dearer,
Yet then my judgement knew no reason why
My most full flame should afterwards burn clearer.
But reckoning time, whose millioned accidents   5
Creep in 'twixt vows, and change decrees of kings,
Tan sacred beauty, blunt the sharp'st intents,
Diverts strong minds to th' course of alt'ring things.
Alas why, fearing of Time's tyranny,
Might I not then say 'Now I love you best',   10
When I was certain o'er incertainty,
Crowning the present, doubting of the rest?
    Love is a babe, then might I not say so,
    To give full growth to that which still doth grow.

8 Diverts] This edition (*conj.* Capell); diuert Q   10 'Now . . . best'] MALONE 1790 (*italic*); ~
. . . ~ Q   11 incertainty] Q (in-certainty)

A version of this sonnet was set to music by Henry Lawes. See Willa McLung Evans, 'Lawes's Version of Shakespeare's Sonnet CXVI', *PMLA* 51 (1936), 120–2. The manuscript is New York Public Library, Music Division, Drexel MS 4257, No. 33.

1–2 **Let me not . . . impediments** Much depends here on which *two minds* are married. If it is the poet and the friend then the sonnet follows on from the declarations of love in 115, and in it the poet is refusing to *admit* ('acknowledge' (*OED* 2b)) that there are any barriers to love, or any changes in his friend which can undo their union. If it refers to a union between the friend and someone else, the poem becomes excessive and potentially ironic in its self-abnegation: 'Do not let *me* become an impediment to your union, because *I* adhere to an elevated and abstract form of love'. *Admit* on this reading means 'To allow of the coexistence or presence' (*OED* 5), or 'To allow to enter, let in, receive (a person or thing)' (*OED* 1).

2 **impediments** echoes the Solemnization of Matrimony in the Book of Common Prayer: 'I require and charge you (as you will answer at the dreadful day of judgement, when the secrets of all hearts shall be disclosed) that if either of you know any impediment, why ye may not lawfully be joined in matrimony, that ye confess it'.

4 **bends . . . remove** yields to change when the loved person ceases to love. See 25.14 n. Disturbingly, *polyptoton* (the repetition

of a word in a different form) is used to insist on constancy: *remover . . . remove* and *alters . . . alteration*. Even words for constancy change form. Compare the proverb 'A perfect love does last eternally' (Dent L539).

5 **mark** landmark (*OED* 9); here probably a star which aids navigation

7 **star** to star that guides, like the pole star
   every wandering barque each small vessel lost at sea

8 **Whose worth's unknown** whose value is untested by actual experience (that is, love is presented as a star which gives a direction, but which is too distant ever to be properly valued by those who steer by it)
   height Q's 'higth' answers the closing consonant of *worth*.

9 **Time's fool** the plaything of Time; almost the slave of Time. Cf. *124.13*.

10 **compass** range. 'A circular arc, sweep, curve' (*OED* 6a) is also germane to Time's scythe. A mariner's compass (only referred to by Shakespeare in *Coriolanus* 2.3.24) is unlikely to be in play, although as Kerrigan points out the sense may be activated by the maritime context.

12 **bears it out** endures

13 **error and upon me proved** The language is of legal testimony: 'a claim subject to procedural irregularity which is proven against me'. (*OED* s.v. 'error' 4c *Law*. 'A mistake in matter of law appearing on the proceedings of a court of record. *Writ of error*: a writ brought to procure the reversal of a judgement, on the ground of error'.)

116

Let me not to the marriage of true minds
Admit impediments; love is not love
Which alters when it alteration finds,
Or bends with the remover to remove.
O no, it is an ever-fixèd mark,   5
That looks on tempests and is never shaken;
It is the star to every wandering barque,
Whose worth's unknown, although his height be taken.
Love's not Time's fool, though rosy lips and cheeks
Within his bending sickle's compass come.   10
Love alters not with his brief hours and weeks,
But bears it out even to the edge of doom.
   If this be error and upon me proved,
   I never writ, nor no man ever loved.

0.1 116] BODLEY-CALDECOTT; 119 Q (*all other copies*)   8 worth's] Q; north's *conj.* Walker
height] Q (higth)

1 **Accuse me thus** continues the legal register of the end of the previous sonnet.
scanted all neglected everything

2 **Wherein** by which

3 **to call** (a) to pay my respects; (b) to visit; (c) to pray (as to a divinity)

4 **all bonds** spiritual and emotional ties; perhaps also bonds of a legal sort, possibly of service, established by the friend's *dear-purchased right* (l. 6).

5 **frequent been with** (a) been familiar with (first citation for *OED* 6c); (b) have often been with (pre-dating the first citation for the adverbial usage of *frequent* by five years)

6 **given to time . . . right** wasted the time for which you have paid dearly. The running metaphor is of a bondsman who has reneged on his obligations of service. *Time* functions here as a voracious consumer of duties which should have been paid to the friend.

9 **Book** record

10 **And . . . accumulate** add imaginary sins to those which you can prove. The suggestion is that the sins which are known about are a good foundation for further suppositions. Q punctuates 'surmise, accumulate'.

11 **within the level of** within the range and aim (as of a gun)

12 **wakened hate** in the first rush of passion

13 **appeal** effort to overturn the findings of a lower court by referring the case to a higher
prove puns on the legal sense of 'to show without reasonable doubt' and to 'try, test'. *Strive* suggests that the case failed, and that the *constancy and virtue* of the friend's love was not or could never be proven.

14 **virtue** (a) power; (b) moral excellence

117

Accuse me thus, that I have scanted all
Wherein I should your great deserts repay,
Forgot upon your dearest love to call,
Whereto all bonds do tie me day by day,
That I have frequent been with unknown minds,   5
And given to time your own dear-purchased right,
That I have hoisted sail to all the winds
Which should transport me farthest from your sight.
Book both my wilfulness and errors down,
And on just proof, surmise accumulate,   10
Bring me within the level of your frown,
But shoot not at me in your wakened hate,
　　Since my appeal says I did strive to prove
　　The constancy and virtue of your love.

10 proof, surmise accumulate] MALONE; ~ ~, accumilate Q

1 **Like as** just as

2 **eager compounds** sharp-tasting mixtures

3 **to . . . purge** we take emetics to purge our-
selves in order to forestall the illnesses
which are not yet *manifest*

5 **ne'er-cloying** Kerrigan suggests that
Benson's 'neare cloying' indicates a pun
on 'never cloying' and 'near cloying'
which Q's 'nere' allows. However, Q fol-
lows a consistent convention (shared by
both compositors) that 'nere' is the con-
tracted form of 'never' and 'neere' is the
equivalent of 'near'. Compare the proverb
'Too much honey cloys the stomach'
(Dent H560).

6 **frame my feeding** i.e. he turned to a diet of
bitter sauces to rid himself of the friend's
sweetness. This defence of infidelity seeks
an antipathetic quasi-medical reason for
turning from the friend's affection. Com-
pare the proverb 'Sweet meat must have
sour sauce' (Dent M839).

7 **welfare** good health
meetness suitableness

8 **To be . . . needing** to make myself ill before
there was a true need to be

9 **policy** cunning (with a suggestion of self-
defeating ingenuity)

9–10 **t' anticipate . . . assurèd** in order to fore-
stall future sicknesses generated real dis-
eases. *Ills* and *faults* can also convey moral
failings. Q punctuates 'Thus pollicie in
love t' anticipate | The ills that were, not
grew to faults assured', which editors
since Gildon have found inadequate.

11 **brought to medicine a healthful state**
(a) reduced to the state of needing
medicine; (b) subjected to medical inter-
ference a state which had formerly been
healthy

12 **rank of goodness** puffed up, gorged with
goodness
would by ill be curèd wished to be cured
by sickness (or by wickedness)

118

Like as to make our appetites more keen
With eager compounds we our palate urge,
As to prevent our maladies unseen
We sicken to shun sickness when we purge;
Even so, being full of your ne'er-cloying sweetness,   5
To bitter sauces did I frame my feeding,
And, sick of welfare, found a kind of meetness
To be diseased ere that there was true needing.
Thus policy in love, t' anticipate
The ills that were not, grew to faults assurèd,   10
And brought to medicine a healthful state,
Which, rank of goodness, would by ill be curèd.
   But thence I learn, and find the lesson true,
   Drugs poison him that so fell sick of you.

5 ne'er-cloying] Q (nere cloying); neare cloying BENSON   10 were not] GILDON; ~,~ Q
assurèd] Q; assur'd MALONE 1790   12 curèd] Q; cur'd MALONE 1790

1 **potions** medicinal or intoxicating drinks
siren tears tears which allure and en-
snare. The Sirens are part women, part
birds who attempt by the sweetness of
their song to lure mariners to their
deaths. See *Odyssey* 12.165–200. Here the
tears are *siren* probably because they are
the tears of lovers who have drawn the
poet away from the friend. Kerrigan notes
links with *147*, in which the mistress is
described as inwardly black as hell.

2 **limbecks** apparatus for distilling. Eyes are
also presented as limbecks which distil out
tears in Thomas Lodge's *Phyllis* (1593),
37.11. In Barnabe Barnes's *Parthenophil
and Parthenophe* 49 there is a similar
conjunction: 'A Siren which within thy
breast doth bath her, | A fiend which doth
in graces garments grath [clothe] her, | A
fortress whose force is impregnable: |
From my love's limbeck still stilled tears,
oh tears!' For a further possible echo of
this passage, see *A Lover's Complaint*, l.
316 n.

3 **Applying . . . fears** The language is medi-
cal, and the processes antipathetic, seek-
ing to drive out one ill by another: *OED*
s.v. 'apply' 3 *trans.* 'to administer a reme-
dy of any kind'. The *antimetabole* (repeti-
tion of *hopes* and *fears* in inverse order)
evokes a hopeless effort to recombine ail-
ments in order to make them into cures.

7 **spheres** The eyes are compared to planets
shaken from their orbits by convulsions.
Cf. *Kinsmen* 5.2.45–6: 'Torturing convul-

sions from his globy eyes | Had almost
drawn their spheres'. There may also be a
play on the social sense of *spheres*, 'their
proper social arena', although this sense
was not fully established *c.*1600, and the
first cited instance of it is still very
strongly linked with its astrological
origins: ' 'Twere all one | That I should
love a bright particular star | And think
to wed it, he is so above me. | In his
bright radiance and collateral light |
Must I be comforted, not in his sphere'
(*All's Well* 1.1.84–8).

7 **fitted** *OED* cites this passage alone to sup-
port 'fit' *v.*[2]: 'forced by fits or paroxysms
out of (the usual place)', which suits the
context of a *madding fever.* Ingram and
Redpath suggest 'displaced from [i.e.
made not to fit into] their proper sphere'.
This is not impossible, since the senses of
'fit' v.[1] were very flexible *c.*1600.

9 **O benefit of ill** What benefit comes of (a)
disease; (b) hardship; (c) wickedness. The
word 'bene*fit*' picks out and renders
beneficial the *fit* of l. 6.

10 **still** continually, with perhaps a trace of
a pun on the *stills* of l. 2. Compare the
proverbs 'A broken bone (leg) is the
stronger when it is well set' (Dent B515)
and 'The falling out of lovers is a renew-
ing of love' (Dent F40).

13 **content** source of content, the friend

14 **spent** (a) paid out; (b) wasted; with a pos-
sible play on the 'spending' or ejaculation
of semen

119

What potions have I drunk of siren tears,
Distilled from limbecks foul as hell within,
Applying fears to hopes, and hopes to fears,
Still losing when I saw myself to win?
What wretched errors hath my heart committed,   5
Whilst it hath thought itself so blessèd never?
How have mine eyes out of their spheres been fitted
In the distraction of this madding fever?
O benefit of ill, now I find true
That better is by evil still made better,   10
And ruined love, when it is built anew,
Grows fairer than at first, more strong, far greater.
   So I return rebuked to my content,
    And gain by ills thrice more than I have spent.

1 siren] Q (*Syren*) 7 fitted] Q; flitted *conj.* Lettsom in Dyce 1866

1–4 The poet's earlier experience of neglect by his friend (35–6, 40–42, 92–6) gives him a means of inferring what the friend may now be suffering, and this in turn makes him appreciate the severity of his transgression.

1 **befriends** is used with a deliberate irony to mean 'is a source of comfort to me' or 'gives a sense of proximity to you through a suffering which we have both endured'.

2 **then** i.e. when I was mistreated by you

3 **bow** stoop penitently as under a weight of sin; 'To bend the body, knee, or head, in token of reverence, respect, or submission; to make obeisance' (*OED* 6).

4 **nerves** sinews

6 **hell of time** hellish time. Cf. *58*.13 and *119*.2 for the poet's experience of hell.

8 **weigh . . . crime** 'consider how I once suffered from your similar wrongdoing'. *Suffered in your crime* would have seemed grammatically odd even to early readers. *Suffer* can mean 'to labour as under a physical weight' (*sub-ferro*), which ties in with *weigh* and the burden which makes the poet *bow*; it can also mean 'to undergo martyrdom'. There is no clear precedent for its use with the preposition *in* (except in adverbial phrases, as in *Macbeth* 2.3.125–6: 'when we have our naked frailties hid, | That suffer in exposure'). This suggests an exceptional union of suffering: 'I suffered the pangs of martyrdom by participating in the experience of your crime'.

9 **night of woe** darkest period of grief. *Our* presents their sorrow as mutual and simultaneous, whereas the rest of the sonnet presents the lovers' several woes as sequential and separate.
rememb'red reminded

10 **deepest sense** most profound level of apprehension. *Sense* unites both tactile, emotional, and rational apprehension.

11–12 **And soon . . . fits!** 'and if only it had prompted me quickly to offer to you, as you had offered to me in our night of woe, the healing balm of a humble apology, the best cure for a wounded heart'. The grammatical subject of *tend'red* is technically *our night of woe*, which prompts a memory of pain from *my deepest sense*, which in turn prompts the offer of an apology. Q has no comma after 'then', but it seems reasonable to supply one to emphasize that the period of earlier separation and reconciliation referred to is the same throughout.

13 **that your trespass** that offence of yours
fee a payment, benefit

14 **Mine . . . me** my trespass pays the debt which was owing as a result of your trespass, and your trespass in the past must serve to annul the debt which is owing as a result of my recent offence. *Ransom* suggests both the mechanical paying of a debt and a wider, potentially theological, sense of 'liberates' or even 'redeems': so 'your earlier trespass serves to liberate me from the burden of guilt which makes me bow'.

120

That you were once unkind befriends me now,
And for that sorrow, which I then did feel,
Needs must I under my transgression bow,
Unless my nerves were brass or hammered steel.
For if you were by my unkindness shaken,   5
As I by yours, y' have passed a hell of time,
And I, a tyrant, have no leisure taken
To weigh how once I suffered in your crime.
O that our night of woe might have rememb'red
My deepest sense how hard true sorrow hits,   10
And soon to you, as you to me then, tend'red
The humble salve, which wounded bosoms fits!
    But that your trespass now becomes a fee;
    Mine ransoms yours, and yours must ransom me.

4 hammered] GILDON; hammered *i.e. hammerèd*) Q   11 you, . . . me then,] STAUNTON (*conj.*
Walker); ~, . . . ~ ~, Q; ~, . . . ~,~, MALONE (*conj.* Capell); ~ . . ~,~, INGRAM AND REDPATH

1–2 **'Tis better . . . being** 'It is preferable actually to be a vile person than to be thought one, when in the eye of the world one receives all the odium of being vile when one is not in fact so.' *Vile* is an extremely strong expression of contempt in the period, which ranges from 'worthless' to 'utterly depraved'. It can carry a charge of sexual sin. Compare the proverb 'There is small difference to the eye of the world in being nought and being thought so' (Dent D336).

3–4 **And . . . seeing** The primary sense is 'and the legitimate pleasure is lost when an affair is termed "vile", not by those who experience it but by those who look on'. Rippling across this are secondary senses: 'and one does not even get the pleasure which is rightfully due to what is termed vile behaviour—what is not felt by us to be vile behaviour, but what is presented as being vile by malevolent observers'. *So deemèd* (termed such) could refer back to *vile* or to *pleasure*. This allows two secondary senses: (a) we do not even feel what they call pleasure as pleasure; (b) those who think a love affair is vile also think (pruriently and erroneously) that pleasure comes from it.

5 **adulterate** (a) defiled, contaminated; (b) adulterous. Sense (b) is given support by *false*, which can mean 'sexually unfaithful' as well as 'inaccurate'.

6 **Give . . . blood** ranges in sense from the morally neutral 'greet my lively spirits' to 'give a knowing wink at my randyness'. For this latter sense (*OED* 2) of *sportive* see *Richard III* 1.1.14–15: 'But I, that am not shaped for sportive tricks, | Nor made to court an amorous looking-glass'.

7 **frailties . . . frailer spies** 'why do those who are more susceptible to sexual failings

than me spy on my failings?' *Frail* implies weakness and susceptibility to passions, especially to sexual desires. *Frailer* means 'people who are frailer than me'.

8 **Which** who
in their wills count in their passionate nature consider. *OED* s.v. 'will' 2 *spec.* 'Carnal desire or appetite', as in *Lucrece* ll. 246–7. The phrase also suggests the arbitrary imposition of a particular value on something which is morally neutral via *OED* 9a: 'Undue assertion of one's own will; wilfulness, self-will'.

9 **I am that I am** alludes to God's mysterious words to Moses in Exodus 3: 14. This is not to claim divinity: rather 'I know in my private counsels what kind of man I am (and I am not perfect, but I am better than they say)'.
level 'To aim (a missile, weapon)' (*OED* 7a)

10 **reckon up their own** count up the sum of their own sins; perhaps also call to judgement or account

11 **bevel** crooked (*OED* 2; first cited usage)

12 **rank** sexually depraved; overabundant to the point of decay

13 **general evil** universal maxim that the world is evil; also with a suggestion that holding such a maxim to be true is itself evil. The phrase hints at the doctrine of original corruption which has been implied in much of the sonnet.

14 **reign** prevail, prosper, flourish (*OED* 2c; almost obsolete by 1600); perhaps also 'glory in'. It is not possible to be sure if the *general evil* is just the first half of this line ('all men are bad'), and that those who utter this maxim are supreme in their badness, or if it extends to include the whole line ('all men are bad and in their badness reign').

121

'Tis better to be vile than vile esteemèd,
When not to be receives reproach of being,
And the just pleasure lost which is so deemèd
Not by our feeling, but by others' seeing.
For why should others' false adulterate eyes   5
Give salutation to my sportive blood?
Or on my frailties why are frailer spies,
Which in their wills count bad what I think good?
No, I am that I am, and they that level
At my abuses reckon up their own;   10
I may be straight though they themselves be bevel.
By their rank thoughts my deeds must not be shown,
    Unless this general evil they maintain:
    All men are bad and in their badness reign.

1 esteemèd] Q; esteem'd GILDON 1714   3 deemèd] Q; deem'd GILDON 1714

1 **thy tables** possibly a commonplace book containing compositions, as in *77*

2 **Full charactered** stamped out in full. The process of writing or printing is here used as an analogy for mental processes, as in *Hamlet* 1.3.58–9: 'And these few precepts in thy memory | See thou character'.

3 **that idle rank** the row of mere physical letters in the book which he was given

5 **Or at the least** Claims that verse gives immortality are often qualified, as when Horace, *Odes* 3.30.8–9, says, 'I shall be read as long as the priest accompanied by the silent virgin ascends the Capitol' (see 55.1–2). This qualification is unusually pointed, however: the immortality offered by the record of memory is as frail as life itself.

6 **Have faculty . . . subsist** Have the ability, given to them by nature, to survive. The senses are referred to in this period as 'corporal faculties', as are the powers of the mind (including memory), which are sometimes presented as having a power of retention akin to print, as in Abraham Fraunce's *Lawyers Logic* (1588), fo. 2ʳ, which describes natural reason as 'that *ingraven* gift and faculty of wit and reason'.

7 **each** both *brain* and *heart*
razed oblivion the flat landscape of oblivion in which all monuments are razed to the ground; also continuing the metaphor of the memory as a text via

OED 'raze' *v.* 3 *spec.* 'To erase or obliterate (writing, etc.) by scraping or otherwise'.

8 **thy record . . . missed** the memory (presented as a written record) of you can never go astray

9 **That poor retention** that weak receptacle of memory, the table book. *OED* cites this passage under 'retention' 2a: 'The fact of retaining things in the mind; the power or ability to do this; memory', which ignores the fact that this sense is made material here ('physical record'). A pun on sense 3a of *retention* is in the air ('The action or fact of keeping to oneself or in one's own hands, under one's power or authority'), since the poet is apologizing for having failed to keep the table book.

10 **tallies** material records (literally, sticks marked with notches to record quantities)

12 **those tables** the tables, or writing tablets, of his memory
receive thee more The general sense is 'retain your image better'. *Receive* unites a range of senses: welcomes you more frequently (*OED* 9a), 'takes your impression more fully' (*OED* 4b: 'To admit (an impression, etc.) by yielding or by adaptation of surface'). This would continue the metaphors of printing and physically recording. Another possibility is 'To take into the mind; to apprehend mentally' (*OED* 7).

13 **adjunct** external aid. See 91.5.

14 **import** (a) cause, introduce (*OED* 4); (b) mean, signify (*OED* 5b)

122

Thy gift, thy tables, are within my brain
Full charactered with lasting memory,
Which shall above that idle rank remain
Beyond all date even to eternity;
Or at the least so long as brain and heart   5
Have faculty by nature to subsist,
Till each to razed oblivion yield his part
Of thee, thy record never can be missed.
That poor retention could not so much hold,
Nor need I tallies thy dear love to score,   10
Therefore to give them from me was I bold
To trust those tables that receive thee more.
   To keep an adjunct to remember thee
   Were to import forgetfulness in me.

1 Thy gift] BENSON; TThy guift Q

1 **No!** The exclamation mark is Q's, one of only five in the volume. The poem may be indebted to Propertius 3.2: 'Not sumptuous Pyramids to skies upreared, | Nor Elean Jove's proud Fane, which heaven compeered | Nor the rich fane of Mausoleus' tomb, | Are privileged from death's extremest doom' (trans. in John Weever, *Ancient Funerall Monuments* (1631), 3).

2 **pyramids** are associated in the period both with pride and with the immortalizing ambitions of artists. Usually the word describes what is now called an obelisk (i.e. a pointed column). See e.g. Ben Jonson's 'Epistle to Elizabeth Countess of Rutland', ll. 83–4: 'There like a rich and golden pyramid, | Borne up by statues, shall I rear your head'. Historical allusions have been sensed: the obelisks erected in Rome in 1586–9 by Pope Sixtus V (Hotson; improbable given the early date), or those erected by the 3,000 carpenters who laboured to create the setting for James I's triumphal entry in to London in 1604 (Alfred Harbage, 'Dating Shakespeare's Sonnets', *Shakespeare Quarterly* 1 (1950), 62–3). However, rebuilding the pyramids was a type of vainly ambitious labour, as in Thomas Storer, *The Life and Death of Thomas Wolsey* (1599), ll. 449–55: 'He might as well appoint some artless swain, | In Pytheas' place to build Mausolus' tomb; | To rear th' Egyptian Pyramids again, | Restore the ruins of declining Rome, | Or put some shepherdess to Arachne's loom'.

4 **dressings of a former sight** (a) mere adornments of what we have already seen; (b) re-erections of things we have already seen. The *pyramids built up with newer might,* apparently ancient structures created anew, initiates the poem's deliberate confusion of what is old and what is new, and of the relative values of each.

6 **foist . . . old** whatever old thing you try to persuade us is new

7 **born to our desire** appear newly created to suit our wishes. Wyndham takes Q's 'borne' as 'bourn' (limit), which makes good sense for l. 7 but not for l. 8.

9 **registers** official written records

10 **Not wond'ring at** refusing to marvel at

11–12 **For thy . . . haste** 'For neither your records of the past nor what we ourselves see are reliable; each changes in its perspective as time passes.' *Made more or less* probably means that the present seems less when it is superseded by the future, and the distant past comes to seem greater than it is by virtue of its antiquity. The phrase also allows for sudden random shifts in value as time passes. *Records* is stressed on the second syllable.

13 **This . . . this** Behind the second *this* one might hear 'this sonnet (which embodies the vow)', harking back to the usage in *18*.14.

14 **true** faithful. The earlier claim that time distorts relative values suggests also 'speak accurately'.

123

No! Time, thou shalt not boast that I do change.
Thy pyramids built up with newer might
To me are nothing novel, nothing strange;
They are but dressings of a former sight.
Our dates are brief, and therefore we admire   5
What thou dost foist upon us that is old,
And rather make them born to our desire
Than think that we before have heard them told.
Thy registers and thee I both defy,
Not wond'ring at the present, nor the past,   10
For thy records, and what we see, doth lie,
Made more or less by thy continual haste.
   This I do vow and this shall ever be:
   I will be true despite thy scythe and thee.

7 born] Q (borne); borne (*i.e. bourn* WYNDHAM

1 **If my . . . state** if my deep affection were merely the product of circumstances. *Dear love* glances at the object of love, its costs and its value. *State* ranges in sense through 'fortune', 'status', 'wealth', 'dignity appropriate to high standing', to 'the body politic'.

2 **It might . . . unfathered** It might be regarded as merely the bastard child of Fortune, denied its true paternity, and rendered subject to time. That is, his love is not simply fathered by accidental circumstances. Q reads 'unfathered' (i.e. 'unfatherèd'), probably because compositor B was thrown by the feminine rhyme.

3 **As subject** (a) and become a creature subject to; (b) as being a creature subject to

4 **among . . . flowers** mingled in aimlessly with weeds and flowers, all subject to Time's scythe. It is likely that the second 'flowers' is disyllabic.

5 **accident** contingency, the influence of chance; secondary attributes rather than primary qualities. *Accidere* means 'that which falls out', and the etymological association with falling is brought out by *builded*: this edifice will not fall.

6 **It suffers . . . pomp** (a) surrounded by the favours of the great it does not deteriorate; (b) in majestic confidence it does not deteriorate. The potentially negative senses of *suffers not* are hard to accommodate here: 'does not endure', 'does not tolerate the presence of' provide a melancholy undertow which is not fully worked into the main argument.

7 **blow of thrallèd discontent** (a) the sudden impact of rebellion by those who are resentfully subject to its power (continuing the metaphor of the love as an unassailable monarch in *smiling pomp*); (b) the spiritually imprisoning effects of melancholy.

8 **Whereto . . . calls** which (i.e. *discontent*) is particularly tempting for men of our type these days. *Fashion* means 'mode of behaviour', hence 'our type of people', but also suggests that time is changing fashions of behaviour more generally. Kerrigan relates to the vogue for melancholy (*discontent*) in the late sixteenth century.

9 **policy, that heretic** self-interested scheming, personified as a betrayer of truths. The standard gloss on *heretic* ('one who holds opinions differing from the established faith', Schmidt) is inadequate: heretics are here associated with political

duplicity and rebellion (*thrallèd discontent*), as Jesuits were widely believed to conceal their true faith and to conspire against the Protestant monarchy. Some commentators detect allusions to the Gunpowder Plot of 1605, but any of the many real or imagined Catholic plots from the 1570s onwards could have prompted this association.

10 **works on . . . hours** 'dissolves leases which are already of too short a date'. The received gloss is 'takes up only short-term commitments'. This is inadequate because *leases* never refer to contracts of employment but always to contracts determining land or property tenure. More probable is Pooler's gloss 'like a tenant on a short lease who exhausts the land in his own immediate interests'. But to *work on* in Shakespeare is often associated with deceptive corruption, as in *Othello* 1.3.383: 'The better shall my purpose work on him', and 4.1.277: 'Or did the letters work upon his blood . . . ?' Policy works to accelerate the end of love before the short lease of life is destroyed.

11 **hugely politic** gigantic in its self-dependent prudence. The opposition between *policy* (scheming short-termism) and being *politic* ('Apt at pursuing a policy; sagacious, prudent, shrewd' (*OED* 2)) is fine, since the word can be used 'in a sinister sense: Scheming, crafty' (*OED* 2d). The love seems to possess to a superior degree the powers of political manipulation of *policy, that heretic*, and so remains ruler over it.

13 **fools of Time** those who are in the service of time (as jesters); hence the objects of both mockery and control. The general sense of the couplet is that the poet has an awareness of the permanent truth of his love which is normally only experienced by those who are about to die and repent of their subservience to time; by calling such changeable beings to witness its truths, however, the poem does end with a decidedly unreliable testimony to permanence.

14 **Which die . . . crime** who die to acquire the reputation of virtuous martyrs, who have committed crimes in their lives. Historical allusions have been found here: the Catholic Gunpowder plotters of 1605, the Earl of Essex, who was executed after his rebellion in 1601, the Protestant Marian martyrs of the 1550s, and the Elizabethan Jesuits are favourites. The reference is more general: prisoners on the scaffold,

124

If my dear love were but the child of state
It might for Fortune's bastard be unfathered,
As subject to time's love, or to time's hate,
Weeds among weeds, or flowers with flowers gathered.
No, it was builded far from accident,   5
It suffers not in smiling pomp, nor falls
Under the blow of thrallèd discontent,
Whereto th' inviting time our fashion calls.
It fears not policy, that heretic,
Which works on leases of short-numb'red hours,   10
But all alone stands hugely politic,
That it nor grows with heat, nor drowns with show'rs.
   To this I witness call the fools of Time,
   Which die for goodness, who have lived for crime.

2 unfathered] Q (vnfathered, i.e. *unfathered*) ∠ gathered] Q (gatherd) 13 fools] Q (foles)

especially those condemned for treason, frequently stated their loyalty and allegiance to the crown after having *lived for crime.*

1 **Were 't . . . canopy** 'Would it mean anything to me if I had carried the ornamental awning borne over the head of a dignitary?' At the coronation the *canopy* was normally carried by members of the aristocracy or favoured courtiers. The first eight lines of the sonnet respond to the accusations levelled at the poet; the person who makes the allegations is referred to as a *suborned informer* in l. 13.

2 **With . . . honouring** honouring with shows of outward respect the public appearance of dignity. This is the *OED*'s only citation for *extern* used as a noun meaning 'outward appearance'.

3 **great bases** (a) substantial foundations; (b) magnificent pedestals (*OED* s.v. 'base' 4), on which eternity, like a statue, could rest

4 **Which proves** (a) referring back to *bases* (a plural subject may concord with a verb ending in 's'); (b) referring (paradoxically) to *eternity*.

5 **dwellers on** (a) those who concentrate on courtly manners and procedures; (b) those who live for beauty and outward appearance

6–7 **paying . . . savour** activates the metaphor of *dwellers on*. Those who pay all they have to live in smart areas give up simple health-giving fare for pleasant-tasting, complex (and implicitly unwholesome) foods. Q has no comma after *rent* and a semicolon after *sweet*, suggesting the rent is paid for the *compound sweet*.

8 **Pitiful thrivers** people who appear to be successful in material matters, but who actually are wretched, and deserving of pity

8 **in their gazing spent** used up by gawping at nobility. *Spent* continues the idea that being *a dweller on form and favour* (someone who is obsessed by and lives on beauty) is expensive. *Gazing* may conceivably mark an allusion to the Book of Common Prayer, which urges believers not to 'stand by as gazers and lookers on them that do Communicate'.

9 **obsequious** one who follows after (in mourning or respect; picking up the metaphor of formalized devotion from l. 1). The sense 'fawning, cringing, sycophantic' (*OED* 2) is emerging in this period, but here is neutralized by the ritual devotions evoked by *oblation* in the next line.

in thy heart that is, internally, privately only

10 **oblation** ritual offering, often to God

11 **mixed with seconds** unadulterated; not a *compound*. Second pressings of oil, and second crops of honey and wheat are inferior to the first (*OED* 3).

11–12 **knows no art, | But mutual render** is capable of no sharp practice, indeed only has the ability to offer what is mine in fair exchange for what is yours (although the exchange seems one-sided: *me for thee* without any clear return). Q follows *art* with a comma, reinforcing the effect of the line ending ('has no ability to deceive') and pushing *But* towards 'but is rather'.

13 **suborned informer** seller of (false) information to the enemy

14 **impeached** accused (usually of a serious crime, sometimes a crime against the state)

125

Were 't aught to me I bore the canopy,
With my extern the outward honouring,
Or laid great bases for eternity,
Which proves more short than waste or ruining?
Have I not seen dwellers on form and favour   5
Lose all and more by paying too much rent,
For compound sweet forgoing simple savour,
Pitiful thrivers in their gazing spent?
No, let me be obsequious in thy heart,
And take thou my oblation, poor but free,   10
Which is not mixed with seconds, knows no art,
But mutual render, only me for thee.
    Hence, thou suborned informer: a true soul
    When most impeached, stands least in thy control.

7 sweet forgoing] MALONE (*conj.* Capell); sweet; Forgoing Q

This poem concludes the Sonnets to the friend in an amputated form (six pentameter couplets followed in Q by two pairs of italic brackets to indicate the expected thirteenth and fourteenth lines). Many editors omit the brackets as compositorial. As a part of the typographical effect of Q they should certainly be retained: they highlight the frustrated expectations created by the poem's form. The curves of the lunulae (or brackets) may graphically evoke both a crescent moon and the curve of Time's sickle. See John Lennard, *But I Digress: The Exploitation of Parentheses in English Printed Verse* (Oxford, 1991), 41–3. The effect is deliberately of abrupt termination, as in Hotspur's dying lines, 'No, Percy, thou art dust, | And food for—' (*1 Henry IV* 5.4.84–5). The numbering of the sonnet is significant, as Graziani points out ('Numbering' (see headnote to Sonnet 60), 79–82), since 126 is double the 'grand climacteric' of 63, in which men were believed to undergo a potentially deadly climax in mental and physical constitution. See headnote to 63.

1 **lovely boy** This form of address (used only here in the Sonnets) is also found in an explicitly homosexual poem in Philemon Holland's translation of Plutarch's *Moralia*: 'So often as these eyes of mine behold | That beardless youth, that smooth and lovely boy, | I faint, I fall: then wish I him to hold | Within mine arms, and so to die with joy', *The Philosophy, Commonly Called the Morals* (1603), 1130. The Indian boy who causes Oberon's jealousy of Titania in *Dream* 2.1.22 is also called a 'lovely boy', as is Cyparissus (who was also loved by a man) in Marlowe's *Hero and Leander* ll. 154–5: 'Sylvanus weeping for the lovely boy | That now is turned into a cypress tree'.

1–2 **power . . . glass** The *glass* is likely to be an hourglass full of sand ('A sand-glass for the measurement of time; *esp.* an hourglass', *OED* 6a), as in *All's Well* 2.1.165–6: 'Or four-and-twenty times the pilot's glass | Hath told the thievish minutes how they pass', and in Time's boast in *Winter's Tale* 4.1.16: 'I turn my glass, and give my scene such growing'. It could also be a 'mirror' reflecting back to the lovers their own ageing (which would fit with *therein show'st*), as in 3.1 and 22.1. The friend's *power* is either way limited by the fickleness of Time's *glass*: controlling an

hourglass does not enable one to alter the flow of its sand, nor does one's ownership of a mirror affect what it reflects.

2 **his sickle hour** the hour in which he uses his sickle, hence the moment of death. Q reads 'fickle glass, his ſickle, hower', which has led editors to give to Time three attributes: a *glass* in the sense of 'mirror', a sickle, and an *hour* in the sense 'hourglass'. However, Time only has two hands, one for a sickle and the other for an hourglass. The lines gain their effect through the uneasy parallelism between the *fickle glass* and the *sickle hour*, juxtaposing mutability and necessary mortality in phrases of which the individual elements seem grammatically deliquescent: the *sickle* functions adjectivally, and through its initial long ſ recalls *fickle*. The *glass* fickly turns from an hourglass to a mirror, the *hour* from a day of reckoning to an hourglass, an emblem of the continuing slippage of time.

3 **by waning grown** by growing old you have become more. *Waning* recalls the cycles of the moon, which *wanes* in order then to wax larger. The word is echoed from 11.1.
   therein (a) in doing so (i.e. in achieving such control over the attributes of Time to which mortals are normally subject); (b) in the glass

4 **lovers withering** your lovers ageing (like plants, recalling 15.5). *Lovers* follows Q, which does not use possessive apostrophes: the form 'louers' also could be read with *withering* as a verbal noun rather than a participle: so 'lover's' and 'lovers''. This variety of senses allows for both a note of personal elegy, and a hint that there have been other lovers.

5 **wrack** destruction, decay. As *sovereign mistress over wrack* Nature can prevent the ageing process; but the same phrase admits the pessimistic interpretation 'sole monarch over what is no more than ruins'.

6 **As thou . . . back** as you proceed towards death [Nature] always will attempt to pull you back. *Still* functions both with *goest* and with *will pluck*; the former battles with the latter, as the friend's progress to death continues always. *Pluck* can denote a violent or destructive action, as when it is used of Time in 19.3.

7 **skill** ability; perhaps 'cleverness, expertness' (*OED* 6a)

8 **wretched minutes kill** Time is represented as a monarch, who has enough initial

126

O thou my lovely boy, who in thy power
Dost hold Time's fickle glass, his sickle hour;
Who hast by waning grown, and therein show'st
Thy lovers withering as thy sweet self grow'st—
If Nature (sovereign mistress over wrack)   5
As thou goest onwards still will pluck thee back,
She keeps thee to this purpose, that her skill
May Time disgrace, and wretched minutes kill.
Yet fear her, O thou minion of her pleasure:
She may detain, but not still keep, her treasure!   10
Her audit (though delayed) answered must be,
And her quietus is to render thee.
(   )
(   )

2 fickle] Q; tickle *conj.* Kinnear in Rollins 2 his sickle hour] TYLER; sickie, hower Q; fickle hower LINTOT; sickle-hour HUDSON 1881 (*conj.* Walker); tickle hour *conj.* Anon. in Rollins 2 8 minutes] MALONE (*conj.* Capell); mynuit Q 11 audit] Q (*Audite*) 12 quietus] Q (*Quietus*) 13–14] *The italic parentheses appear in Q, but are omitted by many editors following Malone*

dignity to be *disgraced* when defeated; the *wretched minutes* are the smallest subservient units of time, which are killed without compunction.

9 **her** i.e. Nature. Anything which *grows* (like a flower) might reasonably fear a hand which *plucks*.
minion 'darling, favourite; . . . c. *esp.* A favourite of a sovereign, prince, or other great person; *esp.* opprobriously, one who owes everything to his patron's favour, and is ready to purchase its continuance by base compliances' (*OED* n.¹ 1).

10 **detain . . . treasure!** To *detain* continues the idea that Nature *plucks back* the friend (*OED* s.v. 'detain' 5 'to hinder; to delay'); it may also mean 'to keep back what is due or claimed' (*OED* 2a), as Nature and Time are struggling for ownership. The opposition between *detain* and *keep* is that between temporary (and perhaps illegitimate) tenure and permanent retention (*keep* meaning 'guard, defend, protect, preserve, save' (*OED* 14); also perhaps 'hold as a captive or prisoner' (*OED* 25)).

10 **still** always (*OED* 3a). 'To pay one's debt to

nature' was a proverbial expression for death (Dent D168).

11 **answered** paid ('To satisfy a pecuniary claim' (*OED* 7))

12 **And her quietus is to render thee.** 'The satisfaction of her debt is to give you up.' *Quietus* is the technical term to mark the settling of a debt, at the time of an *audit*, as in Webster's *Duchess of Malfi* 3.2.186–7: 'You had the trick in audit-time to be sick, | Till I had signed your *quietus*'. Since the friend is merely *detained* (held without proper ownership) the poem prepares for the ruthless justice of its conclusion. The *mutual render* of 125.12 turns into the irrevocable yielding up of the friend, who must pay his debt to Nature like all other mortals ('Thou owest God a death', says Prince Harry to Falstaff and abruptly exits, 1 *Henry IV* 5.1.126, echoing the proverb 'Death pays all debts' (Dent D148)). Although the syntax of the poem is complete, the brackets create the impression that *render* could be functioning as a transitive verb, of which the object is sliced away by the sickle hour of time, bracketed to oblivion.

Sonnet 127 begins a group of sonnets which are chiefly about a mistress with dark hair and dark eyes whom Shakespeare never calls a 'lady', let alone the 'dark lady' favoured by his biographical critics. Scores of women with dark hair and dark eyes who were capable of doing dark deeds have been identified as her historical original (see Samuel Schoenbaum, 'Shakespeare's Dark Lady: A Question of Identity' in Philip Edwards, Inga-Stina Ewbank, and G. K. Hunter, eds., *Shakespeare's Styles: Essays in Honour of Kenneth Muir* (Cambridge, 1980), 221–39). Her appearance is designed to enable the sonnets to dwell on the paradoxes of finding 'fair' (beautiful) something which is 'dark'. This group is likely to contain the earliest Sonnets in the sequence, for two reasons: (a) two of them appear in *The Passionate Pilgrim* of 1598 (*138* and *144*); (b) there are no late rare words in this part of the sequence. On which, see Hieatt, Hieatt, and Prescott, 'When did Shakespeare Write *Sonnets* 1609?' (see headnote to Sonnet *103*).

1 **black . . . fair** Dark colouring (dark hair and dark eyes) was not considered beautiful (with a pun on *fair* meaning 'blonde').

2 Modifies the previous line: 'or if it was called *fair* it wasn't called beautiful'.

3 **successive heir** the true inheritor by blood. *Successive* is a standard term to describe hereditary succession (*OED* 3b) as in *The Spanish Tragedy* 3.1.14: 'Your King, | By hate deprived of his dearest son, | The only hope of our successive line'.

4 **And beauty . . . shame** (a) beauty is declared illegitimate; (a) beauty is publicly shamed with having borne a bastard. The desire for paradox here creates a genealogical problem: *beauty* is both the source of due succession and its own illegitimate offspring.

5 **put on Nature's power** usurped an office which is properly Nature's (through cosmetics)

6 **Fairing the foul** making the foul beautiful (or blonde). The use of *fair* as a transitive

verb is not common, and would have added to the deliberate strangeness here, which anticipates the witches in *Macbeth* 1.1.10: 'Fair is foul, and foul is fair'.

7 **no name . . . bower** no legitimate hereditary title (or reputation) and no sacred inner sanctum. *Bower* is usually glossed as a vague poeticism (so *OED* cites this passage under 1b: 'a vague poetic word for an idealized abode'), but it continues the poem's concern with legitimate succession and bastardy, and means 'a bed-room' (*OED* 2). Not even beauty's bedchamber is safe from profanation.

8 **is profaned** is defiled, perhaps with a suggestion that her holiest places have been invaded

9 **Therefore** because of beauty's profanation (by the abuse of cosmetics) they are black in mourning
raven black Compare the proverb 'As black as a raven' (Dent R32.2).

10 **brows** Q's repetition of 'eyes' has prompted many emendations. Staunton's is the most convincing, since black *brows* (eyebrows) are elsewhere referred to by Shakespeare (*L.L.L.* 4.3.256–8: 'O, if in black my lady's brows be decked | It mourns that painting and usurping hair | Should ravish doters with a false aspect'), and are often treated as expressive (e.g. 'I see your brows are full of discontent', *Richard II* 4.1.320).
so suited and similarly attired, and. *And* may mean 'As if', 'as though' (*OED* 3), as in *Dream* 1.2.77–8: 'I will roar you an 'twere any nightingale'.

11 **At . . . lack** at those who, despite not being born beautiful, do not lack beauty through their use of cosmetics. *Beauty* here almost merits inverted commas, since it has been so thoroughly contaminated by its context.

12 **Sland'ring . . . esteem** giving a bad name to what is natural by making real beauty indistinguishable from false

13 **so** in such a way (leading to *that* in l. 14).
becoming of gracing, suiting so well with that they become beautiful

14 **so** i.e. black like the mistress's eyes

127

In the old age black was not counted fair,
Or if it were it bore not beauty's name;
But now is black beauty's successive heir,
And beauty slandered with a bastard shame:
For since each hand hath put on Nature's power,   5
Fairing the foul with Art's false borrowed face,
Sweet beauty hath no name, no holy bower,
But is profaned, if not lives in disgrace.
Therefore my mistress' eyes are raven black,
Her brows so suited, and they mourners seem   10
At such who, not born fair, no beauty lack,
Sland'ring creation with a false esteem.
    Yet so they mourn, becoming of their woe,
    That every tongue says beauty should look so.

9 mistress'] Q (Mistersse)   9–10 eyes . . . brows] BROOKE (conj. Staunton); eyes . . . eyes Q; eyes . . . hairs CAPELL; hairs . . . eyes conj. Walker; brows . . . eyes GLOBE (conj. Staunton); eyes . . . brow INGRAM AND REDPATH   10 and] Q; that GILDON; as DYCE 1857

The lover who envies the instrument on which his mistress plays is a cliché in the period. Fastidious Brisk in Jonson's *Every Man Out of his Humour* 3.9.101–6 describes his mistress playing the viola de gamba: 'I have wished myself to be that instrument, I think, a thousand times'. E. C.'s *Emaricdulfe* Sonnet 17 ('I am enchanted with thy snow-white hands') dwells with erotic fascination on his mistress's hands and the music they produce. For a discussion and transcription of the version of this sonnet in Bodleian MS Rawl. Poet. 152, see R. H. Robbins, 'A Seventeenth Century Manuscript of Shakespeare's Sonnet 128', *NQ* 212 (1967), 137–8. The variants in this transcription illustrate how seventeenth-century miscellanists modified details which they found obscure or inapplicable to their own circumstances.

1 **music** source of sweetness. Cf. 8.1.
2 **that blessèd wood** the wood of the keyboard, graced by the player's touch
3 **gently sway'st** (a) rule over with gentleness (transitive; the object is *The wiry concord*); (b) move gently in time to the music. The line-ending allows the verb momentarily (and unusually for the period) to be intransitive, 'move gently'.

4 **The wiry . . . confounds** the harmonious sound of the strings which overpowers and amazes my ear
5 **jacks** 'In the virginal, spinet, and harpsichord: An upright piece of wood fixed to the back of the key-lever, and fitted with a quill which plucked the string as the jack rose on the key's being pressed down. (By Shaks. and some later writers erron. applied to the key.)' (*OED* 14); playing on 'a lad, fellow, chap; *esp.* a low-bred or ill-mannered fellow, a "knave" ' (*OED* 2a) **that nimble leap** Like agile courtiers, the jacks leap to kiss the player's hand.
6 **the tender inward of thy hand** Compare Leontes' objections when his wife takes Polixenes' hand: 'But to be paddling palms and pinching fingers, | As now they are . . . Still virginalling | Upon his palm?' (*Winter's Tale* 1.2.117–18; 127–8). To paddle palms is to share a quasi-sexual intimacy.
8 **by** beside
9 **tickled** punning on 'excited, stimulated by touch' and 'to play or operate (the keys of a keyboard instrument or machine)' (*OED* 6a)
10 **dancing chips** the keys
11, 14 **thy** Q reads 'their'. On this recurrent error, see 26.12 n.
13 **saucy jacks** cheeky upstarts (widely used slang)

128

How oft, when thou, my music, music play'st
Upon that blessèd wood whose motion sounds
With thy sweet fingers when thou gently sway'st
The wiry concord that mine ear confounds,
Do I envy those jacks that nimble leap   5
To kiss the tender inward of thy hand,
Whilst my poor lips, which should that harvest reap,
At the wood's boldness by thee blushing stand.
To be so tickled they would change their state
And situation with those dancing chips,   10
O'er whom thy fingers walk with gentle gait,
Making dead wood more blest than living lips.
    Since saucy jacks so happy are in this,
    Give them thy fingers, me thy lips to kiss.

1 my music] Q; deere deerist BOD4   2 motion] Q; mocions BOD4   3 sway'st] Q; swaies BOD4
5 Do I] Q; o how BOD4   jacks] Q; kies BOD4   leap] Q; leapes BOD4   7 reap] Q; reped BOD4
8 wood's] Q; wood BOD4   9 tickled] Q; tuched BOD4   they] Q; the faine BOD4   11 thy]
GILDON; their Q; youre BOD4   13 saucy jacks] Q; then those keyes BOD4   14 thy fingers]
BENSON; their fingers Q; youre fingers BOD4   thy lips] Q; youre lipes BOD4

1–2 **Th' expense . . . action** 'The achieved end of lust is the shameful squandering of vital powers.' *Spirit* (disyllabic here) can mean 'semen' (as in Mercutio's bawdy ' 'Twould anger him | To raise a spirit in his mistress' circle', *Romeo* 2.1.23–4). It could have a more rarefied sense: 'mental energy, vitality'. The *waste of shame* similarly ranges from the extremely carnal (playing on 'waist' to mean 'ejaculating into a shameful waist') to the aridly spiritual ('with the result that one is left in an emptiness of shame').

3 **perjured . . . bloody** false to oaths, prone to kill and maim
full of blame (a) packed with guilt; (b) full of recrimination

4 **extreme** severe, violent
rude brutal, barbarous
not to trust not to be trusted

5 **Enjoyed . . . straight** No sooner does it achieve its ends than it loathes them. *Enjoyed* combines 'To have the use or benefit of' (*OED* 4a) with 4b, 'To have one's will of (a woman)'.

6 **Past reason hunted** sought with an eagerness which is beyond all that is reasonable

8 **On purpose laid** set there with the deliberate desire. *Bait* allures and then kills.

8–9 **mad, | Mad** The *anadiplosis* (repetition at the end of one clause and the beginning of the next) uniquely here bridges the gap between two quatrains. The energy of the poem surges unstoppably. Q reads 'Made', which is an acknowledged sixteenth-century spelling of 'mad'. McLeod (see note on l. 11 below) would retain it. The compulsion evoked by 'Made In pursut' does contribute to the picture of lust in the sonnet, but *so* requires an adjective to refer back to, which must surely be *mad* rather than 'made'.

9 **so the same**, i.e. *mad*

10 **in quest . . . extreme** Q's 'in quest, to haue extreame' is defended by Robert Graves and Laura Riding in *A Survey of Modernist Poetry* (1927), 68–9, on the grounds that Q presents lust as wishing to possess extremity itself. It is unlikely that any early modern reader could have read the line this way, and many read with a quill to hand to correct printers' slips.

11 **A bliss . . . woe** primarily 'A source of delight whilst it is being tried out; once experienced a source of utter misery'. Q's reading, 'A blisse in proofe and proud and very wo', has its champions, notably the tireless anti-editor Randall McLeod, 'Information Upon Information', *Text: Transactions of the Society for Textual Scholarship* 5 (1991), 241–78, who calls the emendation of the second 'and' to 'a' 'stupid' (250). He argues that Q's character string 'proud' could be read as both proud and 'prov'd' by a contemporary reader (compare collation to *Lucrece* l. 712). 'Proud', in the sense of showing pride, does have strong associations with the uncontrollable energies of lust in the Sonnets, but to read 'proud' in a modernized text would be misleading. However, the line in Q is ambiguous. It could, unemended, be read by a seventeenth-century reader as a string of adjectival clauses akin to those in 3–4, making lust 'a bliss in proof and proud and very woe'; or it could reinforce the idea of the previous line that all stages of lust are undifferentiatedly dreadful by reading 'A bliss both while it is being tried out (*in proof*), and when it has been tried out (*proved*), and a source of complete misery'. The chief argument for the emendation of the second 'and' to 'a' is that the line in its emended form moves towards the following line's claim that 'before action lust is a joy; after action it is an insubstantial dream'. Q's lack of pointing is retained here, however: in order to make a link with the previous line it must be possible momentarily to read 'a bliss in proof and proved' as a single unit of sense meaning 'a source of bliss both when one is trying it out and when one has finished trying it out' before the bliss evaporates in woe.

12 **Before . . . dream** in anticipation a joy which is looked forward to; in retrospect an insubstantial dream. Cf. *Lucrece* ll. 211–12.

13 **All this . . . well** Everyone knows this proverbial piece of wisdom; but no one *really* knows when it comes to practice.

14 **hell** (a) hell of guilt; (b) slang for the vagina

129

Th' expense of spirit in a waste of shame
Is lust in action, and, till action, lust
Is perjured, murd'rous, bloody, full of blame,
Savage, extreme, rude, cruel, not to trust,
Enjoyed no sooner but despisèd straight,   5
Past reason hunted, and, no sooner had,
Past reason hated as a swallowed bait
On purpose laid to make the taker mad,
Mad in pursuit, and in possession so,
Had, having, and in quest to have, extreme,   10
A bliss in proof and proved a very woe,
Before, a joy proposed; behind, a dream.
    All this the world well knows, yet none knows well
    To shun the heaven that leads men to this hell.

9 Mad] Q (Made)   11 and proved a] SEWELL: and proud and Q

1 **My . . . sun** *My* is given a proud emphasis to distinguish the poet's mistress from the majority of Elizabethan sonneteers' mistresses. Cf. Henry Constable's *Diana* (1592) 1.7, ll. 9–12: 'No, no, I flatter not, when I thee call | The sun, sith that the sun was never such; | But when thee I thee compared withal | Doubtless the sun I flatterèd too much'. Lynche's *Diella* (1596) 3 is also a fruitful candidate for parody: 'My mistress' snow-white skin doth much excel | The pure-soft wool Arcadian sheep do bear; | Her hair exceeds gold forced in smallest wire, | In smaller threads than those Arachne spun; | Her eyes are crystal fountains, yet dart fire | More glorious to behold than midday sun; | Her ivory front, (though soft as purest silk) | Looks like the table of Olympic Jove, | Her cheeks are like ripe cherries laid in milk, | Her alabaster neck the throne of Love; | Her other parts so far excel the rest, | That wanting words, they cannot be expressed'. Giles Fletcher's *Licia* 45 compares Licia's eyes first to a comet and then to a sun rising in the west. Shakespeare uses the comparison in 49.6.

2 **Coral** is a stock comparison for lips. See for example Lynche's *Diella* 31.2: 'sweet lips of coral hue but silken softness'; *Zepheria* Canzon 23.1: 'Thy coral coloured lips'; Richard Barnfield, *Cynthia*, Sonnet 6.1: 'Sweet coral lips, where Nature's treasure lies'; and *Venus* l. 542.

3 **dun** dingy brown

4 **wires** a traditional comparison in sonnet sequences. Wire, being made of gold, iron, brass, or copper, could not be black unless tarnished, although Barnabe Barnes, when looking for flaws in his mistress, finds 'A mole upon her forehead, coloured pale, | Her hair disordered, brown and crispèd wiry' (*Parthenophil and Parthenophe* 13.10–11). The anonymous *Zepheria* Canzon 17 sets out the orthodox coiffure of the Petrarchan mistress: 'The golden ceiling of thy brows' rich frame | Designs the proud pomp of thy face's architure: | Crystal transparent casements to the same | Are thine eyes' sun, which do the world depure, | Whose silvery canopy gold wire fringes'.

5 **damasked, red and white** OED's definition ('4. Having the hue of the damask rose') is unhelpful, since *Rosa damascena* includes red, white, and parti-coloured varieties. The reference is probably to *R. x damascena* var. *versicolor* ('the York and Lancaster Rose'), which has parti-coloured pink and white petals (and often also pure white or pure pink blooms). *Damasked, red and white* then means 'parti-coloured, I mean red and white on the same rose tree', rather than referring to three separate types of rose. A similar (single) 'rose brier' which bears red and white blooms is referred to in *1 Henry VI* 2.4.0.1.

8 **reeks** rises like smoke. The sense 'to stink' is not recorded before the eighteenth century. However, smoking chimneys 'reek' and so can blood, as in *Lucrece* l. 1377.

11 **go** walk. Goddesses were supposed not to touch the ground, as in *Venus* l. 1028 and n.

13 **rare** exceptional, precious

14 **As any . . . compare** as any woman misrepresented by inaccurate and deceitful comparisons. The poem archly ends with a comparison (*As . . .*). The emphasis falls on *I think*, which confesses a privately held, self-consciously inaccurate belief.

130

My mistress' eyes are nothing like the sun,
Coral is far more red than her lips' red;
If snow be white, why then her breasts are dun;
If hairs be wires, black wires grow on her head.
I have seen roses damasked, red and white,   5
But no such roses see I in her cheeks,
And in some perfumes is there more delight
Than in the breath that from my mistress reeks.
I love to hear her speak, yet well I know
That music hath a far more pleasing sound.   10
I grant I never saw a goddess go:
My mistress when she walks treads on the ground.
   And yet, by heaven, I think my love as rare
   As any she belied with false compare.

1 **tyrannous** Petrarchan mistresses are traditionally *tyrannous*. It implies 'lacking in pity' and 'enjoying absolute control over my emotions'. See e.g. Bartholomew Griffin, *Fidessa* 47.10, Sidney, *Astrophil and Stella* 47.
  so as thou art just as you are (i.e. not 'fair')

3 **dear** functions as both adjective and adverb: tender(ly); expensively.

5 **in good faith** is a reliteralized set phrase. In general conversation it marks a protestation of earnestness; here it also means 'some poor credulous fools genuinely believe that . . .'.

7 **err** stronger than its modern sense: be categorically wrong, or even 'mad'; also with an element of moral disapproval, through *OED* 4, 'To go astray morally; to sin'. The only character in Shakespeare to be told 'Madman, thou errest' is the madly doting Malvolio, *Twelfth Night* 4.2.43.

9 **And to be sure . . . swear** (a) and to testify for certain that what I swear is true . . . ; (b) and certainly what I swear is not false. The absence of punctuation in Q makes (a) the primary sense, but editors often feel a need to draw out (b) by punctuating after *swear*.

10 **but thinking on** just thinking about

11 **One on another's neck** one following rapidly after another, as in Nashe's *Unfortunate Traveller*: 'Passion upon passion would throng one on another's neck', Nashe, ii.262. Compare the proverb 'One misfortune comes on the neck of another' (Dent M1013).

12 **Thy black . . . place** Your blackness is the most beautiful in the eyes of my judgement. The topsyturvyness of *black* being *fairest* is reinforced by the faint suggestion that judgement is put out of its proper *place* by the blackness of the mistress.

13 **deeds** On first reading this means only 'your tyrannical conduct towards me'; if the poem is reread in the light of 133 it might be taken as carrying a wider reference to infidelities.

14 **this slander** the claim that her face *hath not the power to make love groan*. The sonnet has in the background a courtroom drama in which a trial for defamation is being enacted: *swear, witness, judgement,* and finally *slander* contribute to this milieu.

131

Thou art as tyrannous, so as thou art,
As those whose beauties proudly make them cruel,
For well thou know'st to my dear doting heart
Thou art the fairest and most precious jewel.
Yet in good faith some say, that thee behold,   5
Thy face hath not the power to make love groan;
To say they err I dare not be so bold,
Although I swear it to myself alone.
And to be sure that is not false I swear
A thousand groans but thinking on thy face   10
One on another's neck do witness bear
Thy black is fairest in my judgement's place.
  In nothing art thou black save in thy deeds,
  And thence this slander as I think proceeds.

1 **as** as if they were

2 **Knowing . . . disdain** a parenthesis: 'knowing that your heart torments me with its scornful rejection of my suit'. A lady's *disdain* (implying lack of pity and insensibility to the sufferings of the lover) is a standard element in sonnet sequences.

4 **pretty ruth** becoming compassion. That pity was beautiful was a common argument used by sonneteers: the beautiful are supposed also to be pitiful; since the mistress is beautiful she should also be pitiful, and pity consists in yielding to the demands of her lover. See the anonymous *Zepheria* Canzon 7: '(Though by how much the more thou beauteous art, | So much of pity should'st thou more esteem)'. Cf. Donne's 'What if this present were the world's last night?' ll. 9–12: 'but as in my idolatry | I said to all my profane mistresses, | Beauty, of pity, foulness only is | A sign of rigour'.

5 **morning** punning on the eyes as *mourners*

7 **full star** Hesperus the evening star is *full* presumably in the sense 'intense' (*OED* 10b), otherwise not found before 1657.

9 **mourning** Q's 'morning' highlights the pun on 'morning' and 'mourning'.

10 **beseem** suit

12 **And suit . . . pity** and dress your pity in a similar way throughout. That is, make all your body pity me as at present only your eyes do.

14 **And all they foul** and that all of those are ugly who . . .
complexion combines both 'outward appearance' and 'inner mental constitution' through the primary sense of *complexion*, 'the combination of the four 'humours' of the body in a certain proportion' (*OED* 1a), combined with the sense 'skin colour'. Cf. *Merchant* 2.1.1: 'Mislike me not for my complexion, | The shadowed livery of the burnished sun'.

132

Thine eyes I love, and they, as pitying me,
Knowing thy heart torment me with disdain,
Have put on black, and loving mourners be,
Looking with pretty ruth upon my pain.
And truly not the morning sun of heaven   5
Better becomes the grey cheeks of the east,
Nor that full star that ushers in the even
Doth half that glory to the sober west
As those two mourning eyes become thy face.
O, let it then as well beseem thy heart   10
To mourn for me, since mourning doth thee grace,
And suit thy pity like in every part.
    Then will I swear beauty herself is black,
    And all they foul that thy complexion lack.

2 torment] Q; torments BENSON 5 the east] GILDON 1714; th' East Q 9 mourning] Q
(morning)

1 **Beshrew** woe to. A mild imprecation in Shakespeare, often used affectionately, as in Northumberland's rebuke to his daughter-in-law: 'Beshrew your heart, | Fair daughter', *2 Henry IV* 2.3.45–6.

2 **deep wound** grave injury; a wound like that inflicted by Cupid's arrow (with a pun on the 'wound' of the vagina)

4 **slave to slavery** completely dominated; a slave subjected to complete, dominating control

6 **And my . . . engrossèd** 'and you have taken my other self, my friend, from me in an act of even greater cruelty'. *Engrossed* originally means to write out (a name etc.) in large letters on a legal document. Shakespeare uses it to mean 'to seek to establish a monopoly in' like a voracious merchant (*OED* 4). Other germane senses include 9a: 'To make (the body) gross or fat; to fatten'. The modern sense of 'absorb attention of completely' is not recorded before the 1680s.

7 **Of . . . forsaken** both 'left by' and 'deprived of'. *My self* functions as a parenthetical gloss on the friend (he is myself, you know) and to mean that the mistress has enslaved the poet.

8 **thrice threefold** The Trinitarian imagery of *105* is darkly recalled here.
crossèd thwarted (*OED* 14). The thrice threefold torment is likely to have pagan provenance (in classical heroic narratives major actions are often performed three times), but *OED* 'cross' *v.* 1, 'to crucify', may be activated by the triple trinity of woes.

10 **my friend's . . . bail** 'let my heart stand bail for that of my friend and go to prison in his stead'. *OED* cites this passage under the rare 'bail' *v.* 3: 'To confine'. This misses the point: the poet imagines presenting his heart as bail for his friend, being imprisoned for him, and then becoming his protector (*guard*) or his prison (*OED* s.v. 'guard' 17a). Line 11 does not gloss what it is to 'bail', but develops a new conceit: 'regardless of who imprisons me, let my heart be his prison warden'.

12 **use rigour** be as hard as strict application of the law allows

13 **pent** imprisoned (also 'enclosed in a sexual embrace')

14 **and all** and everything (which includes the friend)

133

Beshrew that heart that makes my heart to groan
For that deep wound it gives my friend and me.
Is 't not enough to torture me alone,
But slave to slavery my sweet'st friend must be?
Me from myself thy cruel eye hath taken,   5
And my next self thou harder hast engrossèd.
Of him, myself, and thee I am forsaken,
A torment thrice threefold thus to be crossèd.
Prison my heart in thy steel bosom's ward,
But then my friend's heart let my poor heart bail,   10
Whoe'er keeps me, let my heart be his guard;
Thou canst not then use rigour in my jail.
    And yet thou wilt, for I, being pent in thee,
    Perforce am thine, and all that is in me.

6 engrossèd] Q; engross'd MALONE   8 crossèd] Q; cross'd MALONE

1 **So** Many editors (after Capell) make this into an exclamation by adding a comma after *so*. This marks the connection with the end of the previous sonnet. However, *so* also anticipates an unspoken 'in that case' before *Myself I'll forfeit.*

2 **mortgaged** continues the metaphors of substitutive financial binding from the previous poem: to *mortgage* is 'To make over (property, esp. houses or land) as security for a money debt, on condition that if the debt is discharged the grant shall be void'.

3–4 **Myself I'll forfeit . . . still** 'I shall default on the debt and make myself rather than my friend the surety for the debt, so that the mortgaged property (myself) will never be redeemed from your ownership, while the friend will be returned to me.'

3 **that other mine** (a) that other possession of mine; (b) my other self

5 **wilt not . . . will not** you do not intend to . . . he does not wish to. This is the one point in the sonnet at which the poet confesses that the friend's infidelity is voluntary (*he will not*).

7–8 **He learned . . . bind** 'He meant only to stand as surety in my stead (i.e. as someone who agreed to underwrite my debt, as Antonio does in *Merchant*), but found that he had signed a document that bound him to you as tightly as I am bound to you.' On bonds, see *87.*4 n.

9 **The statute . . . take** you will exact the full

measure of power afforded by your beauty. The *statute* referred to may be a legal instrument which binds all irrespective of whether or not they have consented to it (and so extends the power of the mistress to make her an absolute legislator), or, more probably, 'A statute merchant or statute staple; a bond or recognizance by which the creditor had the power of holding the debtor's lands in case of default' (*OED* 4a).

10 **Thou usurer . . . use** The mistress is a usurer who will lend out anything in order to gain interest, and control over other people's property. To *put forth* means 'To lay out (money) to profit' as in Jonson's *Every Man Out of his Humour* 2.3.245–8: 'I am determined to put forth some five thousand pound, to be paid me five for one, upon the return of myself, my wife, and my dog from the Turk's court' (*OED* s.v. 'put' 43j).

11 **came debtor** (a) who came as a debtor; (b) who became a debtor

12 **unkind abuse** (a) unnaturally harsh mistreatment (at the hands of the mistress); (b) harsh mistreatment of the friend

14 **He . . . free** 'He has paid the whole sum owing, and yet I am still held subject to my bond.' The pun on *whole* (an alternative spelling for 'hole' in this period) might suggest that the friend is paying for sex with the mistress.

134

So now I have confessed that he is thine,
And I myself am mortgaged to thy will;
Myself I'll forfeit, so that other mine
Thou wilt restore to be my comfort still.
But thou wilt not, nor he will not be free,   5
For thou art covetous, and he is kind.
He learned but surety-like to write for me,
Under that bond that him as fast doth bind.
The statute of thy beauty thou wilt take,
Thou usurer that put'st forth all to use,   10
And sue a friend came debtor for my sake:
So him I lose through my unkind abuse.
    Him have I lost, thou hast both him and me;
    He pays the whole, and yet am I not free.

12 lose] Q (loose)

1 **Will** The poem plays insistently on different senses (a figure known as *antanaclasis*): (a) what you want; (b) what you sexually desire; (c) sexual organs (male and female); (d) the poet's first name (which appears nowhere in the book called *Shakespeares Sonnets* except in the 'Will' poems). Some commentators have suggested it may also be the name of the friend. Q italicizes the word (1, 2 (twice), 11 (twice), 12, 14) which is a standard means of indicating a proper name (although italics are also used to emphasize a rare word or an unusual sense, as in 126.11). Q's italics are marked here by an initial capital, since they suggest autobiographical allusion (although they seem insignificant in ll. 11–12). It is easy to criticize the poem as a piece of sexual chortling, which rises to venom through its innuendo (*make thy large will more*, meaning 'stretch your cunt even more'). The final 'Will' of the poem, though, does salvage something wittily self-recriminating from the carnal puns, as the poet becomes one universal appetitive will, uniting all lovers and the organs of both sexes into himself. Compare the proverbs 'Women will have their wills' (Dent W723) and 'Will will have will' (Dent W397).

2 **to boot** in addition. Literally 'to the good'.
overplus excess

3 **vex** annoy, agitate

4 **To thy . . . thus** (a) giving you in this way more than you desire (as an overimportunate suitor); (b) filling up your vagina (*sweet will*) with my penis

6 **to hide . . . thine?** More or less a single entendre. Beyond the obvious bawdy sense ('hide my penis in your vagina'), also 'to unite your wishes with mine'.

7 **Shall will . . . gracious** (a) shall other people's 'wills' seem attractive to you; (b) shall my penis appeal to others . . .

8 **fair acceptance** gracious consent, warm welcome
shine appear

9 **The sea . . . still** Compare the proverbs 'The sea refuses no river', and 'The sea is never full' (Tilley S179 and Dent S181). The passage also recalls Ecclesiastes 1: 7: 'All the rivers go into the sea, yet the sea is not full: for the rivers go unto the place whence they return, and go'.

10 **in abundance** (a) in his abundance; (b) abundantly
store rich supply (*OED* 4b). There are echoes here of 1.5–9.

13 **Let 'no' . . . kill** Let no ungenerous refusal kill any handsome (honest, or earnest) suitors. Q reads 'Let no unkinde, no faire beseechers kill', which could be interpreted as 'Let no unkind mistress kill any handsome suitors' (a standard emphatic use of the double negative) or as 'Let no unkind "no", fair beseechers kill'. The reading offered here is metrically less harsh, although all alternatives would have been possible to an early reader.

14 **Think all but one** Think of all those *fair beseechers* as one man, and think of me as being in that single Will (meaning 'wish, desire, penis and vagina').

135

Whoever hath her wish, thou hast thy Will,
And Will to boot, and Will in overplus;
More than enough am I that vex thee still,
To thy sweet will making addition thus.
Wilt thou, whose will is large and spacious,   5
Not once vouchsafe to hide my will in thine?
Shall will in others seem right gracious,
And in my will no fair acceptance shine?
The sea, all water, yet receives rain still,
And in abundance addeth to his store;   10
So thou, being rich in Will, add to thy Will
One will of mine to make thy large Will more.
   Let 'no' unkind no fair beseechers kill:
   Think all but one, and me in that one Will.

1 Will] Q (*Will; also italicized in 2 twice, 11 twice, 12, and 14*) 13 'no' unkind no] TUCKER; no vnkinde, no Q; no unkind 'No' *conj.* Dowden; Let 'no', unkind, no INGRAM AND REDPATH

I **check** (a) reprimand (*OED* 11); (b) arrest, stop (*OED* 3)

come so near (a) touch you to the quick (Schmidt, s.v. 'near' 4: 'touching, interesting one's intellect or feelings, coming home to one', sometimes with an erotic flavour, as when Malvolio muses, 'Maria once told me she [Olivia] did affect me, and I have heard herself come thus near, that should she fancy it should be one of my complexion', *Twelfth Night* 2.5.22–5); (b) move physically close to you

3 **there** Will is admitted into the soul to communicate with it; also 'Will' is allowed into your body.

4 **Thus far . . . fulfil** The lack of pointing follows Q. Some editors put commas before and after *sweet*, marking it as a vocative. Q allows for this possibility, as well as allowing *sweet* to function as an adjective agreeing with 'love-suit' and perhaps too as an adverb (*OED* B 1) with 'fulfil'.

5 **fulfil** fill up; fill full. Q spells it 'fullfill' in l. 4 but not here.

treasure (a) treasury (*OED* 3; *Lucrece* l. 16); (b) vagina

6 **my will one** (a) my will alone; (b) and my will being one of the many who are allowed to fill up your treasury of love

7 **of great receipt** with a great capacity (*OED* s.v. 'receipt' 15a). The argument here is that 'your sexual organs are like a large exchequer or treasure chest in which a single thing is not worth counting; therefore let me in without telling anyone or counting me as part of the tally'.

7 **prove** demonstrate, i.e. give practical illustration of the abstract mathematical principle that 'one is no number' by seeing a single item vanish into a huge store.

8 **Among a number** (a) among all the numbers only one is not properly speaking a number; (b) among a large number of entities a single one does not matter. That 'One is no number' is proverbial (Dent O52, 54), as in Marlowe's *Hero and Leander* l. 255 and 8.14 n.

9 **untold** (a) uncounted; (b) unrecorded (as a secret)

10 **Though . . . be** although I must be considered as part of your complete tally. *Account* may pun on 'cunt'.

11 **hold . . . hold** consider . . . physically grasp me

so provided that

12 **That nothing . . . thee** regard that inconsiderable thing that I am as sweet. *Hold* and *something sweet* all carry an erotic charge.

14 **my name is Will** So it was, of course. Here, though, the poem approaches a popular riddle cited by Kerrigan, and blurs into anonymous ribaldry: 'My lover's will | I am content to fulfil; | Within this rhyme his name is framed; | Tell me then how he is named?' Will I am (William) is the answer.

136

If thy soul check thee that I come so near,
Swear to thy blind soul that I was thy Will,
And will, thy soul knows, is admitted there:
Thus far for love my love-suit sweet fulfil.
Will will fulfil the treasure of thy love,   5
Ay, fill it full with wills, and my will one.
In things of great receipt with ease we prove
Among a number one is reckoned none;
Then in the number let me pass untold,
Though in thy store's account I one must be;   10
For nothing hold me, so it please thee hold
That nothing me, a something sweet to thee.
   Make but my name thy love, and love that still,
   And then thou lov'st me for my name is Will.

2 Will] Q (*Will; also italicized in 5 and 14*) 6 Ay] Q (I) 12 nothing me] Q; Nothing-me
GILDON; no-thing me INGRAM AND REDPATH something sweet] Q (some-thing sweet); some-
thing (sweet) *conj.* Capell; some-thing, sweet, INGRAM AND REDPATH 14 lov'st]
SEWELL; louest Q

1 **love** Q's 'Thou blinde foole loue' is often modernized as 'Thou blind fool, Love', which makes the addressee unequivocally the blind Cupid. Love is proverbially blind (Dent L506).

3 **lies** The context of deception adds 'deceives' to 'lives'.

4 **Yet what . . . be** Rhetoric was believed to be able to make the worst seem the better course, although passion is proverbially able to make us 'know and see what is better, and yet follow the worse', as Ovid's Medea puts it (Golding 7.24–5): 'Love persuades me one, another thing my skill. | The best I see and like: the worst I follow headlong still'.

5 **corrupt** (*ppl. a.*) contaminated; and, for a moment, a transitive verb

6 **anchored . . . ride** Anchorage can accompany bawdy elsewhere, as in Cleopatra's 'There would he anchor his aspect, and die | With looking on his life' (*Antony* 1.5.33–4). Presumably this is because ships at anchor move up and down on the spot. *Ride* has its nautical sense (*80*.10) but *all men* gives it a bitterly sexual twist.

7 **Why of . . . hooks** It is not clear whose *eyes* are false and therefore forged into hooks (either anchors or hooks for fishing could be meant). Traditionally it would be the eyes of a seductive woman which would

be like baited hooks (as in *FQ* 1.1.49: 'Lo there before his face his Lady is, | Vnder blake stole hyding her bayted hooke'); here it is also the distorted vision of the lover's own eyes, which are transformed into predators by the mistress.

9 **several plot** a separate, individually owned piece of land

10 **common place** a publicly owned area on which anyone might walk or graze their animals. By the later seventeenth century it could be used to refer to a common object of derision (*OED* 5b). It implies prostitution or at least promiscuity here.

12 **To put** in order to put. Compare the proverb 'To set a good face on a bad matter' (Dent F17).

13 **things right true** (a) matters which are indisputably the case; (b) 'chaste cunts' (as Kerrigan elegantly puts it). This is presented as an answer to the questions put in the sonnet, but merely restates their cause.

14 **And . . . transferred** and so they are transformed into this sickness of misjudgement. *Transferred* is unusual in the sense 'transformed' (it is not given this sense by *OED*, although is by Schmidt), and may also mean 'my affections are transferred to this (disease-giving) false woman'. *Plague* may suggest venereal disease.

137

Thou blind fool love, what dost thou to mine eyes
That they behold and see not what they see?
They know what beauty is, see where it lies,
Yet what the best is, take the worst to be.
If eyes corrupt by over-partial looks   5
Be anchored in the bay where all men ride,
Why of eyes' falsehood hast thou forgèd hooks,
Whereto the judgement of my heart is tied?
Why should my heart think that a several plot,
Which my heart knows the wide world's common place?   10
Or mine eyes seeing this, say this is not,
To put fair truth upon so foul a face?
   In things right true my heart and eyes have erred,
   And to this false plague are they now transferred.

11 this is not,] SEWELL; ~ ~ ~ ᴧ Q; '~ ~' TUCKER

For an alternative version of this sonnet, see *P. Pilgrim*, Poem 1. A manuscript version, grouped with poems from *P. Pilgrim*, and probably ultimately deriving from that printed version, is in Folger MS V.a.339, fo. 197ᵛ.

1 **made of truth** composed of fidelity

2 **lies** By l. 13 the sense 'sleeps around' emerges.

3 **That** so that
untutored 'Uneducated, untaught; simple, unsophisticated' (*OED*, which offers the dedication to *Lucrece* and 3 *Henry VI (True Tragedy)* 5.5.32 as earliest citations).

4 **false subtleties** cunning deceptions. *False* also implies sexual infidelity (Schmidt, 6), as it does in 20.4.

5 **vainly** unreasonably, without any effect. The sense 'With personal vanity; conceitedly' (*OED* 3) is emerging *c.*1600, but there is no clear Shakespearian parallel for such a usage (*All's Well* 5.3.122–4 plays on 'vanity' and 'vainly': 'My fore-past proofs . . . | Shall tax my fears of little vanity, | Having vainly feared too little.')

6 **my days are past their best** When the poem was first printed in 1599 Shakespeare was 35. 'Youth' has no fixed limit in the period, but according to many of the established divisions of the ages of man Shakespeare would still have counted as a youth by this date. See 7.6 n. For ageing sonneteers, see *104*.3 n.

7 **Simply** (a) straightforwardly, artlessly; (b) unconditionally; (c) stupidly, like a simpleton (*OED* 5; although not otherwise used by Shakespeare in this sense)

8 **suppressed** (a) left unexpressed (*OED* 4); (b) kept secret (*OED* 3a)

9 **wherefore** why
unjust sexually unfaithful. The usage develops *OED* 2, 'Not upright or free from wrongdoing; faithless, dishonest', and is paralleled in *P. Pilgrim* 18.21, where it also rhymes with 'trust'.

11 **O, love's . . . trust** 'O the best dress for love is the appearance of mutual fidelity.' This answers the questions of the previous lines.

12 **age** personified: aged people
told (a) counted; (b) publicly revealed. Cf. *suppressed*, l. 8 above.

13 **lie** brings out the double meaning latent in l. 2.

14 **And in . . . be** And through our sins and weaknesses we are delightfully misled. *Faults* covers both the act of lying together (and with others) and their reluctance to perceive the truth. *Flattered* means both 'beguiled' and 'pleased'.

138

When my love swears that she is made of truth,
I do believe her though I know she lies,
That she might think me some untutored youth,
Unlearnèd in the world's false subtleties.
Thus vainly thinking that she thinks me young,   5
Although she knows my days are past the best,
Simply I credit her false-speaking tongue.
On both sides thus is simple truth suppressed:
But wherefore says she not she is unjust?
And wherefore say not I that I am old?   10
O, love's best habit is in seeming trust,
And age in love loves not to have years told.
     Therefore I lie with her, and she with me,
     And in our faults by lies we flattered be.

4 Unlearnèd . . . subtleties] Q; Vnskilfull . . . forgeries o1   6 she . . . are] Q; I know my year-
es be o1; I know my yeres are FOL9   7 Simply I] Q; I smiling, o1   8 On . . . suppressed] Q;
Outfacing faults in Loue, with loues ill rest o1   9 she . . . unjust] Q; my Loue that she is young
o1   11 habit is in seeming trust] Q; habit's in an soothing tongue o1; habit is a soothing
tongue o2; habit is a smoothinge tongue FOL9   12 to have] o1; t'haue Q   13 I . . . she] Q; Ile
lye with Loue, and Loue o1   14 And . . . flattered] Q (flattered *i.e. flatterèd*); Since that our
faults in Loue thus smother'd be o1

1-2 O call . . . heart (a) Do not ask me to provide excuses for the harm which your unpleasantness causes me; (b) Do not expect me to provide excuses for the failing which you, through your inhumanity, are imputing to me. To *lay upon* can mean 'To impose (an injunction, penalty, tax); to bestow (a name) upon' (*OED* s.v. 'lay' 55), although these senses were archaic by 1590.

3 Wound me . . . tongue On first reading this might mean 'do not stab my heart with your steely eye', alluding to the convention of the mistress's eyes as sources of pain and rebuke. The couplet returns to the convention that mistresses can murder with a gaze. By l. 5 the chief sense emerges: 'do not wound me by revealing your feelings through glances of your eye, but tell me directly'.

4 Use power with power . . . art use the capacity you have to hurt with direct force, rather than in an underhand way. Cf. *94.1*.

5 in my sight while I can see you

6 forbear restrain yourself from

7 What need'st thou why do you need to

8 o'erpressed overtaxed; overwhelmed

9-12 'Ah . . . injuries' Inverted commas are not used in Q to indicate speech. Q's 'Ah' followed by the defence of the mistress couched in the language of the orthodox besotted sonneteer would mark the lines as speech for early modern readers. What is lost in a modernization is the uncertainty as to when the direct speech ends. The couplet is usually (as here) set apart as a dry coda to the defence of the mistress; for an early reader it would not have been so clearly distinguished.

10 pretty looks (a) charming glances; (b) beautiful appearance

11 my foes i.e. her eyes

13 Yet do not so do not look at others, despite my efforts to justify your conduct

14 rid do away with. In other words, 'look at me and kill me with your eyes'. A desire for a quick death is frequent among sonneteers: as Sidney put it: 'A kind of grace it is to slay with speed', *Astrophil and Stella* 48.14.

139

O call not me to justify the wrong
That thy unkindness lays upon my heart:
Wound me not with thine eye but with thy tongue,
Use power with power, and slay me not by art.
Tell me thou lov'st elsewhere; but in my sight,   5
Dear heart, forbear to glance thine eye aside.
What need'st thou wound with cunning when thy might
Is more than my o'erpressed defence can bide?
Let me excuse thee: 'Ah, my love well knows
Her pretty looks have been mine enemies,   10
And therefore from my face she turns my foes,
That they elsewhere might dart their injuries.'
   Yet do not so, but since I am near slain,
   Kill me outright with looks, and rid my pain.

9–12 'Ah, ... injuries.'] TUCKER; ˏah ... injuries:ˏ Q   13 near] Q (neere)

I **press** subject to pressure. *Tongue-tied* adds an extra element to her cruelty: criminals who refused to plead (especially when charged with treason) could be subjected to *peine forte et dure*: 'Such felons as stand mute and speak not at their arraignment are pressed to death by huge weights laid upon a board that lieth over their breast and a sharp stone under their backs', Harrison, 191. In such a setting even the innocent '*express*', l. 3, acquires a painful suggestion of imposed suffering.

4 **pity-wanting** both lacking and needing pity

5 **wit** common sense, sometimes tending to 'sharpness, canniness' in the period

6 **Though . . . so** to tell me that you love me even though you do not

7 **testy** irritable, querulous; often with a slight suggestion of deficiency in the testy person. Shakespeare uses the word of children (as in *Lucrece* l. 1094) and fools (*Coriolanus* 2.1.43).

11 **ill-wresting** prone to interpret in the worst possible sense (the only instance in *OED*)

13 **so** i.e. a mad slanderer; possibly also 'believed'

belied be slandered

14 **Bear . . . wide** The general sense is 'look honest even if you are not'. A metaphor from archery underlies *straight* and *go wide*: 'Direct your gaze towards the target (me), even though your heart shoots past me to another object'. To *go wide* can mean 'to miss the point of a remark', hence here the association with gently humouring the poet while her thoughts are on another subject.

140

Be wise as thou art cruel; do not press
My tongue-tied patience with too much disdain,
Lest sorrow lend me words, and words express
The manner of my pity-wanting pain.
If I might teach thee wit, better it were,   5
Though not to love, yet, love, to tell me so,
As testy sick men, when their deaths be near,
No news but health from their physicians know.
For if I should despair I should grow mad,
And in my madness might speak ill of thee.   10
Now this ill-wresting world is grown so bad,
Mad slanderers by mad ears believèd be.
    That I may not be so, nor thou belied,
    Bear thine eyes straight, though thy proud heart go wide.

6 yet, love,] MALONE; yet‸ loue‸ C; yet (love) *conj.* Capell   11 Now] Q; Know *conj.* G. B. Evans   13 belied] GILDON; be lyde Q; be-lide BENSON

The sonnet takes as its structural device a combination of the *gradus amoris*, in which sight of the beloved is followed by hearing her, then touching her, and the idea of a 'banquet of sense' by which a lover feasts each of his senses in turn on the beloved. See *Venus* ll. 433–50 and n.

1 **In faith** truly, indeed

2 **errors** (a) physical defects; also (b) mistakes (such as her reluctance to recognize that the poet is old in *138*); (c) sins; (d) wanderings (often with an association of licentiousness)

3 **they** the eyes

4 **in despite of view** (a) despite what it sees; (b) in contempt of mere sight (chiming on *despise*). *View* is quite often used in the poems and Sonnets in *OED* sense 4: 'The exercise of the faculty of sight; the faculty or power of vision', as in *27*.10, *148*.11.

5 **thy tongue's tune** the sound of your voice; not necessarily implying melodiousness, as Coriolanus's gruff words to the plebs reveal: 'if it may stand with the tune of your voices that I may be consul' (2.3.85–6), although counter-examples include Cymbeline's rapt 'The tune of Innogen', *Cymbeline* 5.6.240, and *8*.1.

6 **base touches** (a) ignoble physical contact (possibly sexual, as in *OED* 1b and *Measure* 5.1.140–1: 'Who is as free from touch or soil with her | As she from one ungot'); (b) deep musical sounds (*OED* s.v. 'touch' 8 *Mus.* 'The act or manner of touching or handling a musical instrument, so as to bring out its tones'; cf. *Merchant* 5.1.67–8: 'With sweetest touches pierce your mistress' ear, | And draw her home with music').

8 **sensual feast** The 'banquet of sense' is a literary topos which dwells on the delights afforded each sense in turn by the inviting prospect of a mistress. Ben Jonson's *Poetaster* 4.5.192–9 is representative: 'To celebrate this feast of sense, | As free from scandal, as offence. | Here is beauty, for the eye; | For the ear, sweet melody; | Ambrosiac odours, for the smell; | Delicious nectar for the taste; | For the touch, a lady's waist; | Which doth all the rest excel'. Shakespeare explores the topos in

Timon 1.2.122–4: 'Th' ear, | Taste, touch, smell, all, pleased from thy table rise'. It is typical of the programmatic unconventionality of the sonnets to the mistress that this poem rejects the convention whilst exploiting it, and, through the pun on *touches* above, blurs the neat divisions of the traditional banquet in synaesthetic delight.

9 **five wits** are traditional subdivisions of the inner mental faculties, which correspond to the five outer senses: they are sometimes reckoned to be common sense, imagination, fantasy, right estimation, memory. The broadly Augustinian account in *Batman upon Bartholomew* (1582), fo. 13^{r-v} is closer to Shakespeare's faculty psychology elsewhere, and lists the inner wits as feeling (by means of which the soul 'taketh heed to the bodily wits'), wit (the power of the soul to know corporeal things), imagination ('whereby the soul beholdeth the likeness of bodily things when they be absent'), reason (which adjudicates between good and bad), and intellect (which is the power to understand intellectual and material entities, such as God and his angels).

11–12 **Who leaves . . . to be** 'who leaves uncontrolled the mere outward husk of a man in order to be your abject servant'. That is, the heart has abdicated its sovereignty over the body in order to become the slave of the mistress.

13 **Only** means both 'however' and 'to this extent and no further'.
plague suffering, sickness; often regarded as being inflicted by God, sometimes for a greater good

14 **awards** (a) imposes on me (usually used of judicial sentences); (b) is kind enough to grant me. Samuel Butler suggested that there is an allusion to purgatorial suffering here: the poet rejoices because he is reducing his pain in the afterlife by suffering it now. A simpler, masochistic, pleasure is at work, though: the poet rejoices that he suffers because he would rejoice in anything his mistress makes him do, and being made to suffer is a form of attention. There is also a jaunty 'who cares if I got VD? It was fun' struggling somewhere in there.

141

In faith I do not love thee with mine eyes,
For they in thee a thousand errors note,
But 'tis my heart that loves what they despise,
Who in despite of view is pleased to dote.
Nor are mine ears with thy tongue's tune delighted,   5
Nor tender feeling to base touches prone,
Nor taste, nor smell, desire to be invited
To any sensual feast with thee alone;
But my five wits nor my five senses can
Dissuade one foolish heart from serving thee,   10
Who leaves unswayed the likeness of a man,
Thy proud heart's slave and vassal wretch to be.
   Only my plague thus far I count my gain:
   That she that makes me sin awards me pain.

1 **dear virtue hate** (a) your valued chastity amounts to no more than hatred (of my love); (b) your most prized inner quality is hatred. A compliment to the mistress's chaste resistance to love is almost entirely obscured because of the completion of the clause and the line with 'hate'.

2 **grounded on** built upon. See 62.4 and n. It is left carefully uncertain as to whether *grounded on* agrees with *my sin* or the mistress's *hate*. Both are founded on adulterous love.

3 **but** only

6 **scarlet ornaments** lips. *Scarlet* has strong pejorative associations through the 'scarlet woman' described in Revelation 17–19, who was frequently linked with Catholicism, sexual infidelity, and with misleading the faithful, as in *FQ* 1.8.6. These associations are activated by *profaned*.

7 **sealed false bonds** (a) attached (red wax) seals to testaments of adultery; (b) consummated treacherous liaisons (with kisses)

8 **Robbed . . . rents** by adultery you have stolen the dues of marriage (and robbed others of the children which are the productive yield of their marriage). Beds are presented as estates, or *revenues* (accented on the second syllable), 'The collective items or amounts which constitute an income' (*OED* 4) which yield *rents*, or the payments by tenants. The imagery recalls the sonnets to the friend, which associate good stewardship of an estate, due returns from investments, and procreation.

9 **Be it lawful** Let it be lawful; uttered with some confidence, since the phrase fuses together two formulae widely used in Tudor statutes: 'it shall be lawful' and 'be it enacted'. *Be it* is monosyllabic.

10 **Whom . . . thee** at whom you are gazing amorously even now, while I am beseeching you. Compare the rolling gaze of 139.

12 **pity** On the association of pity with yielding sexual favours, see 132.4 n.

13 **what thou dost hide** i.e. pity

14 **By self . . . denied** you can be refused pity simply on the basis of the example which you yourself are setting. That is, if you want to be pitied, you must pity me.

142

Love is my sin, and thy dear virtue hate,
Hate of my sin, grounded on sinful loving.
O, but with mine compare thou thine own state,
And thou shalt find it merits not reproving,
Or if it do, not from those lips of thine   5
That have profaned their scarlet ornaments
And sealed false bonds of love as oft as mine,
Robbed others' beds' revenues of their rents.
Be it lawful I love thee as thou lov'st those,
Whom thine eyes woo as mine importune thee.   10
Root pity in thy heart, that, when it grows
Thy pity may deserve to pitied be.
    If thou dost seek to have what thou dost hide,
    By self example mayst thou be denied.

8 beds' revenues'] Q (*beds*ᴧ *reuenues*ₐ)

1 **careful** (a) attentive; (b) full of care, anxiety

housewife was pronounced 'hussif'.

2 **One of her feathered creatures** evidently a chicken, but also perhaps, as Kerrigan suggests, an Elizabethan fop in feathers. Feathered hats were voguish in the 1590s.

4 **pursuit** is accented on the first syllable.

5 **holds her in chase** runs after her. A set phrase listed under *OED* 'chase' 1e, and used in *Coriolanus* 1.7.18–19: 'Spies of the Volsces | Held me in chase'.

6 **bent** directed

7 **flies before her face** flees just ahead of her, with a play on flying, which is what the chicken tries to do. The phrase suggests wilful opposition through the phrase 'to fly in the face of', meaning 'openly to oppose' (the phrase is first cited in *OED*, s.v. 'face' 4b, from Thomas Wilson's *Art of Rhetoric*, a work which Shakespeare knew well).

8 **prizing** caring about

10 **thy babe** The comparison of an impotent lover to a baby who is unable to influence his nurse or mother is also used by Fulke Greville, *Caelica* 43.13–14 ('I, like the child, whom Nurse hath overthrown, | Not crying, yet am whipped, if you be known') and 61.5–10.

11 **thy hope** the thing which you are hoping for

13–14 **So will . . . still** 'So I will pray that you will have what you desire (which is a man called Will) if you turn back to me and calm my loud crying.' What she desires, the other lovers whom she pursues, will of course be lost if she stops her pursuit and returns to the poet called Will. It was proverbial that 'Women must have their wills while they live because they make none when they die' (Tilley W715), and, more simply, 'Women will have their wills' (Dent W723).

143

Lo, as a careful housewife runs to catch
One of her feathered creatures broke away,
Sets down her babe and makes all swift dispatch
In pursuit of the thing she would have stay,
Whilst her neglected child holds her in chase.   5
Cries to catch her whose busy care is bent
To follow that which flies before her face,
Not prizing her poor infant's discontent;
So runn'st thou after that which flies from thee,
Whilst I, thy babe, chase thee afar behind.   10
But if thou catch thy hope, turn back to me
And play the mother's part: kiss me, be kind.
    So will I pray that thou mayst have thy Will,
    If thou turn back and my loud crying still.

1 careful] Q (carefull); care-full OXFORD   2 feathered] LINTOT (feth'er'd); fethered (*i.e. feath-erèd*) Q   13 Will] Q (*Will*)

For an alternative version of this sonnet, see *P. Pilgrim*, Poem 2.

1 **Two loves** both 'two kinds of love' and 'two lovers'

2 **suggest** 'To prompt (a person) to evil; to tempt *to* or *to do* something; to seduce or tempt away' (*OED* 2a). The verb is often used of the devil, as in *Merry Wives* 3.3.205: 'what devil suggests this imagination?'

3 **right fair** (a) very beautiful; (b) of a very fair complexion

4 **coloured ill** dark, with a suggestion of evil. The idea that one had a good and a bad angel who argued over one's soul is common in the drama of the period, as in *Dr Faustus* (A Text) 2.3.12 ff. Drayton's *Idea* (1599) 22 provides an analogue in the sonnet tradition. The convention here is transformed into a seduction and corruption of one angel by the other.

5 **hell** The slang sense 'vagina' runs through the poem.

6 **side** Q's 'sight' is probably a compositorial error, although it could mark the survival of an earlier draft.

7 **saint** good angel. Unusual in this sense (although see *OED* 3b and the King James Bible, Jude 14: 'The Lord cometh with ten thousands of his Saints'), and probably resorted to because 'angel' is unmetrical and the monosyllabic 'spirit' has already been used indifferently of both loves.

9 **whether that** whether or not

10 **directly** (a) 'Completely, absolutely, entirely, exactly, precisely' (*OED* 4); (b) 'Immediately (in time); straightway; at once' (*OED* 6a)

11 **from me** away from me

14 **fire my good one out** (a) blasts my good angel to hell (and so rejects him); (b) gives my good angel the flaming irritation of venereal disease; (c) blasts my friend's penis out of her 'hell'. Commentators have also suggested that there is an allusion to the practice of smoking foxes from their holes. It is hard to see how this would help the poet to know whether or not his friends are sleeping together. Compare the proverb 'One fire drives out another' (Dent F277).

144

Two loves I have, of comfort and despair,
Which like two spirits do suggest me still.
The better angel is a man right fair;
The worser spirit a woman coloured ill.
To win me soon to hell my female evil   5
Tempteth my better angel from my side,
And would corrupt my saint to be a devil,
Wooing his purity with her foul pride.
And whether that my angel be turned fiend
Suspect I may, yet not directly tell,   10
But being both from me, both to each friend,
I guess one angel in another's hell.
    Yet this shall I ne'er know, but live in doubt,
    Till my bad angel fire my good one out.

2 Which] Q; That o1   suggest] Q (suggest)   3, 4 The] Q; My o1   6 side] o1; sight Q   8 foul] Q; faire o1   9 fiend] Q (finde)   11 But ... from] Q; For ... to o1   13 Yet ... ne'er] Q; The truth I shall not o1

The octosyllabic form of this poem combined with the surface simplicity of its wordplay has led many to believe that it is early work. See Andrew Gurr, 'Shakespeare's First Poem: Sonnet 145', *Essays in Criticism* 21 (1971), 221–6. 'Hate away' in l. 13 may be a pun on 'Hathaway', the surname of Shakespeare's wife, whom he married in 1582 when she was already pregnant. She was 26 and he was 18.

2 'I hate' Inverted commas are editorial throughout

3 **for her sake** because of her

5 **Straight** immediately

6–7 **that ever sweet . . . doom** which, always mild in sound and tone, was used to give a mild sentence

8 **And taught it . . . greet** her heart decides to greet me in a different way

10–11 Compare the proverb 'After night comes the day' (Dent N164).

11–12 **fiend . . . heaven . . . hell** Although this poem is likely to be very early work, these terms all link it with the previous sonnet.

13 **'I hate' . . . threw** She tore the words 'I hate' away from meaning that she hated me (by adding 'not you' to them).

145

Those lips that love's own hand did make
Breathed forth the sound that said 'I hate'
To me that languished for her sake;
But when she saw my woeful state,
Straight in her heart did mercy come,   5
Chiding that tongue, that ever sweet
Was used in giving gentle doom.
And taught it thus anew to greet:
'I hate' she altered with an end
That followed it as gentle day   10
Doth follow night, who, like a fiend,
From heaven to hell is flown away.
 'I hate' from hate away she threw
 And saved my life, saying 'not you.'

2, 9, 13 'I hate'] MALONE (*italic; conj.* Capell); ˌ~ ~ˌ Q 14 'Not you.'] MALONE (*italic*); ˏ~~·ˏ Q

Sonnets which explored a dialogue between soul and body were not uncommon. See e.g. Sidney, *Astrophil and Stella* (first printed 1591), 110 ('Leave me, O Love, which reachest but to dust | And thou, my mind, aspire to higher things'), and Bartholomew Griffin, *Fidessa* (1596), 28: 'Well may my soul, immortal and divine, | That is imprisoned in a lump of clay, | Breathe out laments, until this body pine, | That from her takes her pleasures all away'. As Vendler notes, however, 'The gloominess of this sonnet has little of the radiance of Christian hope'.

1 **centre** the central, animating principle. The suggestion that the soul is imprisoned by its position is developed in the lines that follow.

2 **Spoiled** by Q's repetition of 'My sinful earth' is hypermetrical and not readily intelligible, since the singular 'sinful earth' becomes a plural *rebel powers*. The compositor appears to have repeated the last three words of the previous line. There is also a possibility that the copy was incomplete or partially revised at this stage of the sequence. The poem comes after a very early work, and in the last but one sonnet, *144*.6, there is a misreading of a rhyme word which could indicate illegible or partially revised copy. Most modern editors simply omit the first three syllables of l. 2 and replace them with square brackets. Emendation is necessarily pure conjecture based on Shakespearian usage elsewhere (see collation). The main alternatives are that the *rebel powers* trick or deceive the soul, hence Malone's 'Fool'd' and Seymour-Smith's 'Gull'd'; or that they attack, control, or otherwise seek to diminish its autonomy, hence B. G. Kinnear's 'thrall to', which has an analogue in *Lucrece* ll. 719–26. Vendler's reading (after Sebastian Evans's conjecture) 'Feeding' merits serious consideration since it contributes (perhaps excessively) to wordplay later in the poem. The central conceit of the poem is that the soul is arrayed by (i.e. 'dressed in'; the possible sense 'to raise in arms' is not elsewhere used by Shakespeare) outer walls (the senses and bodily appetites) which are rebellious to it in that their sensuous ornamentation enmires the soul in mortality. As the soul pines within, like a captive in a siege, it is likely that whatever the poet wrote in l. 2 anticipated this image. 'Sieged by' is one pos-

sibility, but *Spoiled* combines the sense of aggressive attack (*OED* 1a: 'Pillaged, plundered; ravaged') with a diminution in the soul's resources. The word is also associated by Shakespeare with mortality (Cassio's 'O I am spoiled', *Othello* 5.1.55), and when sexual purity has been sullied, as it is in *Lucrece* ll. 1170–3, the closest analogue for this passage. *Spoiled* also suits the concern of the poem with outer garments of doubtful value, via the sense 'to damage, mar or mark' (see Schmidt, 3 and *Troilus* 2.2.68–9: 'We turn not back the silks upon the merchant | When we have spoiled them' (although Q reads 'soiled')). See Wells, 'New Readings' (see 12.4 n.), 318–19.

3 **pine** starve

5 **short a lease** There is no point in expensively decorating a lodging which one is only entitled to occupy for a short period. Compare the proverb 'No man has lease of his life' (Dent M327). Christopher Sutton, *Disce Mori: Learn to Die* (1600), 75, uses a similar image: 'we are but tenants at will in this clay farm . . . howsoever we piece and patch this poor cottage, it will at last fall into the Lord's hands'.

6 **fading mansion** increasingly decrepit body. Cf. 2 Corinthians 5: 1: 'For we know that if our earthly house of this tabernacle be destroyed, we have a building given of God, that is, an house not made with hands, but eternal in the heavens'.

8 **charge** (a) expense; (b) what has been entrusted to you; perhaps also (c) *OED* 8 *fig.* a, 'A burden, load, weight (of trouble, inconvenience, etc.)'

9 **live . . . loss** reverses the predatory relationship with which the poem started: now the soul is exhorted to live upon its subordinates.

10 **that** the body
   aggravate as usually in Shakespeare 'augment, increase' (*OED* 5). The sinister sense 'Of things evil: To increase the gravity of' (*OED* 6a) may be in play, suggesting that a material supply (*store*) can only get worse for getting bigger, as it increases the burden on the soul.

11 **Buy terms divine** (a) purchase long periods (as against a short, mortal *lease*); (b) secure favourable terms from God (by sacrificing hours previously devoted to the decking of the body)
   hours of dross hours which are worthless. Cf. Matthew 6: 20: 'But lay up treasures for yourselves in heaven, where neither

146

Poor soul, the centre of my sinful earth,
Spoiled by these rebel powers that thee array,
Why dost thou pine within and suffer dearth,
Painting thy outward walls so costly gay?
Why so large cost, having so short a lease,   5
Dost thou upon thy fading mansion spend?
Shall worms, inheritors of this excess,
Eat up thy charge? Is this thy body's end?
Then, soul, live thou upon thy servant's loss,
And let that pine to aggravate thy store;   10
Buy terms divine in selling hours of dross;
Within be fed, without be rich no more.
   So shalt thou feed on Death, that feeds on men,
   And Death once dead, there's no more dying then.

2 Spoiled by these] This edition (*conj.* Spence); My sinfull earth Q; Fool'd by those MALONE; Starv'd by the *conj.* Steevens in Malone; Hemmed with these *conj.* Furnivall; Gull'd by these SEYMOUR-SMITH; Feeding these VENDLER (*conj.* Sebastian Evans in Cambridge 1893); Seiged by these *conj.* This edition.

the moth nor canker corrupteth, and where thieves neither dig through, nor steal'.
12 **rich** gorgeous, richly attired
14 **And Death . . . then** Cf. two biblical passages included in the service for the Burial of the Dead: 1 Corinthians 15: 26: 'The last enemy that shall be destroyed, is death', and 15.54 'Death is swallowed up into victory'.

2 **longer nurseth** protracts (despite the expected sense 'helps to cure')

3 **ill** (a) disease; (b) evil

4 **uncertain** intermittent, difficult to please.

5 **prescriptions are not kept** professional recommendations are not followed

7 **desperate** two syllables

8 **Desire . . . except** that which my physician forbade me, Desire, is indeed deadly. Cf. Romans 8: 6: 'For the wisdom of the flesh is death: but the wisdom of the Spirit is life and peace'.

9 **Past cure . . . past care** Compare the proverb 'Past cure is past care' (Dent C921); here, though, Reason simply abdicates, leaving the poet sick beyond the power of medicine.

10 **frantic-mad** insanely active; as opposed to melancholy madness of sullen inactivity
evermore (a) continual; (b) continually increasing. Compare the proverb 'Desire has no rest' (Dent D211).

11 **discourse** my talk, conversation. Accented on the second syllable.

12 **At random . . . expressed** wandering insanely from the truth and ineffectually put

13 **bright** beautiful and of shining moral worth

147

My love is as a fever, longing still
For that which longer nurseth the disease,
Feeding on that which doth preserve the ill,
Th' uncertain sickly appetite to please.
My reason, the physician to my love,　　　　　　　　5
Angry that his prescriptions are not kept,
Hath left me, and I desperate now approve
Desire is death, which physic did except.
Past cure I am, now Reason is past care,
And, frantic-mad with evermore unrest,　　　　　　10
My thoughts and my discourse as madmen's are,
At random from the truth vainly expressed.
　　For I have sworn thee fair, and thought thee bright,
　　Who art as black as hell, as dark as night.

1 **O me!** The exclamation mark is Q's.
love Q does not capitalize, but 'Love' (Cupid the blind god) is fleetingly evoked throughout this poem on the fallibility of love's sight.

2 **have no . . . true sight** (a) do not represent what is actually there; (b) bear no relation to accurate vision. *Sight* is both what is seen (*OED* 1) and the 'sense or power of vision' (*OED* 9a).

4 **censures** 'To form or give a "censure" or opinion of; to estimate, judge of, pass judgement on, criticize, judge' (*OED* 1). In Renaissance faculty psychology the judgement assessed the images presented it by the sight and formed an opinion of what objects they represented. The sense 'criticize adversely' is probably not meant.
falsely both 'inaccurately' and 'in a way that betrays'

6 **What means the world** for what reason does everyone else

7–8 **If it be . . . men's** 'If it is not the case that my mistress is fair, then love clearly proves that the vision of someone who is in love is not as accurate as the vision of the world.' *Denote* usually means to point out or designate with an outward visible sign; hence its usage here to mean 'gives

public proof of'. Q punctuates 'If it be not, then loue doth well denote, | Loues eye is not so true as all mens: no', which prompts some editors to take 'no' as direct speech: 'Love's eye is not so true as all men's "no" '.

9 **true** (a) accurate; (b) faithful

10 **vexed** 'Of diseases, etc.: To afflict or distress physically; to affect with pain or suffering' (*OED* 2)
watching staying up late

11 **I** The first occurrence of the first-person pronoun brings out a subliminal pun on the falsity of the 'eye' and the internal divisions of the 'I'.

13 **love** Again 'Love' (Cupid the blind god) meets 'love' (the emotion) meets 'love' (the object of my affection).
with tears The primary sense is that love blurs the vision by making one cry, but since the addressee of the couplet is left uncertain there are other possibilities: if the mistress is addressed as 'love' (and the next line appears to turn on her), then her tears (of apparent repentance) could play their part in blinding the poet to what is really going on.

14 **thy foul faults** (a) your visible defects in beauty; (b) your disgusting vices

148

O me! What eyes hath love put in my head,
Which have no correspondence with true sight,
Or if they have, where is my judgement fled
That censures falsely what they see aright?
If that be fair whereon my false eyes dote   5
What means the world to say it is not so?
If it be not, then love doth well denote
Love's eye is not so true as all men's: no,
How can it? O, how can love's eye be true
That is so vexed with watching and with tears?   10
No marvel then though I mistake my view:
The sun itself sees not till heaven clears.
   O cunning love, with tears thou keep'st me blind,
   Lest eyes well-seeing thy foul faults should find.

8 men's: no] Q; men's₍ no DYCE 1857 (*conj*. Lettsom)

1 **O cruel** a traditional way of referring to the beloved in sonnet sequences, used here for the first time by Shakespeare. It brings to a climax the increasingly claustrophobic use of the conventional language of sonnet sequences. *Cruel* is used eight times in the sequence and five of those usages occur after *126*. The friend is never called *cruel* (except in *1*.8 where he is urged not to be cruel to himself), although time and age are (*60*.14, *63*.10). In the later part of the sequence cruelty is gradually focused on the mistress: first there is the general 'those whose beauties make them cruel' (*131*.2), then the mistress's eye is called cruel (*133*.5), then she is urged to 'be wise as thou art cruel' in *140*.1.

2 **with thee partake** 'To take part *with* a person, take sides', *OED*, citing this instance alone. Presumably it is the audible similarity of the word to 'part take' which prompts the usage. Elsewhere Shakespeare sometimes uses the word of intimate secret exchanges, as in 'thy bosom shall partake | The secrets of my heart', *Caesar* 2.1.304–5, and 'to your secrecy our mind partakes | Her private actions', *Pericles* Scene 1. 194–5. This might suggest a secondary sense 'When I am intimately close to you against my own interests'.

4 **myself, all tyrant for thy sake** Punctuation follows Q, making the poet become a surrogate tyrant for his mistress's sake. Some editors prefer to add a comma after 'all tyrant', making it a simple vocative. This is possible; but Q's compositors more usually omit a comma *before* a subordinate clause or a vocative rather than after it.

7 **lour'st** frown
spend vent (revenge is presented as a passion like anger). *Spend* can mean 'ejaculate' ('Spending his manly marrow in her arms', *All's Well* 2.3.278): its presence here at the end of the line and in close company with the reflexive *upon myself* and *moan* gives a strong undercurrent of self-mockery: 'I come even when you glare at me'.

9–12 **What merit . . . eyes?** 'What quality do I possess which is proud enough not to want to serve you? All my best qualities lose themselves in abject worship even of your very faults, ordered to do so by the proud glance of your eye.' This extreme of abjection is hard not to take with at least a trace of irony, especially since the sole quality attributed to the mistress is a *defect* (stressed on the second syllable).

13 **thy mind** what you think

14 **Those that . . . blind** You love those who can see (and taken in conjunction with the previous poem this might encompass 'see your faults'); I am not one of those, since I am blinded to your faults by my love. The general sense is that the mistress likes those who see her for what she is, and hates those who are blindly besotted with her.

149

Canst thou, O cruel, say I love thee not
When I against myself with thee partake?
Do I not think on thee when I forgot
Am of myself, all tyrant for thy sake?
Who hateth thee that I do call my friend?   5
On whom frown'st thou that I do fawn upon?
Nay, if thou lour'st on me do I not spend
Revenge upon myself with present moan?
What merit do I in myself respect
That is so proud thy service to despise,   10
When all my best doth worship thy defect,
Commanded by the motion of thine eyes?
    But, love, hate on, for now I know thy mind:
    Those that can see, thou lov'st, and I am blind.

14 see, thou lov'st,] This edition; see, thou lov'st, Q

1 **power . . . powerful** authority . . . strong; pronounced as Q spells them, 'powre' and 'powrefull' respectively.

2 **With insufficiency** through imperfection. *Insufficiency* is not elsewhere used by Shakespeare so it is hard to judge how negatively to take it.

3 **give the lie to** contradict; call a liar

4 **And swear . . . day** Because the mistress is dark, brightness ceases to be an ornament of beauty. Compare *28*.9–10.

5 **becoming of things ill** ability to make ugly (or wicked) things beautiful. Cf. Enobarbus on Cleopatra: 'vilest things | Become themselves in her', *Antony* 2.2.244–5.

6 **refuse of thy deeds** (a) in the meanest, least regarded of your actions (implying that there are other, nobler actions); (b) in the dregs that are your actions (implying that all her actions are such). *Refuse* as a noun, like *insufficiency*, is not elsewhere used by Shakespeare. The following line, with its mention of *warrantise of skill* (guarantee of good workmanship), suggests that *refuse* may correspond to 'seconds', or items of manufacture of poor quality which have been rejected for sale at full price. That sense appears to have been current in the seventeenth-century cloth industry.

11, 12 **abhor** a play on 'whore' or 'turn into a whore' seems likely, as in the name 'Abhorson' (the executioner and son of a whore in *Measure* and in Desdemona's 'I cannot say "whore". | It does abhor me now I speak the word', *Othello* 4.2.165–6. This sense may be picked out by *with others* (by sleeping with others) in the next line.

13–14 **If . . . thee** 'The surface meaning is that in loving even the meanest in her his generosity deserves the return of her love for him; but beneath this there may well lie the harsh innuendo, playing on two senses of "worthy", that in loving someone so foul he shows himself a suitable person (because foul enough) to be loved by the foul one herself' (Ingram and Redpath).

150

O, from what power hast thou this powerful might
With insufficiency my heart to sway,
To make me give the lie to my true sight,
And swear that brightness doth not grace the day?
Whence hast thou this becoming of things ill,   5
That in the very refuse of thy deeds
There is such strength and warrantize of skill
That in my mind thy worst all best exceeds?
Who taught thee how to make me love thee more,
The more I hear and see just cause of hate?   10
O, though I love what others do abhor,
With others thou shouldst not abhor my state.
    If thy unworthiness raised love in me,
    More worthy I to be beloved of thee.

1-2 Love . . . love again plays on the senses 'Cupid' (represented as a child) and 'the emotion of love'.

1, 2 conscience a sense of right and wrong. The French *con* or 'cunt' might be heard in the word, giving a quibble on 'carnal knowledge'. See Partridge, 84-5.

3 urge not my amiss do not charge me with wickedness

4 Lest guilty . . . prove in case you prove yourself to be guilty of the same crimes as me. The next line introduces a sophistical alternative, which seeks to blame the mistress for the poet's lust. Q reads 'Least', which might give its readers a sense that the poet is seeking to exculpate the *gentle cheater*.

5-6 For . . . treason 'We two lovers are one: so when you betray me you are committing a double crime: first, you disloyally betray my faults to the world; secondly you commit treason against our joint state. You, the irrational part, are causing a rebellion against the reason, and are prompting the flesh to become uncontrollable.' *Betraying* may also mean 'when you are unfaithful to me with other men'.

8 stays no farther reason waits for no further excuse. The body, which has no conscience, is told by the soul that it has been victorious in love; the body carnally assumes that this means it should leap into sexual activity.

9 rising at thy name The penis is like a soldier who springs to attention at the mention of the mistress's name.

9 point out thee as a soldier chooses a particular opponent as his prize in battle. A 'point' or tip of the sword could mean the end of the penis (as in *L.L.L.* 5.2.276-7: 'Dumaine was at my service, and his sword: "*Non point*," quoth I'); so, 'fits you out with an erect prick'.

10 pride 'insurgent penis' (Partridge). For other usages which exploit this sexual sense, see 25.7.

11 drudge a contemptible slave of a lover

12 To stand . . . side 'to stand firm like an eager soldier and fight your cause, then to die at your side'. The primary sense is harder to paraphrase than the innuendo: *stand* is also used to mean 'have an erection' in the backchat between Speed and Lancelot in *Two Gentlemen* 2.5.20-4: 'when it stands well with him it stands well with her . . . My staff understands me.' *Fall* describes post-coital detumescence, and between standing and falling the mistress's loyal soldier of love 'dies', or has an orgasm.

13-14 No want . . . fall (a) so do not think that it is lack of a sense of duty that makes me call her 'love', since I, like a good soldier, die for her daily; (b) so it is not because I am a virgin who does not know about cunts that I call her 'love' (for me the word does not mean what it means to soppy innocents), for whose sake I regularly stiffen and detumesce

151

Love is too young to know what conscience is,
Yet who knows not conscience is born of love?
Then, gentle cheater, urge not my amiss,
Lest guilty of my faults thy sweet self prove.
For thou betraying me, I do betray   5
My nobler part to my gross body's treason.
My soul doth tell my body that he may
Triumph in love; flesh stays no farther reason,
But, rising at thy name, doth point out thee
As his triumphant prize. Proud of this pride,   10
He is contented thy poor drudge to be,
To stand in thy affairs, fall by thy side.
   No want of conscience hold it that I call
   Her 'love', for whose dear love I rise and fall.

4 Lest] Q (Least)   14 'love'] DYCE 1857; ‸loue,‸ Q

2 **twice forsworn . . . swearing** you break two vows in swearing love to me. What the two vows are has elicited much debate. The traditional explanation is a wedding vow and a vow of love made to the friend. The most probable explanation is the two kinds of vow described in the next two lines.

3–4 **In act . . . bearing** 'You broke your wedding vows by adultery, and you tore up your more recent commitment to a lover by swearing to hate where you formerly loved.' These are the two acts of being forsworn referred to in ll. 1–2. Q punctuates 'In act thy bed-vow broake and new faith torne, | In vowing new hate after new loue bearing'. The comma at the end of l. 3 would allow that the two breaches of faith are specified in each of the two lines: 'You are forsworn once in action by breaking your wedding vows and in breaking faith, and you are forsworn again in vowing, since you bear new hate after a recent love'. This is superficially tidy since it divides the two infidelities between the two lines, but does not make good sense: tearing up new faith could at a stretch be seen as an *act*, but not really as action which is equivalent to breaking a wedding vow by adultery; similarly it is hard to see how bearing hate can really be a breach in vowing. Hence the modification in Q's punctuation here.

3 **new faith torn** The image is of a contract being torn apart.

4 **new love bearing** (a) after experience of new love, after taking on a new lover; (b) after bearing the weight of a new lover (in bed). For this sense of *bear* see *Shrew* 2.1.200–1: '*Petruccio*: Women are made to bear, and so are you. *Katherine*: No such jade as you, if me you mean.'

5–6 Compare the proverb 'He finds fault with others and does worse himself' (Dent F107).

6 **perjured** forsworn

7 **but to misuse thee** 'To speak falsely of, to misrepresent' (*OED* 5, citing this passage alone); other senses of *misuse* are 'to maltreat' (*OED* 2); 'to violate or ravish' (*OED* 1b); 'To speak evil of; to abuse with words; to revile, deride' (*OED* 4); 'To deceive, delude' (*OED* 6). That is, the poet has made a score of vows that she is honest; since she is not true to him, he is forsworn in his oaths.

8 **All . . . lost** (a) all the simple faith that I had in you has left me; (b) all my capacity for honesty and truth to my word has vanished into you

9 **For I . . . kindness** The kind of oaths sworn have shifted from vows exchanged between lovers to declarations on oath as to the character of a person; hence *deep* on its first occurrence means 'utterly binding', almost 'religious'. On its second occurrence it means 'deep-seated' and has an edge of irony.

11 **enlighten** (a) give you light; (b) render you less dark (physically and morally) **gave eyes to blindness** sacrificed my eyes to the blind (including presumably Cupid); made myself blind.

12 **made them . . . see** The eyes become coerced witnesses, forced to commit perjury. The perjuries alluded to in the poem hitherto at least have the virtue of being voluntary.

14 **more perjured eye** quibbles on 'eye' and 'I'. The poet concludes that the eye has committed the worst perjury of all, but the pun confesses his complicity.

152

In loving thee thou know'st I am forsworn,
But thou art twice forsworn, to me love swearing:
In act thy bed-vow broke, and new faith torn
In vowing new hate after new love bearing.
But why of two oaths' breach do I accuse thee,   5
When I break twenty? I am perjured most,
For all my vows are oaths but to misuse thee,
And all my honest faith in thee is lost.
For I have sworn deep oaths of thy deep kindness,
Oaths of thy love, thy truth, thy constancy,   10
And to enlighten thee gave eyes to blindness,
Or made them swear against the thing they see.
  For I have sworn thee fair: more perjured eye,
  To swear against the truth so foul a lie.

13 eye] Q; I SEWELL   14 so] BENSON; fo Q

The relationship of 153 and 154 to the rest of the sequence is loose. Aetiological tales about the origins of wells are not unusual in sonnet sequences (in Giles Fletcher's *Licia* 27.10–12 the mistress makes a well into a source of health by bathing in it: 'She touched the water, and it burnt with love, | Now by her means, it purchased hath that bliss | Which all diseases quickly can remove'). A significant number of other sonnet sequences end with a similar shift in mood and genre: *Delia* (1592) bridges the gap between its sonnets and the *Complaint of Rosamond* by an Ode; Barnfield's *Cynthia* (1595) has an anacreontic ode between its sonnets and its concluding tale of Cassandra. Spenser's *Amoretti* (1595) are followed by a short group of poems known as 'Anacreontics' which precede the triumphs of the 'Epithalamion'. Sonnets 153 and 154 also follow ultimately a Greek form, the lines by Marianus Scholasticus in the Greek Anthology: 'Beneath these plane trees, detained by gentle slumber, Love slept, having put his torch in the care of the Nymphs; but the Nymphs said to one another "Why wait? Would that together with this we could quench the fire in the hearts of men." But the torch set fire even to the water, and with hot water thenceforth the Love-Nymphs fill the bath.' See James Hutton, 'Analogues of Shakespeare's Sonnets 153–4', *Modern Philology* 38 (1941), 385–403.

1 **brand** firebrand, or flaming torch, one of Cupid's traditional attributes. A Cupid bearing a firebrand is sometimes used to represent Platonic Love, who, in Achilles Bochius, *Symbolicarum quaestionem de universo genere* (Bologna, 1574), is presented as driving away the blind Cupid of corporeal passion. See Erwin Panofsky, *Studies in Iconology*, 2nd edn. (New York, 1962), 128. There may also be phallic overtones here.

2 **maid of Dian's** virginal attendant of the goddess Diana (goddess of chastity)
advantage 'a favourable occasion, an opportunity, a "chance" ' (*OED* 4)

3 **his** functions as both a masculine and neuter pronoun, agreeing with both Cupid and his *brand*.

4 **of that ground** in that vicinity

7 **grew** became. It was transformed into a hot bath of the kind used in the treatment of venereal diseases, as well as other ailments.
prove find by experience to be

8 **sovereign cure** a set phrase, 'Of remedies, etc.: Efficacious or potent in a superlative degree' (*OED* 3)

9 **new fired** relit

10 **The boy for trial needs would touch** Cupid, to test its potency, felt the need to touch. *Touch* can carry the sense 'infect' (Schmidt, 11b), as in *K. John* 5.7.1–2: 'The life of all his blood | Is touched corruptibly'.

11 **the help of bath** A few editors have imagined the poet setting off with his diseases to Bath to take the waters, ignoring the fact that sweating tubs must have been available in London.

12 **distempered** diseased (by the disruption to the temper of the four humours in the body)

153

Cupid laid by his brand and fell asleep.
A maid of Dian's this advantage found,
And his love-kindling fire did quickly steep
In a cold valley-fountain of that ground,
Which borrowed from this holy fire of love   5
A dateless lively heat, still to endure,
And grew a seething bath, which yet men prove
Against strange maladies a sovereign cure.
But at my mistress' eye love's brand new fired,
The boy for trial needs would touch my breast.   10
I, sick withal, the help of bath desired,
And thither hied, a sad distempered guest,
 But found no cure; the bath for my help lies
 Where Cupid got new fire: my mistress' eyes.

8 strange] Q (strang); strong TUCKER (*conj.* Tyler) 14 eyes] BENSON; eye Q

1 **Love-god** Cupid

5 **votary** one bound by vows (here by chastity). Not elsewhere used by Shakespeare of a female, for which he prefers 'votaress'.

6 **legions** a great number

7 **general of hot desire** the commander in chief of passion, i.e. Cupid

9 **quenchèd** put out, extinguished

11 **Growing** becoming

12 **thrall** 'One who is in bondage to a lord or master; a villein, serf, bondman, slave' (*OED* 1); a standard term for the abject sonneteer

13 **this by that I prove** I show the following maxim to be true as a result of my experience

14 **Love's fire . . . love** 'Cupid's brand can heat up water, but the waters to which I resorted cannot cool my love' (nor can they perhaps cure his feverish disease). The dainty classicism and sexually experienced bitterness of this poem are qualified by its concluding allusion to Song of Solomon 8: 6–7: 'for love is as strong as death: jealousy is cruel as the grave: the coals thereof are fiery coals, and a vehement flame. Much water cannot quench love, neither can the floods drown it: if a man should give all the substance of his house for love, they would greatly contemn it.'

154

The little Love-god lying once asleep
Laid by his side his heart-inflaming brand,
Whilst many nymphs, that vowed chaste life to keep,
Came tripping by; but in her maiden hand
The fairest votary took up that fire,   5
Which many legions of true hearts had warmed.
And so the general of hot desire
Was, sleeping, by a virgin hand disarmed.
This brand she quenchèd in a cool well by,
Which from love's fire took heat perpetual,   10
Growing a bath and healthful remedy
For men diseased; but I, my mistress' thrall,
    Came there for cure, and this by that I prove:
    Love's fire heats water; water cools not love.

'Spes Altera' (Manuscript version of 2).
The variants between this and the text in
Q may indicate that this is an early ver-
sion. See Mary Hobbs, 'Shakespeare's
Sonnet 2: "A Sugred Sonnet"?', *NQ* 224
(1979), 112–13 and Gary Taylor, 'Some
Manuscripts of Shakespeare's Sonnets',
Bulletin of the John Rylands Library 68
(1985–6), 210–46, and Introduction, pp.
106–7. It is closer to the source text in
Wilson: *pretty* in l. 10 and *new born* in l. 13
may echo Wilson, 56, 'you shall have a
pretty little boy, running up and down
your house, such a one as shall express
your look, and your wife's look . . . by
whom you shall seem to be new born'.
This is the strongest argument that
the poem reflects an early draft, but nei-
ther of those readings are found in BL3,
nor in BL4 from which it was transcribed.
As the late Jeremy Maule showed in
unpublished research, the majority of the
MS witnesses derive from Westminster
Abbey MS 41 (control text here). There
are several features which suggest that
the process of scribal transmission flat-
tened the text (e.g. *rotten* for Q's 'tattered',
'all-eaten truth' for 'all-eating shame').
The repetition of *account* in ll. 11 and 3
may reflect a transcriber's memory that
the poem contained financial language. It
may be that the variants from Q derive
from one scribally modified exemplar
which was doing the rounds of Christ
Church, Oxford, with which a number of
the MSS have an association. If so this
poem is an illustration of how the Sonnets
were received rather than how they
originated.

TITLE 'Spes Altera' 'another hope'. The
phrase alludes to Aeneas's son Ascanius
(*Aen.* 12.168), who is described as
'another hope for Rome'. Taylor claims it
is 'Shakespearean' ('Some Manuscripts',
236), but Shakespeare is otherwise not
known to have given any lyric poem a
title. Several poems in Benson's 1640 edi-
tion are given similar non-authorial Latin
titles (Sonnet 62 is entitled 'Sat fuisse',
and 61 'Patiens Armatus').

Manuscript Version

[2]

Spes Altera

When forty winters shall besiege thy brow
And trench deep furrows in that lovely field,
Thy youth's fair liv'ry so accounted now
Shall be like rotten weeds of no worth held.
Then, being asked where all thy beauty lies,   5
Where all the lustre of thy youthful days,
To say 'within these hollow sunken eyes'
Were an all-eaten truth, and worthless praise.
O how much better were thy beauty's use
If thou couldst say 'This pretty child of mine   10
Saves my account and makes my old excuse',
Making his beauty by succession thine.
    This were to be new born when thou art old,
    And see thy blood warm when thou feel'st it cold.

Title] BL1, BL3, BL4; Spes Altera A song FOL9; To one y^t would dye a Mayd BL5, BL6, FOL6, W, YALE2; A Lover to his Mistres NOTT.; The Benefitt of Mariage RO 2
1 forty] W, Q; threescore BL1; 40[?] BL5 winters] W; yeares RO 2 2 trench deep furrows] digge deep trenches Q trench] W; drench RO 2 field] W; cheeke BL3, BL4 3 youth's] W; youth BL6 fair] W; proud Q; fairer RO 2 liv'ry] W; field RO 2 accounted] gaz'd on Q; esteemed NOTT. 4 Shall be like rotten weeds] W; Will be a totter'd weed Q; like] W; like like BL6 weeds] W; cloaths FOL6 no] W; small Q 5 being asked] W etc.; if we aske BL3, BL4; askt RO 2 thy] W etc.; this BL4 6 Where] W, Q; Where's BL1, BL3, BL4, FOL9, NOTT. the] W, Q; that BL1 lustre] W; treasure Q youthful] W; lusty Q 7 these hollow sunken] W; thine owne deepe sunken Q these] W; those YALE2; omitted BL5 8 all-eaten truth] W all-eating shame Q; all beaten truth FOL6 worthless] W; thriftless Q praise] W etc.; pleasure BL6 9 O how much better were] W; How much more praise deseru'd Q O] W; omitted BL6 much] W; far YALE2; omitted B5 beauty's] W; beautious YALE2 10 say] W; answer Q pretty] W; faire Q; little BL3, BL4 11 Saves my account] W; Shall sum my count Q; Saud my account YALE2 my] W; mine NOTT. makes my old] W; make my old Q; makes me old BL5; makes no old FOL6; yeilds mee an NOTT.; makes the old RO 2; makes not old YALE2 12 Making] W; Prooving Q 13 new born] W; new made Q; made young BL3, BL4

A Lover's Complaint

A Lover's Complaint

From off a hill whose concave womb reworded
A plaintful story from a sist'ring vale,
My spirits t' attend this double voice accorded,
And down I laid to list the sad-tuned tale;
Ere long espied a fickle maid full pale,   5
Tearing of papers, breaking rings a-twain,
Storming her world with sorrow's wind and rain.

7 sorrow's] GILDON 1714; sorrowes, Q

1 **concave womb** cave or other hollow in the hill. The opening of the poem, with its discontented narrator and its riverside setting, is distinctively the locale of the complaint mode. There are frequent echoes of Spenser's *Ruins of Time* (1591) and of his *Prothalamion* (1596), on which see MacDonald P. Jackson, 'Echoes of Spenser's *Prothalamion* as Evidence Against an Early Date for Shakespeare's *A Lover's Complaint*', NQ 235 (1990), 180–2. The inversion of Spenser's festive riverside scene, which anticipates the marriage of the Earl of Worcester's two daughters, is as notable as the verbal echoes: 'There, in a meadow, by the river's side, | A flock of lovely nymphs I chauncèd to espy, | All lovely daughters of the Flood thereby, | With goodly greenish locks all loose untied, | As each had been a bride, | And each one had a little wicker basket, | Made of fine twigs entraylèd curiously', ll. 19–25.
reworded re-echoed (the only citation for OED 2; the word is used in the sense 'to repeat' in *Hamlet* 3.4.134)

2 **plaintful** signals the genre of the poem. A 'plaint' could be a plangent lament, or suggest that the complainer had been wronged in law. The adjective occurs nowhere else in Shakespeare.

3 **spirits** is monosyllabic.
attend listen to; also wait upon
accorded agreed, perhaps with a suggestion that the spirits of the poet are in harmony with that of the complainer. OED s.v. 'accorded' ppl. a. cites Sidney's *Defence of Poesie*: 'The Lyric, who with his tuned Lyre, and well accorded voice, giveth praise, the reward of virtue, to virtuous acts'. This sense is reinforced by *sad-tuned* in l. 4.

4 **laid to list** lay down to listen to. Both verbs had an archaic flavour by 1609.

5 **fickle** the senses offered by OED seem at first unhelpful ('False, deceitful, treacherous'; 'Changeable, changeful, inconstant, uncertain, unreliable'), and have led editors to gloss as 'moody' or 'fitful'. Given that the maid is destroying potent symbols of sexual fidelity—rings and papers—and given that neither the reader nor the narrator knows anything of her history at this point, the standard Shakespearian sense 'inconstant' is appropriate, although it implies a judgement which awaits later qualification.

6 **a-twain** in two. The only other usage in Shakespeare also concerns the violation of a sacred bond: Kent says 'Such smiling rogues as these, | Like rats, oft bite the holy cords a-twain | Which are too intrince t' unloose', *Lear* (Folio) 2.2.73–5. On a similar use of *twain* see Sonnet 36.1 n.

7 **Storming . . . rain** Sighs and tears become elemental storms which assault the maid, as *Lear* (Quarto), Scene 8.9–10: he 'Strives in his little world of man to outstorm | The to-and-fro-conflicting wind and rain.'

Upon her head a plaited hive of straw,
Which fortified her visage from the sun,
Whereon the thought might think sometime it saw   10
The carcass of a beauty spent and done:
Time had not scythèd all that youth begun,
Nor youth all quit, but, spite of heaven's fell rage,
Some beauty peeped through lattice of seared age.

Oft did she heave her napkin to her eyne,   15
Which on it had conceited characters,
Laund'ring the silken figures in the brine
That seasoned woe had pelleted in tears,
And often reading what contents it bears;
As often shrieking undistinguished woe   20
In clamours of all size both high and low.

14 lattice] Q (lettice)

8 **plaited hive** woven straw hat (*OED* s.v. 'hive' 5a, first cited usage). Elizabethan beehives were often conical and made of straw. The straw hat suggests a pastoral milieu.

9 **fortified** protected

10 **the thought might think** The doubling has a parallel in *Merchant* 1.1.36–7: 'Shall I have the thought | To think on this?' *Thought* is used in *OED* sense 4c, 'conception, imagination, fancy', as in *Lucrece* l. 288.

11 **spent and done** extinguished and finished. On the sexual sense of *spent*, see Sonnet 4.1 n.

12 **Time ... begun** (a) Time had not destroyed all of that newly beginning youth; (b) Time had not destroyed everything which youth had initiated.

13 **Nor youth all quit** nor had youth entirely gone
heaven's is monosyllabic.
fell rage destructive anger

14 **Some beauty ... age** Lattice windows are criss-crossed with lead: some remnant of youth is visible through the wrinkles as a face is just visible through a lattice window. Cf. Sonnet 3.11 n.

15 **napkin** handkerchief
eyne eyes (archaic by 1600)

16 **conceited characters** intricately embroi-

dered images (the *silken figures* of the next line), which might have a hidden significance

17 **Laund'ring** washing with tears. This is the first citation of the verb in *OED*.
the brine i.e. her salt tears. Cf. *All's Well* 1.1.45–6, where tears are 'the best brine a maiden can season her praise in'.

18 **seasoned** (a) matured through time; (b) salted. Compare *Lucrece* l. 796.
pelleted formed into bullet-like spheres (although a *pellet* could also be a meatball, incongruously evoked by some editors here). The former is closer to *Antony* 3.13.168, in which Cleopatra talks of a 'pelleted storm'.

19 **often reading ... bears** The maid repeatedly deciphers the handkerchief's *conceited characters* which presumably recall her lover. *Contents* is stressed on the second syllable.

20 **undistinguished** confused, inarticulate

21 **all size both high and low** (a) both loud and soft; (b) both high- and low-pitched. There may also be a suggestion that the complaints are in both a high and a lower idiom, as *size* can refer to social standing; cf. 'He hath songs for man or woman, of all sizes', *Winter's Tale* 4.4.192.

Sometimes her levelled eyes their carriage ride,
As they did batt'ry to the spheres intend;
Sometime diverted their poor balls are tied
To th' orbèd earth; sometimes they do extend   25
Their view right on; anon their gazes lend
To every place at once and nowhere fixed,
The mind and sight distractedly commixed.

Her hair, nor loose nor tied in formal plait,
Proclaimed in her a careless hand of pride;   30
For some, untucked, descended her sheavèd hat,
Hanging her pale and pinèd cheek beside;
Some in her threaden fillet still did bide,
And true to bondage would not break from thence,
Though slackly braided in loose negligence.   35

A thousand favours from a maund she drew,
Of amber crystal and of beaded jet,
Which one by one she in a river threw,
Upon whose weeping margin she was set,
Like usury applying wet to wet,   40

37 beaded] Q (bedded)

22 **levelled eyes . . . ride** Her eyes are aimed like a cannon which rests on a *carriage* or 'wheeled support on which a piece of ordnance is mounted' (*OED* 27). (*Carriage* is not used to refer to a wheeled vehicle made specifically to carry people before the eighteenth century.)
23 **batt'ry to the spheres** a military assault on the unassailable (because immutable) spheres in which the planets were believed to be housed
24 **balls** (a) cannon-balls; (b) eyeballs
28 **The mind . . . commixed** What is seen and what is imagined blend madly together. Cf. Sonnets *114* and *118*. *Distractedly* is used twice by Shakespeare of those who are mad with love, as when Viola relates how Olivia 'did speak in starts, distractedly', *Twelfth Night* 2.2.21.
29 **plait** This is the only occurrence in Shakespeare of the noun.
30 **careless . . . pride** 'a hand which had no care for pride'; Kerrigan notes that ' "a hand whose pride showed itself in carelessness" is not eclipsed'.

31 **descended** is not otherwise recorded in the sense 'came down below'.
sheaved is the only citation given in *OED* for sense 2, 'made of straw' (i.e. woven like a sheaf of straw).
32 **pinèd** thin with pining
33 **fillet** hair ribbon
34 **true to bondage** Some of the hair breaks out rebelliously; the rest remains dutifully in place.
36 **favours** gifts from a lover (often ribbons or gloves)
maund 'A wicker or other woven basket having a handle or handles' (*OED* 1). They could be given as love-tokens, as in Edward Wilkinson's *Thameseidos* (1600), 1.33–44, in which the Thames carries an elaborately ornamented maund which was originally a love gift from the Ocean to the nymph Doris.
37 **beaded jet** jet beads
39 **weeping** The epithet is transferred from her to the river.
40 **Like usury** The tears augment the already copious streams of the river as interest adds richly to abundant capital.

Or monarch's hands that lets not bounty fall
Where want cries 'some', but where excess begs all.

Of folded schedules had she many a one,
Which she perused, sighed, tore, and gave the flood,
Cracked many a ring of poesied gold and bone,   45
Bidding them find their sepulchres in mud;
Found yet more letters sadly penned in blood,
With sleided silk feat and affectedly
Enswathed and sealed to curious secrecy.

These often bathed she in her fluxive eyes,   50
And often kissed, and often gave to tear,
Cried 'O false blood, thou register of lies,
What unapprovèd witness dost thou bear!
Ink would have seemed more black and damnèd here!'

41 monarch's] Q (Monarches); monarchs' MALONE (*conj.* Capell) 42 'some'] MALONE (*italic*); ˏsomeˏ Q 47 more] Q (mo) 51 gave to tear] Q; gave a tear GILDON; 'gan to tear MALONE

41–2 **Or . . . all** like a rich king who will not give any charity where a needy person cries out for just a little, but who gives instead to one who is already rich, and who demands everything
43 **folded schedules** folded pieces of paper containing writing, as in *Lucrece* l. 1312; presumably here love-letters (*OED* 1), also often used in the seventeenth century of additions to legal documents, such as codicils to wills (*OED* 2)
45 **Cracked many a ring** as in l. 6.
poesied gold and bone The rings, made of gold and ivory, are engraved (like many lovers' rings in the period) with 'poesies' or mottoes.
48 **sleided silk** silk which has been separated into threads. *Sleided* is an unusual variant form of 'sleaved', meaning 'To divide (silk) by separation into filaments'. It is otherwise used by Shakespeare only in the archaizing prologue, *Pericles* Scene 15.21: 'Be 't when they weaved the sleided silk'.
feat becomingly, elegantly (archaic by 1600)
affectedly has a wide range of near-contradictory senses: 'with true intent; intentionally, sincerely, earnestly' (*OED* 1); 'affectionately, lovingly' (*OED* 2); 'With affectation or studied art; artifi-

cially, fancifully. (Opposed to simply or naturally.)' (*OED* 3). Senses 1 and 2 are found in the work of seventeenth-century dramatists, and 'affected' is usually used by Shakespeare to mean 'in love with', but sense 3 is also in play.
49 **Enswathed . . . secrecy** wrapped tightly up and sealed into a state of ingeniously achieved secrecy. This is the first cited usage of *enswathed*.
50 **fluxive** flowing (with tears). The word, of which this is the first cited usage, can also mean 'mutable'.
51 **gave to tear** made show of tearing. Most editors adopt Malone's emendation to ''gan' (began to) on the grounds that 'gave to' is not otherwise found in this sense in Shakespeare. Some interpret Q's 'teare' as an elliptical form of the verb 'to weep'.
52 **register** record. The word has a legal flavour, which is reinforced by *witness*.
53 **unapprovèd** 'Not demonstrated; unproved' (first citation for *OED* 2)
54 **Ink . . . here** The papers are signed in blood, but black ink would have been a more suitably sinister medium. Contracts with the Devil were signed with blood, so the letters could be more diabolical than the woman recognizes.

This said, in top of rage the lines she rents,   55
Big discontent so breaking their contents.

A reverend man that grazed his cattle nigh,
Sometime a blusterer that the ruffle knew
Of court, of city, and had let go by
The swiftest hours observèd as they flew,   60
Towards this afflicted fancy fastly drew,
And, privileged by age, desires to know
In brief the grounds and motives of her woe.

So slides he down upon his grainèd bat,
And comely distant sits he by her side,   65
When he again desires her, being sat,
Her grievance with his hearing to divide,
If that from him there may be aught applied
Which may her suffering ecstasy assuage,
'Tis promised in the charity of age.   70

61 fastly] Q; softly *conj.* Maxwell

55 **top of rage** in the height of anger
  rents rends
56 **Big . . . contents** Her anger destroys what
  the papers contain. *Contents* is accented
  on the second syllable.
58 **Sometime a blusterer** formerly a braggart
  (first cited usage)
  ruffle 'Ostentatious bustle or display'
  (*OED* 3; first recorded usage in this sense)
59–60 **had let go by . . . flew** who had allowed
  the rapidly passing days of youth to slip
  away, but who had drawn instruction
  from them (*observèd*). The reverend man is
  an example of a figure, popular in the
  period 1590–1610, who has withdrawn
  from court life in order to retreat into a life
  of philosophical contemplation. See 'His
  golden locks Time hath to silver turned',
  in which the Queen's former champion
  Sir Henry Lee bids farewell to court life
  and turns to 'feed on prayers', which are
  Age's alms', in John Dowland, *First Book
  of Songs or Airs* (1597), printed in E. H.
  Fellowes, ed., *English Madrigal Verse
  1588–1632*, 3rd edn. (Oxford, 1967),
  464–5.
61 **this afflicted fancy** i.e. the woman, who is
  distressed by love-sickness
  fastly closely; perhaps also 'rapidly' (*OED*
  3), and also suggesting 'steadfastly; with
  confidence' (*OED* 2)

62 **privileged** given the right to speak with-
  out fear of rebuke. Cf. Kent's 'anger hath
  a privilege', *King Lear* (Folio) 2.2.70.
63 **the grounds and motives of her woe** the
  causes and emotional sources
64 **slides he . . . bat** The old man uses his staff
  (*grainèd bat*) to move to join the woman.
  Kerrigan suggests that *slides* is used in the
  sense 'To pass from one place or point to
  another with a smooth and continuous
  movement' (*OED* 1a), but 'down upon'
  suggests that he may, as old men do, slide
  his hands down his stick in order to sit.
  Grainèd may mean that the grain of the
  wood is visible, or it may be the dialect
  word, as *OED* has it (*ppl. a.* 3), meaning
  'Having tines or prongs; forked'. Rustic
  long staffs are often made with a forked
  cleft at the top to help the thumb to grip
  it. *Bat* is used of a shepherd's stick by
  Spenser in *Virgil's Gnat* l. 154, and so rein-
  forces the pastoral and Spenserian mood
  of the opening.
65 **comely distant** at a decent distance
67 **Her grievance . . . divide** to share her sor-
  row with him, and perhaps to diminish it
  by sharing
68 **applied** administered (like a medicine)
69 **suffering ecstasy** frenzy of misery. *Ecstasy*
  means being beside oneself, here with
  misery.

'Father,' she says, 'Though in me you behold
The injury of many a blasting hour,
Let it not tell your judgement I am old:
Not age, but sorrow over me hath power.
I might as yet have been a spreading flower,   75
Fresh to myself, if I had self-applied
Love to myself, and to no love beside.

'But woe is me, too early I attended
A youthful suit—it was to gain my grace;
O one by nature's outwards so commended   80
That maidens' eyes stuck over all his face.
Love lacked a dwelling and made him her place,
And when in his fair parts she did abide
She was new lodged and newly deified.

'His browny locks did hang in crookèd curls,   85
And every light occasion of the wind
Upon his lips their silken parcels hurls.
What's sweet to do, to do will aptly find:

79 suit—it] *marked as a parenthesis by* MALONE; ~ ‸ ~ Q   80 O one] Q; Of one MALONE (*conj.*
Tyrwhitt)   88 will] Q; we'll *conj.* Delius

71 **Father** is used as a respectful form of address, with, as Kerrigan suggests, confessional overtones.
72 **injury** the wrongful hurts inflicted by **blasting** 'blighting, striking with baleful effect' and also, interestingly given the damage suffered by the woman's reputation, 'defaming' (*OED* 1)
75 **spreading** in luxuriant full growth
76–7 **Fresh . . . beside** echoes Sonnet 94.9–10, as well as the narcissism of the young man in Sonnet 3. These arguments are transformed when echoed by a violated woman: the young man's wish to remain sweet only for his own benefit becomes a counsel of prudence.
79 **it was to gain my grace** The aim of the suit was to win her favour, with also an anticipatory sense 'it was in the future to win my favour'.
80 **O** is emended by some editors to 'Of'. Q's exclamation is timely, however: as the woman first mentions the youth she breaks off her syntax.
    nature's outwards external appearance bestowed by nature

80 **so commended** His appearance is like a letter of recommendation which guarantees his character.
81 **That maidens' . . . face** 'Stick' in this period can mean 'to linger over' (*OED* 6c) or 'to remain in one place' (*OED* 6). Shakespeare talks of eyes 'sticking' to their objects usually in contexts which suggest sycophantic adoration, e.g. 'O place and greatness, millions of false eyes | Are stuck upon thee', *Measure* 4.1.58–9, and 'The mouths, the tongues, the eyes and hearts of men | . . . That numberless upon me stuck, as leaves | Do on the oak', *Timon* 4.3.262–5.
82 **Love** Venus
    dwelling permanent place of abode. Compare *Venus* ll. 241–6.
85 **browny** 'inclining to brown' (*OED*). Not otherwise used by Shakespeare.
86 **every light occasion** on every chance movement. *Light* can mean 'nimble' (*OED* 15), or 'wanton, unchaste' (*OED* 14b).
87 **their silken parcels** i.e. the curls
88 **What's sweet . . . find** 'Things that are pleasant will readily find means of being

700

Each eye that saw him did enchant the mind,
For on his visage was in little drawn   90
What largeness thinks in paradise was sawn.

'Small show of man was yet upon his chin:
His phoenix down began but to appear
Like unshorn velvet, on that termless skin,
Whose bare out-bragged the web it seemed to wear;   95
Yet showed his visage by that cost more dear,
And nice affections wavering stood in doubt
If best were as it was, or best without.

'His qualities were beauteous as his form,
For maiden-tongued he was, and thereof free;   100
Yet if men moved him, was he such a storm
As oft 'twixt May and April is to see,

91 sawn] Q; sown *conj.* Boswell; drawn *conj.* Lettsom in Dyce   102 May] Q; March
OXFORD

done.' The curls find a means to kiss the young man's lips, with a secondary suggestion that everyone rapidly finds an excuse to love him.

90–1 **For on his . . . sawn** 'His face is a miniature picture of the beauties which the viewer thinks must have been seen on a broad canvas in paradise.' Boswell suggested that the unusual form *sawn* meant 'sown', and took the phrase as a reference to the abundance of vegetation in paradise.

92 **Small show . . . chin** i.e. he had scarcely any beard

93 **phoenix down** incomparably soft down. The description is formed by analogy with phrases such as 'phoenix-feather' in which 'phoenix' is used adjectivally to imply dazzling uniqueness.

94 **unshorn velvet** The process of finishing velvet involved shaving off loose or long threads to create a nap. Unshorn velvet is softer than the finished product.
termless which had no date given for its expiry, hence *like the phoenix* 'immortal'. Since this is the only occurrence of the word in Shakespeare's oeuvre it may be that it means (as *OED* sense 2 has it) 'incapable of being expressed by terms; inexpressible, indescribable'. This is sup-

ported by analogy with *phraseless* in l. 225.

95–6 **Whose bare . . . dear** 'The bare chin was more impressively beautiful than the delicate fabric (the *web*, or *unshorn velvet*) of the faint trace of beard which it wore; yet none the less his appearance seemed even more richly desirable for its ornament.' *Cost* may, as Mackail suggests, play on the French *côte*, 'silken floss'.

97 **nice affections** (a) people of scrupulous discernment; (b) delicate judges who were enamoured of the youth

98 **If best . . . without** whether he looked better with or without a beard

99 **qualities** accomplishments, manners

100 **maiden-tongued** 'soft-spoken like a woman' and 'chaste in language'
free The sense 'frank, plain-spoken' is just emerging in the period. Pejorative senses 'sexually licentious', 'seductively garrulous') may register.

102 **May and April** the period of early spring. Cf. Sonnet 18.3. Oxford reads 'March and April'. This emendation does not seem necessary: the inversion of the expected progression of the months momentarily suggests a stormy battle for supremacy between (*'twixt*) the incoming May and the outgoing April.

When winds breathe sweet, unruly though they be.
His rudeness so with his authorized youth
Did livery falseness in a pride of truth.   105

'Well could he ride, and often men would say
That horse his mettle from his rider takes,
Proud of subjection, noble by the sway,
What rounds, what bounds, what course, what stop
    he makes.
And controversy hence a question takes   110
Whether the horse by him became his deed,
Or he his manège by th' well-doing steed.

'But quickly on this side the verdict went:
His real habitude gave life and grace
To appertainings and to ornament,   115

107–9 That horse . . . makes] Q; *marked as direct speech (italic) by* MALONE   112 manège]
WYNDHAM; mannad'g Q

104–5 **His rudeness . . . truth** 'His unculti-
vated appeal, combined with the licence
accorded to youth, gave a superficial
appearance of fidelity and integrity to his
false nature.' The young man's appear-
ance of rugged truthfulness was a mere
livery, or outward show of nobility, which
did not alter his sexual duplicity. *Autho-
rized* is accented on the second syllable.
Livery is disyllabic.
107 **That horse . . . takes** Horses and riders
also influence each other's temperament
in Sonnet 50.5–6. Editors often mark ll.
107–9 as direct speech, and take *That* as a
demonstrative pronoun. It is quite pos-
sible however that it introduces indirect
speech, i.e. 'a horse takes its mettle'.
108 **by the sway** by the young man's control
109 **rounds** circuits (as in formal displays of
horsemanship, or manège)
bounds or leaps are the most demanding
elements in manège, which Thomas
Blundeville in *The Art of Riding* (1593)
recommends only to those whose horses
are 'nimble of nature' (fo. 34ʳ).
course 'The action of running; a run; a
gallop on horseback' (*OED* 1). Blundeville
in *The Art of Riding* advises, 'see that as
well in his [the horse's] turns as courses
he keep always like measure' (fo. 28ᵛ).
stop 'In the manège: A sudden check in a
horse's career' (*OED* 21a). In equestrian
displays this manoeuvre was often exe-
cuted at a specific place in the course.

110 **controversy . . . takes** The terminology is
drawn from the arts of rhetorical disputa-
tion: *controversiae* were formal topics
for debate, such as whether Summer
is preferable to Winter; *quaestiones* were
points of dispute, which could be either
infinite (such as whether it is better to
marry or to live single), or finite (such as
whether this person should marry). See
Wilson, 1. The question whether the
youth or the steed provided the skill which
they together display becomes a set topic
for debate (with the assumption that the
quaestio is intrinsically irresolvable).
112 **Or he . . . steed** or whether he acquired
his exceptional control from the skill of
the horse.
113 **this side** i.e. the first option, that the
young man was the cause of the horse's
excellence
114 **real habitude** probably 'regal
disposition' rather than 'true nature',
although *real* in the sense 'royal' (*OED
adj.* 1) is not otherwise used by Shake-
speare and is nearly obsolete by 1609, and
habitude is also not otherwise found in
his works. On Shakespeare's rare and
carefully weighed uses of 'real', see Anne
Barton, *Essays, Mainly Shakespearean*
(Cambridge, 1994), 186–9.
115 **To appertainings . . . ornament** 'to mere
belongings and external embellishments'.
This is the only citation of *appertainings* in
the *OED.*

Accomplished in himself, not in his case;
All aids, themselves made fairer by their place,
Came for additions; yet their purposed trim
Pieced not his grace, but were all graced by him.

'So on the tip of his subduing tongue   120
All kind of arguments and question deep,
All replication prompt and reason strong,
For his advantage still did wake and sleep.
To make the weeper laugh, the laugher weep,
He had the dialect and different skill,   125
Catching all passions in his craft of will;

'That he did in the general bosom reign
Of young, of old, and sexes both enchanted,
To dwell with him in thoughts, or to remain
In personal duty, following where he haunted.   130

118 Came] SEWELL; Can Q

116 **case** (a) external dress; (b) accidental circumstances

118 **Came for additions** presented themselves to act as improvements to the young man's natural grace. Q reads 'Can for addicions', which could mean 'were effective as', were it not for the fact that the next line says that they were not effective. 'Can' for 'came' is an error also found in the Folio *Macbeth* 1.3.96.
purposed trim their intention to act as ornaments

119 **Pieced not** did not supplement. To 'piece' is to mend (Schmidt, 1) or to enlarge or increase (Schmidt, 3). Q's 'Peec'd' could conceivably be modernized as 'peised', hence 'did not equal in weight'.

120 **subduing** conquering

121 **arguments and question deep** persuasive proofs and profound debates. Again the terminology of rhetorical (and forensic) debate is in play.

122 **replication** reply, perhaps with a trace of the legal sense 'The reply of the plaintiff to the plea or answer of the defendant, being the third step in common pleadings' (*OED* 3b)

123 **For his advantage . . . sleep** The techniques of persuasion are completely subject to the young man's interests, so that they will spring into action if he needs

them, or slumber if his adversary could make use of them.

125 **had the . . . skill** he could catch different idioms and different modes of speech. Given that the young man is presented as a rhetorician, *dialect* may mean 'the art of dialectics' or argumentation (*OED* 3). Thomas Wilson uses the form in his *Logic* of 1553 (fo. 2ᵛ): 'Logic otherwise called dialect (for they are both one) is an art to tell the corn from the chaff'.

126 **Catching all passions . . . will** (a) capturing each human emotion in a skilful display of artistry; (b) winning over everyone's feelings in a crafty display of control. *Craft of will* ranges from the artful 'articulation of volition' to the potentially negative 'sly display of sexual desire'.

127 **general bosom** the affections of everyone

129–30 **to remain | In personal duty** This is the literal alternative to remaining with the young man in thought. *Personal duty* means 'service in person' (*OED* s.v. 'personal' 2a: 'Done, made, performed in person'), but may suggest also intimate service.

130 **haunted** frequented. The ghostly overtones to the verb are less pronounced in this period than they are now. Its inviting proximity here to *bewitched* releases some

Consents bewitched, ere he desire, have granted,
And dialogued for him what he would say,
Asked their own wills and made their wills obey.

'Many there were that did his picture get
To serve their eyes, and in it put their mind,   135
Like fools that in th' imagination set
The goodly objects which abroad they find
Of lands and mansions, theirs in thought assigned,
And labouring in more pleasures to bestow them
Than the true gouty landlord which doth owe them.   140

'So many have that never touched his hand
Sweetly supposed them mistress of his heart.
My woeful self that did in freedom stand,
And was my own fee-simple (not in part),
What with his art in youth and youth in art   145
Threw my affections in his charmèd power,
Reserved the stalk, and gave him all my flower.

---

131 Consents] MALONE; Consent's Q   139 labouring] Q; labour OXFORD (*conj.* Wyndham)

of the otherworldly potential which Shakespeare exploited in *Richard II* 3.2.153–4: 'How some have been deposed, some slain in war, | Some haunted by the ghosts they have deposed'.

131 **Consents bewitched . . . granted** People who have fallen under his spell consent to his wishes even before he has formulated them. Q reads 'Consent's bewitcht, ere he desire, haue granted'. This could at a pinch be glossed 'Consent is magically won even before he has deigned to bestow his desire on the person who consents'. This is the only instance in which Q uses an apostrophe to mark an elision of 'is'. It may indicate a compositor's vain attempt to grasp at sense.

132 **dialogued for him** have spoken his side of the conversation on his behalf

134–5 **Many there were . . . mind** 'Many have obtained his portrait in order simply to look at it, but have come to be obsessed by it.'

137 **objects** 'Things placed before the eyes' (*OED* 3a)
abroad in the wide world

138 **theirs in thought assigned** 'which they imagine to be their property'. The legal

sense of *assign* is active: 'To transfer or formally make over to another' (*OED* 2).

139–40 **And labouring . . . owe them** 'expending more pleasurable energy in giving the lands away than the gouty old landlord who really does own them'. *Bestow* may also mean 'to spend or lay out' (Schmidt), or possibly 'administer'. *Owe* is an archaic form of 'own'. *Labouring* is pronounced 'lab'ring', and the line ends with a feminine rhyme.

142 **them** themselves

144 **fee-simple** absolute possession. A *fee-simple* is an absolute right to own a piece of land without any limitations on the class of heirs who can inherit it, and until the then owner dies without heirs.
(not in part) not in part-ownership

146 **affections** primarily *OED* 3: 'Feeling as opposed to reason; passion, lust'; but the young man's control may extend to *OED* 4: 'State of mind generally, mental tendency; disposition'.
charmèd magically attractive

147 **stalk** 'the worthless remnant once the flower has been plucked'. *OED* cites this under 4d 'coarse slang. A penis, esp. one that is erect. Cf. *Pericles* Scene 19.47–8 in which the Bawd refers to Marina as 'a

'Yet did I not, as some my equals did,
Demand of him, nor being desirèd yielded;
Finding myself in honour so forbid,   150
With safest distance I mine honour shielded.
Experience for me many bulwarks builded
Of proofs new bleeding, which remained the foil
Of this false jewel and his amorous spoil.

'But, ah, whoever shunned by precedent   155
The destined ill she must herself assay,
Or forced examples 'gainst her own content
To put the by-passed perils in her way?
Counsel may stop awhile what will not stay;
For when we rage advice is often seen   160
By blunting us to make our wits more keen.

161 wits] Q; wills MAXWELL

rose': 'Here comes that which grows to the stalk, never plucked yet, I can assure you.'

148 **some my equals** some social equals of mine. *Equals* can also (unusually) mean 'of the same age' in the 1590s (*OED* B 1c), although it is not otherwise used by Shakespeare in this sense.

149 **nor being desired yielded** 'nor did I let him sleep with me the moment I was asked'

150 **Finding myself . . . forbid** 'finding that I was forbidden by my sense of honour from doing so'

151 **With safest distance** i.e. by removing myself from his presence. *OED* gives this as the first citation for 8, 'Of relations of personal intercourse: Remoteness in intercourse, the opposite of intimacy or familiarity'. As in l. 237 below, however, either literal or figurative distance could be meant.

152 **bulwarks** defensive earthworks

153 **proofs new bleeding** still-fresh evidence of harm he had done
foil 'A thin leaf of some metal placed under a precious stone to increase its brilliancy' (*OED* 5a), with perhaps a momentary hint of *OED* 'foil' *n* 1, a fencer's sword, or even of 'foil' *n* 2, 'a repulse'.

155 **by precedent** by following prior examples. Many complaints end with an appeal that the example of the heroine's fall will prevent others from undergoing the same ordeal whilst also including within their narrative moments which dramatize the inadequacy of precedent and example to influence conduct. Daniel's Rosamond sees the engraved image of Io immediately before her fall and bewails that 'These precedents presented to my view, | Wherein the presage of my fall was shown. | Might have forewarned me well what would ensue, | And others' harms have made me shun mine own; | But fate is not prevented, though foreknown', ll. 407–11.

156 **assay** try by experience

157–8 **Or forced . . . her way?** 'Or who has ever managed to set past literary examples of the sufferings of other people in the way of what she wants?'

159 **Counsel . . . stay** Good advice may cause something to stop for a moment that does not wish to do so. *Stop* and *stay* are effectively synonyms.

160–1 **For when . . . keen** For the idea that delay serves only to stimulate the appetite, see Sonnet *118*. *Rage* can be used of any passionate frenzy, including sexual desire.

'Nor gives it satisfaction to our blood
That we must curb it upon other's proof,
To be forbod the sweets that seems so good
For fear of harms that preach in our behoof: 165
O, appetite from judgement stand aloof!
The one a palate hath that needs will taste,
Though reason weep and cry "It is thy last."

'For further I could say this man's untrue,
And knew the patterns of his foul beguiling,   170
Heard where his plants in others' orchards grew,
Saw how deceits were gilded in his smiling,
Knew vows were ever brokers to defiling,
Thought characters and words merely but art,
And bastards of his foul adulterate heart.   175

169 For further] Q; For, father, HUDSON 1881 *(conj.* Staunton)   169 this man's untrue] Q (this
mans vntrue); 'this man's untrue' MALONE *(italic)*

162 **blood** the passionate appetites, sexual
desire
163 **upon other's proof** as a result of precepts
which have been experienced by someone
else. As in Sonnet *129, proof* carries an
overtone of 'to have sexual experience of'.
164 **forbod** is a recognized form of 'forbid-
den' in the period, although not other-
wise used by Shakespeare.
seems The singular verb with a plural sub-
ject is common in Shakespeare's English.
165 **in our behoof** for our advantage
166 **stand aloof** keep away from
167 **The one** i.e. the appetite
169 **For further . . . untrue** is usually glossed
as 'I could say more about this man's sex-
ual infidelity'. It is more likely, though,
that it means 'Not only did I have past
examples to guide me, and not only did I
have the voice of Reason warning me
against him, but *(further)* I actually had
knowledge of his conduct which enabled
me to say without doubt "This man is
untrue."' If glossed in this way (after Mal-
one's italics which mark 'This man's
untrue' as direct speech) the phrase
marks the link between the preceding
argument, which dismisses literary
examples as powerless to affect human
conduct, and the next, which lists the
woman's first-hand experience (*knew,
heard, saw, knew*) of the man's actions. It
does require, however, that an apostro-

phe marking the elision of 'is' was omit-
ted from 'man's' in Q (as the compositor
took 'mans' as a possessive form), but
there are two other omissions of apostro-
phes in the poem ('whats sweet to do', l.
88, 'thats to ye sworne', l. 180), as well as
the aberrant contraction in 'Consent's' in
l. 131.
170 **patterns of his foul beguiling** instances
of his wicked ability to charm and
seduce; and perhaps too the formulae
(patterns) which he used in his seductions
171 **his plants . . . grew** i.e. he had affairs with
married women as a result of which his
children were raised as members of other
men's families
172 **gilded** glossed speciously over
173 **Knew vows . . . defiling** knew that oaths
of fidelity have always been the agents of
sexual defilement. *Broker* can mean 'deal-
er in second-hand goods' and convey
all the condemnation which that still
implies, and also (*OED* 4) 'a procurer,
pimp, bawd; a pander generally'. Polo-
nius urges Ophelia, 'Do not believe his
vows, for they are brokers, | Not of that
dye which their investments show, | But
mere implorators of unholy suits', *Hamlet*
1.3.127–9.
174 **characters** written words (of the kind
which the woman has been tearing up)
merely but art nothing more than artifice
175 **bastards** illegitimate offspring, and so,

'And long upon these terms I held my city,
Till thus he gan besiege me: "Gentle maid,
Have of my suffering youth some feeling pity,
And be not of my holy vows afraid.
That's to ye sworn to none was ever said,   180
For feasts of love I have been called unto
Till now did ne'er invite nor never woo.

' "All my offences that abroad you see
Are errors of the blood, none of the mind:
Love made them not; with acture they may be,   185
Where neither party is nor true nor kind.
They sought their shame that so their shame did find,
And so much less of shame in me remains
By how much of me their reproach contains.

' "Among the many that mine eyes have seen,   190
Not one whose flame my heart so much as warmèd,
Or my affection put to th' smallest teen,
Or any of my leisures ever charmèd:
Harm have I done to them but ne'er was harmèd,
Kept hearts in liveries, but mine own was free,   195
And reigned commanding in his monarchy.

182 woo] DYCE 1857 (*conj*. Capell); vovv Q   191 warmèd] Q; warm'd MALONE   194 harmèd] Q; harm'd MALONE

like the Bastard in *K. John* and Edmund in *Lear*, likely to deceive.
175 **adulterate** impure, contaminated, as well as 'adulterous'

176 **my city** Cf. *Lucrece* ll. 469 and 1547.
177 **gan** began to
178 **feeling pity** On the association between pity and accepting a lover's suit, see Sonnet 132.4 n.
180 **That's . . . said** 'that which is sworn to you was never uttered to anyone else'
182 **woo** Q reads 'vovv', which appears to be the result of eyeslip from l. 179.
183 **that abroad you see** which have become public knowledge
185 **with acture they may be** 'they may be held to be simply actions, rather than expressions of deliberate volition' (and so may be disregarded). The most probable explanation for the coinage *acture* (the only cited instance in the OED) is that the

young man is inventing legalese terms to obscure a bogus argument.
186 **Where neither . . . kind** 'in cases where neither party in the relationship is faithful nor loyally familial in their behaviour towards the other'. This argument requires the youth to confess that both he and his lovers were unkind and untrue.
187 **They sought . . . find** 'The women who were shamed by me were asking for it.'
188–9 **And so . . . contains** 'and the more they reproach me the less I am to blame'
192 **teen** suffering, hurt. A poeticism, favoured by the archaizing Spenser.
193 **leisures** periods of leisure. The plural is unusual, but is also found in *Timon* 2.2.124.
195 **Kept hearts in liveries** The hearts of his other lovers were, like feudal retainers, clothed in livery which showed that they were in service.

' "Look here what tributes wounded fancies sent me
Of pallid pearls and rubies red as blood,
Figuring that they their passions likewise lent me
Of grief and blushes, aptly understood   200
In bloodless white and the encrimsoned mood:
Effects of terror and dear modesty,
Encamped in hearts but fighting outwardly.

' "And lo, behold these talents of their hair,
With twisted metal amorously impleached,   205
I have received from many a several fair,
Their kind acceptance weepingly beseeched
With the annexions of fair gems enriched,
And deep-brained sonnets that did amplify
Each stone's dear nature, worth, and quality.   210

198 pallid] Q (palyd); palèd MALONE   204 talents] Q; talons DUNCAN-JONES   204 hair] Q
(heir)   208 the annexions] MALONE (*conj.* Capell); th' annexions Q; th' annexations OXFORD

195 **free** echoes the former freedom of the
woman, ll. 143–4.

197 **tributes** fits the feudal imagery of the
previous lines: 'rent or homage paid in
money or an equivalent by a subject to his
sovereign or a vassal to his lord' (*OED*).
wounded fancies doting women, whose
imaginations have been wounded by love

198 **pallid** Not otherwise used by Shake-
speare. Some editors modernize Q's
'palyd' as 'palèd'. The word 'pallid'
appears to have been introduced by
Spenser, a poet to whom *A Lover's Com-
plaint* is more deeply indebted than to any
other. The opening of this poem may echo
that of Spenser's *Prothalamion*, which
describes 'the Violet pallid blew' in l. 30.

199 **Figuring** covertly signifying

200 **aptly understood** appropriately inter-
preted and represented. *Understood*
applies both to the giver and to the
recipient, who share a private code.

201 **encrimsoned mood** both 'the emotional
state (of embarrassment) which turns
bright red', and 'the red form' of the ruby.
Encrimsoned is the first citation of the
form.

202 **Effects** manifestations

203 **but fighting outwardly** which are only
pretending outwardly to resist

204 **talents** are literally units of measure-
ment or a coin; here figuratively 'valuable

tokens'. The intertwining of metal and
hair makes the tokens costly, and prompts
the image.

205 **impleached** intertwined. This is the first
cited usage of the verb. The im- prefix
intensifies the sense of 'pleached', or
woven.

206 **many a several fair** many different beau-
tiful women

207 **Their kind acceptance** that I should
accept them with affection

208 **the annexions** the addition (*OED* 2; first
citation). Q reads 'th' annexions', which
produces a metrically defective line. Roe's
suggestion that the word is stressed on the
first and third syllables does not tally with
other Shakespearian usage: 'ion' if disyl-
labic is usually stressed on the 'on' (see
Abbott §479). Wells and Taylor emend to
'th'annexations'. Elision of 'the' before
initial 'a' is rare in Q (it occurs only at
Sonnet 58.3 and here), and so cannot
readily be attributed to a compositorial
tic. However, Capell's emendation to *the
annexions* runs with the normal practice
of not eliding before an initial vowel (pro-
clitic 'th' before a vowel is found on only
three other occasions in the poem: ll. 25,
136, 318), and so is the least obtrusive
emendation.

209 **deep-brained** ingeniously profound
amplify develop. In classical rhetoric
amplificatio was the art of redescribing an

' "The diamond? Why, 'twas beautiful and hard,
Whereto his invised properties did tend;
The deep-green em'rald in whose fresh regard
Weak sights their sickly radiance do amend;
The heaven-hued sapphire and the opal blend   215
With objects manifold; each several stone
With wit well-blazoned, smiled or made some moan.

' "Lo, all these trophies of affections hot,
Of pensived and subdued desires the tender,
Nature hath charged me that I hoard them not,   220
But yield them up where I myself must render:
That is to you, my origin and ender;

object or action in such a way as to make
it appear to be as good or as bad as
possible. See Quintilian 8.4.

212 **Whereto his ... did tend** (a) to which (i.e.
the immediately apparent properties of
hardness and beauty) the unseen quali-
ties of the diamond also contributed; (b)
to which (beauty and hardness) the as yet
unseen moral qualities of the youth
tended. This secondary sense requires
that the line be read as an aside by the
woman. There are two uncertainties here:
his could be either a neuter or a masculine
possessive pronoun; and the sense of
invised (for which this is the only citation
in the *OED*) is not clear. The word could
conceivably also mean 'seen within' (as
the sparkle of a diamond is often matched
by an inner almost invisible glow) if *his*
were taken as a neuter pronoun.

213 **in whose fresh regard** in looking at the
fresh appearance of which

214 **Weak sights ... amend** The emerald was
believed to restore the sight: 'if the sight
hath been wearied and dimmed by
intentive poring upon anything else, the
beholding of this stone doth refresh and
restore it again', Pliny, ii.611. *Sickly radi-
ance* refers to the weakening of the eye-
beams after prolonged study or reading.
The emerald was supposed to augment
the eye-beam: 'as they ever send out their
own rays by little and little, so they enter-
tain reciprocally the visual beams of the
eye', Pliny, ii.611.

215 **heaven-hued** Sapphires are sky-blue.

215–16 **the opal blend| ... manifold** If *blend*
is a verb, then this means 'the sapphire

and opal combine themselves with many
things which are presented to the view'.
This presumably refers to the multiple
reflections from the surface of the gems. If
blend is a past participle ('blended') the
sense is probably that the opal is a gem
which is blended with an eye-catching
multiplicity of colours. The opal was
widely described as resembling a mixture
of other precious stones: 'In the Opal you
shall see the burning fire of the Carbuncle
or Ruby, the glorious purple of the
Amethyst, the green sea of the Emerald,
and all glittering together mixed after an
incredible manner' (Pliny, ii.614).

217 **wit well-blazoned** The *deep-brained son-
nets* describe the properties and appear-
ance of the gems with such vividness that
the gems themselves appear to smile or
complain.

219 **Of pensived ... tender** 'the offerings (*ten-
der*) of melancholy and humbly repressed
desires'. *Pensived* is not otherwise
recorded in *OED*.

220–1 **Nature ... render** The young man is
echoing arguments familiar well before
the exhortations in Sonnets 4 and 11 not
to hoard Nature's goods by continued vir-
ginity; here the wealth which he is offer-
ing up is not his own natural qualities but
gems given to him by earlier unhappy
lovers. On *render*, see 126.12 n. *Audit*, l.
231, also recalls Sonnet 126. The youth in
this poem is yielding all to his mistress;
readers of the preceding sequence would
recall that he owes a larger debt to nature.

222 **my origin and ender** source of my life
and death

For these of force must your oblations be,
Since I their altar, you enpatron me.

' "O then advance (of yours) that phraseless hand,   225
Whose white weighs down the airy scale of praise.
Take all these similes to your own command,
Hallowed with sighs that burning lungs did raise:
What me, your minister, for you obeys,
Works under you, and to your audit comes   230
Their distract parcels in combinèd sums.

' "Lo, this device was sent me from a nun,
Or sister sanctified of holiest note,
Which late her noble suit in court did shun,
Whose rarest havings made the blossoms dote;   235
For she was sought by spirits of richest coat,

---

228 Hallowed] MALONE (*conj.* Capell); Hollowed Q   229 me, your minister, for you] COLLIER;
~ ~ ~ ~ ~ ~ Q; ~, ~ ~ ~ ~, OXFORD   233 Or] Q; A DYCE 1866 (*conj.* Malone)

223 **of force** of necessity
   oblations religious offerings
224 **Since I . . . me** 'I am the altar on which
   such offerings are set; you are my patron
   saint to whom the offerings are made.'
   Enpatron is recorded as 'impatron' in the
   OED, and the first citation given is from
   1642.
225 **phraseless** which cannot be described in
   words (the only example in *OED*)
226 **Whose white . . . praise** whose whiteness
   is so perfect that it outweighs all the
   praise, mere air, that could be lavished
   on it
227 **these similes** presumably the com-
   parisons made in the *deep-brained sonnets*
228 **Hallowed** made holy. Q's 'Hollowed' (i.e.
   'hollowèd') may suggest that the compos-
   itor was thinking of the form '*hallowèd*',
   used in the Lord's Prayer, even as he mis-
   took the initial vowel. It also may indicate
   that he took the suggestion that this airy
   praise is indeed a little hollow. If Q is cor-
   rect then an improbable image from glass-
   blowing is in play, in which air from
   burning lungs inflates praise as a blower
   his molten glass.
229 **What me . . . obeys** 'whatever obeys me,
   your servant or priest, also obeys you'.
   Editors have sometimes added punctua-
   tion to the line on the grounds that 'for
   you' is better taken as intensifying 'your

minister'. It seems more likely to be
an ellipsis which is clarified in the next
line.
230 **audit** (a) final account (in which the
   woman is presented as the lord of a
   household who summons all her agents
   to reckoning); (b) hearing
231 **distract parcels** separate parts. *Distract* is
   stressed on the first syllable.
232 **device** emblematic figure or design (*OED*
   9)
233 **sanctified of holiest note** consecrated as
   one of the most notably holy. *Sanctified*
   may indicate that the woman, unlike
   Isabella in *Measure*, is not a novice but has
   taken her full vows. The gloss which the
   young man gives to *nun* may indicate that
   he is correcting himself: *nun* can mean
   'prostitute', as he realizes and then anx-
   iously tries to put the cat back into the
   bag.
234 **her noble suit** the wooing of her by noble
   courtiers
235 **rarest havings** unique qualities
   blossoms dote both literally, and figura-
   tively (referring to the courtiers)
236 **spirits** men (of noble animation). The
   word is monosyllabic.
   richest coat primarily 'of the highest
   birth' (with *coat* referring to heraldic
   coats of arms); also 'most sumptuously
   attired'

But kept cold distance, and did thence remove
To spend her living in eternal love.

' "But, O, my sweet, what labour is 't to leave
The thing we have not, mastering what not strives,   240
Paling the place which did no form receive,
Playing patient sports in unconstrainèd gyves?
She that her fame so to herself contrives
The scars of battle scapeth by the flight,
And makes her absence valiant, not her might.   245

' "O pardon me in that my boast is true:
The accident which brought me to her eye
Upon the moment did her force subdue,
And now she would the cagèd cloister fly:
Religious love put out religion's eye.   250

241 Paling] MALONE 1790; Playing Q; Planing OXFORD (conj. Capell)   242 unconstrainèd]
GILDON 1714; unconstraind Q   242 gyves] Q (giues)

237 **distance** See l. 151 and n.
238 **spend her living** waste her life, with a
secondary sense of 'waste her livelihood'
(on rich gems and tokens). *Living* in this
sense was an archaism by 1609.
240 **mastering what not strives** 'overcoming
that which does not resist us'; i.e. it is
harder to overcome a love for someone
who is not there than a love for someone
who is present and resistant.
241 **Paling** enclosing. Two senses are pos-
sible: (a) 'building a protective barrier
around (*paling*) the heart into which no
image of a lover (*form*) now comes'; (b)
'embracing the air which holds no physi-
cal presence (*form*) of a lover'. The second
alternative is supported by *Venus* ll.
229–31. The combination of the two sug-
gests that the disappointed lover both tries
to insulate her heart against love and
vainly hugs the air. 'Pale' is used as a verb
in *Antony* 2.7.67. Q's 'Playing', which
anticipates the start of the next line, is
very likely to be a compositor's error.
Capell's 'playning' ('smoothing [the place
on the pillow, or in the heart' which had
received no impression') requires only
that the compositor missed a tilde above
the 'y' of his copy, but yields weak sense,
since 'plane' is almost invariably used in
the period to describe a process of
smoothing that involves physical modifi-
cation (destroying trees or shaving the
surface of wood), and nothing in the con-

text invites such rough treatment. A
tempting alternative would be 'plaining'
(complaining of the place, or filling the
place with complaint), were the first cita-
tion of the transitive verb in *OED* not as
late as it is (1855). The verbal noun is
found in the form 'playning' in *Richard II*
1.3.169 and in *Lucrece* l. 559.
242 **unconstrainèd gyves** manacles which
we put on voluntarily. Cf. Posthumus,
imprisoned by the British: 'Must I repent,
| I cannot do it better than in gyves |
Desired more than constrained', *Cymbe-
line* 5.5.108–9.
243 **She that . . . contrives** The self-
imprisoning woman avoids damage to her
reputation by retiring from the fray into
herself.
245 **And makes . . . might** 'and is considered
valiant because of absence from the fight
rather than participation in it'. Compare
the proverb 'Discretion is the better part of
valour' (Dent D354).
248 **Upon the moment** instantaneously
249 **the cagèd cloister** the cloister which
imprisons her
250 **put out religion's eye** blinded religious
devotion. Cf. Sonnet 31.6. Kerrigan
detects a secular inversion of Mark 9: 47:
'And if thine eye cause thee to offend,
pluck it out: it is better for thee to go into
the kingdom of God with one eye, than
having two eyes, to be cast into hell fire'.

Not to be tempted would she be immured,
And now to tempt all liberty procured.

' "How mighty then you are, O hear me tell:
The broken bosoms that to me belong
Have emptied all their fountains in my well,   255
And mine I pour your ocean all among.
I strong o'er them, and you o'er me being strong,
Must for your victory us all congest,
As compound love to physic your cold breast.

' "My parts had power to charm a sacred nun,   260
Who disciplined, ay, dieted, in grace,
Believed her eyes when they t' assail begun,
All vows and consecrations giving place.

251 immured] GILDON; enur'd Q   252 now to tempt all] Q; ~, ~ ~, ~ GILDON; ~, ~ ~ ~,
MALONE   procured] BENSON; procure Q   260 nun] DYCE 1857 (conj. Capell); Sunne Q   261
ay] Q (I)

251 **immured** imprisoned, walled in. See
Sonnet 84.3–4 n. Q reads 'enur'd'. It is pos-
sible that she 'wished to be habituated
(this is the sense in which Shakespeare
uses 'inured' in *Lucrece* l. 321) in the art of
not being tempted', but the emended ver-
sion provides a more exact antithesis
between her former imprisonment and
her subsequent liberty. In Q1 of *L.L.L.*
3.1.121 'immured' is spelt 'emured', and
the prologue of *Troilus* l. 8 describes Troy's
walls as 'strong emures'. Consequently a
simple minim error of 'n' for 'm' is likely
to have led to Q's reading. The fact that a
final 'd' is omitted at the end of the follow-
ing line may imply that the copy at this
point was hard to read or heavily revised.
252 **to tempt all liberty procured** (a) to assay
all forms of freedom she procured liberty
for herself (taking *all* as qualifying *lib-
erty*); (b) to tempt everyone she procured
liberty for herself (taking *all* as the object
of *tempt*). The various attempts to punc-
tuate the line (see collation) needlessly
limit the alternatives which Q offers. *Pro-
cure* had by 1609 acquired the sense (*OED*
5b) 'To obtain (women) for the gratifica-
tion of lust', a sense activated by the prox-
imity of *tempt* and *liberty* (both suggestive
of sexual licence).
256 **your ocean all among** into the wide
expanse of your bosom
258 **Must for ... congest** 'Since I have con-

quered all my former mistresses, and you
have conquered me, the terms of your vic-
tory require that we must all combine into
one force.' Cf. Sonnet 31.10–12. *Congest*,
used here for the only time by
Shakespeare, means 'to collect; to heap
up, to mass' (*OED* 1).
259 **compound** love a love made up, like a
medicine, of many distinct elements. See
Sonnet 76.4 n.
to physic to act as a cure for
cold unresponsive; but the young man
plays on the medicinal sense 'lacking
in heat and vitality, and so in need of
physic'
260 **parts** attributes
nun Q reads 'Sunne'. While the reminder
that the young man's prime victim was a
nun seems a shade awkward, nothing in
the context develops the comparison with
the sun, which would mean presumably
'the brightest luminary of the cloister'
(Malone).
261 **disciplined ... grace** subjected to the dis-
cipline of grace, which implies the morti-
fication of the flesh. To *diet* in this period
can mean to subject oneself to any sort of
regimen of moral or physical health, as
well as to restrict one's intake of food.
262 **t' assail** to attack (her resolve by present-
ing her with images of the young man)
263 **giving place** making room, yielding
ground

O most potential love; vow, bond, nor space
In thee hath neither sting, knot, nor confine,   265
For thou art all, and all things else are thine.

' "When thou impressest, what are precepts worth
Of stale example? When thou wilt inflame
How coldly those impediments stand forth
Of wealth, of filial fear, law, kindred fame.   270
Love's arms are peace 'gainst rule, 'gainst sense,
    'gainst shame,
And sweetens in the suff'ring pangs it bears
The aloes of all forces, shocks and fears.

' "Now all these hearts that do on mine depend,
Feeling it break, with bleeding groans they pine,   275

270 kindred fame] Q; ~, ~ BENSON   271 peace] Q; proof MALONE (*conj.* Capell)

---

264 **potential** powerful

264–5 **vow, bond . . . confine** 'oaths, legal obligations, and physical constrictions do not have purchase on the conscience, binding power, nor the ability to contain a person who is in love'. *Space* here implies physical constriction, *sting* implies bitterly remorseful consequences (*OED* 5, as in 'O death, where is thy sting? O grave where is thy victory? The sting of death is sin: and the strength of sin is the law', 1 Corinthians 15: 56–7).

267 **thou impressest** 'when you (Love) force someone into your service'. The first citation in *OED* is from *1 Henry IV* 1.1.20–1: 'under whose blessèd cross | We are impressèd and engaged to fight'.

267–8 **precepts . . . example** What is the value of musty old examples of what is good and bad? Cf. the woman's arguments at l. 155.

268 **wilt** implies deliberate volition: when you want to

269 **impediments** obstacles. The word is used in the Solemnization of Matrimony in the Book of Common Prayer: 'I require and charge you both . . . if either of you know any impediment, why ye may not be lawfully joined together in Matrimony, ye do now confess it'.

269 **stand forth** 'To step forward (in order to do something, make a speech, face a company, etc.)' (*OED* 93a). The *impediments* are presented as unenthusiastic soldiers, or as public speakers, who are reluctant to confront the power of Love. The reminiscence of the marriage service may continue: the lover is too overwhelmed by love to *stand forth* boldly and declare that there are impediments to the union.

270 **filial fear** a daughter's fear of disobeying her father. *Filial* is disyllabic.

kindred fame The reputation of the family was thought to be smirched by illegitimate unions. Editors since Benson have often added a comma between *kindred* and *fame*, but Q's form probably indicates an uninflected genitive.

271 **peace** i.e. capable of subduing even adversaries as strong as law, reason, and shame into a state of peace. Capell's emendation to 'proof' too easily replaces this startlingly compressed image.

272 **sweetens** Love is the subject of the verb.

suff'ring pangs suggest the pains of childbirth, which are so great as to render all other sufferings insignificant.

273 **aloes** 'A drug of nauseous odour, bitter taste, and purgative qualities, procured from the inspissated juice of plants of the genus Aloe' (*OED* 3). *Forces, shocks* (military assaults), and *fears* would normally act as bitter medicinal deterrents, but love takes their bitterness away.

275 **bleeding groans** For the notion that sighs consumed the blood, see *2 Henry VI* (*Contention*) 3.2.60–1: 'Might liquid tears, or heart-offending groans, | Or blood-consuming sighs recall his life'.

And supplicant their sighs to you extend
To leave the batt'ry that you make 'gainst mine,
Lending soft audience to my sweet design,
And credent soul to that strong bonded oath
That shall prefer and undertake my troth."   280

'This said his wat'ry eyes he did dismount,
Whose sights till then were levelled on my face,
Each cheek a river running from a fount,
With brinish current downward flowed apace:
O how the channel to the stream gave grace!   285
Who glazed with crystal gate the glowing roses
That flame through water which their hue encloses.

'O father, what a hell of witchcraft lies
In the small orb of one particular tear?
But with the inundation of the eyes   290
What rocky heart to water will not wear?

276 **supplicant** a humble petitioner. This is
the first cited usage of the variant form of
'suppliant' as an adjective.

277 **leave** desist
batt'ry military assault (continuing the
image of a city under siege from l. 176).
mine i.e. my heart

278 **Lending soft audience** giving a recep-
tively mild hearing

279 **credent** believing, trusting. The first
recorded usage is also associated with
dangerous gullibility: in *Hamlet* 1.3.29–
30 Laertes warns Ophelia: 'Then weigh
what loss your honour may sustain | If
with too credent ear you list his songs'.
strong bonded oath an oath which is
attached to a bond, or contract promising
forfeits for its breach. See Sonnet 87.4 n.
This is the first cited usage of *bonded* as a
participle-adjective. Many editors after
Capell hyphenate *strong bonded*, which
draws the emphasis away from the fact
that this is an oath tied to a legal bond, as
well as being simply a strong one.

280 **prefer** give advancement to
undertake act as surety for (*OED* 10)

281 **dismount** the first citation for *OED* 8: 'To
set, put, or bring down from an elevated
position; to lower'. There may be a mili-
tary sense, 'to remove a gun from its
mounting', which is developed in the next
line.

282 **sights . . . were levelled** whose gaze was
directed. By 1590 *sights* could refer to the
aiming mechanism of a gun, and *level* is
often used in descriptions of people taking
aim. The young man has been gazing like
a marksman at his prey.

285 **O how . . . grace** i.e. the cheeks (the
channel) lend their beauty to the *stream*
of tears

286–7 **Who glazed . . . encloses** The tears
create a glazed barrier (*gate*) over the red
roses of the cheeks, which glow out
like roses through water. Gates made of
transparent crystal are rarities in the
literature of the period, though, and it is
possible that *gate* is (as Malone suggested)
a contracted form of 'begat'. *Who* would
then refer to the cheeks, which, glazed
with crystal, begot the glowing roses
which shine through the glaze of
tears.

287 **hue** See Sonnet 20.7 n.

288 **father** See l. 71 and n.
hell of witchcraft a mass of wickedly
bewitching torments

289 **particular** single, distinct

291 **to water . . . wear?** For the slow erosion of
stone (suggesting resistant obduracy) to
water (suggesting mutability) see e.g.
Venus l. 200, *Lucrece* ll. 560, 592, and 959,
and the proverb 'Constant dropping will
wear the stone' (Dent D618).

What breast so cold that is not warmèd here?
O cleft effect! Cold modesty, hot wrath,
Both fire from hence and chill extincture hath.

'For lo, his passion, but an art of craft,   295
Even then resolved my reason into tears.
There my white stole of chastity I daffed,
Shook off my sober guards and civil fears,
Appear to him as he to me appears,
All melting, though our drops this difference bore: 300
His poisoned me, and mine did him restore.

'In him a plenitude of subtle matter,
Applied to cautels, all strange forms receives,
Of burning blushes, or of weeping water,
Or sounding paleness: and he takes and leaves   305
In either's aptness as it best deceives,
To blush at speeches rank, to weep at woes,
Or to turn white and sound at tragic shows;

293 O] MALONE (conj. Capell); Or Q

293 **O cleft effect!** 'What divided conse-
quences!' That is, tears warm the resis-
tant chill of modesty and chill the heat of
anger. Q reads 'here, | Or cleft effect,' in
which the compositor may have mistaken
'h' for 'r'.
294 **extincture** extinction. The form is re-
corded only here.
295 **passion** emotion; but also 'A poem, liter-
ary composition, or passage marked by
deep or strong emotion; a passionate
speech or outburst' (*OED* 6d), with poten-
tially a theatrical edge to it, as when in
Dream 5.1.310 Theseus says of Flute play-
ing Thisbe, 'Here she comes, and her
passion ends the play'.
art of craft a skilled display of
dissembling
296 **resolved** dissolved. The sense 'resolute,
determined' is pointedly secondary here.
297 **daffed** is the first cited usage of the
Shakespearian variant of 'doffed', put off.
298 **guards** defences
civil fears the scruples which guarantee
life in civil society
300 **All melting** with tears; also continues
the force of *resolved* from l. 296.
drops tears. Kerrigan notes the frequent

conjunction of teardrops and poison in
Shakespeare, especially in *Cymbeline*
4.2.296–333, and *Lear* (Folio) 4.6.22–71,
and suggests that medicinal drops may be
referred to. Compare *Venus* l. 1074 and n.
301 **restore** 'To bring (a person or part of the
body) back to a healthy or vigorous state'
(*OED* 4c).
302–5 **in him ... paleness** The young man
possesses a mass of ingenious ability (*sub-
tle matter*), which he devotes to trickery
(*cautels*), and which takes on a multiplici-
ty of novel and surprising shapes (*strange
forms*): blushes, weeping, and swooning
pallor (*sounding paleness*). *Sounding* was
by 1609 a slightly archaic variant of
'swooning'.
305–6 **takes and leaves ... aptness** 'he uses
or does not use each device as it best
suits'. *Aptness* is also used of a time-
serving suitor in *Cymbeline* 2.3.46–8:
'Frame yourself | To orderly solicits, and
be friended | With aptness of the season.'
307 **speeches rank** gross remarks
308 **tragic shows** events that seem tragic
(rather than 'theatrical performances':
the young man extends theatricality into
the responses of an audience).

'That not a heart which in his level came
Could 'scape the hail of his all-hurting aim, 310
Showing fair nature is both kind and tame;
And, veiled in them, did win whom he would maim.
Against the thing he sought he would exclaim:
When he most burnt in heart-wished luxury
He preached pure maid, and praised cold chastity. 315

'Thus merely with the garment of a grace
The naked and concealèd fiend he covered,
That th' unexperient gave the tempter place,
Which like a cherubim above them hovered.
Who, young and simple, would not be so lovered? 320
Ay me, I fell; and yet do question make
What I should do again for such a sake.

'O that infected moisture of his eye;
O that false fire which in his cheek so glowed;
O that forced thunder from his heart did fly; 325

309 **level** aim. See ll. 282 n., and Sonnet
117.11.
310 **hail** volley of shot. This is the first cited
usage in this sense.
311 **Showing fair . . . tame** proving that a
gentle disposition is generous and
tractable. *Fair nature* implies a necessary
relation between 'beautiful' and 'good',
hence acquiescent' characters. The
woman has here adopted a typical
argument used by male seducers: that
beauty is necessarily accompanied by a
pitiful susceptibility to the sufferings of a
lover. *Showing* implies duplicity.
312 **veiled in them** disguised in the feigned
passions described in the previous stanza
314 **heart-wished luxury** the sensual aban-
donment for which he most wished. *Luxu-
ry* in Shakespeare always implies 'lust'.
315 **preached pure maid** he preached
chastely. Cf. *As You Like It* 3.2.209–10:
'Speak sad brow and true maid.'
316 **merely** both 'only' and 'completely'
the garment of a grace the outward
appearance of beauty (or sanctity).
Cf. Barnabe Barnes, *Parthenophil and
Parthenophe* Sonnet 49: 'A fiend which
doth in grace's garments grath [clothe]
her'. The same sonnet has parallels
with Shakespeare's Sonnet 119.2 (see
note, and MacDonald P. Jackson,

'Shakespeare's "Sonnets", "Parthenophil
and Parthenophe", and "A Lover's Com-
plaint" ', *NQ* 217 (1972), 125–6).
317 **concealèd** is proleptic: the naked fiend is
to be covered by the outward dress of
sanctity.
318 **unexperient** inexperienced people.
This is the first citation of this form in
OED.
gave . . . place let him in
319 **like a cherubim** like a guardian angel.
Q's 'Cherubin' is Shakespeare's usual
(archaic) form of 'cherubim'.
320 **so lovered** accept such a man as a lover.
This is the first citation of the form in
OED.
321 **question make** pose the question
322 **for such a sake** for the sake of one like
him
323–9 O Exclamations of this kind were
termed 'ecphonesis', 'when through
affection either of anger, sorrow, glad-
ness, marvelling, fear, or any such like,
we break out in voice with an exclama-
tion' (Peacham, sig. K4ʳ). Early readers
might have found it especially hard
here to distinguish between sorrow and
gladness.
323 **infected** infectious; morally
contaminated
325 **from** that from

O that sad breath his spongy lungs bestowed;
O all that borrowed motion, seeming owed,
Would yet again betray the fore-betrayed,
And new pervert a reconcilèd maid.'

FINIS.

326 **spongy** His lungs, like a sponge, can squeeze out the sighs stored in them. *Spongy* is an epithet widely used of tissue which can absorb fluid or air: see Joshua Sylvester's 'Hymn of Alms' (1621), ll. 55–6: 'The spongy lungs with gentle sighs inspire | The vital air our little worlds require'.

327 **borrowed motion, seeming owed** that feigned emotion which appeared genuine. *Motion* primarily means emotion (*OED* 9a, as in 'But we have reason to cool our raging motions', *Othello* 1.3.329–30), but can also mean 'puppet show' (as in *Winter's Tale* 4.3.95–6). *Owed* is the archaic form of 'owned'. Although Q reads 'bestowed' and 'owed' a feminine rhyme on 'owèd' is not intended, since the char-

acter string 'owed' is invariably monosyllabic in Q.

328 **fore-betrayed** who had already been betrayed

329 **pervert** lead astray, corrupt. The verb was sometimes used of Catholics who sought to lead members of the English Church to Roman Catholicism, which ties in with the young man's repeated claims that his love is holy.

reconcilèd reformed, repentant. *OED* sense 5a of 'reconcile' may be germane, given that the 'father' to whom the confession is made has priestly overtones (he is *a reverend man* at l. 57): 'To bring back, restore, or readmit to the Church, *spec.* the Church of Rome'.

717

POEMS ATTRIBUTED TO SHAKESPEARE
IN THE SEVENTEENTH CENTURY

'Shall I Die?'

1

Shall I die? Shall I fly
    Lovers' baits and deceits,
      sorrow breeding?
Shall I tend? Shall I send?
Shall I sue, and not rue   5
      my proceeding?
In all duty her beauty
Binds me her servant for ever.
    If she scorn, I mourn,
I retire to despair, joining never.   10

2

Yet I must vent my lust
And explain inward pain
      by my love breeding.
If she smiles, she exiles
All my moan; if she frown,   15
      all my hope's deceiving.
Suspicious doubt, O keep out,
For thou art my tormentor.
    Fly away, pack away;
I will love, for hope bids me venture.   20

Title 'Shall I die?'] This edition; A Song OXFORD 5 sue] BOD5 (shewe); YALE1 (shew) 10 joining] YALE1; Joying BOD5 13 by my] BOD5, YALE1; by *conj.* Jackson breeding] BOD5; bred YALE1; conceiving OXFORD 16 all my hope's] BOD5, YALE1; hope's *conj.* Jackson deceiving] BOD5; dead YALE1 17 Suspicious doubt, O] BOD5; O suspitious doubt YALE1 19 Fly] BOD5; Fie YALE1

'SHALL I DIE?'
    The poem is known in two MSS: Bodleian MS Rawl. Poet. 160, and Beinecke Library MS Osborn b.197. The latter MS gives no attribution. The former is the control text here. For discussion of the arguments for and against attributing this poem to Shakespeare, see Introduction, pp. 148–52.

4 tend wait in expectation
4 send (a messenger)
5 sue make a direct approach for favour (like a litigant)
10 joining (a) physically uniting with her; (b) joining battle (picking out the military sense of *retire*)
11 vent my lust express my desire
19 pack away get packing!

3

'Twere abuse to accuse
My fair love, ere I prove
   her affection.
Therefore try! Her reply
Gives thee joy or annoy,   25
   or affliction.
Yet howe'er, I will bear
Her pleasure with patience, for beauty
   Sure will not seem to blot
Her deserts; wronging him doth her duty.   30

4

In a dream it did seem—
But alas, dreams do pass
   as do shadows—
I did walk, I did talk
With my love, with my dove,   35
   through fair meadows.
Still we passed till at last
We sat to repose us for pleasure.
   Being set, lips met,
Arms twined, and did bind my heart's treasure.   40

5

Gentle wind sport did find
Wantonly to make fly
   her gold tresses.
As they shook I did look,
But her fair did impair   45
   all my senses.
As amazed, I gazed
On more than a mortal complexion.
   You that love can prove
Such force in beauty's inflection.   50

21 accuse] BOD5; excuse YALE1   27 I will] BOD5; Ile YALE1   28 pleasure] BOD5; pleasures YALE1   29 will] YALE1; wit BOD5   blot₊] ~. BOD5; ~, YALE1   30 doth] BOD5; to doe YALE1   31 it] BOD5; I YALE1   38 pleasure] YALE1; our pleasure BOD5   41 did find] BOD5; it fine YALE1   49 You] YALE1; Then BOD5   50 force] BOD5; forces YALE1

22 **prove** test out

28–30 **for beauty . . . duty** The sense is strained: 'Beauty can't be a reason for timidly failing to recognize her deserts and so diminishing them; doing a wrong to beauty (by direct courtship) is an expression of honour due to her'.

45 **fair** beauty

50 **beauty's inflection** The word *inflection* does not occur in the canon of works safely attributable to Shakespeare; here it may mean 'yielding' (through the sense 'The action of inflecting or bending' (*OED* 1), or 'modulation of the voice' (*OED* 5); with perhaps a sinister undertone of 'a mental or moral bending or turning' (*OED* 1c).

6

Next her hair, forehead fair,
Smooth and high; next doth lie,
   without wrinkle,
Her fair brows; under those,
Star-like eyes win love's prize   55
   when they twinkle.
In her cheeks who seeks
Shall find there displayed beauty's banner;
   O admiring desiring
Breeds, as I look still upon her.   60

7

Thin lips red, fancy's fed
With all sweets when he meets,
   and is granted
There to trade, and is made
Happy, sure, to endure   65
   still undaunted.
Pretty chin doth win
Of all that's called commendations;
   Fairest neck, no speck;
All her parts merit high admirations.   70

8

Pretty bare past compare
Parts, those plots which besots
   still asunder.
It is meet naught but sweet

---

52 next] BOD5, YALE1; neat OXFORD   55 win] BOD5; winns YALE1   61 Thin] BOD5; Then YALE1   68 that's called] BOD5, YALE1; their culled OXFORD   70 admirations] BOD5 (admiracons); admiration YALE1   71 pretty] YALE1; A pretty BOD5   72 which] BOD5; witte YALE1   73 asunder] BOD5; sunder YALE1   74 It is] BOD5; is it YALE1

---

61 **fancy's fed** i.e. when the imagination is allowed to dwell on the lady's lips he feeds himself full of all delights

68 **that's called commendations** Oxford's emendation to 'culled commendations' means praises choicely gathered ('like flowers'). The emendation makes the poem better, which is a reason for resisting it.

71–3 The grammar here is awkward, and is intelligible only if one assumes the lover is enraptured into using asyndeton: the *parts* are presumably the bosom of the lady, since the lover's eye is in traditional manner tending downwards: they are *pretty* and *bare* and *past compare*, and are places (*plots*) which entrance and beguile, and are *still asunder* (which presumably refers both to the separateness of the breasts and to the fact that they are more desirable if the lover is separated from them). To insert a comma after *Pretty bare* (as Oxford does) suggests 'she is prettiest when she is naked', while to treat *bare* as a substantive (which Oxford also does) gives the poem an explicitness with which it only flirts.

Should come near that so rare   75
   'tis a wonder.
No mis-shape, no scape
Inferior to nature's perfection;
   No blot, no spot:
She's beauty's queen in election.   80

9

Whilst I dreamt, I, exempt
From all care, seemed to share
   pleasure's plenty;
But awake, care take
For I find to my mind   85
   pleasures scanty.
Therefore I will try
To compass my heart's chief contenting.
   To delay, some say,
In such a case causeth repenting.   90

Upon a Pair of Gloves that Master Sent to his Mistress

The gift is small,
The will is all:
Alexander Aspinall

75 so rare] BOD5; so | so rare YALE1   77 mis-shape] BOD5 (mishap), YALE1 (mishappe)   82
From] OXFORD; for BOD5, YALE1   83 plenty] YALE1; in plenty BOD5

75 **that** that thing which is
77 **scape** defect (used both of inadvertent errors—'nature has made no slips here'—and of moral blemishes—'there is no sin here')
80 **in election** she has been carefully chosen as the queen of beauty
88 **compass** achieve

UPON A PAIR OF GLOVES
  The poem is found in Shakespeare Birthplace Trust MS ER.93, p. 177 (control text here), a poetical miscellany compiled in around 1629 by Sir Francis Fane (1611–80; brother of the poet Mildmay Fane), where it is followed by a prose note: 'Shakespeare upon a pair of gloves that master sent to his mistress'. For a full discussion of the MS, see E. M. Martin, 'Shakespeare in a Seventeenth Century Manuscript', *English Review* 51 (1930), 484–9. Alexander Aspinall was schoolmaster at Stratford 1582–1624. He married the widow Shaw in 1594. E. I. Fripp has it that Aspinall bought gloves from Shakespeare's father to present to his fiancée, and Shakespeare accompanied the gift with an epigram (*Shakespeare: Man and Artist*, 2 vols. (1938), i.401–2). This is speculation. The pun on 'Will' may support the attribution to Shakespeare, as the Oxford editors suppose. The echo of *Pericles* 14.17, 'Yet my good will is great, though the gift small', provides scanty additional support for the attribution since the thought was proverbial (cf. Dent G97). However, Mistress Shaw had two sons, William and July (the latter a friend of Shakespeare). William Shaw was a glover. The apparent play on 'will' there-

Verses upon the Stanley Tomb at Tong (East End)

Ask who lies here, but do not weep.
He is not dead; he doth but sleep.
This stony register is for his bones;
His fame is more perpetual than these stones,
And his own goodness, with himself being gone,   5
Shall live when earthly monument is none.

STANLEY TOMB (EAST END)
1 weep] TONG; peep BOD3   3 stony] TONG; earthly BOD3   is] TONG; his BOD3

fore may have nothing to do with Shakespeare: it is conceivable that Aspinall ordered gloves from Mistress Shaw's son William, who sent them to his mother with this poesy as an indication of his support for the match; it is also possible, given that 'Alexander Aspinall' ends the poem almost as a signature, that the poem was written by Aspinall (it appears to have become a general assumption by 1630 that any poem with a Stratford connection must have been by Shakespeare; there is nothing in this poem which would have been beyond the powers of any literate person in the period) If the gloves which it accompanied were made by Mistress Shaw's son William 'the will is all' would be Aspinall's joke at his own expense: 'these cost me hardly anything and your son Will made them'. So fancy weaves its webs. On Aspinall see Mark Eccles, *Shakespeare in Warwickshire* (1961), 57–8.

STANLEY TOMB (EAST END)

In the south transept of St Bartholomew's church at Tong in Shropshire is a fine monument in the Italian style to members of the Stanley family (Sir Thomas Stanley, his wife Margaret Vernon, and their son Sir Edward Stanley). It was originally on the north side of the altar. It is undated. This and the following poem are engraved on either end of the tomb, and the inscription is control text here. The poem(s) exists in College of Arms MS C.35, Church Notes Section, p. 20, a MS based on the visitation of the church on 23 September 1663, probably in the hand of the antiquary William Dugdale or of a closely supervised amanuensis. (The original visitation notebook, which might provide clues to the origins of the

attribution, has not been located.) The margin reads 'Shakespeare', the text 'These following verses were made by William Shakespeare the late famous Tragedian'. Another unascribed version is found later in the same MS, p. 41, along with an illustration of the tomb in its original state, surrounded by obelisks. The poem is also found ascribed in Folger MS V a.103. Pt. 1, fo. 8 and in University of Nottingham Portland MS Pw.V.37, p. 12, and (unattributed and with many variants) in Bodleian MS Rawl. Poet. 117, fo. 269ᵛ. Full transcriptions are given in Gordon Campbell, 'Shakespeare and the Youth of Milton', *Milton Quarterly* 33 (1999), 95–105. It is not clear when the tomb was constructed. Nor is it entirely clear to which Stanley or Stanleys this and the following poem are addressed. The Nottingham MS and Folger entitle this poem 'On Sir Thomas Standley' and the following poem 'An Epitaph on Sʳ Edward Standly Igraven on his Toombe in Tong'. Thomas Stanley, second son of the third Earl of Derby, died in 1576, before Shakespeare was active as a poet; his son Edward died in 1632, sixteen years after Shakespeare's death. It is possible that the monument was erected *c.*1602 by the Stanley family as a memorial to Sir Thomas and in anticipation of the death of Edward (as John Weever notes, 'It was usual in ancient times, and so it is in these our days, for persons of especial rank and quality to make their own Tombs and Monuments in their life-time', *Ancient Funeral Monuments* (1631), 18). This would explain why Edward is not referred to as 'Sir Edward', since he was knighted in 1603 (Chambers, i.553). It is also possible, as Campbell suggests, that the effigy of Sir Edward was added to

Verses upon the Stanley Tomb at Tong (West End)

Not monumental stone preserves our fame,
Nor sky-aspiring pyramids our name.
The memory of him for whom this stands
Shall outlive marble and defacers' hands.   5
When all to time's consumption shall be given,
Stanley for whom this stands shall stand in heaven.

STANLEY TOMB (WEST END)
1 stone preserves] TONG; stones preserved BOD3; stones preserves FOL2   1, 2 our] TONG; thy
BOD3   3 memory] TONG; monument BOD3   4 and] TONG; or BOD3   6 When all to time's
consumption] And when to tyme confusion BOD3

the monument after his death, in which
case both poems may be addressed to
Sir Thomas. Shakespeare may have had
some links with the Stanley family: Fer-
dinando Stanley, Lord Strange, was the
patron of Lord Strange's Men, and was
the cousin of Edward Stanley (Honig-
mann, 80). 'Let the bird of loudest lay'
appeared in a volume dedicated to Sir
John Salusbury, who in 1586 married
Ursula Stanley, illegitimate daughter of
Henry Stanley, fourth Earl of Derby.
However, if the monument had been
erected after the death of Edward in
1632 then any connection with Shake-
speare would vanish. It may be that Dug-
dale or his informant for the attribution
noticed a similarity between the second
poem and Milton's epitaph on Shake-
speare (first printed with the second Folio
of 1632) and assumed Shakespearian
authorship of these poems. Campbell has,
however, argued that this poem and its
attribution was known to Milton, and
that he imitated it in 1630. Further in-
formation about the monument can be
found in G. Griffiths, *A History of Tong,
Shropshire, with Notes on Boscobel* (1894)
and D. H. S. Cranage, *Architectural Ac-
count of Churches in Shropshire* (1901),
i.42. This gives a picture of the tomb as
plate VIII facing p. 48, which is rather
larger than the illustrations given by
Campbell. The engraving is illustrated in
Stanley Wells and Gary Taylor, *William
Shakespeare: A Textual Companion* (Oxford,
1987), 25.

1 **Ask who** The first line plays on a tradi-

tional formula for epitaphs, many of
which begin by asking who is buried in
the tomb on which they appear. See John
Scattergood, 'A Graveyard Formula in
Hamlet V.i.115–31', *NQ* 233 (1988),
470–1.

3 **register** written record. Compare Sonnet
123.9.

STANLEY TOMB (WEST END)
For MSS and attribution, see headnote to
previous poem.

2 **sky-aspiring pyramids** The Stanley tomb
is ornamented by four large obelisk
columns which in this period would have
been classed as pyramids. The illustra-
tion in Dugdale's visitation (College of
Arms, MS C.35, Church Notes Section,
p. 41) shows that the obelisks were origi-
nally set at the four corners of the tomb
at ground level. Now they are mounted
on top of the tomb at its corners. Com-
pare Milton's 'On Shakespeare' (1632),
which presents the memory as a better
medium of record than a 'star-ypointing
pyramid'.

6 **Stanley** Either Sir Thomas Stanley
(d.1576), his son Sir Edward Stanley
(d.1632), or Sir Edward the brother of Sir
Thomas (d.1609) (see headnote to previ-
ous poem). There is a pun on 'Standley',
which is how the inscription spells the
name. Funerary poems in the period
frequently played on the name of the
deceased, as does the epitaph on Hero in
Much Ado 5.3.3–4: 'Done to death by slan-
derous tongues | Was the Hero that here
lies.'

On Ben Jonson

Master Ben Jonson and Master William Shakespeare being merry
at a tavern, Master Jonson having begun this for his epitaph:

> Here lies Ben Jonson
> That was once one,

he gives it to Master Shakespeare to make up who presently writes:

> Who while he lived was a slow thing,
> And now, being dead, is no thing.

An Epitaph on Elias James

> When God was pleased, the world unwilling yet,
> Elias James to nature paid his debt.
> And here reposeth. As he lived, he died,
> The saying strongly in him verified:
> 'Such life, such death'. Then, a known truth to tell,   5
> He lived a godly life, and died as well.

ON BEN JONSON

Master . . . epitaph] BOD 1; *not in* FOL7, FOL8   1 lies Ben] BOD 1, FOL7, PLUME 1 & 2; lieth FOL8
2 That] BOD 1, FOL8; Who FOL7, PLUME 1 & 2   2 was once] BOD 1, FOL7, PLUME 1; once was
FOL8, PLUME 2   he gives . . . writes] *not in* FOL7, FOL8   3 Who while he lived] BOD 1, PLUME; In
his life FOL7; while he lived FOL8   4 being dead] BOD 1; hee's dead FOL7; hee is dead is worth
FOL8; he's b(urie)d is PLUME 1; he is b(urie)d is PLUME 2

EPITAPH ON ELIAS JAMES

3 reposeth] BOD 5; reposes STOW   4 strongly in him] STOW; in him strongly BOD 5   5 a] STOW;
the BOD 5

ON BEN JONSON

Ascribed to Shakespeare in Bodleian MS Ashmole 38, p. 181 (c.1650), the control text here, and in Archbishop Plume's MS 25 in Maldon, Essex, where it appears twice (fo. 77 and fo. 51). It is also found in Folger MS V.a.180, fo. 79', and in Folger MS V.a.275, fo. 177. One could contentedly believe that Shakespeare and Jonson drank and rhymed together without having the least doubt that this particular exchange is a piece of mid-seventeenth-century apocrypha. Its main joke is familiar, but also Shakespearian: compare *Dream* 5.1.302–4: '*Demetrius*: No die but an ace for him; for he is but one. *Lysander*: Less than an ace, man; for he is dead; he is nothing'.

EPITAPH ON ELIAS JAMES

This inscription was in the south aisle of the church of St Andrew by the Wardrobe, which was destroyed in the great fire of London. The augmented

Appendix

An Extemporary Epitaph on John Combe, A Noted Usurer

Ten in the hundred here lieth engraved;
A hundred to ten his soul is ne'er saved.
If anyone ask who lieth in this tomb,
'O ho!' quoth the devil, ''tis my John-a-Combe.'

EPITAPH ON JOHN COMBE

1–2 Ten . . . saved] FOL3; *not in* BOD1, FOL7, FANE; Ten in the Hundred the Devill allowes | But
Combe will have twelve he swears and vowes: BOD2; Ten in' th hundred by ye lawes you may
haue | But Twenty in' th hundred the diuel doth craue FOL 10   I here lieth] FOL3; lies here
ROWE; in his grave BRATHWAIT   2 A] FOL3; 'Tis ROWE; but BRATHWAIT   his soul is ne'er
saved] FOL3, ROWE; whether God will him have? BRATHWAIT   ne'er] FOL3 (nere); not OXFORD
3 If . . . lies] FOL3; Hay hay sayth Tom toule who is FANE; FOL7   anyone] FOL3, BOD2; any
man ROWE; any FOL 10   lieth] FOL3, FOL7; lies BOD1, BOD2, FOL 10   4 Oh ho] FOL3, ROWE;
Ho ho FANE, FOL 10; Oh BRATHWAIT; hough BOD1; Hoh! BOD2; Baw wough FOL 10   4 'tis
my] FOL3, FOL 10; my BRATHWAIT; t'is my sonne BOD1

edition of John Stow's *Survey of London*
(1633), 825, sig. Aaaa3, records the
inscription (which is unascribed and in
the company of many very similar anony-
mous epitaphs). In Bodleian MS Rawl.
Poet. 16c, fo. 41, the poem is ascribed
to Shakespeare. Elias James was a brewer
with premises close to Shakespeare's re-
sidence in Puddle Dock Hill. This gives
some additional circumstantial weight to
the attribution. James died a bachelor,
and left £10 to the poor of his parish. His
will was proved 26 September 1610, and
he was buried 24 September 1610. The
fullest account of his life and his pos-
sible connections with Shakespeare is in
Leslie Hotson, *Shakespeare's Sonnets Dated*
(1949), 111–24; see also Hilton Kelliher,
letter to *The London Review of Books* vol. 8,
no. 9 (22 May 1986).

2 **paid his debt** That 'you owe God a death'
was commonplace.
5 **'Such life, such death'** proverbial (Tilley
L263)

EPITAPH ON JOHN COMBE

John Combe died 10 July 1614, and was
buried in Stratford (Eccles, *Shakespeare in
Warwickshire*, 119–20). He and his family
were close to Shakespeare: he left the poet
£5 in his will, and his monument was
made by the same stonemason as Shake-
speare's. Shakespeare left his sword to
John's brother Thomas. The earliest texts
of this poem do not mention Shakespeare,
and it is likely that it came to be attributed
to him later in the seventeenth century as
he became known as the only famous poet
from Stratford. So in Richard Brathwait,
Remains after Death (1618), sig. L2^v, as

reissued with Patrick Hannay, *A Happy
Husband* (1619), the poem is described
as 'An Epitaph upon one John Combe of
Stratford upon Avon, a notable usurer,
fastened upon a Tomb that he had caused
to be built in his lifetime'. A version from
the commonplace book of Sir Francis
Fane (*c.*1629) is in Shakespeare Birthplace
Trust MS ER.93, p. 177: 'Hay Hay sayth
Tom toule who is in this tome | ho ho
quoth the deuill tis my Johna Come' (see E.
M. Martin, 'Shakespeare in a Seventeenth
Century Manuscript', *English Review* 51
(1930), 484–9). In 1634 it was ascribed to
Shakespeare by Hammond (BL MS Lans-
downe 213, fo. 332^v); in Bodleian MS Ash-
mole 38, p. 180 (*c.*1650) and in Bodleian
MS Aubrey 6, fo. 109, Folger MS V.a.345,
p. 232 it is also attributed to Shakespeare.
Aubrey claims the poem was made ex-
tempore. Robert Dobyns claimed to have
transcribed the poem from the tomb in
Folger MS V.a.147 (1673), control text
here, and that after his visit the Combe
family had the lines expunged. An unat-
tributed version is in Folger MS V.a.180,
fo. 79^v. The fact that it is founded on a
familiar joke about usurers (see note to
l. 1) means that either Shakespeare was
recycling an old gag or that he did not
write it.

1 **Ten in the hundred** 'Mr 10 per cent'.
Eccles records of Combe that 'lending
money at the usual ten in the hundred
made him the richest man in Stratford'
(*Shakespeare in Warwickshire*, 119). The
joke was common in the seventeenth
century (Chambers, ii.140): in H[enry]
P[arrot]'s *The More the Merrier* (1608)
there is a usurer's epitaph: 'Ten in the

Another Epitaph on John Combe

Howe'er he livèd judge not,
John Combe shall never be forgot
While poor hath memory, for he did gather
To make the poor his issue; he, their father,
As record of his tilth and seed   5
Did crown him in his latter deed.

Upon the King

Crowns have their compass, length of days their date,
Triumphs their tombs, felicity her fate:
Of more than earth, can earth make none partaker,
But knowledge makes the KING most like his maker.

hundred lies under this stone, | And a hundred to ten to the devil he's gone'. The same formula, as Chambers shows, was used as part of generic epitaphs for usurers and for epitaphs on specific usurers including Edward Stanhope, Sir John Spencer, and Dr Pearse.

2 **A hundred to ten** i.e. I'll give odds of a hundred to ten on
ne'er Oxford's emendation 'not' rests on what appears to be a mistranscription of Folger MS V.a.147's 'nere' as 'now'.

3 **If anyone ask** For this formula, see 'Verses upon the Stanley Tomb at Tong (East End)' l. 1 n.

ANOTHER EPITAPH ON JOHN COMBE
The attribution is in Bodleian MS Ashmole 38, p. 180, which heads the poem 'He being dead, and making the poor his heirs, hee [i.e. Shakespeare] after writes this for his epitaph'. The poem is then subscribed 'W. Shak'. Combe's will, made on 28 January 1612–13, left a legacy of £5 to Shakespeare and £30 to the poor. His tomb records that he left 'Six pounds, thirteen shillings and four pence to buy ten gowns for the poor . . . and one hundred pounds to be lent unto fifteen poor tradesmen . . . more, he gave to the poor of Stratford twenty pounds', J. Q. Adams, 'Shakespeare as a Writer of Epitaphs', in *The Manly Anniversary Studies in*

Language and Literature (Chicago, 1923), 85–6.

3 **gather** both 'accumulate wealth' (*OED* 3b) and 'collect grain in the harvest' (*OED* 4b), which anticipates *tilth and seed.*

UPON THE KING
The poem appears below a picture of James I prefixed to his *Works* (1616). It is attributed to Shakespeare in Folger MS V.a.160 (c.1633–4) and Folger MS V.a.262 (c.1650). These attributions are likely to derive simply from the knowledge of the compilers that Shakespeare was the leading playwright of the King's Men, and are contradicted by Bodleian Ashmole 38, which entitles the poem 'Certain verses written by Mr Robert Barker | His Majesty's printer under his Majesty's picture'. This reproduces the information from the title-page of James I's *Works* (1616; printed by Robert Barker and John Bill), in which the poem first appeared (control text here), but may well be a true indication of the poem's authorship. Had the poem been by Shakespeare it is likely the fact would have been recorded in the engraving. There is no evidence beyond the late MS ascriptions that by 1616 Shakespeare was engaged in any literary activity; to suppose that he was called out of retirement to compose an epigram for the King's book is at best a pleasing fancy.

Epitaph on Himself

Good friend, for Jesus' sake forbear
To dig the dust enclosèd here.
Blessed be the man that spares these stones,
And cursed be he that moves my bones.

EPITAPH ON HIMSELF
1–2 Good friend . . . here] TOMB; *Not in* FOL7   3 spares] TOMB; shades FOL7   4 my bones]
TOMB; these stones FOL7

EPITAPH ON HIMSELF
Shakespeare died on 23 April 1616. These lines are carved on the stone slab covering his grave in Stratford. The lines were presumably intended to prevent his bones being added to the large charnel house at Stratford Church. William Segar, *The Book of Honour and Arms* (1602), 231, notes: 'the violation of Monuments funeral, have ever been reputed a crime infamous: and every generous mind desiring to eternize the memory of his own virtue, or the honour of his noble Ancestors, cannot endure so great indignity'. These lines are attributed to Shakespeare himself in Folger MS V.a.180, fo. 79^v (c.1655–6), and in Folger MS V.a.232, p. 63. A version is in Shakespeare Birthplace Trust MS ER.93, p. 177: 'Blest be the man that shaides these Bones | And Curst be hee that moues these stones'. Whether or not they are by Shakespeare, they are the most practically effective lines attributed to him, since no one has yet opened his grave. Dowdall, who visited the church in 1693, quotes the church clerk as saying that the sextons did not dare touch Shakespeare's grave (Adams, 'Shakespeare as a Writer of Epitaphs', 80), and William Hall in 1694 notes: 'there is in this Church a place which they call the bone-house, a repository for all bones they dig up . . . The Poet being willing to preserve his bones unmoved, lays a curse on him that moves them . . . Nor has the design missed of its effect' (Bodleian Rawlinson MS D.377, fo. 90, quoted in *Allusion Book*, i, p. xiv).``

INDEX

This is a selective guide to points made and glosses given in the commentary and introduction. An asterisk indicates that the entry supplements the information provided by *OED*.

The following abbreviations are used in the index: 'Jonson' = 'Upon Ben Jonson'; 'James' = 'Epitaph on Elias James'; 'Epitaph' = 'Epitaph on himself'; 'Combe' = 'Epitaph on John Combe'; 'Combe 2' = 'Another Epitaph on John Combe'; 'Let the Bird' = 'Let the Bird of Loudest Lay'; *LC* = *A Lover's Complaint*; *PP = The Passionate Pilgrim*; 'Shall I' = 'Shall I die?'; 'Stanley' = 'Upon the Stanley Tomb at Tong (East End)'; 'Stanley 2' = 'Upon the Stanley Tomb at Tong (West End)'; 'Gloves' = 'Upon a Pair of Gloves'; 'King' = 'Upon the King'.

anon, Sonnet 33.4
answer, *v. Lucrece* 83; Sonnet 126.11
anthem, *Venus* 839; 'Let the Bird' 21
antics, *Lucrece* 459
antique, Sonnet 19.10
apology, *Lucrece* 31
aposiopesis, Lucrece 666
appaid, *Lucrece* 914
appal, *Venus* 882
apparel, *sb.* Sonnet 26.11
appeal, *sb.* Sonnet 117.13
appertainings, *LC* 115
apply, *Lucrece* 531; Sonnet 119.3; *LC* 68
approve, Sonnet 42.9
apt, *Venus* 254
aptly, *Venus* 716
aptness, *LC* 306
aqua fortis, Lucrece 755
Ardea, *Lucrece* Arg. 7
argued, *Lucrece* 65
argument, Sonnet 38.3
arms,crossed, *Lucrece* 793
arrest, *Lucrece* 1780; Sonnet 74.1
ask who, 'Stanley' 1
askance, *Venus* 342; Sonnet 110.6
askance, *v. Lucrece* 637
aspect, *Lucrece* 14; Sonnet 26.10
Aspinall, Alexander, 'Gloves' headnote
aspire, *Lucrece* 5
aspiring, *Lucrece* 548
assay, *Lucrece* 1720; *LC* 156
assign, *v. LC* 138
assured, Sonnet 92.2
astonished, *Venus* 825; Sonnet 86.8
astronomy, Sonnet 14.2
Atalanta, pp. 20–1
attaint, *sb. Venus* 741; *Lucrece* 825;
    Sonnet 82.2
attainted, Sonnet 88.7
attend, *Lucrece* 330; Sonnet 66.12; *LC* 3
attorney, *Venus* 335
atwain, *LC* 6
*audaciously, *Lucrece* 1223
audience, *LC* 278
audit, Sonnet 4.12; *LC* 230
augurs, Sonnet 107.6
Augustine, St., pp. 45–6, 100
*auspicious, *Lucrece* 347
authority, *Lucrece* 620
avaunt, *Lucrece* 274
azure, *Lucrece* 419

babe, lover as, Sonnet 143.10
back, *v. Lucrece* 622
backed, *Venus* 419; *Lucrece* 352
badge, *Lucrece* 1054; Sonnet 44.14
*bail, Sonnet 74.2; *Sonnet 133.10
Baines, Richard, p. 125

balk, *Lucrece* 696
balls, *LC* 24
balm, *Lucrece* 1466
ban, *v. Venus* 326; *Lucrece* 1460; *PP*
    18.32
banquet of sense, Sonnet 141.8
bar, *v.* Sonnet 46.3
bare, *a. Venus* 188
bareness, Sonnet 5.8
Barker, Robert, 'King' headnote
barn, *v. Lucrece* 859
Barnfield, Richard, pp. 23, 76, 78, 80, 81,
    127
barque, Sonnet 80.7
barren, *Lucrece* 81; Sonnet 12.5
base, *a. Lucrece* 93
base, *sb. Venus* 303
basest, Sonnet 33.5
bastard, *LC* 175
bastardy, *Lucrece* 522
bat, *LC* 64
bate-breeding, *Venus* 655
bateless, *Lucrece* 9
battery, *Venus* 426; *LC* 277
battle, *sb. Venus* 619
bawd, *Venus* 792
bay, *sb. Venus* 877; *PP* 11.13
beaded, *LC* 37
bear, *v.* Sonnet 152.3
bear with, *Lucrece* 612
beated, Sonnet 62.10
Beaumont, Francis, pp. 16, 21
beck, Sonnet 58.5
bedrid, *Lucrece* 975
begetter, Sonnets Ded. 1
beguild, *Lucrece* 1544
behaviour, Sonnet 79.10
behests, *Lucrece* 852
behoof, *LC* 165
beldam, *Lucrece* 953
bells, *Lucrece* 511
belly, *Venus* 594
Benson, John, pp. 93–4, 151
bent, *Venus* 618; Sonnet 143.6
bereave, *Lucrece* 373
bereft, *Lucrece* 835
beset, *Lucrece* 444
beshrew, Sonnet 133.1
bestow, *LC* 139
bethink, *Venus* 1024
*bett'ring, Sonnet 32.5
betumbled, *Lucrece* 1037
bevel, Sonnet 121.11
bewray, *PP* 18.54
bewrayed, *Lucrece* 1698
bias, *PP* 5.5
biding, *Lucrece* 550
bier, Sonnet 12.8

INDEX OF FIRST LINES

The Oxford World's Classics Website

www.worldsclassics.co.uk

- Browse the full range of Oxford World's Classics online

- Sign up for our monthly e-alert to receive information on new titles

- Read extracts from the Introductions

- Listen to our editors and translators talk about the world's greatest literature with our Oxford World's Classics audio guides

- Join the conversation, follow us on Twitter at OWC_Oxford

- Teachers and lecturers can order inspection copies quickly and simply via our website

www.worldsclassics.co.uk

American Literature

British and Irish Literature

Children's Literature

Classics and Ancient Literature

Colonial Literature

Eastern Literature

European Literature

Gothic Literature

History

Medieval Literature

Oxford English Drama

Poetry

Philosophy

Politics

Religion

The Oxford Shakespeare

A complete list of Oxford World's Classics, including Authors in Context, Oxford English Drama, and the Oxford Shakespeare, is available in the UK from the Marketing Services Department, Oxford University Press, Great Clarendon Street, Oxford OX2 6DP, or visit the website at www.oup.com/uk/worldsclassics.

In the USA, visit www.oup.com/us/owc for a complete title list.

Oxford World's Classics are available from all good bookshops. In case of difficulty, customers in the UK should contact Oxford University Press Bookshop, 116 High Street, Oxford OX1 4BR.

An Anthology of Elizabethan Prose Fiction

An Anthology of Seventeenth-Century Fiction

Early Modern Women's Writing

Three Early Modern Utopias (Utopia; New Atlantis; The Isle of Pines)

FRANCIS BACON   Essays

APHRA BEHN   Oroonoko and Other Writings
                     The Rover and Other Plays

JOHN BUNYAN   Grace Abounding
                     The Pilgrim's Progress

JOHN DONNE   The Major Works
                     Selected Poetry

BEN JONSON   The Alchemist and Other Plays
                     The Devil is an Ass and Other Plays
                     Five Plays

JOHN MILTON   Selected Poetry

SIR PHILIP SIDNEY   The Old Arcadia

IZAAK WALTON   The Compleat Angler

Women's Writing 1778–1838

WILLIAM BECKFORD	**Vathek**
JAMES BOSWELL	**Life of Johnson**
FRANCES BURNEY	**Camilla** **Cecilia** **Evelina** **The Wanderer**
LORD CHESTERFIELD	**Lord Chesterfield's Letters**
JOHN CLELAND	**Memoirs of a Woman of Pleasure**
DANIEL DEFOE	**A Journal of the Plague Year** **Moll Flanders** **Robinson Crusoe** **Roxana**
HENRY FIELDING	**Joseph Andrews and Shamela** **A Journey from This World to the Next and** **The Journal of a Voyage to Lisbon** **Tom Jones**
WILLIAM GODWIN	**Caleb Williams**
OLIVER GOLDSMITH	**The Vicar of Wakefield**
MARY HAYS	**Memoirs of Emma Courtney**
ELIZABETH HAYWOOD	**The History of Miss Betsy Thoughtless**
ELIZABETH INCHBALD	**A Simple Story**
SAMUEL JOHNSON	**The History of Rasselas** **The Major Works**
CHARLOTTE LENNOX	**The Female Quixote**
MATTHEW LEWIS	**Journal of a West India Proprietor** **The Monk**
HENRY MACKENZIE	**The Man of Feeling**
ALEXANDER POPE	**Selected Poetry**